CHORAL MUSIC

CHORAL MUSIC

History, Style, and Performance Practice

ROBERT L. GARRETSON
Professor Emeritus
Colorado State University, Fort Collins

PRENTICE HALL, Englewood Cliffs, New Jersey 07632

Library of Congress Cataloging-in-Publication Data

GARRETSON, ROBERT L.
   Choral music : history, style, and performance practice / Robert
L. Garretson.
     p. cm.
   Includes bibliographical references and index.
   ISBN 0-13-137191-6 (case)
    1. Choral music—History. 2. Performance practice (Music)
   3. Choral singing—Interpretation (Phrasing, dynamics, etc.)
   I. Title.
   ML1500.G37   1993
   782.5'09—dc20   92-35478
                                       CIP
                                       MN

Acquisitions Editor: Bud Therien
Editorial/production supervision: Hilda Tauber
Cover design: Ben Santora
Prepress buyer: Herb Klein
Manufacturing buyer: Robert Anderson
Editorial Assistant: Lee Mamunes

© 1993 by Prentice-Hall, Inc.
A Simon & Schuster Company
Englewood Cliffs, New Jersey 07632

Printed in the United States of America

10 9 8 7 6 5 4 3 2 1

ISBN 0-13-137191-6

Prentice-Hall International (UK) Limited, *London*
Prentice-Hall of Australia Pty. Limited, *Sydney*
Prentice-Hall Canada Inc., *Toronto*
Prentice-Hall Hispanoamericana, S.A., *Mexico*
Prentice-Hall of India Private Limited, *New Delhi*
Prentice-Hall of Japan, Inc., *Tokyo*
Simon & Schuster Asia Pte. Ltd., *Singapore*
Editora Prentice-Hall de Brasil, Ltda., *Rio de Janeiro*

Contents

Preface

This book is intended primarily for conductors of choral music in schools, churches, colleges, and universities. I hope it will also serve as a text for students in choral literature and choral conducting classes.

For many years there has been a need for an authoritative text on choral music performance practices to which conductors might refer for specific information relating to the preparation and performance of their choral music programs. This book addresses that need, providing an immediate and reliable source to which conductors may turn for the information they seek.

Although numerous articles have been published in scholarly journals, the problem is having access to them when the need arises. In addition, the majority of these articles focus on the Renaissance and Baroque periods. Scholarship has tended to concentrate on these earlier periods because it was not until the Classical period that composers began to indicate clearly in their scores the manner in which their music should be performed.[1] Much more remains to be said, especially with regard to the Classical, Romantic, and Modern periods. I hope this book will provide at least a starting point for these efforts.

---

[1]For a discussion of the historical and philosophical aspects of the authenticity movement, see *Authenticity and Early Music: A Symposium,* edited by Nicholas Kenyon (Oxford/New York: Oxford University Press, 1988).

Choral Music is divided into five chapters corresponding to the major periods: Renaissance, Baroque, Classical, Romantic, and Modern. Each chapter begins with an introduction and presents background information about the society of the period, the major choral composers, and the status and makeup of choirs. The central focus in each chapter is on musical style and performance practice. In these sections you will find information on meter and stress, tempo, dynamics, tone quality, pitch, texture, and expressive aspects of the music of the period.

Every chapter includes biographical information on the more prominent composers. This information is useful to choral conductors, because an understanding of the composer's background, attitudes, and opinions can contribute significantly to one's interpretation of the music. Additionally, conductors have a responsibility to provide their singers with background information about the music being studied.

As a firm believer that all the arts are an outgrowth and reflection of their culture, I include in each chapter a section on the related arts of painting, sculpture, and architecture. I hope this information will remind choral conductors that music does not exist in a vacuum, that it reflects the historical period that gave it birth. Because music and painting share some common terms such as form, rhythm, texture, and color, it is sometimes helpful to draw analogies between music and art in order to clarify to choral singers the stylistic characteristics of the music they are performing.

Four appendixes contain valuable reference materials. Appendix A lists the choral composers by period, and gives their dates and birthplaces. Choral octavo publications are listed alphabetically by composer in Appendix B. Appendix C lists extended choral works and publishers alphabetically by composer. Finally, Appendix D provides names and addresses of music publishers and distributors. Rather than include all the choral output of each composer, I have selected the most appropriate music for college and university study, making sure it is available from the sources indicated.

For permission to include excerpts from their choral publications, I am indebted to the following music publishers: A.M.S.I., Augsburg Fortress Publishing House, Bourne Company, Concordia Publishing House, CPP/ Belwin, Inc., Mark Foster Music Company, Hal Leonard Publishing Corporation, Edward B. Marks Music Corporation, Music Press, Northern Music Corporation, Novello & Company, Otto Heinrich Noetzel Verlag, C. F. Peters Corporation, G. Schirmer, Inc., Walton Music Corporation, Warner/ Chappell Music, and World Library Publications.

I am also indebted to the following museums and galleries for permission to include illustrations of paintings and sculptures in their collections: The Louvre, Paris; Metropolitan Museum of Art, New York; Museum of Modern Art, New York; National Gallery, Washington, D.C.; Philadelphia Museum of Art; The Wadsworth Atheneum, Hartford; and the Wallace Collection, London. I am also grateful for permission to include illustrations of art works in

Antwerp Cathedral, Belgium and the Cornaro Chapel of Santa Maria della Vittoria, Rome.

Special appreciation is expressed to those faculty members at Colorado State University who critiqued the manuscript: Kenneth Rock, Professor of History, for his helpful suggestions regarding the life and times in each historical period; Patricia Coronel, Professor of Art, for her helpful comments on the Music and the Related Arts sections; and John N. Parsons, Professor of Music History, who perused the entire manuscript and offered many valuable suggestions. To each of these persons I owe a very special debt of gratitude.

R. L. G.

The Renaissance Period

Cultural change is a slowly moving process, and ascribing particular dates to certain periods is often arbitrary. Notwithstanding, the period of approximately 200 years that we call the *Renaissance* (ca. 1400–1600) does have certain salient characteristics. In some circles of European society, religious orientation declined in the face of rising secular interests. Ultimately this shift was to culminate in the development of modern scientific inquiry in the seventeenth century. Renaissance intellectuals began to emphasize their destinies here on earth, rather than considering life only as a prelude to the hereafter. They developed new confidence in their ability to solve their own problems and to determine their own fate. The wisdom of the Church usually was not denied, but the claims of other sources of truth were staked out.

Considerable discussion has taken place as to the beginning of the Renaissance period in music. Although no exact date can be affirmed, the year 1400 seems to be the most suitable. Jeppesen concurs on this point and offers the following well-founded reasons:

> As far as can be discerned at present, there is a marked and very significant boundary line, especially in a musico-technical respect, at about the transition from the 14th to the 15th century. What happened at that time may be characterized as a change in the conception of consonance—the definite, practical recognition of the 3rd and 6th as not only having privileges in musical

1

art equal to the 4th, 5th and 8th, but moreover as main consonants—tonal combinations decidedly preferred above all others, and regarded as fundamental factors in musical composition.[1]

RENAISSANCE SOCIETY

"Renaissance" means rebirth, and certainly many new beginnings occurred during the Renaissance period. Also referred to as the "Age of Humanism," the Renaissance was a time of rediscovery of the worth of human beings and their achievements past and present. As the term implies, "humanism" is an interest in human achievement. This new interest reflected a change from the primacy of matters spiritual that was prevalent during the Middle Ages. Humanism—both secular and Christian—is often called "the heart and soul of the Renaissance."

One writer characterizes the Renaissance as an age of scientific inquiry, a "quest for truth":

> The history of science might be defined as the history of the discovery of objective truth, of the gradual conquest of matter by the human mind; it describes the age-long and endless struggle for the freedom of thought—its freedom from violence, intolerance, error, and superstition.[2]

During the Renaissance, geographical discoveries of immense importance were made. By the year 1600, the known surface of the earth had doubled. Expeditions supported by the ruling classes of Portugal, Spain, and Italy led to the discovery of many new lands, and the names of explorers such as Christopher Columbus and Ferdinand Magellan became widely known. The invention of the compass and of gunpowder had obvious effects in spurring exploration. In addition to new continents and numerous islands, the high Alps were explored—earlier Europeans had feared climbing them because of the superstition that devils existed there. By the end of the sixteenth century, some 47 summits had been reached. During the Renaissance there was an intense rivalry among various nations to colonize parts of the newly discovered world and thus to expand their influence on the world. Scientific contributions to navigation increased the accuracy of sailing and minimized the dangers of world travel.

Banking systems were initiated, and bankers found ways to overcome the old objections to the charging of interest on loans. They also served as agents in the handling of accounts resulting from the sale and exchange of goods with

---

[1]Knud Jeppesen, *The Style of Palestrina and the Dissonance*, 2nd ed. (Copenhagen: Ejnar Munksgaard, Publisher, and New York: Oxford University Press, Inc., 1946), p. 222.

[2]George Sarton, "The Quest for Truth: Scientific Progress during the Renaissance," in *The Renaissance* (New York: Harper & Row, Publishers, Inc., 1962), p. 55.

businessmen in various parts of Europe. Bankers also introduced the first insurance policies.

In any period of change, education assumes great importance. In the Netherlands, the Brothers of Common Life had established themselves toward the end of the fourteenth century. Their thrust was to reconcile the humanities with Christianity. By the end of the fifteenth century, they had established about 150 schools in the Netherlands, France, and Germany. The Protestant point of view held that all Christians should be able to read the scriptures by themselves. As a result, Martin Luther was very concerned about public education; by 1524 new schools were established in many German cities, and schooling became available to children on a gradually increased basis. In the second half of the sixteenth century, the Brothers of Common Life were replaced and their work surpassed by the Jesuit colleges.[3]

The advancement of mathematics was of particular importance during the Renaissance. During the fifteenth and sixteenth centuries algebra and trigonometry made great strides. The introduction of operational symbols led to the writing of equations. Efforts by the Italians, French, and Flemish produced important achievements in mathematics by the end of the sixteenth century.

In 1543, the Polish astronomer Copernicus completed his treatise on the new astronomy, which involved explaining the relationship of the Earth to the sun. Copernicus was a canon of the cathedral of Frombork, and had a close working relationship with his pupil and disciple, George Joachim Rheticus, a professor of mathematics at the Protestant University of Wittenberg. This relationship is striking, since both Catholic and Protestant theologians of the sixteenth century were opposed to the Copernican theory, which conflicted with the scriptures. Copernicus and Rheticus, however, influenced the thinking of later astronomers, leading to the rejection of the Julian calendar by the Catholic Church.

One of the greatest developments of the Renaissance was the invention of printing, which occurred in Germany in about the middle of the fifteenth century (1445 has been cited as the most likely date). The printing of multiple copies of information allowed for a wider distribution of knowledge and provided the opportunity for scholars in all countries to "compare notes" and thus to broaden their knowledge and understanding. Johannes Gutenberg (ca. 1400–1468), a German printer, was reputedly the first European to print with movable type. Also, the invention of engraving contributed to the graphic arts and to the publication of books with illustrations of plants, and anatomical or surgical drawings were of immense importance.

Scientists of the age had a similar interest in the study of animals, and the discovery of new lands and new species engendered the traveling scientist who was willing to undergo hardships to broaden knowledge. Paralleling this

---

[3]Ibid., p. 60.

research was an equally strong interest in mineralogical investigation. Study of both of these areas contributed immensely to the knowledge of those scientists and scholars who were unable to travel.

The study of anatomy came into existence during the Renaissance largely through the efforts of Leonardo da Vinci in Italy and Andrea Vesalius in Belgium. Leonardo devoted an extraordinary amount of time to dissection and created remarkable drawings of the human body. Vesalius published his treatise *Fabrica* in 1543 and thus marked the beginning of anatomical studies.

The field of medicine advanced considerably—particularly the concept that diseases could be transmitted from one person to another. The epidemic called the Black Death was so severe that from 1348 to 1352 it destroyed one fourth of the population of Europe and demoralized the rest. Syphilis first appeared in Naples in 1495, believed to have been brought back to Europe from the West Indies.

The Renaissance produced many famous artists, but perhaps the two best known are Leonardo da Vinci (1452–1519) and Albrecht Dürer (1471–1528). Leonardo devoted much of his time to science; Dürer concentrated on printing and engraving and excelled in the production of woodcuts and engraving. Leonardo, who embraced both Oriental and Western thought, has been called the "Prince of Painters." Some of the other famous artists of the period are Michelangelo (1475–1564), Andrea del Sarto (1486–1531), Antonio Allegri da Correggio (1494?–1534), Titian (1490?–1576), the master of Venetian colorists, and Tintoretto (1518–1594), a master of technique. In Flanders, Holland, and Germany, other outstanding artists besides Dürer are Jan van Eyck (??–1441) and the younger Hans Holbein (ca. 1497–1543).

During the Renaissance there was no unified Italy as we know it today; the peninsula consisted of separate kingdoms, duchies, republics, and the Papal States (see map).

RENAISSANCE COMPOSERS

The Renaissance gave rise to a multitude of talented composers, a number of whom stand out because their unique contributions had a significant influence on other musicians. The first Renaissance composer of note is the Englishman JOHN DUNSTABLE (1370–1453), who was born in Dunstable, Bedfordshire, and died in London. Although known as the founder of the Continental School of English music, he spent considerable time in France and Burgundy. Dunstable's music is known for its original creative style, simple beauty, flowing lines, and free treatment of borrowed melodies.[4]

[4]Don C. Walter, *Men & Music in Western Culture* (New York: Appleton-Century-Crofts, 1969), p. 54.

Italy during the Renaissance

Heavy line indicates limits of the Papal States

The Duchy of Burgundy flourished during the fifteenth century; it included what is now Belgium, the Netherlands, and part of eastern France. The name *Burgundian* is used to describe a school of composers whose leader was GUILLAUME DUFAY (1400–1474). Born in Hainaut, Belgium, Dufay wrote music utilizing the intervals of thirds and sixths and with a well-defined bass part. GILLES BINCHOIS (1400–1460) was born in Mons, Belgium. His greatest contribution was in the development of secular music, including the *rondeau,* the *ballade,* and the *chanson.*

During the Renaissance, the country called Flanders extended along the North Sea from the Strait of Dover to the Scheldt River. Today, the region includes the provinces of East Flanders and West Flanders and adjacent parts of the Netherlands and northern France. Flemish musicians contributed greatly to the development of such forms as the French *chanson,* the English and Italian *madrigal,* and the German *Lied.* Flemish composers were the first to have their music printed with movable type. The earliest-known printing of music was in 1476 by Ulrich Hahn of Rome; music was printed by Jörg Reyser of Wurzburg in 1481 and by Ottavio Scatto of Venice in the same year.[5]

JOHANNES OKEGHEM (ca. 1430–1495), born in East Flanders, Belgium, was the leader of the Flemish School of composition, and studied with and was influenced by both Binchois and Dufay. Okegham developed imitative devices that served as models for later *a cappella* music. Innumerable composers of the succeeding generation studied with him, and they affectionately bestowed upon him the title "Prince of Music."[6]

JACOB OBRECHT (1452–1505) was born in Berg-op-Zoom, Netherlands. Obrecht's music displayed an artistic use of phrase and cadence following the meaning of the text. He normally wrote for four voices, the lowest one being a true bass line.

JOSQUIN DESPRÉS (ca. 1450–1521) was born in Hainaut, Belgium. His music may be divided into two categories: (1) works in which elaboration is a principal feature and (2) music in which the sentiment of the text is given expression. Both Obrecht and Després were fortunate in that most of their music was published, and thus they became widely known. Both spent time in Italy, Obrecht in the court chapels of Italy and Després from 1486 to 1494 in the Papal Chapel.

During the fifteenth century, most creative efforts in Italy were directed toward sculpture and painting. It was not until the sixteenth century that music expression in Italy peaked, and then particularly in Venice and Rome. In Venice, the Cathedral of St. Mark was an important musical center. St. Mark's was built in the form of a cross, and multiple choirs singing from the arms of the cross performed antiphonal music. Organs and various other instruments gradually came into use. ANDREA GABRIELI (1517–1595) and his nephew

[5]Ibid., pp. 56–57.
[6]Ibid., p. 58.

Giovanni Gabrieli (1555–1612) composed antiphonal music for brass instruments combined with one or more choirs and an organ to create exciting effects. Giovanni Gabrieli's *Sacrae Symphoniae* utilized several organs, four choirs of singers, a large group of recorders, and a brass choir.

The other important center of Italian music was Rome, where Giovanni Pierluigi da Palestrina (ca. 1525–1594) was choirmaster at St. Peter's. Complaints stemming from the Reformation about complicated polyphony that made words unintelligible and about the use of "noisy instruments" resulted in a directive from the Council of Trent to correct abuses so that the church could properly be called a house of prayer. Palestrina, therefore, composed music for the church that was in keeping with the purity and simplicity of its earlier music. He was able to achieve this goal while working within the framework of the highly developed style of his predecessors.[7] Tomás Luis de Victoria (ca. 1549–1611) and Orlando di Lasso (1532–1594) were both contemporaries of Palestrina. Victoria represented the Roman School in Spain. Orlando di Lasso, born in Belgium, represented the Flemish School, but spent his formative years in Italy and his later years in Bavaria.

While the primary thrust of Renaissance music was liturgical, there was an increasing demand for secular music, particularly by the many groups of amateur performers, both among the aristrocracy and the upper middle class. One of the marks of the cultivated lady or gentleman of the Renaissance was his or her ability to sing or play an instrument. Madrigals, performed in courtly social gatherings, were quite popular, and had texts that dealt with sentimental and sometimes erotic love.

One of the finest madrigalists was Luca Marenzio (1553–1599), who was born in Coccaglio, Italy. He developed an expressive, polished style that raised the techniques of word painting to the level of sophisticated art.[8] Although the madrigal was an Italian development, it became very popular in England after about 1588, and was often accompanied in performance by either the lute or the harpsichord. The best-known English madrigal composer during the latter part of the sixteenth century was Thomas Morley (1557–1602). The popularity of madrigal singing in England continued into the seventeenth century, and other well-known composers of this genre were William Byrd (1543–1623), Peter Philips (ca. 1561–1628), John Dowland (1562–1626), Francis Pilkington (1562–1638), Thomas Tomkins (ca. 1572–1656), John Wilbye (1574–1688), Thomas Weelkes (ca. 1575–1625), and Orlando Gibbons (1583–1625).

Another important secular form was the *chanson* (French for song). During the fifteenth century, the chanson's character was an expression of dignity and intimacy. Composers of this genre were Johannes Okeghem, Jacob Obrecht, Heinrich Isaac (ca. 1450–1517), Pierre de La Rue (ca. 1430–1518),

---

[7]Ibid., p. 65.
[8]Arthur Jacobs, *Choral Music* (Baltimore: Penguin Books, 1963), p. 48.

and Josquin Després. During the sixteenth century, the chanson was written in the imitative style of the motet; however, it had a quicker rhythm, a more homophonic texture, and phrases in which all the parts ended together. Sixteenth-century chansons have been described as nimble and frivolous. Composers of this era were CLÉMENT JANEQUIN (ca. 1485–1560), CLAUDIN DE SERMISY (ca. 1490–1562), and PIERRE CERTON (1510–1572).[9]

RENAISSANCE CHOIRS

Traditionally, the Church has taken in, sheltered, and educated orphans. As part of their training, some of these children were prepared for participation in the solemn rites and services of their churches. Initially, boys were used to perform ceremonial rather than musical functions—as altar servers, holy water bearers, and so on. In time, however, the more musically talented boys were given intensive music instruction and participated along with men in the performance of church music of the early Renaissance. Schools for the training of choristers had their beginnings as early as the fourth century. These *scholae cantorum* were sometimes called *orphanotropia* in reference to the orphan children that they sheltered and trained. During the early Renaissance, men singing in their falsetto voices were often used to reinforce the boys' voices. As might be expected, problems arose because the boys were sometimes rowdy and because their voices changed too soon after they had been properly trained.[10] Also, during the latter part of the fifteenth century, the range of polyphonic music increased beyond the range that Italian falsettists could readily sing. The Spanish, in the meantime, devised a special system of training the falsetto voice that improved both its quality and range. However, the Spanish refused to share their training secrets with the papal music masters, and thus forced the Italians into a pact that assured them monopolistic control of the falsettist supply.[11]

During the sixteenth century, many Spanish falsettists were exported to Italy, and many were employed in the Papal Choir, where they sang the treble or upper two parts of the motets and masses. It should be understood that the male alto voice is developed from the natural baritone voice, while the soprano falsetto is developed from a naturally high, light tenor voice.[12] Falsettists

---

[9]For a complete list of Renaissance composers, with their dates and places of birth, see Appendix A.

[10]Nan Cooke Carpenter, *Music in the Medieval and Renaissance Universities* (Norman, OK: University of Oklahoma Press, 1958), p. 85.

[11]Sol Landon, "When Singing Was a Monster's Art," *High Fidelity*, Vol. 8, No. 2 (February 1958): 42.

[12]Ronald Stuart Tatnell, "Falsetto Practice: A Brief Survey," *The Consort*, Vol. 22 (Summer 1965): 32.

An early English choir as portrayed in a fourteenth-century woodcut.

eventually supplanted boy singers in the cathedrals.[13] They were exceedingly popular, and the supply could not meet the demand; therefore, in many parish churches it may be assumed that boys continued to sing the treble parts, with only some falsettists reinforcing them in those instances where they were available.[14]

In addition to cathedrals and parish churches, the aristocracy often had its own private chapels, and dukes often spent considerable sums for a choirmaster, a choir of men and boys, and the creative efforts of composers. Additionally, a priest was also generally available for all services.

In the fifteenth century, the number of singers in a choir probably depended to a considerable extent on the size of the music manuscript; scholars do not always agree on precise numbers, except that as time passed choirs gradually became larger. According to Bukofzer, during the early part of the Renaissance, music manuscripts were only large enough for three or four persons to sing from. However, in about the middle of the fifteenth century, manuscripts became larger, and the so-called "giant" choir books that could be

[13]Francis Rogers, "The Male Soprano," *Musical Quarterly*, Vol. 5, No. 3 (July 1919): 413–414.

[14]For further information on the Renaissance falsettists, see Robert L. Garretson, "The Falsettists," *The Choral Journal*, Vol. XXIV, No. 1 (September 1983): 5–9.

Celebration of Mass with full choral accompaniment, 1595. Engraving by Adrian Collaert after a drawing by Johannes Stradarus.

read from a distance by a relatively large group came into existence. The staff lines were from one to two inches apart and the dimensions of the page varied from 20 by 14 inches to 28 by 19 inches.[15] Although these large music books could accommodate more singers, the size of the choirs should not be overestimated. Bukofzer states that the Papal Chapel had only nine singers for polyphonic performances in 1436; however, the number was gradually increased from twelve to sixteen, and finally to twenty-four persons in the second half of the century.[16]

According to Brown, choirs or groups of singers in churches in northern Italy increased in size from about six men in the first part of the fifteenth century to about twenty late in the century. Additionally, he states that there were an undetermined number of choirboys.[17]

References in the diaries of the Sistine Chapel and in the establishment book of the Chapel Royal indicate that the minimum number of singers required for a full choral service in the sixteenth century was from 12 to 16. As

[15]Manfred F. Bukofzer, *Studies in Medieval and Renaissance Music* (New York: W. W. Norton, 1950), p. 181.

[16]Ibid., p. 189.

[17]Howard Mayer Brown, "Choral Music in the Renaissance," *Early Music*, Vol. 6, No. 2 (April 1978): 164.

to the maximum size, this was probably determined by the amount of money the choir owner could afford in supporting it. For example, on special occasions, such as the wedding celebrations of the Medici family in Florence, records indicate that fairly large numbers of singers and instrumentalists were employed. In fifteenth- and sixteenth-century secular music, including madrigals, *chansons,* and *frottolas,* the evidence, primarily paintings of the period, indicates that only a small number of solo performers, and never choirs, were used.[18]

In reflecting on the size of Renaissance church choirs in relationship to the size of their music manuscripts, two other factors should perhaps be considered: (1) the amount of rehearsal time devoted to preparing the music for performance, and (2) the ability of some singers to memorize the music more quickly. Adequate rehearsal time, coupled with astute and capable singers who memorized their music, would have allowed additional singers to be within a good viewing distance of the music manuscript positioned in front of the choir.[19]

Toward the end of the sixteenth century, the Counter-Reformation, through which the Church endeavored to gain back its "lost sheep," gave rise to a greater splendor and magnificence in music, painting, sculpture, and architecture. While falsettists continued to sing the alto parts, *castrati* began to take over the soprano parts. According to one scholar, "While several writers name *castratos* in the Sistine Choir between 1565–98, the first unequivocal reference in the Sistine Diary is the entry for 22 April, 1599."[20] However, in 1589, Pope Sixtus V issued the Bull *Cum pro nostro pastorali munere,* in which he reorganized the Capella Julia, the group of clerics and singers at St. Peter's Basilica. The duties of the choir are detailed as follows:

"12 singers: four basses, four tenors, and four contraltos (i.e., falsettists), and in addition for the voice which is called soprano, four eunuchs, if skilled ones can be found; if not, six boys. These singers, according to the custom of the basilica, shall be present at the whole of the day and night office and at Mass, every day."[21]

To avoid any confusion with the *castrati,* the falsettists at this time were referred to as *"voci naturali."*[22] The church, however, referred to the *castrati*

[18]Thurston Dart, *The Interpretation of Music* (New York: Harper & Row Publishers, 1963), pp. 51–52.

[19]For additional information on the sizes of choirs during the Renaissance in various parts of Europe, see Christopher A. Reynolds's article "Sacred Polyphony" in *Performance Practice: Music Before 1600,* edited by Howard Mayer Brown and Stanley Sadie (New York/London: W. W. Norton, 1989), pp. 187–189.

[20]Anthony Milner, "The Sacred Capons," *The Musical Times,* Vol. 114, No. 1561 (March 1973): 250.

[21]Ibid., 250.

[22]V. E. Negus and Owen Jander, "Falsetto," in *The New Grove Dictionary of Music and Musicians* (London: Macmillan Publishers, 1980, Vol. 6), p. 375.

voices as *sopranisti,* while in the theatre they were called *musico* and *envirato.*

The number of singers in today's choirs may vary considerably, and Renaissance music may be performed by a choir of any size. However, conductors will want to restrain or limit the sound of larger choirs to make it more in keeping with the Renaissance sound.

MUSICAL STYLE AND PERFORMANCE PRACTICE

The following discussion of Renaissance musical style and performance practices focuses on certain basic elements of the music that generally are dealt with in interpretative situations. They include meter and stress, tempo, dynamics, tone quality, pitch, texture, and expressive aspects of the music.

Meter and Stress

Most of the music of the Renaissance period was unmetered, with stress occurring only through the emphasis on particular syllables in important words. The bar line, with its resultant stress on the first beat of the measure, generally was not used during this period. Although the bar line did come into being during the latter part of the period, it was utilized only as a "measure" of elapsed time and as a means of keeping the singers together. When metrical stress is used for music of this period, the inherent beauties and flow of the vocal lines are destroyed. MICHAEL PRAETORIUS (1571–1621) utilized short vertical dashes outside the staff as orientation marks. But even when bar lines did come into use, they were actually orientation marks and did not imply accentual patterns.[23]

Notwithstanding this important difference in metrical stress, editors of many current editions of Renaissance music often insert regularly spaced bar lines, presumably as a guide to the eye, because today's singers are used to them. The problem, however, is that singers are inclined to stress those notes immediately following the bar line. This response should be strictly avoided as it usually distorts the natural syllabic accent of words in the text. The best way to determine the natural emphases in a Renaissance work is by reciting the text aloud until the emphases become clear, and then marking the stressed syllables in one's score.

In Figure 1a, an excerpt from Palestrina's *Missa Papae Marcelli* is shown illustrating the use of the traditional bar lines. The normal syllabic accents occurring on the words "*Ple*-ni sunt *coe*-li et *ter*-ra" are obscured, and the rhythmic counterpoint so necessary to the music does not occur with this manner of barring. Figure 1b, however, is barred according to the natural

[23]Curt Sachs, *Rhythm and Tempo: A Study in Music History* (New York: W. W. Norton, 1953), pp. 257–258.

FIGURE 1 Excerpt from *Missa Papae Marcelli* by Palestrina. (a) illustrates the use of traditional bar lines; (b) is barred according to the natural accent of the text.

accent of the text, thus revealing the beauties of the rhythmic complexity of the music.

Some editors have tried to avoid the unnatural stress of syllables following a bar line by using one of the following means:

1. Editions are published in which bar lines are placed between the staves, as an indication of elapsed time, with the hope of avoiding unnecessary emphases on unaccented syllables. (See Figure 2, an excerpt from "Adoramus Te" by Orlando di Lasso, edited by Robert Hufstader.) To be further helpful, this editor has placed a stroke (−) mark over syllables that are to be stressed.

FIGURE 2 Excerpt from "Adoramus Te" by Orlando di Lasso, edited by Robert Hufstader. Bar lines are placed between staves to indicate elapsed time, and strokes (−) are placed over syllables to be stressed. Copyright © 1946 Mercury Music Corporation. Used by permission of the publisher.

2. Certain other editors use what they call a varia-bar system, in which bar lines are placed immediately before syllables they feel should receive an accent of pressure, i.e., a momentary stretching or slight elongation of a note. (See Figure 3, an excerpt from "Kyrie Eleison" by Tomás Luis de Victoria, edited by James McKelvy.)

3. While some editors choose to include meter changes and regular bar lines immediately before any natural syllabic accents, as illustrated in Figure 1b, still other editors prefer to use dotted rather than solid bar lines before the meter changes to indicate only an accent of pressure or a lesser accent than might occur following a traditional bar line. (See Figure 4, an excerpt from "Ave Maria" by Tomás Luis de Victoria, edited by Max T. Krone.)

FIGURE 3 Excerpt from "Kyrie Eleison" by Tomás Luis de Victoria, edited by James McKelvy. Note use of the varia-bar system, with bar lines placed before those notes to receive an emphasis or accent of pressure. Copyright 1972 by Mark Foster Music Company. Used by permission.

FIGURE 4 Excerpt from "Ave Maria" by Tomás Luis de Victoria, edited by Max T. Krone. Note use of dotted lines before meter changes to indicate an accent of pressure. Copyright © 1933 Warner Bros. Inc. (renewed). All rights reserved. Used by permission.

As to notation, it was common practice for composers to uniformly give a short note to a short syllable and one twice its length to a long syllable.[24] And, as Thomas Morley stated, "We must also have a care so to applie the notes to the wordes as in singing there be no barbarisme committed; that is, that we cause no syllable that is by nature short, to be expressed by many notes, or one long note, nor so long a syllable to be expressed with a short note."[25] The practice of giving twice the time value to long as to short syllables resulted in music with irregular and constantly shifting accents.[26] Perhaps the best illustration of this is Le Jeune's "Revecy venir du printans" ("Here Comes Springtime Once Again"), in which the metrical pattern shifts between 6/4 and 3/2 time (a rhythm known as *hemiola*), which was a favorite rhythm of composers of *chansons* up until the end of the Baroque period (see Figure 5).[27] Obviously, not all editions will be edited with the meter signatures and stress marks as illustrated in Figure 5. Therefore, conductors will necessarily have to study and analyze their scores carefully.

The conductor should always be alert to the tendency of singers to stress certain figures or rhythmic groupings in a manner that is inimical to their proper interpretation. For example, in the motet *Cantantibus Organis* by Marenzio (Pustet, No. B32), there often exists a tendency for some singers to stress, in a somewhat mechanical manner, the first and third of each group of four eighth notes (Figure 6). This practice should be avoided, as stress should occur only through the natural accent of particular syllables in important words. The sacred music of this period, in particular, should be performed in a smooth, flowing manner, and phrases should be thought of in terms of long ascending and descending lines.

The conductor should remind singers always to think melodically and never chordally, except when tuning various intervals, and to avoid the regular recurring accents common to barred music. To help achieve the correct syllabic stress, singers should be asked to read the text aloud with accents in the correct place and in accordance with the rise and fall of the various vocal lines. The conductor should utilize the *tactus*, or downward and upward movement of the hand and arm, to minimize any tendency toward metrical stress and to allow for the interplay of rhythmic polyphony. Each *tactus* has two beats in opposite directions: up–down or down–up (usually the latter is employed), each one at a tempo ranging between M.M. = 60–80. This tempo was related to the normal human heartbeat during quiet respiration or leisurely walking stride; thus the tempo of Renaissance music remained relatively steady. Both tactus

---

[24] Ibid., p. 250.

[25] Thomas Morley, A *Plaine and Easie Introduction to Practical Musicke*, 1597, edited by R. A. Harmon (New York: W. W. Norton, 1953).

[26] See, for example, Le Jeune's "O rôze, reyne des fleurs" ("O rose, queen of flowers") and "D'une coline" ("As I walk upon a hill").

[27] Arthur Jacobs, ed., *Choral Music* (Baltimore: Penguin Books, 1966), pp. 46–47.

FIGURE 5 This excerpt from "Revecy venir du printans" by Claude Le Jeune illustrates the alteration of stressed (−) and unstressed (˘) syllables.

movements were made with equal force whether it was conceived as down−up or up−down.[28] Tactus, which means literally touching or beating, is not concerned with the actual rhythm, i.e., with grouping or accent. It maintains the even pulsation of units, and nothing else.[29]

Tempo

The tempo of Renaissance music is determined largely by the syllabic setting of the text and the mood of the music. When one syllable is set to a melodic figure (*melisma*), the tempo should be restrained so that the inherent

[28]Sachs, *Rhythm and Tempo*, p. 219.
[29]Ibid., p. 242.

FIGURE 6   Excerpt from the serie *Cantantibus Organis*, madrigal by Luca Marenzio, edited by E. Kraus. Mechanical stress should be avoided in the eighth-note groupings in measures 2, 3, and 4, and the music should be performed in a smooth, flowing manner. Used by permission of Otto Heinrich Noetzel Verlag, Wilhelmshaven, Germany.

beauty of the vocal line may be revealed. On the other hand, when each syllable is set to a different note, of a comparatively longer duration, the tempo may be pushed slightly forward.

Careful analysis of the spiritual and poetic content of the text will help the conductor to determine a suitable tempo. Also, the overall complexities in a score should be carefully considered. Complex music necessitates a somewhat slower tempo than simple, straightforward music, so that all the intricacies in the score may be given ample attention and treatment.

The tempo should remain relatively steady throughout the composition, or at least throughout a particular section. Any change in tempo should result only through a contrasting change in the mood of the text and a resultant change in the musical texture. Changes in tempo within a given section should be extremely gradual and subtle, lest the symmetry of the music be destroyed.

Rallentando, as we know it today, did not exist in the music of the Renaissance period. Composers of the period were, however, aware of this effect, and when it was felt desirable they made it a part of the music itself. That is, they achieved the effect by simply broadening or lengthening the musical notation. Therefore, conductors should avoid the deliberate use of *rallentando*, as this would only distort the musical interpretation.[30] See, for example, the ending of Jacob Arcadelt's madrigal, "Il bianco e dolce cigno" (Figure 7).

FIGURE 7 Excerpt from Jacob Arcadelt's "Il bianco e dolce cigno," in which a *ritardando* is "built into" the ending.

A somewhat greater freedom, however, may be said to exist in the performance of madrigals and related genres than with the masses and motets of the Renaissance period. Madrigal composers were captivated by the expressive qualities of the words. The mood of the text, therefore, is an essential determining factor in the selection of the correct tempo (and the proper dynamics). Restraint and avoidance of extremes, however, should always be paramount in the conductor's mind.

The conductor should remember that the English madrigal is essentially chamber music, and that it was sung by a relatively small group in a social setting. Therefore, modern performances should show intimacy and restraint.

Dynamics

Selection of the proper dynamic levels is most important to an effective musical interpretation. According to Dorian, in Renaissance music, "dynamics must be analogous to the text, must deepen the content of the underlying

[30]*Cf.* Sachs, *Rhythm and Tempo*, pp. 218–219.

affection—a law from which very fine dynamic shadings of the performance may be deduced."[31]

The dynamics of the music of this period is related to and is dependent upon any changes of mood in the text. Changes in dynamics would occur only as with changes in tempo—that is, with a contrasting mood between sections of the music. Within the overall framework of the music, however, dynamic levels should be moderate; extremes should seldom occur. Owing to the high degree of consonance, the pervading imitation, the lack of harmonic complexity, and the restraints inherent in the style, a climax seldom occurred and was not even sought by composers of the period.[32]

Through the use of the "seamless" technique, there was an overlapping or dovetailing of cadences; that is, one phrase ended in two or more of the parts, while another began in the other parts. Through this technique many cadences were minimized, thus lessening the necessity for dynamic changes. It should be added, however, that dynamics, especially in the madrigal, *frottola,* and *canto carnascialesco,* may be realized simply through the natural *tessitura* of the voices, as well as in the intensity of the word symbolism.

Tone Quality

Choral directors generally believe in the performance of music in an authentic style and use the term "tonal ideal" in reference to the tone appropriate to a given style of music, as well as that utilized during a particular historical period. Singing in the early church was limited to the voices of men and boys. During the early part of the Renaissance period, men singing in their falsetto voices often were used to reinforce the boys' voices, and sang the treble or upper two voice parts. Today, these voices are called *countertenors.* An excellent example of their use and of how these voices might have sounded during the Renaissance is demonstrated by the King's Singers (see the Schwann Record Catalog for a listing of their available recordings). Since choral conductors are concerned with authentic performance practices, and choirs today use women on the treble parts (rather than falsettists), the tone quality should be light and clear, with a minimum of vibrato—if any is used at all. Perhaps the best model of mixed voices performing Renaissance motets was the Roger Wagner Chorale in their album "Echoes from a 16th Century Cathedral" (Angel S-36013). While this long-playing record is no longer on the market, it may be located in some university or community music libraries. The Tallis Scholars, Peter Phillips, Conductor, has recorded a number of albums of Renaissance choral music, and the Schwann Catalog, Artist Issue, 17th edition (1991–92) indicates that eleven CD's (compact discs) are currently available.

[31]Frederick Dorian, *The History of Music in Performance* (New York: W. W. Norton, 1942), p. 40.

[32]*Cf.* Robert Stevenson, *Music Before the Classic Era* (London: Macmillan & Co. Ltd., 1955), p. 42.

There seems to be general but perhaps not total agreement among scholars on the tonal quality to be achieved, as the following quoted statements will reveal:

"Polyphonic music should be sung with a light, clear voice. To sing with a vibrato would destroy the clarity of the various vocal lines and reduce the effectiveness of the performance."[33]

"In recent decades many choirs which specialize in Renaissance music seem to be developing a rather light sound, produced far forward in the mask and with little or no vibrato. That sort of sound produces to many ears the best results—a clear texture in which all of the polyphonic strands are clearly audible—but the justifications for such a solution are empirical rather than historical."[34]

"Tone quality should not be approached mechanistically, but should result from an understanding of the overall musical style, texture, and intent of the music. Approached in this manner Renaissance music will be sung with a lighter, straighter tone, but not one that is stark and totally vibratoless."[35]

"Vibrato needed to be controlled and was considered relatively unimportant in the early motets (1350) and the madrigal, and frottola."[36]

"Avoid a flat or straight tone at the one extreme and the 19th century operatic style on the other. The voices should be vibrant, but under control."[37]

"Importance of a clear, natural and unforced tone with clarity of diction was the ideal."[38]

"The high, clear sound associated with the male falsetto continued to grow in popularity and during the last half of the 16th century some boys were replaced by adult singers who had undergone the 'secret' training in Spain."[39]

Van Eyck's famous painting *Adoration of the Lamb* shows young singers with strained facial expressions. This painting has led some observers to assume that the singers performed with a nasal quality.[40] Such an assumption is not warranted, especially when one realizes that the painting is not a photograph but a representation based on an artist's perception. Van Eyck might just as well have recalled the faces of boys playing in the street as of them singing in

[33]Peter Phillips, "Performance Practice in 16th Century English Choral Music," *Early Music,* Vol. 6, No. 2 (April 1978): 195–199.

[34]Brown, "Choral Music": 167.

[35]William H. Bartells, "Problems of Choral Interpretation and Technique," *The Choral Journal,* Vol. 13, No. 1 (September 1972): 19–21.

[36]Andrea Von Ramm, "Style in Early Music Singing," *Early Music,* Vol. 8, No. 1 (January 1980): 17.

[37]Fausto Razzi, "Polyphony of the Seconda prattica: Performance Practice in Early Italian Vocal Music of the Mannerist Era," *Early Music,* Vol. 8, No. 3 (July 1980): 303.

[38]N. Joel Kramme, "Notes on Renaissance Performance Practice," *American Choral Review,* Vol. XIX, No. 3 (July 1971): 10.

[39]Ibid., 11.

[40]See, for example, Dart, *The Interpretation of Music,* p. 50.

church. An artist's objective, above all, is to make the painting intriguing to the observer.

Now, while there is a strong preponderance of opinion that advocates a light, clear tone with a minimum of vibrato, there are bound to be contrary opinions, as the following statement would indicate:

> The traditional mellow tone is not the only sound a boy can make . . . many of us remember recordings of Palestrina's "Tu es Petrus" sung by a continental choir with voices that revelled in the lines in an almost operatic way and that were not afraid of all things—vibrato! The boys' tone that goes with this style is certainly a full-blooded sound, harsh, even to English ears attuned to our traditional sound.[41]

Pitch

During the Renaissance the only pitch reference available was from church organs, and their pitches varied considerably from church to church and from country to country.[42] Praetorius describes two types of pitches in use during the sixteenth century—choir pitch, which was in use in most churches, and chamber pitch. Choir pitch was said to be a whole tone lower than chamber pitch (hence the low pitch of old church organs). In the sixteenth to seventeenth centuries, pitch seems to have been very high in Germany, as appears from the pitch of old organs, which are about a whole tone higher than our chamber pitch.[43]

Praetorius stated in his *Syntagma Musicum* in 1619, "In former times, choir pitch was originally one tone lower and deeper than now, as can be observed in old organs and other wind instruments. And then it was raised, year after year, to the point at which it now stands in Italy and England, as well as the princely courts of Germany."[44]

According to Bowers, however, no element in the notation of fifteenth-century vocal music represented any attempt to convey to the performers an exact point of reference from which to deduce the intended sounding pitch and no fixed relationship between source pitch and modern performing pitches can be postulated.[45] Also, Kinkeldey states "there was no standard pitch in the

---

[41]Alan Luff, "The Authentic Sound," *The Musical Times*, Vol. CX, No. 15 (March 1969): 308.

[42]The tuning fork was invented by John Shore in 1711 and was improved by Rudolph Konig in about 1850.

[43]Arthur Mendel, "Pitch in the 16th and Early 17th Centuries—Part I," *Musical Quarterly*, Vol. 34, No. 1 (January 1948): 28.

[44]Arthur Mendel, "Pitch in the 16th and Early 17th Centuries—Part II," *Musical Quarterly*, Vol. 34, No. 2 (April 1948): 199–221.

[45]Roger Bowers, "The Performing Pitch of English 15th Century Polyphony," *Early Music*, Vol. 8, No. 1 (January 1980): 27.

Renaissance. Choirmasters took a higher or lower pitch, within wide limits, to suit the convenience of their choirs."[46]

While the papal choir performed in the Sistine Chapel, they sang without any instrumental accompaniment; thus there was no way of instruments giving the pitch to the choir. According to Arthur Mendel and others, for music performed during the Renaissance era, "the pitch level was left entirely to the discretion of the performers and had nothing to do with notated pitch."[47] "References in the *Diarii Sistini* of the early 18th century . . . show that the word 'intonare' is to be read in its usual sense. All pieces, whether chant or polyphony apparently began with an intonation, that is, the senior bass intoned the beginning of the chant (although sometimes the chant was intoned by sopranos or contraltos), and the senior singer of whichever part began the polyphony sang the first few notes as a means of giving the pitch (rather than humming or singing a single note as might be done today); this was followed by a new start from the beginning by the whole choir for chant or by all the singers of the appropriate part for polyphony."[48] "The senior singers would be experienced enough to know what a comfortable pitch level was, although . . . sometimes they erred and chose a pitch level that was not practicable. At that point . . . they were supposed to stop, tell the choir they were beginning the intonation again, and start on a different pitch."[49]

In summary, therefore, a conductor should feel free to choose a pitch that is comfortable for the singers and that also achieves the desired musical effect.

Texture

The music of the Renaissance was primarily contrapuntal in texture; that is, the various vocal lines were conceived as horizontal in nature. Composers wrote using anywhere from three to six or more parts. Upon first examining music of the period, one might feel that some compositions or portions of others were conceived harmonically rather than contrapuntally. Upon careful examination, however, one will often discover, for example, that the third in a particular part may be omitted in an effort to achieve the best movement in the various vocal lines.[50]

Imitation as a contrapuntal device was used by composers from Dufay throughout the remainder of the period. The term "point of imitation" pertains to the introduction of a figure or motive in one part, which is taken up

---

[46]Otto Kinkeldey, "Equal Voices in the A Cappella Period," in *Essays in Honor of Archibald T. Davison* (Cambridge, MA: Harvard University Press, 1957), pp. 101–109.

[47]Kenneth Kreitner, "Very Low Ranges in the Sacred Music of Ockeghem and Tinctoris," *Early Music*, Vol. 14, No. 4 (November 1986): 467.

[48]Richard Sherr, "Performance Practice in the Papal Chapel in the 16th Century," *Early Music*, Vol. 15, No. 4 (November 1987): 454–455.

[49]Ibid., 455.

[50]See, for example, Jeppesen, *The Style of Palestrina*, p. 92.

successively in the other parts. These points of imitation should be emphasized slightly. The entrances need to be definite and precise, but vigorous accents are out of place and should be avoided. These entering parts should be brought out slightly, but should never overshadow the other contrapuntal lines. As other parts enter, they should then recede into the background.

Renaissance polyphony was not always performed as written, but was usually made "ornate" through the use of florid embellishments. From the beginning of the sixteenth century, manuals were available that included information on the technique of improvising embellishments. The first such manual was the *Opera intitulata Fontegara* by Sylvestro di Ganassi, published in Venice in 1535. Through considerable practice, performers developed a vocabulary of melodic patterns that could be used between the melodic intervals of a given composition. When, for example, the performer observed a particular interval, he could use one of these figures instead of the simple interval skip.[51] It has been suggested that instruction on embellishments be included in courses on Renaissance music. However, a performance without ornamentation would not be considered incorrect, especially when more than one singer is on one part, as is the case with today's choruses.[52]

Expressive Aspects

The sacred music of the Renaissance period sounds remote and restrained, primarily because of the large degree of consonance. There was a wide use of unisons, thirds, fifths, sixths, octaves, and triad sounds. Dissonance of the unprepared variety was used sparingly and was considered something "vehement and violent." Therefore, the objective was to conceal or muffle it insofar as was possible.[53]

Renaissance music possesses very subtle points of harmonic arrival. As previously mentioned, with the "seamless" technique there existed an overlapping or dovetailing of phrases; that is, one phrase ended in two or more parts, while another began in the other parts. Through this technique many cadences were somewhat obscured and the tension of the cadence was minimized. The conductor should search out all the suspensions in Renaissance music, mark them in the score, and have the chorus "lean" on them ever so slightly during performance.

The masses and motets of the Renaissance are impersonal in nature and should be performed with an atmosphere of quiet reflection and sincerity of feeling—in other words, as a prayer to God, and not as a concert. The tone quality, therefore, should be kept light. Heavy dramatic quality and excessive

---

[51]Imogene Horsley, "Improvised Embellishment in the Performance of Renaissance Music," *Journal of the American Musicological Society*, Vol. IV, No. 1 (Spring 1951): 3–4.

[52]Ibid., 7–15.

[53]Jeppesen, *The Style of Palestrina*, p. 108.

vibrato in the voices are inimical to the expressive character of the music; both should be eliminated.

As previously mentioned, Renaissance music, when performed correctly, sounds remote and restrained. The resonance in the church or hall in which it was originally performed contributed substantially to this effect. The impersonal quality of Renaissance sacred music is comparable to the detachment that may be observed in certain paintings of the period.[54]

A somewhat greater freedom existed with the madrigals and related secular styles of the period. Composers were well aware of the expressive qualities of the text, and often employed word painting in their music. That is, they used the music to portray, in a variety of ways, the character of certain words. For example, leaps in the melody were often used to depict joy, while the voices might ascend on such words as "heaven" and descend on words such as "earth." To depict grief and sadness, a diminished or augmented triad was often used, and dissonance was employed to represent such words as "sadness" and "pain."

The conductor should study the score and identify the various word-painting devices employed by the composer and, for an effective performance, the singers must be led to an understanding of them. The music must be sung with an emotional expressiveness that can result only through proper understanding of it. Secular music of the period, although light in texture, should never be sung in an insipid manner. The rhythmic interplay among the voices should be emphasized somewhat, and the text articulated in a crisp manner, especially in English secular music. While a firmness of approach is necessary to performance, the inherent emotion in the music should not be allowed to run rampant; rather, the music should be performed with a certain degree of restraint.[55]

MUSIC AND THE RELATED ARTS

All of the arts reflect the culture of which they are an outgrowth. Therefore, it behooves choral conductors to be reasonably knowledgeable about all the arts. Thus they will be in a position to relate information to their singers about the general cultural life that existed during any given period, but particularly during the life of the composer whose music is being studied. Also, concepts of musical performance may be strengthened by an understanding of parallel art forms. Paintings of the masters provide ample opportunities for such comparisons.

In Renaissance music the dynamics are quite restrained; colors in early Italian Renaissance style were likewise restrained, with pastels and a liberal use of gold. As to line and shape, paintings were contained and orderly, balanced

---

[54]See, for example, Raphael's painting *The Niccolini-Cowper Madonna*, on page 29.

[55]For a further discussion on the interpretation of madrigals, see Charles Kennedy Scott, *Madrigal Singing* (London: Oxford University Press, 1931).

Enguerrand Quarton, *The Lamentation of Christ, with a Donor*, known as the *Pietà of Villeneuve-lès-Avignon*. Wood, 64¼ × 86¼ in. From the Church at Villeneuve-lès-Avignon. Given to the Louvre in 1905 by Les Amis du Louvre.

and symmetrical, generally restful, with clarity of definition and minimal tension. Later Renaissance paintings displayed similar characteristics; however, the themes or subject matter were more evenly balanced between sacred and secular subjects. There was more celebration of the sensual world, and paintings were more realistic.

The Lamentation of Christ, known as the *Pietà of Villeneuve-lès-Avignon,* is considered one of the finest examples of art during the waning Middle Ages and early Renaissance. This masterwork is by the noted painter Enguerrand Quarton, who was born in Laon about 1410. He became an established artist by 1447 at Avignon and was active in Provence from 1444 to 1466. In the painting, the figures are grouped with a rounded contour that is both delicate and massive. The painting assumes an almost secular form—"that of a Lady mourning the Champion dying on her lap—with its overtones of courtly love."[56] *The Lamentation* reflects an agony with a rare restraint and a simplicity of sorrow.

[56]Laurence Gowing, *Paintings in the Louvre* (New York: Stewart, Tabori & Chang, Inc., 1987), p. 72.

Leonardo da Vinci, *The Madonna of the Rocks*, ca. 1485. Panel, 75 × 43½ in. The Louvre, Paris.

Leonardo da Vinci's *Madonna of the Rocks* (ca. 1485) "creates a remote, dreamlike quality and makes the picture seem a poetic vision rather than an image of reality pure and simple . . . the infant St. John adoring the Infant Christ in the presence of the Virgin and an angel—is mysterious in many ways . . . few pictures cast a more enduring spell."[57]

[57]H. W. Janson, *History of Art* (Englewood Cliffs, N.J.: Prentice Hall, 1972), p. 349.

Jacopo Bellini, *The Virgin and Child Adored by Leonello d'Este*. Wood, 23½ × 15½ in. The Louvre, Paris.

The Virgin and Child Adored by Leonello d'Este by Jacopo Bellini has been on display in the Louvre since 1873. Bellini was active as an artist in Florence in 1423 and Venice in 1470. Note in the painting the soft formal beauty expressed in the face of the Madonna.

The *Niccolini-Cowper Madonna* by Raphael (1483–1520), signed and dated 1508, is on display in the National Gallery in Washington, D.C. Its simple composition made it a model for early sixteenth-century Florentine painters. Note in the painting the soft formal beauty expressed in the face of the Madonna. Also, note that the Madonna is not caressing her child, but is

Raphael, *The Niccolini-Cowper Madonna*, 1508. Oil on wood, 32¾ × 22⅝ in. National Gallery of Art, Washington, D.C.

maintaining a distance between Him and herself. This painting belonged to the Niccolini family of Florence and is reputed to have once been in the possession of Lord Cowper, hence the name.

EPILOGUE

Changes from one stylistic period to another occur gradually, and the seeds of one style or movement are sown in the preceding period. At this point it is important to consider the Reformation and the effect it had upon the entirety of Europe. It has been called a turning point in history.

An important event relating to the Protestant Reformation was a decision around 1500 by the Church in Rome to build a new basilica, St. Peter's, an architectural monument that exists today. To help finance this large undertaking, church officials were authorized to collect fees in exchange for the granting of indulgences, or remissions of the punishments due for sins committed. This was a multinational effort, with Catholic communities all over the world participating. Martin Luther was much opposed to this practice and felt it was a manifestation of corruption, and that the church hierarchy had exceeded its authority in interpreting the Bible.[58]

It is known that the Renaissance did foster some religious skepticism, and perhaps motivated some churchmen to criticize the administration of the Roman Catholic Church and some of its lax practices. Martin Luther (1483–1546) became the leader of the Reformation in Germany. In 1517 Luther wrote his Ninety-Five Theses against indulgences and, according to legend, nailed them to the door of the church in Wittenberg.[59] Luther rejected the authority of the Pope and substituted the Bible as the sole source of Christian truth. Other scholars who helped to spread the Reformation were Philipp Melanchthon, Luther's colleague at the University of Wittenberg, Johann Reuchlin of Heidelberg, who fostered the study of Hebrew and Greek, thus enabling people to read the Bible in its original form, and Johann Tauler of Strasbourg. Reformers in other countries were Erasmus in Holland, Lefèvre d'Étaples in France, Zwingli in Switzerland, John Colet in England, John Calvin, who made Geneva the world center of the Presbyterian Church, and John Knox in Scotland.

Luther was successful in his attempt to break with the established church partly because Johannes Gutenberg had invented printing with movable type around the middle of the fifteenth century and had begun to print bibles around 1458. Without printed bibles, Luther's argument for individual interpretation

---

[58] Andy Larkin, *Varieties of Economic Experiences,* unpublished manuscript (St. Cloud, MN: St. Cloud State University, 1989), pp. 4–18.

[59] There is no hard evidence that Luther actually nailed his Ninety-Five Theses to the door of the church in Wittenberg.

of the Bible would have been invalid, as before that time there were only enough bibles for the church leaders and not enough for the common man.[60]

A number of wars broke out as one unfortunate result of the Reformation; however, peace treaties followed each of the conflicts. The most important treaty was the Peace of Augsburg in 1555, which granted the ruler of each German state the right to choose Catholicism or Lutheranism. The Lutheran faith soon spread to northern Germany and to Scandinavia. A generation later, John Calvin led a movement that spread Protestantism to France and Holland, and John Knox brought Presbyterianism to Scotland. The English Reformation began when King Henry VIII broke relations with the Pope and declared himself supreme head of the Church of England.

It took some time for the Roman Catholic Church to react to the Reformation; however, action was finally taken. From 1545 to 1563 the Council of Trent issued decrees to correct known abuses and to reaffirm ancient traditions. This movement has been called the Catholic Counter-Reformation. As part of this movement there was a strong effort to regain the "lost sheep" who had strayed from the Church, and various means were utilized for this purpose; perhaps the most notable was the use of the arts, including music, painting, architecture, and design, to attract people back to the Catholic Church. From this effort rose the spirit of the Baroque.

REFERENCES

Bartels, Williams H. "Problems of Choral Interpretation and Technique." *The Choral Journal*, Vol. 13, No. 1, September 1972, pp. 19–21.

Bastian, James. "The Cappella Musicale at San Marco in the Late Sixteenth Century." *American Choral Review*, Vol. XII, No. 1, January 1970, pp. 3–14.

Beckmann-Collier, Aimee. "Performance Practices of Sacred Polyphony in Rome and Madrid at the Time of Tomás Luis de Victoria." *Choral Journal*, Vol. XXVIII, No. 7, February 1988, pp. 13–20.

Biggs, John. "Some Information and Ideas About Contemporary Performance of Early Music." *The Choral Journal*, Vol. XIV, No. 3, November 1973, pp. 8–15.

Bixler, Martha. "An Interpretation to Renaissance Ornamentation." *The American Recorder*, Vol. VIII, No. 4, 1967, pp. 107–109, and Volume IX, No. 4, 1968, pp. 108–112.

Blackburn, Bonnie J. "On Compositional Process In The Fifteenth Century." *Journal of the American Musicological Society*, Vol. XL, No. 2, Summer 1987, pp. 210–284.

Bowers, Roger. "The Performing Pitch of English 15th-Century Church Polyphony." *Early Music*, Vol. 8, No. 1, January 1980, pp. 21–28.

Brown, Earle. "The Notation and Performance of New Music." *The Musical Quarterly*, Vol. LXXII, No. 2, 1986, pp. 180–201.

Brown, Howard Mayer. "Choral Music in the Renaissance." *Early Music*, Vol. 6, No. 2, April 1978, pp. 164–169.

———. *Embellishing Sixteenth Century Polyphonic Music*. London: Oxford University Press, 1977.

———. "Embellishment in Early Sixteenth-Century Italian Intabulations." *Proceedings of the Royal Music Association*, Vol. 100, 1973–74, pp. 49–83.

[60]Larkin, *Varieties of Economic Experiences*, pp. 4–19.

———. "Guillaume Dufay and the Early Renaissance." *Early Music*, Vol. 2, No. 4, October 1974, pp. 219–233.

———. "On the Performance Of Fifteenth-Century Chansons." *Early Music*, Vol. 1, No. 1, January 1973, pp. 3–10.

———. "Performing Practice," in *Grove's Dictionary of Music and Musicians*, 5th ed., Eric Blom, Editor. London: Macmillan & Co., Ltd., 1954, p. 378.

Brown, Howard Mayer, and Stanley Sadie, eds. *Performance Practice: Music Before 1600*. New York: W. W. Norton & Company, 1990.

Bryant, James R. "Musica Ficta in Renaissance Choral Music." *The Choral Journal*, Vol. XVIV, No. 2, October 1978, pp. 20–25.

Bukofzer, Manfred F. "On the Performance of Renaissance Music." MTNA Proceedings for 1941 (Music Teachers National Association, Pittsburgh, 1942).

———. *Studies in Medieval and Renaissance Music*. New York: W. W. Norton, 1950, p. 181.

Carapetyan, Armen. "Some Remarks on Current Performance of Early Music." *Musica Disciplina*, Vol. XXV, 1971, pp. 5–16.

Carey, Frank. "Composition for Equal Voices in the Sixteenth Century." *The Journal of Musicology*, Vol. IX, No. 3, Summer 1991, pp. 300–342.

Carpenter, Nan Cooke. *Music in the Medieval and Renaissance Universities*. Norman, OK: University of Oklahoma Press, 1958.

Carter, Tim. "Music-Selling In Late Sixteenth Century Florence: The Bookshop of Piero Di Giuliano Morosi." *Music and Letters*, Vol. LXXVI, No. 4, November 1989, pp. 483–504.

Collins, Michael B. "The Performance of Sesquialtera and Hemiola in the 16th Century." *Journal of the American Musicological Society*, Vol. XVII, No. 1, Spring 1964, pp. 5–28.

Cooper, Timothy G. "Two Neglected Aspects of Renaissance Motet Performance Practice." *Choral Journal*, Vol. XXVII, No. 4, November 1986, pp. 9–12.

Crawford, David. "A Chant Manual In Sixteenth-Century Italy." *Musica Disciplina*, Vol. XXXVI, 1982, pp. 175–190.

Cummings, Anthony M. "Towards An Interpretation of the Sixteenth-Century Motet." *Journal of the American Musicological Society*, Vol. XXXIV, No. 1, Spring 1981, pp. 43–59.

Dart, Thurston. "How They Sang in Jena in 1598." *Musical Times*, Vol. 108, No. 1490, April 1967, pp. 316–317.

———. *The Interpretation of Music*. New York: Harper & Row, 1953.

Day, Thomas. "The Organ and Choral Music of the Renaissance." *Diapason*, Vol. LXIX, No. 1, December 1977, p. 1.

Dean, Jeffrey J. *The Scribes of the Sistine Chapel, 1501–1527*. Ph.D. dissertation, The University of Chicago, 1984.

Dixon, Graham. "G. F. Anerio (1567–1630) and the Roman School." *The Musical Times*, Vol. 121, No. 1648, June 1980, pp. 366–367.

———. "The Cappella of S. Maria In Trastevere (1605–45): An Archival Study." *Music and Letters*, Vol. 62, No. 1, January 1981, pp. 30–40.

Dolmetsch, Carl. "Interpretation." *The Consort*, No. 5, 1948, pp. 7–12.

Dolmetsch, Cecile. "Ornamentation in Singing." *The Consort*, No. 9, 1952, pp. 21–23.

Dorhout, Albert. "Out of the Past: A Conversation with Four Renaissance Composers." *American Music Teacher*, Vol. 31, No. 1, September–October 1981, pp. 29–31.

Dorian, Frederick. *The History of Music in Performance*. New York: W. W. Norton, 1942.

———. *The History of Music in Performance: The Art of Musical Interpretation from the Renaissance to Our Day*. Westport, CT: Greenwood Press, 1981.

Edwards, Warwick, A. "The Performance of Ensemble Music in Elizabethan England." *Royal Music Association* (Proceedings, 1970–1971), Vol. 97, pp. 113–123.

Einstein, Alfred. *The Italian Madrigal*. Translated by Alexander H. Krappe, Roger H. Sessions, and Oliver Strunk. 3 vols. Princeton, NJ: Princeton University Press, 1971.

Elias, Cathy Ann. "Musical Performance in 16th Century Italian Literature: Straparola's Le Piacevole Notti." *Early Music*, Vol. 18, No. 2, May 1989, pp. 161–173.

Fellowes, Edmund, H. *The English Madrigal*. London: Oxford University Press, 1925.

Fenlon, Iain. *The Renaissance*. Englewood Cliffs, NJ: Prentice Hall, 1990.

Fenlon, Iain (ed). *The Renaissance: From the 1470's to the End of the 16th Century*. Basingstoke, England: Macmillan, 1989.

Fenlon, Iain, and James Haar. *The Italian Madrigal in the Early Sixteenth Century: Sources and Interpretation*. New York: Cambridge University Press, 1988.

Ferand, Ernest T. "Improvised Vocal Counterpoint in the Late Renaissance and Early Baroque." *Annales Musicologiques*, Vol. IV, 1956, pp. 129–174.

Fischer, Gary. "Renaissance Vocal Technique for the Choral Conductor." *Choral Journal*, Vol. XXIX, No. 1, August 1989, pp. 15–23.

Flood, Gordon. "Extemporaneous Ornamentation of Renaissance Polyphonic Music." *Choral Journal*, Vol. XII, No. 6, February 1972, pp. 12–18.

Forester, Donald W. "Conducting Practice in the Spanish Polyphonic Choral Tradition." *Choral Journal*, Vol. XV, No. 2, October 1974, pp. 7–8.

Garretson, Robert L. "The Falsettists." *The Choral Journal*, Vol. XXIV, No. 1, September 1983, pp. 5–9.

Godt, Irving. "The Motets in the Josquin Edition—A Contribution to Performance." *American Choral Review*, Vol. XVII, No. 1, January 1946, pp. 17–20.

Grout, Ronald J. "On Historical Authenticity in the Performance of Old Music," in *Essays on Music in Honor of Archibald T. Davison*. Cambridge, MA: Harvard University Press, 1957.

Haar, James. *Essays on Italian Poetry and Music in the Renaissance*. Berkeley and Los Angeles: University of California Press, 1986.

Haberlen, John B. "Microrhythms: The Key to Vitalizing Renaissance Music." *The Choral Journal*, Vol. XIII, No. 3, November 1972, pp. 11–14.

Haggh, Barbara. "Itinerary to Residency: Professional Careers and Performance Practices in 15th Century Sacred Music." *Early Music*, Vol. 17, No. 3, August 1989, pp. 359–366.

Hamburger, Paul. "The Ornamentation in the Works of Palestrina." *Acta Musicologica*, Vol. XXII, 1950, pp. 128–147.

Harding, Rosamond E. M. *Origins of Musical Time and Expression*. London: Oxford University Press, 1938.

Hickman, Joe. "Performance Practice in the Anthems of Orlando Gibbons." *The Choral Journal*, Vol. XXII, No. 9, May 1982, pp. 5–7.

Horsley, Imogene. "Improvised Embellishment in the Performance of Renaissance Music." *Journal of the American Musicological Society*, Vol. IV, No. 1, Spring 1951, pp. 3–19.

Igoe, James Thomas. *Performance Practices in the Polyphonic Mass of the Early Fifteenth Century*. Ph.D. dissertation, University of North Carolina, 1971, p. 169.

Jackson, Roland. *Performance Practice, Medieval to Contemporary: A Bibliographic Guide*. New York: Garland Publishing, 1988.

Jacobs, Arthur. *Choral Music*. Baltimore: Penguin Books, 1963.

Jeppesen, Knud. *The Style of Palestrina and the Dissonance*, 2nd ed. Copenhagen: Ejnar Munksgaard, Publishers, and New York: Oxford University Press, Inc. 1946.

Kenyon, Nicholas, ed. *Authenticity and Early Music: A Symposium*. New York: Oxford University Press, 1989.

Kinkeldey, Otto. "Equal Voices in the A Cappella Period," in *Essays in Honor of Archibald T. Davison*. Cambridge, MA: Harvard University Press, 1957, pp. 107–109.

Kirby, F. E. "Herman Finck on Methods of Performance." *Music and Letters*, Vol. XLII, July 1961, pp. 212–220.

Kite-Powell, Jeffery T., ed. *A Practical Guide to Historical Performance: the Renaissance*. New York: Early Music Press, 1989.

Kohn, Karl. "The Renotation of Polyphonic Music." *The Musical Quarterly*, Vol. LXVII, No. 1, January 1981, pp. 29–49.

Kramme, Joel. "Notes on Renaissance Performance Practice." *American Choral Review*, Vol. XIX, No. 3, July 1977, pp. 7–12.

Kreitner, Kenneth. "Very Low Ranges in the Sacred Music of Ockeghem and Tinctoris." *Early Music*, Vol. 14, No. 4, November 1986, pp. 467–479.

Landon, Sol. "When Singing Was a Monster's Art." *High Fidelity*, Vol. 8, No. 2, February 1958, pp. 41–44, p. 124.

Larkin, Andy. *Varieties of Economic Experience.* Unpublished manuscript. St. Cloud, MN: St. Cloud State University, 1989.

Lionnet, Jean. "Performance Practice in the Papal Chapel During the 17th Century." *Early Music,* Vol. 15, No. 1, February 1987, pp. 4–15.

Lowinsky, Edward E. "On the Use of Scores by Sixteenth-Century Musicians." *Journal of the American Musicological Society,* Vol. 1, No. 1, Spring 1948, pp. 17–23.

———. *Tonality and Atonality in Sixteenth-Century Music* (Foreword by Igor Stravinsky). New York: Da Capo Press, 1990.

Luff, Alan. "The Authentic Sound." *Musical Times,* Vol. 110, No. 1513, March 1969, p. 308.

Macey, Patrick. "Savonarola and the Sixteenth-Century Motet." *Journal of the American Musicological Society,* Vol. XXXVI, No. 3, Fall 1983, pp. 422–452.

Mendel, Arthur. "Pitch in the 16th and Early 17th Centuries—Part I." *Musical Quarterly,* Vol. 34, No. 1, January 1948.

———. "Pitch in the 16th and Early 17th Centuries—Part II." *Musical Quarterly,* Vol. 34, No. 2, April 1948, pp. 199–221.

———. "Pitch in Western Music Since 1500: A Re-examination." *Acta Musicologica,* Vol. L, 1978, pp. 1–93.

Menerth, Edward F. "Singing in Style: Renaissance." *Music Educators Journal,* Vol. 52, April/May 1966, pp. 56–57.

Milner, Anthony. "The Sacred Capons." *The Musical Times,* Vol. 114, No. 1561, March 1973, pp. 250–252.

Morely, Thomas. *A Plain and Easie Introduction to Practicall Musicke,* 1597, edited by R. A. Harmon. New York: W. W. Norton, 1953.

Negus, V. E., and Owen Jander. "Falsetto," in *The New Grove Dictionary of Music and Musicians.* London: Macmillan Publishers, 1980, Vol. 6, p. 375.

Neumann, Frederick. *New Essays on Performance Practice.* Ann Arbor, MI: UMI Research Press, 1989.

Paine, Gordon, ed. *Five Centuries of Choral Music: Essays in Honor of Howard Swan.* Stuyvesant, NY: Pendragon Press, 1988.

Palisca, Claude V. *Humanism in Italian Renaissance Musical Thought.* New Haven, CT: Yale University Press, 1986.

Phillips, Peter. "Performance Practice in 16th Century English Choral Music." *Early Music,* Vol. 6, No. 2, April 1978, pp. 195–199.

Powers, Harold S. "Tonal Types and Modal Categories in Renaissance Polyphony." *Journal of the American Musicological Society,* Vol. XXXIV, No. 3, Fall 1981, pp. 428–470.

Prizer, William. "Performance Practices in the Frottola." *Early Music,* Vol. 3, No. 3, July 1975, pp. 227–235.

Razzi, Rausto. "Polyphony of the Seconda Prattica: Performance Practice in Early Italian Vocal Music of the Mannerist Era." *Early Music,* Vol. 8, No. 3, July 1980, pp. 298–311.

Reese, Gustave. *Music In The Renaissance,* rev. ed. New York: W. W. Norton & Company, 1959.

Roche, Jerome. *The Madrigal.* London: Hutchinson University Library, 1972.

Rogers, Francis. "The Male Soprano." *Musical Quarterly,* Vol. 5, No. 3, July 1919, pp. 413–424.

Ruff, Lillian M. "Josquin Des Prez: Some Features of His Motets." *The Consort,* No. 28, 1972, pp. 106–118.

Rumery, Leonard R. "Music at Seville Under a Renaissance Master." *American Choral Review,* Vol. XXIII, No. 2, April 1981, pp. 11–17.

Sachs, Curt. *Rhythm and Tempo: A Study in Music History.* New York: W. W. Norton & Company, 1953.

Sarton, George. "The Quest for Truth: Scientific Progress during the Renaissance," in *The Renaissance.* New York: Harper & Row, Publishers, Inc., 1962.

Sawkins, Lionel. "For and Against the Order of Nature: Who Sang the Soprano?" *Early Music,* Vol. 15, No. 3, August 1987, pp. 315–324.

Scott, Charles Kennedy. *Madrigal Singing.* London: Oxford University Press, 1931.

Seay, Albert. "The Setting of Tempo by Proportions in the Sixteenth Century." *The Consort,* No. 37, 1981, pp. 394–398.

Shearer, C. M. "Dynamic Inflection of Renaissance Polyphony." *Choral Journal*, Vol. XXI, No. 2, October 1980, pp. 10–14.

Sherr, Richard. "From the Diary of a 16th-Century Papal Singer." *Current Musicology*, No. 25, 1978, pp. 83–98.

———. "Josquin's *Missa Lingua:* A Note on *Agnus Dei* III." *Early Music*, Vol. 18, No. 2, May 1989, pp. 271–275.

———. "Performance Practice in the Papal Chapel in the 16th Century." *Early Music*, Vol. 15, No. 4, November 1987, pp. 453–462.

———. "The Performance of Josquin's *L'Homme armé* Masses." *Early Music*, Vol. 19, No. 2, May 1991, pp. 261–268.

Stevens, Denis. "Choral Dialogues of the Renaissance." *The Musical Times*, Vol. 122, No. 1664, October 1981, pp. 667–670.

Stevenson, Robert. *Music Before the Classic Era*. London: Macmillan & Co., Ltd., 1955.

———. *Spanish Music in the Age of Columbus*. The Hague: Martinus Nijhoff, 1960.

Strunk, Oliver. *Source Readings in Music History*. New York: W. W. Norton & Company, 1950.

Tatnell, Ronald. "Falsetto Practice: A Brief Survey." *The Consort*, Vol. 22, Summer 1965, p. 32.

Thomas, Bernard. "Renaissance Music in Modern Notation." *Early Music*, Vol. 5, No. 1, January 1977, pp. 4–11.

Thommessen, Olav Anton. "The Significance of Culture." *The Musical Times*, Vol. 131, No. 1772, October 1990, pp. 528–529.

Toft, Robert. "Traditions of Pitch Content In The Sources of Two Sixteenth-Century Motets." *Music and Letters*, Vol. LXIX, No. 3, July 1988, pp. 334–344.

Tolin, Craig. "An Outline of Performance Practices in Late Fifteenth- and Early Sixteenth Century Sacred Choral Music." *Choral Journal*, Vol. XXVII, No. 3, October 1986, pp. 5–14.

Tomasello, Andrew. "Ritual, Tradition, and Polyphony at the Court of Rome." *The Journal of Musicology*, Vol. IV, No. 4, Fall 1985–86, pp. 447–471.

Tomlinson, Gary. *Monteverdi and the End of the Renaissance*. Berkeley, CA: University of California Press, 1987.

Trowbridge, Lynn M. "Style Change in the Fifteenth-Century Chanson: A Comparative Study of Compositional Detail." *Journal of Musicology*, Vol. IV, No. 2, Spring 1985–86, pp. 146–170.

Uberti, Mauro. "Vocal Techniques in Italy in the Second Half of the Sixteenth Century." *Early Music*, Vol. 9, No. 4, October 1981, pp. 486–495.

Von Ramm, Andrea. "Singing Early Music." *Early Music*, Vol. 4, No. 1, January 1976, pp. 12–15.

———. "Style in Early Music Singing." *Early Music*, Vol. 8, No. 1, January 1980, pp. 17–20.

Walter, Don C. *Men & Music in Western Culture*. New York: Appleton-Century-Crofts, 1969.

Wegman, Rob C. "Concerning Tempo in the English Polyphonic Mass, c. 1420–70." *Acta Musicologica*, Vol. LXI, 1989, pp. 40–65.

Wright, Craig. "Musicology and Fifteenth-Century Music." *Journal of Musicology*, Vol. I, No. 1, January 1982, pp. 39–43.

———. "Performance Practices at the Cathedral of Cambrai 1475–1550." *The Musical Quarterly*, Vol. LXIV, No. 3, July 1978, pp. 295–328.

Wulstan, David. "The Problem of Pitch in Sixteenth-Century English Vocal Music." *Proceedings of the Royal Music Association*, Vol. 93, 1966–67, p. 97–112.

Young, Percy. "Reformation and Renaissance." *American Choral Review*, Vol. XXIII, No. 3, July 1981, pp. 12–16.

The Baroque Period

The Baroque period began toward the end of the sixteenth century, and is generally considered to have ended by 1750 — the year of the death of Johann Sebastian Bach. The word *baroque* is said to have originated from *barrôco,* a Portuguese word meaning "a pearl of irregular form." In the nineteenth century, the term *baroque* was used in a pejorative manner, implying that the exceptionally ornate style of the arts of this period was in poor taste and a debasement of the Renaissance style. Today, however, such a connotation of the word has largely disappeared, and the Baroque is considered to be one of the greatest periods of dramatic expression.

The art forms of the Baroque period were characterized by expansiveness, grandeur, and impressiveness. Baroque architecture was expansive and monumental; paintings were dynamic, alive with color, and filled with the tension of opposing masses; and the interior decoration of churches was highly ornate and dramatic.

Through the Counter-Reformation, beginning about the middle of the sixteenth century, the papacy, utilizing all its resources, set out to regain the faith of the people previously lost to Protestantism. The Counter-Reformation sought converts by trying to reach the spiritual through the senses. A vigorous program, incorporating the most impressive aspects of all the arts, was put into action. As a result, cultural forms were developed that were both grandiose and sublime.

The period of the early Baroque began to take form during the pontificate of Sixtus V (1585–1590), and the new Catholicism was reflected in all the arts.

> The early baroque was, at first, a period of Catholic churchly art, and it was again the Society of Jesus which gave this art its peculiar traits of character. From the sphere of quiet devotion, the faithful were lifted into the world of the triumphant Church whose cult was celebrated by richly decked clergy under the vaults of a mighty architecture, surrounded by statues and pictures, before scintillating altars ornamented with gold and silver, to the accompaniment of the impressive and resonant music of multiple choirs, orchestras, and organs. In elaborate processions with flags, candles, and torches, triumphal carriages, floats, and arches, with the marchers singing, accompanying soldiers' bands blaring forth with their trumpets, the bells tolling and cannon booming, priests and students, guilds and corporations with their emblems, princes and the populace all united to demonstrate their adherence to the regenerated triumphal Church.[1]

Whereas the Counter-Reformation prompted the creation of a vast amount of sacred art, Protestantism, on the other hand, showed little interest in pictorial and decorative art, presumably because such churchly ornamentation would be contrary to the evangelical precepts of the church.[2] Protestant piety held that the proper reverence to God's word would be weakened if the congregation's attention were diverted by ornaments and decorations. In the main, therefore, the Protestant churches remained relatively simple, their architecture merely imitating that of pre-Reformation times. Although music also suffered as a result of this artistic hostility, it was the one art form that eventually became an integral part of the reformed faiths. After a while music came to epitomize the highest degree of artistic expression in Protestantism.[3]

While the Counter-Reformation may have ignited the Baroque spirit, it certainly did not perpetuate it; from 1565 to 1572 the Church under the leadership of Pope Pius V became increasingly conservative. It outlawed nudity, and established rules for the use of secular melodies in composition.[4] It also enforced an Index of prohibited books that was widely used against both Protestant and and scientific "heresy."[5]

[1]From *Music in Western Civilization* by Paul Henry Lang. By permission of W. W. Norton & Company, Inc. Copyright 1941 by W. W. Norton & Company, Inc. Copyright renewed 1968 by Paul Henry Lang. Page 319.

[2]Extreme Calvinists sometimes went so far as to destroy stained-glass windows and smash religious statues in their rejection of traditional symbolism.

[3]Lang, *Music in Western Civilization*, pp. 320–321.

[4]Carl J. Friedrich, *The Age of the Baroque* (New York: Harper & Row, 1962), p. 40.

[5]The Index grew out of the Council of Trent, which convened from 1545 to 1563. The Index remained in existence until 1965, when it was dropped by the order of the Second Vatican Council.

LIFE DURING THE BAROQUE ERA

The Baroque period is viewed by some people as a "middle" period between the Renaissance and the modern age. As previously indicated, the term *baroque* is said to be derived from the Portuguese word *barrôco*, meaning an irregularly shaped pearl. Some historians, however, believe it stems from the Italian term *baroco*, a stumbling-block in medieval scholastic logic. In either case, however, the word came to mean any contorted idea, or tortuous, involved process of thought. It also described elaborate, voluptuous, tension-filled art and architecture. This application of meaning, however, did not begin until the second half of the eighteenth century, when it was applied to indicate contrast with classical values.

Shortly after the beginning of the Baroque period, the Thirty Years' War (1618–1648) broke out. It began as a conflict between Protestants and Catholics. In Bohemia, the Protestant nobility refused to recognize the Catholic Ferdinand II, who shortly thereafter became Holy Roman Emperor, as their king. The nobility chose Frederick V; this resulted in a war between the Bohemian estates and the Holy Roman Empire. The war eventually embroiled the Catholic forces of Germany, Spain, and France against the Protestant forces of Holland, Denmark, and eventually Sweden. From 1634 to 1648 fighting continued in Germany, Italy, and Flanders.

The ravages of war reduced the population of Germany by more than half, and education, commerce, and agriculture came to a halt. For many years there were not enough people to rebuild the cities or replant the fields. As to patronage for the arts, the middle class gradually throughout the years began to play an increasingly important part. In Holland, this was the brilliant era of the Dutch republic, with its merchants and traders who patronized Rembrandt.

Diseases were a continuing and troublesome problem to the populace in Europe for centuries. Among the most prevalent diseases were the plague, which swept Europe until the early eighteenth century; typhus; typhoid and smallpox; tuberculosis, a scourge up through the nineteenth century; and syphilis, which was particularly virulent when varieties combined after the discovery of America. Contaminated drinking water and poor hygiene contributed to difficulties. Autopsies dating back to the sixteenth century describe malformations, wasting illnesses, skin ailments, and abnormally large colonies of parasites in lungs and intestines.[6] With the populace living perpetually on the brink of disaster, it is readily understandable why religion was such an important aspect of peoples' lives. When the plague, or "Black Death," reached Oberammergau, Germany in 1634, the townsfolk vowed that those whose lives were spared would present every ten years a Passion play depicting Christ's last days on earth. The event is still held today; it is

[6]Fernard Braudel, *Afterthoughts on Material Civilization and Capitalism* (Baltimore: The Johns Hopkins University Press, 1977), p. 10.

presented in an open-air theater, occurs in decimal years, and attracts thousands of visitors from May through September.

A belief in sorcery and witchcraft was quite prevalent among the intellectual elite of the seventeenth century. This appears to be contrary to the growing scientific spirit of the times. In England, Scotland, Germany, Spain, and elsewhere, witches were burned by the hundreds. Such superstitious practices resulted from the multitude of unexplainable calamities that struck the populace, involving sickness, madness, and death. This was an era of religious tension, warfare, hatred, suspicion, and hysteria. Witchcraft was part of popular culture and was used by the elite, both Catholic and Protestant, to further their own ends.[7] King James I, Charles I, the Puritan Matthew Hopkins, and even scientific men like Boyle and Sir Francis Bacon, subscribed to beliefs in witchcraft. Another superstition that was still prevalent was the belief that the Earth was the center of the universe. This view was common throughout the seventeenth century.[8]

Oswald Spengler has suggested that Baroque is in fact the fulfillment of the "Faustian soul" of Western man.[9]

> The Baroque sought to give literary and artistic expression to an age that was intoxicated with the power of man. . . . At the height of the Baroque, architects, sculptors, painters, poets and musicians strove to accomplish the impossible in *all* directions. Hence materialism vied with spiritualism, radical naturalism with extreme formalism, the most terrifying realism with the most precious illusionism. . . . Poetry sought to probe into ultimate mysteries, and voluptuous and lascivious erotic poetry violated all canons of good taste.[10]

In Baroque art

> monarchs, cardinals, and princesses, devout nuns and praying saints competed with beggars, miscreants and cripples in the paintings of Velasquez, Rubens, and Rembrandt; highly ornamented altars decorated in gold contrast with severe church interiors, colorful and dramatic murals with geometrically rigid gardens.[11]

As to personal behavior, the wig is said to be probably the most revealing symbol of the Baroque. It was an attempt to cultivate the theatrical exaggeration of reality. As the seventeenth century progressed, hair gradually became shorter and beards and mustaches became smaller and then disappeared, since they hid the face rather than setting it off as a wig does. Louis XIV

---

[7]Alchemy was more "popular" than "science." This was the era of Faust—the hero of several medieval legends—an old philosopher who sells his soul to the devil in exchange for knowledge and power.

[8]Friedrich, *Age of Baroque*, pp. 105–106.

[9]Oswald Spengler, *Der Untergang des Abendlandes*, in Friedrich, *Age of Baroque*, p. 44.

[10]Ibid., p. 44.

[11]Ibid., p. 44.

was proud of his youthful locks—and subsequently needed a wig to maintain his majestic image. The defense of one's honor became a most sought-after sign of individual power and resulted in endless quarreling and dueling among the aristocracy. Excesses in eating and drinking were extreme, particularly in Germany, as was violent sexual debauchery among both men and women. Indications are that this sexual behavior was as prevalent among the common folk as it was in the aristocracy. The Baroque embued people with a new sense of their power to shape their own society and their own destiny. The emphasis was on action, personal success, constant combat, and the resulting heightening of one's sense of worthiness.[12] Religious passions were prevalent and tension and struggle was everywhere. And, as previously discussed, resurgent Catholicism versus stalwart Protestantism led to the senseless Thirty Years' War, which ended in a stalemate.

The population of London grew from about 70,000 people in the year 1500, to some 450,000 in 1650, to over 500,000 by the end of the seventeenth century. London was at that point the largest, busiest, and wealthiest metropolis in the world, and Samuel Johnson wrote that "when a man is tired of London, he is tired of life, for there is in London all that life can afford."[13] It was into this economic and social climate that George Frideric Handel continued his famous career.

BAROQUE COMPOSERS

Composers of the Baroque period were often associated with the localities in which they lived and worked. Some of the composers of the seventeenth century were CLAUDIO MONTEVERDI (1567–1643) of Venice; GIACOMO CARISSIMI (1605–1674) of Rome; HEINRICH SCHÜTZ (1585–1672) of Saxony, a region in southeast Germany; DIETRICH BUXTEHUDE (1637–1707) of Lübeck; JEAN-BAPTISTE LULLY (1632–1687) of Paris and Versailles; and HENRY PURCELL (1659–1695) of London. The year 1685 marked the birth of the two giants of the Baroque period: JOHANN SEBASTIAN BACH (1685–1750), and GEORGE FRIDERIC HANDEL (1685–1759). Important as they were, Bach and Handel had some important contemporaries who made significant contributions to choral music—in particular, ALESSANDRO SCARLATTI (1660–1725) and GIOVANNI PERGOLESI (1710–1736). The Baroque period is considered to have ended upon the death of Handel in 1759.

CLAUDIO MONTEVERDI was born in Cremona in 1567. As a young man he was sent to a technical school to study engineering, but later decided to study music. He was employed in his early years at the court of the Gonzagas at

---

[12]Ibid., pp. 45–46.

[13]Carlo Cipolla, *Before the Industrial Revolution: European Society and Economy, 1000–1700* (New York: W. W. Norton & Company, 1975), p. 293.

Mantua, but in 1613 he became *maestro di cappella* at St. Mark's Cathedral in Venice, Italy. At St. Mark's, Monteverdi was asked to restore the prestige of the church by writing in the older polyphonic style *(prima prattica)* of Palestrina.

Monteverdi was also a successful composer of opera, as well as masses, but perhaps his greatest contribution lies in his madrigals, of which he composed eight books, the first in 1587, when he was 20 years old, and the last in 1638. One of his best-known madrigals is "Lasciate mi morire" (from his Sixth Book of Madrigals, 1614), in which he shows "consideration for the word, the new tendency to think harmonically and the power of chromatic and discordant departure from the norm."[14] Monteverdi has also been described as a revolutionary and as "the creator of modern music."[15]

Most composers of the Baroque era were quite subservient to their patrons and eager to please. Claudio Monteverdi was at the court of Mantua under the Gonzaga regime from 1590 until 1612, and seems to have been exceptionally subservient, as illustrated by the following letter:[16]

Your Highness, My Lord and Benevolent Patron:

Ten days ago I received the most recent letter from your Highness, which commanded me to prepare two *entrate*—one for the stars that are to follow the moon, and the other for the shepherds that accompany Endymion; likewise, two balletti: one for the stars alone, and the other for the stars and shepherds together. Thus, with a most ardent desire to obey and fulfill as quickly as possible the commands of your Highness, as I have always done and will always do until I die, I first began to work on that of the stars. . . .

I have done this, my most Serene Lord, with my usual good will and ready desire to serve you that I have always had and always will have. . . .

If, Most Serene Highness, my lord, you find yourself not well served by me, nor with the beauty and swiftness that perhaps you expected and as it was my desire to serve, as I likewise have always desired to do, do not blame my good will nor my spirit, since both the one and the other will always receive the greatest grace and highest favor if you Your Highness deigns to command them; to whom, bowing, I make the humblest reverence and pray Our Lord will give you all happiness.

From Cremona
December 1604

Most humble and devoted servitor
Claudio Monteverdi

[14]Percy M. Young, *The Choral Tradition* (New York: W. W. Norton, 1962), p. 62.

[15]Stanley Sadie, *Music Guide: An Introduction* (Englewood Cliffs, NJ: Prentice Hall), p. 145.

[16]G. P. Malipiero, *Claudio Monteverdi* (Milan, 1929), from Carol MacClintock, *Readings in the History of Music in Performance* (Bloomington, IN: Indiana University Press, 1979), pp. 176–177.

GIACOMO CARISSIMI was exclusively a church composer, and in 1628 he became *maestro di cappella* at the church of St. Apollinare. Most of Carissimi's predecessors in the *nuove musiche* movement were seemingly oblivious to the importance of the bass part. Carissimi "gave momentum to melody by setting it over a moving bass" part. He described the bass as "the axis whereon a melody turns. . . . Likewise, he gave musical purposiveness to melody by making it self-sufficient yet flexible to verbal intention."[17] ALESSANDRO SCARLATTI (1660–1725) was a pupil of Carissimi who was widely known even though he appears never to have left Rome.

Among the published choral works of Carissimi are four oratorios: *Jephte, Judicium Salomonis, Jonas,* and *Balthazar;* two collections of motets (1664, 1667); and masses (1663, 1667).

HEINRICH SCHÜTZ was born in 1585 in Kostritz, Germany. He was a pupil of Giovanni Gabrieli between 1609 and 1612 in Venice, where he became well aware of the Venetian musical tradition. Schütz was later a law student at the University of Marburg and did not decide to follow music as a vocation until 1614, when he became Kapellmeister at the Electoral Court of Dresden. Schütz was known for his boldness in coloring and for his fine polyphony.

Among the choral works of Schütz are three passions: *St. Matthew* (1666), *St. Luke* (1666), and *St. John* (1666); oratorios: *Christmas Oratorio* (1664), *Seven Words from Christ on the Cross* (1657), and Resurrection oratorios; collections of motets: *Cantiones sacrae* (1625), *Symphoniae sacrae* (1629, 1647, 1650), *Geistliche Konzerte* (1636, 1639); psalm settings: *Psalmen Davids* (1619, 1628); and Italian madrigals (1611).

DIETRICH BUXTEHUDE was born in Helsingborg, Denmark, in about 1637. He was organist in Helsingør for eight years beginning in about 1660, and in 1668 he became organist at St. Mary's in Lübeck (a city and port in northwest Germany). Buxtehude was highly successful while at Lübeck, had fine support from his fellow citizens, and developed Lübeck into a great musical center. Its reputation was so great that both J. S. Bach and G. F. Handel made a pilgrimage to the Marienkirche there. Buxtehude was a famous organist, and his development of various instrumental forms was of considerable importance to his successors. In his choral compositions, he drew upon varied methods of treatment, including the use of "southern brilliance," the solo voice, and even the classical polyphonic style, all within a framework of a modern technique. A complete edition of Buxtehude's vocal music was published in seven volumes (1925–37).

JEAN-BAPTISTE LULLY was born in 1632 in Florence, Italy, and was taught the elements of music by a Franciscan monk. While still a young boy he was taken to Paris to become a page to Mademoiselle d'Orléans, a young cousin of Louis XIV. He later entered the service of Louis XIV, where he rose fast in royal favor and became a favorite composer for the court ballet. In 1661 he

---

[17]Arthur Jacobs, *Choral Music* (Baltimore: Penguin Books, 1963), p. 59.

received the post of composer to the king, and in 1662 was appointed *maître de musique* of the royal family.

Among Lully's choral works are a *Te Deum*, a *Miserere*, a four-part Mass, *a cappella*, and many motets. Lully's motets, however, were really cantatas for solo, chorus, and orchestra, thus differing from the sixteenth-century motet, as well as from other church music. Lully, however, was primarily concerned with the development of French opera, in which he made extensive use of the chorus. Lully was highly sensitive to the French language in setting his texts to music and imparted a strong dramatic interest to his choral ensembles. His death in 1687 resulted from an accident. While conducting he struck his foot with a sharp-pointed cane that he used as a baton; gangrene set in, and he died of blood poisoning.

HENRY PURCELL is regarded as one of the finest of English composers. Purcell was organist at Westminster Abbey from 1679 until his death in 1695. He was not a prolific composer, but wrote music when he was required to do so. Purcell is known for establishing the English secular cantata. His operas are really considered masques, or plays with music. Purcell is also known for his anthems, two of the best known of which are "Rejoice in the Lord" and the eight-part work "Hear My Prayer."

JOHANN SEBASTIAN BACH was born in Eisenach, Germany in 1685. Bach began his schooling in Eisenach; however, both his mother and his father died when he was nine. He then went to live with his older brother Johann Christoph in Ohrdruf, where he continued his schooling and was taught to play keyboard instruments by his brother. In 1700, when he was fifteen, Johann went to Lüneberg, where he became a chorister at St. Michael's Church and also received a scholastic education. In 1717 Bach was appointed Kapellmeister and director of the "Kammermusik" to Prince Leopold of Anhalt at Cöthen. In 1723 he was appointed cantor at the Thomasschule in Leipzig, where he also became organist at two churches—Thomaskirche and Nicolaikirche. He further received the appointment of honorary Kapellmeister to the Duke of Weissenfels. In 1736 he was appointed court composer to the King of Poland, Elector of Saxony, which involved occasional visits to Dresden. He remained at his post in Leipzig, however, for twenty-seven years until his death in 1750.

Among Bach's choral works are 190 sacred cantatas; the *St. Matthew Passion*; the *St. John Passion*; oratorios for Christmas, Easter, and Ascension (the latter known as Cantata No. 11); two Magnificats; *Grand Mass in B minor*; several short masses; five Sanctus; many motets; and a number of secular cantatas, including *Dramma per musica*, *Der Streit zwischen Phoebus und Pam*, the *Coffee Cantata*, and the *Cantata en burlesque* (Peasant Cantata).

During Bach's time it was the custom to add instruments with considerable freedom and to the extent that they were available and made musical sense. Instruments doubled the choral parts or embellished them by diminutions. They were used to add festive brilliance, to replace missing choral parts, to reinforce the *cantus firmus*, or to emphasize contrast in the multichoral works. Instruments could also add symbolic meaning or intensify the sound. Groups of instruments were used for "registration" effects, like the stops of an organ.[18] The lower wind instruments and the low strings doubled the middle and low vocal parts, and the high strings and high winds played *obbligato* parts. The harpsichord at that time was used as the conductor's instrument to support the choir and to help keep it together. It was not used simply as an accompaniment instrument.[19] "The use of brass instruments in a chorale signifies a symbolic underlining of the word of God."[20]

GEORGE FRIDERIC HANDEL was born in Halle in southeast Germany in 1685. As a young boy he studied music with Friedrich Wilhelm Zachow, who was organist at the Church of Our Lady near Handel's home. When he was seventeen, Handel became a law student at Halle University. The following year, 1703, he went to Hamburg, where he was employed as a violinist and harpsichordist in a Hamburg opera orchestra. In 1706 he went to Florence, Italy upon the invitation of a prince of the Medici family. While in Italy he divided his time between Florence, Rome, and Venice. He had great success there as an opera composer—in Florence in 1707, and in Venice in 1709–10, where his *Agrippina* was presented twenty-seven times. In 1711 Handel moved to London, where he composed and presented his opera *Rinaldo*. Audiences in general were delighted with it and it was a great success; however, some English intellectuals were highly critical of his use of *castrati* in the production, as well as of various theatrical aspects, and of the use of the Italian language. Handel then went to Hanover for more than a year, but in 1712 he returned to London, where he remained for the rest of his life.[21]

In 1719 Handel was appointed director of the newly formed Royal Academy of Music, which was supported by money raised through subscription as well as the patronage of the king. Handel auditioned singers all over Europe to locate the performers he wanted. In the late 1730s his interest in opera lessened, and he turned to other large-scale vocal forms, principally oratorio. Handel composed his *Messiah* in six weeks during the summer of 1741. Opera was now behind him, and his main interest was the presentation of oratorio at the Covent Garden Theater. His largest audience now was not the aristocratic class, but the broadly based middle class that was created by the commercial and industrial activity that made London the biggest and most prosperous city in the world.[22]

Among Handel's oratorios are *Esther* (revised, 1732); *Acis and Galatea* (1732); *Deborah* (1733); *Athalia* (1733); *Saul* (1739); *Israel in Egypt* (1739); *Ode*

[18]Wilhelm Ehmann, "Performance Practice of Bach's Motets," *American Choral Review*, Vol. XV, No. 2 (April 1973): 10.

[19]Ibid., p. 12.

[20]Ibid., p. 14.

[21]Sadie, *Music Guide*, pp. 205–207.

[22]Ibid., p. 215.

for St. Cecilia's Day (1739); L'allegro, il pensiero, ed il moderato (1740); Messiah (1742); Sampson (1743); Dettingen Te Deum, Semele (1744); Joseph and His Brethren (1744); Belshazzar (1745); Occasional Oratorio (1746); Judas Maccabaeus (1747); Joshua (1748); Susanna (1749); Solomon (1749); Theodora (1750); The Choice of Hercules (1751), and Jeptha (1752).

ALESSANDRO SCARLATTI was born in Palermo, Italy in 1660. In 1672 he went to Rome, where he became a pupil of Carissimi. When he was about twenty, Scarlatti served as maestro di cappella to Queen Christine of Sweden. In 1694 he was made maestro to the viceroy at Naples. In 1703 Scarlatti became assistant maestro to Foggia at Santa Maria Maggiore in Rome, and in 1707 he became first maestro. In 1709 Scarlatti returned to Naples to become maestro of the royal chapel. Scarlatti also taught briefly at the Conservatorio di Santa Maria di Loreto in Naples (1689). Scarlatti enhanced religious music as he imbued sacred texts with lyrical commentary.[23]

Scarlatti's choral works include 14 oratorios, about 85 motets, over 200 masses, numerous madrigals, and a vast number of cantatas (600 with basso continuo and 61 with instruments).

GIOVANNI PERGOLESI was born in Jesi, near Ancona, Italy in 1710. He studied music with Francesco Santi, choir director at Jesi Cathedral. He later entered the Conservatorio dei Poveri at Naples, where he studied violin with Domenico de Matteis and theory with Gaetano Greco. As a highly proficient violinist, he played periodically during the carnivals. As a young adult, his health deteriorated because of tuberculosis, and he died in 1736 at the age of 26. Among Pergolesi's choral works are La Conversione di S. Giglielmo d'Aquitania, oratorio (1731); La Frate sul rogo, oratorio (1731); Mass (1732); and Stabat Mater (1735–1736).

BAROQUE CHOIRS

References to the size of choirs during the Baroque period generally indicate that they were comparatively small. For example, one scholar says that "in Handel's day, the oratorios were sung by comparatively small choirs. The soprano part was sung by boys and all the others by men."[24] Basal Lam, however, states that "Bach's choirs numbered around 20 singers."[25] Even music for double choir did not necessitate the use of many more voices. The evidence indicates that the motet "Singet dem Herrn" was originally performed a cappella, and for the first performance Bach used his best choirs—each choir numbered about 12 voices, 24 in all, with three singers on a part. According

[23]Young, Choral Tradition, p. 107.

[24]Jens Peter Larsen, "Messiah Performance Traditions," American Choral Review, Vol. XIV, No. 1 (January 1972).

[25]Basil Lam, "Authenticity and the St. John Passion," Early Music, Vol. 5, No. 1 (1977): 45–49.

to Young, however, in the performance of his *St. John Passion* (for double choir), Bach used his sixteen best singers for chorus I, and his eighteen less proficient singers for chorus II.[26]

In an endeavor to achieve authentic performance conditions, today's choirs need not be reduced in size at all, as long as the conductor is careful about the balance between voices and solo parts. While the size of choirs will vary, a conductor's important objective is to achieve clarity in the contrapuntal lines, coupled with a strength of sound.

As previously indicated, the practice of using *castrati* in church choirs began toward the end of the sixteenth century, and in the seventeenth and eighteenth centuries it dominated serious opera. The combination of a boy's vocal quality with the strength of a man's lungs and body is said to have produced a sound of exquisite beauty, power, and flexibility. *Castrato* singers took the roles in opera of heros, warriors, and lovers for about two centuries. These singers had a vocal range similiar to that of a mezzo soprano, and the roles they took during their time are now performed by women.[27]

Music history books seldom refer to the *castrato* voice. The word may be mentioned in the text in relation to a particular work or composer, but it is hardly ever included in the index. While most people today regard castration as barbaric, it must be remembered that the castrato voice was used in church, opera, and oratorio music for a very long time and that composers wrote specific parts for this voice. Furthermore, audiences of the past reveled in the performances of *castrati*. This is indeed a reflection of the Baroque audiences' musical tastes, and more specifically of their attraction to the agility, power, and wonder of the voices.

One of the more exciting pieces of Baroque church music is the "Miserere Mei" by GREGORIO ALLEGRI (1582–1652). The music alternates between full chorus and a group of four soloists. The soprano soloist's part, originally sung by a *castrato*, soars to a high C and must have had a highly emotional effect on congregations of the time. The solo parts and the traditional *abbellimenti* or embellishments occur in verses 2, 6, 10, 14, and 18. This music was periodically performed in the Sistine Chapel in Rome, and for many years the church kept these ornamented passages a closely guarded secret; only a few highly prized copies were made before 1770, when the English historian Charles Burney discovered it. When Mozart was 14 he attended a service at the Sistine Chapel, heard the music, and then went home and copied it out from memory. Both Goethe and Mendelssohn admired the piece when earlier music was attracting the attention of composers and musicians. There are several editions of this work. In one, the Latin text is used throughout, but without the *abbellimenti*. Another edition includes the *abbellimenti*, but is set to English words (Figure 8). An edition using both the original Latin text and the

---

[26]Young, *Choral Tradition*, p. 130.
[27]Sadie, *Music Guide*, p. 34.

FIGURE 8 Excerpt from "Miserere Mei" by Gregorio Allegri. The parts shown are for four solo voices from one of five identical sections, each 14 measures in length. The written-out embellishments in the soprano part occur in verses 2, 6, 10, 14, and 18. © 1951 Novello & Company Ltd. Used by permission of the publisher. Sole U.S.A. representative, Theodore Presser Co.

abbellimenti is edited by George Guest, published by Chester Music, and available through the Music Sales Corporation. A beautiful recording of this work by the Choir of King's College, Cambridge, directed by Stephen Cleobury is available on EMI Records, Ltd., Hayes Middlesex, England. A vocally talented boy soprano performs the highest part. How it might have sounded as sung by a *castrato* will have to be left to the reader's imagination. *Castrati* were highly popular in the theater during the seventeenth and eighteenth centuries, and, as mentioned in Chapter 1, were referred to as *musico* or *envirato*.

When one reads about the *castrati,* one wonders what they went through emotionally. It is known that even though they were admired in the theater, they were despised in some segments of society. Their lives were not easy, but they managed to survive, and they made a strong imprint in particular on seventeenth- and eighteenth-century musical culture.

The most famous of the *envirati* was Carlo Broschi, known as Farinelli. Born in 1705, Carlo underwent castration to preserve his promising soprano voice. He studied with Niccolo Porpora, made his debut in 1720 at the age of 15, and astonished Europe from that time on. Farinelli appeared for three seasons in London and is said to have been so popular that he reduced Handel's rival opera company to ruins.

In 1737 Farinelli went to Madrid to perform privately every evening for Philip V of Spain. He is said to have cured Philip of his afflictions through the power of his voice alone. This has been referred to as the "miracle." After Philip's death, Farinelli remained in Spain until expelled unceremoniously by Charles, Ferdinand's successor. He lived out his life in a village near Bologna until his death in 1782.

In his administration of the Royal Academy of Music, Handel was free to engage any singers he might choose for his opera productions. In the second season, Handel hired in 1719 the "superb" *castrato* Senesino, whose powerful alto voice is said to have made him an ideal singer for the big heroic roles.[28]

For readers who are curious about the life of a *castrato,* his attitudes and feelings, his place in society, and how he was generally treated, I recommend *The Castrato* by Lawrence Louis Goldman (New York: The John Day Company), 1973. This book, although a novel, is based on the life of Farinelli. Goldman has researched this topic thoroughly, and he lists 59 scholarly works in his bibliography.

MUSICAL STYLE AND PERFORMANCE PRACTICE

Meter and Stress

The bar line and metered music came into being during the Baroque period; accentuations, therefore, generally occur at regularly spaced intervals. To evoke these accentuations in the performance of Baroque music, the

[28]Ibid., p. 209.

conductor should utilize a definite and precise beat. This approach is particularly appropriate for music such as, for example, Schütz's "Cantate Domino Canticum Novum" (Bourne, No. ES 33). The conductor, however, should avoid a mechanical, machinelike stress following each bar line. For example, in Carissimi's "Plorate Filii Israel" (Bourne, No. ES 34; E. C. Schirmer, No. 1172), a broad *legato* style is needed with a minimum degree of stress. The conductor should analyze each selection under consideration, and particularly each phrase, to determine those places requiring greater stress— sometimes those notes at the peak of the phrase. [29]

The frames of Baroque paintings usually did not encompass the entirety of a particular scene, but often cut through various objects, thus giving the illusion of boundless space. [30] Composers achieved a similar effect by often beginning their music on a beat following a rest, thus giving the listener the feeling that the music was a continuation of something that had already been underway. This delayed entrance effected a tension and rhythmic drive leading to the nearest downbeat. [31]

As to the articulation of late Baroque music, while some of it is to be performed *legato*, i.e., in a smooth and connected way, a much greater proportion of it should be detached, with a slight separation between the notes, as in, for example, certain phrases in "And the Glory of the Lord," from Handel's *Messiah*. There is often a tendency for performers to sing music of this period in a too *legato* or connected style, particularly when it should be detached. This results in an undesirably sluggish effect. As regards late Baroque articulation, Quantz's words are strikingly revealing—"The notes must not seem stuck together." [32] Donington also addresses this matter: "A slight silence or rather a new silence may occur between every two notes. . . . It is less articulate than the staccato, but more so than the legato, and it must be consciously cultivated for Baroque music." [33] In passages necessitating a separation between the notes, singers should be advised to exaggerate their enunciation of words, with precise lip and jaw movements.

As to the matter of dotted notes, Sir Charles Mackerras, in an interview with Bernard Jacobson, comments that Handel presents an intriguing problem

---

[29]It should be mentioned that, in the Baroque period, two basic stylistic practices existed—the *stilo antico* and the *stilo moderno*. In the *stilo antico*, or old style, which was suitable for the church, the music dominated the text. In the *stilo moderno*, or new style, the text dominated the music. These styles are sometimes referred to as *strict style* and *free style*. Some composers (Eberlin, for example) mixed these styles, rather than keeping them separate.

[30]See, for example, the painting *Landscape with the Chateau of Steen* (1636) by Peter Paul Rubens (1577–1640).

[31]Curt Sachs, *Rhythm and Tempo: A Study in Music History* (New York: W. W. Norton & Company, 1953), p. 266.

[32]Don V. Moses, with Robert W. Demarec, Jr., "Articulation in Late Baroque Choral Music," *The Choral Journal*, Vol. XXVII, No. 10 (May 1987): 18.

[33]Robert Donington, "Baroque Interpretation," in *Grove's Dictionary of Music and Musicians*, 5th ed., Eric Blom, ed. (London: Macmillan & Co., Ltd., 1954).

in his work "The Trumpet Shall Sound" (from *Messiah*). First he writes dotted notes (in the orchestral accompaniment), and then he writes them even, and then he writes them dotted again. They question whether he meant to indicate a difference, or whether he just got lazy at a certain point. Mozart, however, in his interpretation, took the notation literally, and performed it as written.[34] But then again, that was a judgment made some 200 years ago, so it behooves current-day musicians to consider such matters of interpretation carefully.

The practice of lengthening the dotted note and shortening the complementary note is an important consideration in the proper interpretation of Baroque music, particularly during the last half of the seventeenth century. This is generally referred to as double-dotting. For example, the rhythm

$\mathbf{C}$ ♪. ♫ ♩ | should often be performed as $\mathbf{C}$ 𝄾 𝄾 ♫.. ♩ |

and

$\frac{6}{8}$ ♫ ♫ | as $\frac{6}{8}$ ♩..♪ ♩..♪ | .

Quantz in his *Versuch* (Berlin, 1752) stated that "the length of every note was altered in performance to bring out the good notes."[35] Michael L'Affiland wrote in the late seventeenth century, "In singing, one holds the (dotted) eighth note a little longer (*un peu plus longtemps*) and passes over quickly (*passer viste*) the sixteenth note."[36] Why is it that the composers did not indicate what they wanted? Simply because it was easier to *tell* the performers how the music should be performed than to write out the notation. This treatment of the dotted note began during the early part of the seventeenth century and carried through to the beginning of the nineteenth century. The music of Monteverdi, Purcell, Bach, and Handel (as well as the later music of Haydn, Mozart, and Beethoven) all necessitate this treatment.[37] During the latter part of the eighteenth century, however, composers began to indicate more carefully their desired intentions in the music.

There are those, however, who prefer the term *overdotting* to double-dotting, because they feel that in some instances more than double-dotting is involved, and that in others less than double-dotting is appropriate. Neuman states that "the complexity of the issue . . . cannot be reduced to a single

[34] Bernard Jacobson, *Conductors on Conducting* (Frenchtown, NJ: Columbia Publishing Company, Inc., 1979), p. 79.

[35] Sol Babitz, "Concerning the Length of Time that Every Note Must Be Held," *Music Review*, Vol. 28, No. 1 (February 1967): 21–37.

[36] Michael L'Affiland, *Principes très faciles pour bien apprendre la musique* (Paris, 1694), 2nd ed., 1697.

[37] Thurston Dart, *The Interpretation of Music*, rev. ed. (London: Hutchinson Publishing Group Ltd., 1960), pp. 81–82.

convention with a clear-cut set of rules. Overdotting certainly was practised (and so was underdotting), but it was done under various musical categories."[38]

Certainly, in view of these diverse opinions, the conductor is left with some latitude in which to use his or her musical judgment within the parameters of accepted musical practice during the Baroque period.

The purpose of this practice is the achievement of a crisp, clear manner of articulation, as opposed to a lazy and sluggish treatment. This manner of articulation also minimizes the tendency for performers to rush their parts.

Fuller states that musicians should "keep an open mind . . . and play the music the way we think it sounds best . . . the vigour of dotted rhythms is as much a function of articulation—particularly the sharpness with which the short note is delivered—as it is of the proportion of values. If the short note is delayed so much that there is not time to make it speak properly, the effect will be flabby and neurotic rather than energetic."[39] Of course, conductors should utilize discretion in applying this convention. One criterion for consideration is the general character of the music; that is, the lengthening of the dotted notes would be more appropriate to brilliant and majestic music and somewhat less appropriate to music of a lilting, graceful character.

According to Campbell, "the use of *notes inégales* is appropriate in music that is martial and maestoso in character, but not for music (or sections of a piece) that is of a serene *cantabile* nature."[40]

Donington states, "No one seems to question the idea of inequality, the only difference might be when it is to be applied." Notes in phrases that move stepwise and fall into pairs are most likely to be performed unequally. Exceptions to this practice are in marchlike melodies, melodies with leaps, groups of notes that do not fall into pairs, or music that moves much faster or slower than moderate tempi.[41] Further evidence to support this opinion is as follows: "Double-dotting was widespread, if not universal, and there is no doubt it applies to Bach. The only question is exactly where? To a large extent it is for the performers to find the answer by trial and error. . . . If a conductor thinks a double-dotted performance is too extreme, let him find a happy mean."[42]

---

[38]Frederick Neumann, "Facts and Fiction About Overdotting," *Musical Quarterly*, Vol. LXII, No. 2 (April 1977): 155–185.

[39]David Fuller, "Dotting the 'French Style,' and Frederick Neumann's Counter-Reformation," *Early Music*, Vol. V, No. 4 (October 1977): 527.

[40]Margaret Campbell, "To Dot or Double Dot: The Eternal Question," *The Consort*, Vol. 31 (July 1975): 142–147.

[41]Robert Donington, "A Problem of Inequality," *Musical Quarterly*, Vol. 53, No. 4 (October 1967): 503–517.

[42]Walter Emery, "The Interpretation of Bach," *The Musical Times*, Vol. XCVI (April 1955): 190–193.

There are also musicians who believe that the dotted quarter note should also be double-dotted. For example:

notated   *performed*

| ♩ ♩. ♪ | o ‖ | ♩ ♩.. ♪ | o ‖

L'Affiland stated during the latter part of the seventeenth century, "to render the dots in their proper value one has to sustain (*suspendre*) the dotted quarter and pass quickly the eighth note."[43] Again, in making a judgment regarding the treatment of the dotted quarter note, the conductor will also want to consider the nature and character of the music, as was done with the dotted eighth note.

A different treatment of dotted rhythms, however, should occur with trochaic rhythms in compound triple meter, which are sometimes written as dotted rhythms. For example, the rhythm notated as $\frac{3}{4}$ ♫ ♫ ♫♫ | should be performed as $\frac{9}{8}$ ♩ ♪ ♩ ♪ ♫♫ | . To determine the proper handling of these rhythms the conductor should analyze the music; when the dominant rhythm is compound triple meter (often determined by the triplet groupings), then the passage should be performed as indicated in the latter example above.[44]

A somewhat more controversial problem is encountered in the handling of dotted eighth notes against triplets. An example of this occurs in the Bach sacred cantata No. 4, *Christ lag in Todesbanden* ("Christ Lay in Death's Dark Prison"), *Versus VI* (see Figure 9).[45] The dotted rhythm ♪.♪ ♪.♪ in the bass line of the orchestral accompaniment (*continuo*) occurs against the triplet figure ♫♩♩♩ in the parts for soprano and tenor. As a general rule, duplets should yield to triplets.[46] In this case the dotted eighth note should coincide with the first two triplets and the sixteenth note with the last triplet (see Figure 10).[47] Also, in reference to this type of notation, Neumann states, "the vertical alignment of the notation can give a clue to the proper interpretation. For example, it seems clear that in this instance, the dotted eighth and sixteenth notes were meant to be synchronized with the triplets."[48]

[43]Michael L'Affiland, *Principes très faciles.*

[44]Ibid., p. 89.

[45]Another example of this problem occurs in Bach's *Jesu, Joy of Man's Desiring* (E. C. Schirmer, No. 317).

[46]For an example of the suggested interpretation, listen to the recording by the Robert Shaw Chorale, RCA Victor LSC-2273.

[47]For a further discussion of dotted rhythms, see Sachs, *Rhythm and Tempo,* pp. 303–306, and Thurston Dart, *The Interpretation of Music* (New York: Harper & Row, 1953), pp. 81–83, 88–89, 111, 125–126, and 171.

[48]Frederick Neumann, "External Evidence and Uneven Notes," *The Musical Quarterly,* Vol. LII, No. 4 (October 1966): 450.

Versus VI

FIGURE 9   Excerpt from Versus VI of *Christ lag in Todesbanden* by J. S. Bach. As the triplets are the dominant rhythm in the accompaniment, the dotted eighth note should coincide with the first two triplets and the sixteenth note with the last triplet. This treatment of the dotted eighth and sixteenth note figures should be continued in all subsequent measures.

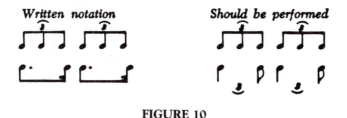

FIGURE 10

Another example of the importance of duplets yielding to triplets occurs in the organ accompaniment to "Jesu, Joy of Man's Desiring," by J. S. Bach. Perhaps some readers will recall, in the not-too-distant past, church organists endeavoring to play the sixteenth note following the last eighth note in a triplet figure and before the next downbeat. How they struggled at that time! If only they knew then that duplets yielded to triplets, their frustrations could have been lessened considerably. In later editions of this work, however, the original notation is altered so that each sixteenth note coincides with the last note in each triplet figure.

An *appoggiatura* is an ornamental note, usually a second, that is melodically connected with the main note that follows and is sung in the same breath. It is indicated by a small note, but in the seventeenth century was often introduced extemporaneously during performance. The duration of the *appoggiatura* is proportionate to the main note according to the following rules: (1) if the main note can be divided into two equal parts, the *appoggiatura* takes half its value; (2) an *appoggiatura* to a dotted note takes two thirds of the main note's value. For example, the *appoggiatura* in the following second measure is notated as

but when performed, the main note (C) is divided into two equal parts as follows:

In the excerpt from "Alleluia" by J. S. Bach (see Figure 11), rule 2 applies and the *appoggiatura* to the dotted note takes two thirds of the main note's value. In other words, the original notation of

would be performed as

Some conductors, however, perform the notation as

Although they presumably know rule 2 on the preferred treatment of *appoggiaturas*, some conductors are instead inclined to follow their own musical instincts as to the interpretation that seems best to them under the circumstances of performance.

Metric Alterations

Perhaps the best-known means of rhythmic alteration during the Baroque period is Sesquialtera. *Sesquialtera* is that proportion which arises when three semibreves (half notes) appear in the time of two semibreves. The sign

FIGURE 11 Excerpt from "Alleluia" by J. S. Bach. The *appoggiatura* to the dotted note takes two thirds of the main note's value.

designating this proportion is 3/2. *Hemiolia* is exactly the same as sesquialtera except that all the notes are blackened. Sesquialtera and hemiolia are identical in function. The changes may occur at any portion of a work and are generally indicated by a change in meter from 4/4 to 3/2 with the directions above the new meter signature of, for example, o = o· , or from 4/4 to 6/4, with the directions of ♩ = ♩· . Examples of these changes occur in "Tröstet, tröstet mein Volk" (Comfort Ye My People) by Heinrich Schütz (see Figure 12), and "For God So Loved the World" by Heinrich Schütz (see Figure 13). In other instances, the directions may be reversed, as ♩· = ♩ preceding, as occurs in the example in Figure 14, "Jubilate Deo" from *Sacrae Symphoniae* by Giovanni Gabrieli. In other words, the notation in each measure of 3/4 meter (♩♩) would receive the same time limit as a half note in the preceding section, thus resulting in a somewhat faster-moving pace in the new section.

When encountering the meter signature 3/1, the 3/1 indication is not a real time signature, but a sign of proportions. It does not mean three whole notes per measure, but that the tempo should be three times as fast. In other words, three semibreves (whole notes) have the same time value as one semibreve had before.[49] (See Figure 15.)

In preparing any work with metrical alteration, first try to analyze the metrical proportions. In a work, for example, with the directions o = o· or

[49]Arthur Mendel, "A Brief Note on Triple Proportion in Schütz," *The Musical Quarterly*, Vol. XLVI, No. 1 (January 1960): 67–70.

FIGURE 12 Excerpt from "Tröstet, tröstet, mein Volk" (Comfort Ye My People) by Heinrich Schütz, edited by C. Buell Agey. Note the directions at the meter change: (o = o.) or C ♩♩ = 3/2 ♩♩♩. Copyright © 1966 G. Schirmer, Inc. International copyright secured. All rights reserved. Used by permission.

FIGURE 13 Excerpt from "For God So Loved the World" by Heinrich Schütz, edited by C. Buell Agey. Note the directions at the meter change (𝅗𝅥 = 𝅘𝅥.) Copyright © 1959 Concordia Publishing House. Used by permission.

FIGURE 14　Excerpt from "Jubilate Deo" from *Sacrae Symphoniae* by Giovanni Gabrieli, edited and arranged by Norman Greyson. Note the directions given at the meter change (♩. = ♩ preceding). Copyright 1963 by Bourne Co. Used by permission.

♩ = ♩. in contrast with the established rhythm, it might be helpful to think of the notation at the metrical change as delayed triplets. After analyzing the rhythmic change, try playing it on the piano and then singing the change until it seems smooth and natural. Then determine the appropriate conducting gestures and try to practice the change without and then with the music.

Tempo

The tempo of Baroque music should generally be somewhat moderate and deliberate, and extremes should be avoided. Even fast tempi should be performed with some restraint. Donington states, "No slow movement should

FIGURE 15 Excerpt from "And Take Heed to Yourselves" by Heinrich Schütz, edited by Denis Stevens. Note the meter change from C to 3/1 and the marking *L'istesso tempo* ♩ = ♩ . Copyright © 1966 by C. F. Peters Corporation. Used by permission.

make us think of it as slow, nor fast movement as fast. A certain pulse should keep the slow movement alive; a certain ampleness should keep the fast movement from sounding hurried.[50] During the Baroque period, Italian terms such as *allegro* and *largo* were used to indicate the character of the music, rather than as specific directions as to tempo. As a result some conductors, misunderstanding the meaning of these terms, are inclined to rush the music marked *allegro* and *vivace*, and to conduct too slowly music marked *adagio* and *largo*. Italian markings should be considered as an indication of mood rather than of tempo. *Allegro* should be interpreted literally, as merry, lively, brisk, rather than as fast, while *largo* should be considered as simply broad, rather than as very slow.[51]

Handel often wrote the Italian marking *largo* at the end of many of his sacred choruses. The composer's intent in adding this marking at the end of a chorus implies simply that the quarter note for the *allegro* becomes exactly twice as long for the *largo*; for example, if the *allegro* has been conducted at $\downarrow = 120$, then the *largo* will be conducted at $\downarrow = 60$. He also, however, sometimes wrote notes of a larger or greater value as a means of achieving the desired intention of *largo*, that is, simply broad. For the conductor to further slow down the pulse of the music would make the ending too slow and thus distort the desired effect.[52]

Of the music that doubles in time values at the portion marked *adagio*, certainly the most familiar is the final measures of the "Hallelujah Chorus" from *Messiah* by G. F. Handel. This may serve as a model when dealing with other pieces marked *adagio* in the closing measures (see Figure 16). Another work similarly marked is the final measure of "Zadok the Priest," also by Handel (see Figure 17). Doubling the time length should be limited to those pieces marked *adagio*, as other music often necessitates a different treatment. For example, in the closing measures of "All Breathing Life, Sing and Praise Ye the Lord," from the motet *Sing Ye to the Lord*, by J. S. Bach, the tempo should gradually be held back and ritarded to the final chord beginning with the part marked *largamente* (broadly) (see Figure 18). A similar treatment is needed in the final measures of "Hallelujah Amen" from *Judas Maccabaeus* by G. F. Handel, beginning with the part marked *maestoso* (majestic) (see Figure 19). In the final measures of "Alleluia" by J. S. Bach, the tempo should be gradually held back beginning with the last Alleluia (see Figure 20).

In the early Baroque monody, a considerable flexibility existed in the tempo so that the emotions in the text and the music might be fully expressed. In the late 1630s, however, a reversal of this trend occurred and the tempi of

---

[50]Robert Donington, *The Interpretation of Early Music,* 2nd ed. (London: Faber and Faber, 1965), p. 317.

[51]Richard T. Gore, "The Performance of Baroque Church Music," *Music Teachers National Association, Volume of Proceedings,* 1950 (Pittsburgh: The Association, 1953), pp. 156–157.

[52]Ibid., p. 157.

FIGURE 16 Excerpt from the final measures of "Hallelujah Chorus" from *Messiah* by G. F. Handel. The portion beginning with the measures marked *Adagio* are meant to be conducted and performed at a tempo twice as slow as in the preceding *Allegro*.

FIGURE 17 Excerpt from the final measures of "Zadok the Priest" by G. F. Handel. The portion beginning with *Adagio* is performed at a tempo twice as slow as in the preceding *Allegro moderato*.

FIGURE 18 Excerpt from the closing measures of "All Breathing Life, Sing and Praise Ye the Lord," from the motet *Sing Ye to the Lord* by J. S. Bach. Beginning with the measure marked *largamente* (broadly), the tempo should gradually be held back and ritarded to the final chord.

FIGURE 19 Excerpt from the last score of "Hallelujah, Amen" from *Judas Maccabaeus* by G. F. Handel. Beginning with the part marked *Maestoso* (majestic), the tempo should be held back and gradually ritarded to the end.

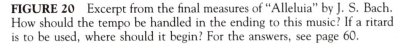

FIGURE 20 Excerpt from the final measures of "Alleluia" by J. S. Bach. How should the tempo be handled in the ending to this music? If a ritard is to be used, where should it begin? For the answers, see page 60.

music became more strict and restrained.[53] The relative freedom of emotional expression gave way to rhythmical shifts within a stricter tempo.

According to Machlis, one of the most notable characteristics of Baroque music is its steady pulsation or unflagging rhythm.[54]

> The Baroque, with its fondness for energetic movement, demanded a dynamic rhythm based on the regular recurrence of accent. The bass part became the carrier of the new rhythm. Its relentless beat is an arresting trait in many compositions of the Baroque. This steady pulsation, once under way, never slackens or deviates until the goal is reached. It imparts to baroque music its unflagging drive, producing the same effect of turbulent yet controlled motion as animates baroque painting, sculpture, and architecture.[55]

Although a steady pulsating drive is important to proper interpretation, this does not mean that the tempo should be completely unyielding. For instance, at cadences immediately prior to subsequent sections, a slight holding back of the tempo is often desirable. The exact treatment of each cadence, however, will vary according to the music itself.[56] In reference to the handling of cadences, *Grove's* states:

> Each needs its own natural flexibility, though this may vary according to circumstances from the merest easing scarcely consciously perceptible, at the one extreme, to a majestic broadening at the other. It is for the performer to judge on the merits of each case between sentimental excess and self-conscious rigidity.[57]

The long, gradual *accelerando* and *ritardando* (or *rallentando*) are inappropriate and out of place in Baroque music, principally because these concepts of gradually increasing or gradually decreasing the tempo did not exist in this period. These concepts grew out of the Mannheim school in the latter part of the eighteenth century. Another concept often misunderstood is the treatment of the *fermata*. A *fermata* in Baroque music simply indicates the end of a phrase and a point at which the singers may take a breath. The concept of the *fermata* as an untimed hold developed during the latter part of the eighteenth century, as did also the modern concept of *accelerando* and *ritardando*.

---

[53]Sachs, *Rhythm and Tempo*, pp. 265–266.

[54]Exceptions to this general characteristic of Baroque music are the *recitative*, which is sung in a declamatory style with stress or accent occurring as a result of important words or particular syllables, and the *arioso*, which in style lies somewhere between the recitative and the aria and possesses some of the characteristics of each.

[55]Joseph Machlis, *The Enjoyment of Music*, 3rd reg. ed. (New York: W. W. Norton & Company, Inc., 1970), p. 397. Used with permission.

[56]For a discussion of conflicting viewpoints in regard to tempo changes, see Sachs, *Rhythm and Tempo*, pp. 277–280.

[57]*Grove's Dictionary of Music and Musicians*, ed. Eric Blom, Vol. II (New York: St. Martin's Press, Inc., Macmillan & Co. Ltd., 1954), p. 986. Used by permission of Macmillan, London and Basingstoke.

Cadences are extremely numerous in Baroque music and it is in the nature of a cadence to be acknowledged by a *rallentando*. One needs, however, to distinguish cadences that pass on at once from those that bring some portion of the music to an end.[58] In other words, one must differentiate between internal cadences, where only a slight *rallentando* would be appropriate, and a final cadence where a more deliberate slowing down of the tempo contributes to the finality of the work.

A rather conflicting opinion as to the necessity for *rallentando* is expressed by Paul H. Lang. "Cadences were indeed slowed down, especially at the ends of sections, because an improvised ornamental embellishment was usually executed at such points. Our musicians are no longer trained in this art of improvisation (though some able harpsichordists are bringing it back), therefore the main reasons for the *ritard* no longer exists."[59] Lang's statement, however, was made over 17 years ago, and today's musicians *are* well trained. Things have changed!

It is hoped that this information will not leave the choral conductor in a quandary. It should simply reaffirm the fact that in interpreting Baroque music, conductors must rely upon their innate musical judgment as to the rendition that feels and sounds best. The point of view has been expressed that the text of the music often holds the clue to identifying the correct tempo.[60]

Another factor affecting tempo and discussed in the preceding section is the effect of metrical alteration. Metrical changes of, for example, 4/4 to 3/2, with the directions of o = o. or ♩ = ♩. result in a faster-moving tempo in the new section. Also, metrical changes of 4/4 to 3/1 result in a new tempo that is three times as fast as in the preceding section.

Dynamics

The concept of *crescendo* and *decrescendo* did not exist widely during the Baroque period, principally because the instruments of the period did not have the necessary flexibility to achieve these ends. The organ, for example, did not possess swell shutters until 1712, and the piano was not invented until the latter part of the period. Therefore, contrast was sought by other means.[61] Contrast in dynamics was achieved by adding or dropping out various instruments or voice parts. This was referred to as *terraced dynamics*, meaning various levels or plateaus of dynamics. Extremes in dynamics, therefore, should

---

[58]Donington, *Early Music*, p. 367.

[59]Paul H. Lang, "Performing Bach," *American Choral Review*, Vol. XVII, No. 4 (October 1975): 17–21.

[60]Jean Colleen Bicknell, "On Performing Purcell's Vocal Music: Some Neglected Evidence," *Music Review*, Vol. 25, No. 1 (February 1964): 27–33.

[61]According to *Grove's Dictionary of Music and Musicians*, *crescendo* and *decrescendo* were not entirely unknown to Baroque composers, as written indications of it are found in the mid-seventeenth-century music of the Italian composer Mazzochi (*Grove's*, Vol. II, p. 988).

be avoided, as the concept of terraced dynamics would render them undesirable.[62] Usually the music itself will take care of the often slight dynamic changes in terraced dynamics, and one should question editorial markings that seem to place undue emphasis upon these changes. Terraced dynamics is only part of the change, however, the other being in the density due to the increase or decrease of the number of voices participating. Composers up through J. S. Bach generally did not include dynamic markings, but in those instances where they did, it was to make clear a change that might not have been recognized in the performance practice of the time or where an absolute insistence of change seemed necessary by the composer. The conductor should utilize a dynamic range only from *piano* to *forte*. Extending the dynamics above or below these levels is inappropriate and should generally be avoided except on rare occasions.

Exceptions to rules often exist, however, and Boyden cites two examples in music of the period: "dying away to nothing" (Mazzochi, 1638 in a madrigal), and Leonard Lechter (ca. 1640), who uses the signs *p, pp, ppp,* and *pppp.*"[63]

Regarding the clarity of entering parts in polyphonic music, Lodovico Zacconi in *Prattica di Musica*, Venice, 1592, states, "Entries should be emphasized a little so as to be instantly and clearly perceived by the hearer".[64]

To achieve the proper balance among the parts, however, Boyden advises: "In polyphonic music, when the entries follow closely one upon another, it may be necessary to reduce the volume and significance of the part almost as soon as the entry has been made, in order to get out of the way of the next entry."[65]

Tone Quality

An exact reconstruction of an original performance is probably not possible, but we can strive for a reasonable achievement of the older traditions. Certainly one elusive aspect of performance is vocal tone quality. As to timbre, "the sound ideal of the Baroque period was not the full, rich, vibrant sonority that is cultivated by modern instruments and singers. It was a thin, clear, somewhat piercing tone . . . inherent in most of the instruments of the period—the viols, recorders, cornetti, high trumpets, harpsichord, the stops of the Baroque organ, and even the seventeenth-century violins."[66]

---

[62]Gore, *Baroque Church Music*, pp. 157–158.

[63]David D. Boyden, "Dynamics in Seventeenth- and Eighteenth-Century Music," in *Essays on Music in Honor of Archibald T. Davison* (Cambridge, MA: Harvard University Press, 1957), pp. 185–193.

[64]Donington, *Early Music*, p. 426.

[65]Boyden, "Seventeenth- and Eighteenth-Century Music," p. 418.

[66]Putman Aldrich, "The Authentic Performance of Baroque Music," in *Essays on Music in Honor of Archibald T. Davison* (Cambridge, MA: Harvard University Press, 1957), p. 162.

Because of the ornateness of some musical passages, a heavy, weighty tone quality would prohibit a singer from properly articulating the music. Modern voice training often places heavy emphasis upon the fullness and vibrancy of sustained tone quality. In the Baroque period, in contrast, the emphasis was upon agility and the clear execution of graces, trills, and rapid scale passages.[67]

The Italian vocal technique widely used during the seventeenth century was *bel canto* (Italian for "beautiful singing"). Its emphasis was on beauty of sound and brilliancy of performance, as well as on an elegant vocal style. It has also been described as a light and florid vocal delivery. As to vibrato, it has been stated that in late Baroque vocal performance a freely produced, resonant voice will have a certain amount of vibrato as it is part of the technique.[68]

The Counter-Reformation that developed during the latter part of the sixteenth century and its desire to impress, gave rise to the use of castrati in the performance of choral music in the church, as well as in the theatre. One of the most famous castrati of the eighteenth century was Farinelli, whose coloratura was said to be remarkable.

Pitch

According to Mendel, the pitch levels at which Baroque music was performed varied considerably. They were different from town to town and even from church to church. During the Baroque period there were two principal terms for identifying pitch standards: *Kammerton* (chamber pitch) and *Chorton* (choir pitch). In 1619, Michael Praetorius (1571–1621) stated that *Chorton* was a major second above *Kammerton*, which was the practice in Germany in his time. However, in Prague and other Catholic courts the usage was reversed, with *Kammerton* being the higher pitch and *Chorton* the lower of the two pitches. It is said that Praetorius preferred this latter scheme and recommended its adoption.[69] Twenty-three years later, however, Mendel states,

> To musicians before 1750, the notes on the staff, and the names by which they
> were referred to, represented degrees in a gamut that had no permanent anchor
> at a standard pitch level, but was freely moveable up and down according to the
> nature of the voices or instruments involved on any given occasion. This attitude
> was the same as that of the present-day tonic *sol-fa* system, with its moveable *do*.
> The gamut itself was at first of small compass, and the limit within which it might
> move up or down entirely undefined. But as the compass of the gamut was
> extended, these limits gradually narrowed, until in our own day the amount of

[67]Ibid., p. 163.

[68]Anthony Ransome, "Towards an Authentic Vocal Style and Technique in Late Baroque Performance," *Early Music*, Vol. 6, No. 3 (July 1978): 417–419.

[69]Arthur Mendel, "On the Pitch in Use in Bach's Time—I," *Musical Quarterly*, Vol. XLI, No. 3 (July 1955): 335–336.

variation is slight. . . . For the musicians before 1750 "A" meant any tone related to a given pattern of tones, and semitones to the other tones in use, the actual pitch (varying over the distance of a major third or more) being determined by the convenience or necessity of the moment.[70]

There are still those authorities, however, who believe that there was a standard pitch of A = 422, which is about a semitone below A = 440, and known as low pitch during the Baroque period. While some authorities feel that this was considered a standard pitch between 1600 and 1820, others disagree and feel this pitch had no greater usage than other pitches during the period.[71] However, if one believes this premise, then to perform Baroque music in as authentic a manner as possible, one ought to lower the pitch a half step to return it to its original key. Of course, practical considerations, such as the difficulty of transposing the orchestral parts, or even the piano or organ accompaniment, often make this practice unfeasible. Another argument, however, against this practice is the additional brilliance which is often achieved through performance in the higher key. On the other hand, when the *tessitura* of the various parts appears to be too high and thus negatively influences the tone quality, the conductor may consider lowering the pitch. If he elects to do so, he then will have at least two justifications for his decision. By and large, however, the conductor will find his problems minimized if he performs the music in the key in which it is presently written.

Texture

The beginning of the Baroque period ushered in a change from a texture of independent but interrelated parts to a single melody or voice part supported by chords or chordal combinations. This change from modal polyphony to a homophonic style necessitated a change in the harmonic system—from the medieval church modes to a system of major and minor tonality. Whereas the polyphony of the Renaissance symbolized the submissiveness of the individual, the new style fulfilled the need for greater individual expression. Secular music gained vastly in importance, and the new style allowed for a greater emotional expression of the text. When polyphony returned, after a brief lapse, it did so within a different harmonic framework, that is, the system of major–minor tonality.[72] Even when the new harmonic counterpoint came into vogue, some composers continued to write in the old-style polyphony (*stile antico*),

---

[70]Arthur Mendel, "Pitch in Western Music Since 1500, A Re-examination," *Acta Musicoligica*, Vol. L (1978): 1–93.

[71]Donington, *Early Music*, p. 445.

[72]While polyphony was rejected by most composers during the early Baroque period, it was never abandoned by the famous three S's: Johann Herman Schein (1586–1630), Samuel Scheidt (1587–1654), and Heinrich Schütz (1585–1672).

sometimes called the Palestrina style. Conductors, therefore, need to recognize and treat each style accordingly.

As Baroque polyphony functions within a harmonic framework of tonality and generally well-defined chord progressions, cadences are important aspects of arrival but may be different according to the overall texture of the music, i.e., some may be lighter and others heavier (see section on tempo for a discussion on the treatment of cadences). Also, the complexity of the texture, as well as the complexity of the chords, especially when some have been chromatically altered, may have an influence on the tempo of the music. In lighter textures the tempo may be pushed slightly forward, while in denser textures the tempo may be held back somewhat. As to imitations, answering voices should be replicas of the announcing voice's treatment of the subject, including specific rhythmic patterns, trills, and so on.

As to the practice of ornamentation, Aldrich states, "the intervals between the notes of the given melody are filled in more or less completely with free melodic ornaments, scalewise or *arpeggio* figures beginning and ending on the given notes. This type of ornament was known as *passaggio*. It had no fixed form; nevertheless its use was taught systematically, as follows: the instructor took up each possible interval that could occur in a basic melody (i.e., unison, ascending 2nd, 3rd, 4th, etc.). The student was required to memorize a large number of *passaggi*, in various rhythms that could be used appropriately to fill out each interval. The number of possibilities is, of course, infinite, and the student, after having become proficient at introducing a good number of representative patterns, was encouraged to invent his own."[73]

An example of how written music might be embellished in performance is illustrated in Figure 21, an excerpt from "Funeste piaggie" by the early Baroque composer JACOPO PERI (1561–1633).[74]

Expressive Aspects

In contrast to the Renaissance composer, who expressed emotion with considerable restraint, the Baroque composer gave freer vent to his emotions. Nevertheless, his music was still somewhat impersonal, with the emotion stemming not from an individual struggle, as in the Romantic period, but from the tumultuous and dramatic forces affecting all mankind.[75]

Within the new system of major–minor tonality, each chord assumed a definite relationship to the others. Harmonic tension and repose were well understood by composers of the period and were used as devices in composition.

---

[73]Putman Aldrich, "Bach's Technique of Transcription and Improvised Ornamentation," *Musical Quarterly*, Vol. XXXV, No. 1 (January 1949): 32.

[74]From Donington, *Early Music*, p. 105.

[75]George Howerton, *Technique and Style in Choral Singing* (New York: Carl Fischer, Inc., 1957), p. 133.

FIGURE 21   Excerpt from "Funeste piaggie" by Jacopo Peri. (a) Music as written, (b) how the music might be performed, and (c) how the music might be performed as the end of a piece.

There were fewer but stronger cadences, and the drive to the keynote was apparent. There was a considerable increase in the intensity of the music and in the amount of dissonance that was used for the purpose of achieving emotional intensity. Whereas in the Renaissance period dissonance was permissible only when prepared—that is, when first heard with a consonant interval and introduced through a suspension—the use of unprepared dissonance became accepted and widely used as an expressive device.[76]

Tone painting, or the way in which the music portrayed the words, was increasingly given attention by composers of the period. Bach, for example, advised his students to "play the chorale [prelude] according to the meaning of the words." It must be understood, however, that although the text gave birth to the musical idea, it was the music itself that ultimately reigned supreme.[77]

The Baroque period marked the first time in history that instrumental music assumed an equal position with vocal music. The spirit of the times prompted the development of new instruments and improvements in the old. The new status of instrumental music has caused certain people to say that some music was conceived instrumentally rather than vocally. The performance of Baroque music, therefore, necessitates a most exacting rhythmic precision. Singers should thus be as exacting as instrumentalists. They should also maintain a steadiness and purity of vocal line, devoid of excessive vibrato, as this may adversely affect the intonation and thus blur the polyphonic

[76]Claudio Monteverdi (1567–1643) is often credited with the first wide use of unprepared dissonance.

[77]Machlis, *Enjoyment of Music*, p. 355.

structure. These qualities are especially important in singing contrapuntal music.

According to Manfred Bukofzer, one of the fundamental aspects of Baroque music is the musical expression of the text. He states:

> The means of verbal representation in Baroque music were not direct, psychological, and emotional, but indirect, that is, intellectual and pictorial. The modern psychology of dynamic emotions did not yet exist in the Baroque era. Feelings were classified and stereotyped in a set of so-called affections, each representing a mental state which was itself static. It was the business of the composer to make the affections of the music correspond to that of the words according to the lucid rationalism of the time. The composer had at his disposal a set of musical figures which were pigeonholed like the affections themselves and were designed to represent these affections in music.[78]

Perhaps the most obvious types of musical expression were the setting of such words as "ascendit" with a rising and "descendit" with a falling melodic line.

MUSIC AND THE RELATED ARTS

The Baroque style in all the arts extended from about the middle of the sixteenth century to the middle of the eighteenth century. The essence of the Baroque feeling focused on movement, intensity, tension, and force. Baroque art found its greatest fulfillment in the castle and in opera. In architecture the Baroque created a richly ornamented facade, and in the theater it depicted intense emotional states and sentiments, particularly in the ornate embellishments by soloists in opera and oratorio.

In architecture, sculpture and painting, as well as in the music of the Counter-Reformation, the aim was to dazzle and bewilder the spectator or listener.[79] In painting, artists employed curvaceous lines, strong diagonal lines, and bold extreme contrasts of light and shade that created tension and excitement, tonal gradation rather than clear colors, limitations of distinct outlines and the merging of objects into the surrounding background, and the use of large quantities of pigment and the resultant visibility of brush strokes.

Giovanni Lorenzo Bernini (1598–1680) is considered to be the greatest of Baroque sculptors and architects and was a distinguished painter as well. Bernini's lifesize sculpture *The Ecstasy of Saint Teresa* is in the Cornaro Chapel of Santa Maria della Victoria in Rome. Bernini also contributed the baldacchino, a fanciful structure over the high altar (1627–1633) of St. Peter's Basilica in Rome (St. Peter's was completed in 1612). Considered the greatest

---

[78]Qtd. in Glen Haydon, "On the Problem of Expression in Baroque Music," *Journal of the American Musicological Society*, Vol. III, No. 2 (Summer 1950): 113–119.

[79]Dart, *Interpretation of Music*, p. 109.

achievement of Baroque city architecture, the Piazza di San Pietro in Rome was built by Bernini between 1656 and 1667. In this work two vast semicircles of colonnades enclose a space that provides a striking setting of the portal to St. Peter's Basilica.

Other well-known sculptors of the time were Francesco Borromini (1599–1667) and Guarino Guarini (1624–1683) among the Italians; François Mansart (1598–1666) and Claude Perrault (1613–1680), who designed the Louvre, among the French; the architects Johann Fischer von Erlach (1656–1723) and Balthasar Neumann (1607–1753), who helped shape

Gianlorenzo Bernini, *The Ecstasy of Saint Teresa* 1645–52. Marble, lifesize. Cornaro Chapel of Santa Maria della Vittoria, Rome. Alinari-Scala/Art Resource.

Vienna, Dresden, Würzburg, and Munich; and Christopher Wren (1632–1723), who received his opportunity after the great fire of London in 1666.

Bernini's *The Ecstasy of Saint Teresa* is a lifesize white marble sculpture that shows an extraordinary animation of all the surfaces and creates a vivid play of light and dark, imparting a vibrant and ethereal quality to the clothing, the hair, and the angel's feathery wings.[80]

The angel is holding a golden spear that he has plunged into the saint's heart.

> The dart wherewith he wounded me
> Was all embarked with love
> And thus my spirit came to be
> One with the Maker, God above.

Perhaps the most outstanding painter of the Baroque era was Peter Paul Rubens (1577–1640). Among his most celebrated works are *Garden of Love* (1615), *The Conversion of St. Paul* (ca. 1616), *Fall of the Damned* (1620), *Henry IV Receiving the Portrait of Maria de' Medici* (1622–1625), *Garden of Love* (ca. 1632–1634), and *The Adoration of Kings* (1634). One of Rubens' greatest followers was Anthony van Dyck (1599–1641), who was most renowned for his portraits, particularly of the British aristocracy. Diego de Silva y Velasquez (1599–1660) was known for his portraits of King Philip IV, and of Olivarez. The two greatest French painters of the time were Nicolas Poussin (1593–1665) and Claude Lorrain (1660–1682). Poussin is known for his scenes of earthy and sensuous pleasure, and of the mighty clash of arms. *The Rape of the Sabine Women* (1637–1639) is at the Metropolitan Museum of Art in New York, and *The Triumph of Pan* is at the Louvre. Claude Lorrain was a master of sunsets and their sheen upon the waters of harbors, of the indirect light through a mist, and of ships with their masts and sails. Some of his finest works are *Harbor in Mist* (1646), *Landscape with Flight to Egypt* (1647), and *Adoration of the Golden Calf* (1653).

In 1503, the city of Florence commissioned Leonardo da Vinci to do a mural for the council chamber of the Palazzo Vecchio that depicted some historical event. Leonardo chose the Battle of Anghiari where the Florentine forces had once defeated the Milanese army. Leonardo had completed the cartoon and had just begun the mural when his work was interrupted by his return to Milan thus necessitating his abandonment of the project. Today the cartoon is known only through some preliminary sketches by Leonardo, but primarily from a drawing by Peter Paul Rubens, which he completed in about 1605. The savage fury and tension shown in the drawing has seized the animals as well as the men. The battle scene is not uncontrolled, but stabilized by the hexagonal outline (a figure with six angles and six sides).[81]

---

[80]Henri Dorra, *Art in Perspective* (New York: Harcourt Brace Jovanovich), p. 147.

[81]H. W. Janson, *History of Art* (New York: Harry N. Abrams, Inc., 1973), p. 351.

Peter Paul Rubens, *Drawing after Leonardo's Cartoon for "The Battle of Anghiari,"* ca. 1605. The Louvre, Paris.

The idea of expressing emotion originated in the Renaissance and was taken up in the seventeenth century by Baroque artists. Charles Lebrun, Director of the French Academy of Painting and Sculpture, 1663–90, endeavored to formulate rules, and his drawings of the head show the way in which a person's facial muscles contract while under the stress of terror. This was one of a series of drawings done to illustrate his lecture on "The Expression of the Passions," which was probably first given in 1668.[82]

As will be noted in the painting *The Tiger Hunt* by Peter Paul Rubens, Baroque art possesses a turbulent, yet controlled motion that parallels the rhythm in Baroque music.

The most noted of the Dutch artists were Franz Hals (1584–1666) and Rembrandt Harmensz von Rijn (1616–1669). Hals's work was representational of the lust for life and for nature of the Baroque age. His painting style was lively and vivacious, with the use of brilliant but fused colors. One of his outstanding works is *The Women Regents of the Old Men's Home at Haarlem* (1664), the place where he spent his final years. Rembrandt's *The Night Watch* (1641) has been called the greatest painting of the Baroque era.

[82]Michael Kitson, *The Age of the Baroque* (New York: McGraw-Hill Book, Co., 1966), p. 12.

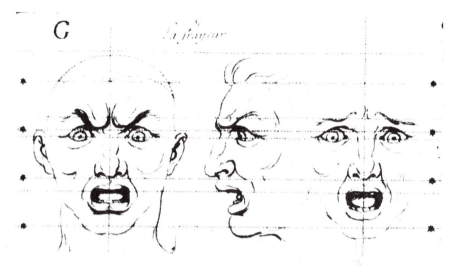

Charles Lebrun, *The Expression of Terror,* 1668? Pen and black ink over a sketch in black chalk. 7¾ × 10 in. The Louvre, Paris.

Peter Paul Rubens, *The Tiger Hunt,* ca. 1616. Panel, 38 × 48 in. The Wadsworth Atheneum, Hartford.

REFERENCES

Aldrich, Putman. "The Authentic Performance of Baroque Music," in *Essays on Music in Honor of Archibald T. Davison.* Cambridge, MA: Harvard University Press, 1957.

——. "Bach's Technique of Transcription and Improvised Ornamentation." *Musical Quarterly,* Vol. XXXV, No. 1, January 1949, pp. 26–35.

Anderson, Nicholas. "Performing Style in Bach Cantatas—1." *Early Music,* Vol. 6, No. 1, January 1978, pp. 89–93.

——. "Performing Style in Bach Cantatas—2." *Early Music,* Vol. 6, No. 3, July 1978, pp. 421–427.

——. "Performing Style in Bach Cantatas—3." *Early Music,* Vol. 7, No. 1, January 1979, pp. 99–102.

Babitz, Sol. "Concerning the Length of Time that Every Note Must be Held." *Music Review,* Vol. 28, No. 1, February 1967, pp. 21–27.

——. "A Problem of Rhythm in Baroque Music." *Musical Quarterly,* Vol. 33, No. 3, July 1952, pp. 533–565.

——. "Restoring Baroque Inequality." *American Recorder,* Vol. IX, 1968, p. 7.

Babitz, Sol, J. Byrt, and Michael Collins. "Three Further Views on Notes Inégales." *Journal of the American Musicological Society,* Vol. XX, 1967, p. 473.

Bicknell, Jean Colleen. "On Performing Purcell's Vocal Music: Some Neglected Evidence." *Music Review,* Vol. 25, No. 1, February 1964, pp. 27–33.

Blom, Eric, Editor. *Grove's Dictionary of Music and Musicians,* 5th ed. Vol. II. New York: St. Martin's Press, Inc., Macmillan & Co. Ltd., 1954.

Borge, Dale. "Gaffurius on Pulse and Tempo: A Reinterpretation." *Musica Disciplina,* Vol. XXXVI, 1982, pp. 167–174.

Borroff, Edith. *The Music of the Baroque.* Dubuque, IA: Wm. C. Brown Company, 1970.

Bowman, David D. A Study of the Castrati Singers and Their Music. Ph.D. dissertation, Indiana University, 1952.

Boyden, David D. "Dynamics in Seventeenth- and Eighteenth-Century Music," in *Essays on Music in Honor of Archibald T. Davison.* Cambridge, MA: Harvard University Press, 1957.

Braudel, Fernard. *Afterthoughts on Material Civilization and Capitalism.* Baltimore: The Johns Hopkins University Press, 1977.

Brooke, Barry S. "Pergolesi: Vindication After 250 Years." *The Musical Times,* Vol. 127, No. 1717, March 1986, pp. 141–145.

Brown, Howard Mayer, and Stanley Sadie, eds. *Performance Practice: Music After 1600.* Basingstoke, Hampshire, England: Macmillan; New York: W. W. Norton, 1990.

Buelow, George J. "A Schütz Reader: Documents on Performance Practice." *American Choral Review,* Vol. XXVII, No. 4, October 1985, pp. 5–35.

——. "A Study in Baroque Performing Practice." *The Musical Times,* Vol. CXX, No. 1638, August 1979, pp. 625, 638–639.

——. "Vocal Ornamentation in the Sacred Music of the Schütz Era." *American Choral Review,* Vol. XXIV, No's 2 and 3, April and July 1982, pp. 5–13.

Bukofzer, Manfred F. *Music in the Baroque Era: From Monteverdi to Bach.* New York: W. W. Norton and Company, 1947.

Campbell, Margaret. "To Dot or Double Dot? The Eternal Question." *The Consort,* Vol. 31, July 1975, pp. 142–147.

Charteris, Richard. "The Performance of Giovanni Gabrieli's Vocal Works: Indications in the Early Sources." *Music and Letters,* Vol. 71, No. 3, August 1990, pp. 336–351.

Cipolla, Carlo. *Before the Industrial Revolution: European Society and Economy, 1000–1700.* New York: W. W. Norton and Company, 1975.

Collins, Michael B. "Correspondence on The Performance of Coloration, Sesquialtera and Hemiola (1450–1750)." *Current Musicology,* Vol. 5, 1967, pp. 128–130.

——. *The Performance of Coloration, Sesquialtera and Hemiola (1450–1750).* Ph.D. dissertation, Stanford University, 1963.

——. "The Performance of Triplets in the 17th and 18th Centuries." *Journal of the American Musicological Society,* Vol. XIX, Fall 1966, pp. 281–328.

——. "A Reconsideration of French Overdotting." *Music and Letters,* Vol. 50, 1969, p. 111–123.

Crookes, David Z. "Small As a Eunuch: A Problem in Coriolanus, Act III, Scene 2." *Music and Letters*, Vol. LXVII, No. 2, April 1986, pp. 159–161.

Dart, Thurston. *The Interpretation of Music*. New York: Harper & Row, Publishers, 1963.

Dolmetsch, Arnold. *The Interpretation of the Music of the XVIIth & XVIIIth Centuries*. London: Oxford University Press, 1946.

Dolmetsch, Carl. "Interpretation." *The Consort*, No. 5, 1948, pp. 7–12.

Dolmetsch, Cecile. "Ornamentation in Singing." *The Consort*, No. 9, 1952, pp. 21–23.

Donington, Robert. "Baroque Interpretation," in *Grove's Dictionary of Music and Musicians*, 5th ed. Eric Blom, Editor. London: Macmillan & Co., Ltd., 1954.

————. *Baroque Music: Style and Performance*. New York: W. W. Norton, 1982.

————. "The Choice of Instruments in Baroque Music." *Early Music*, Vol. 1, No. 3, July 1973, pp. 131–146.

————. *The Interpretation of Early Music*, 2nd ed. London: Faber and Faber, 1965.

————. "On Interpreting Early Music." *Music and Letters*, Vol. XXVII, No. 1, January 1947, pp. 223–241.

————. *A Performer's Guide to Baroque Music*. New York: Charles Scribner's Sons, 1973.

————. "A Problem of Inequality." *Musical Quarterly*, Vol. 53, No. 4, October 1967, pp. 505–517.

————. "What Is Rhythmic Alteration?" *Early Music*, Vol. 5, No. 4, October 1977, pp. 542–544.

Dorian, Frederick. *The History of Music in Performance*. New York: W. W. Norton & Company, 1942.

Dorra, Henri. *Art in Perspective*. New York: Harcourt Brace Jovanovich.

Durr, Alfred. "Performance Practice of Bach's Cantatas." *American Choral Review*, Vol. XVI, No. 2, April 1974, pp. 5–33.

Eckersley, Kate. "Some Late Chamber Cantatas of Domenico Scarlatti: A Question of Style." *The Musical Times*, Vol. 131, No. 1773, November 1990, pp. 585–591.

Ehman, Wilhelm. "Performance Practice of Bach's Motets." *The American Choral Review*, Vol. XV, No. 2, April 1973, p. 10.

Elvers, Rudolf. "The Interpretation of Bach. A Note on Additional Ornaments and Rhythmic Alteration." *The Musical Times*, Vol. XCVI, 1955, pp. 190–193.

Emery, Walter. "The Interpretation of Bach." *The Musical Times*, Vol. XCVI, April 1955, pp. 190–193.

Fenlon, Iain. "Production and Distribution of Music in 16th- and 17th-Century European Society." *Acta Musicologica*, Vol. LIX, January–April 1987, pp. 14–18.

Fernad, Ernest, T. "Improvised Vocal Counterpoint in the Late Renaissance and Early Baroque." *Annales Musicologiques*, Vol. IV, 1956, pp. 129–174.

Fischer-Dieskau, Klaus. "The Employment of Dynamics in Interpreting the Music of Heinrich Schuetz and Hugo Distler." Translated by Martyn Clarke and Harold A. Decker. *The Choral Journal*, Vol. XIV, No. 2, October 1973, pp. 14–19.

Fleming, William, and Abraham Veinus. *Understanding Music: Style, Structure, and History*. New York: Holt, Rinehart and Winston, 1958.

Friedrich, Carl J. *The Age of the Baroque*. New York: Harper & Row, 1962.

Fuller, David. "Dotting, the 'French Style,' and Frederick Neumann's Counter-Reformation." *Early Music*, Vol. V, No. 4, October 1977, pp. 517–543.

————. "Notes and Inégales Unjoined: Defending a Definition." *Journal of Musicology*, Vol. 7, No. 1, Winter 1989, pp. 21–28.

————. "Notes Inégales," in *The New Grove Dictionary of Music and Musicians*. Edited by Stanley Sadie. London: Macmillan Publishers, Ltd., 1980, pp. 420–427.

Garong, William F. *Review of Medical Physiology*, 3rd ed. Los Angeles, CA: Appleton & Lange, 1967, p. 358 (on the physical characteristics of the castrati).

Goldman, Lawrence Louis. *The Castrato* (a novel). New York: The John Day Company, 1973.

Gore, Richard T. "The Performance of Baroque Church Music." *Music Teachers National Association, Volume of Proceedings*, 1950. Pittsburgh: The Association, 1953, pp. 156–157.

Harding, Rosamond E. M. *Origins of Musical Time and Expression*. London: Oxford University Press, 1938.

Harmon, R., Alec, and Anthony Milner. *Late Renaissance and Baroque Music*. London: Barrie & Rockliff, 1959.

Haskell, Harry. *The Early Music Revival*. London: Thames and Hudson, Ltd., 1988.

Hawthorne, Walter. "The Choral Conductor and Proportio Sesquialtera." *Choral Journal*, Vol. XXII, No. 7, March 1982, pp. 19–24.

Haydon, Glen. "On the Problem of Expression in Baroque Music." *Journal of the American Musicological Society*, Vol. III, No. 2, Summer 1950, pp. 113–119.

Heriot, Angus. *The Castrati in Opera*. London: Secker and Warburg, 1956.

Herz, Gerhard. "Bach Sources in America." *American Choral Review*, Vol. XXV, No. 2, April 1983, pp. 5–51.

———. "The Performance History of Bach's B Minor Mass." *American Choral Review*, Vol. XV, No. 1, January 1973, pp. 5–21.

Hiley, David. "Sesquialtera" in *The New Grove Dictionary of Music and Musicians*. Edited by Stanley Sadie. Vol. 17. London: Macmillan Publishers, Ltd., pp. 192–193.

Horsley, Imogene. "Improvised Embellishment in the Performance of Polyphonic Music." *Journal of the American Musicological Society*, Vol. IV, No. 1, Spring 1951, pp. 3–10.

Houle, George. "Meter and Performance in the Seventeenth and Eighteenth Centuries." *Historical Performance: The Journal of Early Music America*, Vol. 2, No. 1, Spring 1989, pp. 11–15.

Howerton, George. *Technique and Style in Choral Singing*. New York: Carl Fischer, 1957.

Jacobs, Arthur. *Choral Music*. Baltimore: Penguin Books, 1963.

Jacobson, Bernard. "Nikolaus Harnoncourt on Bach," in *Conductors on Conducting*. Frenchtown, NJ: Columbia Publishing Co., 1979, pp. 51–69.

———. "Sir Charles Mackerras on Handel," in *Conductors on Conducting*. Frenchtown, NJ: Columbia Publishing Co., 1979, pp. 75–97.

Kenyon, Nicholas, Editor. *Authenticity and Early Music: A Symposium*. Oxford/New York: Oxford University Press, 1988.

Kirby, F. E. "Herman Finck on Methods of Performance." *Music and Letters*, Vol. XLII, No. 1, 1961, pp. 212–220.

L'Affiland, Michael. *Principes très faciles pour bien apprendre la musique*. Paris, 1694 (2nd ed., 1697).

Lam, Basil. "Authenticity and the St. John Passion." *Early Music*, Vol. 5. No. 1, 1977, pp. 45–49.

Lang, Paul Henry. *Music in Western Civilization*. New York: W. W. Norton & Company, 1941.

———. "Performing Bach." *American Choral Review*, Vol. XVII, No. 4, October 1975, pp. 17–21.

Larsen, Jens Peter. "Handel Studies." *American Choral Review*, Vol. XIV, No. 1, January 1972, pp. 7–49.

———. "Messiah Performance Traditions." *American Choral Review*, Vol. XIV, No. 1, January 1972, pp.

Linfield, Eva. "Formal and Tonal Organization in a 17th Century Ritornello/Ripiero Structure," *The Journal of Musicology*. Volume IX, No. 2, Spring, 1991, pp. 145–164.

Lionnet, Jean. "Performance Practice in the Papal Chapel During the 17th Century." *Early Music*, Vol. 15, No. 1, February 1987, pp. 4–15.

Lowinsky, Edward. "On the Use of Scores by Sixteenth Century Musicians." *Journal of the American Musicological Society*, Vol. I, No. 1, Spring 1948, pp. 17–23.

MacClintock, Carol. *Readings in the History of Music in Performance*. Bloomington, IN: Indiana University Press, 1979.

Machlis, Joseph. *The Enjoyment of Music*. 3rd reg. ed. New York: W. W. Norton & Company, 1970.

Mackerras, Charles. "Sense About the Appoggiatura." *Opera*, Vol. XIV, 1963, pp. 669–678.

Marshall, Robert L. "Bach's Chorus: A Preliminary Reply to Joshua Rifkin." *The Musical Times*, Vol. 124, No. 1679, January 1983, pp. 19–22.

———. "Bach's Choruses, Reconstituted." *High Fidelity*, October 1982.

Matthews, Betty. "Handel and the Royal Society of Musicians." *The Musical Times*, Vol. 125, No. 1692, pp. 79–82.

Mendel, Arthur. "A Brief Note on Triple Proportion in Schuetz." *The Musical Quarterly*, Vol. XLVI, No. 1, January 1960, pp. 67–70.

———. "On the Pitches in Use in Bach's Time." *Musical Quarterly*, Vol. XLI, No. 3, July 1955, pp. 332–354, 466–480.

———. "Pitch in the 16th and Early 17th Centuries." *Musical Quarterly*, Vol. 34, No. 2, April 1948, pp. 28–45, 199–221, 336–357, 575–593.

———. "Pitch in Western Music Since 1500, A Re-examination." *Acta Musicoligica*, Vol. L, 1978, pp. 1–93.

Moses, Don V., with Robert W. Demarec, Jr. "Articulation in Late Baroque Choral Music." *The Choral Journal*, Vol. XXVII, No. 10, May 1987, pp. 17–30.

Neumann, Frederick. "External Evidence and Uneven Notes." *Musical Quarterly*, Vol. LII, No. 4, October 1966, pp. 448–464.

———. "Facts and Fiction About Overdotting." *Musical Quarterly*, Vol. LXIII, No. 2, April 1977, pp. 155–185.

———. *New Essays on Performance Practice*. Ann Arbor, MI: UMI Research Press, 1989.

———. "The Notes inégales Revisited." *The Journal of Musicology*, Vol. VI, No. 2, Spring 1988, pp. 137–149.

———. "Notes on 'Melodic' and 'Harmonic' Ornaments." *The Music Review*, Vol. 29, No. 4, November 1968, pp. 249–256.

———. "Once More: The 'French Overture Style'." *Early Music*, Vol. 7, No. 1, January 1979, pp. 39–45.

———. "Ornament and Structure." *Musical Quarterly*, Vol. LVI, No. 2, April 1970, pp. 153–161.

———. *Ornamentation in Baroque and Post-Baroque Music With Special Emphasis on J. S. Bach.* Princeton/Guildford: Princeton University Press, 1978.

———. "The Overdotting Syndrome: Anatomy of a Delusion." *The Musical Quarterly*, Vol. 67, No. 3, July 1981, pp. 305–347.

———. "The Use of Baroque Treatises on Musical Performance." *Music and Letters*, Vol. XLVIII, 1967, p. 315.

Palisca, Claude. "Baroque," in *The New Grove Dictionary of Music and Musicians*. Vol. II. London: Macmillan Publishers, Ltd., 1980, pp. 172–178.

———. *Baroque Music*, 2nd ed. Englewood Cliffs, NJ: Prentice Hall, 1981.

Pont, Graham. "Handel and Regularization: A Third Alternative." *Early Music*, Vol. 13, No. 4, November 1985, pp. 500–505.

Rangel-Ribeira, Victor. *Baroque Music: A Practical Guide*. New York: Schirmer Books, 1981.

Rifkin, Joshua. "Bach's Chorus: A Preliminary Report." *The Musical Times*, Vol. 123, No. 1677, November 1982, pp. 747–754.

———. "Bach's Chorus: A Response to Robert Marshall." *The Musical Times*, Vol. 124, No. 1681, March 1983, pp. 161–162.

———. "Towards A New Image of Heinrich Schutz—1." *The Musical Times*, Vol. 126, No. 1713, November 1985, pp. 651–658.

———. "Towards a New Image of Heinrich Schutz—2." *The Musical Times*, Vol. 126, No. 1714, December 1985, pp. 716–720.

Rosseli, John. "The Castrati as a Professional Group and a Social Phenomenon." *Acta Musicologa*, Vol. LX, May–August 1988, pp. 143–179.

Rothchild, Fritz. *The Lost Tradition in Music: Rhythm and Tempo in J. S. Bach's Time.* Westport, CT: Hyperion Press, 1979.

Sachs, Curt. *Rhythm and Tempo: A Study in Music History.* New York: Columbia University Press, 1988. (Originally published: New York: Norton, 1953).

Sadie, Stanley, Editor. *The New Grove Dictionary of Music and Musicians.* London: Macmillan Publishers, Ltd., 1980.

Samuel, Harold E. *The Cantata in Nuremberg During the Seventeenth Century.* Ann Arbor, MI: UMI Research Press, 1982.

Sawkins, Lionel. "For and Against the Order of Nature: Who Sang the Soprano?" *Early Music,* Vol. 15, No. 3, August 1987, pp. 315–324.

Schulze, Hans-Joachim. "Johann Sebastian Bach's Orchestra: Some Unanswered Questions." *Early Music,* Vol. 17, No. 1, February 1989, pp. 3–15.

Schütz, Heinrich. *Letters and Documents of Heinrich Schutz, 1656–1672: An Annotated Translation.* Gina Spagnoli. Ann Arbor, MI: UMI Research Press, 1990.

Wolff, H. C. *Original Improvisations from the 16th–18th Centuries.* Translated by A. C. Howie. Cologne: Arno Volk Verlag, 1972.

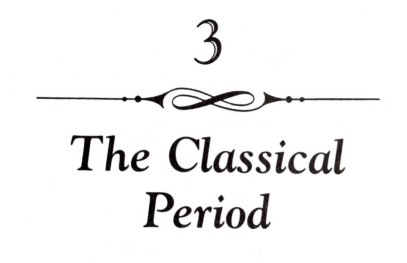

The Classical
Period

While Bach and Handel were carrying the Baroque style to its culmination in the first half of the eighteenth century, forces were already at work leading toward the formulation of a new style. The Classical era, generally considered to cover the period from 1750 to 1820, includes such diverse aesthetic trends as the Rococo (*Stile galant*), *empfindsamer Stil* (literally, "sensitive" style), Enlightenment, and *Sturm und Drang* (storm and stress). The Classical period thus lacked any unifying social and aesthetic philosophy like the one that shaped artistic expression in the Baroque period. Although each of these aesthetic trends had its proponents, it was the master composers of the period—Haydn, Mozart, and Beethoven—who were able to synthesize the elements of each into their music.

The Rococo style (ca. 1720–ca. 1770) repudiated the massive forms of the Baroque. The Rococo has been described as a "a lighter and more gracious Baroque."[1] The endless vistas gave way to intimate glimpses; the grandeur of Baroque decoration changed to delicate, often unnecessary, ornamentation; monumental sculpture decreased in size to figurines for the mantle; the center of life moved from the ballroom to the boudoir; and the grandiloquent language of the Baroque changed in manner and tone to witty, tête-à-tête conversations.[2] The expansiveness, grandeur, and impressiveness of Baroque music gave

[1]Carl J. Friedrich, *The Age of the Baroque* (New York: Harper & Row, 1962), p. 58.
[2]William Fleming and Abraham Veinus, *Understanding Music: Style, Structure, and History* (New York: Holt, Rinehart and Winston, Inc., 1958), pp. 309–310.

way to an expression of elegance in delicate proportions. The polyphony of the later Baroque was abandoned in favor of a homophonic style, with interest focused on the soprano line that often was adorned with a proliferation of ornamentation.

Whereas the music of Rococo was elegant and ornate, and written to please the aristocracy, the *empfindsamer Stil* (or expressive style) was more the music of the middle class. This bourgeois style reflected the attitudes of honesty and goodness and often approached the borders of sentimentality. It is reflected, for example, in the title of a collection of songs by the German composer J. F. Reichardt, "Lullabies for Good German Mothers."[3]

The eighteenth-century Enlightenment, or Age of Reason, began as a reaction against supernatural religions, formalism, and authority. The underlying philosophical belief was that humans should be "natural" in all respects—that is, they should value natural behavior as opposed to formality, and individual freedom as opposed to submission to authority.[4] Denis Diderot's *Encyclopédie*, or *Classified Dictionary of Sciences, Arts, and Trades*, was published serially beginning in 1751 and symbolizes rationalism and the spirit of scientific inquiry. Thomas Paine's book *The Age of Reason* also reflects such rationalism. The Marquis de Condorcet's book *The Progress of the Human Spirit* (1774) set forth ten stages through which humans had progressed from primitive life to nearly ultimate perfection. This philosophy expressed the belief that humans, through the use of their rational and moral powers, could ultimately control their environment. Jean Rameau was an outstanding exponent of rationalism and sought to restore reason to musical thought. There is evidence of this philosophy in the optimism expressed in some of the music of Beethoven, who was the movement's most articulate spokesman.[5]

Although the eighteenth century has been referred to as the Age of Reason, it was in reality a time when people began to talk a lot about reason, and about the hope that enlightenment might bring about an improvement in human affairs. This does not mean that individuals before or after this time were unreasonable or were incapable of reasoning.[6]

The *Sturm und Drang* (storm and stress) movement in Germany ran counter to the elegance of the Rococo, the optimism of the Enlightenment, and the restricted emotionalism of the *empfindsamer Stil*.[7] These aesthetic trends were rejected in favor of a search for emotional truth and a more flexible

---

[3]Ibid., p. 312.

[4]Donald Jay Grout, *A History of Western Music* (New York: W. W. Norton & Company, Inc., 1960), p. 411.

[5]Fleming and Veinus, *Understanding Music*, p. 313.

[6]Jacques Barzun, *Classic, Romantic and Modern* (Garden City, New York: Anchor Books, 1961), p. 4.

[7]Some authorities feel that the *empfindsamer Stil* and the *Sturm und Drang* are only different manifestations of an overall Classical-Romantic style.

use of the imagination. This philosophy may be seen in the literary works of both Goethe and Schiller. The best-known literary example is Goethe's *Faust*. Faust rejects the tenets of the Age of Reason, ceases to search for nature's secrets in books, and seeks the ultimate truth in experiences and emotion. Some authorities point out that Haydn, Mozart, and Beethoven were all influenced by this philosophy, as indicated by the pathos and occasional outbursts in their music.[8]

CLASSICAL SOCIETY

During the Classical period the aristocracy strove to attain the "ideal" of the gentleman. Self-control was a guiding factor, and "for the sake of decency, certain feelings were exhibited—pleasure, amusement, ridicule, surprise—and these in their mildest form. . . . gestures, fervor, eccentricity were suppressed so that the social stage—the salon or court—is occupied with persons whose manner is perfectly smooth. With this ideal . . . go some admirable rules of conversation."[9]

The center of cultural life in the Classical period was the palace. There, members of the ruling aristocracy steeped themselves in the arts, which they claimed as their right and privilege. Beauty of expression and elegance of manner became formalized, and permeated all aspects of aristocratic life. Artists of the period created works for their patrons, who far outranked them in the social hierarchy. Composers were employed for what they could contribute to their employer's cultural surroundings. In general, the patron was more interested in the artistic creations rather than in the artist himself. A certain degree of reserve existed between patron/employer and artist/employee. In this social setting, with its emphasis on courtly manners and decorum, the artist avoided an overtly personal style because this would have been considered in poor taste. Consequently, objectivity and reserve became the essential characteristics of Classical expression.

In commenting about Classicism, Barzun calls it "an . . . original movement of reaction aiming at uniformity. . . . All these writers speak of the 'improvement and refinement' of their speech over that of the previous age, of 'harmonious numbers,' of 'art calling imagination to the aid of reason,' of 'charm and correctness.' "[10]

Individuals were concerned with king-worship, love-making, intrigue, etiquette, and dueling. Outlets for these feelings were the theater (or the playhouse), and watching public executions. The life of leisure and

[8]Barzun, *Classic, Romantic, and Modern*, p. 314.
[9]Ibid., p. 44.
[10]Ibid., p. 188.

the constraints of politeness encouraged activities such as gaming, hunting, and the playing of practical jokes, as well as extremely lavish entertainment.[11]

The so-called cultural elite are generally believed to have been rather impolite and inconsiderate during the Classical era. Supporting this idea is a statement by Leopold Mozart in which he criticized Viennese taste and attitudes in a letter written to Lorenz Hagenauer at the end of January, 1768:[12]

> That the Viennese, generally speaking, do not care to see serious and sensible performances, have little or no idea of them, and only want to see foolish stuff, dances, devils, ghosts, magic, Hanswurst, Lipperl, Bernardon, witches and apparitions is well known; and their theatres prove it every day. A gentleman, even a nobleman with decorations, will clap his hands and laugh so much over some ribald or naive joke of Hanswurst as to get short of breath; during the most serious scenes, however, . . . he will prattle so loudly to his lady that other honest people in the audience cannot understand a word.[13]

As to the demeanor of the composer in the presence of his patron, or others of high social standing, Mozart's letter to his father of January 17, 1778 is revealing.

> About eleven in the morning the Herr Councillor came to see me bringing Herr Vogler. . . . After dinner, he sent to his house for two claviers . . . and for his tedious published sonatas. I was forced to play them and he accompanied me on the other clavier. At his request I was then obliged to send for my own sonatas. . . . Before dinner he bungled through my concerto *prima vista*, the first movement went *prestissimo*, the andante *allegro* and the rondo still more *prestissimo*. . . . You may easily conceive how insupportable it was, for I could not well say to him, Much too fast![14]

The *castrati* have an amazing history throughout the seventeenth and eighteenth centuries. In seventeenth-century Italy, falsettists continued to sing the alto part, while the *castrati* took over the soprano part. In Northern Europe, however, falsettists singing the alto part continued to be used along with boy sopranos. This practice continued until the nineteenth century, when it became acceptable to allow women to sing in Protestant church choirs.

---

[11]Ibid., p. 46.

[12]It is interesting to speculate on how this might have influenced the compositional attitudes of composers, as well as the performers, of that time. Consider, for example, the quotation from Diderot's *Rameau's Nephew* in *Authenticity and Early Music*, ed. Nicholas Kenyon (Oxford/New York: Oxford University Press, 1988), p. 80.

[13]Eva Badura-Skoda, "The Influence of the Viennese Popular Comedy on Haydn and Mozart," *Proceedings of the Royal Music Association*, Vol. 100 (1973–74), p. 196.

[14]From Carol MacClintock, *Readings in the History of Music in Performance* (Bloomington, IN: Indiana University Press, 1979), p. 382.

COMPOSERS OF THE CLASSICAL PERIOD

The Classical period is generally considered to have lasted from 1750 to around 1820, and its paramount composers were FRANZ JOSEPH HAYDN (1732–1809), WOLFGANG AMADEUS MOZART (1756–1791), and LUDWIG VAN BEETHOVEN (1770–1827). As Beethoven lived well into the nineteenth century, many writers consider the Classical period to have extended to 1820 or 1825; however, it would be more realistic if they would terminate the period around the turn of the century and then explain that Beethoven changed his compositional style at about that time and began to write music more aligned with the romanticists. (There are some authorities, however, who believe that Beethoven became more classical as he grew older.)

FRANZ JOSEPH HAYDN was born in Rohrau, in Lower Austria, in 1732. As a young boy Haydn was a choirboy at St. Stephen's Cathedral in Vienna for nine years—from 1740 to 1749. From 1755 to 1759, he studied with Nicola Porpora. This was a period of great musical development for Haydn. In 1759, he became Kapellmeister to Count Morzin, and in 1766, Haydn accepted the post of Kapellmeister to Prince Nikolaus Esterhazy at the new palace on the Neusiedler lake called Esterháza. In 1795 he entered the service of the younger Prince Nikolaus Esterhazy, and remained at this post for the remainder of his musical career. While in this later position he composed a mass each year for Eisenstadt—*The Creation* in 1798 and *The Seasons* in 1801.

One of Haydn's outstanding works was the *Applausus* Cantata, which is about two hours in length, and was composed in 1768 for the birthday celebrations of the Abbot of Zwetti monastery in Lower Austria. *Applausus* was a generic name for a cantata of this type, and as Haydn was not invited for the first performance he sent detailed instructions as to how the music should be performed (see page 97 for details). Haydn's first oratorio was *The Return of the Tobias*, written in 1775; however, a work of much more interest is *The Creation*, written in 1798, which had more performances than all Haydn's other choral works combined. *Missa in Angustiis in D minor*, No. 9 (*Mass in Time of Peril*), written in 1798 and better known as the *Nelson* or *Imperial Mass*, is considered Haydn's supreme masterpiece in the choral field.[15] Two of Haydn's shorter works worthy of mention are the *Te Deum in C*, written in 1799 (about ten minutes in length), and his *Salve Regina in C minor* (about twenty minutes in length), which is quite poetic and intense.

WOLFGANG AMADEUS MOZART was born in Salzburg in 1756. As a child prodigy, playing the harpsichord, he was taken on tours by his father Leopold and performed in various European musical centers—Paris in 1763 and 1765, and London in 1764–65. Mozart's father gave young Mozart composition lessons, but the quick, impressionable boy learned primarily by listening to

[15]Arthur Jacobs, *Choral Music* (Baltimore: Penguin Books, 1963), p. 172.

other composers' music and imitating what he liked; therefore, his early compositions are comparatively conventional.

Mozart was also a fine violinist, and at the age of 13 he took on the job of concertmaster with the orchestra of Prince-Archbishop of Salzburg. Although Wolfgang was interested in obtaining a position elsewhere than in provincial Salzburg, he remained there, and from 1773 to 1777 was primarily concerned with church and lighter orchestral music. In 1777, however, when Mozart was only 21 years old, he went to Munich and Mannheim, where he found no open positions, then finally to Paris, where he wrote a symphony for the Paris Orchestra, considered to be one of the finest in Europe. In 1779 he returned to Salzburg for a more senior concertmaster position, and there he continued to compose church music as well as orchestral works. In late 1780, when he was 25, he was invited to Munich to compose an opera for the court theater. The result was *Idomeneo*, which was highly successful and is considered to be one of his finest works.

While Mozart was still in Munich, he was instructed by the Archbishop of Salzburg to go to Vienna to "attend" on him. While there he was denied the opportunity to play for other noblemen, and at mealtime was seated at a table with the valets and cooks. Furious at this treatment, he asked the Archbishop to discharge him from his duties. The Archbishop finally complied, as Mozart later wrote, "with a kick on my arse . . . by order of our worthy Prince-Archbishop." This behavior seems very much in line with that portrayed in both the Broadway play and the movie *Amadeus*. While in Vienna Mozart took on several pupils, thus assuring himself of an income. He also wrote, "Vienna was the land of the piano," and composed several piano sonatas and piano and violin sonatas followed by three concertos. Mozart's middle years in Vienna were a time when the Viennese public recognized and admired his genius as a pianist and a composer and eagerly attended his concerts. Mozart composed for every medium; however, his chief interest was opera, which he infused with a new humanity and depth of feeling.[16]

Mozart's church music was mostly written early in his career. As the Archbishop of Colloredo did not wish the Mass to last longer than 45 minutes, this limited Mozart's music to about 20 minutes. While at Salzburg, Mozart composed 17 masses, all of which are on a much smaller scale than Haydn's.

LUDWIG VAN BEETHOVEN was born in Bonn in 1770. In 1792, he studied piano with Franz Joseph Haydn in Vienna for a relatively brief period and then later with J. G. Albrechtsberger. Beethoven made his piano debut in Vienna in 1795. At the age of 30 his hearing began to deteriorate and he developed periods of depression. The year 1803 was the beginning of his heroic middle

---

[16]Stanley Sadie, *Music Guide: An Introduction* (Englewood Cliffs, NJ: Prentice Hall, 1986), pp. 245–258.

period when he composed his *Eroica Symphony* (No. 3). This was also the time when he substantially changed his style and began to write in a manner more aligned with the romanticists. A number of authorities mark this change as the end of the Classical period (1803); however, others will extend it to 1825. Beethoven wrote his oratorio *Christ on the Mount of Olives* in 1803, his opera *Fidelio* in 1805 (later revising it in 1806 and 1814), the *Mass in C* (*Missa Solemnis*) in 1819–23, and finished his *Choral Symphony* (No. 9) in early 1824, with its first performance in May of that year.

CHOIRS FOR HAYDN'S CREATION

The number of singers in choirs during the Classical period varied considerably, as they often did in previous eras, depending upon the circumstances, and on the financial support available. At the Esterházy Palace in Eisenstadt there were in September of 1800, according to pay lists, no more than eight singers and about 24 instrumentalists employed. This, however, was not Haydn's preferred arrangement.

The first performance of Haydn's *Creation* was in Vienna on April 28, 1798, when Haydn was at the pinnacle of his international fame. In Vienna, 45 performances were given between 1798 and 1810. Haydn himself conducted the first 14 of these public performances and a number of later concerts. For some of the later performances Antonio Salieri served as conductor.

The concerts in Vienna employed a relatively large number of performers, and the stage was reported to be in the form of an amphitheater with various levels of seating. On the lowest level, the chorus was seated, along with the pianoforte player; on the next higher level was the conductor—Haydn himself with conductor's baton. On the next higher level were the violins, and the lower strings and double basses. On the next higher level were the woodwinds, and at the top level were the trumpets, trombones, and timpani. This is reported to have been the preferred arrangement for the later performances of the *Creation* in London.

In the London concerts of the *Creation*, Haydn assumed the musical leadership as conductor, while the concertmaster and the keyboard player served as subconductors. As to the total number of performers, the actual number varied; however, 180 were most frequently used. It has been estimated that 120 of this number were orchestral musicians and about 60 participated in the chorus. This seeming imbalance between singers and orchestral musicians was somewhat rectified by the fact that the chorus was placed in front of the orchestra, and not behind as is currently the practice.[17]

[17]Frederick Neumann, *New Essays on Performance Practice* (Ann Arbor/London: U.M.I. Research Press, 1989), pp. 229–230.

MUSICAL STYLE AND PERFORMANCE PRACTICE

Meter and Stress

The art of the Classical era, the Rococo style in particular, strove for elegance and more delicate proportions. These general characteristics were also reflected in the music of the period. Therefore, the pulsation of the music was more delicately marked than in the Baroque period. In order to convey clearly this style to the performers, the conductor should, therefore, utilize a lighter beat, yet with a definite or marked precision to delineate the crisp rhythmic patterns of the music.[18]

In his 1789 treatise *Klavierschule*, Daniel Gottlob Türk stated that dotted notes require a different execution with respect to the rhythmic pattern and to a heavy or light execution. Dotted notes are usually prolonged, with the following notes being played correspondingly quicker (see Figure 22). The notation in (a) is performed as in (b) if the music is serious or solemn, and applies to music marked *grave*, as well as to music marked *sostenuto*. The dotted notes are performed with "weight" and thus somewhat sustained. In performing music that is gay or cheerful, the execution should be somewhat lighter, as illustrated in (c). When the music is passionate or defiant, or marked *staccato*, it is to be performed as in (d).[19]

While one usually gives a slight stress to the first beat in a measure, it is desirable to give a slightly heavier emphasis to the first regularly stressed tone of a new section or period. As Türk states, "the beginning tone of every period and the like must be given an even more marked emphasis than an ordinary

FIGURE 22   Dotted notes (a) as written; (b), (c), and (d), as performed (see text).

---

[18]George Howerton, *Technique and Style in Choral Singing* (New York: Carl Fischer, Inc., 1957), p. 142.

[19]Fritz Rothchild, *Musical Performance in the Times of Mozart and Beethoven: The Lost Tradition in Music*, Part II (London: Oxford University Press, 1961), pp. 71–72.

strong beat. Strictly speaking, these beginning tones are themselves stressed to a greater or lesser degree according to whether they begin a larger or smaller part of the whole, that is, after a full cadence, the beginning tone (of the following section) must be more strongly marked than after a half cadence, or merely after a phrase division."[20]

As to the performance of duplets against triplets, the same treatment should be given as with Baroque music. (For a discussion of this topic, see pp. 52–53.) The comments of eighteenth-century composers and theorists, however, are appropriate and revealing. Carl Philipp Emanuel Bach in 1753 stated, "With the advent of an increased use of triplets in common 4/4 time, as well as in 2/4 and 3/4, many pieces have appeared which might be more conveniently written as 12/8, 9/8, or 6/8."[21] The musical example that accompanies the preceding statement adopts the dotted group to the triplet, and the short note after the dot is to coincide with the last note of the triplet. The theorist Fredrich Wilhelm Marpurg stated in 1755 that "the two first notes of a triplet are always played against the first note of a duplet . . . even if the first of the two binary notes happens to be dotted."[22] Stated another way, the two notes of a duplet should coincide with the first and last note of the triplet, even if the first note of the duplet is dotted. While one may find some conflicting opinion to the preceding approach, the rationale is based on its practicality.

Tempo

The Classical period generally favored moderate tempi and avoided extremes. More and more, composers indicated tempo markings on their scores and often included correct phrasing and desired tonal quality as well. Tempo was often indicated through the use of Italian words (i.e., *allegro, adagio,* etc.), and signs indicating dynamic changes were written in.[23] In the waning years of the Classical period, composers, Beethoven in particular, were able to prescribe the desired tempo of their compositions through the use of metronome markings (the metronome was invented by Mälzel in 1816).

In a manual on how to play the transverse flute, published in Berlin in 1752, Quantz states with regard to determining tempo: "It is the pulse beat at the hand of a healthy person."[24] We do not know the actual pulse beat Quantz

[20]Daniel Gottlob Türk, *Klavierschule* (1789), trans. Raymond H. Haggh (Lincoln and London: University of Nebraska Press, 1982).

[21]Carl Philipp Emanuel Bach, *Essay on the True Art of Playing Keyboard Instruments,* trans. William J. Mitchell (New York: W. W. Norton, 1949), p. 160.

[22]F. W. Marpurg, *Anleitung zum Clavierspielen* (Berlin, 1755), p. 24.

[23]Frederick Dorian, *The History of Music in Performance* (New York: W. W. Norton & Company, Inc., 1942), p. 155.

[24]Johann Joachim Quantz, *Versuch ein Anweisung die Flöte traversiere zu spielen* (Berlin, 1752), trans. E. R. Reilly, unpublished Ph.D. dissertation, University of Michigan, 1958.

may have meant, but today's average normal pulse is between 60 and 80 beats per minute.

A fairly wide variety of tempi were in use during the Classical period. Leopold Mozart mentions the following in his *Versuch einer gründlichen Violinschule*[25]:

Prestissimo: the fastest tempo, *presto assai* about the same

Presto: fast, *allegro assai* about the same

Allegro: lively but not overly fast

Allegro, ma non troppo: fast, but do not exaggerate the speed

Vivace: lively

Moderato: temperately, moderately, neither too fast nor too slow

Tempo commodo and *tempo giusto:* neither too fast nor too slow; in the proper, suitable, and natural tempo

Sostenuto: sustained, held back

Maestoso: with majesty, deliberately

Andante: (*"gehend"*) going, let the piece take its natural pace

Lento: very moderately, comfortably

Adagio: slowly

Adagio pesante: a melancholy *adagio*, somewhat slower and reserved

Largo: still slower

Grave: melancholy and serious, very slow

According to music historian Curt Sachs, the eighteenth century "was an age of almost foamy decoration, of light, silvery colors, of pastels pale and frail, of a general dislike for anything ponderous."[26] In view of this attitude, it seems logical that music tempi were more likely to be on the bright side, and overly slow tempi were avoided.

Tempo rubato originated from the vocal art and eventually was utilized as a device in the interpretation of instrumental music. It was first discussed in a book on singing by Pier Francesco Tosi, published in 1723. The letters of Mozart reveal that he was well aware of the device and used it in his piano performances.

Although Wolfgang Amadeus Mozart was perhaps the first well-known composer to utilize *tempo rubato* in his performances, evidence indicates that other concert performers also did so during Mozart's time. In a letter to his father dated October 24, 1777, the 21-year-old Mozart states: "I . . . still play *espressivo*. . . . I always play accurately in time. No one seems to understand the *tempo rubato* in an adagio, where the left hand does not know anything about it." In the same letter Mozart indicates that the function of the left hand

---

[25]Leopold Mozart, *Versuch einer gründlichen Violinschule* (Augsburg: J. J. Lotter, 1756).

[26]Curt Sachs, *Rhythm and Tempo: A Study in Music History* (New York: W. W. Norton & Company, 1953), p. 317.

is to provide an accompaniment in strict time, and that the function of the right hand is to play *expressivo*, performing the melody somewhat like a singer. *Rubato* was, therefore, used when a specific musical phrase necessitated an expressive emphasis. This, of course, was done by increasing or decreasing the value of notes in the melody line, with the bass line maintaining its regular, established tempo. Finally, it should be pointed out that *tempo rubato* originated in the vocal tradition and was carried over and used by instrumentalists of the time.[27]

As to the effect on tempo of expression and manner, Türk states:

> Certain thoughts which are repeated in a more intensified manner (generally higher) require that the speed be increased to some extent. Sometimes when gentle feelings are interrupted by a lively passage, the latter can be played somewhat more rapidly. A hastening of the tempo may also take place in a passage where a vehement effect is unexpectedly to be aroused. For extraordinary tender singing, or melancholy passages, in which the emotion, as it were, is concentrated in one point, the effect can be very much intensified by an increasing hesitation. The tempo is also taken gradually slower for tones before certain fermatas . . . as if the powers were gradually being exhausted. The passages toward the end of a composition . . . which are marked diminuendo can also be played in a somewhat more lingering manner.[28]

Certainly a practice that is intuitively understood by most musicians is that sixteenth or thirty-second notes must be clearly articulated and not performed as fast as in slower tempi. According to Türk, "An allegro with some thirty-second notes intermingled should not be played as fast as when its most rapid passages consist of only eighth notes."[29]

Also, the place of performance or the circumstances of the performance have an affect upon tempi. For example, Türk states, "An allegro for the church or in ecclesiastical cantatas . . . must be given a far more moderate tempo than an allegro for the theatre or in the so-called chamber style."[30]

As to the use of *tempo rubato* in Beethoven's music, Dorian states, "It is only in places of agitated emotion, of intense expression, that we are obliged to perform with an appropriate amount of *tempo rubato*. Such slight and controlled *rubato* would coincide with the style of Beethoven's own rendition, as described by those who were privileged to hear him."[31]

Philipp Emanuel Bach (1714–1788) discussed *tempo rubato* in Volume Two of his *Versuch*.[32] It is reasonable to assume that other composers of the

---

[27]Dorian, *History of Music*, pp. 188–190.
[28]Türk, *Klavierschule*.
[29]Ibid.
[30]Ibid.
[31]Dorian, *History of Music*, p. 207.
[32]Ibid., pp. 186–193.

period were also aware of this interpretative device. It is suggested, however, in performing music of this period, that *tempo rubato* be used with discretion and restraint, and that its more exaggerated use, as in the subsequent Romantic period, be avoided. In general, the principle of strict time should be followed. The exceptions where *tempo rubato* seems desirable will usually be dictated by the poetical aspects of the text.[33] The use of *ritardando* and *accelerando* became more frequent, especially during the latter part of the period. In accordance with the general characteristics of the music of the period, such alterations in tempi should be slight and should be performed with restraint.

Dynamics

Although dynamic contrast was an important part of the music of the period, composers did not seek the extremes that occurred during the later periods.

By the middle of the eighteenth century, however, a considerable number of dynamic markings were known and in use. They are recorded by the music theorist Friedrich Wilhelm Marpurg (1718–1795) in his *Anleitung zum Klavierspielen* (1755). The markings include *forte*, loud (*f*); *più forte* (*ff*); *fortissimo*, very loud (*fff*); *piano*, soft (*p*); *più piano*, softer (*pp*); *pianissimo*, very soft (*ppp*); *poco piano*; *poco forte*; *meno piano*; *meno forte*; *mezzo piano*; *mezzo forte*; *piano assai*; and *forte assai*.[34]

One of the most significant developments growing out of the latter part of the eighteenth century was that of *crescendo–decrescendo*. Such a concept was in marked contrast to the terraced dynamics of the earlier Baroque period. While the concept of *crescendo–decrescendo* was not entirely unknown and had been utilized to some degree in Italy from the beginning of the century, it had not been widely used elsewhere. Through the efforts of Stamitz, the precision of the orchestra at Mannheim was developed to such a high degree that this carefully controlled *crescendo* became known as the *Mannheim crescendo*. In choral performances the *crescendo–decrescendo* should be performed with some restraint, considering the general dynamic level of the passage. The *crescendo* should not begin from as low a dynamic level, nor reach as high a level, as it would during the Romantic period. Generally, in *crescendo* and *decrescendo*, the dynamic level should change gradually just one degree higher or lower—for example, from *p* ===== *mp*; and rarely from *p* ========== *f*.

The *forte–piano* contrast was an unwritten law of dynamic execution; that is, repeated phrases and/or periods should be performed *piano*, as in an echo. Periods performed *piano* the first time should be performed *forte* on the

---

[33]For a further discussion of *tempo rubato*, see Sachs, *Rhythm and Tempo*, pp. 306–310.
[34]Rothchild, *Musical Performance in the Times of Mozart and Beethoven*, p. 32.

repetition.[35] The harmony itself will provide the conductor with further clues for the treatment of dynamics.

> Philipp Emanuel Bach points out that every tone foreign to the key can very well stand a *forte*, regardless of whether it occurs in dissonance or consonance. . . . Quantz distinguishes clearly three classes of dissonances, to be played *mezzo forte*, *forte*, and *fortissimo*, respectively. He also explains that the theme of the composition calls for dynamic emphasis. Likewise, all other notes of importance (in a theme, in a contrapuntal passage, or in a harmonic structure) must be stressed by means of dynamics. The notes introducing the theme must be marked; the dissonance must be made stronger than its resolution.[36]

It is also often necessary and desirable to adjust the dynamics to the acoustical conditions of the performance hall. The conductor needs to consider the character of the music, the number and maturity of the performers, and the size and the acoustical conditions of the performance hall or auditorium. To maintain the classical proportions of the music, it should never become overbearing from the dynamic standpoint. An overly large musical organization, coupled with an auditorium with exceptionally live acoustical properties, can create a dynamic level that is much too high; to be effective, the dynamic level must be reduced in size and/or scope.

It is not possible for a composer to indicate through words or symbols every conceivable degree of loudness or softness. Therefore, it is up to the performer to make numerous judgments regarding the dynamics of particular portions of the music. As to this point Türk states:

> Concerning the intensity of tone required in any given case, I content myself in remarking that, generally, compositions of a spirited, happy, lively, sublime, magnificent, proud, daring, courageous, serious, fiery, wild, and furious character all require a certain degree of loudness. This degree must even be increased or decreased according to whether the feeling or passion is represented in a more vehement or more moderate manner. What a number of degrees of loudness are thus required for all this![37]

Choral conductors who prepare large choruses for performances with symphony orchestras are often concerned that the chorus is overshadowed or overbalanced by the orchestra. This concern is well-founded in many instances; however, in some cases the conductor's concern may be affected by his feeling that the dominant part of the work *is* the chorus. In respect to this situation,

---

[35]Dorian, *Music in Performance*, p. 166.

[36]From *The History of Music in Performance* by Frederick Dorian. New York: W. W. Norton & Company, Inc., 1942, p. 168. Copyright renewed 1970 by Frederick Dorian.

[37]Türk, *Klavierschule*. 1789.

the opinion of Franz Joseph Haydn is relevant, as he believed the chorus is conceived as part of the total mass and should not be regarded by those who sing it as the dominant partner.[38]

Tone Color and Vibrato

During the eighteenth century, tone color was relatively important to the music of Mozart, but not so much with the music of Bach, where line was more important. Had tone color been of concern to Bach he would have prescribed the registrations for his organ works, which he never did. Mozart's operas exude warmth, and tone color is a natural part of projecting the characterization of a role. Vibrato develops naturally in most trained voices, and consists of fast, regular oscillations in pitch with about seven pulsations per second. On string instruments, the oscillations seldom exceeded a quarter tone in pitch deviation.[39] A similar model for singers during the Classical period appears to be desirable. Wide variations in pitch need to be guarded against, and the straight vibratoless tone of boys' voices need not be emulated by adult singers.[40] Mozart in a letter to his father from Paris on June 12, 1778 wrote:

> Meissner, as you know, has the bad habit of purposely pulsating the voice, marking on a long-held note all the quarters and sometimes even the eights—and that manner of his I have never been able to tolerate. It is truly abominable and such singing runs counter to nature. The human voice vibrates by itself, but in a way and to a degree that is beautiful—this is the nature of the voice, and one imitates it not only on wind instruments, but also on strings, and even on the clavichord, but as soon as one carries it too far, it ceases to be beautiful, because it is unnatural.[41]

Texture

Composers of the Classical period sought lightness and simplicity in their music. In place of the heavy Baroque texture, there was a combination of textures in which chordal patterns, running figures, unsupported melodies, and other devices were used alternately, depending upon the expressive intentions of the composer. Contrapuntal devices were also sometimes used, particularly in the masses; however, polyphony was generally not sought by composers of the period. During the Baroque period a polarity existed between the melody and the bass parts. The bass supported the melody, while the inner voices

---

[38]Percy M. Young, *The Choral Tradition* (New York: W. W. Norton & Company, 1962), p. 189.

[39]Frederick Neumann, *Performance Practice*, p. 171.

[40]One source states that vibrato in the eighteenth century was used only on long notes. See Bernard Jacobson, "James Levine on Verdi and Mozart," in *Conductors on Conducting* (Frenchtown, NJ: Columbia Publishing Co., 1979), p. 43.

[41]Frederick Neumann, *Performance Practice*, p. 172.

sometimes only completed the harmonies. During the Classical period, the inner voices assumed greater importance, and the previous supporting function of the bass part gave way to one of greater flexibility and interplay with the inner voices.[42]

The practice of singing *appoggiaturas* at the cadences of eighteenth-century recitative was thought to be universal. The omission of *appoggiaturas* does not ruin the music—it merely has the effect of making it sound different.[43]

The *appoggiatura* of today is very short and stressless, with little duration given to the first note, which then snaps or bounces into the following or main note. In the eighteenth century, however, the *appoggiatura* fell upon the beat, carried the accent, and took an essential part from the following note. For examples of *appoggiaturas* as written and as played, see Figure 23. The examples are from Quantz's *Versuch einer Anweisung die Flöte traversiere zu spielen* (1752) and will provide an idea of the interpretation of *appoggiaturas* around the middle of the eighteenth century.

Expressive Aspects

In contrast to the late Baroque period, when the cadences were relatively infrequent and somewhat inconspicuous, and the phrases were "spun-out," the composers of the Classical period utilized phrases of a regular two- or four-bar length that were shorter and more distinct. There were generally rather strong points of harmonic arrival, and the period structure was well defined. Although the harmonic vocabulary did not differ substantially from that used in the late Baroque period, the harmonic progressions were certainly less weighty.[44] Melody reigned supreme; the other parts served to support and enhance it, and were often subordinate to it. Ornamentation developed to its fullest bloom. This embellishment of the melodic line, however, was only reflective of the spirit of the times, where elegance and grace were considered highly important, particularly to the patrons of the arts.

The music of the Classical period was generally abstract in nature and "discreet" in taste and was an integral part of a sophisticated mode of living. It was moderate in style, avoiding the extremes of the later Romantic period. Emotional content was less important, and unity of design became the composer's goal. Form served to eliminate personal qualities and universalized the style. Symmetry, balance, clarity, and restraint summarized the composer's artistic creations.

---

[42]Homer Ulrich and Paul A. Pisk, *A History of Music and Musical Style* (New York: Harcourt Brace Jovanovich, Inc., 1963), pp. 322–323.

[43]Jack Westrup, Editorial, *Music and Letters*, Vol. XLIX, No. 4 (October 1968): 313–316.

[44]Grout, *Western Music*, p. 417.

As written :

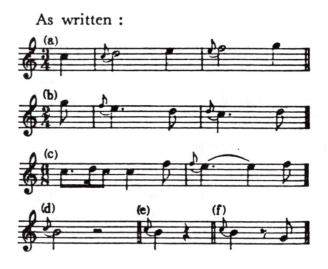

As played :

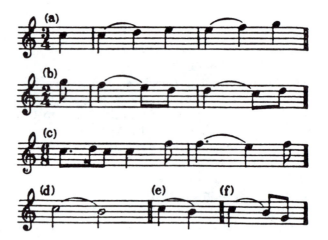

FIGURE 23 Examples of eighteenth-century appoggiaturas as written and as played.

Proper diction was seemingly just as important in the mid-eighteenth century as it is today. In discussing the "Requirements of a Good Singer," Quantz writes, "In producing the words he must take care not to change one vowel into another, such as to transform *e* into *a* and *o* into *u*; for example, in

Italian pronouncing *genitura* instead of *genitore,* causing laughter among those who understand the language."[45]

All composers, of course, have concerns that their music be performed appropriately, and are generally desirous of assisting the performers in whatever ways possible. Haydn was certainly no exception, and for the first performance of his work *Applausus* he was unable to attend, so he sent a list of specific instructions for the Kapellmeister's information:

> The composer asks that his indication of tempo be carefully observed and that, in accordance with the festive character of the text, the allegro be taken a little faster than usual.
>
> The composer requires the dynamic signs to be strictly observed and points out that there is a great difference between piano and pianissimo, forte and fortissimo, crescendo and sforzando.
>
> He requests a good and slow diction of the soloists, so that every syllable may be understood.
>
> He hopes that at least three or four rehearsals be given to his composition.[46]

MUSIC AND THE RELATED ARTS

In painting and architecture, the Rococo style was in vogue during a good part of the eighteenth century, from about 1722 to 1770. This lighter style was characterized by free, graceful movement, a playful line with curlicues and decorative variations, and lighter colors. Ornaments were delicate, curved and asymmetrical, and colors leaned toward pastel shades. The subject matter of painting emphasized carefree youth and love, replacing the battles, history, and morality subjects of Baroque art.[47]

The painting *The Toilet of Venus,* 1751, by François Boucher, displays the eighteenth-century boudoir ideal of feminine charm. Love is no longer the great passion it was with Peter Paul Rubens, but has become sophisticated flirtation. Voluptuous womanhood has been replaced by slender girlish forms.[48]

Jean-Honoré Fragonard was Boucher's successor as the leader of the French Rococo movement. His painting *The Swing* portrays the frivolous, pleasure-seeking pursuits of the upper class. The person in the lower left of the painting has bribed his servant in the lower right of the painting to conceal him in the shrubbery while his lady love indulges in her amusement. Fragonard's sensitive feeling for color and the artistic manner in which he develops his composition contributes to its artistic merit.

---

[45]Quantz, *Versuch einer Anweisung die Flöte traversiere zu spielen,* Ch. XVIII, sec. 11.

[46]Young, *Choral Tradition,* p. 174.

[47]Benjamin Rifkin, *Art History* (New York: Monarch Press, Inc., 1964), p. 100.

[48]William Fleming, *Art, Music & Ideas* (New York: Holt, Rinehart and Winston, 1970), p. 274.

François Boucher, *The Toilet of Venus*, 1751 Oil, 42⅝ × 33½ in. The Metropolitan Museum of Art, New York.

EPILOGUE

The French Revolution began in 1789 when the French people overthrew their government and adopted the phrase *"Liberté, Egalité, Fraternité"* (liberty, equality, fraternity). The French people wanted equality with the nobles and the clergy—privileged classes that were exempt from land taxes. In addition to taxes they paid to the king, the peasants had to pay dues to the Church. All these obligations seemed senseless to a people who were beginning to believe in the "Age of Reason." The writers of the time had a considerable influence on the attitudes of the people. The nobles reluctantly gave up their feudal rights, and the entire feudal system was abolished. France became a limited monarchy

Jean-Honoré Fragonard, *The Swing,* ca. 1766. Oil, 32 ×25 in. Wallace Collection, London.

with a one-house legislature. The Assembly completed a constitution that included a Declaration of the Rights of Man. On August 10, 1792, however, royalty was abolished, a republic was proclaimed, and a new constitution was prepared. After 1794 the Convention prepared a third constitution. The new government, the Directory, was unable to solve the varied problems of a disorganized France, so in 1799 Napoleon Bonaparte replaced it with a Consulate of three members. He, however, was the actual ruler of France. In 1804, Bonaparte discarded all pretense and declared himself "Napoleon I, Emperor of the French." While liberty thus vanished, the people still had equality.

REFERENCES

Bach, Carl Philipp Emanuel. *Essay on the True Art of Playing Keyboard Instruments.* Translated by William J. Mitchell. New York: W. W. Norton & Company, 1949.

Badura-Skoda, Eva. "The Influence of the Viennese Popular Comedy on Haydn and Mozart." *Proceedings of the Royal Music Association,* Vol. 100, 1973–74, pp. 185–199.

Barbour, J. Murray. "Billings and the Barline." *American Choral Review,* Vol. XVIII, No. 4, October 1976, pp. 37–49.

Barzun, Jacques. *Classic, Romantic, and Modern.* Garden City, NY: Anchor Books, 1961.

Bauer, Wilhelm A., and Otto Erich Deutsch, eds. *Mozart: Brief und Aufzeichnungen.* London: Cassel & Co., 1962.

Boomgaarden, Donald R. *Musical Thought in Britain and Germany During the Early Eighteenth Century.* New York: P. Lang, 1987.

Braudel, Fernand. *Afterthoughts on Material Civilization and Capitalism.* Baltimore: The Johns Hopkins University Press, 1977.

Brown, A. Peter. "Options: Authentic, Allowable, and Possible in Performing Haydn's *The Creation.*" *The Musical Times,* Vol. 131, No. 1764, February 1990, pp. 73–76.

———. *Performing Haydn's Creation: Reconstructing the Earliest Renditions.* Bloomington, IN: Indiana University Press, 1986.

Brown, Clive. "Perspectives on Beethoven." *The Musical Times,* Vol. 129, No. 1747, pp. 448–452.

Brown, Howard Mayer, and Stanley Sadie, eds. *Performance Practice: Music After 1600.* New York: W. W. Norton & Company, 1989.

Campbell, Margaret. "To Dot or Double Dot? The Eternal Question." *The Consort,* No. 31, 1975, pp. 142–147.

Cassel, David C. "Some Performance Suggestions for the Mozart Missae Breves and Others of His Works." *The Choral Journal,* Vol. XXVI, No. 1, August 1985, pp. 7–11.

Churgin, Bathia. "Beethoven and Mozart's Requiem: A New Connection." *Journal of Musicology,* Vol. V, No. 4, Fall 1987, pp. 457–477.

Collins, Michael B. "The Performance of Triplets in the 17th and 18th Centuries." *Journal of the American Musicological Society,* Vol. XIX, Fall 1966, pp. 281–328.

Corri, Domenico. *A Treatise on the Art of Singing.* London: Metzler & Co., 1799.

Cowart, Georgia J. "Sense and Sensibility in Eighteenth-Century Musical Thought." *Acta Musicologica,* Vol. LXI, July–December 1984, pp. 251–266.

Davies, Peter J. "Mozart's Manic-Depressive Tendencies—1." *The Musical Times,* Vol. 128, No. 1729, March 1987, pp. 123–126.

———. "Mozart's Manic-Depressive Tendencies—2." *The Musical Times,* Vol. 128, No. 1730, April 1987, pp. 191–126.

Dolmetsch, Arnold. *The Interpretation of the Music of the XVII & XVIII Centuries.* London: Oxford University Press, 1946.

Dorian, Frederick. *The History of Music in Performance.* New York: W. W. Norton & Company, Inc., 1942.

Federhofer, Hellmut. "Johann Joseph Fux: Choral Styles and the Gradus ad Parnassum." *American Choral Review,* Vol. XXIV, Nos. 2 and 3, April and July 1982, pp. 14–26.

Fleming, William, and Abraham Veinus. *Understanding Music: Style, Structure and History.* New York: Holt, Rinehart and Winston, 1950.

Flothuis, Marius. "Mozart and the Human Voice." *American Choral Review,* Vol. XXIV, Nos. 2 and 3, April and July 1982, pp. 61–66.

Forbes, Elliot. "Beethoven As a Choral Composer." *Royal Music Association* (Proceedings, 1970–1971), Vol. 97, pp. 69–82.

———. "Beethoven's Choral Music." *American Choral Review,* Vol. XXIV, Nos. 2 and 3, April and July 1982, pp. 67–82.

Grout, Donald Jay. *A History of Western Music,* 4th ed. New York: W. W. Norton & Company, 1988.

Hitchcock, H. Wiley. *Music in the United States: A Historical Introduction*, 3rd ed. Englewood Cliffs, NJ: Prentice Hall, 1988.

Howerton, George. *Technique and Style in Choral Singing*. New York: Carl Fischer, Inc., 1957.

Jacobs, Arthur. *Choral Music*. Baltimore: Penguin Books, 1963.

Jacobson, Bernard. "James Levine on Verdi and Mozart," in *Conductors on Conducting*. Frenchtown, NJ: Columbia Publishing Co., 1979, pp. 33–45.

Kerst, Friedrich. *Mozart: The Man and the Artist Revealed in His Own Words*. Translated and edited by Henry Krehbiel. New York: Dover Publications, Inc., 1965. (First published by Geoffrey Bles, London, in 1926.)

Kolisch, Rudolph. "Tempo and Character in Beethoven's Music." *Musical Quarterly*, Vol. XXIX, 1943, pp. 169–187, 291–312.

Larsen, Jens Peter. *Handel, Haydn and the Viennese Classical Style*. Translated by Ulrich Krämer. Ann Arbor, MI: UMI Research Press, 1988.

———. "Haydn's Early Masses: Evaluation of a Genre." *American Choral Review*, Vol. XXIV, Nos. 2 and 3, April and July 1982, pp. 48–60.

———. "Haydn: Repertory, Interpretation, Image." *The Musical Times*, Vol. 123, No. 1669, March 1982, pp. 163–166.

Leppert, Richard. "Imagery, Musical Confrontation and Cultural Difference in Early 18th Century London." *Early Music*, Vol. 14, No. 3, August 1986, pp. 323–345.

MacClintock, Carol. *Readings in the History of Music in Performance*. Bloomington, IN: Indiana University Press, 1979.

Marpurg, F. W. *Anleitung zum Clavierspielen*. Berlin, 1755.

Mersman, Hans, ed. *Letters of Wolfgang Amadeus Mozart*. New York: Dover Publications, Inc., 1972. (Original publication, 1928.)

Nathan, Hans. "The Sense of History in Musical Interpretation." *Music Review*, Vol. XIII, 1952, pp. 85–100.

Neumann, Frederick. *New Essays on Performance Practice*. Ann Arbor, MI: UMI Research Press, 1989.

———. *Ornamentation and Improvisation in Mozart*. Princeton, NJ: Princeton University Press, 1986.

———. "The Overdotting Syndrome: Anatomy of a Delusion." *Musical Quarterly*, Vol. 67, No. 3, July 1981, pp. 305–347.

O'Neal, Melinda. "An Introduction to Performance Practice Considerations for the Mozart Requiem." *Choral Journal*, Vol. XXXI, No. 9, April 1991, pp. 47–56.

Pauly, Reinhard G. *Music in the Classic Period*, 3rd ed. Englewood Cliffs, NJ: Prentice Hall, 1988.

Quantz, Johann Joachim. *Versuch ein Anweisung die Flöte traversiere zu spielen*. Berlin, 1752. Translation and study by E. R. Reilly. Unpublished Ph.D. dissertation, University of Michigan, 1958.

Ratner, Leonard G. *Classic Music: Expression, Form, and Style*. New York: Schirmer Books, 1980.

Rifkin, Benjamin. *Art History*. New York: Monarch Press, Inc., 1964.

Rosen, Charles. *Classic Style*. New York: The Viking Press, 1971.

Rothchild, Fritz. *Musical Performance in the Times of Mozart and Beethoven: The Lost Tradition in Music*. Part II. London: Oxford University Press, 1961.

Sachs, Curt. *Rhythm and Tempo: A Study in Music History*. New York: W. W. Norton & Company, 1953.

Sadie, Stanley. *Music Guide: An Introduction*. Englewood Cliffs, NJ: Prentice Hall, 1986.

Schenbeck, Lawrence. "Baroque Influences in Mozart's Masses: Later Works." *American Choral Review*, Vol. XX, No. 4, October 1978, pp. 3–16.

Slotterbach, Floyd. "Mozart's Requiem: History, and Performance." *American Choral Review*, Vol. XXVI, No. 2, April 1984, pp. 5–30.

Sonneck, O. G. *Beethoven: Impressions By His Contemporaries*. New York: Dover Publications, Inc., 1967.

Steptoe, Andrew. "Mozart and Poverty: A Re-examination of the Evidence." *The Musical Times*, Vol. 125, No. 1694, pp. 196–201.

Stolzfus, Fred. "Beethoven's Mass in C: Notes on History, Structure, and Performance Practice." *Choral Journal*, Vol. XXIII, No. 3, November 1982, pp. 26–30.

Strunk, Oliver, ed. *Source Readings in Music History*. New York: W. W. Norton & Company, 1950.

Sutcliff, W. Dean. "Haydn's Musical Personality." *The Musical Times*, Vol. 130, No. 1756, pp. 341–344.

Temperley, Nicholas. "Haydn's Tempos in *The Creation*." *Early Music*, Vol. 19, No. 2, May 1991, pp. 235–245.

Türk, Daniel Gottlob. *Klavierschule* (1789). Translated with notes by Raymond H. Haggh. Lincoln and London: University of Nebraska Press, 1982.

Ulrich, Homer, and Paul A. Pisk. *A History of Music and Musical Style*. New York: Harcourt Brace Jovanovich, 1963.

Van Camp, Leonard, and John Haberlen. "On Performing the Music of William Billings—Part I." *The Choral Journal*, Vol. XIV, No. 3, November 1973, pp. 18–22.

Walker, Ernest. "The Appoggiatura." *Music and Letters*, Vol. V, No. 1, January 1924, pp. 121–144.

Walter, Hawthorne. "The Choral Conductor and Proportio Sesquialtera." *The Choral Journal*, Vol. XXII, No. 7, March 1982, pp. 19–23.

Westrup, Jack. Editorial. *Music and Letters*, Vol. XLIX, No. 4, October 1968, pp. 313–316.

Young, Percy. *The Choral Tradition*. New York: W. W. Norton & Company, 1962.

Zaslaw, Neal. *The Classical Era: From the 1740's to the End of the 18th Century*. Englewood Cliffs, NJ: Prentice Hall, 1990.

The Romantic Period

The French Revolution, beginning in 1789, resulted in the breakdown of the aristocratic way of life and led to the development of nineteenth-century liberalism. In the world of the arts, it was paralleled by the rise of the Romantic movement, in essence a revolt against formality and authority. Previously, composers had for many centuries worked under the patronage of either the Church or princely courts. Under this system, composers generally wrote music to please their patrons. They were careful not to let their music become too personal in nature. With the breakdown of the patronage system, composers were free to express themselves individually. They were no longer inhibited or restricted by a patron's demands, and were able to please their equals—the general public. With their greater freedom, composers sought out new and unique means of expression. This led to a greater display of emotion, heretofore largely restrained.

Although the composer, no longer bound to his patron, was able to express himself more freely, his financial insecurity often caused him to withdraw from the world around him. He sometimes became preoccupied with his own inner problems and even became pessimistic about the future. Nevertheless, composers' withdrawal and escape into mysticism and religion, as well as their need for self-expression, all were often reflected in their music, and the repertoire was enriched as a result.

The term "romanticism," as it pertains to the nineteenth century, is inexact and somewhat misleading. The Romantic period contained many diametrical differences, which seemingly run counter to its name. According to Machlis:

> The nineteenth century included many opposites: liberalism and reaction, idealism and the crassest materialism, bourgeois sentimentality and stark realism, mysticism and scientific inquiry, democratic revolution and royalist restoration, romantic optimism and no less romantic despair. [1]

The word "romantic" is derived from "romance"—a type of story named after the romance languages in which they were originally written. Since these stories were mostly about love and adventure, the word romantic became associated with these two subjects. The stories often had attractive natural settings, so the phrase "romantic spot" came to be used as the opposite of ugly and commonplace. Gradually there developed five variants of the original meaning of romantic: it came to be applied to love, adventure, scenic beauty, improbability, and make-believe. These meanings are not necessarily interrelated or bound together. [2]

One of the great escapes of the Romantic era was to fantasize a return to the Middle Ages—a time when, nostalgically, order and tranquility prevailed—but this was an attempt to escape the rapid pace of changing times brought about by the French and Industrial Revolutions.

In the musical style of the Romantic period, everything was bigger, phrases were longer, dynamic changes were greater, and there was more emotionalism and excitement, as well as a heavier orchestration.

SOCIETY IN THE NINETEENTH CENTURY

The American Revolution and the birth of the United States in 1776, and the French Revolution of 1789, brought to the fore a concept of democracy that was welcomed by the rising middle class of Europe. No single European court or political system dominated Europe, thus allowing for greater individual expression than ever before. This was the era of the classic "balance of power" or "Concert of Europe" after 1815.

Another equally important development was the Industrial Revolution— the change in social and economic organization brought about by the replacement of hand tools by machine and power tools and the development of

---

[1]Joseph Machlis, The Enjoyment of Music, reg. rev. ed. (New York: W. W. Norton & Company, Inc., 1963), p. 85. Used with permission.
[2]Jacques Barzun, Classic, Romantic, and Modern (Garden City, New York: Anchor Books, 1961), p. 74.

large-scale production in industry. These changes began to occur about 1760; however, by 1800 many new and faster processes were in operation. For example, the invention of the spinning jenny by James Hargreaves in 1770 enabled a single worker to run eight spindles instead of only one. In 1763, James Watt, a Scottish mechanic, adapted the power of the steam engine to run factory machinery—a process that accelerated during the nineteenth century. Pack horses and wagons were an inefficient means of transporting goods, so Thomas Tilford and John MacAdam developed an improved method of road construction. Also, many canals were dug, which connected the main rivers and provided a network of waterways for transporting coal and other heavy goods. In the early nineteenth century came George Stephenson's locomotive and Robert Fulton's steamboat. These developments marked the beginning of modern transportation.

During the earlier part of the nineteenth century there existed throughout Europe a feeling of political and cultural inferiority and the desire for a national means of expression. This was a reaction to the widespread cultural and, since 1789, political and military domination of France, the French language, and Napoleon Bonaparte. As countries gradually developed, however, a spirit of nationalism burgeoned throughout Europe as well as in America. This was in contrast to the previous suppression of indigenous ethnic and linguistic groups. Out of these groups emerged strong literary and musical voices that expressed themselves freely. There were basically two types of nationalism—defensive and aggressive. Defensive nationalism was dedicated to achieving a cultural identity and emphasized the arts. It was quite idealistic in nature and may be observed in some of the music of Guissepi Verdi and Anton Dvořák. Aggressive nationalism, on the other hand, sought to impose a specific cultural identity upon other societies or groups of people. Historians often speak of these two forces as "cultural nationalism" and "political nationalism." They consider the first half of the nineteenth century the high point of a cultural and romantic type of nationalism, while in the second half of the century a more belligerent, martial nationalism gradually developed. During the latter period there also occurred a widespread shift in mood, from romanticism to realism.

Composers were as concerned about the status of their countries as other citizens, and their music often reflected their feelings. For example, Johannes Brahms composed his *Triumphlied* (for eight-part chorus and orchestra, Opus 55) in 1871 to celebrate the German victory over the French in the Franco-Prussian War in 1871. This date (1871) has been identified as the time when a complete shift from defensive to aggressive nationalism occurred. This latter type may be identified in the music of Bizet, Tchaikovsky, and Elgar, and in the marches of John Philip Sousa that accompanied America's aggressive debut as a world power in 1898.[3]

---

[3]Rey M. Longyear, *Nineteenth-Century Romanticism in Music* (Englewood Cliffs, NJ: Prentice Hall, 1973), p. 7.

World economics have a center of importance and influence. This center has shifted over the centuries from place to place. In Europe in the 1380s the center was in Venice, Italy. In about 1500 the center shifted to Antwerp. Then from about 1550 to 1560 it returned to Genoa, Italy. In the years 1590 to 1610, the center moved to Amsterdam, and it remained there for almost two centuries. Between 1780 and 1815 it moved to London, and then finally to New York in 1919, following World War I (1914–18).[4] So throughout most of the nineteenth century London was economically very strong, and this may have contributed to the group of strong middle-class English citizens who made music a part of their lives. From 1815 to 1914 the city of London was the economic and financial hub of the world. It encompassed the prosperous Victorian era: 1837–1901.

Opera during the Romantic period found a newly broadened audience, particularly among the increasingly wealthy emerging middle class. A popular genre growing out of the French Revolution was "rescue opera," of which good examples are Cherubini's Le Deux Journées (1800) and Beethoven's Fidelio (1805). At the beginning of the nineteenth century, the production of castrati temporarily ceased, but resumed in about 1815. The practice finally ended in 1878. Sometime thereafter, the Catholic Church in Italy again advocated the use of boys and men in cathedral choirs.

In contrast to eighteenth-century composers, whose primary focus was their music and whose efforts were normally supported by patrons, nineteenth-century composers had strong interests and capabilities in other fields. For example, Hector Berlioz and Richard Wagner were important literary figures. Robert Schumann was a competent author; Felix Mendelssohn was a gifted painter; and Johannes Brahms, Peter Tchaikovsky, and Camille Saint-Saens edited early music. Most nineteenth-century composers were well-read and literately sensitive to a greater extent that ever before.[5]

COMPOSERS OF THE ROMANTIC ERA

The Romantic era had a multitude of successful composers. Among the most renowned are GIOACCHINO ROSSINI (1792–1868), FRANZ SCHUBERT (1797–1828), HECTOR BERLIOZ (1803–1869), FELIX MENDELSSOHN (1809–1847), ROBERT SCHUMANN (1810–1856), FRANZ LISZT (1811–1886), RICHARD WAGNER (1813–1883), GIUSEPPI VERDI (1813–1901), ANTON BRUCKNER (1824–1896), JOHANNES BRAHMS (1833–1897), and EDWARD ELGAR (1857–1934).

GIOACCHINO ROSSINI was born in Pesaro, Italy, in 1792. As a young boy Rossini was often left in a home while his parents traveled and performed in

---

[4]Fernard Braudel, *Afterthoughts on Material Civilization and Capitalism* (Baltimore: The Johns Hopkins University Press, 1977), pp. 85–86.

[5]Longyear, *Nineteenth-Century Romanticism*, p. 11.

various theaters in Italy. While there he learned to play the harpsichord and acquired some knowledge of music. At 15 Rossini entered the Liceo Communali of Bologna, where he studied theory with Padre Mattei and cello with Cavedagni. On August 8, 1808, his cantata *Il Pianto d'armonia per la morte* was performed at Liceo and won a prize. Over the years he composed 22 other cantatas, the last in 1861, seven years before his death. This is interesting, as he ceased composing operas at age 37, but apparently felt compelled to continue the writing of cantatas. His other cantatas are *La Morte di Didone* (1811), *Egle ed Irene* (1814), *Inno agli Italiani* (1815), *Le Nozze di Teli e Peleo* (1816), *Igea* (1819), *Partenope* (1819), *Voto filiale* (1820), *La Riconoscinza* (1821), *La santa alleanza* (1822), *Il vero omaggio* (1822), *L'Augurio felice* (1822), *Il Bardo* (1822), *Omaggio pastorale* (1823), *Il Pianto della muse in morte di Lord Byron* (1824), *I Pastori* (1825), *Il Serto votivo* (1829), *Giovanna d'Arco* (1832), *Inno popolare* (1846), *Inno nazionale* (1848), *Inno alla pace* (1848), *Il Faciollo smarrito* (1861), and *Coro di cacciatori* (1861).

FRANZ SCHUBERT was born in Lichtenthal near Vienna in 1797. His father taught him to play the violin, and his older brother taught him the piano. At the age of 11 Schubert became a choirboy in the Imperial Chapel in Vienna and also entered the "Konvict," the training school for the court singers, where one of his teachers was Antonio Salieri. In 1813 his voice changed, so he left the "Konvict" and began to prepare himself as an elementary school teacher. He taught in his father's school in 1815–16. Schubert wrote eight or nine symphonies, 15 string quartets, 21 piano sonatas, two operas—*Alfonso und Estrella* (1822) and *Fierabras* (1823)—and various pieces of sacred choral music, including seven masses. However, his most outstanding contributions are his songs, of which a number have been arranged for chorus.

HECTOR BERLIOZ was born in La Côte-Saint-André, Isère, France, in 1803. His father, a physician, encouraged Berlioz to enter the medical profession, and from 1821 to 1824 he was a medical student in Paris and at the same time studied composition with Jean Le Sueur. Berlioz found the practice of medicine to be too distasteful, so he turned his energies full-time to music. During his lifetime Berlioz wrote music of various forms, including three operas, orchestral symphonies, choral music both sacred and secular, and vocal solo music. Berlioz also earned part of his living as a journalist and contributed many works to Parisian periodicals. Berlioz's early musical training was on flute and guitar. As he was not a pianist, he was unused to the movement of nineteenth-century harmonic patterns. This, it is believed, is the reason he turned to unused sequences of harmony and rhythm. Berlioz was considered a master of orchestration and wrote a treatise on the subject. In attendance at the first performance of his dramatic symphony *Romeo and Juliet* in 1839 was Richard Wagner, who was much impressed not only by the music, but by the composer's artistic ideals. The *Grand messe des morts* (Requiem) was conceived on a large scale, since musical events during that time were written to appeal to large audiences. Berlioz's work uses 16 timpani and brass bands located in four

A caricature of Berlioz by Cajetan, based on Grandville's view of Berlioz's flamboyant conducting style and his use of a large orchestra with its presumed deafening effects.

corners of the church. The work is strident in some places, but stark and austere in others.[6]

In 1842 Berlioz made his first tour of Europe as a conductor; he continued to do this, and in 1848 he began to concentrate less on composition and more on conducting. His conducting style is reputed to have been highly flamboyant, and along with his music motivated an intriguing caricature by Cajetan. Berlioz did indeed use large forces in his works. For example, in his *Te Deum* he employed a children's choir of 600 voices. At the other extreme, however, is his gentle oratorio *L'Enfance du Christ* (The Childhood of Christ).

[6]Stanley Sadie, *Music Guide: An Introduction* (Englewood Cliffs, NJ: Prentice Hall, 1986), p. 328.

Of his orchestral works, the *Symphonie Fantastique* (Fantastic Symphony) is most renowned. It tells the story of a young musician who takes opium and plunges into a deep sleep that is accompanied by strange visions. A beloved woman becomes a melody, a fixed idea that is heard everywhere. The *Symphonie Fantastique* is in five movements: (1) "Reveries, Passions," (2) "A Ball," (3) "Scene in the Fields," (4) "March to the Scaffold," and (5) "Dream of a Witches' Sabbath." The first performance was given in Paris on December 5, 1830. Among Berlioz's choral works are *Lélio* (a sequel to *Symphonie Fantastique*) (1832), *Grande messe des morts* (Requiem) (1837), *La Damnation de Faust* (1846), *Te Deum* (1849), and *L'Enfance du Christ* (1854). Berlioz also wrote a number of motets.

FELIX MENDELSSOHN was born in Hamburg, Germany, in 1809 into a family with a strong cultural and intellectual background. Mendelssohn's family moved to Berlin when he was an infant, and there he received a very thorough education. When he was a young boy, Mendelssohn's teacher was the composer Zelter, who was director of the Berlin Choral society, the *Singakademie*. At the age of 12 Mendelssohn was taken to meet Goethe, and at 16 he was taken to Paris, where the composer Luigi Cherubini encouraged him to pursue a musical career.

In 1835, Mendelssohn was appointed conductor of the Gewandhaus in Leipzig, and he held the post for the remainder of his life. During this time he did much to revive the music of older composers, and presented concerts performing the music of J. S. Bach, W. A. Mozart, and Beethoven, as well as introducing the music of Carl Maria von Weber (1786–1826) and Franz Schubert. On one of his many trips to London, Mendelssohn became friends with Queen Victoria. He was much admired by the English choral societies of the time, for one of which he composed the oratorio *Elijah*. It was first performed in 1846 at a music festival in Birmingham.

Among Mendelssohn's choral works are the oratorios *St. Paul* and *Elijah;* the symphony-cantata *Lobgesang* (Opus 52); *Die erste Walpurgisnacht* (Opus 60), for soli, chorus, and orchestra; *"Festgesänge,"* An die Künstler, for men's chorus and brass; *Zur Säcularfeier der Buchdruckerkunst* ("Gutenberg cantata") for men's chorus and orchestra; *Hymn,* for alto solo, chorus, and orchestra (Opus 96); *Lauda Sion,* for chorus and orchestra (Opus 73); *Tu es Petrus,* for chorus and orchestra (Opus 111); Psalms 115 (Opus 31) and 95 (Opus 46) for soli, chorus, and orchestra; Psalms 114 (Opus 51) and 98 (Opus 91), for men's chorus and orchestra; the prayer *Verleih' uns Frieden,* for chorus and orchestra; Psalm 42, for chorus and organ; Psalms 2, 22, and 43, for chorus *a cappella; Funeral Song,* for mixed chorus (Opus 116); *Kyrie eleison,* for double chorus; six anthems ("Sprüche") for eight-part chorus (Opus 79); three motets for soli, chorus, and organ (Opus 23); and three motets for women's chorus and organ (Opus 39).

ROBERT SCHUMANN was born in Zwickau in Saxony in 1810. His first lessons on piano were taught by the organist at the Zwickau Marienkirche. In

1828, at age 18, he entered Leipzig University and two years later began to apply himself more seriously to his musical studies. In 1843 he assumed a teaching position at the Conservatorium in Leipzig. The following year he moved to Dresden, where he lived until 1850. In 1848, he organized the "Chorgesang-Verein." In 1850 he moved to Düsseldorf to assume the post of town musical director, a position he held until 1853, when he became seriously ill.

Among Schumann's choral works are cantata *Das Paradies und die Peri*, for soli, chorus, and orchestra (Opus 50); *Adventlied*, for soprano, chorus, and orchestra (Opus 71); *Beim Abschied zu singen*, for chorus with woodwinds or piano (Opus 84); *Requiem für Mignon* (Opus 98b); *Nachtlied*, for chorus and orchestra (Opus 108); cantata *Der Rose Pilgerfahrt* (Opus 112); ballade *Des Sängers Fluch* (Opus 139); four ballades *Vom Pagen und der Konigstochter* (Opus 140); ballade *Das Glück von Edenhall*, for men's chorus and orchestra (Opus 143); *Missa sacra*, for chorus and orchestra (Opus 147); *Requiem Mass*, for chorus and orchestra (Opus 148); and numerous choruses for mixed voices, and men's and women's voices.

FRANZ LISZT was born in Raiding, near Ödenburg, Hungary, in 1811. He began receiving instruction in piano at age six and progressed so rapidly that he presented a public concert in Ödenburg at age nine. Hungarian aristocrats financed his musical education for six years. Liszt and his family moved to Vienna in 1821, where Liszt studied piano with Czerny and theory with Salieri. His career was interrupted by a liaison with the Countess d'Agoult (1835–39), with whom he had three children. Cosima, the youngest of his two daughters, grew up to become the wife of Richard Wagner. Liszt was considered the greatest piano virtuoso of the nineteenth century. As a pianist Liszt was quite a showman, and gave the public what it wanted—for example, he often placed two pianos on the stage and alternated between them so that the entire audience could see his hands. He enjoyed performing flamboyant arrangements of excerpts from popular operas. He was also a glamorous figure who was highly attractive to women. His status prompted the caricature by Boland Istók on March 25, 1876. Liszt was allied with Wagner in the movement called "Zukunftsmusik"—the music of the future—and in 1848 he accepted the position of court Kapellmeister at Weimar, with the understanding that he would direct his efforts toward the progress of modern musical art. Liszt experimented with new melodic progressions, including the whole-tone scale, and with harmonic combinations using dissonant notes produced by suspensions, with long-delayed resolutions creating an impression of atonality and of polytonality. Liszt also built large sonorities through his use of a large orchestra, thus following the precedent set by Berlioz.

Liszt's choral works include *Missa solemnis* (the Grand Festival Mass); *Hungarian Coronation Mass*; *Mass in C minor*, with organ; *Missa choralis in A minor*, with organ; *Requiem*; three oratorios—*Die Legende von der Heiligen Elisabeth*, *Christus*, and *Stanislaus*; *Die Seligkeiten*, for baritone solo, chorus and

LISZT és a NŐK

Franz Liszt idolized by female admirers after a concert. Caricature by Boland Istók, March 25, 1876.

organ; *Pater noster*, for mixed chorus; *Pater noster* and *Ave Maria* for men's chorus and organ; *Psalm 13*, for tenor solo, chorus and orchestra; *Psalm 18*, for men's chorus, orchestra and organ; *Psalm 116*, for soli and men's or mixed chorus; *Christus ist geboren*, for chorus with organ; *An den heiligen Franziskus*, for men's chorus, organ, trombones, and percussion (drums); *Les Morts*, for men's chorus and orchestra; the cantatas *Die Glocken des Strassburger Münsters*; *Die heilige Cäcile*, *An die Künstler*, for soli, men's chorus, and orchestra; *Hungaria*, for soli, mixed chorus, and orchestra; *Zur Säcular-Feier Beethovens*; *Festalbum*; *Festchor*; and numerous four-part works for men's choruses.

RICHARD WAGNER was born in Leipzig, Germany, in 1813. His family moved to Dresden, where he attended the foremost church school, and then in 1827 back to Leipzig, where he went to the Nikolaisschule and later to

Thomasschule. In his schooling he studied piano, violin, and harmony. In 1831 he entered Leipzig University; however, his main musical studies were with the Kantor of the Thomasschule. Throughout his career, Wagner seemed plagued with financial problems. Wagner, of course, is best known for his operas. For these he wrote his own librettos. His music is marked by its grandeur of conception, originality, boldness of execution, vividness of characterization, and intensity of expression.

Wagner's choral works include *Neujahrskantate,* for mixed chorus and orchestra (1834); *Volkshymme,* for mixed chorus and orchestra (1837); *La Descente de la Courtille,* for mixed chorus and orchestra (1840); *Weihegyuss,* for men's chorus and orchestra; *Das Liebesmahl der Apostel,* for men's chorus and orchestra (1843); *Grüss seiner Treuen an Friedrich August den Geliebten,* for men's chorus *a cappella* (1843); and *An Webers Grabe,* for men's chorus *a cappella* (1844), written for Carl Maria Weber's burial.

GIUSEPPI VERDI was born in 1813 in Le Roncole, near Busseto in northern Italy. His early education was in Busseto, where he also studied organ with the church organist. At age 18 he moved to Milan, where he studied for several years, but then he returned to Busseto in 1835 when he became town music-master and taught at the music school. While Verdi is perhaps best known for his much-admired operas, 14 in all, he also composed some fine works for chorus. They include the *Requiem Mass* ("Manzoni Requiem," 1874); *Quattro Pezzi sacri* (1898); *Ave Maria* and *Stabat Mater,* for mixed chorus *a cappella; Laudi alla Vergine Maria,* for female chorus *a cappella; Te Deum,* for double chorus and orchestra; *Inno della Nazioni;* and *Pater Noster,* for five-part chorus *a cappella* (1880).

ANTON BRUCKNER was born in Ansfelden, near Linz, Austria, in 1824, the son of a schoolmaster-organist. Orphaned early in life, he learned to play the organ primarily by his own efforts. Bruckner eventually became a cathedral organist at Linz in 1856. He then studied composition with Kitzler and Sechter. In 1867, he became court organist in Vienna and also instructor of organ and harmony at the Vienna Conservatory. In 1875, Bruckner obtained the post of Lecturer of music at Vienna University. Although widely known for his orchestral compositions, Bruckner also wrote choral compositions, including *Missa Solemnis* in B flat Major (1854); *Germananzug* (1863); *Abendzauber* (1878); *Helgoland* (1893); three masses (1864, 1866, 1871); *Te Deum* (1881); and *105th Psalm* (1892).

JOHANNES BRAHMS was born in Hamburg, Germany, in 1833. Brahms's first teacher was his father, who was a double-bass player at the Hamburg opera. Later Brahms studied with Otto Cossel, and in his early teens was sent to Eduard Marxsen, who helped develop his proficiency as a pianist. At age 14 he presented a public concert in Hamburg that included his own variations on a folk tune. Brahms became a close friend of Robert and Clara Schumann, and when Brahms was 20, Schumann hailed him as the coming genius of German music. In 1859, Brahms founded and conducted a women's choir in Hamburg. In 1860, he signed a manifesto opposing the so-called "Music of the Future," as promulgated by Franz Liszt and Richard Wagner. In 1863, Brahms became conductor of the Vienna Singakademie. From 1864 to 1871 he was a freelance teacher in Hamburg and also completed his *German Requiem*, on which he worked from 1857 to 1868. From 1872 to 1875 Brahms served as conductor of the Vienna Philharmonic.

Brahms wrote many works for chorus, among which are *Ave Maria*, for women's voices, organ, and orchestra, Opus 12 (1858); *Funeral Hymn*, for chorus and wind orchestra, Opus 13 (1858); *Four Songs* for women's voices, two horns, and harp, Opus 17 (1860); *Marienlieder*, for mixed voices, Opus 22 (1859); *13th Psalm*, for women's voices and organ, Opus 27 (1859); two motets for five-part *a cappella* chorus, Opus 29 (1860); *Lass dich nur nichts dauern*, for four-part chorus with organ, Opus 30 (1856); choruses for women's voices, *a cappella*, Opus 37 (1859–63); *Five Soldatenlieder*, for four-part male chorus, Opus 41 (1861–62); three songs for six-part mixed chorus, *a cappella*, Opus 42 (1859–61); twelve songs and romances for women's voices, *a cappella*, Opus 44 (1859–63); *Ein deutsches Requiem*, for soli, chorus, and orchestra, Opus 45 (1857–68); *Rinaldo*, cantata for tenor, male chorus, and orchestra, Opus 50 (1863–68); *Rhapsodie*, for alto, male chorus, and orchestra, Opus 53 (1869); *Schicksallied*, for mixed chorus and orchestra, Opus 54 (1871); *Triumphlied*, for eight-part chorus and orchestra, Opus 55 (1870–71); seven songs for *a cappella* chorus, Opus 62 (1874); two motets for *a cappella* chorus, Opus 74 (1863–77); *Nänie* for chorus and orchestra, Opus 82 (1880–81); *Gesang der Parzen*, for six-part chorus and orchestra, Opus 89 (1882); six songs and romances for four-part *a cappella* chorus, Opus 93a (1883–84); *Tafellied*, for six-part chorus with piano, Opus 93b (1884); five songs for *a cappella* chorus, Opus 104 (1888); *Deutsche Fest-und Gedenksprüche* for double *a cappella* chorus, Opus 109 (1886–88); three motets for four- and eight-part *a cappella* chorus, Opus 110 (1889); and thirteen canons for women's voices and piano, Opus 113 (1863–90).

EDWARD ELGAR was born in Broadheath, near Worcester, England, in 1857. Elgar had little formal training in music; however, from his mid-teens on he made a living as a violinist, organist, bassoonist, conductor, and music teacher. As he built his personal compositional style he drew equally from Brahms and Wagner in composing a number of oratorios, cantatas, and choral works with orchestra.

The oratorios were *The Light of Life*, Opus 29 (1890); *The Dream of Gerontius*, Opus 38 (1900); *The Apostles*, Opus 49 (1903); and *The Kingdom*, Opus 5 (1906). The cantatas were *The Black Night*, Opus 25 (1893); *Scenes from the Saga of King Olaf*, Opus 30 (1896); *The Banner of St. George*, Opus 33 (1897); *Caractacus*, Opus 35 (1898); *Coronation Ode*, Opus 44 (1902); and *The Music Makers*, Opus 69 (1912). Choral works with orchestra are *Star of the*

Summer Night, Opus 23 (1892); *Scenes from the Bavarian Highlands,* Opus 27 (1896); and *The Spirit of England,* Opus 80 (1916).

CHORAL SOCIETIES IN THE ROMANTIC ERA

In the nineteenth century there was a tremendous growth of choral societies. In Britain, Germany, the Scandinavian countries, and America, choral singing became an important activity for many people, particularly those living in industrial communities and large cities. Many great new halls were built to accommodate the large choirs. The *Singakademie* was founded in 1791 in Berlin and became a pattern for many choral societies. The Singakadamie was not only a choral society, but a school of music as well. In 1810 a performance of Mozart's *Requiem* was presented there, and two years later the choir numbered 200 members. In 1815, *Judas Maccabaeus* was performed; in 1815, *The Creation;* in 1829, the *St. Matthew Passion;* and in 1834, Beethoven's *Ninth Symphony* and the "Kyrie" and "Gloria" from the *Missa Solemnis.* [7]

Vienna supported many choral societies. In 1812, *The Gesellschaft der Musikfreunde* was founded, and vast numbers of singers participated in an annual Musicfest. In about the middle of the nineteenth century the *Singverein* and the *Wiener Singakademie* were also established. In England the Three Choirs Festival was founded in 1737, and Edward Elgar, Gustav Holtz, and Ralph Vaughan Williams all maintained close connections with the organization. In London, the *Aristocratic Ancient Concerts* existed from 1776 to 1848 and the last conductor was the Duke of Wellington. In 1813, the Philharmonic Society was founded by Vincent Novello, Thomas Attwood, and others. [8]

In America, William Billings formed a singing class in Stoughton, Massachusetts, that became the Stoughton Musical Society, which is today the oldest musical organization in continuous existence in the United States. In Boston, the Handel and Haydn Society was formed in 1815. In New York, a Sacred Music Society was established that performed *Messiah* in 1831 and Mendelssohn's *St. Paul* in 1838. [9] The success of any choral organization is dependent upon high quality published music being available. Shortly after 1800, the firm of Breitkopf and Härtel began to publish editions of the music of Handel, Mozart, Clementi, and Dvořák. Vincent Novello (1781–1861) made an important contribution to English culture in the nineteenth century. In 1829 his eldest son (Joseph) Alfred began the publishing of the works of Handel, Mendelssohn, Beethoven, Haydn, and Mozart. [10]

---

[7]Percy M. Young, *The Choral Tradition* (New York: W. W. Norton & Company, 1962), pp. 192–193.

[8]Ibid., p. 194.

[9]Ibid., pp. 195–196.

[10]Ibid., p. 197.

MUSICAL STYLE AND PERFORMANCE PRACTICE

Meter and Stress

Composers during the Romantic period, in their search for freedom from rules, often sought to break the strictness of the rhythm, yet remain within the time-honored rules. A widely used device to achieve this objective was the use of meter changes without changing the meter signature.[11] An example of this device may be found in the Brahms *Requiem*. Such metric alteration results in displaced accents—that is, accents where they are not normally expected—in a relatively short space of time. Whereas Romantic composers achieved these unique rhythmic effects within the boundaries of the accepted rules, the modern-day composer would normally utilize alternately different meter signatures (see Chapter V, "The Modern Period," and the discussion on meter and stress later in this chapter, for examples). Other varied means of syncopation also became widely used during this period as an expressive device and as a means of evoking interest. Intricate rhythmic patterns and rhythmic surprise were characteristic of the music of the period. Composers sometimes used a phrase structure that was irregular, that is, of varying lengths. Brahms in particular was noted for his elongated or extended phrases; in some cases they were absorbed into contrapuntal textures so that it is difficult to determine where they actually do end.[12]

Tempo

The restraint typical of the Classical period was abandoned during the Romantic era. It was a period of extremes—fast tempi were often performed exceptionally fast and slow tempi exceptionally slow. Tempo was closely aligned with mood, and as the composer was often expressing varying moods within a composition, extreme, abrupt changes in tempo often occurred. *Accelerando* and *ritardando* became more frequently used than in the previous period. As an element of expressiveness *tempo rubato* was developed to its ultimate.

Nineteenth-century composers, however, indicated their desired tempos much more precisely than did earlier musicians. Short Italian phrases helped to indicate both the tempo and the character of the music. It should also be remembered that the metronome, invented by Mälzel in 1816, helped composers to indicate their desired tempi more precisely.

---

[11]Curt Sachs, *Rhythm and Tempo: A Study in Music History* (New York: W. W. Norton & Company, 1953), p. 344.

[12]Homer Ulrich and Paul A. Pisk, *A History of Music and Musical Styles* (New York: Harcourt Brace Jovanovich, 1963), p. 485.

As to tempo modifications, Joseph Czerny stated: "Every composition must be played in the tempo prescribed by the composer and adhered to by the executant, notwithstanding, however, that in almost every line there are certain notes and passages where a little *ritardando* or *accelerando* is necessary, to beautify the reading and to augment the interest."[13]

In about 1825, Czerny itemized, in his authoritative *Klavierschule*, the following eleven situations in which the use of a *ritardando* or *rallentando* is appropriate. These rules were applicable to the performing style used in the first half of the nineteenth century.[14]

1. At the return of the principal subject.
2. When a phrase is to be separated from the melody.
3. On long notes strongly accented.
4. At the transition to a different time.
5. After a pause.
6. On the *diminuendo* of a quick, lively passage.
7. Where the ornamental note cannot be played *a tempo giusto*.
8. In a well-marked *crescendo* serving to introduce or to terminate an important passage.
9. In passages where the composer or the performer gives free play to his fancy.
10. When the composer marks the passage *espressivo*.
11. At the end of a shake or cadence.

During the Romantic period two diametrically opposed schools of interpretative thought existed. One, represented by Mendelssohn, was based on classical principles; the other was the highly romantic style, sometimes called the "Neo-German" type of interpretation, which was initiated by Liszt and exemplified by Wagner. The Mendelssohn school sought to preserve the Classical tradition and to eliminate some of the practices which they felt were extreme. Mendelssohn was an exponent of regularity of rhythm and fluency of tempo. Some of the composers of this school may have even sought to solidify or strengthen their conservative views in the latter part of their lives. Barzun states that only "in the second half of their careers did Johannes Brahms and César Franck seek to restore purity and 'form' to their music." By this they generally meant aloofness or piety combined with academicism.[15] Wagner, on the other hand, favored broad, singing melody, and considerable liberty in tempi.[16] He felt that the correct tempo could be determined only through "a proper understanding of the melos."[17]

---

[13]Frederick Dorian, *The History of Music in Performance* (New York: W. W. Norton & Company, 1942), p. 205.

[14]Ibid., p. 206.

[15]Barzun, *Classic, Romantic, and Modern*, p. 110.

[16]Dorian, *Music in Performance*, pp. 230–231.

[17]Ibid., p. 281.

In addition to his disagreement with Mendelssohn, Wagner criticized not only the compositions of Johannes Brahms, but his interpretations as well, which he assailed as "woodenness and primness."[18] Wagner was also critical of the conducting interpretations of Hector Berlioz and his fluent moving tempi. As to the manner in which Berlioz conducted the Mozart Symphony in G Minor, Wagner stated in a letter to Franz Liszt, "I heard him conduct some classical works, and was amazed to find a conductor who was so energetic in the interpretation of his own compositions sinking into the commonest rut of the vulgar time-beater."[19]

Although composers may be said to have had tendencies toward one or the other of the above positions, and certainly were influenced in one way or another, it would be unwise, as well as impossible, to categorize them all in either group. The music of each composer must be considered individually. Only through a thorough analysis and study of the music will a proper tempo be determined. For example, music with a light texture may be performed in a faster tempo than should music with a heavy, sonorous texture. The latter should be performed somewhat slower if it is to be effective. Relating to this point, the following statement by Robert Schumann is both interesting and revealing:

> You know how I dislike quarreling about tempo, and how for me only the inner measure of the movement is conclusive. Thus, an allegro of one who is cold by nature always sounds lazier than a slow tempo by one of sanguine temperament. With the orchestra, however, the proportions are decisive. Stronger and denser masses are capable of bringing out the detail as well as the whole with more emphasis and importance; whereas, with smaller and finer units, one must compensate for the lack of resonance by pushing forward in the tempo.[20]

Dynamics

In contrast to the restraint of the Classical period, composers of the Romantic period often used extremes in dynamics ranging from *fff* to *ppp*, but with a slight leaning toward the use of the lower dynamic levels. Some editions of the Verdi *Requiem*, it may be noted, even contain dynamic markings of *ppppp*.

Crescendo and *decrescendo*, or the gradual swelling and diminishing of tone, became an expressive device widely used by nineteenth-century composers. In certain compositions it was used to create the illusion of

---

[18]Ibid., pp. 289–291.

[19]Ibid., p. 247.

[20]From *The History of Music in Performance* by Frederick Dorian (New York: W. W. Norton & Company, Inc.), p. 227. *Cf.* Sachs, *Rhythm and Tempo: A Study in Music History* (New York: W. W. Norton & Company, 1953), p. 379.

distance—that is, of a group or object gradually coming closer and then receding into the distance.

Some composers employed a slight *accelerando* with a *crescendo* and a slight *ritardando* with a *decrescendo*. Rossini, in particular, was noted for his combining "a gradual dynamic increase with a great rhythmic momentum."[21]

Composers in the nineteenth century endeavored to indicate their intentions more clearly on their scores through the use of a variety of tempo and dynamic markings. Some of these terms encompassed both tempo and dynamics. For example, *morendo* (dying away) indicates that the music should be both slower and softer, and *andante maestoso* (moderately slow and majestic) implies a moderate tempo yet with a full sonority.

In addition to *crescendo* and *decrescendo*, the use of more sudden climaxes also became a common practice. Grieg, for example, employs this device to a considerable extent in his *Psalms* (C. F. Peters). The use of dynamic accents, such as *sforzando* (*sfz*) and *sforzato* (*sf*), occurred with much greater frequency. See, for example, the Choral Finale to the *Ninth Symphony* by Beethoven (H. W. Gray; G. Schirmer), *Elijah* by Mendelssohn (G. Schirmer), the *Requiem Mass* and the *Stabat Mater* by Dvořák (G. Schirmer), and the *29th Psalm* by Elgar (Novello). In contrast to the moderately sized ensembles utilized in the various princely courts of the Classical era, the combined forces of large orchestras and choirs became the ideal medium for the expression of the dynamic extremes of the Romantic period.

A slight *crescendo*–*decrescendo* within a musical phrase is a quite natural means of musical expression, especially on melodically ascending and descending phrases. Nineteenth-century composers, and the editors of their works, have tended to use this expressive device to a more marked degree. Examples of this occur throughout the "Kyrie" from *Mass in G* by Franz Schubert (see Figure 24), and "Create in Me, O God, a Pure Heart" (Schaffe in mir, Gott ein rein Herz, Opus 29, No. 2) by Johannes Brahms (see Figure 25). The effective achievement of this dynamic effect is partially dependent upon beginning the phrases very softly (almost at a whisper), so the dynamic changes become more apparent.

Texture

New harmonic relationships were explored by composers of the Romantic period. Dissonance became more widely used and an increasing use of melodic and harmonic chromaticism gave the composer a wider range of expressive devices.[22] There was a lessening of harmonic drive, with an increased tendency toward the use of deceptive resolutions and obscured cadences. That is,

[21]Ulrich and Pisk, *History of Music*, p. 455.

[22]The effectiveness of dissonance is certainly related to tempo, as the listener's aural comprehension of a complex and dissonant passage may be blurred by a tempo that is too rapid.

FIGURE 24 Excerpt from "Kyrie" from *Mass in* G by Franz Schubert, illustrating phrase-wise *crescendo–decrescendo*. Copyright 1986 by Hal Leonard Publishing Corporation. Used by permission.

FIGURE 25 Excerpt from the motet "Create in Me, O God, a Pure Heart" (Schaffe in mir, Gott, ein rein Herz) (Op. 29, No. 2) by Johannes Brahms, illustrating phrase-wise *crescendo–decrescendo*. Copyright 1931 by G. Schirmer, Inc. Used by permission.

cadences were sometimes avoided, or resolved deceptively. In contrast to "wandering" chromaticism, composers sometimes utilized sudden harmonic and enharmonic changes, or shifts of tonal center.

Although a balance between harmony and counterpoint is said to have existed during the late Baroque period, the nineteenth-century Romanticist altered the balance in favor of harmony. The Romantic composer, however, often alternated the texture within a short time span. Counterpoint, when used, focused upon the opposition of masses, rather than upon vocal lines. In contrast to the light and clear texture of the Classical period, the texture of music in the Romantic period was often somewhat dense and heavy.

Expressive Aspects

During the Romantic period some composers expressed their opposition to formality, convention, authority, and tradition, while some others expressed a longing for the past—the "golden age"—and made efforts to recapture it in some way. Whereas the Classical composer was highly concerned with expression within a particular form, the Romanticist was not to be restricted by it. He was not to be bound by the previous forms and strove to develop a freer form through which he might better express himself.

Individual expression became the composer's principal goal. To express emotion freely, the composer drew on all the multitude of musical resources at his command. As a means of creating tension and expressing emotion, composers of this period experimented considerably in the field of harmony. Unusual harmonic effects, as well as unusual rhythmic effects, wide contrasts in dynamics, changing moods, and varying textures, were all used as expressive devices.

While tone color has always existed as an integral aspect of music, it took on a new importance during the Romantic period. Through tone color composers sought to express sensuous beauty and tonal enchantment. Musical terms, such as *con amore* (with love), *con fuoco* (with fire), *con passione* (with passion), *dolce* (sweetly), *gioioso* (joyous), and *mesto* (sad) were increasingly used by composers as an indication of their intention to the performers. These terms, in addition, indicate the frame of mind of the composers of the period. Music of this period, both vocal and instrumental, was influenced by the lyricism of the human voice. It is notable that many of the themes of instrumental music of the period have been adapted into popular songs. Their popularity is, in part, affected by their singability.[23]

As to ornamentation, opera composers, such as Rossini, wrote out the ornaments and coloratura passages in full to limit the unwanted liberties often taken by singers of the time.[24]

Composers often write music to be performed *a cappella*, i.e., without accompaniment; however, they often show concern about the singers' ability to maintain the correct and proper pitch. GUSTAV MAHLER (1860–1911), who anticipated all performance problems, provided in the finale of his Second Symphony "a discreet instrumental accompaniment to protect the *a cappella* chorus from falling in pitch."[25] Sometime later, ARNOLD SCHOENBERG (1874–1951) suggests for his *a cappella* chorus *Peace on Earth* "the use of one or two clarinets for the soprano and alto sections each, and one or two bassoons for tenor and bass." These instruments were suggested for the purpose of helping to maintain the proper pitch during performance.[26]

[23]Machlis, *Enjoyment of Music*, pp. 86–88.
[24]Dorian, *Music in Performance*, p. 287.
[25]Ibid., p. 321.
[26]Ibid., p. 321.

The center of musical life in the nineteenth century was the concert hall, rather than the palace or the church. Because of the lack of restrictions in regard to size of performance organizations, composers during the latter part of the period increasingly wrote for larger groups and in a more colorful and grandiose style than was characteristic of the earlier part of the period.[27]

MUSIC AND THE RELATED ARTS

Romanticism in art involves an emotional appeal to the viewer through the senses. The imaginative was accepted over the rational, the individual sensibility over the dogmatic formula. Whereas the Neo-Classicist stressed order, reason, and balance, the Romantic placed importance on the senses, emotions, and irrational balance.[28]

Two outstanding Romantic painters were Théodore Géricault (1791–1824) and Eugène Delacroix (1798–1863). Géricault's painting *The Raft of the Medusa* (1818–19) was drawn from an actual event—the sinking of the ship *Medusa* off the coast of West Africa. The painting shows desperation in its twisted gestures and is arranged on two diagonals. The first diagonal stretches along the line of action from the outstretched corpse in the lower left to the raised arm at the upper right. The second diagonal begins with the second corpse in the lower right and runs up the mast at the upper left. The theme is one of basic human emotions.[29]

Delacroix was impressed with the concept of monumental themes and compositions, and with "poetic truth" rather than illustrating a specific event. His paintings *The Collision of Moorish Horsemen*, *The Arab Attacked by a Lion*, and *A Reclining Tiger* show a romantic interest in nature.

"Romanticism (in France) was swept in on a wave of political unrest culminating in the July Revolution of 1830 . . . Delacroix's painting *Liberty Leading the People* is dominated by the fiery allegorical figure of Liberty . . . seen as the spirit of the French people whom she leads onward to triumph . . . Her muscular arms are strong enough to hold both a bayoneted rifle and the tricolored banner of the Republic . . . she betrays no sign of softness or sensuality . . . as she leads her followers through the oncoming barrage . . . her followers include both impetuous students and battle-scarred soldiers who have heeded her call rather than that of their reactionary king."[30]

Auguste Rodin (1840–1917) is considered to be the finest sculptor since Bernini. Rodin's objective was not to simply capture elusive optical effects, but

---

[27]Machlis, *Enjoyment of Music*, p. 88.

[28]Benjamin Rifkin, *Art History* (New York: Monarch Press, 1963), pp. 109–110.

[29]Ibid., p. 109.

[30]William Fleming, *Art, Music & Ideas* (New York: Holt, Rinehart and Winston, Inc., 1970), p. 293.

Théodore Géricault, *The Raft of the Medusa*, 1818–19. Oil, 16′1″ × 23′6″. The Louvre, Paris.

Eugène Delacroix, *Liberty Leading the People*, 1830. Oil, 8′6″ × 10′10″. The Louvre, Paris.

to emphasize the process of growth—the miracle of dead matter coming to life in the artist's hands. Rodin's famous work *The Kiss* is an over-lifesize group in marble. The contrast of textures emphasizes the veiled, sensuous softness of the bodies.

Other Nineteenth-Century Art Styles

Neo-Classicism.   This style was in vogue from about the middle of the eighteenth century to the middle of the nineteenth century and focused upon historical subjects as favored by Napoleon, mythological, classical, and Oriental subjects, and religious paintings. Outstanding exponents of this genre were Jacques Louis David (1748–1825) and Jean-Auguste Dominigue (1780–1867).

Realism.   This style focuses on naturalistic landscapes and the realistic representation of subjects in contemporary life. Outstanding exponents of this genre were François Millet (1814–1875), Camille Corot (1796–1875), Gustave Courbet (1819–1877), and Edouard Manet (1832–1883). The political cartoon (caricature) that satirized political and social topics was the medium of Honoré Daumier (1808–1879). Other artists who utilized this

Claude Monet, *Regatta at Argenteuil*, ca. 1873–74. Oil, 18¾ × 28½ in. The Louvre, Paris.

means of expression were Gustave Doré, Boland Istók, and Cajetan.[31] Hector Berlioz seemed to be a favorite target, as shown by Doré's caricature of Berlioz conducting a giant chorus, and Cajetan's caricature of Berlioz in *A Concert in the Year 1846*. See also the caricature by Boland Istók of Franz Liszt being idolized by female admirers following a concert.

Impressionism. This style flourished between 1870 and 1885 and is characterized by (a) the stress on the effects of natural light; (b) contemporary scenes; (c) the use of color opposites, such as red and green; (d) the use of small brush strokes or dabs of paint (or broad flat brush strokes), thus leaving the "mixing" to be done by the viewer's eyes; (e) informal composition by painting directly from life. Outstanding exponents of Impressionist art were Claude Monet (1840–1926), Auguste Renoir (1841–1919), and Edgar Degas (1834–1917). The name *impressionism* was coined when a critic viewed Monet's work entitled *Impression: Sunrise,* and commented "That's not a painting, but an impression of a painting!"

The boldest of the Impressionists was Claude Monet, whose *Regatta at Argenteuil,* ca. 1873–74, is an outstanding example. Monet used "intense hues applied in distinct strokes, and he varied the size and shape of the strokes according to the objects he depicted; the waves and the reflections on the water have been rendered in long, horizontal strokes, the trees and greenery . . . in multidirectional dabs . . . and the sails and sky in streaky impasto."[32]

REFERENCES

Artz, Frederick. *From the Renaissance to Romanticism.* Chicago: University of Chicago Press, 1962.

Badura-Skoda, Eva. "On Schubert's Choral Works." *American Choral Review,* Vol. XXIV, Nos. 2 and 3, April and July 1982, pp. 83–90.

Barzun, Jacques. *Berlioz and His Century: an Introduction to the Age of Romanticism.* Chicago: University of Chicago Press, 1982.

———. *Classic, Romantic, and Modern.* Garden City, NY: Anchor Books, 1961.

Braudel, Fernard. *Afterthoughts on Material Civilization and Capitalism.* Baltimore: The Johns Hopkins University Press, 1977.

Brown, Clive. "The Orchestra in Beethoven's Vienna." *Early Music,* Vol. 16, No. 1, February 1988, pp. 4–20.

Brown, Howard Mayer, and Stanley Sadie, eds. *Performance Practice: Music After 1600.* New York: W. W. Norton & Company, 1989.

Calvocoressi, M. D. *A Survey of Russian Music.* Baltimore: Penguin Books, 1944.

Cole, Hugo. "Composers, Performers, and Interpreters." *The Musical Times,* Vol. XCIX, July 1958, pp. 366–368.

[31]Ibid., pp. 112–113.

[32]Henri Dorra, *Art in Perspective: A Brief History.* New York: Harcourt Brace Jovanovich, p. 206.

Dahkhaus, Carl. *Romanticism and Modernism: Four Studies in the Music of the Later Nineteenth Century.* Munich, 1974. Translated from the German by Mary Whittall. Berkeley and Los Angeles: University of California Press, 1980.

Dane, Jeffrey. "If Brahms Had Lived. . . A Conjectural Obituary." *The Musical Times,* Vol. 131, No. 1769, July 1990, pp. 358–360.

Delisi, Daniel. "Mendelssohn's *Elijah:* Dramatic and Musical Structure, Possible Cuts and Excerpts." *Choral Journal,* Vol. 31, No. 10, May 1991, pp. 27–32.

Donington, Robert. "The Search for Redemption in Wagner." *The Musical Times,* Vol. 130, No. 1751, pp. 20–22.

Dorian, Frederick. *The History of Music in Performance.* New York: W. W. Norton & Company, 1942.

Einstein, Alfred. *Music in The Romantic Era.* New York: W. W. Norton & Company, 1947.

Ellison, Ross Wesley. "Mendelssohn's Elijah: Dramatic Climax of a Creative Career." *American Choral Review,"* Vol. XXII, No. 1, January 1980, pp. 3–9.

Elvers, Rudolph, ed. *Felix Mendelssohn: A Life in Letters.* Translated Craig Tomlinson. New York: Fromm International Publishing Corp., 1986.

Finson, Jon. "Performing Practice in the Late Nineteenth Century, with Special Reference to the Music of Brahms." *Musical Quarterly,* Vol. 70, 1984, pp. 457–475.

Geiringer, Karl. *Brahms, His Life and Work,* 3rd ed. New York: Da Capo Press, 1982.

Guthmiller, John. "The Choral Music of Antonín Dvořák." *Choral Journal.* Vol. XXXII, No. 3, October 1991, pp. 7–14.

Howerton, George. *Technique and Style in Choral Singing.* New York: Carl Fischer, 1957.

Jacobson, Bernard. "Bernard Haitink on Mahler," in *Conductors on Conducting.* Frenchtown, NJ: Columbia Publishing Co., 1979, pp. 125–151.

———. "Carlo Maria Giulini on Brahms," in *Conductors on Conducting.* Frenchtown, NJ: Columbia Publishing Co., 1979, pp. 213–227.

———. "Colin Davis on Berlioz," in *Conductors on Conducting.* Frenchtown, NJ: Columbia Publishing Co., 1979, pp. 103–119.

———. "James Levine on Verdi and Mozart," in *Conductors on Conducting.* Frenchtown, NJ: Columbia Publishing Co., 1979, pp. 33–45.

———. "Sir Adrian Boult on Elgar," in *Conductors on Conducting.* Frenchtown, NJ: Columbia Publishing Co., 1979, pp. 189–207.

Kross, Siegfried. "The Choral Music of Johannes Brahms." *American Choral Review,* Vol. XXV, No. 4, October 1983, pp. 5–30.

Leonard, Richard. *A History of Russian Music.* New York: Macmillan Publishing Co., 1957.

Longyear, Rey M. *Nineteenth-Century Romanticism in Music.* 3rd ed. Englewood Cliffs, NJ: Prentice Hall, 1988.

Machlis, Joseph. *The Enjoyment of Music.* 5th ed. New York: W. W. Norton & Company, 1984.

Minchin, Leslie. "Schubert and Language." *The Musical Times,* Vol. 125, No. 1699, September 1984, pp. 497–498.

Moerk, Alice A. "The Musicologist Looks at Style in the Interpretation of Choral Music." *The Choral Journal,* Vol. XV, No. 1, September 1974, pp. 5–11.

Musgrave, Michael. "Brahms the Progressive: Another View." *The Musical Times,* Vol. 124, No. 1683, May 1983, pp. 291–294.

Nathan, Hans. "The Sense of History in Musical Interpretation." *Music Review,* Vol. XIII, 1952, pp. 85–100.

Plantinga, Leon. *Romantic Music.* New York: W. W. Norton & Company, 1984.

Prout, Ebenezer. "The Proper Balance of Chorus and Orchestra." *Monthly Musical Record,* Vol. XXXI, 1901, pp. 26–27, 51–53.

Ringer, Alexander. *The Early Romantic Period.* Englewood Cliffs, NJ: Prentice Hall, 1990.

Sachs, Curt. *Rhythm and Tempo: A Study in Music History.* New York: W. W. Norton & Company, 1953.

Sadie, Stanley. *Music Guide: An Introduction.* Englewood Cliffs, NJ: Prentice Hall, 1986.

Sheets, Thomas. "Antonín Dvořák's *Requiem:* An Introduction." *Choral Journal,* Vol. XXXII, No. 3, October 1991, pp. 17–23.

Slonimsky, Nicholas. *Baker's Dictionary of Musicians*, 8th ed. New York: Schirmer Books, 1992.

Temperly, Nicholas, ed. *Music in Britain: The Romantic Age, 1800–1914*. London: Athlone Press, 1981.

Temperly, Nicholas. "Tempo and Repeats in the Early Nineteenth Century." *Music and Letters*, Vol. XLVII, No. 4, October 1966, pp. 326–336.

Ulrich, Homer, and Paul A. Pisk. *A History of Music and Musical Styles*. New York: Harcourt Brace Jovanovich, 1963.

Wagner, Richard. *Wagner On Conducting*. Mineola, NY: Dover Publications, Inc., 1989. (Originally published by William Reeves, London, in 1887).

Walker, Ernest. "The Appoggiatura." *Music and Letters*, Vol. 5, No. 2, April 1924, pp. 121–144.

Wood, Ralph W. "Putting in the Expression." *Music and Letters*, Vol. XI, No. 4, October 1930, pp. 375–382.

Young, Percy. *The Choral Tradition*. New York: W. W. Norton & Company, 1962.

The Modern
Period

Toward the end of the nineteenth century the subjective expression of Romanticism had run its course. Some composers, however, continued to write in a modified Romantic style. Among the more notable of this group of late Romanticists were SERGEI TANEYEV (1856–1915), EDWARD ELGAR (1857–1934), GUSTAV MAHLER (1860–1911), RICHARD STRAUSS (1864–1949), ALEXANDER GRETCHANINOV (1864–1956), ENRIQUE GRANADOS (1867–1916), MAX REGER (1873–1916), and SERGEI RACHMANINOFF (1873–1943). Most composers, however, began to seek new means of expression. The main currents of musical expression in the Modern period are quite diverse. They include Impressionism, Expressionism, Neo-Classicism, Neo-Romanticism, the Nationalists, avant-garde music, and Eclecticism.

Impressionism

Impressionism developed as a reaction against the emotionalism and subjective aspects of Romanticism. It emerged during the last quarter of the nineteenth century and was exemplified in the music of CLAUDE DEBUSSY (1862–1918) and MAURICE RAVEL (1875–1937). Debussy was strongly influenced by the Impressionist painters and the Symbolist poets, who avoided an exact and clear-cut representation of things, but sought rather to create a momentary impression of them. The painters often did not mix their paints, but juxtaposed daubs of pure color on the canvas, with the "mixing" left to the eye of the viewer. Also seeking new paths, the Symbolist poets rejected emotionalism and turned to nebulous suggestion and dreamlike evocation of mood.[1]

Expressionism

Appearing about 1910 as a reaction against the "vagueness" of Impressionism, Expressionism is sometimes referred to as the German answer to French Impressionism. Expressionism also received its impetus from painting and poetry. Artists, perhaps influenced by Sigmund Freud's work in psychology, endeavored to capture on canvas the myriad thoughts of the unconscious. Distorted images, expressing the artist's inner self, took the place of the traditional concepts of beauty. Composers also rejected older aesthetic concepts and sought new means of expression.[2] Expressionistic music is characterized by its continuous intensity, high level of dissonance, angular melodic fragments, complex rhythms, and fluctuating tempi. The Expressionist composer utilized all the devices at his command to express the conflicts, fears, and anxieties of the inner self. The outstanding exponents of Expressionism are ARNOLD SCHOENBERG (1874–1951), ALBAN BERG (1885–1935), ANTON WEBERN (1883–1945), and ERNST KRENEK (1900–1991).

Neo-Classicism

In the phase of musical expression called Neo-Classicism, which appeared after World War I, composers sought to recapture the ideals of the eighteenth century, when the emphasis was on craftsmanship rather than on emotional expression. They sought to restore the proper balance between form and emotion and rejected the excesses of the Romantic period. The return to form was a primary consideration in composition, with emotional expression being a secondary factor. The Neo-Classicists decried the idea of program music and gave more stress to the intellectual aspects of music. Composers who have written in this style include IGOR STRAVINSKY (1882–1971), PAUL HINDEMITH (1895–1963), DARIUS MILHAUD (1892–1974), FRANCIS POULENC (1899–1963), WILLIAM HOWARD SCHUMAN (1910–1992), BENJAMIN BRITTEN (1913–1976), IRVING FINE (1914–1962), VINCENT PERSICHETTI (1915–1987), and LUKAS FOSS (b. 1922).

Some musicologists have applied the labels of Neo-Classicism and Neo-Romanticism to specific composers, most of whom have written in various styles. It is impossible to categorize the works of all composers in this manner.

---

[1]Joseph Machlis, *Introduction to Contemporary Music* (New York: W. W. Norton & Company, Inc., 1961), pp. 111–112.

[2]Ibid., p. 335.

Each student will need to analyze each work under consideration to determine the "tag" that most appropriately applies.

Neo-Romanticism

Twentieth-century composers have not all found the styles of Impressionism, Expressionism, or Neo-Classicism to their liking. Some, therefore, have utilized means of expression more closely aligned with the ideas of the Romanticists. This group has been referred to as the Neo-Romanticists. Music in the Neo-Romantic style is usually rich in sonorities, contains frequent climaxes, and is comparatively easy for the nonmusician to listen to. The Neo-Romantic composers utilize many of the tonal and rhythmic devices of the Neo-Classicist, but they convey it in a subjective manner—in such a way as to instill emotion and warmth in their music.

While, during the first part of the twentieth century, the majority of composers had rejected the ideals of the nineteenth century in favor of other modes of expression, the political and economic situation of the second quarter of the century led the way to a more emotional means of expression. World War II, in particular, created an atmosphere more receptive to romantic ideals, and a need in some composers for a more personal means of expression, in which greater emphasis is placed upon the poetic and dramatic aspects of music.[3] Some representative composers of this style are ERNST TOCH (1887–1964), CARL ORFF (1895–1982), HOWARD HANSON (1896–1981), WILLIAM WALTON (1902–1983), PAUL CRESTON (1906–1985), SAMUEL BARBER (1910–1981), GIAN CARLO MENOTTI (b. 1911), NORMAN DELLO JOIO (b. 1913), and WILLIAM BERGSMA (b. 1921).

The Nationalists

In addition to the styles of musical expression just discussed, separate consideration must be given to those composers who utilize folk material in their music. This group has often been referred to as the Nationalists. Among the more prominent are ERNEST BLOCH (1880–1959), ZOLTÁN KODÁLY (1882–1967), RALPH VAUGHAN WILLIAMS (1872–1958), CHARLES IVES (1874–1954), RANDALL THOMPSON (1899–1984), AARON COPLAND (1900–1990), HEITOR VILLA-LOBOS (1887–1959), CARLOS CHÁVEZ (1899–1978), and ALAN HOVHANESS (b. 1911).

Whereas the nineteenth-century composer utilized folk material more for color effects and altered it when it did not fit his compositional scheme, the twentieth-century Nationalist incorporated more of the flavor of the original

[3]Ibid., p. 314.

folk idiom in his music. Modal music and material with asymmetrical rhythms were often used to create fresh, new effects.[4]

Avant-Garde Music

Avant-garde music is that which cannot be shown in standard notation. It is in a sense a new type of romanticism through which composers may personally express themselves. All types of sounds may be used and can become meaningful music. Thus, a composer is limited only by the extent of his or her imagination.

Eclecticism

Finally, some contemporary composers write music that does not fit neatly into any of the aforementioned categories. These composers draw from a variety of systems or sources for the purpose of best expressing their particular compositional ideas. Their music thus may be best categorized as "eclectic" in nature.

SOCIETY IN THE TWENTIETH CENTURY

It is with some hesitation that one writes about the society in which the reader lives and presumably is most familiar with; however, the following observations and comments seem pertinent to a clearer understanding of our immediate past and our current societal situation. Of particular importance are the changing attitudes and values of society over the years.

The first decade of the twentieth century has been referred to as a "man's world." Men ran the world's business, cast its votes, and were masters of their own households. With few exceptions—Australia, Norway, and the state of Wyoming—women were banned from voting booths, and were kept out of clubs, saloons, tobacco shops, and "respectable" restaurants unless escorted by a man. This is in great contrast to the women's liberation movement of recent years. Most men sought the company of other males in barbershops, clubs, and saloons. Barbershops were not just places to get a shave or a haircut, but retreats in which men could socialize. Barbershop quartet singing had its beginnings in this manly retreat. The most democratic gathering places in this decade were the saloons, which numbered in the hundreds of thousands in the United States.

After the turn of the century, America became a most attractive place for Europeans to begin life anew, and between 1900 and 1910 some nine million

[4]Ibid., p. 257.

immigrants came to the United States, taxing the facilities of Ellis Island in New York to the limit. Immigrants were welcomed by most Americans, but also met with some prejudice. Disillusioned by bigotry and poverty, many immigrants returned home—390,000 left in the year 1908. On December 17, 1903, Orville and Wilbur Wright successfully launched their flying machine—on a flight lasting 59 seconds and covering 852 feet. In 1908 the Wright brothers demonstrated an improved version of their aircraft to U.S. government officials. Following this a number of other persons developed and exhibited their aircraft in Europe and America.

There were two related conditions prevalent in Europe that led to the outbreak of World War I in 1914— nationalism and militarism. Nationalism was considered the "religion of the fatherland," and it was a strong belief held by most Europeans at the beginning of the twentieth century. "Each nation viewed itself as the chosen instrument of God; its founders and heroes were the apostles and martyrs; its political charters were revered as holy texts. The flag was the sacred symbol of each nation, and pledging allegiance to the flag—and visiting historic shrines—were honored rituals."[5] These attitudes had a considerable effect on a group of composers who utilized folk material in their music (see p. 130).

"The armed forces of each European nation became the principal embodiment of its sovereign spirit and honor."[6] National pride motivated the public to respect and strengthen its army and navy. "Militarism is the belief that preparation for war provides sound moral training and is the best safeguard of peace and the national interest."[7] The objective then became to build the strongest possible military power—one that was greater than any combination of possible enemies. This attitude, of course, led to an unrestricted arms race in Europe during the period that led up to World War I. The establishment of peacetime alliances in Europe prevailed. Germany arranged an alliance with Austria-Hungary, and later Italy joined this pact, making it a Triple Alliance. France allied itself with Russia in 1894, and after 1907 Britain joined the dual alliance of France and Russia, thus creating the Triple Entente.

World War I was the greatest conflict the world had ever seen. Initially the United States held to a pacifist philosophy; however, American public opinion slowly turned against Germany. Finally, Congress declared war on April 6, 1917, and the first American troops landed in France on June 26, 1917. After lengthy fighting and huge casualties, an armistice was signed on November 11, 1918. During the war there were a number of army regimental bands in the European theater whose task it was to provide ceremonial music for various army functions. The band members, however, also served as litter

[5]Thomas H. Greer, A Brief History of the Western World, 5th ed. (New York: Harcourt Brace Jovanovich, 1987), p. 488.

[6]Ibid., p. 489.

[7]Ibid., p. 489.

bearers on the front lines, and many bandsmen perished in this hazardous duty. This use of bandsmen in the armed services changed drastically in later years. World War I brought forth such memorable patriotic songs as "Over There" and "You're a Grand Old Flag" by George M. Cohan. Other memorable songs were the sentimental "Its a Long Way to Tipperary" and "Mademoiselle from Armentières—Parlez Vous!"[8]

While the first decade of the century may have belonged to men, the second was one of women declaring their independence and equality with men. They discarded corsets and petticoats and went off to make their living. The former male business world was now engulfed by female secretaries, salespeople, and telephone operators. In 1910 there were 7.5 million women gainfully employed, but by 1920 the number had increased to more than 8.5 million. This was quite understandable, since the men had gone to war! Throughout the decade from 1910 to 1920, women protested not being allowed to vote and participated in many suffrage rallies and parades. Finally, on June 4, 1919, Congress passed the Nineteenth Amendment to the Constitution, stating that no citizen could be denied the right to vote on account of sex. Twenty-six million newly enfranchised voters were the result.[9]

The early motion picture companies were located in New York and Chicago; however, by the beginning of the second decade many began to move to Hollywood. Whereas previous productions were often only ten-minute flickering sequences of faked newsreels, vaudeville shots, and travelogues, one reel in length, Hollywood began to produce elaborate two-hour features. Also, during this decade Henry Ford's Model T automobile transformed a horse and buggy society into a mobile, modern nation. In 1914 his factory produced 240,700 automobiles. A Ford that sold for $850 in 1908 could be purchased for $360 in 1916. Ford stated that every time he lowered the price a dollar he gained a thousand new buyers.

During the second decade Broadway was the entertainment capital of the world, with at least three dozen shows on the boards each night. In 1916, only three shows were serious dramas; the remainder were musicals, comedies, and revues. The master of the revue was Florenz Ziegfeld, with his famed Ziegfield Follies productions. Irving Berlin came to fame in 1911, with his song "Alexander's Ragtime Band." Berlin was highly prolific, and composed over 300 songs during this era. George M. Cohan was the most active person in show business in the decade, during which he wrote, produced, or directed 19 shows.

The decade of the 1920s was noted for Prohibition as well as for the flirtatious flapper girls. Within the first two weeks of the 1920s, the Eighteenth

---

[8]Tipperary is a county in South Ireland in Munster province, and Armentières is a town in northern France near the Belgian border.

[9]Similar movements took place in Britain, France, Germany, Czechoslovakia, and various other countries.

Amendment, outlawing the manufacture and sale of liquor, beer, and wine, was passed. This national prohibition act, however, did little to change the tastes and habits of the public. The speakeasy took the place of the saloon and by 1925 it is estimated that there were over 100,000 in New York City alone. Bootleggers prospered and found many ways to deliver booze to their customers. Some years later one professional person related to the writer that during Prohibition, liquor was left for him by a bootlegger in the cells of an old automobile battery on his front porch. Who would have guessed? President Herbert Hoover called the Prohibition Amendment "a great social and economic experiment noble in motive." That it was! The first Miss America pageant was held in Atlantic City in 1921. Women, in general, wanted to break free of the restraints of the past and become more independent, wearing shorter skirts, sporting bobbed hair, smoking if they wished, and participating in so-called scandalous dances. Thus came the term "flapper," defined as a young girl considered bold and unconventional in actions and dress in the 1920s.

The 1920s has also been called the Jazz Age, and in 1923 the best jazz group was considered to be King Oliver's Creole Jazz Band. The renowned trumpeter Louis Armstrong joined the group in 1923. It has been said that the most celebrated musical event of the decade in the United States was the premiere performance of George Gershwin's *Rhapsody in Blue* in the winter of 1924 by Paul Whiteman and his orchestra.[10]

Some of Gershwin's most memorable songs were "Lady Be Good," "I've Got a Crush on You," and "The Man I Love." As a home entertainment item the radio was a spectacular success. Gross yearly sales increased from $2 million in 1920 to $600 million in 1929. A perusal of old program listings reveals a comparatively large amount of classical music being broadcast. The first sound motion picture—*The Jazz Singer*, featuring Al Jolson, and referred to as a "talkie"—came out in 1927. In the first half of the decade there was a resurgence of the Ku Klux Klan, and by 1924 the membership totaled four million persons.

The high fling of the 1920s ended in 1929 with the crash of the stock market. An economic depression followed that began in the United States, was exported to rest of the world, and lasted throughout the decade of the 1930s. The number of jobless persons in the United States reached huge propor-tions—estimated to be between 13 and 15 million, or 25 percent of the labor force. The Prohibition Act, popularly called the Volstead Act for its author and referred to as the "noble experiment," was repealed in December of 1933. During the Great Depression, individuals sought a variety of means to make a living. To help the vast numbers of jobless, the federal government, under the leadership of President Franklin Delano Roosevelt, set up new far-reaching

---

[10]Editors, Time-Life Books, *This Fabulous Century—1920–30*, Volume III (New York: Time-Life Books, 1970), p. 91.

programs. The Civilian Conservation Corps (CCC) recruited young men to live and work on government land in comparatively isolated areas, where they built trails and undertook forest conservation plans. The Works Progress Administration (WPA) sought to improve conditions more closely connected with urban life and even assisted, to some extent, various arts programs. The decade of the 1930s saw the implementation of the Social Security program that many retirees are dependent upon today. During the mid-thirties the price of a hamburger was only five cents at many local stands, and the admission price to movie theaters was from 15 to 25 cents. A new Chevrolet sold for $650 and a house for around $3500 midway in the decade. The salary for some music teaching positions in the year 1939–40 ranged from $1200 to $1300 for the school year. In such poor economic conditions people desired and needed some emotional relief. The movie industry helped fill this need by producing numerous musicals, some featuring the talents of Nelson Eddy and Jeannette MacDonald and others starring Fred Astaire and Ginger Rogers. The comic strips also provided diversion. "Blondie and Dagwood" debuted on September 8, 1930. Dagwood's riotous courtship of Blondie Boopadoop culminated in their marriage on February 13, 1933.

The 1930s was the era of the swing bands that played orchestrated or special arrangements of current popular tunes in a jazz style. As indicated, the music was written out, and the only improvised portions were the instrumental solos that were played on the second chorus. Popular tunes of the day were 32 bars or measures in length. A standard swing band arrangement generally included a four- to eight-measure introduction, followed by the playing of the first chorus or melody in a straightforward manner, usually by the saxophone section. The second chorus, or repetition of the tune, often featured an improvised solo by one of the instrumentalists, or a featured singer, while the third or final chorus employed all of the instruments of the group, including both brass and woodwinds. The last chorus was called the shout chorus, or out chorus, or the "anything goes" chorus. Popular swing bands of the era were those of Benny Goodman, Glenn Miller, Artie Shaw, Count Basie, Duke Ellington, Harry James, and Jimmy Lunceford. The cost of supporting such bands was considerable, however, and by the late 1940s they gave way to smaller jazz combos.

In classical music, the combined effects of the 1930s Depression in the United States and the beginning of World War II in 1940 brought about a change in some composers' artistic endeavors that gave rise to a genre known as Neo-Romanticism. The war years brought forth patriotic songs, such as "God Bless America" by Irving Berlin, and sentimental songs, such as "Don't Sit Under the Apple Tree," "You'd Be So Nice To Come Home To," and "White Christmas," as first sung by the memorable crooner Bing Crosby in 1942. In contrast to World War I, Army bandsmen during World War II were assigned largely to ceremonial duties and to providing entertainment for servicemen, including bands that played for dances for both officers and enlisted men (each was a separately scheduled affair). The change in the duties of bandsmen recognized the value of music to the morale of our armed forces. Additionally, there were over 1,000 army regimental bands of 28 members each stationed throughout the world. The other armed services also had many bands on duty.

Following World War II, the United States and the Soviet Union (USSR) became the two leading superpowers, and thus began the long cold war between these rival states. (On December 21, 1991, the Soviet Union became the Commonwealth of Independent States.) Korea was divided after World War II, with the USSR occupying the north and the United States the south. The Republic of Korea was founded in 1948, and the United States withdrew its forces in 1949. In 1950, North Korean communists invaded South Korea and the United Nations chose to defend the country. Nearly 150,000 Americans were killed or wounded in this so-called "police action." An armistice was finally declared on July 27, 1953. One can say that nothing really good came out of this war, and the only lasting memory of it was from the TV series "M*A*S*H," with its nightly reruns being broadcast up through the mid-1980s.

Television, initially in black and white, made its public debut in the United States in about 1946. Color TV became available in 1958. Technical improvements were made gradually; however, in 1964 breakthroughs were achieved that prompted a big boom in sales. Following World War II broadcast facilities expanded rapidly. By 1961 there were 548 commercial and 55 noncommercial education television broadcasting stations. The first message of a president to Congress over network TV was given by Harry S. Truman in 1950. The first TV debate between presidential candidates took place in 1960 between John F. Kennedy and Richard M. Nixon. The first presidential message to Congress that was televised in color was that of Lyndon B. Johnson in 1966.

Rock music was first brought to the attention of the writer in the spring of 1955 by a neighbor who asked, "Have you heard that new kind of music on the radio? I understand they call it rock music!" The term "rock and roll," coined by a New York disc jockey, Alan Freed, was inspired by a raunchy old blues lyric, "My Baby Rocks Me with a Steady Roll."[11] Sometime later the writer heard this music on a car radio and commented, "This music will never last!" How wrong he was![12]

During World War II, German scientists devoted considerable research to rocket engineering. At the conclusion of the war, these scientists, mostly nonpolitical individuals, left Germany and were employed by various govern-

[11]Editors, Time-Life Books, This Fabulous Century—1950–60, Vol. VI (New York: Time-Life Books, 1970), p. 136.

[12]There has been, however, relatively recent speculation that the popularity of rock music is on the decline. See, for example, Dave Marsh, "The Death of Rock," Entertainment Weekly, January 25, 1991, pp. 56–58.

ments. Thus began the race for the conquest of space. In 1957, the Soviet Union achieved the first success by launching Sputnik. This aroused considerable jealousy among people in the United States, and the question was asked, "What has gone wrong? How could the Soviet Union beat us this way?" The result was considerable criticism directed against American public education. While quality education has always been the goal of educators, this was not immediately achievable to the extent everyone desired. Many teachers responded to the criticism by striving for "quality" in the classroom through additional homework assignments for children in the elementary schools—individual assignments, as well as group projects. The United States, however, finally regained its self-respect when in July 1969 American astronauts made the first successful mission to the moon.

The recording industry has mushroomed—the past 40 years have seen a change from 78 RPM records to long-playing (33⅓ RPM) records, cassette tapes, and digital compact discs. The communications media, including radio, television, newspapers, magazines, fax machines, and computers, have become a giant industry. Since World War II, there has been a tremendous growth in the music industry in terms of the publishing of choral and instrumental music, and in the manufacture and sales of band and orchestra instruments, band and orchestra uniforms, choir robes or formal wear, choir and instrumental music risers and platforms, acoustical shells, office and storage equipment, and audiovisual equipment, including microphones, recording equipment, record players, tape recorders, CD players, and video equipment.

In the 1960s a movement began that emphasized conceptual learning, with the stress on basic ideas rather than simply the accumulation of additional facts. While the 1960s began with such optimism, the mood was dramatically changed with the assassination of President John F. Kennedy in 1963. The sense of loss was further reinforced with the assassination of Robert Kennedy and Martin Luther King, Jr. in 1968. The decade of the 1960s brought forth the English rock group The Beatles, who created a sensation among American youth. Who can forget them? Some of their music was even relatively sensitive! In choral music education, a greater stress was put on the importance of achieving authentic performance practices, i.e., performing early music in the style or manner originally intended. Additional scholarly research was stimulated as a result of this attitude.

Whereas most wars involving the United States have had general public support, this was not the case with the Vietnam War. There were more conscientious objectors than ever before, and protests were held on many college and university campuses and elsewhere. Favorite chants at such protests were "Hey, hey, L.B.J. / How many kids did you kill today?" and "Hell no, we won't go."[13] Such was the scene at Kent State University in Ohio in the spring

---

[13]Chants continue to be a favorite means of verbal expression; shortly after the beginning of the Persian Gulf War on January 16, 1991, protesters were heard in prominent gathering places chanting: "No, no, we won't go! We won't fight for Texaco!"

of 1970. The situation troubled the governor of Ohio so much that he called out the National Guard to maintain control. Several misdirected rifle shots, presumably to control the crowd, unfortunately struck and killed several students. This quite understandably caused a public furor—to the extent that a number of other universities canceled their spring graduation ceremonies, and sent diplomas through the mail. All these protests were quite naturally echoed in the current pop/rock music of the time.

Music and the other arts first entered the school curriculum in the U.S. as extracurricular subjects, but over the years the arts became a regular and integral part of the school curriculum. Nevertheless, some individuals labeled these programs frills. During the decade of the 1970s and 1980s some school board members opted to solve their budgetary problems by either reducing or in some cases eliminating arts programs. Because of public pressures, these bans were in some cases short-lived; however, they disrupted the education of many students. From the 1960s on, public education seemingly became the whipping boy or the institution to blame for many of society's problems, and a number of books and articles were written on the subject. This criticism has naturally been difficult for teachers to understand or accept when they have basically dedicated their lives to working at substandard wages for the betterment of our country's children. It is suggested that music educators totally familiarize themselves with the multiple benefits of music participation in the schools and share these ideas with their school administrators, who hopefully will do likewise with all the school board members.[14]

The decade of the 1980s in particular has seen numerous newspaper reports about the falling college entrance scores (SATs or ACTs) of high school students. Jane Healy, in her book The Two-Minute Mind, expresses concern because so many of today's youth speak in short, visceral sentences that don't say much. Another educator, Priscilla Vail, calls it McLanguage— verbal fast food made up of inflection, gesture, and condensation. Healy refers to these "two-minute minds" as those that are nourished on the rapid-fire, frenetic images of TV programs, especially "Sesame Street," or on video games that may help hand-to-eye coordination but do little to improve language and analytical thinking skills. Healy is concerned that parents often have little time to talk to their children, who spend their school hours involved in rote learning or watching a video teacher on TV. She suggests that parents turn off the TV and read and reason with their children. Teachers, she suggests, should teach children to reason, to see the logic of relationships, to generate new ideas, and to solve problems in the real world.[15]

---

[14]For a recommended source article on the values of music participation, see Robert L. Garretson, "Music Curricula," in the International Encyclopedia of Education (Oxford, England: Pergamon Press, 1985), Vol. 6, pp. 3457–3463.

[15]Jane Healy, The Two-Minute Mind (New York: Simon & Schuster, 1990).

In terms of individual values, young persons have been labeled the "me too" generation. Much concern has been expressed about the values of young people today, and particularly about the promiscuity of teenage students and the high pregnancy rate among young unmarried girls, who often end up being supported by public welfare. This brings us to the most volatile issue of our times (the late 1980s and the 1990s), and that is the matter of abortion. On the one hand we see the issue of women's rights, and on the other the issue of saving potential human lives. Certainly both sides have their merits; however, this presumably unresolvable issue will continue to plague the conscience of American citizens for decades to come.

Affirmative action in the 1980s and 1990s has afforded women and minorities greater access to the job market, which is commendable. However, some people feel that in certain instances the law gets carried too far; for example, in the freedom of female sportswriters and TV commentators to roam the locker rooms of collegiate and professional sports teams following games. The idea that athletes should all wear bathrobes to and from their showers has been proposed as a solution to possible embarrassing situations; however, this seemingly reasonable idea has yet to be adopted.

As to the matter of the attitude of the younger generation toward sexual activity, some say it is merely a reflection of the broader values of current-day society. What we see on the current scene is public figures, including TV ministers, who display promiscuous behavior—certainly an undesirable model. Additionally we see porn shops in every community of a considerable size, and numerous pornographic magazines that are widely available throughout the world. TV videos of sexual behavior are also widely available. Motion pictures and public television present material today that would have been totally unacceptable to previous generations. Many educators have expressed their concerns about these negative influences, but to little avail. Interestingly, the veteran entertainer Steve Allen expressed his concerns about television trends toward stronger language and adult-oriented themes in an opinion piece published in the *Los Angeles Times* on September 17, 1990. The article stated that the "flow is carrying us all along right into the sewer. The very sort of language parents forbid their children to use is now being encouraged not only by anything goes cable entrepreneurs, but the once high-minded networks."

An assessment of the current situation leaves one with a rather helpless feeling. However, it is encouraging to know that there is an increasing groundswell of public opposition to the unacceptable on TV, in museums, at the movies, and over the radio. A Gallup poll taken in June, 1990 noted that 71 percent of adults surveyed felt that obscenity in the arts and entertainment was on the rise. Futurists and sociologists predict that attacks on so-called freedom of expression will gradually increase. Also, parents and educators can stress the importance of all those activities that bring young people together in socially desirable situations. Certainly no better activity is available to young people than participating in a choral music group. While they cannot be expected to solve these gigantic problems, choral musicians can rest assured that they are at least contributing to the betterment of current societal problems, if only to a minimal extent.

CHORAL MUSIC IN AMERICA

The growth of choral music education in the schools in the United States in the twentieth century has been phenomenal, and it is appropriate to take a backward look at aspects of this development.

On April 10–12, 1907, a group of 104 music supervisors met in Keokuk, Iowa. This group was the nucleus for the Music Supervisors National Conference, and this name was officially adopted at a meeting in Cincinnati in 1910. Their official publication was the *Music Supervisors Journal,* first established in 1914. The group's membership gradually grew; over 4,600 attended the meeting in Chicago on April 15–20, 1928, and the total membership of the organization was up to 5,400. After hearing the performances of three National High School choruses under the direction of Hollis Dann at Chicago in 1928 and 1930 and in Detroit in 1931, music educators began to realize the great possibilities of adolescent choral performance.[16]

In 1934 the Music Supervisors National Conference became the Music Educators National Conference, and the name of the official journal changed to the *Music Educators Journal.* The organization currently has 60,000 members, all dedicated to the musical education of young students.

The National Association of Schools of Music (NASM), founded in 1924, has been designated as the agency responsible for the accreditation of music curricula in higher education, and by the United States Department of Education as the agency responsible for the accreditation of all music curricula. There are currently 531 colleges and universities in the United States that are members and are accredited by NASM. While there are far more colleges and universities in the United States that are not members, it is well known that these accredited institutions have quality curricula and particularly fine choral organizations that are making substantial contributions to choral music education.

Significant developments in choral music education have occurred each decade from 1930 to the present, and they are worth reviewing. In the 1930s there was a considerable emphasis on *a cappella* performance by choral groups. To some directors, maintaining appropriate pitch became almost a fetish. The leader of this movement was the renowned conductor F. Melius Christiansen (1871–1955) of St. Olaf College in Northfield, Minnesota.

---

[16]Edward Bailey Birge, *History of Public School Music in the United States* (Philadelphia: Oliver Ditson Company, 1937), pp. 245–273.

World War II interrupted the first half of the decade of the 1940s; however, choral music education in the schools continued to flourish. Fred Waring and "The Pennsylvanians" were heard on weekly radio broadcasts. This group performed music of a semipopular style and emphasized the importance of good diction and words being understood by the listeners. Fred Waring's booklet on *Tone Syllables* made an important contribution to the improvement of choral singing in the United States.

The decade of the 1950s in choral music education belonged to the eminent Harry Robert Wilson, Professor of Music at Teachers College, Columbia University, in New York City. Dr. Wilson placed great emphasis on tone production and quality, and used unique and pedagogically sound methods of achieving effective results. This emphasis, coupled with his ingratiating manner, made him a popular conductor at all-state choirs throughout the country. For quite a number of years Dr. Wilson served as conductor of the choir for the annual meetings of Phi Mu Alpha Sinfonia fraternity, held at that time in the Netherland Hilton Hotel in Cincinnati. Dr. Wilson is also the author of the book *Artistic Choral Singing* (New York: G. Schirmer, 1959), and is considered by many to be the preeminent choral music educator of the 1950s.

Also beginning in the 1950s, the eminent conductor Robert Shaw began to have a profound influence on choral music educators which has continued until the present time. His Robert Shaw Chorale delighted audiences throughout the 1950s with its fine artistic singing. Favorite recordings of the Robert Shaw Chorale include *Christmas Hymns and Carols,* Volume I, recorded in December, 1945 and June, 1946 (RCA Victor LM-1112), *Christmas Hymns and Carols,* Volume II (RCA Victor LM-1711), *Great Sacred Choruses* (RCA Victor LM-1117), *Hymns of Thanksgiving* (RCA Victor LM-108), and Bach's *Passion According to St. John* (RCA Victor LM-6103). These recordings have all been favorites of the American public for many years. Through his many public appearances, Shaw has been an inspiration to many directors and singers. The Roger Wagner Chorale, founded in 1946, has also delighted audiences through both its concert tours and its recordings. One exceptionally fine recording was *Echoes from a 16th Century Cathedral* (Capitol P8460), which has served as a model for the interpretation of Renaissance choral singing.

On Tuesday, February 24, 1959, the first organizational meeting of the American Choral Directors Association took place in Kansas City, Missouri, and 130 persons became charter members. In 1990, the organization numbered 15,019 members and continues to be a guiding influence on choral music in America. Its official journal is *The Choral Journal,* with headquarters, along with ACDA, in Lawton, Oklahoma. The decade of the 1960s also saw an emphasis on the importance of authenticity of choral music performance. Articles on this subject have appeared in scholarly professional journals since the 1920s; however, particular attention has been focused on them during the 1960s. The first textbook to include a discussion of this topic was *Technique and Style in Choral Singing* by George Howerton (New York: Carl Fischer, 1957).

The book *Conducting Choral Music*, by the author of this book, Robert L. Garretson, introduced a chapter on this topic in the second edition, published by Allyn and Bacon in 1965. The first edition of this book was published in 1961 and it has now been in continuous print for over 30 years. Prentice Hall took over the second printing of the fifth edition of the book in 1987, and subsequently published the sixth edition in 1988, and the seventh edition in 1993.

In 1967, the first well-known work for choir and electronic tape made its appearance, and made a great impression on musicians at the March, 1968 meeting of the Music Educators National Conference held in Seattle, Washington. The decade of the 1970s was the heyday of music of this genre, and a number of composers chose to write in this style. Toward the end of the decade, however, this means of expression ran its course, and composers turned to other compositional approaches.

Since World War II, colleges and universities in particular have utilized concert tours throughout the United States as a means of student recruitment, as well as a motivational learning experience for the singers. The decade of the 1980s has seen an exciting movement in that high school, college and university, and community choruses have taken tours to many parts of Europe, as well as to the Orient. Performances in European cathedrals and Baroque churches have, in particular, been highly rewarding experiences to all involved.

Individual changes in clothing tastes and other matters are known to be affected by economic and societal influences. Reports and surveys of the early 1990s reveal that individuals are moving to more conservative styles. What, if any, effect this may have on musical tastes in the future remains to be seen.

LATE NINETEENTH- AND TWENTIETH-CENTURY COMPOSERS

In the late nineteenth and twentieth centuries there appear to be more successful composers than ever before. Speculation might lead one to surmise that the increase in world population had a statistical influence on this, but perhaps it is a result of the improvement of educational systems and communications media. Some of the more renowned composers are CLAUDE DEBUSSY (1862–1918), MAURICE RAVEL (1875–1937), RALPH VAUGHAN WILLIAMS (1872–1958), ARNOLD SCHOENBERG (1874–1951), CHARLES IVES (1874–1954), ZOLTÁN KODÁLY (1882–1967), IGOR STRAVINSKY (1882–1971), PAUL HINDEMITH (1895–1963), FRANCIS POULENC (1899–1963), RANDALL THOMPSON (1899–1984), AARON COPLAND (1900–1990), SAMUEL BARBER (1910–1981), WILLIAM HOWARD SCHUMAN (1910–1992), BENJAMIN BRITTEN (1913–1976), NORMAN DELLO JOIO (b. 1913), and LEONARD BERNSTEIN (1918–1990). While a number of these composers were born in the nineteenth century, they lived into, and made their musical contributions during, a good part of the twentieth century.

CLAUDE DEBUSSY was born at St. Germain-en-Laye, France in 1862 during a German bombardment of the city. Mme. Maute de Fleurville, a pupil of Chopin, prepared him for the Paris Conservatory, which he entered at age 11. While there he studied piano with Marmontet and harmony with Emile Durand (1876–80). After graduation, Debussy assumed a position with Mme. Nadezhda von Meck, Tschaikovsky's patroness, as household pianist and to teach piano to her children. Throughout his career, Debussy traveled to European centers where he met composers and/or heard their music. He was in Switzerland and Moscow in 1881 and 1882; in Rome in 1882 and 1884; in London in 1887; in Paris in 1888, where he became an intimate of a group of French poets of the Symbolist school; and in Bayreuth, Germany in 1888, where he heard Wagner's *Parsifal*. His early enthusiasm for Wagner's music soon ended, and he even became strongly opposed to Wagner's musical concepts.

Debussy is considered to be the creator of Impressionism in music, although he denied any role in the movement. His music has been compared to the paintings of Monet, with a style of musical mezzotint using a palette of half-lit colors. To achieve his desired results, Debussy used various devices including the pentatonic scale, the whole-tone scale, modal scales, and dissonances of unresolved chords following one another.[17]

Debussy's choral works include *Printemps*, for women's voices (1882); *Invocation*, for men's voices (1883); *L'Enfant prodigue*, cantata (1884); *La Demoiselle élue*, for soli, chorus, and orchestra (1887–88); *Trois Chansons de Charles d'Orléans*, for unaccompanied chorus (1908); *Ode à la France*, for soli, chorus, and orchestra (1916–17); and a work for orchestra and a wordless choir of women's voices, *Sirènes* (1901).

MAURICE RAVEL was born in Ciboure, Basses-Pyrénées, France in 1875. He began piano study at age seven with Henri Ghiv and harmony with Charles-René at age 12. Ravel entered the Paris Conservatory at age 14, where he studied piano with Anthiome and Charles Bériot and harmony with Émile Pessard. In 1897, when he was 22, Ravel began the study of composition with Gabriel Fauré. During this time he wrote his enchanting *Pavanne pour une Infante défunte* for piano (1899), later adapted for chorus.

Like Debussy, Ravel also used the modes, the whole-tone scale, and augmented triads, but much less frequently. Ravel's textures are very precise and his forms very clear, and he often employs considerable repetition, as in his *Boléro* of 1928. Inspired evocation of the past is but one aspect of Ravel's style, for example in *La Valse* and *Pavanne pour une Infante défunte*. Another stylistic aspect is his use of exotic colors in *Daphnis et Chloë*. In some other

---

[17]Nicolas Slonimsky, *Baker's Biographical Dictionary of Musicians*, 5th ed. (New York: G. Schirmer, 1958), p. 358.

compositions, however, his style is quite austere. Among his choral works are *Trois chansons*, for mixed chorus *a cappella* (1916); *Daphnis et Chloë* (1909–11); and *Pavanne pour une Infante défunte* (1899).

RALPH VAUGHAN WILLIAMS was born in Down Ampney, Gloucestershire, England in 1872. He was educated at Charterhouse School in London (1887–90) and at Trinity College in Cambridge (1892–95). He received his B.M. degree in 1894, and his B.A. in 1895. A Mus. Doc. was earned at Cambridge in 1901. He also studied at the Royal College of Music in London from 1890–92 and in 1895–96. As a composer, Vaughan Williams is noted for the use of English folk tunes in his music. In his later works he utilized large agglomerations of chordal sonorities and parallel progressions of triads.

Among his choral works are *Willow Wood*, for baritone, women's chorus, and orchestra (1903); *Towards the Unknown Region*, for chorus and orchestra (1905, revised 1918); *A Sea Symphony* (Symphony No. 1) for soprano, baritone, chorus and orchestra (1910); *Five Mystical Songs*, for baritone, chorus and orchestra (1911); two motets for double chorus (1913); *Mass in G minor* (1923); *Sancta Civitas*, oratorio (1926); *Te Deum*, for mixed chorus and organ (1928); *Benedicite*, for soprano, chorus, and orchestra (1929); *Magnificat,*, for contralto, women's chorus and orchestra (1932); *Dona nobis pacem*, for soprano, baritone, chorus and orchestra (1936); *Tudor Portraits*, for contralto, baritone, chorus and orchestra (1936); *Thanksgiving for Victory*, for soprano, speaker, chorus and orchestra (1945); *The Sons of Light*, for children's chorus and orchestra (the first performance on May 6, 1951 featured a chorus of 1,000 schoolchildren and the London Philharmonic Orchestra); *Epithalamion*, cantata (1953); *Hodie*, cantata (1954); and *A Vision of Aeroplanes*, motet for chorus and organ (1956).

ARNOLD SCHOENBERG was born in Vienna in 1874. As a young boy he learned to play the violin and the cello. At age 16, he became a bank clerk, but continued his musical studies. At 20, he began the study of counterpoint with Alexander von Zemlinsky and played the cello in Zemlinsky's orchestra. About 1900, Schoenberg became conductor of several amateur choral groups in Vienna, thus stimulating his interest in vocal music. He soon began work on his *Gurre-Lieder*, which called for five solo voices, a speaker, three male choruses, an eight-part mixed chorus, and a very large orchestra. In about 1907 Schoenberg adopted the tenets of Expressionism and as a leading modernist began to attract the attention of a number of "progressive" students, including Alban Berg and Anton Webern.

In 1910 Schoenberg became a teacher of composition at the Vienna Academy. He soon began to appear as a conductor of his own music in various cities: Amsterdam in 1911, St. Petersburg in 1912, and London in 1914. In 1924, Schoenberg established a new principle of tonal relationships, i.e., a method of composing with twelve tones. Thematic material was thus based on twelve different notes stated in a particular order. Development of this material was based on presenting the basic series in inversion, retrograde (backwards), and retrograde inversion. In 1925 Schoenberg became a professor at the Prussian Academy of Arts in Berlin; however, he was dismissed from the position in May, 1933 by the order of the German Ministry of Education under the Nazi regime. Schoenberg then moved to the United States, where in 1935 he became a professor of music at the University of Southern California, and in 1936 assumed a similiar position at the University of California at Los Angeles.

Among his choral works are *Gurre-Lieder*, for soli, mixed chorus and orchestra (1901–13); *Friede auf Erden*, Opus 13 (1907); four pieces for mixed chorus, Opus 27 (1925); *Three Satires*, Opus 28 (1925); six pieces for men's chorus, Opus 35 (1930); *Kol Nidre*, for speaker, chorus and orchestra, Opus 39 (1938); *A Survivor from Warsaw*, cantata for narrator, chorus and orchestra, Opus 46 (1947); *Three German Folksongs*, for chorus *a cappella*, Opus 49 (1948); *Dreimal Tausend Jahre*, for chorus *a capella*, Opus 50a (1949); *De Profundis*, for chorus *a capella*, Opus 50b (1951); and *Die Jacobsleiter*, oratorio, begun in 1913 but unfinished.

CHARLES IVES was born in Danbury, Connecticut in 1874. Ives's father was a bandleader and gave young Charles instruction in piano and cornet. At age 12 he played drums in his father's band, and at 13 played organ at the Danbury church. Charles attended Danbury High School and then entered Yale University in 1894, where he studied with Horatio Parker and Dudley Buck. He was organist at the Central Presbyterian Church in New York City from 1899 to 1902. In 1907 he entered into a partnership with Julian Myrick in an insurance agency, from which he retired in 1930. Ives was considered a pioneer in American music and employed compositional techniques far in advance of his time, such as dissonant harmonies, simultaneous conflicting rhythms, and a highly complex polytonal and polyrhythmic texture. Among his choral works are *The Circus Band*, for mixed chorus and four-hands piano (ca. 1894); *Psalm 67* (1898); *The Celestial Country*, cantata (1899); *Three Harvest Home Chorales*, for mixed chorus, brass, double bass, and organ (1898–1912); and *General William Booth's Entrance Into Heaven*, for chorus with brass band (1914).

ZOLTÁN KODÁLY was born in Kecskemet, Hungary in 1882. Kodály attended high school in Magyszombat and concurrently studied both piano and violin. He then entered the University of Budapest, and also studied composition with Hans Koessler at the Budapest Academy of Music. Kodály exhibited a strong interest in folk music and made use of folk melodies in his own compositions. In 1919 Kodály became assistant director of the Academy of Music in Budapest, a position which he held for only a short time. He resumed teaching, however, in 1922. During the World War II years of 1939–1945, Kodály stayed in Budapest and continued work on his compilation of folk songs. Among his choral works are *Psalmus Hungaricus*, for tenor solo, chorus, and orchestra (1923); *Te Deum*, hymn for soli, chorus, and orchestra (1936);

Missa Brevis, for chorus and orchestra (1945); *Kallo,* folk dances for mixed chorus and small orchestra (1951); and numerous choruses including "Transylvania Lament," "Jesus and the Traders," and "Ode to Franz Liszt."

IGOR STRAVINSKY was born in Oranienbaum, near St. Petersburg, Russia, in 1882. As the son of a bass singer at the Imperial opera, he grew up in a musical atmosphere. Stravinsky became a law student; however, when he was 19, after a meeting with Rimsky-Korsakov, he was encouraged to study composition. He then began the study of theory with Kalafati. In 1907, Stravinsky began private lessons with Rimsky-Korsakov. Because of the interest shown in his compositions by the impresario Diaghilev, Stravinsky moved to Paris in 1911. His work *Sacre du printemps* (Rite of Spring), produced by Diaghilev, was presented by the Ballet Russe in Paris on May 29, 1913. In this work Stravinsky severed all ties with traditional harmony. Although there were demonstrations against it by the general public, the music had a great impact on the music world and was considered the beginning of a new era. Toward the end of World War I in about 1917–18, Stravinsky determined that economy in musical settings was important in the war-torn world; this led to his work *Histoire du Soldat.* Stravinsky's religious feelings found expression in his *Symphony of Psalms* written for the fiftieth anniversary of the Boston Symphony in 1930. Stravinsky became a French citizen in 1934; however, in 1939 he moved to Hollywood, California, and he became an American citizen in 1945.

Among his works for chorus are *Funeral Chant on the Death of Rimsky-Korsakov,* for chorus and orchestra (1908); *The Saucer,* four Russian songs for women's chorus (1914–17); *Paternoster,* for mixed chorus, *a cappella* (1926); *Symphony of Psalms,* for chorus and orchestra (1930); *Credo,* for mixed chorus, *a cappella* (1932); *Ave Maria,* for mixed chorus, *a cappella* (1934); *Mass* for men's and boy's voices and 10 instruments (1948); *Cantata* on four poems by anonymous English poets of the 15th and 16th centuries (1952); *Canticum sacrum ad honorem Sancti Marci nominis,* for tenor, baritone, chorus and orchestra (1956); and *Threni,* for solo voices, chorus and orchestra (1956).

PAUL HINDEMITH was born in Hanau, near Frankfurt, Germany in 1895. As a young boy, he learned to play several musical instruments. In his teens he entered the Hoch Conservatory in Frankfurt, where he studied with Bernhard Seples and Arnold Mendelssohn. As a professional violinist, he became concertmaster of the Frankfurt opera orchestra (1915–23). He then switched his instrument to viola, organized the Amar-Hindemith string quartet, and concertized throughout Europe. He taught a master class in composition at the Berlin Hochschule für Musik from 1925 to 1935. At about that time his ideals came in conflict with the National Socialist government in Germany, and he finally decided to leave the country in 1935. Hindemith then accepted an assignment in Turkey to organize all branches of music study in the country. He performed his viola sonata at the Coolidge Festival at the Library of Congress in 1937, toured the United States in 1938–39, taught at the Berkshire Music Center at Tanglewood in 1940, and then was appointed in that year to the music faculty of Yale University. He became an American citizen in 1946. In 1953 he returned to Switzerland, where he taught at the University of Zurich.

In his early years, Hindemith's compositional style reflected an opposition to previous traditions. Hindemith cultivated the so-called "Gebrauchsmusik," or music for use, and championed "Hausmusik," i.e., music to be performed at home by amateurs. Hindemith used atonal melodies freely; however, he avoided the twelve-tone method. He composed music of a neo-archaic nature, thus utilizing elements of the old polyphonic style in a modern manner. Hindemith wrote music for all genres. Among his choral works are *Das Unaufhörliche*, oratorio (1931); *When Lilacs Last in the Door-Yard Bloom'd*, a requiem for chorus and orchestra (1946); *Apparebit Repentina Dies*, for chorus and brass (1947); *The Demon of the Gibbet*, for chorus a cappella (1949); *Cantique de l'Espérance*, for mezzo soprano, chorus, and two orchestras; six chansons for mixed voices (1939); five songs on old texts, for mixed voices (1943).

FRANCIS POULENC was born in Paris in 1899. He studied piano with Ricardo Vĭnes and composition with Charles Koechlin. At the age of 18, Poulenc became associated with a group of progressive French musicians who identified themselves as "Nouveaux Jeunes," from which the "Groupe des Six" later developed. Poulenc was considerably influenced by both Eric Satie and Maurice Ravel. Among his choral works are *Mass* (1937); *Quatre motets pour un temps de pénitence*, for mixed chorus a cappella (1939); *Exultate Deo*, for mixed chorus, a cappella (1941); *Salve Regina*, for mixed chorus a cappella (1941); *Un Soir de neige*, for chorus a cappella (1945); two books of traditional French songs, for chorus a cappella (1945), and *Stabat Mater*, for soprano solo, mixed chorus, and orchestra (1950).

RANDALL THOMPSON was born in New York City in 1899. He was educated at Harvard University, receiving his B.A. degree in 1920 and his M.A. in 1922. While there he studied with Walter Spalding, E. B. Hill, and Archibald T. Davison. He was also a student of Ernest Bloch. Thompson was an assistant professor of music at Wellesley College from 1927 to 1929, and later from 1936 to 1937. He was Professor of Music at the University of California at Berkeley from 1937 to 1939, and Director of the Curtis Institute of Music in Philadelphia from 1939 to 1941. Thompson was head of the Music Division of the School of Fine Arts at the University of Virginia from 1941 to 1946, and Professor of Music at Princeton University from 1946 to 1948. In 1948 he became a faculty member at Harvard University.

Among his choral works are *Five Odes of Horace*, for mixed chorus (1924); *Pueri Hebraeorum*, for women's voices, a cappella (1929); *Rosemary*, for women's voices, a cappella (1929); *Americana*, for chorus and piano or orchestra (1932); *The Peaceable Kingdom*, for chorus a cappella (1936); *Tarantella*, for men's voices and piano (1937); *The Lark in the Morn*, for chorus a cappella (1938); *Alleluia*, for chorus a cappella (1944); and *The Testament of Freedom*, for men's voices and piano or orchestra (1945).

AARON COPLAND was born in Brooklyn, New York in 1900. He attended Boys' High School in Brooklyn and began piano studies at age 13. His piano teachers were Victor Wittgenstein and Clarence Adler. In 1917 he studied music theory with Rubin Goldmark. In 1921 he went to Paris, where he studied harmony and counterpoint with Nadia Boulanger. Copland was a lecturer at Harvard University in 1935, 1944, and in 1951–52. In 1956 Princeton University awarded him the honorary degree of Doctor of Music. Among his choral works are *What Do We Plant?*, for chorus (1939); *Lark*, for mixed chorus (1939); *Las Agachadas* (the shake-down song) for mixed chorus (1942); and *In the Beginning*, for mezzo soprano and chorus (1947).

SAMUEL BARBER was born in West Chester, Pennsylvania, in 1910. Barber came from a musical family and began the study of piano at the age of six. In 1924, he entered the Curtis Institute of Music in Philadelphia and studied piano with Isabelle Vengerova and composition with Rosario Scalero. Barber traveled extensively throughout Europe beginning in 1928, and in 1935–36 received a Pulitzer Traveling Scholarship. From 1939 to 1942 Barber was a faculty member of the Curtis Institute of Music, where he conducted a chorus and taught a course in orchestration. Barber served in the Army Air Corps from 1942 to 1945 and wrote special music for the armed services. Barber's music is highly lyrical and basically tonal, although he uses chromatic techniques that verge on atonality in his later works. Among his choral works are *A Stopwatch and an Ordinance Map*, for men's chorus and three kettledrums (1940); *The Lovers*, for baritone, mixed chorus, and orchestra; and *Prayers of Kierkegaard*, for mixed chorus. G. Schirmer has published a number of Barber's shorter, octavo publications. These works are "The Virgin Martyrs," for four-part women's chorus, *a capella*, Opus 8 (1939); "Let down the bars, O Death," for four-part mixed chorus, *a cappella* (1942); *Reincarnations* (1. "Mary Hynes," 2. "Anthony O Daly," 3. "The Coolin"), for four-part mixed chorus (1942); "Sure on This Shining Night," for four-part mixed chorus with piano (1956); "A Nun Takes the Veil" (Heaven-Haven), for four-part mixed chorus, four-part women's chorus, or four-part men's chorus, Opus 13, No. 1 (1961); "Under the Willow Tree" (from *Vanessa*), for soprano solo, four-part mixed chorus and piano (1961); "The Monk and His Cat" (from "Hermit Songs"), for four-part mixed chorus and piano, Opus 29 (1967); "Lamb of God" (transcribed from *Adagio for Strings*, Opus 11), for mixed chorus and organ or piano (1967) (Latin text available under the title of "Agnus Dei"); two choruses from *Anthony and Cleopatra*, Opus 40 (1968) (1. "On the Death of Anthony," for three-part women's chorus and piano, 2. "On the Death of Cleopatra"), for mixed chorus and piano; and "Twelfth Night," for four-part mixed chorus, *a cappella*, Opus 42, No. 1 (1969).

WILLIAM HOWARD SCHUMAN was born in New York City in 1910. He first studied harmony with Max Persin at the Malkin Conservatory in New York, then later pursued the study of counterpoint with Charles Haubiel. In 1933, he began studies at Teachers College, Columbia University in New York, and received his B.S. degree in 1935 and his M.A. degree in 1937. Schuman became an instructor of music at Sarah Lawrence College in 1935, a position he held until 1945. In 1936 Schuman began study with Roy Harris at the Juilliard School of Music. In 1945 Schuman became president of the Juilliard School of Music. Schuman's music possesses great emotional tension and rhythmic vitality, and his contrapuntal music can be quite complex. His choral works include *Four Canonic Choruses*, for mixed chorus (1932–33); *Pioneers*, for eight-part mixed chorus (1937); *Choral Etude*, for mixed chorus (1937); *Prologue*, for mixed chorus and orchestra (1939); *Prelude*, for women's chorus (1939); *This is Our Time*, secular cantata for mixed chorus and orchestra (1940); *Requiescat*, for women's chorus (1942); *Holiday Song*, for mixed chorus (1942); *A Free Song*, secular cantata for mixed chorus and orchestra (1943); *Te Deum*, for mixed chorus (1944); *Truth Shall Deliver*, for men's voices (1946); *Four Rounds on Famous Words* (1957); and *The Lord Has a Child*, hymn (1950).

BENJAMIN BRITTEN was born in Lowestoft, Suffolk, England in 1913. As a young boy he played piano and composed. He received a scholarship at the Royal College of Music in 1930, where he studied piano with Arthur Benjamin and Harold Samuel, and composition with John Ireland. He graduated in 1934. During World War II Britten was exempt from service as a conscientious objector. Britten's first great opera success was *Peter Grimes*, which premiered in London on June 5, 1945. He is also widely known for his composition *The Young Person's Guide to the Orchestra, Variations and Fugue on a Theme by Purcell*, written in 1945. Among his choral works are *Hymn to the Virgin* (1930); *A Boy Was Born* (1933); *Friday Afternoons*, for children's voices (1934); *Ballad of Heroes* (1939); *A Ceremony of Carols*, for chorus and harp (1942); *Hymn to St. Cecilia* (1942); *Rejoice in the Lamb*, cantata (1943); *Festival Te Deum* (1945); *St. Nicolas*, cantata (1948); *Spring Symphony*, for soloists, chorus and orchestra (1949).

NORMAN DELLO JOIO was born in New York City in 1913. He came from a musical family and first studied with his father, an organist, and then with his godfather, Pietro Yon. He later studied with Bernard Wagenaar and Paul Hindemith. Dello Joio taught at Sarah Lawrence College from 1944 to 1950. Among his choral works are *Vigil Strange* (1942); *Mystic Trumpeter*, cantata (1943); *Western Star*, for soloists, narrator, and orchestra (1944); *A Jubilant Song* (1946); *A Fable* (1947); and *Psalm of David*, for chorus, brass, and percussion (1950). Additional extended choral works, all published by G. Schirmer, are *As of a Dream*, for narrator, soloists, mixed chorus, orchestra, and optional dancers; *Hymns Without Words; Love Songs at Parting; Mass in Honor of the Blessed Virgin Mary; Mass in Honor of the Eucharist; Proud Music of the Storm; The Psalmist's Meditation*; and *Years of the Modern*. Dello Joio has also written quite a number of shorter octavo works that are published by G. Schirmer, Carl Fischer, and Marks Music Corporation.

LEONARD BERNSTEIN was born in Lawrence, Massachusetts in 1918. He studied with Walter Piston and E. B. Hill at Harvard University and graduated in 1939. He then went to the Curtis Institute of Music in Philadelphia and studied piano with Isabelle Vengerova, conducting with Fritz Reiner, and orchestration with Randall Thompson. During the summers of 1940 and 1941 he enrolled in Serge Koussevitzky's master class at the Berkshire Music Center at Tanglewood, and in 1942 he became Koussevitzky's assistant. In 1943 Bernstein was appointed assistant conductor of the New York Philharmonic Orchestra, and on November 14th of that year he was called on to substitute for the ill Bruno Walter. His debut was a great success and led to engagements by other major symphony orchestras. Bernstein became regular conductor of the New York Philharmonic in 1958, a position he held until 1969.

Bernstein's compositional talents are many-faceted. He wrote both symphonic and popular music, and had several highly successful Broadway musicals, among them *On the Town* (1944); *Candide* (1956); and *West Side Story* (1957). Excerpts from these works are available in various choral arrangements. Bernstein's more serious choral works with orchestra include *Jeremiah Symphony* (1943); *Symphony No. 3*, "Kaddish" (1963); *Chichester Psalms* (1965); and *Mass* (1972).

MUSICAL STYLE AND PERFORMANCE PRACTICE

Meter and Stress

Impressionistic music possesses less tension and rhythmic drive than does music in the Romantic period. Impressionist music, particularly that of Debussy, gives the impression of being "suspended in space." While Impressionistic music may give the feeling of vagueness, it is, however, quite precise. The conductor should avoid any exaggeration of tempo fluctuations, and the beat should be clear and precise but flexible and responsive to all the subtle nuances in the music.

In contrast to Impressionism, Expressionistic music possesses considerable rhythmic incisiveness; that is, the rhythm is even more clear-cut. The rhythm of the music is generally aligned with the durational values of the text; however, as a means of achieving tension, the Expressionists often distorted the normal accentuations of words. This alteration usually necessitated the use of changing meter to accommodate the resultant rhythm.

A particular characteristic of Neo-Classical music is its rhythm. As a means of avoiding the monotony of the regular stress following the bar line, composers employ various devices. One procedure is to alter the meter with each measure. The same effect, however, may be achieved by simply shifting the stresses or accents from point to point within the measure, but without changing the meter signature. In conducting rhythmic patterns with shifting accents, the conductor should limit the scope of his patterns and utilize a precise rebound to each beat. On accented notes—whether on a downbeat or an upbeat—the stress should be reflected in the tension of the arms and shoulders, whereas limited, yet precise, movements should occur on the unaccented notes.

Still another rhythmic device is the use of traditional rhythmic patterns in nonsymmetrical forms. For example, in 4/4 meter the eighth notes might be divided as 3 + 3 + 2, or 3 + 2 + 3, rather than 4 + 4. (Another way of stating these rhythmic groupings is 1 2 3 1 2 3 1 2, or 1 2 3 1 2 1 2 3.) In 6/8 meter, a two-measure pattern might be alternately written as 3 + 3 + 2 + 2 + 2. In conducting rhythms in nonsymmetrical forms, the conductor must alter his patterns to conform to the basic rhythm of the music.[18]

Although the Neo-Romantic composer will use many of the rhythmic devices of the Neo-Classicist, he will do so in moderation. He places a greater emphasis on the poetic aspects of music and on a means of personal expression that is more universally understood. When modern-day rhythmic devices contribute to this end they are used, and when they do not they are avoided.

Tempo

With Impressionistic music most tempi tend toward the moderate and the slow, with exceptionally fast tempi usually being avoided. A considerable degree of modern music following this period, however, exhibits a strong rhythmic drive. As movement and speed are an integral part of our modern-day life, so too are these characteristics reflected in much of our modern-day music. The rhythm of Expressionistic music is generally somewhat irregular and rather complex. As a result of the normal accent of words being sometimes deliberately distorted, the tempo often fluctuates, with the use of pauses, *ritardandos*, and *accelerandos*.

Tempo, of course, is related to both rhythm and mood, and, in determining the proper tempo, the conductor should consider both of these factors carefully. As clarity of line is essential to the performance of Neo-Classical music, a tempo that is too fast will impede the articulation, whereas a tempo that is too slow will sometimes lessen the intensity and rhythmic drive. Mood is an important consideration in determining the tempi of Neo-Romantic music. With emotional expression being relatively important, the projection of textual meanings often necessitates a greater flexibility in tempi.

Dynamics

In contrast to music of the Romantic period, Impressionistic music possesses a relatively low level of dynamic intensity. *Fortissimo* occurs rather infrequently, with the medium and lower dynamic levels, *mezzo forte*, *piano*, and *pianissimo*, being used primarily. *Crescendo* and *decrescendo*, when

---

[18]See, for example, various works by Jean Berger: "It Is Good to Be Merry" (Kjos), "The Good of Contentment" (Presser), "Lift Up Your Heads" (Summy-Birchard), and "Seek Ye the Lord" (Augsburg).

employed, should be used with considerable care and restraint. In performing music from this period, the conductor should take care to adapt the scope of his beat to the dynamic levels of the music. In conducting a *pianissimo* passage, for example, the movements should be very slight.

Following the Impressionistic period there has gradually developed an increasing use of dynamic extremes. Contrast is often achieved through a rapid change from an extremely low dynamic level to one of great intensity and volume. Modern composers are inclined toward using a multiplicity of dynamic effects in their music, including extreme contrast in dynamic levels, rapid *crescendos* and *decrescendos*, dynamic accents, and uniform levels of intensity. [19]

Texture

Composers of the Romantic period were highly interested in harmonic experimentation. This interest was intensified by composers of the Modern period. The Impressionists sought to escape the restrictions of the major–minor system of tonality. In the process, Debussy used a variety of devices, including the church modes, the whole-tone scale, and the pentatonic scale. Parallel fourths, fifths, and octaves were often used above a pedal point, which resulted in unusual effects from the clash between the sustained and the moving harmonies. Another device used by Debussy was to construct a chord that was static and was interesting to him. He often let it stand—thus his so-called "standing chords." When encountering such chords, a conductor should not rush the tempo, but let these chords "shimmer." When he was a student of César Frank, in a keyboard instrumentation class, Debussy infuriated his teacher, who cried, "Modulate, modulate!" as he pounded on the lid of the pianoforte. Debussy replied, "Why should I modulate? I am perfectly happy where I am." After class he commented, "César Frank is a modulating machine."[20]

Although previous harmonic systems focused on the relationship of chords and their progression from one to another, the Impressionists utilized individual chords for the sonorous and coloristic effects they created. Thus the tendency for chord resolution was certainly lessened. While triads were sometimes used, seventh, ninth, and eleventh chords were frequently employed either separately or in succession. Composers, furthermore, often utilized these chords on various scale degrees by shifting them up and down without alteration. This "gliding" use of chordal movement, utilizing blocklike chords in parallel motion, was an integral stylistic feature of Impressionism. Escaped chords—that is, those that are not resolved, but seem to "escape" to

[19]George Howerton, *Technique and Style in Choral Singing* (New York: Carl Fischer, 1957), pp. 179–180.

[20]Richard L. Crocker, *A History of Musical Style* (New York: McGraw-Hill Book Company, 1966), p. 479.

another key—were also an important characteristic of Impressionistic music. Impressionist composers often achieved a feeling of rest, or point of harmonic arrival, by simply using a less dissonant chord than those preceding it. Tonal color became equated with melody, harmony, and rhythm during this era.

Debussy often deliberately created a vagueness within his music, coupled with an indefiniteness of phrase structures. Ravel, on the other hand, utilized traditional forms and phrases to a much greater extent. The whole-tone scale was not utilized by Ravel, as it was by Debussy, as he desired a more definite triad outline, clearer phrase structures, and more functional harmony.

Expressionism is generally considered to have begun with Schoenberg, and, as twelve-tone music is associated with him, the two terms have become somewhat synonymous. It should be understood, however, that all Expressionist music is not twelve-tone music, as the Expressionistic movement began before this development. In Schoenberg's earlier works (his oratorio *Gurre-Lieder* [Universal], for example) he developed his use of chromaticism to its maximum potential. He then began to seek new means of expression.

Schoenberg's experimentation led to the development of the *twelve-tone method* or *serial technique* about 1924. With this method, all compositions are based upon an arbitrary arrangement or *set* of the twelve chromatic tones. Each tone row or set is handled in such a manner that no particular tone becomes any more important than the others. After a tone has been introduced, it may not be used again until every other tone in the series has been used at least once. This is in marked contrast to the conventional major–minor tonal system. The row or set serves as a unifying factor in the music. After the basic set has been introduced, it may be repeated through a variety of means. It may be inverted—that is, turned upside down—it may be performed backwards (retrograde), or inverted and performed backwards (a retrograde of the inversion). The tone row is a type of variation technique in which great variety is achieved with only a minimum of material.[21] The guiding thought is that no idea should be repeated except in a new form. The older style of repetition and sequence, and balanced phrases and cadences, was rejected by the Expressionists.

In the nineteenth century, rhythm, harmony, and tone color were often considered entities unto themselves, whereas Neo-Classicism considered each of these separate elements as subservient to the whole. The use of counterpoint by the Neo-Classical composers became increasingly important. To differentiate it, however, from the "harmonic" counterpoint of the Romantic era, this new polyphony is often referred to as "dissonant counterpoint." It is often marked by its transparency of texture and its dissonance and driving rhythm. While striking dissonance often occurs as a result of clashes between vocal lines, each line must maintain its forward drive or thrust.

In the music of the Neo-Romanticists, extreme harmonic complexity is usually avoided. Their music is generally characterized by its sensuous lyricism

---

[21]Machlis, *Contemporary Music*, pp. 340–342.

and its richness of harmony. It is often simply and directly stated, although some music possesses considerable rhythmic drive and intensity. Neo-Romantic music is primarily tonal in nature. Dissonance is used, but generally for comparatively brief periods to highlight the emotional and poetical aspects of the text. Although a considerable portion of Neo-Romantic music is harmonically conceived, some composers utilize contrapuntal devices as well. While their compositional techniques vary considerably, their one common characteristic is a more personal means of expression.

Expressive Aspects

The Impressionistic composer's aim was simply to suggest rather than boldly to state. Music of this period, therefore, should be approached in an objective manner and performed with considerable restraint. The excesses and extremes of the Romantic period should be avoided.

Expressionistic and Neo-Classical music should be approached with an even more objective point of view. Perhaps the most outstanding characteristic of Expressionistic music is its continuous dissonance (and lack of consonance that would allow for a lessening of the tension). Dissonance, along with such other devices as angular melodic fragments, irregular rhythm, and abrupt changes in tempi, are used as a means of expressing the conflicts of the inner self. The composer's concern is the use of these varied devices to portray these inner feelings, rather than the expression of pure emotion in itself.

The Neo-Classicist is concerned largely with craftsmanship and with the statement of his material in an impersonal, objective manner. Emotional expression is minimized. Although it will vary from composer to composer, it is always carefully controlled. The Neo-Classicist endeavors to recapture the classic spirit by striving for symmetry and balance in his music, by utilizing more transparent textures, and by limiting the size of his musical forces.

The Neo-Romanticist, however, seeks a more universalized type of expression. His goal is different from that of the Neo-Classicist, as he desires his means of communication to be more personal in nature. Although he uses many musical devices similar to those of the Neo-Classical composer, since his purpose is different he uses them in a different way. The conductor should analyze his music and determine the raison d'être for each device if he is to employ it for its intended purpose.

In performing music of the Modern period, particular attention should be given to the tone quality and the manner of articulation. With Impressionistic music, the singers need to use a legato style of diction so as not to disturb the smooth flow of the carefully voiced chords often moving in parallel motion.

The melody of Expressionistic music often moves in wide angular leaps, thus creating some serious intonation problems for the performers. Singers, obviously, need to listen carefully. And as any rigidity in the jaw will inhibit proper articulation, they need to maintain a rather relaxed jaw to facilitate a cleaner articulation of the various interval leaps.

In Neo-Classical music it is usually desirable to lessen the dramatic qualities of the voice so that the clarity of the structure may be brought out. Voices with excessive vibrato or tremolo are particularly detrimental to the interpretation of this style of music. In performing music in a Neo-Romantic style, the voice quality should be warm and expressive so as to convey best the subjective aspects of the music.

Avant-Garde Music

As we stated earlier in the chapter, avant-garde music is defined as that which cannot be shown in standard notation. Avant-garde represents a new type or vein of romanticism that is indicated by a composer's desire for personal expression, individuality, freedom of form, and in certain instances, love of emotion.[22] All types of sounds can become meaningful music; therefore a composer is limited only by the fertility of his or her own imagination.

Sprechstimme

Sprechstimme means "speaking voice" and the recitation of words with a musical inflection. One type of notation is used to indicate speaking at an approximate notated pitch . For a musical example, see the excerpt from "Psalm 27" by Robert Karlen (Figure 26). Another means of notation is the use of regular notes on a one-line staff. Ernst Toch utilizes this latter means in his *Gesprochene Musik* (spoken music) in the works "Valse" and "Geographical Fugue" (see Figure 27). In preparing works such as these, the conductor

FIGURE 26 Excerpt from "Psalm 27" (Part III) by Robert Karlen. Notation indicates, as closely as possible, the pitch of the spoken sounds. Copyright 1968 by A.M.S.I. Used by permission.

[22]Broch McElheran, "Beginner's Guide to the Avant-Garde," *Choral Journal*, Vol. 13, No. 8 (April 1973): 19.

FIGURE 27 Excerpt from "Geographical Fugue" by Ernst Toch. Copyright 1957 by Mills Music, Inc. Used by permission.

should stress careful articulation of the words and achieving a special unique sound that stems from the combination of vowels and consonants, and the inherent meaning of the text. Concentrate not on volume, but on quality and uniqueness of sound. All rhythmically intricate patterns must necessarily be practiced slowly until the singers can articulate the words ably, and until the rhythm is internalized. Then, of course, the music may be gradually taken at a faster tempo.

Still another device is a chart designed to elicit irregular, nonsynchronized speech sounds as used by Richard Felciano in his "Pentecost Sunday" (see Figure 28). Knut Nystedt in his "All the Ways of a Man" (see Figure 29) gives the rhythm and the text, and shows pitch changes (see example A) by ascending and descending lines. Dynamic accents or "shouts" are indicated by special notation (see example B).

Sprechstimme has been used by such well-known composers as Luigi Dallapiccola, Arthur Honneger, Charles Ives, Gian Carlo Menotti, Darius Milhaud, Vaclav Nelhybel, Knut Nystedt, Carl Orff, Krzysztof Penderecki, William Walton, Richard Felciano, Lloyd Pfautsch, Karlheinz Stockhausen, William Schuman, and Ernst Toch.[23]

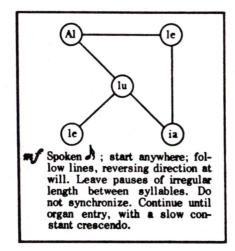

FIGURE 28 Excerpt from *Pentecost Sunday* by Richard Felciano. Chart designed to elicit irregular, nonsynchronized speech sounds. Copyright 1967 by World Library Publications, Inc., Schiller Park, IL. All rights reserved. Used by permission.

[23]Hugh Sanders, "Sprechstimme in Choral Music," *Choral Journal*, Vol. 11, No. 2 (October 1970): 7–10.

FIGURE 29   Excerpt from *All the Ways of a Man*, by Knut Nystedt. Note in (A) pitch changes indicated by ascending and descending lines; in (B) dynamic accents or "shouts" indicated by /fz\. Copyright 1971, Augsburg Publishing House. Copyright assigned 1989 to Norsk Musikforlag A/S, Oslo. Used by permission.

Music with Electronic Tape and/or Nonconventional Notation

The continued search for new means of musical expression has brought forth, particularly during the decade of the 1970s, a variety of types of new choral music, including voices combined with electronic tape sounds, choric speech with singing, aleatoric (chance) music, and multimedia presentations. (We are currently in the midst of many new developments and therefore lack the perspective that we have of earlier music. It thus seems appropriate to include this material in a section separate from other twentieth-century music.)

Conventional notation for the vocal parts is usually employed in choral music with electronic tape. In some music, the time for specific cues is indicated in the score, and a stopwatch is necessary to coordinate the two separate sound sources. In other instances, a graphic illustration of the electronic sound is indicated in the score, thus assisting both the conductor and the singers to coordinate their efforts and making the use of a stopwatch unnecessary. Examples of both types are presented in Figures 30, 31, and 32.

As composers continue to explore new means of musical expression, they find that the conventional means of music notation do not allow them sufficient flexibility, nor do symbols always exist for the expression of their musical ideas. This has resulted in the creation of an entirely new means of notation. Specific notation now has been devised for spoken pitches, raising and lowering the pitch of the voice, shouts, screams, laughter, varying dynamic levels, tone clusters, staccato pronunciations, whispers, various lip sounds, tongue clicks, coughs, hissing sounds, giggles, hand claps, glissandos, vibrato,

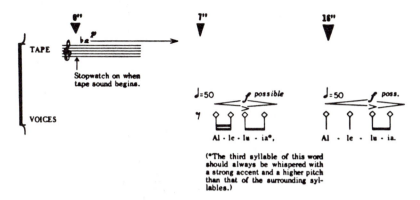

tempo, duration, *accelerando*, *ritardando*, and various other tonal effects.[24] Excerpts from a number of compositions representing this type of notation are shown in Figures 33–36.

[24]For a helpful and useful compilation of all these symbols, along with explanations, see Frank Pooler and Brent Pierce, *New Choral Notation* (New York: Walton Music Corporation, 1971).

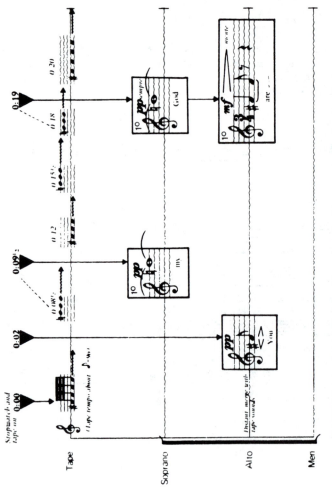

FIGURE 32 Excerpt from *Hymn of the Universe* by Richard Felciano. Score indicates the elapsed time in seconds for coordination of the tape with the choral parts. The vertical lines with the arrows indicate the conductor's cue to the singers. The small notes indicated on the tape line part provide the pitches for the entering voice parts. Copyright 1974 by E. C. Schirmer Company, Boston. Used by permission.

FIGURE 33 Excerpt from *Pshelley's Psalm* by Richard Felciano. Note combination of designated pitches with other sounds, including hisses, shouts, and hand claps. Copyright 1974 by E. C. Schirmer Company, Boston. Used by permission.

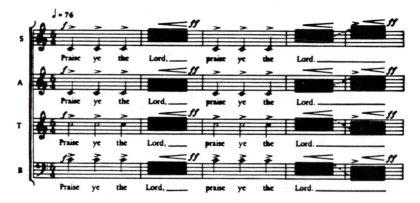

FIGURE 34 Excerpt from *Aleatory Psalm* by Gordon H. Lamb. The black box represents a tone cluster within the confines of the symbol (in this instance—a minor seventh in each part). Singers should endeavor to avoid a pitch sung by another person. Copyright 1973 by World Library Publications, Inc., Schiller Park, IL. All rights reserved. Used by permission.

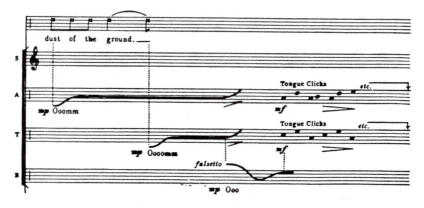

FIGURE 35 Excerpt from "The Creation" from *The Family of Man* by Michael Hennagin. Note how approximate pitch level of vowel sound is indicated by lines; note also special effects such as tongue clicks. Copyright 1971 by Walton Music Corporation. Used by permission.

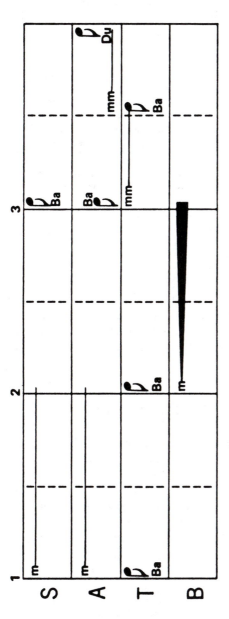

FIGURE 36 Excerpt from *Two Moves and the Slow Scat* by Dennis Kam. Dotted lines divide measures into two parts, with the solid line indicating the cue for the downbeat and the dotted line the cue for the upward beat. The size of each notehead indicates the relative dynamic level (*p*, *mf*, *f*) and their location within the box for each part indicates the pitch range (high, middle, low). The thickening of a line indicates a crescendo. Copyright 1973 Belwin-Mills Inc., c/o CPP/Belwin, Inc. Miami, FL. International copyright secured. Used by permission.

The first step that a conductor desiring to perform music of this type must take is a careful analysis of the choral score. Most of this music will include explanatory information concerning the notational symbols and how to interpret them. While the types of notation are so diverse as to require an array of gestures to indicate the intentions of the musical score, at least some of the basic movements may be categorized as follows:

1. Cueing entrances at designated points in time. Such cues are necessary in a variety of choral selections, particularly music with electronic tape to coordinate the ensemble. For example, a selection may necessitate conducting with a stopwatch in one hand and cueing voices at certain intervals (7", 16", 26", etc.) to coordinate the chorus with the tape (see Figure 30).

2. Indicating the rise and fall of sung or spoken pitches by raising and lowering the hands.

3. Indicating duration ranging from short staccato sounds to long sustained pitches. Gestures might include a wiggling of the fingers for "boxed staccato" and a broad sweep of the arm for long sustained sounds.

4. Indicating the beginning tempo and various tempo changes within a selection, often through conventional means.

5. Indicating dynamic levels through the size of the gestures coupled with appropriate facial expressions.

Obviously, the above generalizations are meant only to illustrate the types of nonconventional gestures that may be used. They will, of course, vary from conductor to conductor depending upon the individual interpretation and the effects desired. Observation of other conductors, and experimentation during rehearsals, based on singers' reaction and input, can lead to more effective and meaningful performances.

THE JAZZ/POP IDIOM

The twentieth century has seen many composers utilizing popular music and the rhythm of various dances as raw material for the more serious expression of their music. As the American composer Douglas Moore points out, we must acknowledge "popular forces, such as jazz, as typical American music products, which, despite their divided allegiance between commerce and art, are of much greater cultural value than the average American suspects."[25] The reason for the use of the elements of ragtime (the forerunner of jazz) and jazz is the composer's attempt to move away from the rhythmic sterility of post-Romanticism, and particularly its divisive even beats that were no longer in vogue.[26]

[25]Frederick Dorian, *The History of Music in Performance* (New York: W. W. Norton & Company, 1942), p. 353.
[26]Curt Sachs, *Rhythm and Tempo: A Study in Music History* (New York: W. W. Norton & Company, 1953), p. 368.

The use of ragtime occurred in "Golliwogs Cakewalk" from *Children's Corner* by Claude Debussy (1908), in one of the dances in *Histoire du Soldat* by Igor Stravinsky (1918), and in one of the dances in *Suite für Klavier* by Paul Hindemith (1922). The jazz idiom appears in numerous twentieth-century works, including *Parade* by Eric Satie (1917); *La Création du Monde* by Darius Milhaud (1923); the opera *Jonny spielt auf* by Ernst Krenek (1926); *Rio Grande*, for chorus, orchestra, and solo pianoforte, by Constant Lambert (1928); *Suite for jazz orchestra* by Dimitri Shostakovich (1934); and *Ebony Concerto* for clarinet and swing band by Igor Stravinsky (1945).

Since World War II, many of the popular tunes from the 1920s and 1930s now known as "golden oldies" have been rearranged for, and performed by, the many jazz/show choirs prevalent in high schools and colleges throughout the United States. Many of these works have also been performed by modern concert choirs as encores, or as part of a closing set of American music.

The use of the elements of jazz in contemporary music does *not* make it unacceptable, as some choral conductors presumably believe. Such music should never be given the status of an "unwanted child." Rather, in view of the respectability given this idiom by numerous serious and highly regarded contemporary composers, it seems fitting and proper to urge that choral musicians endeavor to better understand the jazz idiom. To help them achieve this objective is the thrust or basic purpose of the following section of this book.

In the interpretation of popular music, the conductor who has had no experience performing in an ensemble of this type, or in playing in a jazz ensemble, is somewhat at a disadvantage. His interpretation may be tabbed as somewhat "square" — in other words, too stiff and unyielding or too loose and "sloppy." The effect in either case is unmusical. The same criticism has been leveled at instrumentalists during their initial experiences in playing in a jazz ensemble. The choral conductor who has had no experience with jazz or popular music, however, can, with diligent study, develop proficiency in this area.

Rhythm

A basic aspect of interpretation pertains to the treatment of eighth notes. In most pop/rock tunes they are usually performed with equal duration and are generally notated that way; for example:

The underlying even eighth-note pattern in the percussion part of the combo accompaniment is an integral part of the style and helps to perpetuate the rhythmic drive. (Certain performers even say that they feel the music in eight,

[27]From "Streets A-fire!" by Mark Brymer (Hal Leonard Publishing Co.).

or at least a strong *and*, or second half of the beat.) Some publications provide directions in various ways. For example, in "Crazy Rhythm" by Meyer and Kahn, arr. Ellis Bretton (Warner Bros.), the initial directions are "Funky Rock (equal eighth notes)." In "Sausalito Strut" by Carl Strommen (Alfred Publishing Co.), the music is marked "Bright Rock ($\quarternote = 120$)" and the drum part is notated | ♩♪♪♪ ♪♪♪♩ | . In "Just the Way You Are" by Billy Joel, arr. Ed
Light Rock beat
Lojeski (Hal Leonard), under "Performance Notes" is the comment, "Rehearse slowly, counting each eighth note," and at measure 21 the percussion part includes the directions "Bossa Nova–rock feeling."[28] Eighth notes are also generally of equal length in music of a particularly slow tempo. Textual cues and notation within the total configuration of the music will usually enable the director to determine the proper desired effect. Directions and clues for performance in a pop/rock style may be found at various places in the music, and if none are there, then the director must make his own assessment of the musical style, listen to a current recording of the music, or both.

Singers should always strive to feel and respond to the pulse or forward drive of the music. Particularly after a rest, $\frac{4}{4}$ ⁃ ♪ ♩ | , the entrance of the group must be together, which is not likely to occur unless the singers feel the pulse of the third beat and respond precisely on the rebound, or second half of the beat (pop/rock style).

In performing offbeat rhythms, $\frac{4}{4}$ ♪ ♩ ♪♪ ♪♩♪♪ ♪♪ ♪♩♪ , for example, such as occur in "Just the Way You Are" by Billy Joel, arr. Ed Lojeski (Hal Leonard) and "Baby Come Back to Me" by Nick Santamaria, arr. Jerry Nowak (Hal Leonard), singers should avoid simply trying to read individual notes and should try to develop a feel for the entire phrase. In pop/rock music the offbeat accents occur on the second half of the beat, while in vocal jazz they usually are held back and performed on the last third of the beat (see the following discussion on swing style). Directors should, therefore, determine the basic style and then assist their singers in its interpretation accordingly.

In music with a moderate tempo, there is a tendency for some singers to rush the figure ♪ ♩ ♪♩ , particularly the eighth followed by the quarter note, thus creating a stiff or square effect. [29] Singers should be advised to stretch out or "lay back" on these two notes to create a more relaxed (and less corny) style.

In swing style, both equal eighth notes and dotted eighth and sixteenth notes are performed with a two-to-one, rather than a three-to-one, ratio. For example, the dotted-eighth-and-sixteenth-note pattern in the old standard "Louise," notated as $\frac{4}{4}$ ♪. ♪. ♩ ♪. | ♪. ♪. ♩ | , is not sung as indicated, but as

---

[28]For an interpretation of this song by the singer/composer, see the album *The Stranger*, Columbia, 34987.

[29]See, for example, "Georgia on My Mind" by Hoagy Carmichael, arr. Gene Puerling (Studio P/R).

$\frac{12}{8}$♩♪♩♪♩. ♩♪|♩♪♩♪♩|. The three-to-one durational pattern would create a stiff or "square" effect, whereas the two-to-one relationship (as indicated in the example) makes the choir "swing." Another way of notating the two-to-one relationship is as follows: ♩ ♩♪♩ ♪♩ ♩ ♩♪|♩ ♪♩ ♪♩|. However, in certain instances this notation can be somewhat difficult to read. An increasing number of arrangers are indicating on the score the style they desire. For example, in "I Hear Music" by Loesser and Lane, arr. Larry Lapin (Warner Bros.), the directions "Moderate Swing" (♫ = ♩ ♪) are indicated. While all the eighth notes in this arrangement are written equally, the directions clearly indicate to the director that a two-to-one relationship is necessary in performance. If the music is not marked "swing style," then one may be inclined to assume that equal eighth notes should be performed as written. However, there can be exceptions to this, and the director must use his own musical judgment. In swing style, the dotted quarter note is similarly performed as: ♩. ♪ = ♩♩ ♪ . Also in swing style, one may periodically encounter the rhythmic figure ♩♩ ♩ ♩.♩ ♫|. As to the last two equal eighth notes, they have been performed in three ways: ♫, ♩ ♪ , and ♪ ♩. In such situations, try the pattern several ways; that is, experiment, think about what you feel is the most effective or sensitive way, and then do it!

In the first measure of the introduction to the arrangement of "I Hear Music," each chord (syllable) is notated on the second half of the first, second, and fourth beats, respectively; however, they are performed on the last one-third of each of the beats indicated. (Note the directions by the arranger—"Moderate Swing ♫ = ♩ ♪ .") For the singers to respond to the rhythm accurately, they must feel the beginning of each beat and "bounce off," so to speak, so the accents are as precise as possible.

The question is often asked why arrangers don't notate the music the way they would like it to sound. Figure 37 shows the notated rhythm of an excerpt from "I Hear Music" followed by notation indicating the correct performance style. The latter two ways are obviously more difficult to read than the first. For this reason the traditional means of musical notation is generally used, with an indication of "swing style" given. Once a person comprehends the basic swing style, he or she can usually read the notation quite easily.

In interpreting jazz rhythms, the director will encounter innumerable patterns. For further study, the reader is referred to Clark Terry and Phil Rizzo, *The Interpretation of the Jazz Language*, M.A.S. Publishing Co., Bedford, Ohio, 1977. In this publication, various rhythmic patterns are notated with a suggested appropriate jazz interpretation included on a line underneath.

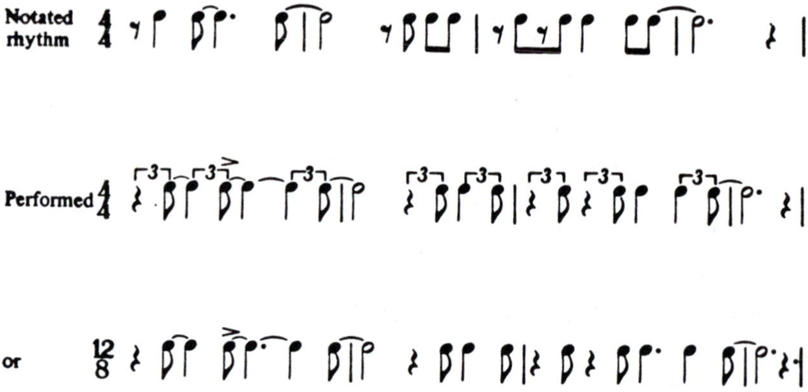

FIGURE 37   Notated rhythm from "I Hear Music" by Loesser and Lane, arr. Larry Lapin. Warner Bros. No. CH 0926. Note how this rhythm is acutally performed.

Tempo

In the rendition of any vocal jazz or pop tune, the finding of the "right groove" is essential for the most precise articulation and overall impact of music. Directors will find the metronome markings helpful, but they should experiment a bit because, for example, the personnel of a group and the acoustics of the performance hall may have a subtle effect on the tempo that will seem right for the group. Once this is determined and marked on the conductor's score, many conductors like to refer to a pocket metronome to make certain of the tempo before it is given to the group. Performance conditions can have subtle effects on the groups, and they should be advised to hold rigidly to the given tempo—that is, don't rush and don't drag; keep on the beat!

On up-tempo tunes, there is often a tendency for the group to drag, or sing behind the beat. Conversely, on medium to slow tempos there is sometimes a tendency for a group to rush the tempo. As previously mentioned, an inward response to the pulse of the music is essential to maintaining a steady beat. On up-tempo tunes the singers should keep on top of the beat, so to speak, and have a feeling of leaning forward; that is, they should anticipate and respond to the "front" side of the beat. (However, they should avoid rushing up-tempo tunes to the extent that articulation becomes blurred.) On slow tempos, singers should be advised to "lay back," relax, and respond to the back side of the beat.

Sometimes there is a tendency for singers to rush staccato notes that fall on the beat—for example, ♩. They should be advised to "lay back" and allow for the separation that should occur between the quarter notes.

Tone Quality

In vocal jazz, as well as in most pop tunes, singers should be advised to sing with a straight tone during all unison passages and in those with close or tight harmony; otherwise, the intonation and the blend will be adversely affected. Note, for example, the voicing in measure 2 of the excerpt from "When I Fall in Love" shown in Figure 38. With the bass, tenor, and alto parts an interval of a major second apart, the clarity of the chord structure would most certainly be "muddled" were any vibrato to be used. Some vibrato, however, may be used occasionally for coloring purposes, but primarily on solo passages.

The same basic principles of correct tone production as utilized by choral singers in general applies to pop singing. As to diction, initial consonants should be clearly and precisely articulated, though the intensity of middle and final consonants should be minimized. The consonant *t*, in particular, needs to be softened. For example, on the final consonant in *doot*, minimize the *t* and keep the tongue in contact with the palate. Also, the function of the *t* in *doot* is to stop the sound.

As to the treatment of diphthongs, the second vowel will usually be omitted or at least softened. One of the most troublesome problems of choral singers, regardless of the music style, seems to be their dogged determination to anticipate the second vowel in diphthongs and, of course, not all at the same time, thus resulting in problems with choral blend. Pop singers, however, have numerous models to whom they listen regularly, so the director can perhaps more readily make his point. In summary, tone and diction in pop style should not be forced, but should be somewhat relaxed and easygoing.

Vocal Jazz Articulations and Inflections

The following symbols are generally accepted as standard articulations and inflections for arrangements of vocal jazz ensemble music.[30]

Accent Markings

$\bar{\hat{\rho}}$ = heavy accent held to fullest value. May occur on or off the beat.

$\hat{\rho}$ = heavy accent, usually on the beat and held less than full value.

$\hat{\rho}$ = heavy accent, but short as possible.

---

[30]For further performance suggestions, see Kirby Shaw's *Vocal Jazz Style*, 2nd ed. (Milwaukee: Hal Leonard Publishing Corp.), 1990.

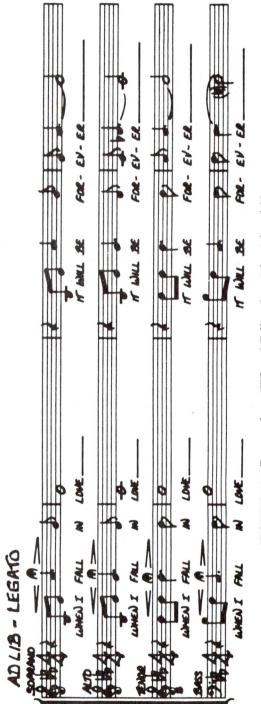

FIGURE 38 Excerpt from "When I Fall in Love" by Adward Heyman and Victor Young, arranged by Phil Azelton. © Copyright 1952, 1973 by Northern Music Corp., a division of MCA Entertainment, Inc., and Victor Young Publications. Used by permission.

Tenuto and staccato

      = note held to fullest value.

      = short and detached.

Shake

      = a rather fast alternation between the written pitch and minimally a major second above. Some directors prefer a minor third or even a major third. Shakes need not be synchronized within the group.

Flip

      = sound first note written and just before its release raise the pitch and drop quickly to the next note.

Smear

      = a slide into a note from below, reaching the pitch just before the next note. The length of the smear, then, depends on the length of the note.

Falloff

      = a descending slide that may be either short or long, depending on the style and the tempo of the music. (The sigh is the essence of the falloff.)

Doit

      = an ascending slide of one to five steps.

Plop

      = a descending slide to the indicated note. Sing the main note at the last instant and "land" with force.

Indefinite sound (ghost notes)

      = an indefinite pitch for notes needing a soft but vital sound.

Glissando (Gliss)

= a slide from one pitch to another that may be up, down, short, or long. Some arrangers simply mark the music as 〽 .

Downward turn or dip

$\tilde{P}$ = an inflection, generally occuring on the first beat of a measure, in which the singers bend a note downward, usually a half step, and resume the original pitch.

In rehearsing the jazz/show choir, the choral director should be aware of many subtleties of interpretation. Conductors can develop greater sensitivity by (1) listening to and analyzing recordings of outstanding popular groups; (2) discussing with colleagues various matters of interpretation (most school systems have at least one person who has had experience with instrumental or vocal jazz ensembles); (3) attending concerts of other jazz/show choirs in the area; and (4) openly discussing interpretative matters with the students in the ensemble. Their younger ears generally are tuned to the current popular music on radio and TV, and as a result, they often quite naturally interpret popular music in an acceptable manner, which, although perhaps not perfect, is stylistically preferable to the approach of the uninitiated conductor.

The following are performing groups whose recordings are suggested for listening and study: The Four Freshmen, Manhattan Transfer, Singers Unlimited, The Hi Lo's, Rare Silk, Phil Mattson & the P.M. Singers, Seawind, and Swingle II.

ART IN THE TWENTIETH CENTURY

Modern art in the twentieth century embraces a number of styles, including Expressionism, Cubism, Fauvism, Futurism, Surrealism, Abstract Expressionism, Pop Art, and Op Art.

Expressionism. This is an emotional style using distortion, exaggeration, and color to express very personal feelings of fear, anxiety, love, and anger, and was most popular among German artists of the World War I period (1914–1918). Outstanding exponents of Expressionism are Chaim Soutine (1894–1943), Edvard Munch (1863–1944), Max Beckman (1884–1950), and Emil Nolde (1867–1956).

Cubism. This style viewed objects simultaneously from different angles and abstracted their form into various geometric shapes. Outstanding expo-

Pablo Picasso, *Three Musicians*, 1921. Oil on canvas, 80 × 74 in. The three masked musicians are commedia dell'arte figures that reflect Picasso's love of the circus and theatrical performances of clowns in gay carnival costumes. Philadephia Museum of Art, The A. E. Gallatin Collection.

nents of Cubism were Pablo Picasso (1881–1973) and Georges Braque (1882–1963). In his work *Three Musicians* (1921), Picasso's concern was not with the surface patterns, but rather with the image of the three musicians—traditional figures of the comedy stage.[31]

[31]H. W. Janson, *History of Art*, rev. ed. (Englewood Cliffs, NJ: Prentice Hall, 1973), p. 528.

Fauvism.   This style was characterized by bold distortion of form and the use of strong, pure colors. The first works so shocked and outraged the public that the artists who painted in this style were called *"fauves"* (French for wild beasts). The leading exponent of Fauvism was Henri Matisse (1869–1954). Upon viewing his painting *The Joy of Life* (1905–06), one might wonder what it means. The answer is exactly what the title says. The purpose of Matisse's painting was to give pleasure. Another important member of the Fauvist group was Georges Rouault (1871–1958). In his painting *Head of Christ* (1905), Rouault emphasizes "the passion mirrored upon a human face." The slashing brush strokes reflect the artist's rage and compassion.[32]

Futurism.   This genre was an attempt to capture motion and time, as the Cubists captured space. Umberto Boccioni (1882–1916) painted trains and machinery in motion, catching several successive stages at one time.[33]

Surrealism.   This genre has two main streams: (a) the "psychic automation" that utilizes accidental and chance effects of the paint to express odd moods, and (b) the "dream school," which endeavored to reproduce the fantasies of the unconscious mind. Max Ernst (1891–1976) was an outstanding exponent of the first style, and Salvador Dali (1904–1909) of the second.

Abstract Expressionism.   This genre, initially developed by Vassily Kandinsky (1866–1944), focuses on rhythmic motion and color. A well-known exemplar of Abstract Expressionism is Jackson Pollack (1912–1956). Using a unique approach, he created his painting *One* (1950) by pouring and spattering his colors, instead of applying them with a brush.

Pop Art.   Pop Art began in London in the mid-1950s and was based mostly on the American mass media that had flooded England since 1945. It views commercial culture, including photography, advertising, magazine illustration, and comic strips, as a broad source of pictorial subject matter, rather than as something to be criticized. Pop art has been referred to as the New Realism. Among the well-known artists of this genre are Jasper Johns (b. 1930), Roy Lichtenstein (b. 1923), and Andy Warhol (1931–1987). Lichtenstein has utilized the imagery of comic strips on the themes of action and love, as in his work *Girl at Piano* (1963). Some artists feel the flat surface of the canvas to be too confining, so they often introduce three-dimensional objects into their pictures and sometimes actually construct models of various objects using all types of materials. This approach was utilized by Edward Kienholz (b. 1927) in his work *The State Hospital.*

---

[32]Ibid., p. 521.
[33]Benjamin Rifkin, *Art History* (New York: Monarch Press, Inc., 1964).

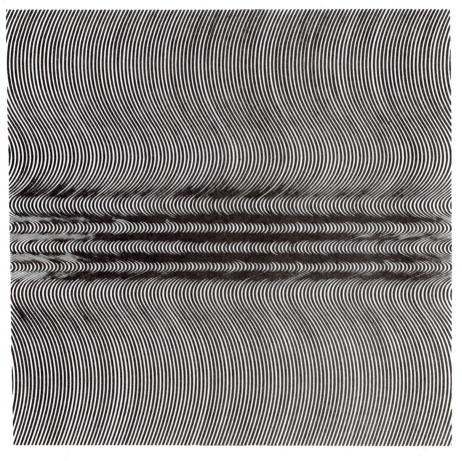

Bridget Riley, *Current*, 1964. Synthetic polymer paint on board, 58⅜ × 58⅞ in. Note how lines seem to shift and equivocate and how the eye moves from one part to another. The Museum of Modern Art, New York, Philip Johnson Fund.

Op Art.   A trend related to Pop Art is Op Art, known as such because of its focus on optics, i.e., the physical and psychological aspects of vision. Op Art is more akin to the sciences than to the humanities. If one considers the mind as a computer into which information is fed, then perception is the answer the computer provides after analyzing the data. A most fascinating work of Op Art is *Current* by Bridget Riley. In this work, stable lines seem to shift and equivocate. Since it is difficult to perceive the entire work at once, the eye moves from one part to another, giving the viewer a feeling of faster–slower perception and forward–backward movement. *Current* intrigues and grasps the viewer, and perhaps may make one think of electronic music or of the compositions for chorus and electric tape that were so much in vogue during the decade of the 1970s.

EPILOGUE—SOME CONCLUDING THOUGHTS

Certainly one characteristic of twentieth-century music is its wide diversity of musical styles. It is often difficult to place composers neatly in the previously mentioned categories, as some change their styles during their composing years. Other composers might be said to possess an "eclectic" style; that is, they draw from the techniques and devices of various schools, depending upon the musical thought to be expressed. The conductor, therefore, if he or she is to interpret properly the works of any particular modern-day composer, should study and analyze the writings as well as the music of the composer under consideration. What a composer says about his own music has obvious implications for the conductor seeking the proper interpretation. Whenever such writings do not exist, or are unavailable, the conductor may well turn to the vast number of books on twentieth-century composers (as well as those of other periods). What others have written about the lives and music of particular individuals will often provide the inquiring, analytical reader with fresh insights into the interpretation of music.

The study of style and interpretation is not a subject to be dealt with on a one-time basis—it should be studied throughout one's musical career. The intent of this book has been to provide a summary of the most salient points for consideration. To be most meaningful, however, they must be studied in connection with actual music. With this background information, the conductor should carefully study and analyze scores. Only through reflective thought on the composer's intentions will the proper interpretation be achieved. The choral conductor should also listen critically to the interpretations of various choral organizations—on recordings and in the concert hall. The listener will most likely find that the interpretation of a particular composition will vary somewhat from one conductor to another. "What is stylistically correct and what is incorrect about these performances?" and "What do I like and dislike about the performances?" These questions must be always present in the listener's mind if he or she is to make the proper evaluation essential to further musical growth. Young conductors must give these questions careful consideration if they are ultimately to achieve the correct interpretation for their own choral groups.

Finally, the effective conductor must also be a scholar. Conductors should devote considerable time to further reading in various sources of the main points discussed in each chapter. They should also develop a broad historical understanding of the various periods of artistic achievement. For these purposes, a selected list of publications recommended for further study is included at the end of each chapter.

REFERENCES

Apel, Willi. *Harvard Dictionary of Music*, 2nd ed. Cambridge, MA: Harvard University Press, 1969.

Banks, Timothy. "Use of Timbre in Igor Stravinsky's Mass." *Choral Journal*, Vol. 20, No. 8, April 1980, pp. 29–36.

Berthiaume, Denny. *Contemporary Musical Styles: Rock, Pop, and Jazz.* Dubuque, IA: Kendall/Hunt Publishing Co., 1983.

Birge, Edward Bailey. *History of Public School Music in the United States.* Philadelphia: Oliver Ditson Company, 1937.

Brand, Juliane, Christopher Hailey, and Donald Harris, eds. *The Berg-Schoenberg Correspondence: Selected Letters.* New York: W. W. Norton, 1987.

Brown, Howard Mayer, and Stanley Sadie, eds. *Performance Practice: Music After 1600.* New York: W. W. Norton & Company, 1989.

Burkholder, J. Peter. "Musical Time and Continuity as a Reflection of the Historical Situation of Modern Composers." *The Journal of Musicology*, Vol. IX, No. 4, Fall 1991, pp. 412–429.

Byrnside, Ronald L. "Musical Impressionism: The Early History of the Term." *The Musical Quarterly*, Vol. 66, No. 4, October 1980, pp. 522–537.

Clark, Walter, J. "Problems in Contemporary Choral Music." *Journal of Church Music*, Vol. 17, No. 7, September 1975, pp. 11–14.

Copland, Aaron. *Copland on Music.* New York: W. W. Norton & Co., Inc., 1963.

Copland, Aaron, and Vivian Perlis. *Copland: 1910 through 1942.* New York: St. Martin's/Marek, 1984.

Crocker, Richard L. *A History of Musical Style.* New York: McGraw-Hill Book Company, 1966.

Cross, Anthony. "Kodaly and Folk Music." *The Musical Times*, Vol. 123, No. 1678, December 1982, pp. 839–841.

Curtis, Marvin V., and Lee V. Cloud. "The African-American Spiritual: Traditions and Performances Practices." *Choral Journal*, Vol. XXXIII, No. 4, November 1991, pp. 15–22.

Dahlhaus, Carl. *Romanticism and Modernism: Four Studies in the Music of the Later Nineteenth Century.* Munich, 1974. Translated from the German by Mary Whittall. Berkeley and Los Angeles: University of California Press, 1980.

Daniel, Keith W. *Francis Poulenc: His Artistic Development and Musical Style.* Ann Arbor, MI: UMI Research Press, 1982.

———. "The Choral Music of Francis Poulenc." *American Choral Review*, Vol. XXIV, No. 1, January 1982, pp. 5–37.

Debussy, Claude. *Debussy on Music: The Critical Writings of the Great French Composer Claude Debussy.* Collected and introduced by Francois Lesure, translated and edited by Richard Langham Smith. Ithaca, NY: Cornell University Press, 1987.

Dennis, Brian. "Metamorphosis in Modern Culture: The Parallel Evolution of Music and Painting in the Twentieth Century." *Tempo*, No. 78, Autumn 1966, pp. 12–20.

Dickinson, Peter. "Copland: Early, Late and More Biography." *The Musical Times*, Vol. 131, No. 1773, November 1990, pp. 582–585.

Dorian, Frederick. *The History of Music in Performance.* New York: W. W. Norton & Company, 1942.

Editors, Time-Life Books. *This Fabulous Century.* Volumes I-VII. New York: Time-Life Books, 1970.

Engen, David P. "The Choral Psalms of Charles Ives: A Performer's Analysis of Psalm 90." *Church Music*, Vol. 8, No. 1, 1976, pp. 20–27.

Ewen, David. *Composers Since 1900, First Supplement: A Biographical and Critical Guide.* New York: H. W. Wilson, 1981.

Folstrom, Roger. "The Choral Warmup: A Look at Avant-Garde Music." *The Choral Journal*, Vol. XIV, No. 8, April 1974, pp. 22–23.

Garcia, Antonio J. "Pedagogical Scat." *Music Educators Journal*, Vol. 77, No. 1, September 1990, pp. 28–34.

Garretson, Robert L. *Conducting Choral Music*, 7th ed. Englewood Cliffs, NJ: Prentice Hall, 1993.
————. "Music Curricula," in the *International Encyclopedia of Education*. Oxford, England: Pergamon Press, 1985, Vol. 6, pp. 3457–3463.
Green, Randall L. "Unsingable Contemporary Music." *Southwestern Musician*, Vol. 40, No. 1, August 1971, pp. 20–22.
Griffiths, Paul. *The Avant Garde Since 1945*. London: J. M. Dent & Sons, 1981.
Hansen, Peter. *An Introduction to Twentieth Century Music*, 2nd ed. Boston: Allyn and Bacon, 1967.
Harvey, Jonathan. "The Composer's View: Atonality." *The Musical Times*, Vol. 122, No. 1653, November 1980, pp. 699–700.
Healy, Jane. *The Two-Minute Mind*. New York: Simon & Schuster, 1990.
Hines, Robert, ed. *The Composer's Point of View*. Westport, CT: Greenwood Press, 1977.
Hienz, William Jr. "New Light on Samuel Barber's Reincarnations." *The Choral Journal*, Vol. XXV, No., 3, November 1984, pp. 25–27.
Hill, Peter. "Authenticity in Contemporary Music." *Tempo*, No. 159, December 1986, pp. 2–8.
Holst, Imogen, *Holst*, 2nd ed. London and Boston: Faber & Faber, 1981.
————. "Holst In the 1980's." *The Musical Times*, Vol. 125, No. 1695, May 1984, pp. 266–269.
————. "Holst's Music: Some Questions of Style and Performance at the Centenary of his Birth." *Proceedings of the Royal Music Association*, Vol. 100, 1973–74, pp. 201–207.
Honert, Peter van den. "American Folk Songs as an Alternative in Programming," *The Choral Journal*, Vol. XXVII, No. 8, March 1977, pp. 31–33.
Howerton, George. *Technique and Style in Choral Singing*. New York: Carl Fischer, 1957.
Jacobson, Bernard. "Jose Serebrier on Ives," in *Conductors on Conducting*. Frenchtown, NJ: Columbia Publishing Co., 1979, pp. 157–183.
Janson, H. W. *History of Art*. Englewood Cliffs, NJ: Prentice Hall, 1973.
Kostelanetz, Richard, ed. *Conversing With Cage*. New York: Limelight Editions, 1988.
Kupkovic, Ladislav. "The Role of Tonality in Contemporary and 'Up-to-Date' Composition," *Tempo*, No. 135, December 1980, pp. 15–19.
Lang, Paul H. "Choral Music in the Twentieth Century." *American Choral Review*, Vol. XIX, No. 2, April 1977, pp. 7–18.
Lerner, Alan Jay. *The Musical Theatre: A Celebration*. New York: McGraw-Hill, 1986.
Lessem, Alan. "Schoenberg, Stravinsky, and Neo-Classicism: The Issues Reexamined." *The Musical Quarterly*, Vol. LXXIII, No. 4, October 1982, pp. 527–542.
Lesure, François, and Roger Nichols, eds. *Debussy's Letters*. London: Faber, 1987.
Lockspeiser, Edward. "Debussy's Concept of the Dream," *Royal Music Association* (1962–1963 Proceedings), Vol. 89, March 21, 1963, pp. 49–56.
Machlis, Joseph. *Introduction to Contemporary Music*. New York: W. W. Norton & Company, 1961.
May, James D. *Avant-Garde Choral Music*. Metuchen, N.J.: The Scarecrow Press, 1977.
McGray, James. "Stravinsky's Cantata—Notes on Structure and Performance." *American Choral Review*, Vol. XXI, No. 1, January 1979, pp. 23–26.
McElheran, Brock. "Beginner's Guide to the Avant-Garde." *Choral Journal*, Vol. 13, No. 8, April 1973, pp. 19–24.
Mellers, Wilfred. "The Avant-garde in America." *Proceedings of the Royal Music Association*, 90th Session, 1963–64, pp. 1–13.
————. "A Minimalist Definition." *The Musical Times*, Vol. 125, No. 1696, June 1984, pp. 328.
Messing, Scott. *Neoclassicism in Music from the Genesis of the Concept Through the Schoenberg/Stravinsky Polemic*. Ann Arbor, MI: UMI Research Press, 1988.
Moses, Don V. *A Conductor's Analysis of the Mass (1948) by Stravinsky; A Conductor's Analysis of the Mass (1963) by Hindemith*. D.M. dissertation, Indiana University, 1968.
Olmstead, Andrea. *Roger Sessions and His Music*. Ann Arbor, MI: UMI Research Press, 1985.
Perrin, Maurice. "Stravinsky in a Composition Class." *The Score*, No. 20, June, 1957, pp. 44–46.
Pleasants, Henry. "Bel Canto in Jazz and Pop Singing." *Music Educators Journal*, Vol. XLIX, No. 9, May 1973, pp. 54–59.

Pooler, Frank, and Brent Pierce. *New Choral Notation*. New York: Walton Music Corporation, 1971.

Rorem, Ned. *Settling the Score: Essays on Music*. San Diego, CA: Harcourt Brace Jovanovich, 1988.

Sachs, Curt. *Rhythm and Tempo: A Study in Music History*. New York: W. W. Norton & Company, 1953.

Salzman, Eric. *Twentieth Century Music: An Introduction*, 3rd ed. Englewood Cliffs, NJ: Prentice Hall, 1988.

Sanders, Hugh. "Sprechstimme in Choral Music." *Choral Journal*, Vol. 11, No. 2, October 1970, pp. 7–10.

Satie, Erik. *The Writings of Erich Satie*. Edited and translated by Nigel Wilkins. New York: DaCapo Press, 1982.

Schuller, Gunther. "Conducting Revisited," in Carl Bamberger, *The Conductor's Art*. New York: McGraw-Hill, 1965.

———. *The Swing Era: The Development of Jazz, 1930–1945*. New York: Oxford University Press, 1989.

Sellers, H. "Francis Poulenc and His Sacred Choral Music." *Choral Journal*, Vol. 17, No. 6, 1977, pp. 19–22; No. 7, pp. 19–22; No. 8, pp. 11–14; No. 9, pp. 9–11.

Sessions, Roger. *Conversations with Roger Sessions*. Boston: Northeastern University Press, 1987.

Shaw, Kirby. *Vocal Jazz Style*, 2nd ed. Milwaukee: Hal Leonard Publishing Corp., 1990. (Includes Teacher's Manual, student books, and cassette tape.)

Shearin, Arthur. "Choral Music of Debussy and Ravel." *Choral Journal*, Vol. 19, No. 6, February 1979, pp. 7–9.

Skinner, Howard. "Words and Music." *The Choral Journal*, Vol. VII, No. 5, May–June 1967, pp. 6–9, and No. 6, pp. 13–15.

Skowronski, Joann. *Aaron Copland: A Bio-Bibliography*. Westport, CT: Greenwood Press, 1985.

Slonimsky, Nicholas, ed. *Baker's Biographical Dictionary of Musicians*, 7th ed. New York: Schirmer Books, 1984.

Stravinsky, Igor. *Stravinsky, Selected Correspondence*. New York: Knopf, 1982.

Stravinsky, Igor, and Robert Craft. *Memories and Commentaries*. Berkeley, CA: University of California Press, 1981.

Terry, Clark, and Phil Rizzo. *The Interpretation of the Jazz Language*. Bedford, OH: M.A.S. Publishing Co., 1977.

Thompson, Edgar J. "Comments on Avant-Garde Choral Music: An Interview with Frank Pooler," *The Choral Journal*, Vol. XII, No. 4, December 1971, pp. 9–14.

Thompson, Virgil. *Selected Letters of Virgil Thompson*. Edited by Tim Page and Vanessa Weeks Page. New York: Summit Books, 1988.

Tipton, Julius R. "Some Observations on the Choral Style of Charles Ives." *American Choral Review*, Vol. XII, No. 3, July 1970, pp. 99–105.

Toch, Ernst. *The Shaping Forces in Music*. New York: Criterion Music, 1953.

White, J. Perry. *Twentieth-Century Choral Music: An Annotated Bibliography of Music Suitable for Use by High School Choirs*. Metuchen, NJ: Scarecrow Press, 1982.

Whittall, Arnold. "Webern and Atonality: The Path from the Old Aesthetic," *The Musical Times*, Vol. 124, No. 1690, December 1983, pp. 733–737.

Wishart, Trevor. "The Composer's View: Extended Vocal Technique." *The Musical Times*, Vol. 121, No. 1647, May 1980, pp. 313–314.

Wood, Ralph W. "Putting in the Expression." *Music and Letters*, Vol. XI, No. 4, October 1930, pp. 375–382 (on dynamics).

Yates, Peter. *Twentieth Century Music*. New York: Random House, 1967.

APPENDIX A

Choral Composers

This chronological list gives the birthplaces and dates for most of the major contributors to choral literature, arranged by period, from ca. 1400 to the present. Although some composers may be known principally for compositions other than choral music, all have made choral contributions significant enough to justify inclusion herein. For representative compositions of these composers, see Appendix B, Choral Octavo Publications, and Appendix C, Extended Choral Works.

PRE-RENAISSANCE (ca. 1200–1400)

Perotin (Perotinus Magnus)	France	ca. 1183–ca. 1238
Adam de la Halle	Arras, France	ca. 1240–1287
Guillaume de Machaut	France	ca. 1304–1377

RENAISSANCE PERIOD (ca. 1400–1600)

John Dunstable	Dunstable, England	ca. 1370–1453
Gilles Binchois	Mons, Belgium	ca. 1400–1460
Guillaume Dufay	Hainaut, Belgium	ca. 1400–1474
Johannes Okeghem	East Flanders, Belgium	ca. 1430–1495
Pierre de La Rue	Tournai, Belgium	ca. 1430–1518
Heinrich Isaac	Brabant, Belgium	ca. 1450–1517
Josquin Després	Hainaut, Belgium	ca. 1450–1521
Jacob Obrecht	Berg-op-Zoom, Netherlands	ca. 1452–1505
Loyset Compère	(unknown)	ca. 1455–1518
Jean Mouton	Haut-Wignes, France	ca. 1470–1522
Antoine Brumel	Flanders	ca. 1475–1520
Martin Luther	Eislenben, Germany	1483–1546
Clément Janequin	Châtellerault, France	ca. 1485–1560
Ludwig Senfl	Zurich, Switzerland	ca. 1490–ca. 1543
Costanzo Festa	Rome, Italy	ca. 1490–1545
Nicolas Gombert	Flanders	ca. 1490–1556

Thomas Créquillon	Ghent, Belgium	?–1557
Claudin de Sermisy	France	ca. 1490–1562
Passereau	France	early 16th c.
Adrian Willaert	Bruges, Belgium	ca. 1490–1562
Robert Carver	Scotland	ca. 1491–ca. 1546
Johann Walther	Kahler, Thuringia	1496–1570
Cristóbal Morales	Seville, Spain	ca. 1500–1553
Christopher Tye	England	ca. 1500–ca. 1572
Jacob Arcadelt	Liège, Belgium	ca. 1505–1560
Claude Goudimel	Besançon, France	ca. 1505–1572
Mattheus Le Maistre	near Liège, Belgium	ca. 1505–1577
Thomas Tallis	Leicestershire (?), England	ca. 1505–1585
Jacobus Clemens	Ypres, Belgium	ca. 1510–1556
Pierre Certon	Paris?, France	ca. 1510–1672
Antonio Scandello	Brescia, Italy	1517–1580
Noé Falgnient	Flanders, Belgium	?–1595
Hubert Waelvant	Tongerloo, Belgium	ca. 1517–1595
Andrea Gabrieli	Venice, Italy	ca. 1520–1586
Philippe de Monte	Mons, Belgium	1521–1603
Fernando Franco	La Serena, Mexico	ca. 1525–1585
Giovanni Pierluigi da Palestrina	Palestrina, Italy	ca. 1525–1594
Claude Le Jeune	Valenciennes, France	1528–1600
Costanzo Porta	Cremona, Italy	1529–1601
Richard Farrant	England	ca. 1530–1581
Baldassari Donati (Donato)	Venice, Italy	ca. 1530–1603
Guillaume Costeley	Pont-Audemer, France	1531–1606
Orlando di Lasso	Mons, Belgium	1532–1594
Cornelius Freundt	Plauen, Germany	1535–1591
Giaches de Wert	Weert, Netherlands	ca. 1535–1596
Andries Pevernage	Courtral, Belgium	1543–1591
William Byrd	Lincolnshire (?), England	ca. 1543–1623
Marco Antonio Ingegneri	Verona, Italy	1545–1592
Giovanni Maria Nanino	Tivoli, Italy	1545–1607
Giulio Caccini	Rome, Italy	ca. 1546–1618
François-Eustache Du Caurroy	Beauvais, France	1549–1609
Tomás Luis de Victoria	Avila, Spain	ca. 1549–1611
Francesco Surlano	Sorlano, Italy	1549–ca. 1621
Jacobus Gallus (Jacob Handl)	Reifnitz, Austria	1550–1591
Orazio Vecchi	Modena, Italy	ca. 1550–1605
Giovanni Matteo Asola	Verona, Italy	1550–1609
Giovanni Macque	Valenciennes, France	ca. 1550–1614
Luca Marenzio	Coccaglio, Italy	1553–1599
Johannes Eccard	Mühlhausen, Germany	1553–1611
Giovanni Gabrieli	Venice, Italy	ca. 1555–1612
Bartholomeus Gesius	Müncheberg, Germany	ca. 1555–1613
Sethus Calvisius	Gorsleben, Germany	1556–1615
Giovanni Gastoldi	Caravaggio, Italy	ca. 1556–1622
Thomas Morley	England	1557–1602
Jacques Mauduit	Paris, France	1557–1627
Jacopo Corsi	Florence, Italy	ca. 1560–1604
Giovanni Croce	Chioggia, Italy	ca. 1560–1609
Don Carlo Gesualdo	Naples, Italy	ca. 1560–1613
Felice Anerio	Rome, Italy	ca. 1560–1614
Melchior Vulpius	Wasungen, Germany	ca. 1560–1615
Hieronymus Praetorius	Hamburg, Germany	1560–1629

Peter Philips	England	ca. 1561–1628
Jacobo Peri	Florence, Italy	ca. 1561–1633
Jan Pieterszoon Sweelinck	Deventer, Netherlands	1562–1621
John Dowland	County Dublin ? Ireland	ca. 1562–1626
John Bull	Somersetshire, England	ca. 1562–1628
Francis Pilkington	England	ca. 1562–1638
Gregor Aichinger	Regensburg, Germany	1564–1628
Ludovico da Viadana	Viadana, Italy	1564–1645
Michael Cavendish	England	ca. 1565–1628
Peter Philips	England	ca. 1565–1638
Thomas Campion	London, England	1567–1620
Giovanni Gastoldi	Caravaggio, Italy	15?–1622
Adriano Banchieri	Bologna, Italy	1568–1634
Paul Peurl	Austria	ca. 1570–1624
Salamone Rossi	Mantua, Italy	1570–ca. 1630
Thomas Bateson	Cheshire, England	1570–1630
Christian Erbach	Hesse, Germany	1570–1635
Thomas Tomkins	St. David's, England	ca. 1572–1656
John Wilbye	Diss, England	1574–1638
Thomas Weelkes	England	ca. 1575–1623
Steffano Bernardi	Verona, Italy	1576–1636
Francisco Correa	Seville, Spain	ca. 1576–?
Melchior Franck	Zittau, Germany	ca. 1579–1639
Michael East	London, England	ca. 1580–ca. 1648
Thomas Ford	England	ca. 1580–1648
Orlando Gibbons	Oxford, England	1583–1625
Adrian Batten	London, England	ca. 1585–1637

BAROQUE PERIOD (ca. 1600–1750)

Giulio Caccini	Rome, Italy	ca. 1546–1618
Giovanni Gabrieli	Venice, Italy	ca. 1557–1612
Hans Leo Hassler	Nuremberg, Germany	1564–1612
Claudio Monteverdi	Cremona, Italy	1567–1643
Michael Praetorius	Kreuzberg, Germany	ca. 1571–1621
Richard Deering	Kent, England	ca. 1580–ca. 1630
Gregorio Allegri	Rome, Italy	1582–1652
Melchior Teschner	Fraustadt, Austria	1584–1635
Adrian Batten	England	1585–1637
Heinrich Schütz	Kostritz, Germany	1585–1672
Johann Hermann Schein	Grünhain, Germany	1586–1630
Salamone Rossi	Mantua, Italy	ca. 1587–ca. 1630
Samuel Scheidt	Halle, Germany	1587–1654
Thomas Ravenscroft	England	ca. 1590–ca. 1633
Thomas Vautor	England	1590–16?
Johann Crüger	Grossbreece, Germany	1598–1662
John Hilton	Oxford, England	1599–1657
Pier Francesco Cavalli	Crema, Italy	1602–1676
Orazio Benevoli	Rome, Italy	ca. 1605–1672
Giacomo Carissimi	Marino, Italy	ca. 1605–1674
Andreas Hammerschmidt	Brüx, Bohemia	1612–1675
Guillaume Bouzignac	France	early 17th c.

Franz Tunder	Burg auf Fehmarn, Germany	ca. 1614–1667
Christoph Bernard	Danzig, Germany	1627–1692
Matthew Locke	Exeter, England	ca. 1630–1677
George Jeffries	England	?–1685
Jean-Baptiste Lully	Florence, Italy	ca. 1632–1687
Johann Christoph Wagenseil	Nuremberg, Germany	1633–1708
Marc-Antoine Charpentier	Paris, France	ca. 1634–1704
Dietrich Buxtehude	Helsingborg, Denmark	ca. 1637–1707
Johann Christoph Bach	Erfurt, Germany	ca. 1642–1703
Johann Wolfgang Franck	Unterschwaningen, Germany	1644–ca. 1710
Pelham Humfrey	England	1647–1674
Michael Wise	Salisbury, England	ca. 1648–1687
Johann Michael Bach	Arnstadt, Germany	ca. 1648–1694
John Blow	Newark-on-Trent, England	1649–1708
Johann Pachelbel	Nuremberg, Germany	1653–1707
George von Reutter	Vienna, Austria	1656–1738
Philipp Heinrich Erlebach	Esens, Germany	1657–1714
Giuseppe Pitoni[1]	Rieti, Italy	1657–1743
Henry Purcell	London, England	1659–1695
Johann Kuhnau	Leipzig, Germany	1660–1722
Alessandro Scarlatti	Palermo, Italy	1660–1725
Gregor G. Gorczycki	Cracow, Poland	ca. 1664–1734
Antonio Lotti	Venice, Italy	1667–1740
Francesco Gasparini	Camaiore (near Lucca), Italy	1668–1727
François Couperin	Paris, France	ca. 1668–1733
Antonio Vivaldi	Venice, Italy	ca. 1669–1741
Antonio Caldara	Venice, Italy	1670–1736
D. Pompeo Canniciari	Rome, Italy	ca. 1670–1744
William Croft	Nether Ettington, England	ca. 1678–1727
Georg Philipp Telemann	Magdeburg, Germany	1681–1767
Jean-Philippe Rameau	Dijon, France	1683–1764
Bohuslav Cernohorsky	Nimburg, Czechoslovakia	1684–1742
Francesco Durante	Frattamaggiore, Italy	1684–1755
Johann Sebastian Bach	Eisenach, Germany	1685–1750
George Frideric Handel	Halle, Germany	1685–1759
Benedetto Marcello	Venice, Italy	ca. 1686–1739
Niccola Antonio Porpora	Naples, Italy	1686–1768
Johan Helmich Roman	Stockholm, Sweden	ca. 1694–1758
Maurice Green	London, England	1696–1755
Francesco Antonio Vallotti	Vercelli, Italy	1697–1780
Georg Gottfried Wagner	Mühlberg, Germany	ca. 1698–1756
Johann Adolf Hasse	Bergedorf, Germany	1699–1783
Johann Ernst Eberlin	Jettingen, Germany	1702–1762
Karl Heinrich Graun	Wahrenbrück, Germany	ca. 1704–1759
Frantisek Ignac Antonin Tuma	Kostelec nad Orlici, Bohemia	1704–1774
Giovanni B. Martini	Bologna, Italy	1706–1784
Giovanni Battista Pergolesi	Jesi, Italy	1710–1736
Thomas Arne	London, England	1710–1778

[1]Although Pitoni lived during the Baroque period, he was of the Roman school, which rejected the styles and forms of Baroque music and directed their efforts toward composing liturgical music in the style of Palestrina.

CLASSICAL PERIOD (1750–1820)

Wilhelm Friedemann Bach	Weimar, Germany	1710–1784
Gottfried August Homilius	Rosenthal, Germany	1714–1785
Christoph Willibald Gluck	Erasbach, Germany	1714–1787
Carl Philipp Emanuel Bach	Weimar, Germany	ca. 1714–1788
Georg Christoph Wagenseil	Vienna, Austria	1715–1777
James Nares	Middlesex, England	1715–1783
Johann Heinrich Rolle	Quedinburg, Germany	1716–1785
Johann Christoph Altnikol	Berna (Silesia)	1719–1759
Johann Ernst Bach	Eisenach, Germany	1722–1777
Christian Friedrich Gregor	Dirsdorf, Germany	1723–1801
Johann Adam Hiller	Wendisch-Ossog, Germany	1728–1804
Johann C. Geisler	Germany	1729–1815
Johann C. F. Bach	Leipzig, Germany	1732–1795
Franz Joseph Haydn	Rohrau-on-the-Leltha, Austria	1732–1809
Carl Friedrich Christian Fasch	Zerbst, Germany	1736–1800
Johann George Albrechtsberger	Klosterneuburg, Austria	1736–1809
Michael Haydn	Rohrau, Austria	1737–1806
Carl Michael Bellman	Stockholm, Sweden	1740–1795
Quirino Gasparini	Bergamasco, Italy	?–1778
John Antes	Frederickstownship, Pennsylvania	1740–1811
Luigi Boccherini	Lucca, Italy	1743–1805
William Billings	Boston, Massachusetts	1746–1800
Johann Friedrich Peter	Heerendijk, Holland	1746–1813
Abbé Vogler	Würzburg, Germany	1749–1814
Andrew Law	Milford, Connecticut	1749–1821
Dimitri S. Bortniansky	Glukhov, Russia	1751–1825
Jacob French	Early American composer	1754–18?
Wolfgang Amadeus Mozart	Salzburg, Austria	1756–1791
Carl Friedrich Zelter	Berlin, Germany	1758–1832
Johann Rudolph Zumsteeg	Sachsenflur, Odenwald, Germany	1760–1802
Luigi Cherubini	Florence, Italy	1760–1842
Joseph Eybler	Schwechat (near Vienna), Austria	1764–1846
Thomas Attwood	London, England	1765–1838
John Wall Callcott	London, England	1766–1821
Samuel Wesley	Bristol, England	1766–1837
Ludwig van Beethoven	Bonn, Germany	1770–1827
Johann Christian Heinrich Rinck	Elgersburg, Germany	1770–1846

ROMANTIC PERIOD (1800–1900)

Ignaz von Seyfried	Vienna, Austria	1776–1841
Johann Neopmuk Hummel	Pressburg, Czechoslovakia	1778–1837
Johann Kaspar Aiblinger	Wasserburg, Germany	1779–1867
Konradin Kreutzer	Messkirch, Germany	1780–1849
Anton Diabelli	Mattee (near Salzburg), Austria	1781–1858
Vincent Novello	London, England	1781–1861
Konrad Kocher	Ditzinger, Germany	1786–1872
Gioacchino Rossini	Pesaro, Italy	1792–1868
Lowell Mason	Medfield, Massachusetts	1792–1872
Franz Schubert	Lichtenthal, Austria	1797–1828
Alexis F. Lvov	Reval, Russia	1798–1870

John Goss	Fareham, England	1800–1880
Gustav Wilhelm Teschner	Magdeburg, Germany	1800–1883
Hector Berlioz	Côte-Saint-André, France	1803–1869
Mikhail Glinka	Novosspaskoye, Russia	1804–1857
Felix Mendelssohn	Hamburg, Germany	1809–1847
Edward L. White	Boston, Massachusetts	1809–1851
Robert Schumann	Zwickau, Germany	1810–1856
Samuel Sebastian Wesley	London, England	1810–1876
Franz Liszt	Raiding, Hungary	1811–1886
Richard Wagner	Leipzig, Germany	1813–1883
Guiseppe Verdi	Le Roncole, Italy	1813–1901
Robert Franz	Halle, Germany	1815–1892
Charles François Gounod	Paris, France	1818–1893
Jacques Offenbach	Cologne, France	1819–1880
Franz Abt	Eilenburg, Germany	1819–1885
Louis Lewandowski	Wreschen (near Posen), Poland	1821–1904
César Franck	Liège, Belgium	1822–1890
Peter Cornelius	Mainz, Germany	1824–1874
Anton Bruckner	Anstelden, Austria	1824–1896
Johann Strauss (Jr.)	Vienna, Austria	1825–1899
Stephen Collins Foster	Pittsburgh, Pennsylvania	1826–1864
François Auguste Gevaert	Huysse, Belgium	1828–1908
Anton Grigorievitch Rubenstein	Vykhvatinetz Podolia, Russia	1829–1894
Jean-Baptiste Fauré	Mouline, France	1830–1914
Johann von Herbeck	Vienna, Austria	1831–1877
August Soderman	Stockholm, Sweden	1832–1876
Alexander Borodin	St. Petersburg, Russia	1833–1887
Johannes Brahms	Hamburg, Germany	1833–1897
César Antonovitch Cui	Vilna, Russia	1835–1918
Camille Saint-Saëns	Paris, France	1835–1921
John Farmer	Nottingham, England	1836–1901
Mily A. Balakirev	Nizhny-Novgorod, Russia	1837–1910
Alfred Robert Gaul	Norwich, England	1837–1913
Theodore Dubois	Rosnay, France	1837–1924
Georges Bizet	Paris, France	1838–1875
Modest P. Moussorgsky	Karevo, Russia	1839–1881
Peter Ilich Tchaikovsky	Kamsko-Votkinsk, Russia	1840–1893
John Stainer	London, England	1840–1901
Antonin Dvořák	Mühlhausen, Czechoslovakia	1841–1904
Arthur Sullivan	London, England	1842–1900
Edvard Grieg	Bergen, Norway	1843–1907
Herman Schroeder	Quedlinburg, Germany	1843–1909
Nikolai A. Rimsky-Korsakov	Tikhvin, Russia	1844–1908
Gabriel Urbain Fauré	Pamiers, France	1845–1924
Alexander Arkhangelsky	Penza, Russia	1846–1924
Gustav Schreck	Zeulenroda, Germany	1849–1918
Mikhail M. Ivanoff	Moscow, Russia	1849–1927
Vincent D'Indy	Paris, France	1851–1931
Hugo Jungst	Dresden, Germany	1853–1923
Alexander A. Kopylov	St. Petersburg, Russia	1854–1911
Engelbert Humperdinck	Siegburg, Germany	1854–1921
Leoš Janáček	Hukvaldy, Moravia	1854–1928
Stevan S. Mokranjac	Negotin, Yugoslavia	1855–1914
Sergei I. Taneyev	Vladimir, Russia	1856–1915
Alexander Kastalsky	Moscow, Russia	1856–1926

Edward Elgar	Broadheath, England	1857–1934
Reginald De Koven	Middletown, Connecticut	1859–1920
Mikhail M. Ippolitov-Ivanov	Gatchina, Russia	1859–1935
Hugo Wolf	Windischgraz, Austria	1860–1903
Gustav Mahler	Kalischt, Bohemia	1860–1911
Edward MacDowell	New York, New York	1861–1908
Horatio Parker	Auburndale, Massachusetts	1863–1919
Pietro Mascagni	Leghorn, Italy	1863–1945
Frederick F. Bullard	Boston, Massachusetts	1864–1904
Richard Strauss	Munich, Germany	1864–1949
Alexander T. Gretchaninov	Moscow, Russia	1864–1956
Jean Sibelius	Tavastehus, Finland	1865–1957
Vassili S. Kalinnikov	Voin, Russia	1866–1901
Enrique Granados	Lérida, Spain	1867–1916
Granville Banlock	London, England	1868–1946
Louis Vierne	Pointiers, France	1870–1937
Franz Lehar	Komorn, Hungary	1870–1948
Henry Hadley	Somerville, Massachusetts	1871–1937
F. Melius Christiansen	Eidsvold, Norway	1871–1955
Max Reger	Brand, Germany	1873–1916
Sergei V. Rachmaninoff	Oneg, Russia	1873–1943
Hugh S. Roberton	Glasgow, Scotland	1874–1952
Samuel Coleridge-Taylor	London, England	1875–1912
Nikolai D. Leonlovich	Monastirsh, Russia	1877–1921
Paul G. Tschesnokov	Vladimir, Russia	1877–1921

MODERN PERIOD (1890 TO PRESENT)

Claude Debussy	St. Germain-en-Laye, France	1862–1918
Frederick Delius	Bradlord, England	1862–1934
Erik Satie	Honfleur, France	1866–1925
Vladimir Ivanovitch Rebikov	Krasnoyarsk, Siberia	1866–1920
Henry Thacker Burleigh	Erie, Pennsylvania	1866–1949
F. Melius Christiansen	Eidsvold, Norway	1871–1955
Ralph Vaughan Williams	Down Ampney, England	1872–1958
Gustav Holst	Cheltenham, England	1874–1934
Arnold Schoenberg	Vienna, Austria	1874–1951
Paul Pierné	Metz, France	1874–1952
Charles Edward Ives	Danbury, Connecticut	1874–1954
Maurice Ravel	Ciboure, France	1875–1937
Martin Shaw	London, England	1875–1958
Pablo Casals	Vendrell, Catalonia	1876–1973
Ernest Bloch	Geneva, Switzerland	1880–1959
Healey Willan	Balham, England	1880–1968
Ferdinand Hiller	Frankfurt, Germany	1881–1885
Béla Barlók	Nagy Szent Miklós, Rumania	1881–1945
Robert Nathaniel Dett	Drummondville, Quebec, Canada	1882–1943
Zoltán Kodály	Kecskemet, Hungary	1882–1967
Igor Stravinsky	Oranienbaum, Russia	1882–1971
Anton Webern	Vienna, Austria	1883–1945
Alban Berg	Vienna, Austria	1885–1935
Deems Taylor	New York, New York	1885–1966
Marcel Dupré	Rouen, France	1886–1971

Konstantin N. Shvedov	Moscow, Russia	1886–?
Sigmund Romberg	Szeged, Hungary	1887–1951
Norris Lindsay Norden	Philadelphia, Pennsylvania	1887–1956
Heitor Villa-Lobos	Rio de Janerio, Brazil	1887–1959
Ernst Toch	Vienna, Austria	1887–1964
Hall Johnson	Athens, Georgia	1887–1970
Božidar Sirola	Zakanj, Yugoslavia	1889–1956
Joseph W. Clokey	New Albany, Indiana	1890–1960
Heinrich Lemacher	Solingen, Germany	1891–1966
Arthur Honegger	Le Havre, France	1892–1955
Darius Milhaud	Aix-en-Provence, France	1892–1974
Felix Labunski	Ksawerynów, Poland	1892–1979
John Jacob Niles	Louisville, Kentucky	1892–1980
Bernard Rogers	New York, New York	1893–1968
Peter Warlock (Philip Heseltine)	London, England	1894–1930
Walter Piston	Rockland, Maine	1894–1976
Paul Hindemith	Hanau, Germany	1895–1963
Albert Hay Malotte	Philadelphia, Pennsylvania	1895–1964
Malcolm Sargent	London, England	1895–1967
Leo Sowerby	Grand Rapids, Michigan	1895–1968
William Grant Still	Woodville, Mississippi	1895–1978
Carl Orff	Munich, Germany	1895–1982
Gordon Jacob	London, England	1895–1984
Richard Kountz	Pittsburgh, Pennsylvania	1896–1950
Howard Hanson	Wahoo, Nebraska	1896–1981
Virgil Thomson	Kansas City, Missouri	1896–1989
Henry Cowell	Menlo Park, California	1897–1965
Alexander Tansman	Lodz, Poland	1897–1986
George Gershwin	Brooklyn, New York	1898–1937
Roy Harris	Lincoln County, Oklahoma	1898–1979
William L. Dawson	Anniston, Alabama	1898–1990
Hugh Ross	Langport, England	1898–1990
Francis Poulenc	Paris, France	1899–1963
Carlos Chávez	Mexico City, Mexico	1899–1978
Alexander Tcherepnin	St. Petersburg, Russia	1899–1977
Randall Thompson	New York, New York	1899–1984
George Antheil	Trenton, New Jersey	1900–1959
Aaron Copland	Brooklyn, New York	1900–1990
Ernst Krenek	Vienna, Austria	1900–1991
Edmund Rubbra	Northamptom, England	1901–1986
Jester Hairston	North Carolina	1901–
Nikolai Rimsky-Korsakov	Tikhvin (near Novgorod), Russia	1844–1908
Otto Luening	Milwaukee, Wisconsin	1900–
Gerald Finzi	London, England	1901–1956
Harry Robert Wilson	Salina, Kansas	1901–1968
Olaf C. Christiansen	Minneapolis, Minnesota	1901–1984
William Walton	Oldham, England	1902–1983
Maurice Duruflé	Louviers, France	1902–1986
Jenö Takács	Siegendorf, Austria	1902–
Luigi Dallapiccola	Pisino, Italy	1904–1975
Undine Smith Moore	Jarrett, Virginia	1905–
Paul Creston	New York, New York	1906–1985
Dmitri Shostakovitch	St. Petersburg, Russia	1906–1975
Normand Lockwood	New York, New York	1906–
Henk Badings	Bandoeng, Java	1907–1987

Miklos Rozsa	Budapest, Hungary	1907–
Hugo Distler	Nuremberg, Germany	1908–1942
Elliot Carter	New York, New York	1908–
Olivier Messiaen	Avignon, France	1908–1992
Halsey Stevens	Scott, New York	1908–1989
Jean Berger	Hamm, Germany	1909–
Samuel Barber	West Chester, Pennsylvania	1910–1981
Julius Chajes	Lwow, Poland	1910–1985
William Howard Schuman	New York, New York	1910–1992
Franz Reizenstein	Nuremberg, Germany	1911–1968
Alan Hovhaness	Somerville, Massachusetts	1911–
Gian Carlo Menotti	Cadegliano, Italy	1911–
Benjamin Britten	Lowestoft, England	1913–1976
Norman Dello Joio	New York, New York	1913–
Morton Gould	New York, New York	1913–
Jan Meyerowitz	Breslau, Germany	1913–
Gardner Read	Evanston, Illinois	1913–
Leland B. Sateren	Everett, Washington	1913–
Irving Fine	Boston, Massachusetts	1914–1962
Gail Kubik	South Coffeyville, Oklahoma	1914–1984
Cecil Effinger	Colorado Springs, Colorado	1914–1990
David Diamond	Rochester, New York	1915–
Knut Nystedt	Oslo, Norway	1915–
Vincent Persichetti	Philadelphia, Pennsylvania	1915–1987
Houston Bright	Midland, Texas	1916–1970
Alberto Ginastera	Buenos Aires, Argentina	1916–1983
Gordon Binkerd	Lynch, Nebraska	1916–
Scott Huston	Tacoma, Washington	1916–1991
Ulysses S. Kay	Tucson, Arizona	1917–
Norman Luboff	Chicago, Illinois	1917–1987
Leonard Bernstein	Lawrence, Massachusetts	1918–1990
Vaclav Nalhybel	Czechoslovakia	1919–
Dave Brubeck	Concord, California	1920–
Paul Fetler	Philadelphia, Pennsylvania	1920–
Edwin Fissinger	Chicago, Illinois	1920–1990
William Bergsma	Oakland, California	1921–
Lloyd Pfautsch	Washington, Missouri	1921–
Ariel Ramirez	Santa Fe, Argentina	1921–
Lukas Foss	Berlin, Germany	1922–
George Walker	Washington, D.C.	1922–
Anton Heiller	Vienna, Austria	1923–1979
Peter Mennin	Erie, Pennsylvania	1923–1983
Daniel Pinkham	Lynn, Massachusetts	1923–
Ned Rorem	Richmond, Indiana	1923–
Kirke Mechem	Wichita, Kansas	1925–
Gunther Schuller	New York, New York	1925–
Friedrich Cerha	Vienna, Austria	1926–
Carlisle Floyd	Latta, South Carolina	1926–
Arnold Freed	New York, New York	1926–
Frank Pooler	La Crosse, Wisconsin	1926–
Dominick Argento	York, Pennsylvania	1927–
Emma Lou Diemer	Kansas City, Missouri	1927–
Donald Erb	Youngstown, Ohio	1927–
Samuel H. Adler	Mannheim, Germany	1928–
Lena J. McLin	Atlanta, Georgia	1928–

Karlheinz Stockhausen	Mödrath (near Cologne), Germany	1928–
Ron Nelson	Joliet, Illinois	1929–
Richard Felciano	Santa Rosa, California	1930–
Gilbert Trythall	Knoxville, Tennessee	1930–
Wendell P. Whalum	Memphis, Tennessee	1931–
Krzysztof Penderecki	Debiça, Poland	1933–
Nicolas Roussakis	Athens, Greece	1934–
Eugene Butler	Durant, Oklahoma	1935–
David Eddleman	Winston-Salem, North Carolina	1936–
Michael Hennigan	The Dalles, Oregon	1936–
Dede Dusan	El Campo, Texas	1938–
James E. McCray	Kankakee, Illinois	1938–
Brent Pierce	Odgen, Utah	1940–
John Rutter	London, England	1945–
Henry Mollicone	Providence, Rhode Island	1946–
Libby Larsen	Wilmington, Delaware	1950–
Z. Randall Stroope	Albuquerque, New Mexico	1953–
Steven Curtis Lance	Santa Ana, California	1954–

APPENDIX B

Choral Octavo Publications

The following list of choral music for mixed voices is arranged alphabetically by composer. Each work has been carefully perused and selected by the author as appropriate for use with school, church, community, and college/university choruses. After each title, an arranger or an editor's name (if any) is given, followed by the publisher, catalog number, whether the music is to be performed *a cappella* or accompanied, and the degree of performance difficulty.

ADLER, SAMUEL H.
   Autumn Rain. Associated No. A-263. *A cappella.* Medium.
   Strings in the Earth. Associated No. A-264. *A cappella.* Medium.

ALBERTI, DOMENICO
   O Jesu, Salvator. ed. Boyd. Lawson-Gould No. 51843. Accompanied. Medium.

ALBRECHTSBERGER, JOHANN GEORG
   De profundis. ed. Martin Banner. Carl Fischer No. CM 8316. Accompanied. Moderately difficult.

ALCOCK, JOHN
   Voix Célestes (humming chorus). Chappell No. 2055. *A cappella.* Medium.

ALTNIKOL, JOHANN CHRISTOPH
   To Him Who Never Faileth. ed. Frank. Sam Fox No. MM 3. Accompanied. Moderately easy.

AMRAM, DAVID
   Rejoice in the Lord. C. F. Peters No. 66517. *A cappella.* Medium.

ANDERSON, LEROY
   Sleigh Ride. arr. Hawley Ades. Shawnee Press No. A-669. Piano and sleigh bells. Moderately easy.

ANERIO, FELICE
   Alleluia! Christus surrexit. ed. Percy M. Young. Broude Brothers No. MGC 43. *A cappella.* Moderately difficult.

ANTES, JOHN
   Our Soul Doth Wait Upon the Lord. arr. Kroeger. Boosey & Hawkes No. 5941. Organ accompaniment. Medium.

190

ARGENTO, DOMINICK
Party of Lovers at Tea, A. Boosey & Hawkes No. 5712. *A cappella.* Medium.

ARKHANGELSKY, ALEXANDER
Incline Thine Ear, Oh Lord. Witmark No. 5-W2689. *A cappella.* Medium.
Lend Thine Ear to My Prayer. arr. Wilhousky. Carl Fischer No. CM 613. *A cappella.*
Moderately difficult.
We Have No Other Help. arr. Gnotov. Witmark No. 5-W3005. *A cappella.* Moderately
easy.

ATTWOOD, THOMAS
O Lord, We Beseech Thee. ed. Percy M. Young. Broude Bros. No. MGC 44. Organ
accompaniment. Medium.

BACH, JOHANN SEBASTIAN
All Breathing Life (from the motet *Sing Ye to the Lord*). G. Schirmer No. 7470. Optional
accompaniment. Difficult.
Alleluja. C. F. Peters No. 6106a. Accompanied. Medium.
Ave Maria. Arr. Tolmadge. Staff No. 243. Accompanied. Easy.
Break Forth, O Beauteous Heavenly Light. Oliver Ditson No. 13744. Accompanied. Easy.
Break Forth, O Beauteous Heavenly Light. G. Schirmer. SATB—for chorus and orchestra
(orchestra parts available from publisher on rental only).
Chorale: King of Glory. Staff. SATB—for chorus and band; chorus and orchestra; chorus,
band, and orchestra.
Come, Blessed Rest. Kjos No. 2004. *A cappella.* Medium.
Come Thou, O Savior. Summy-Birchard No. 5203. *A cappella.* Moderately easy.
Crucifixus (from Mass in B minor). Hope Publishing Co. No. CY 3356; E. C. Schirmer
No. 1174. Accompanied. Medium.
Das neugeborne Kindelein (The Newborn Child). National Music Publishers No. NMP-
175. Piano or organ accompaniment. Medium.
Four Chorales from the *Saint Matthew Passion.* ed. Walter Ehret. Lawson-Gould No. 686. A
cappella. Moderately easy.
Gloria (from Mass No. 3 in G minor). Gentry No. JG2021. Accompanied. Medium.
Glory and Honor Are Before Him. Kjos No. 5150. *A cappella.* Medium.
Glory to God. ed. Harry R. Wilson. Ricordi No. NY1397. Optional accompaniment.
Moderately difficult.
Honor and Glory. Plymouth No. SC10. Accompanied. Moderately easy.
In Thee Is Joy. Somerset Press No. MW 1229. Accompanied. Moderately easy.
Jesu, Joy of Man's Desiring. E. C. Schirmer No. 317. Organ accompaniment. Moderately
easy.
My Savior Dear, What Woe of Soul. arr. Lundquist. Willis No. 5503. *A cappella.* Medium.
O Rejoice, Ye Christians, Loudly. Carl Fischer No. CM 6600. *A cappella.* Moderately easy.
Praise Him. arr. Steele. Raymond A. Hoffman No. 11-2005. Accompanied. Moderately
easy.
Sanctus (from B Minor Mass). G. Schirmer No. 5654. Accompanied. Difficult.
Sheep May Safely Graze (from *Was mir behagt*). arr. Julia Morgan. Beckenhorst No. BP
1369. Accompanied (piano and two flutes). Moderately easy.
Sheep May Safely Graze. arr. James Winfield. Somerset No. MW 1244. Accompanied
(organ and two flutes). Moderately easy.
Sicut locutus est (Sing Joyful Songs to God). ed. Gerald R. Mack and Martha Banzhaf.
Optional accompaniment. Medium.
Song of Repentance. Broude Bros. No. 65. *A cappella.* Medium.
Von Himmel hoch (From Highest Heav'n). Lawson-Gould No. 903. *A cappella.* Medium.
We Pledge You Forever (from Cantata No. 208). ed. Malin. Belwin Mills No. 2406.
Accompanied. Moderately difficult.

Ye Are Not of the Flesh (from the motet *Jesu meine Freude*). Lawson-Gould No. 785. Accompanied. Difficult.

BACH, CARL PHILLIP EMANUEL

Humility before Thee. arr. Walter Ehret. Elkan-Vogel No. 1268. Piano or organ accompaniment. Medium.

With Sorrow Shaken. Elkan-Vogel No. 362-01303. Piano or organ accompaniment. Alto solo. Moderately easy.

BARBER, SAMUEL

Anthony O Daly. G. Schirmer No. 8909. A *cappella*. Medium.

Coolin, The. G. Schirmer No. 8910. A *cappella*. Moderately difficult.

Sure on This Shining Night. G. Schirmer No. 10864. Accompanied. Moderately easy.

Under the Willow Tree (from *Vanessa*). G. Schirmer No. 10861. Accompanied. Soprano solo. Moderately difficult.

BASSETT, LESLIE

Collect. World Library Publications No. CA2000-8. SATB, electronic tape.

BEETHOVEN, LUDWIG VAN

Dona nobis pacem. National Music Publishers No. WHS-143. A *cappella*. Medium.

Hallelujah (from *Mount of Olives*). G. Schirmer No. 2215. Accompanied. Difficult.

Heavens Are Declaring, The. G. Schirmer No. 3032. Accompanied. Easy.

Kyrie (from *Mass in C Major*). ed. K. Lee Scott. Carl Fischer No. CM 8213. Accompanied. Medium.

Lord, Have Mercy Upon Us (Kyrie Eleison) from Mass in C. ed. John Kingsbury. Plymouth No. PCS-175. Accompanied. Medium.

My Peace I Leave With You. arr. Lon Beery. Beckenhorst No. BP 1329. Accompanied. Easy.

O Swiftly Glides the Bonny Boat. National Music Publishers No. CMS-126. Violin, cello, and piano accompaniment. Moderately easy.

Sanctus (from C Major Mass). Walton No. 6014. Accompanied. Medium.

BERGER, JEAN

If I Flew to the Point of Sunrise. Kjos No. ED 5992. A *cappella*. Medium.

It Is Good to Be Merry. Kjos No. 5293. A *cappella*. Medium.

Twilight. John Sheppard No. 2011. A *cappella*. Moderately easy.

BERLIN, IRVING

Alexander's Ragtime Band. arr. Simeone. Shawnee Press No. 0638. Piano accompaniment. Moderately easy.

Blue Skies. arr. Roger Emerson. Jenson No. 403-02094. Piano and optional rhythm section. Medium.

Give Me Your Tired, Your Poor (patriotic or commencement). arr. Roy Ringwald. Shawnee Press No. A 0119. Accompanied. Medium.

There's No Business Like Show Business. arr. Hawley Ades. Shawnee Press No. A-0637. Piano accompaniment. Medium.

BERLIOZ, HECTOR

Glory and Triumph. Mercury. SATB, for chorus and band; chorus and orchestra.

Religious Meditation. ed. Prussing. Tetra No. AB 833. Organ accompaniment. Medium.

Thou Must Leave Thy Lowly Dwelling (from *Childhood of Christ*). Gray No. 1898. Accompanied. Medium.

BERNSTEIN, LEONARD

Almighty Father (Chorale from *Mass*). G. Schirmer No. 11948. A *cappella*. Moderately easy.

Life Is Happiness Indeed (from *Candide*). arr. Robert Page. G. Schirmer No. 12024. Accompanied. Medium.

One Hand, One Heart (from *West Side Story*). arr. William Stickles. G. Schirmer No. 10606. Accompanied. Easy.

This World (from *Candide*). arr. Robert Page. G. Schirmer No. 12027. Accompanied. Medium.

West Side Story *(Choral Selections)*. arr. William Stickles. G. Schirmer No. 10703. Accompanied. Medium.

BILLINGS, WILLIAM

David's Lamentation. C. F. Peters No. 66336. Optional accompaniment. Moderately easy.

Modern Music. C. F. Peters No. 66340. *A cappella*. Medium.

BORTNIANSKY, DIMITRI S.

Cherubim Song No. 7. arr. Peter I. Tchaikovsky. G. Schirmer No. 2560. *A cappella*. Easy.

Glory to God. Witmark No. 5-W2743. *A cappella*. Moderately easy.

This Is the Day Which the Lord Hath Made. Bourne No. BL3041. *A cappella*. Medium.

BRAHMS, JOHANNES

Angelic Greeting, The. ed. Mattfeld. E. C. Schirmer No. 2477. *A cappella*. Medium.

As Long As Beauty Shall Remain. arr. Van Christy. Schmitt, Hall & McCreary No. 1172. *A cappella*. Easy.

Ave Maria. C. F. Peters No. 66136. Accompanied. Medium.

Call to Mary. ed. Mattfeld. E. C. Schirmer No. 2480. *A cappella*. Medium.

Create in Me, O God, a Pure Heart. ed. John Finley Williamson. G. Schirmer No. 7504. *A cappella*. Moderately easy.

Der Gang zum Liebchen (Journey to My Love). National Music Publishers No. WHC-132. Accompanied. Medium.

Falcon, The. ed. Terry Eder. Greystone Press No. GRP-1001. *A cappella*. Medium.

Farewell, The (Horch, der Wind klagt in den Zweigen). Sam Fox No. RC 2. Accompanied. Moderately easy.

Grant unto Me the Joy of Thy Salvation. G. Schirmer No. 7506. *A cappella*. Moderately difficult.

How Lovely Is Thy Dwelling Place. G. Schirmer No. 5124. Accompanied. Moderately difficult.

Hunter, The. E. C. Schirmer No. 1680. *A cappella*. Moderately easy.

Hymn of Freedom. arr. Tolmadge. Staff. SATB—for chorus and band.

If All My Heartfelt Thinking. Associated No. A-407. *A cappella*. Medium.

In Silent Night. G. Schirmer No. 5848. *A cappella*. Easy.

Let Nothing Ever Grieve Thee. C. F. Peters No. 6093. Accompanied. Moderately easy.

Lo, How a Rose E'er Blooming (Rhineland folk melody). arr. Arthur Frackenpohl. Mark Foster No. MF 563. Accompanied. Moderately easy.

Lost Youth (Verlorene Jugend). Presser No. 312-40946. *A cappella*. Medium.

Love Song. arr. Harry R. Wilson. Ricordi No. NY1475. Optional accompaniment. Moderately easy.

Magdalena. G. Schirmer No. 9953. *A cappella*. Medium.

O Cast Me Not Away from Thy Countenance. G. Schirmer No. 7505. *A cappella*. Moderately difficult.

O Lovely May (O Süsser Mai). Belwin Mills No. 2174. *A cappella*. Moderately easy.

On the Way to My Sweetheart. arr. Matesky. Gentry No. G-4007. Accompanied. Moderately easy.

O Savior, Throw the Heavens Wide (Motet, Op. 74, No. 2). G. Schirmer No. 8545. *A cappella*. Moderately difficult.

Sigh Goes Stirring Through the Wood, A. Associated No. A-379. *A cappella*. Medium.

Six Love Songs. Summy-Birchard. Four-hand accompaniment. Moderately difficult.

Thought like Music, A. arr. Suchoff. Plymouth No. A. S. 103. Accompanied. Moderately easy.

Trysting Place, The (Der Gang zum Liebchen). E. C. Schirmer No. 391. Accompanied. Medium.

Wie Melodien zieht es mir. arr. Gregory Vancil. Southern Music No. SC 223. Moderately easy.

BRIGHT, HOUSTON
Fall, Leaves, Fall. Shawnee Press No. A-945. A cappella. Medium.
Hodie nobis coelorum Rex. Shawnee Press No. A-812. Accompanied. Medium.
Sing a Song of Sixpence. Shawnee Press No. A-851. A cappella. Medium.
Sunrise Alleluia. Shawnee Press No. A-852. Accompanied. Moderately easy.

BRITTEN, BENJAMIN
As Dew in Aprille (from A Ceremony of Carols). arr. Julius Harrison. Boosey & Hawkes No. 1829. Accompanied. Medium.
Ballad of Green Broom. Boosey & Hawkes No. 1875. A cappella. Moderately difficult.
Boy Was Born, A. Oxford No. X92. A cappella. Medium.
Hymn to Saint Peter. Boosey & Hawkes. Organ accompaniment. Soprano solo. Moderately difficult.
Old Abram Brown. Boosey & Hawkes No. 1786. Accompanied. Easy.
Old Joe Has Gone Fishing (from Peter Grimes). Boosey & Hawkes No. 1784. Accompanied. Moderately difficult.
This Little Babe (from A Ceremony of Carols). arr. Julius Harrison. Boosey & Hawkes No. 1830. Harp or piano accompaniment. Moderately easy.
Whoso Dwelleth Under the Defence of the Most High (from The Company of Heaven). Farber Music No. 50481206. A cappella. Difficult.

BRUCKNER, ANTON
Ave Maria. Edw. B. Marks No. 47. A cappella. Moderately easy.
Christus factus est pro nobis. C. F. Peters No. 6316. A cappella. Moderately difficult.
Locus iste a Deo factus est. C. F. Peters No. 6314. A cappella. Easy.
Music the Comforter (Trösterin Musik). Sam Fox No. MM 12. Accompanied. Moderately easy.
Os justi. G. Schirmer No. 8121. A cappella. Medium.

BUXTEHUDE, DIETRICH
Alleluia, Alleluia. Presser No. 312-40668. Accompanied. Medium.
Every Thing You Do. Sam Fox No. CM 19. Accompanied. Medium.
Magnifican—My Soul Doth Magnify the Lord. C. F. Peters No. 66288. Accompanied. Moderately difficult.
O Lord, Have Mercy on Us (Kyrie eleison). Sam Fox No. CM 6. Optional accompaniment. Medium.

BYRD, WILLIAM
Ave verum corpus. Bourne No. ES44. A cappella. Moderately easy.
Haec dies. Oxford No. TCM 50. Optional accompaniment. Moderately difficult.
Iustorum animae. E. C. Schirmer No. 327. A cappella. Medium.
Ne irascaris. Alexander Broude No. 216-9. A cappella. Moderately difficult.
O God Who Reigns in Heav'n Above. arr. Walter Ehret. Gentry No. JG-439. Optional accompaniment. Moderately easy.
When the Bright Sun. Belwin Mills No. A-202. A cappella. Moderately easy.

CALDARA, ANTONIO
Praise Him, Praise Ye the Lord. ed. Walter Ehret. Elkan-Vogel No. 362-03145. Piano or organ accompaniment. Soprano, alto, tenor, and bass solos. Moderately easy.
Sanctum Domini Dei nomen est (Lord, God, We Praise Thy Holy Name). E. C. Schirmer No. 3076. Optional Organ accompaniment. Moderately difficult.
Serve the Lord With Gladness. ed. Benjamin Suchoff. Plymouth No. SC-120. Accompanied. Easy.
Si consistant adversum me (Lord, from Thee Comes Our Strength). E. C. Schirmer No. 3075. Optional organ accompaniment. Moderately difficult.

CALVISIUS, SETHUS
Joseph Dear, Oh Joseph Mild. Associated No. A-396. A cappella. Medium.

CAMPRA, ANDRÉ
In omnem terram (In Every Land). arr. Castle. Wood No. 44-964. Organ or piano accompaniment. Moderately difficult.

CARISSIMI, GIACOMO
Plorate filii Israel (from *Jeptah*). Bourne No. ES 34; Kjos No. ED 29; E. C. Schirmer No. 1172. Accompanied. Medium.

CARMICHAEL, HOAGY
Georgia on My Mind. arr. Kirby Shaw. Hal Leonard No. 08657630. Piano, with optional guitar, bass and drums. Moderately easy.
Georgia on My Mind. arr. Gene Puerling. Studio P/R No. VGP 8001. Piano, bass, and drums. Moderately difficult.
Stardust. arr. Roy Ringwald. Shawnee Press No. A-0689. Piano accompaniment. Medium.
Stardust. arr. Chuck Cassey. CPP/Belwin No. 64414. A *cappella*. Medium.

CARTER, ELLIOT
To Music. Peer International. A *cappella*. Moderately difficult.

CASALS, PABLO
O vos omnes (O Ye People). Tetra/Continuo No. TC 1103. A *cappella*. Moderately easy.

CHAJES, JULIUS
Song of Galilee (El Yivnch Hagalil). Transcontinental No. TCL 214. Accompanied. Medium.

CHAVEZ, CARLOS
Three Nocturnes. G. Schirmer No. 9522. A *cappella*. Moderately difficult.
Tree of Sorrow. Mercury No. MP-113. A *cappella*. Difficult.
Woman Is a Worthy Thing, A. G. Schirmer No. 9611. A *cappella*. Medium.

CHERUBINI, LUIGI
Jesus, Now to Thee I Turn Me. arr. Lundquist. Elkan-Vogel No. 1159. A *cappella*. Easy.
Lacrymosa. ed. De Pietto. Lawson-Gould No. 51853. Accompanied. Medium.
Veni Jesu. arr. Riegger. Flammer No. 84189. Accompanied. Medium.

CHRISTIANSEN, F. MELIUS
Beautiful Savior (Silesian folk tune). C. Augsburg No. 51. A *cappella*. Medium.
From Grief to Glory (Verse II—Love in Grief). Augsburg No. 175. A *cappella*. Difficult.
Hosanna (Palm Sunday). Augsburg No. 57. A *cappella*. Difficult.
Lamb of God (Chorale 1540). C. Augsburg No. 133. A *cappella*. Easy.
Lost in the Night (Finnish folk melody). C. Augsburg No. 119. A *cappella*. Soprano solo. Moderately difficult.

COLERIDGE-TAYLOR, SAMUEL
Lift Up Your Heads. ed. William Tortolano. Broude Bros. No. CR 61. Organ accompaniment. Medium.

COPLAND, AARON
Las Agachadas. Boosey & Hawkes. A *cappella*. For solo group and eight-part chorus. Moderately difficult.
Promise of Living, The (from *The Tender Land*). Boosey & Hawkes No. 5020. Piano duet accompaniment. Moderately difficult.
Stomp Your Foot (from *The Tender Land*). Boosey & Hawkes No. 5019. Piano duet accompaniment. Moderately difficult.
Younger Generation. arr. Swift. Boosey & Hawkes No. 1723. Accompanied. Moderately easy.

CORNELIUS, PETER
Lord of Love, to Thee I Flee. Sam Fox No. MM 26. Accompanied. Medium.

CORREA DE ARAUJO, FRANCISCO
O vos omnes. Lawson-Gould No. 52225. A *cappella*. Easy.

CORSI, JACOPO
Adoramus Te. arr. Norman Greyson. Bourne No. ES15. *A cappella.* Moderately easy.

COSTANTINI, ALESSANDRO
Praise the Lord in Song. arr. Elwood Coggin. Music 70 No. M70-341. *A cappella.*
Moderately easy.

COURTNEY, CRAIG
Thine, O Lord. Beckenhorst No. BP 1276. Accompanied. Moderately easy.

CRESTON, PAUL
Here Is Thy Footstool. G. Schirmer No. 11146. *A cappella.* Medium.

CRUGER, JOHANN
Now Thank We All Our God (Thanksgiving). arr. Gustav Holst. Kjos No. 5138.
Accompanied. Moderately easy.

CUNDICK, ROBERT
An American Tribute. TRO No. S7067. Accompanied. Moderately easy.

DAWSON, WILLIAM L.
Mary Had a Baby. Kjos No. T118. *A cappella.* Soprano solo. Medium.

DE KOVEN, HENRY LOUIS REGINALD
Recessional (Memorial Day). Presser No. 322-35015. Accompanied. Moderately easy.

DELLO JOIO, NORMAN
Fable, A. Carl Fischer No. CM 6299. Accompanied. Moderately easy.
O Star That Makes the Stable Bright (from *Nativity*). Associated No. 50488442.
Accompanied. Medium.

DE MONTE, PHILIPPE
Once I Had Hoped from Thee. Piedmont No. 4427. *A cappella.* Medium.

DES PRÉZ, JOSQUIN
Ave Christe, immolate. Editions Salabert No. MC 531. *A cappella.* Medium.
Ave Maria, gratia plena. Associated No. 28. *A cappella.* Medium.
Ave Maris Stella. Associated No. 35. *A cappella.* Medium.
Nune dimittis. ed. James Erb. Lawson-Gould No. 52251. *A cappella.* Medium.
Tu solus qui facis mirabilia. Mercury No. 352-00045. *A cappella.* Medium.

DIAMOND, DAVID
Warning. Elkan-Vogel No. 362-03143. Accompaniment. Moderately difficult.

DIEMER, EMMA LOU
I Myself When Young Did Eagerly Frequent. Boosey & Hawkes No. 5778. *A cappella.*
Medium.

DONATO, BALDASSARI
Three Italian Partsongs (*Viva Sempre* by Donato; *Basciami, Vita Mia* by Hassler; *Chi La
Gagliarda* by Donato). ed. Victoria Glaser. E. C. Schirmer No. 3042. *A cappella.*
Medium.

DURANTE, FRANCESCO
Kyrie eleison. Pro Art No. 2279. *A cappella.* Moderately easy.

DVOŘÁK, ANTONIN
Largo from *New World Symphony* (choral parts: "Behold Our God"). Belwin Mills. SATB,
for chorus and band.
Songs Filled My Heart. Presser No. 312-40813. Accompanied. Moderately easy.
Up Sprang a Birch Tree Overnight. Mercury No. 312-40816. *A cappella.* Medium.
When Evening Comes Chimes Fill the Forest. Mercury No. 312-40814. Accompanied.
Medium.

EDDLEMAN, DAVID
Clap Your Hands. Carl Fischer No. CM 8039. Optional percussion. Moderately easy.

ELGAR, EDWARD
As Torrents in Summer. arr. Noble Cain. Flammer No. 81068. *A cappella.* Moderately easy.
My Love Dwelt in a Northern Land. G. Schirmer No. 2366. *A cappella.* Moderately easy.

ELLINGTON, DUKE
Come Sunday (from *Black, Brown and Beige*). arr. Alice Parker. G Schirmer No. 50481495. Alto solo. Accompanied. Medium.
It Don't Mean A Thing (If It Ain't Got That Swing). arr. Paris Rutherford. CPP/Belwin No. 64402. Accompanied. Medium.
Mood Indigo. arr. Harry Simeone. Shawnee Press No. A-0800. Piano and optional guitar, string bass, and drums. Medium.
Mood Indigo. arr. Paris Rutherford. CPP/Belwin No. 64395. Piano, guitar, percussion and bass. Moderately easy.
Solitude. arr. Paris Rutherford. CPP/Belwin No. 64401. Piano, and optional guitar, bass and drums. Medium.

EMMETT, DANIEL
Dixie. arr. Norman Luboff. Walton No. 3004. *A cappella.* Medium.

ERB, DONALD
God Love You Now. Merion No. 342-40099. SATB, speaker, assorted instruments, reverberation device.
Kyrie. Merion No. 342-40026. SATB, piano, percussion, electronic tape.

ELGAR, EDWARD
Hail, Glorious Day. arr. Schaefer. Boosey & Hawkes. SATB, for chorus and band.
Land of Hope and Glory (commencement). Boosey & Hawkes No. 1161. Accompanied. Moderately easy.
Pomp and Circumstance. Staff. SATB, for chorus and band; chorus and orchestra; chorus, band, and orchestra.

FARRANT, RICHARD
Call to Remembrance. arr. Norman Greyson. Bourne No. ES 17. *A cappella.* Moderately easy.

FAURÉ, GABRIEL
Cantique de Jean Racine. Broude Bros. No. 801. Accompanied. Moderately easy.
Cantique de Jean Racine. ed. James Laughlin. Tetra/Continuo No TC 882. Accompanied. Medium.
Comfort All Ye My People. arr. Hal H. Hopson. Carl Fischer No. CM 8017. Piano or organ accompaniment. Moderately easy.
Libera me. Belwin Mills No. 2032. Accompanied. Medium.
Palms, The (Palm Sunday). arr. Howorth. Belwin Mills No. 790. Accompanied. Medium.
Sanctus (from *Requiem*). Fitzsimons No. 2119. Accompanied. Easy.

FELCIANO, RICHARD
Hymn of the Universe. E. C. Schirmer No. 2944. SAB and electronic sounds.
Out of Sight. E. C. Schirmer No. 2909. SATB, organ, and electronic tape.
Pentecost Sunday. World Library Publications No. EMP-1532-1. Unison male chorus, organ, electronic tape.
Pshelley's Psalm. E. C. Schirmer No. 2930. SATB.
Sic transit. E. C. Schirmer No. 2903. SAB chorus, organ, electronic tape, light sources.
Signs. E. C. Schirmer No. 2927. SATB, electronic tape and one, two, or three film strip projectors.
Susani. E. C. Schirmer No. 3002. Mixed voices, organ, percussion, and electronic tape.
Three-in-One-in-Three. E. C. Schirmer No. 2910. Chorus, organ, tape.
Two Public Pieces. E. C. Schirmer No. 2937. Unison voices and electronic sounds.
Words of St. Peter. World Library Publications No. CA-2093-8. Mixed voices, organ, and electronic tape.

FILZER, ALBERT VON
Take Me Out To the Ball Game. arr. Donald Moore. Mark Foster No. MF 3033. Accompanied. Easy.

FINZI, GERALD
All This Night. Boosey & Hawkes No. 5127. A cappella. Medium.

FISSINGER, EDWIN
No Man Is an Island. Walton No. WW1141. A cappella. Moderately difficult.

FORD, THOMAS
Almighty God, Who Hast Me Brought. C. F. Peters No. 1558. A cappella. Moderately easy.

FOSTER, STEPHEN
My Old Kentucky Home. arr. Donald P. Moore. Mark Foster No. MF 3028. A cappella. Moderately easy.

FRANCK, CESAR
Ave Maria. arr. Borucchia. McLaughlin & Reilly No. 1072. Organ accompaniment. Moderately easy.
Let Every Nation His Praises Sing. Sam Fox No. CM 20. A cappella. Medium.
O Lord Most Holy (Panis angelicus). Summy-Birchard No. 396. Accompanied. Medium.
Psalm CL (Praise Ye the Lord). Oliver Ditson No. 332-14082. Organ accompaniment. Medium.

FRANZ, ROBERT
Dedication. arr. Rieger. Flammer No. 81043. A cappella. Medium.

FREED, ARNOLD
Dance Alleluia. Hansen Publications No. C566. Accompanied (piano, string bass, bongos, and wood block). Moderately easy.

GABRIELI, GIOVANNI
Angelus ad pastores ait. C. F. Peters No. 5930. Two choirs, 12 parts. Optional accompaniment. Difficult.
Benedixisti (Thou Hast Been Gracious, Lord). G. Schirmer No. 7625. A cappella. Medium.
Magnificat. Curwen No. 10565. A cappella. Three choirs. Difficult.

GASPARINI, FRANCESCO
Adoramus Te. Belwin Mills No. 2148. A cappella. Medium.

GASTOLDI, GIOVANNI
Come, Let Your Hearts Be Singing. arr. Norman Greyson. Bourne No. ES 26. A cappella. Moderately easy.
In You Is Gladness (In Dir ist Freude). ed. Edward W. Klammer. G.I.A. No. G-3526. A cappella. Moderately easy.
Look Upon Me, My Beloved. ed. Francis J. Guentner. CPP/Belwin No. SV8719. A cappella. Medium.
Six Balletti. C. F. Peters, Set I, No. 6877a. A cappella. Moderately easy. Set II, No. 6877b. A cappella. Medium.

GERSHWIN, GEORGE
Embraceable You. arr. Steve Zegree. Warner Bros. No. 43509052. A cappella. Moderately easy.
Fascinating Rhythm (from A Gershwin Portrait). arr. Mac Huff. Warner Bros. No. 08721792. Piano with optional instrumental accompaniment. Moderately easy.
Gershwin in Love (from A Gershwin Portrait). arr. Mac Huff. Warner Bros. No. 08721785. Piano, with optional instrumental accompaniment. Medium.
A Gershwin Portrait. arr. Mac Huff. Warner Bros. No. 08721797. A medley of thirty arrangements organized into six categories: I. Opening, II. Gershwin At The Opera, III. A Gershwin Swing Set, IV. Fascinating Rhythm, V. Gershwin In Love, VI. Sing A Gershwin Show Stopper. Piano, with optional instrumental accompaniment including

Trumpets I & II, Tenor Sax/Flute/Clarinet, Trombone, Synthesizer, Guitar, Bass, and Drums. Medium.

Let's Call the Whole Thing Off. arr. Anita Kerr. Hal Leonard No. 08565696. Piano, guitar, bass and drums. Moderately easy.

Love Walked In. arr. Steve Zegree. Hal Leonard No. 08704361. *A cappella.* Moderately easy.

Rhapsody in Blue (choral finale). arr. Clay Warnick. Harms, Inc. SSATTBB, for chorus and band; chorus and orchestra.

Sing of Spring. Lawson-Gould No. 51964. Accompanied. Medium.

Summertime. arr. Kirby Shaw. Hal Leonard No. 08664217. Piano, electric bass, and drums. Medium.

GESUALDO, DON CARLO
Madrigal. Edw. B. Marks No. 52. *A cappella.* Medium.

GEVAERT, FRANÇOIS AUGUSTE
Slumber Song of the Infant Jesus. E. C. Schirmer No. 1163. *A cappella.* Easy.

GIBBONS, ORLANDO
Almighty and Everlasting God. Bourne No. ES35. *A cappella.* Moderately easy.
Almighty and Everlasting God. ed. James McKelvy. Mark Foster No. MF 2032. *A cappella.* Moderately easy.
This Is the Record of John. ed. Parker and Shaw. Lawson-Gould No. 550. Organ accompaniment. Tenor solo. Medium.

GILBERT, W. S. AND SULLIVAN, SIR ARTHUR
Gondoliers, The (Finale). E. C. Schirmer No. 356. Four-hand piano accompaniment. Medium.

GLINKA, MIKHAIL
Cherubim Song. Music 70 No. M70-423. *A cappella.* Moderately easy.

GOLDMAN, MAURICE
O Mighty Hand (Dot Nifia). Transcontinental No. 991033. Organ or piano accompaniment. Moderately easy.

GORCZYCKI, GRZEGORZ G.
In Virtute Tua. ed. William Bausano. Mark Foster No. MF 2008. Organ and two violins. Moderately difficult.

GOULD, MORTON
Walkin' On Air (from *Quotations*). G. Schirmer No. 12535. For double chorus and wind orchestra. Moderately difficult.

GOUNOD, CHARLES FRANÇOIS
Hosanna in excelsis Deo. Gentry No. G-136. Accompanied. Medium.
Je serais enchanté (I Would Be Overjoyed). Alexander Broude No. 252-3. Accompanied. Moderately easy.
Lovely Appear (from *The Redemption*). G. Schirmer No. 2013. Accompanied. Medium.
O Divine Redeemer. arr. Noble Cain. Schmitt, Hall & McCreary No. 1602. Accompanied. Moderately easy.
We Praise and Bless Thee (from *Messe Solennelle*). arr. Witford. Oliver Ditson No. 332-40049. Accompanied. Moderately easy.

GRAUN, KARL HEINRICH
Lord, We Love the Place. Sam Fox No. MM 6. Accompanied. Medium.

GRETCHANINOV, ALEXANDER
Cherubim Song. arr. Noble Cain. Hoffmann No. 46012A. *A cappella.* Medium.
Gloria—Only Begotten Son. arr. Tellep. Boosey & Hawkes No. 5097. *A cappella.* Medium.
Hail, Thou Gladdening Light. Wood No. 594. *A cappella.* Moderately difficult.
Lord, How Lovely Is Your Dwelling Place. arr. Hopson. Carl Fischer No. CM8214. *A cappella.* Medium.

O Glorious One. arr. Noble Cain. Hoffman No. 46,339. *A cappella.* Moderately easy.

Our Father. English text by Kimball. Presser No. 332-13000. *A cappella.* Moderately difficult.

Simeon's Song. arr. Curtis Hansen. Curtis No. C9018. *A cappella.* Medium.

Vouchsafe, O Lord. Galaxy No. 1356. Optional accompaniment. Medium.

We Praise Thee. arr. Noble Cain. Hoffman No. 46,335. *A cappella.* Easy.

GRUBER, FRANZ

Silent Night. arr. David Conte. E. C. Schirmer No. 4562. Accompanied. Moderately easy.

Silent Night. arr. Gene Puerling. Shawnee Press No. A-1315. *A cappella.* Optional soprano and tenor solos. Moderately difficult.

HAMLISCH, MARVIN

One (from *A Chorus Line*). arr. Anita Kerr. Edwin H. Morris No. 08565753. Piano, guitar, bass and percussion. Moderately easy.

They're Playing Our Song (choral medley). arr. Ed Lojeski. Hal Leonard No. 08240600. Piano, electric guitar, electric bass, and percussion. Medium.

HANDEL, GEORGE FRIDERIC

All the Earth Doth Worship Thee. Ricordi No. NY2030. Accompanied. Moderately easy.

And Draw a Blessing Down (from *Theodora*). arr. Don Malin. Edw. B. Marks No. 4535. Accompanied. Medium.

Be Ye Sure That the Lord, He Is God (from *Utrecht Jubilate*). arr. Walter Ehret. Carl Fischer No. CM 8295. Accompanied. Medium.

Day by Day We Magnify Thee. Lawson-Gould No. 797; Edw. B. Marks No. 4516. Accompanied. Medium.

Glory to God (from *Judas Maccabaeus*). arr. Noel Goemanne. Neil A. Kjos No. ED. GC149. Organ accompaniment. Easy.

Glory to God. Lawson-Gould No. 796. Accompanied. Medium.

Hallelujah, Amen (from *Judas Maccabaeus*). G. Schirmer No. 9835. Optional accompaniment. Medium.

Hallelujah Chorus (from *Messiah*). Carl Fischer. SATB, for chorus and orchestra; chorus and band.

How Beautiful Are the Feet (from *Messiah*). arr. Arthur Frackenpohl. Mark Foster No. MF 566. Accompanied. Easy.

Jesus, the Christ, Is Risen Today. arr. Hal H. Hopson. Hope No. AA 1687. Accompanied. Moderately easy.

Joyful Day. National Music Publishers No. NMP-143. Accompanied. Medium.

Let Their Celestial Concerts All Unite (from *Samson*). E. C. Schirmer No. 312. Accompanied. Moderately difficult.

May We Ever Praise the Father. Lawson-Gould No. 52235. Optional accompaniment. Moderately easy.

Oh Love Divine (from *Theodora*). Carl Fischer No. ZCM108. Accompanied. Medium.

O, Lord, in Thee Have I Trusted. Kjos No. 5481 C. Accompanied. Medium.

O, Love Divine (from *Theodora*). arr. Don Malin. Edw. B. Marks No. 4543. Accompanied. Moderately difficult.

Serve the Lord with Gladness. Lawson-Gould No. 794. Accompanied. Medium.

So Are They Blest Who Fear the Lord. arr. Robert S. Hines. Neil A. Kjos. No. ED 8699. Accompanied. Medium.

Surely He Hath Borne Our Griefs (from *Messiah*). G. Schirmer No. 6598. Accompanied. Medium.

Thou Art the King of Glory. Kjos No. 5481A. Accompanied. Moderately easy.

To All Our Hearts Are Now Returning (from *Julius Caesar*). Belwin Mills No. 2404. Accompanied. Medium.

We Will Rejoice in Thy Salvation. ed. Don Malin. Belwin Mills No. 2407. Accompanied. Moderately difficult.

Your Voices Tune (from *Alexander's Feast*). ed. Don Malin. Belwin Mills No. 2408.
  Accompanied. Medium.

HANDL, JACOB
  Alleluia. ed. Daniel Pinkham. E. C. Schirmer No. 3007. For double chorus. A *cappella*.
    Moderately difficult.
  Behold a Hallowed Day. Concordia No. 98-1690. A *cappella*. Medium.
  Ecce, quomodo moritur. G. Schirmer No. 8424. A *cappella*. Moderately easy.
  Kyrie. ed. Rod Walker. CPP/Belwin No. SV8738. A *cappella*. Moderately easy.
  Natus est nobis. Arista No. AE 286. A *cappella*. Medium.
  O magnum mysterium. ed. Vahe Aslanian. Lawson-Gould No. 51893. Double chorus. A
    cappella. Moderately difficult.
  Orietur stella. ed. Lee Egbert. Broude Brothers No. CR 54. Organ ad libitum. Medium.
  Three Christmas Motets. ed. Lee Egbert. Broude Brothers No. CR 57. A *cappella*. Medium.

HASSE, JOHANN ADOLF
  Confitebor Tibi. ed. Martin Banner. Carl Fischer. No. CM 8271. Accompanied. Medium.

HAYDN, FRANZ JOSEPH
  Awake the Harp (from *The Creation*). ed. Don Neuen. Lawson-Gould No. 51982.
    Accompanied. Medium.
  Blest Be the Lord. McLaughlin & Reilly Co. No. 2217. Accompanied. Medium.
  Eloquence (Die Beredsamkeit). Elkan-Vogel No. 1133. Accompanied. Medium.
  Gloria (from the *Heiligmesse*). ed. Bennett Williams. Plymouth No. FS-104. Accompanied.
    Easy.
  Gloria in excelsis (from *Harmoniemesse*). Hal Leonard No. 08679600. Accompanied.
    Medium.
  Great and Glorious. Wood No. 316. Accompanied. Medium.
  Heavens Are Telling, The (from *The Creation*). arr. Charles Phillips. Carl Fischer No. CM
    127. Organ accompaniment. Moderately difficult.
  Holy, Holy, Holy (Sanctus and Hosanna). Mercury No. 352-00469. Accompanied.
    Moderately easy.
  Kyrie eleison. arr. Walter Ehret. Heritage No. 11 94. Accompanied. Moderately easy.
  Lord God, in Power and Glory. Curwen No. 80782. Optional accompaniment. Moderately
    easy.
  Old Man, The (Der Greis). Associated No. A-618. A *cappella*. Medium.
  O Wondrous Harmony. Lawson-Gould No. 52065. Accompanied. Medium.
  Sanctus (from 16th Mass). arr. Hilton. Mercury No. MC 399. Accompanied. Medium.
  Sing to the Lord (Gloria in excelsis Deo). G. Schirmer No. 5414. Accompanied.
    Moderately easy.
  Thou Art Worthy of Praise. Sam Fox No. MM 13. A *cappella*. Moderately easy.

HAYDN, MICHAEL
  Sleep in Peace, O Heavenly Child. G. Schirmer No. 11043. Accompanied. Moderately
    easy.

HASSLER, HANS LEO
  Agnus Dei. Shawnee Press No. A-1482. A *cappella*. Easy.
  Agnus Dei. ed. Rod Walker. CPP/Belwin No. SV8918. A *cappella*. Easy.
  Ah, Love, to You I'm Crying. ed. Walter Ehret. Tetra No. A.B. 759. A *cappella*. Medium.
  Ave Maris Stella. Kjos No. 5012. A *cappella*. Moderately easy.
  Blessed Savior, Our Lord Jesus. G. Schirmer No. 7563. A *cappella*. Medium.
  Christ Is Arisen. Edw. B. Marks No. 26. A *cappella*. Moderately easy.
  Come Let Us Start a Joyful Song. Bourne No. ES 74. A *cappella*. Moderately easy.
  Good News Is in the Air. arr. Hal H. Hopson. Hope Publishing No. AA 1686. Optional
    accompaniment. Moderately easy.
  Kyrie eleison (Lord Have Mercy On Us). ed. Patrick M. Liebergen. Carl Fischer No. CM
    8325. A *cappella*. Medium.

Lamb of God. Lawson-Gould No. 800. *A cappella.* Moderately easy.

Laudate Dominum (O Praise the Lord, Our God). ed. Patrick M. Liebergen. Tetra/Continuo No. TC 1104. Optional accompaniment. Moderately difficult.

O, Dearest Love of Mine (Herzlieb zu Dir allein). Boston Music Co. No. 13703. *A cappella.* Medium.

O Sing Unto the Lord. G. Schirmer No. 10872. *A cappella.* Moderately easy.

HAYDN, JOHANN MICHAEL

Sing a New Song. Flammer No. A-5970. Accompanied. Moderately easy.

Veni Creator Spiritus. ed. Martin Banner. Carol Fischer No. CM 8317. Accompanied. Medium.

HELFMAN, MAX

Mi Yemalel (Who Can Retell?). Transcontinental No. 991500. *A cappella.* Moderately easy.

HENNAGIN, MICHAEL

Creation, The (from *The Family of Man*). Walton No. W2186. SATB.

Walking on the Green Grass. Boosey & Hawkes No. 5443. *A cappella.* Medium.

HILLER, FERDINAND

Unto Thee I Lift My Spirit (Ich erhebe mein Gemute). Sam Fox No. MM 7. Accompanied. Moderately easy.

HINDEMITH, PAUL

In Winter. Associated No. AS 19432V. *A cappella.* Medium.

Since All Is Passing. Schott No. AP 37. *A cappella.* Moderately easy.

Springtime. Schott No. 19432, IV. *A cappella.* Moderately difficult.

Swan, A. Schott No. 19432, II. *A cappella.* Medium.

HOLST, GUSTAV

Christmas Day. Gray. SATB, for chorus and orchestra (orchestral parts available from publisher on rental only).

Let All Mortal Flesh Keep Silence. Galaxy No. 3.2309.1. Accompanied. Medium.

Psalm 148. Galaxy No. 1.5015. Organ and strings, or brass choir accompaniment. Moderately difficult.

Three Old English Carols. arr. Schmidt No. APS 15171. Accompanied. Moderately easy.

Turn Back, O Man. Galaxy No. 6. Accompanied. Medium.

HOMILIUS, GOTTFRIED AUGUST

Be Joyful, Be Joyful. Sam Fox No. MM5. Accompanied. Moderately easy.

HOVHANESS, ALAN

Psalm 61. C. F. Peters No. 6255. Organ accompaniment. Medium.

INGEGNERI, MARC ANTONIO

Tenebrae factae sunt. ed. Harold A. Decker. National Music No. 140. *A cappella.* Moderately easy.

IPPOLITOV-IVANOV, MICHAEL MIKHAILOVITCH

In Solemn Silence (memorial anthem). arr. Peter J. Wilhousky. Carl Fischer No. 635. *A cappella.* Medium.

ISAACSON, MICHAEL

Light the Legend (A Song for Chanukah). Transcontinental No. 991024. Accompanied. Moderately easy.

ISAAC, HEINRICH

O Bread of Life from Heaven. ed. Hal H. Hopson. Carl Fischer No. CM 8206. Optional accompaniment. Moderately easy.

O World, I Now Must Leave Thee (Innsbruck, ich muss dich lassen). Alexander Broude No. 251-3. *A cappella.* Medium.

IVES, CHARLES EDWARD

Sixty-seventh Psalm. Associated No. A-274. *A cappella.* Moderately difficult.

JACOB, GORDON
Brother James' Air (Marosa). Carl Fischer No. OCS763. *A cappella.* Easy.

JACOBSON, JOSHUA R.
Mi Zeh Y'maleil. Transcontinental No. 992016. Baritone solo. Tof (an Arab clay drum) and tambourine accompaniment. Medium.

JANEQUIN, CLEMENT
Je ne fus jamais si aise. arr. William D. Hall. National Music Publishers No. CMS-117. Brass, woodwind, or recorder accompaniment. Medium.

JOPLIN, SCOTT
Entertainer, The. arr. Ed. Lojeski. Hal Leonard No. 08214000. Piano, guitar, string bass and percussion. Moderately easy.

KALINNIKOV, VASSILI SERGEIVITCH
Let All Creatures of God His Praises Sing (Thanksgiving). arr. Noble Cain. Boosey & Hawkes No. 1801. *A cappella.* Medium.
O Lamb of God. arr. Walter Ehret. Pro Art No. 1513. *A cappella.* Moderately easy.

KAM, DENNIS
Two Moves and the Slow Scat. Belwin Mills No. 2282. SATB.

KARLEN, ROBERT
Dialogue. A.M.S.I. No. AMS 175. SATB, tape recorder.
Psalm 27 (Part III). A.M.S.I. No. 160. SATB.

KERN, JEROME
All the Things You Are (from *Very Warm For May*). arr. Kirby Shaw. Hal Leonard No. 08720244. *A cappella.* Solo. Medium.

KODÁLY, ZOLTÁN
Evening. Boosey & Hawkes No. 1710. *A cappella.* Difficult.

KOPYLOV, ALEXANDER A.
Hear My Prayer. Boston Music Co. No. 1294. *A cappella.* Medium.
Heavenly Light. arr. Wilhousky. Carl Fischer No. CM 497. *A cappella.* Moderately easy.
Hymn to the Trinity. Kjos No. 5337. *A cappella.* Easy.

KRENCK, ERNST
I Heard an Angel. Rongwen No. 3540. *A cappella.* Medium.

LAMB, GORDON H.
Aleatory Psalm. World Library Publications No. CA-4003-8. SATB.

LARSEN, LIBBY
Pluck the Fruit and Taste the Pleasure. E. C. Schirmer No. 4291. *A cappella.* Medium.
Shepherds All Are Waking, The (16th Century carol). E. C. Schirmer No. 4205. String orchestra and handbells accompaniment.

LASSUS, ROLAND DE (LASSUS, ORLANDUS; LASSO, ORLANDO DI)
Adoramus Te. Music Press No. MP-76. *A cappella.* Medium.
Adoramus Te. ed. John B. Haberlein. Mark Foster No. MF 921. *A cappella.* Easy.
Agnus Dei (Lamb of God). Raymond A. Hoffman No. R-2002. *A cappella.* Moderately easy.
Agnus Dei. arr. Robert S. Hines. Music 70 No. M70-589. *A cappella.* Easy.
Ave Regina Coelorum. Associated No. A-406. *A cappella.* Medium.
Chanson on *Dessus le Marche d'Arras.* Associated No. NYPM 32. *A cappella.* Medium.
Factus est Dominus. Arista No. AE 306. *A cappella.* Medium.
Fair Is the Crystal. Piedmont No. 4384. *A cappella.* Medium.
Hear, O Lord, Hear My Prayer. arr. Lundquist. Elkan-Vogel No. 1110. *A cappella.* Moderately easy.
Jubilate Deo. Mercury No. MP-80. *A cappella.* Moderately easy.
Jubilate Deo (Alleluia! Praise God). ed. Elwood Coggin. Lawson-Gould No. 52438. *A cappella.* Moderately easy.

Lord Christ, Son of God (Christe Dei Soboles). G. Schirmer No. 9414 *A cappella.* Medium.

Matona, Lovely Maiden. Carl Fischer No. CM 4637. *A cappella.* Moderately easy.

Oh, When My Husband Comes Back Home. Pro Art No. 2365. *A cappella.* Moderately easy.

O occhi manza mia. Arr. Walter Ehret. Walton No. 800463. SATB.

Resonet in laudibus (Let Praise Sound from Heav'n on High). ed. Harold Schmidt. C. F. Peters No. 66221. *A cappella.* Medium.

Salve Regina. Music Press No. MP-73. *A cappella.* Medium.

Surgens Jesus. Arista No. AE 309. *A cappella.* Medium.

Surrexit Pastor bonus (The Shepherd Has Arisen). G. Schirmer No. 7685. *A cappella.* Medium.

Three Chansons. ed. Francis J. Guentner. Broude Brothers No. CR 60. *A cappella.* Medium.

Timor et Tremor (Trembling and Terror). ed. Maynard Klein. G. Schirmer No. 12129. *A cappella.* Medium.

Welcome Sweet May (Wohl kommt der Mai). Carl Fischer No. CM 7566. *A cappella.* Moderately easy.

LE JEUNE, CLAUDE

Je pleure (I Weep). Editions Salabert No. 23-6. *A cappella.* Moderately easy.

LEKBERG, SVEN

Weep, O Willow (mountain tune). Summy-Birchard No. 5009. *A cappella.* Soprano solo. Medium.

LENNON, JOHN, AND PAUL MCCARTNEY

Michelle. arr. Gene Puerling. Shawnee Press No. A-1344. *A cappella.* Soprano and tenor solos. Difficult.

Yesterday. Shawnee Press No. A-1338. *A cappella.* Medium.

LEWANDOWSKI, LOUIS

Psalm 150 (Hallelujah, Praise Ye the Lord). Schmitt, Hall & McCreary No. 1640; Transcontinental No. 990792. Optional *a cappella.* Medium.

LISICKY, PAUL

Break Out Shouting Joy (Psalm 100). World Library No. 7993. Cantor and piano. Moderately easy.

LOCKWOOD, NORMAN

Monotone. Kjos No. 8. *A cappella.* Medium.

LOTTI, ANTONIO

Agnus Dei. Edw. B. Marks. No. 4365. *A cappella.* Moderately easy.

Glory. Edw. B. Marks No. 4366. *A cappella.* Moderately easy.

Holy, Holy, Holy (Sanctus). E. C. Schirmer No. 2216. *A cappella.* Medium.

Miserere mei. Boosey & Hawkes No. 1938. *A cappella.* Easy.

Sanctus (from Mass VII). G. Schirmer No. 9407. *A cappella.* Moderately easy.

We Adore Thee (Adoramus Te). Chappell No. 6149. *A cappella.* Moderately easy.

LUBOFF, NORMAN

A Capital Ship. Walton No. WW 1081. 2-Piano accompaniment. Medium.

Still, Still, Still. Walton No. 3003. Accompanied. Easy.

When the Saints Go Marching In (spiritual). Walton No. 3068. Accompanied. Moderately easy.

LULLY, JEAN-BAPTISTE

Au clair de la lune. arr. Stone. CPP/Belwin No. 2156. Medium.

LUTHER, MARTIN

Mighty Fortress Is Our God, A. Witmark No. 5W2835. Optional accompaniment. Moderately easy.

Mighty Fortress Is Our God, A. Staff. SATB, for chorus and band; chorus and orchestra; chorus, band, and orchestra.

LUTKIN, PETER C.
Lord Bless You and Keep You, The. Summy-Birchard No. 1089. *A cappella*. Easy.

LVOV, ALEXEY FEODOROVITCH
Hospodi Pomilui. ed. Wilhousky. Carl Fischer No. CM 6580. *A cappella*. Medium.

MADDY, JOSEPH
Festival Finale. Kjos. SATB, for chorus and band; chorus and orchestra; chorus, band, and orchestra.

MANDEL, JOHNNY
Shadow of Your Smile, The (from *The Sandpiper*). Arr. Gene Puerling. CPP/Belwin No. SVGP501. Piano or vocal solo. Piano, bass and drums. Medium.

MARENZIO, LUCA
O voi che sospirate a migliore note. Dartmouth Publications No. A-977. *A cappella*. Medium.
See How Aurora Comes with Brow All Glowing. Piedmont No. 4438. *A cappella*. Medium.
Tribus miraculis. Available—World Library. *A cappella*. Medium.
Warm Was the Sun (Scaldava il sol). Piedmont No. 4545. *A cappella*. Medium.
While As a Stone, Yet Living. Piedmont No. 4485. Optional accompaniment. Moderately easy.

MASCAGNI, PIETRO
Light Divine (scene and prayer from *Cavalleria Rusticana*). G. Schirmer No. 5959. Accompanied. Moderately difficult.

McCRAY, JAMES
Child Said, A. National Music Publishers No. NMP-151. Piano and oboe. Optional solo. Moderately easy.
Love Is a Blue Star. National Music Publishers No. WHC-137. *A cappella*. Medium.
Praise Ye the Lord. Music 70 No. M70-374. *A cappella*. Medium.
Songs of Love. Mark Foster No. MF 3037. *A cappella*. Medium.
Sweet Day. J. Fischer No. 10132. *A cappella*. Moderately easy.

MECHAM, KIRKE
Island in Space. G. Schirmer No. 50481434. *A cappella*. Moderately difficult.

McELLERAN, BROCK
Etude and Pattern. Oxford. SSAATBB unaccompanied.
Etude and Scherzo. Oxford. SSAATBB unaccompanied.

MENDELSSOHN, FELIX
Auf dem See (On the Lake). National Music Publishers No. NMP-184. *A cappella*. Medium.
Behold a Star from Jacob Shining. arr. Davison. E. C. Schirmer No. 1683. Organ accompaniment. Medium.
Early Spring. Music 70 No. M70-259. *A cappella*. Medium.
Festival Song of Praise. arr. M. R. Wilson and Harris. Bourne. SATB, for chorus and orchestra.
Frühzeitiger Frühling (Early Spring). National Music Publishers No. NMP-167. *A cappella*. Medium.
Herbstlied (Autumn Song). Lawson-Gould No. 52180. *A cappella*. Medium.
He Watching over Israel (from *Elijah*). G. Schirmer No. 2498. Accompanied. Moderately difficult.
Hundredth Psalm, The. ed. Hines. Concordia No. 98-2215. *A cappella*. Moderately difficult.
Hunting Song. Sam Fox No. RC 9. *A cappella*. Medium.
In the Forest. ed. Frank Mueller. Music 70 Publishers No. M70-604. *A cappella*. Medium.

Justice, O God (Richte mich, Gott). ed. Kenneth Jennings. Neil A. Kjos No ED. 8694. A
cappella. Medium.

Lark, The (Lerchengesang). Music 70 Publishers No. M70-252. A cappella. Moderately
easy.

Lord, Remember Not. Walton No. 6010. Optional accompaniment. Medium.

Nightingale, The. ed. Mason. Walton No. 7010. Optional accompaniment. Moderately
easy.

Peaceful Vale. ed. Frank Mueller. Music 70 No. M70-603. A cappella. Moderately easy.

Primrose, The (Die Primel). Associated No. A-382. A cappella. Medium.

Prayer and Chorale. Lawson-Gould No. 849. A cappella. Moderately easy.

Psalm 43. Hope Publishing Co. No. APM 006. A cappella. Medium.

Skylark's Song, The. Belwin Mills No. 2181. Optional accompaniment. Moderately easy.

Song of the Lark (Lerchengesang). Sam Fox No. RC 11. A cappella. Moderately easy.

There Shall a Star from Jacob. Carl Fischer No. CM 6228. Accompanied. Medium.

MENNIN, PETER

In the Quiet Night. Carl Fischer No. CM 6417. A cappella. Medium.

MENOTTI, GIAN CARLO

Shepherds' Chorus (from Amahl and the Night Visitors). G. Schirmer No. 10801.
Accompanied. Soprano and bass solos. Medium.

MOE, DANIEL

Glory of This Day, The. Augsburg Fortress No. 11-0542. A cappella. Medium.

MOLLICONE, HENRY

Send Forth, O God, Thy Light and Truth. E. C. Schirmer No. 3083. A cappella. Medium.

When the Stars Are Gone. E. C. Schirmer No. 4510. Accompanied. Easy.

MONTEVERDI, CLAUDIO

Anima mia perdona. ed. Don Malin. Belwin Mills No. 2380. A cappella. Medium.

If I Should Part from You. Presser No. 312-40939. A cappella. Moderately easy.

Lasciatemi morire. Ricordi No. NY841. A cappella. Moderately easy.

O Death, Pray Come. Boston Music Co. No. 2890. A cappella. Medium.

MORALES, CRISTÓBAL DE

Salva Nos, Stella Maris (Save Us, Star of the Sea). ed. Martin Banner. Lawson-Gould No.
51971. A cappella. Medium.

MORLEY, THOMAS

Agnus Dei. arr. Greyson. Bourne No. ES36. A cappella. Medium.

April Is in Her Lovely Face. Ricordi No. 1398; E. C. Schirmer No. 1612. A cappella.
Moderately easy.

'Tis the Time of Yuletide Glee. Music 70 No. M70-235. A cappella. Moderately easy.

MOUTON, JEAN

Ave Maria. Music Press No. DCS 40. A cappella. Moderately easy.

MOZART, WOLFGANG AMADEUS

Adoramus Te. G. Schirmer No. 9932. Optional accompaniment. Moderately easy.

Alleluia (from the motet Exsultate, Jubilate). arr. Rosenberg. Carl Fischer No. 541.
Accompanied. Medium. (Soprano solo, difficult.)

Ave verum corpus. G. Schirmer No. 5471. Organ accompaniment. Moderately easy.

A Warning. arr. Ernest Gold. Lawson-Gould No. 52518. Accompanied. Moderately easy.

Bless the Lord for Ever and Ever. arr. Hilton. Mercury No. 352-00459. Accompanied.
Moderately difficult.

Contentment. Lawson-Gould No. 937. Accompanied. Soprano solo. Moderately easy.

Crucifixus. National Music Publishers No. WHC-141. Accompanied. Medium.

Dies irae (from Requiem). G. Schirmer No. 10016. Accompanied. Medium.

Farmer's Wife Lost Her Cat. Edw. B. Marks No. 1. A cappella. Moderately difficult.

Gloria in excelsis. G. Schirmer No. 3515. Accompanied. Medium.

Graduale—Sancta Maria. Broude Bros. No. 77. Accompanied. Medium.

Hear Our Supplication. Arr. Hilton. Mercury No. 352-00378. Accompanied. Medium.
Hymn of Praise. arr. Tolmadge. Staff. SATB—for chorus and band.
In excelsis Deo (from Mass in C). Presser No. 312-41198. Accompanied. Medium.
Jubilate (O Be Joyful). ed. Patrick M. Liebergen. Carl Fischer No. CM 8324.
    Accompanied. Medium.
Jubilate Deo. Pro Art No. 1007. *A cappella.* Moderately easy.
Justum deduxit Dominus (Lord, God Has Led the Righteous Man). Lawson-Gould No.
    52137. Accompanied. Moderately difficult.
King of Glory. ed. Walter Ehret. Gentry No. G-345. Accompanied. Medium.
Kyrie, K. 341. ed. Jonathan Barnhart. E. C. Schirmer No. 4131. Accompanied. Medium.
Kyrie. ed. Landon. G. Schirmer No. 12067. Accompanied. Medium.
Lacrymosa (from *Requiem*). G. Schirmer No. 10017. Accompanied. Medium.
Laudate pueri. Lawson-Gould No. 51166; Associated No. A-683. Accompanied. Medium.
Lullaby (Wiegenlied). Associated No. A-84. Accompanied. Soprano solo. Moderately easy.
O Be Joyful! (Freut euch. freut euch). Sam Fox No. MM 9. Accompanied. Medium.
Placido e il mar (from *Idomenco*). Belwin Mills No. 2403. Accompanied. Medium.
Pleasure Awaits Us (from *La Finta Gardiniera*). Belwin Mills No. 2403. Accompanied.
    Medium.

NARES, JAMES
    Call to Remembrance. ed. Percy M. Young. Broude No. MGC 48. Organ accompaniment.
    Moderately difficult.

NYSTEDT, KNUT
    All the Ways of a Man. Norsk Musikforlag, Oslo, Norway. *A cappella.* Medium.
    If You Receive My Words. Norsk Musikforlag No. N.M.O. 9814. *A cappella.* Moderately
    difficult.
    Praise to God. Associated No. A-597. *A cappella.* Medium.

OFFENBACH, JACQUES
    Beggar's Canon (from *The Brigands*). Broude Bros. No. 117. Accompanied. Medium.
    Chorus of the Office Clerks (from *Fortunia's Song*). Broude Bros. No. 4066. Accompanied.
    Medium.
    Neighbors' Chorus. Broude Bros. No. 130. Accompanied. Medium.

PACHELBEL, JOHANN
    Sing Ye to the Lord (Jauchzet dem Herrn). Music 70 No. M70-192. Accompanied.
    Moderately easy.

PALESTRINA, GIOVANNI PIERLUIGI DA
    Adoramus Te, Christe. Carl Fischer No. CM 6578. *A cappella.* Easy.
    Come, Then, O Holy Breath of God. Piedmont No. 4414. *A cappella.* Medium.
    Corporis mysterium (Sacrament of Priceless Worth). Ricordi No. NY1852. *A cappella.*
    Moderately easy.
    Dies sanctificatus. National Music Publishers No. RCS-102. *A cappella.* Medium.
    Exaltabo Te, Domine. G. Schirmer No. 7620. *A cappella.* Medium.
    Exultate Deo (Sing and Praise Jehovah). G. Schirmer No. 7672. *A cappella.* Medium.
    Gloria Patri (Glory to God). arr. Norman Greyson. Bourne No. ES46. *A cappella.* Easy.
    Like as the Hart. G. Schirmer No. 3509. *A cappella.* Moderately easy.
    O bone Jesu (O Blessed Jesus). ed. Patrick M. Liebergen. Carl Fischer No. CM 8299. *A
    cappella.* Easy.
    O bone Jesu. Oliver Ditson No. 332-03070. *A cappella.* Easy.
    Praise Be to Thee. arr. Lundquist. Willis No. 5678. *A cappella.* Easy.
    These Are My Heartfelt Tears (madrigal). Lawson-Gould No. 51029. *A cappella.*
    Moderately easy.
    Tu es Petrus. Arista No. AE 378. *A cappella.* Medium.
    Tu es Petrus. National Music No. RCS-100-9. *A cappella.* Medium.

PERGOLESI, GIOVANNI
    Agnus Dei. Mercury No. MC 147. Accompanied. Medium.

Glory to God in the Highest. Wood No. 289. Organ accompaniment. Moderately difficult.
Glory to God in the Highest. arr. Houseknecht. Kjos. SATB, for chorus and band.
Miserere mei. Walton No. 6011. Accompanied. Medium.
Requiem aeternam. ed. James McCray. Music 70 No. M70-610. Accompanied. Medium.
Sanctus and Hosanna. Music 70 No. M70-405. Accompanied. Medium.
Sing unto the Lord Most High. Boosey & Hawkes. A cappella. Easy.

PETER, JOHANN FRIEDRICH
I Will Clothe Thy Priests with Salvation. arr. Kroeger. Boosey & Hawkes No. 6004.
Accompanied. Medium.

PFAUTSCH, LLOYD
Love Came Down at Christmas. Lawson-Gould No. 52278. A cappella. Medium.

PILKINGTON, FRANCIS
Look, Mistress Mine. ed. John Kingsbury. Music 70 No M70-239. A cappella. Moderately
easy.
Rest, Sweet Nymphs. National Music Publishers No. CMS-121. String quartet or recorder
consort accompaniment. Moderately easy.

PINKHAM, DANIEL
Alleluia, Acclamation and Carol. E. C. Schirmer Nos. 2954 and 2955. SATB, timpani,
percussion, and electronic tape.
Amens. E. C. Schirmer No. 3016. SATB and electronic tape.
And Peace Attend Thee. E. C. Schirmer. No. 4036. Organ or piano accompaniment.
Medium.
Call of Isaiah, The. E. C. Schirmer No. 2911. SATB with organ and electronic tape.
Evergreen. E. C. Schirmer No. 2962. Unison chorus, electronic tape, and optional
instruments (autoharp, bells, harp, guitar, piano, and organ).
In the Beginning of Creation. E. C. Schirmer No. 2902. Mixed chorus, electronic tape.
I Saw an Angel. E. C. Schirmer No. 2973. SATB and electronic tape.
Three Lenten Poems of Richard Crashaw. E. C. Schirmer No. 2693. Accompanied.
Medium.

PISTON, WALTER
O Sing Unto the Lord a New Song. Associated No. A-640. Accompanied. Moderately
difficult.

PITONI, GIUSEPPE OTTAVIO
Cantate Domino. ed. Patrick M. Liebergen. Carl Fischer No. CM 8274. A cappella.
Moderately easy.
Cantate Domino. Bourne No. ES 5. A cappella. Moderately easy.
Laudate Dominum (Praise Ye the Lord with Song). ed. Patrick M. Liebergen. Carl Fischer
No. CM 8255. A cappella. Moderately easy.
Tarry Here and Watch. arr. Kingsbury. Tetra No. A.B. 757. A cappella. Medium.

PORTER, COLE
Another Op'nin', Another Show (from Kiss Me Kate). Arr. Howard Cable. Hal Leonard
No. 00346038. Piano accompaniment. Moderately easy.
Blow, Gabriel, Blow. arr. Roy Ringwald. Shawnee Press No. A-1638. Accompanied.
Medium.
Friendship. Arr. Norman Leyden. Plymouth Music No. CP 101. Accompanied. Moderately
easy.
I've Got You Under My Skin. arr. Phil Mattson. Hal Leonard No. 08603340. Piano, bass,
and drums. Medium.
Just One of Those Things. arr. Roger Emerson. Warner Bros. No. 403-10104. Piano
accompaniment. Easy.

POTE, ALLEN
Break Forth into Song. Hope No. A 639. Keyboard and optional percussion. Moderately
easy.

PRAETORIUS, HIERONYMUS
Lo, How a Rose E'er Blooming. G. Schirmer No. 2484. *A cappella.* Easy.
Psallite. arr. Norman Greyson. Bourne No. ES 21. *A cappella.* Easy.
Rise Up, Oh Flame. arr. Harley and Aschenbrenner. Carl Fischer No. CM 4712. *A cappella.* Moderately easy.
Sing dem Herrn. Arr. Wallace DePue. CPP/Belwin No. SV8640. *A cappella.* Medium.
Sing We All Now with One Accord. G. Schirmer No. 7543. Accompanied. Moderately easy.
PUCCINI, GIACOMO
Requiem. Ricordi No. 50481477. Organ accompaniment, with solo viola. Medium.
PURCELL, HENRY
Glory and Worship. E. C. Schirmer No. 1108. Organ accompaniment. Moderately easy.
In These Delightful, Pleasant Groves. Novello No. M.T.I. *A cappella.* Medium.
Let My Prayer Come Up (Offertorium). Gray No. 1527; Mercury No. 352-00440. Accompanied. Moderately easy.
Magnificat and Nunc dimittis. C. F. Peters No. 66266. Optional accompaniment. Medium.
O Be Joyful Ye Lands. Gentry No. JG-459. Accompanied. Easy.
O Sing Unto the Lord. E. C. Schirmer No. 1103. Organ accompaniment. Moderately easy.
Rejoice in the Lord Always. Novello No. 1581. Accompanied. Moderately easy.
Trumpet Voluntary. Staff. SATB; SAB, SSA; SA—for chorus and band; chorus and orchestra; chorus, band, and orchestra.
RACHMANINOFF, SERGEI V.
Ave Maria. Oliver Ditson No. 332-14564; Lawson-Gould No. 52344. *A cappella.* Medium.
Glory Be to God. arr. Peter Tkach. Kjos No. 6528. *A cappella.* Medium.
RAMIREZ, ARIEL
Los reyes magos (The Three Kings). Lawson-Gould No. 51748. Harpsichord, percussion, and guitar accompaniment. Moderately easy.
Zamba for You. Lawson-Gould No. 52242. *A cappella.* Medium.
RAVEL, MAURICE
Pavane pour une infante défunte. Broude Bros. No. 100. Accompanied. Moderately difficult.
REUTTER, GEORG VON
Veni virgo sacrata. ed. Young. Broude Bros. No. MGC 21. Organ accompaniment. Medium.
REYNOLDS, ROGER
Emperor of Ice Cream, The. C. F. Peters. Eight singers, piano, percussion, bass; multimedia.
RIESE, MARK
A Choral Fantasy (God Rest Ye Merry, Gentlemen). E. C. Schirmer No. 4059. Chamber orchestra or keyboard accompaniment. Medium.
I Saw Three Ships. E. C. Schirmer No. 4391. Chamber orchestra or keyboard accompaniment. Medium.
RIMSKY-KORSAKOV, NIKOLAI
Glory. Witmark. SSAATTBB—for chorus and orchestra.
ROGERS, RICHARD
Getting to Know You (from *The King and I*). arr. Gene Puerling. Hal Leonard No. 07359124. Piano with optional rhythm section. Medium.
If I Loved You (from *Carousel*). arr. Kirby Shaw. Hal Leonard No. 08665939. *A cappella.* Moderately easy.
It Might as Well Be Spring (from *State Fair*). arr. Kirby Shaw. Hal Leonard No. 08657871. *A cappella.* Moderately easy.
Johnny One Note. arr. Gene Puerling. Hal Leonard No. 08624171. Piano and rhythm section, with optional jazz ensemble. Medium.

King and I Medley, The. arr. Anita Kerr. Hal Leonard No. 08565671. Piano and optional instrumental accompaniment. Moderately easy.

My Funny Valentine (from *Babes In Arms*). arr. Roger Emerson. Jenson No. 40326051. A *cappella*. Moderately easy.

Rorem, Ned

He Shall Rule from Sea to Sea. Boosey & Hawkes No. 5651. Accompanied. Medium.

O magnum mysterium. Boosey & Hawkes No. 6006. A *cappella*. Medium.

Rossini, Gioacchino

Quando corpus (from *Stabat Mater*). ed. Leonard Van Camp. Music 70 No. 205. A *cappella*. Medium.

Sanctus. ed. Ferguson. Lawson-Gould No. 51890. Accompanied. Moderately difficult.

Sanctus and Benedictus. arr. Robert N. Roth. Tetra No. TC 1108. Soprano and tenor solos. Optional accompaniment. Medium.

Rowley, C. E.

Italian Salad. G. Schirmer No. 10625. Baritone solo. A *cappella*. Medium.

Jig for Voices. Boosey & Hawkes No. 1699. Optional accompaniment. Medium.

Rubenstein, Anton Grigorievitch

Voice of Freedom. arr. Lucien Caillet. Boosey & Hawkes. SATB; TTBB—for chorus and band; chorus and orchestra.

Rutter, John

Blow, Blow, Thou Winter Wind. Oxford No. 52.024. Accompanied. Moderately easy.

O Be Joyful in the Lord. Oxford No. A 346. Accompanied. Medium.

Saint-Saens, Camille

Chorale from *Organ Symphony No. 3*. Staff. SATB, for chorus and band.

Sandberg, Rhonda

Americana Medley. Aberdeen Music No. 1088. Accompanied. Moderately easy.

Sargent, Malcolm

Three Far-Eastern Carols. Oxford No. X73. A *cappella*. Moderately easy.

Two Folk Carols (Star in the South and Zither Carol). Oxford No. X50. A *cappella*. Moderately easy.

Sateren, Leland B.

This Is the Night. Neil A. Kjos No. C9012. A *cappella*. Moderately easy.

Scarlatti, Alessandro

Amen. arr. Walter Ehret. European American No. EA 231. Organ or piano accompaniment. Moderately easy.

Exultate Deo. G. Schirmer No. 11001. A *cappella*. Medium.

Holy, Holy, Holy. Chappell No. 6141. A *cappella*. Medium.

Scheidt, Samuel

Puer natus in Bethlehem. arr. Rod Walker. CPP/Belwin No. SV 8712. Optional accompaniment. Medium.

Schein, Johann Herman

Who With Grieving Soweth. Mercury No. 19. A *cappella*. Moderately difficult.

Schoggl, Franz

Trout As You Like It (Variations on Schubert's Song). English version by Eugene Hartzell. Doblinger No. D.17.269. A *cappella*. Medium.

Schubert, Franz

Agnus Dei (from *Deutsche Messe*). Piedmont No. 4449. Accompanied. Medium.

Christ Is Arisen. E. C. Schirmer No. 2686. A *cappella*. Moderately easy.

Christ ist erstanden (Christ Is Arisen). National Music Publishers No. CII-4. A *cappella*. Medium.

Dona nobis pacem. arr. Carl J. Nygard. Beckenhorst No. BP 1359. Accompanied. Easy.

Glaube, Hoffnung und Liebe (Faith, Hope and Love). National Music Publishers No. NMP-185. Accompanied. Medium.

Happiness (O Seligkeit). ed. Freed. Sam Fox No. RC 4. Accompanied. Moderately easy.

Holy Is the Lord. Presser No. 312-21416. Accompanied. Easy.

Joy of Living. ed. Cennen Gordon. Tetra/Continuo No. TC 258. Accompanied. Medium.

Kyrie (from Mass in G). Kjos No. ED 5989. Accompanied. Soprano solo. Medium.

Lebenslust (Joy of Living). Alexander Broude No. 258. Accompanied. Medium.

O Hear Me When I Call on Thee. E. C. Schirmer No. 2684. Accompanied. Medium.

O Jesus, Crucified for Man. National Music Publishers No. CH-10. Accompanied. Medium.

Omnipotence, The. G. Schirmer No. 10146. Accompanied. Medium.

Osterlied (Easter Song). National Music Publishers No. CH-9. Accompanied. Easy.

Psalm 92. Alexander Broude No. AB 823. A *cappella*. Baritone solo. Moderately difficult.

Sanctus (Holy Is the Lord). ed. Don Craig. Plymouth No. DC-109. Optional accompaniment. Easy.

Sound the Cymbal. Schmitt, Hall & McCreary No. 1745. Accompanied. Medium.

Sound the Trumpet (from *Miriam's Song of Triumph*). arr. Hal H. Hopson. Carl Fischer No. CM 8321. Piano accompaniment, with optional Bb trumpet. Medium.

Stabat Mater. Belwin Mills No. 2161. Accompanied. Moderately easy.

To Music (commencement). arr. Harry R. Wilson. Schmitt, Hall & McCreary No. 1070. Accompanied. Moderately easy.

Tones Enchanted (Dutch der Töne). Kenbridge Music No. K-103. Accompanied. Medium.

Wonderful Life, A (Lebenslust). Sam Fox No. MM 8. Accompanied. Medium.

SCHUETKY, FRANZ JOSEPH

Send Out Thy Light (Emitte Spiritum Tuum). Carl Fischer No. CM 548. A *cappella*. Moderately easy.

SCHULLER, GUNTHER

O Lamb of God. Margun No. MM-26. A *cappella*, with optional organ or piano accompaniment. Difficult.

O Spirit of the Living God. Margun No. MM-27. A *cappella*, with optional organ or piano accompaniment. Moderately difficult.

SCHUMAN, WILLIAM HOWARD

Prelude. G. Schirmer No. 8929. A *cappella*. Soprano solo. Moderately difficult.

Requiescat. G. Schirmer No. 8926. Accompanied. Medium.

Te Deum. G. Schirmer No. 9453. A *cappella*. Medium.

To All, To Each. Presser No. 342-40013. A *cappella*. Medium.

SCHUMANN, ROBERT

Lonely Boat Drifts Slowly, A. Broude Bros. No. 135. Soprano solo, flute, and horn. Medium.

O God, I Thank Thee. arr. Lundquist. Willis No. 8466. A *cappella*. Easy.

O Lord, Hear Thou My Prayer. arr. Goldman. Lawson-Gould No. 51968. Piano or organ accompaniment. Soprano solo. Medium.

So wahr die Sonne scheinet (As Surely as the Sun Shines). National Music Publishers No. WHC-117. Accompanied. Medium.

Zigeunerleben (Gypsy Life). Walton No. 2706. Accompanied. Moderately easy.

SCHÜTZ, HEINRICH

Blessed Are the Faithful. ed. Robert Shaw and Klaus Speer. G. Schirmer No. 10114. A *cappella*. Moderately difficult.

Cantate Domino. Arista No. AE 356; Bourne No. B201889. A *cappella*. Moderately difficult.

Ehre sei Dir, Christe (Christ, Be Thine the Glory!). G. Schirmer No. 10123. Optional accompaniment. Medium.

He Who with Weeping Soweth. G. Schirmer No. 10115. Optional accompaniment. Moderately difficult.

In Thee, O Lord, Do I Put My Trust (In Te Domine speravi). arr. John Kingsburg. Plymouth No. SC-117. Accompanied. Medium.

Lo, I Am the Voice of One Crying in the Wilderness. G. Schirmer No. 10116. Optional accompaniment. Moderately difficult.

Sicut Moses serpentem. Associated No. A-412. Accompanied. Difficult.

Who Shall Separate Us. Chantry Music Press. Organ or piano accompaniment. Medium.

SCHWARTZ, STEPHEN

Beautiful City (from Godspell). arr. Ed. Lojeski. Hal Leonard No. 08200630. Piano with optional percussion, guitar, and string bass. Moderately easy.

Corner of the Sky (from Pippin). Arr. Cacavas. Belwin Mills No. OCT 02288. Piano accompaniment. Moderately easy.

Day By Day (from Godspell). arr. Norman Leyden. CPP/Belwin No. 0014DC1X. Piano, drums, and electric and bass guitars. Medium.

SHAW, MARTIN

Fanfare for Christmas Day. G. Schirmer No. 8745. Optional organ accompaniment. Moderately easy.

With a Voice of Singing. G. Schirmer No. 8103. Accompanied. Moderately easy.

SHOSTAKOVITCH, DMITRI

Face to Face (from Ten Songs). G. Schirmer No. 12121. A cappella. Moderately difficult.

Have Courage, Friends (from Ten Songs). G. Schirmer No. 12118. A cappella. Medium.

SIBELIUS, JEAN

Onward, Ye Peoples!. arr. Lefebvre. Galaxy No. 938-10. Accompanied. Moderately easy.

STAINER, JOHN

God So Loved the World. G. Schirmer No. 3798. A cappella. Easy.

Grieve Not the Holy Spirit of God. ed. James McKelvy. Mark Foster No. MF 2029. Optional accompaniment. Medium.

STEFFE, WILLIAM

Battle Hymn of the Republic (patriotic). arr. Roy Ringwald. Shawnee Press No. A 0028. Accompanied. Moderately easy.

Battle Hymn of the Republic (patriotic). arr. Peter J. Wilhousky. Carl Fischer No. CM 4743. Accompanied. Medium.

STRAUSS, JOHANN

Come and Sing (from Die Fledermaus). Carl Fischer No. CM 4628. Accompanied. Moderately difficult.

Roses of the South. arr. Gibb. Homeyer No. 437. Accompanied. Moderately easy.

Sängerlust-Polka. Doblinger No. D.17636. Accompanied. Medium.

STRAVINSKY, IGOR

Pater Noster. Boosey & Hawkes No. 1833. A cappella. Medium.

STROMMEN, CARL

Homeward Bound. CPP/Belwin No. SV 9060. Accompanied. Moderately easy.

STROOPE, Z. RANDALL

Cantate Domino. Mark Foster No. MF 2016. A cappella, with tambourine. Moderately difficult.

STROUSE, CHARLES

Choral Highlights from Annie. arr. Roger Emerson. Jenson No. 403-01084. Piano, guitar, bass and drums. Moderately easy.

You're Never Fully Dressed Without a Smile (from Annie). arr. Frank Metis. CPP/Belwin No. T6540YC1. Piano, with optional guitar, percussion and bass. Moderately easy.

SWEELINCK, JAN PIETERSZOON

Hodie Christus natus est. Edw. B. Marks No. MC 4301. A cappella. Moderately difficult.

Laudate Dominum. Concordia No. 97-5450. Optional accompaniment. Medium.

Sing with Gladness. ed. Leland Sateren. AMSI No. 337. A cappella. Moderately difficult.

Venite, exultemus Domino (O Come Let Us Praise God). Summy-Birchard No. 5517. Optional accompaniment. Medium.

TALLIS, THOMAS
If Ye Love Me, Keep My Commandments. ed. Brian Busch. CPP/Belwin No. 02515. A cappella. Moderately easy.
If Ye Love Me, Keep My Commandments. E. C. Schirmer No. 2269. A cappella. Medium.

TANEYEV, SERGEI I.
Sunrise. G. Schirmer No. 2623. A cappella. Difficult.

TAYLOR, DEEMS
Waters Ripple and Flow (Czechoslovakian folk song). J. Fischer No. 5675. Accompanied. Soprano and baritone solos. Moderately difficult.
Well-Beloved, The (Armenian folk song). J. Fischer No. 4844. Accompanied. Soprano solo. Moderately easy.

TCHAIKOVSKY, PETER ILICH
Ave Maria. Boston Music Co. No. 1064. A cappella. Moderately easy.
Cherubim Song No. 3. G. Schirmer No. 2561. Piano or organ accompaniment. Moderately difficult.
Hail, Thou Holy One. arr. Cain. Boosey & Hawkes No. 1979. A cappella. Medium.
Nuptial Chorus (from The Guardsman). ed. Don Malin. Belwin Mills No. 2405. Accompanied. Medium.
O Blessed Lord. Wallace Gillman No. 4001. Optional accompaniment. Moderately easy.
Oh, Blest Are They. arr. Noble Cain. Remick No. 3024. A cappella. Moderately difficult.
Pater Noster (Our Father). G. Schirmer No. 5475. A cappella. Moderately easy.

TELEMANN, GEORG PHILIPP
Der Gott, unsers Herrn, Jesu Christi (To God, Our Lord and Saviour). Lawson-Gould No. 52207. Accompanied. Medium.

TESCHNER, GUSTAV WILHELM
All Glory, Laud and Honor (Palm Sunday). Arr. Noble Cain. Flammer No. 81127. Accompanied. Easy.

THOMPSON, RANDALL
Alleluia. E. C. Schirmer No. 1786. A cappella. Moderately difficult.
Best of Rooms, The. E. C. Schirmer No. 2672. A cappella. Medium.
Choose Something Like a Star. E. C. Schirmer No. 2487. Accompanied. Moderately easy.
De profundis (Out of the Deep). Weintraub. A cappella. Moderately difficult.
Glory to God in the Highest. E. C. Schirmer No. 2470. A cappella. Medium.
Last Words of David, The. E. C. Schirmer No. 2294. Accompanied. Medium.
Lord Is My Shepherd, The. E. C. Schirmer No. 2688. Accompanied. Moderately easy.
Lord Shall Be Unto Thee, The (from Requiem). E. C. Schirmer No. 2641. A cappella. Medium.
Now Thank We All Our God (from A Psalm of Thanksgiving). E. C. Schirmer No. 4008. Accompanied (keyboard or orchestra). Moderately easy.
Ride On! Ride On! (Palm Sunday). Gray No. GMR 1154. A cappella. Medium.
Road Not Taken, The. E. C. Schirmer No. 2485. Accompanied. Moderately easy.
Twelve Canticles. E. C. Schirmer. 1. Praise Ye the Lord. No. 4100. 2. God Is a Spirit. 3. When Thou Liest Down. No. 4101. 4. My Grace Is Sufficient. No. 4102. 5. The Old and the Young. 6. I Call to Remembrance. No. 4103. 7. Arise, Shine. 8. The Past of the Just. No. 4104. 9. Face Answereth to Face. 10. Fear Thou Not. No. 4105. 11. Farewell. 12. Amen. No. 4106. All Canticles are of medium difficulty.
Two Worlds. E. C. Schirmer No. 3041. Accompanied. Medium.

THOMSON, VIRGIL
Tribulationes civitatum. Weintraub. A cappella. Moderately difficult.

TOCH, ERNST
Geographical Fugue (speaking chorus). Belwin Mills No. 347. Difficult.
Valse (Speaking Chorus). Belwin Mills No. 60564. Optional percussion. Medium.

TOMKINS, THOMAS
Absalom. Chappell No. 6140. A cappella. Medium.

TORME, MEL AND ROBERT WELLS
Christmas Song, The (Chestnuts Roasting on an Open Fire). arr. Walter Ehret. Edwin H.
Morris No. E9822a. Accompanied. Solo. Moderately easy.
Christmas Song, The (Chestnuts Roasting on an Open Fire). arr. Gene Puerling. Edwin H.
Morris No. 07359063. Piano, bass and drums. Medium.

TRYTHALL, GILBERT
In the Presence. Edw. B. Marks No. 4495. SATB, electronic tape.
Time to Every Purpose, A. Edw. B. Marks No. 4586. SATB, electronic tape.

TSCHESNOKOV, PAUL G.
Let Thy Holy Presence. arr. Cain. Summy-Birchard No. 12. A cappella. Medium.
Salvation Is Created. arr. Norden. J. Fischer No. 4129. A cappella. Medium.

TYE, CHRISTOPHER
All Earth, Sing Forth Your Joyful Praise (Laudate Nomen Domini). ed. Hal H. Hopson.
Augsburg Fortress No. 11-4676. Optional accompaniment. Easy.

VASQUEZ, JUAN
En la fuente de rosel. Lawson-Gould No. 51376. SATB.

VAUGHAN WILLIAMS, RALPH
All Hail the Power. Oxford. Accompanied. Moderately difficult.
Dark Eyed Sailor, The (English folk song). Galaxy No. 1.5097. A cappella. Medium.
Fantasie on Christmas Carols. Galaxy. SATB, with baritone solo—for chorus and orchestra
(orchestra parts available from publishers on rental only).
Just as the Tide Was Flowing (English folk song). Galaxy No. 1.5020. A cappella. Medium.
Magnificat. Oxford. SSA, with contralto solo—for chorus and orchestra (orchestral parts
available from publisher on rental only).
O Clap Your Hands. Galaxy No. 222. Organ accompaniment. Moderately difficult.
O Mistress Mine. Galaxy No. 1.5017 A cappella. Moderately easy.
Spring Time of the Year, The (English folk song). Galaxy No. 1.5013. A cappella.
Medium.
Wassail Song. Galaxy No. 1.5008. A cappella. Medium.
Whether Men Do Laugh or Weep. Oxford No. X66. Accompanied. Medium.

VECCHI, ORAZIO
Fa una canzona. Lawson-Gould No. 556. SATB.

VERDI, GUISEPPE
Ave Maria. C. F. Peters No. 4256a. A cappella. Moderately difficult.
Chorus of the Hebrew Captives (from Nabucco). Music 70 No. 224. Accompanied.
Medium.
Glory (March from Aida). Willis No. 2892. Accompanied. Moderately difficult.
Lord, Hear Our Prayer (from Otello). Arr. Huguelet. Carl Fischer No. CM 616. Optional
accompaniment. Medium.
We Are Brave Matadors (from La Traviata). G. Schirmer No. 5435. Accompanied.
Medium.

VIADANA, LODOVICO
Exultate justi. ed. Maynard Klein. G.I.A. No. G-2140. A cappella. Medium.

VICTORIA, TOMÁS LUIS DE
Agnus Dei (from Missa Simile est Regnum coelorum). ed. Walter Ehret. European American
No. B 232. A cappella. Medium.
Agnus Dei. Lawson-Gould No. 925. A cappella. Medium.
Ave Maria. Music Press No. MP-79. A cappella. Moderately easy.
Ave Maria. arr. Max T. Krone. M. Witmark No. W 2712. A cappella. Medium.
Gaude Maria Virgo. ed. James McKelvy. Mark Foster No. MF 153. A cappella. Medium.
Jesu dulcis memoria. G. Schirmer No. 5573. A cappella. Easy.

Kyrie (*Missa: O quam gloriosum*). ed. Robert S. Hines. Plymouth No. SC-52. A cappella. Medium.

O magnum mysterium (O Wondrous Nativity). G. Schirmer No. 7626. A cappella. Medium.

O vos omnes. Ricordi No. NY1875. A cappella. Medium.

Sancta Maria, succurre miseris (Holy Mother, Succor the Wretched). ed. Martin Banner. Lawson-Gould No. 51980. A cappella. Medium.

Sanctus. Music 70 No. M70-212. A cappella. Medium.

Sanctus. ed. Robert S. Hines. Music 70 No. M70-212. A cappella. Medium.

Surely, He Bore Our Sorrows (Lent). E. C. Schirmer No. 2217. A cappella. Medium.

VILLA-LOBOS, HEITOR
Ave Maria No. 20. new text by Harry R. Wilson. Consolidated. A cappella. Medium.

VIVALDI, ANTONIO
Et misericordia. arr. Lee Kjelson. Belwin Mills No. 2236. Accompanied. Moderately easy.

Gloria. National Music Publishers No. NMP-132. Accompanied. Medium.

Gloria in excelsis (from *Gloria*). ed. Mason Martens. Walton No. W2043. Accompanied. Medium.

In memoria aeterna (from *Beatus Vir*). ed. McEwen. Hinshaw No. HMC-179. Accompanied. Medium.

VON FILZER, ALBERT (SEE FILZER, ALBERT VON)

VULPIUS, MELCHIOR
Christ Is the King. arr. Carolyn Jennings. Neil A. Kjos No. ED C8702. Organ and optional trumpet. Moderately easy.

Now God Be Praised in Heav'n Above. E. C. Schirmer No. 1693. Optional accompaniment. Moderately easy.

WAGENSEIL, GEORG CHRISTOPH
Magnificat. ed. Martin Banner. Carl Fischer No. CM 8293. Accompanied. Medium.

WALKER, W.
Amazing Grace. arr. Richard Wienhorst. Mark Foster No. MF 2010. Two flutes or keyboard. Moderately easy.

WARD, SAMUEL A.
America the Beautiful. arr. John Ness Beck. Beckenhorst Press No. BP 1370. Accompanied. Moderately easy.

America the Beautiful. arr. Robert Berglund. Neil A. Kjos No. C8822. Accompanied (optional band or full orchestra). Moderately easy.

WEBERN, ANTON
In Swift Light Vessels Gliding (Opus 2). Universal No. E6643A. A cappella. Moderately difficult.

WEBBER, ANDREW LLOYD
Phantom of the Opera (medley). arr. Ed. Lojeski. Hal Leonard No. 08252941. Accompanied. Medium.

Phantom of the Opera (title song). arr. Ed. Lojeski. Hal Leonard No. 08252881. Accompanied. Medium.

WEELKES, THOMAS
O Care, Thou Wilt Despatch Me. Boston Music Co. No. 13705. A cappella. Moderately easy.

WERT, GIACHES DE
Lady, So Fair Thou Seemest. Belwin Mills No. 60778. A cappella. Moderately easy.

WESTENDORF, OMER
Sent Forth by God's Blessing (Welsh folk song). arr. John Schiavone. World Library No. 8517. Organ accompaniment with trumpet. Easy.

WILLAERT, ADRIAN
Ave Regina coclorum. Ricordi No. NY1887. A cappella. Medium.

WILLAN, HEALEY
Three Kings, The. Carl Fischer No. OCS 718. *A cappella.* Medium.

WILLBYE, JOHN
Adieu, Sweet Amarillis. ed. Kaplan. Lawson-Gould No. 51865. *A cappella.* Medium.

WILSON, HARRY ROBERT
Twenty-Third Psalm, The. Bourne No. 703. *A cappella.* Medium.

YOUMANS, VINCENT
More Than You Know. arr. Steve Zegree. Hal Leonard No. 08704491 *A cappella.*
Moderately easy.

ZELTER, CARL FRIEDRICH
Tenebrae factae sunt. E. C. Schirmer. No. 4121. *A cappella.* Moderately easy.

APPENDIX C

Extended Choral Works

All choral conductors should familiarize themselves with the extended choral works of various composers. For if conductors are not familiar with major choral works, which in certain instances represent the crowning achievement of a composer, their picture or concept of choral literature is incomplete. Although an advanced high school choir could perform some of these works in their entirety, some works would be too difficult for even an advanced choir. Conductors of college, university, and adult community choruses should examine all these works for possible use by their groups.

AHLE, JOHANN RUDOLF
　Be Not Afraid — Concordia
ANTHEIL, GEORGE
　Cabeza de Vaca — Templeton Pub. Co.
BACH, JOHANN CHRISTOPH
　Childhood of Christ, The — J. Fischer
BACH, JOHANN SEBASTIAN
　Beautify Thyself, My Spirit (Cantata No. 180) — G. Schirmer
　Be Not Afraid (Motet IV) — C. F. Peters
　Christ Lay in Death's Dark Prison (Cantata No. 4) — Breitkopf & Härtel; G. Schirmer

　Christmas Oratorio — G. Schirmer
　Coffee Cantata, The (3-part chorus) — G. Schirmer
　Come, Jesus, Come (Motet V) — H. W. Gray; C. F. Peters
　Come, My Spirit, Come Exalt (Cantata No. 189) — Breitkopf & Härtel
　Come, Thou Lovely Hour (Cantata No. 161) — E. C. Schirmer
　Deck Thyself, My Soul, with Gladness (Cantata No. 180) — E. C. Schirmer
　For As the Rain and Snow from Heaven Fall (Cantata No. 18) — G. Schirmer
　For the Righteous, Wedding Cantata (No. 195) — Breitkopf & Härtel
　For Us a Child Is Born (Cantata No. 142) — Galaxy; Mark Foster
　From Depths of Woe (Cantata No. 38) — E. C. Schirmer
　Gerechten muss das Licht, Dem (Cantata No. 195) — Breitkopf & Härtel
　Gloria in excelsis Deo (Cantata No. 191) — G. Schirmer
　God, the Lord Is Sun and Shield (Cantata No. 79) — G. Schirmer
　God Is My King (Cantata No. 71) — Breitkopf & Härtel

God's Time Is the Best (Cantata No. 106)	G. Schirmer
Great David's Lord and Greater Son (Cantata No. 23)	E. C. Schirmer
Heavens Declare the Glory of God, The (Cantata No. 76)	Breitkopf & Härtel
Heavens Laugh, the Earth Exults, The (Cantata No. 31)	G. Schirmer
How Brightly Shines Yon Morning Star (Cantata No. 1)	E. C. Schirmer
If Thou Wilt Suffer God To Guide Thee (Cantata No. 93)	G. Schirmer
In God I Place My Faith and Trust (Cantata No. 188)	G. Schirmer
I Suffered with Great Heaviness (Cantata No. 21)	G. Schirmer
It Is Enough (Cantata No. 82)	Breitkopf & Härtel
Jesus, My Great Pleasure (Motet III)	C. F. Peters
Jesus, Thou My Constant Gladness (Cantata No. 147)	H. W. Gray
Jesus, Thou My Wearied Spirit (Cantata No. 78)	G. Schirmer
Kantate	Breitkopf & Härtel
King of Heaven, Come in Triumph (Cantata No. 182)	E. C. Schirmer
Kyrie in D Minor	G. Schirmer
Let Songs of Rejoicing Be Raised (Cantata No. 149)	H. W. Gray
Lord, Enter Not into Wrath (Cantata No. 105)	E. C. Schirmer
Magnificat	Breitkopf & Härtel; C. F. Peters; G. Schirmer
Mass in B Minor	G. Schirmer
Messe No. 4 in G Major	C. F. Peters
Missa Brevis in G	H. W. Gray
My Soul Doth Magnify the Lord (Cantata No. 10)	G. Schirmer
My Soul Exalts the Lord (Cantata No. 10)	E. C. Schirmer
New-Born Babe, The (Cantata No. 122)	G. Schirmer
Now Thank We All Our God (Cantata No. 192)	G. Schirmer
Nun ist das Heil und die Kraft (Cantata No. 50)	Breitkopf & Härtel
O Christ, My All in Living (Cantata No. 95)	Novello
Ode of Mourning (Cantata No. 198)	G. Schirmer
O God, How Grievous (Cantata No. 3)	E. C. Schirmer
O Jesus Christ, My Life and Light (Cantata No. 118)	G. Schirmer
O Light Everlasting (Cantata No. 34)	E. C. Schirmer
O Lord, Relent, I Pray (Cantata No. 135)	E. C. Schirmer
O Lord, This Grieving Spirit (Cantata No. 135)	G. Schirmer
O Praise the Lord for All His Mercies (Cantata No. 28)	H. W. Gray
Out of Darkness Call I Lord to Thee (Cantata No. 131)	Breitkopf & Härtel
Passion According to St. John, The	Breitkopf & Härtel; G. Schirmer
Passion According to St. Mark, The	Chantry Music Press
Passion According to St. Matthew, The	Breitkopf & Härtel; G. Schirmer
Peasant Cantata, The	Paterson's Pub. Ltd.
Praise Him, the Lord, the Almighty King (Cantata No. 137)	Breitkopf & Härtel
Praise Our God in All His Splendor (Cantata No. 11)	G. Schirmer
Praise the Lord, All Ye Nations (Motet VI)	C. F. Peters
Sheep May Safely Graze (Cantata No. 208)	G. Schirmer
Sing Ye to the Lord (Motet I)	C. F. Peters
Sleepers, Wake! (Cantata No. 140)	H. W. Gray
Spirit Also Helpeth Us, The (Motet II)	H. W. Gray; C. F. Peters
Stronghold Sure, A (Cantata No. 80)	G. Schirmer
There Uprose a Great Strife (Cantata No. 19)	G. Schirmer
Thou Guide of Israel (Cantata No. 104)	H. W. Gray
Thou Very God and David's Son (Cantata No. 23)	G. Schirmer
To Us a Child Is Given (Cantata No. 142)	G. Schirmer
Weeping, Crying, Sorrow, Sighing (Cantata No. 12)	G. Schirmer

We Must through Great Tribulations (Cantata No. 146)	G. Schirmer
When Will God Recall My Spirit? (Cantata No. 8)	E. C. Schirmer
BACH, CARL PHILIPP EMANUEL	
Holy Is God	Concordia
Magnificat	G. Schirmer
BADINGS, HENK	
Missa Antiphonica	Harmonia (Foreign Music Distributors)
BARBER, SAMUEL	
Prayers of Kirkegaard	G. Schirmer
BARTÓK, BÉLA	
Cantata Profana	Boosey & Hawkes
Shepherd's Christmas Songs	Boosey & Hawkes
BEETHOVEN, LUDWIG VAN	
Cantata on the Death of Emperor Joseph II	G. Schirmer
Choral Fantasia	Edwin F. Kalmus
Choral Finale to the Ninth Symphony	H. W. Gray; G. Schirmer
Christ on the Mount of Olives	Edwin F. Kalmus
Mass in C Major	Edwin F. Kalmus
Mass in D	Novello
Missa Solemnis, Op. 123	G. Schirmer
BERGER, JEAN	
Brazilian Psalm	G. Schirmer
Fiery Furnace, The	G. Schirmer
Psalm 57	Presser
Vision of Peace	Broude Bros.
BERLIOZ, HECTOR	
Childhood of Christ	G. Schirmer
Childhood of Christ (abridged version)	H. W. Gray
Choral Suite from Benvenuto Cellini	Oxford
Grand Death Mass, Op. 5	Breitkopf & Härtel
Requiem	G. Schirmer
Te Deum	G. Schirmer
BERNSTEIN, LEONARD	
Chichester Psalms	G. Schirmer
Choruses from The Lark	G. Schirmer
Kaddish	G. Schirmer
BLITZSTEIN, MARC	
Airborne, The (cantata)	Chappell
BLOCH, ERNEST	
Sacred Service	Broude Bros.
BOITO, ARRIGO	
Prologue in Heaven (from Mefistofele)	G. Schirmer
BORODIN, ALEX	
Polovetzian Dance and Chorus (from Prince Igor)	G. Schirmer
BRAHMS, JOHANNES	
Love-Song Waltzes (Liebeslieder Walzer)	Associated
Marienlieder	Breitkopf & Härtel; C. F. Peters; E. C. Schirmer
Motet from Psalm LI, Op. 29, No. 2	G. Schirmer
Nänie	G. Schirmer; E. C. Schirmer
Neue Liebeslieder	Lawson-Gould
Requiem, Op. 45	Edwin F. Kalmus; G. Schirmer

Schicksalslied (Song of Destiny)	H. W. Gray; E. C. Schirmer; Belwin Mills
Triumphal Hymn, Op. 55	G. Schirmer; Kalmus
BRITTEN, BENJAMIN	
A.M.D.G. (Ad majorem Dei glorium)	Faber Music
Ballad of Heroes	Boosey & Hawkes
Cantata Misericordium	Boosey & Hawkes
Ceremony of Carols, A (SATB; SSA)	Boosey & Hawkes
Company of Heaven, The	Faber Music
Festival Te Deum	Boosey & Hawkes
Hymn to St. Cecilia	Boosey & Hawkes
Rejoice in the Lamb	Boosey & Hawkes
Saint Nicolas	Boosey & Hawkes
Spring Symphony	Boosey & Hawkes
Voices for Today	G. Schirmer
War Requiem	Boosey & Hawkes
Wedding Anthem, A (Amo, ergo sum)	Boosey & Hawkes
BRUCKNER, ANTON	
Mass in E minor	Broude Bros.
Mass No. 1 in D minor	C. F. Peters
Mass No. 3 in F minor	C. F. Peters
Psalm 150	Musikwissenschaftlicher Verlag
Te Deum laudamus	G. Schirmer; C. F. Peters
BUXTEHUDE, DIETRICH	
Aperite mihi portas justitiae (Open to Me Gates of Justice)	C. F. Peters
Good Christian Men, with Joy Draw Near	Concordia
Jesu, Joy and Treasure	C. F. Peters
Laudia Sion Salvatorem	Chantry Music Press
Missa Brevis	Mercury
Open to Me Gates of Justice	C. F. Peters
Rejoice, Earth and Heaven	C. F. Peters
Sing to God the Lord	Concordia
What Is the World to Me	Concordia
BYRD, WILLIAM	
Magnificat and Nunc dimittis	Oxford
Mass for Five Voices	Galaxy: Stainer & Bell
Mass for Four Voices	Galaxy: Stainer & Bell
Mass for Three Voices	Galaxy
CALDARA, ANTONIO	
Credo	E. C. Schirmer
CARISSIMI, GIACOMO	
Jephte	Ricordi
CERHA, FRIEDRICH	
Rubaijat des Omar Khajjam	Doblinger
CHARPENTIER, MARC-ANTOINE	
Midnight Mass for Christmas	Elkan-Vogel
Venite ad me	G. Schirmer
CHERUBINI, LUIGI	
Requiem in D Minor	C. F. Peters
Requiem Mass in C Minor	G. Schirmer
COLERIDGE-TAYLOR, SAMUEL	
Hiawatha's Wedding Feast	G. Schirmer
COLLINS, DON L.	
Huckleberry Finn	Cambiata Press

COMES, JUAN BAUTISTA
  Beatus vir — G. Schirmer
  Lamentación — G. Schirmer
  Magnificat — G. Schirmer
COPLAND, AARON
  Canticle of Freedom — Boosey & Hawkes
  In the Beginning — Boosey & Hawkes
CRESTON, PAUL
  Celestial Vision, The — Shawnee Press
  Isaiah's Prophecy — Franco Colombo
  Missa Solemnis, Op. 44 — Belwin Mills
DEBUSSY, CLAUDE
  Blessed Damoiselle, The — G. Schirmer
  L'Enfant Prodigue — Elkan-Vogel
  Ode à la France — Elkan-Vogel
DELIUS, FREDERICK
  Appalachia — Boosey & Hawkes
  Mass of Life, A — Universal
  Sea Drift — Boosey & Hawkes
  Songs of Farewell — Boosey & Hawkes
DELLO JOIO, NORMAN
  Mystic Trumpeter, The — G. Schirmer
  Psalm of David, A — Carl Fischer
  Psalm of Peace — Edw. B. Marks
  Song of Affirmation — Carl Fischer
  Song of the Open Road — Carl Fischer
  To St. Cecilia — Carl Fischer
  Years of the Modern — Edw. B. Marks
DIAMOND, DAVID
  This Sacred Ground — Southern Music
DORATI, ANTAL
  Missa Brevis — Belwin Mills
DUBOIS, THEODORE
  Seven Last Words of Christ, The — G. Schirmer
DURUFLÉ, MAURICE
  Requiem — Durand
DVOŘÁK, ANTON
  Stabat Mater, Op. 58 — G. Schirmer
EFFINGER, CECIL
  Invisible Fire, The — H. W. Gray
  St. Luke Christmas Story, The — G. Schirmer
  Set of Three — Elkan-Vogel
EINEM, GOTTFRIED VON
  Missa Claravallensis, Op. 83 — Doblinger
ELGAR, EDWARD
  Dream of Gerontius — Novello
  48th Psalm — Novello
  29th Psalm — Novello
ETLER, ALVIN
  Ode to Pothos — Associated
FAURÉ, GABRIEL
  Requiem — H. T. Fitzsimons
FETLER, PAUL
  Now This Is the Story (SSA) — Carl Fischer
  Te Deum — Augsburg

FOSS, LUKAS
 Parable of Death, A   Carl Fischer
 Prairie, The   G. Schirmer
 Psalms   Carl Fischer
FRANCK, CÉSAR
 Beatitudes, The (oratorio)   G. Schirmer
 Communion Service in A Major Op. 12 E. C. Schirmer
GABRIELI, GIOVANNI
 Jubilate Deo   Bourne; G. Schirmer
 Timor et tremor   Annie Banks
GALUPPI, BALDASSARE
 Kyrie   Lawson-Gould
GESUALDO, CARLO
 Illumina nos   Boosey & Hawkes
 Tres sacrae cantiones   Boosey & Hawkes
GINASTERA, ALBERTO
 Lamentations of Jeremiah, The Mercury
GOUDIMEL, CLAUDE
 Messe audi filia   Éditions Salabert
GOUNOD, CHARLES
 Gallia   G. Schirmer
 Mass in C   G. Schirmer
 Mess Solennelle (St. Cecilia) G. Schirmer
 Missa Choralis   E. C. Schirmer
 Missa Paschalis   E. C. Schirmer
GRIEG, EDVARD
 Choral Suite   Hinrichsen & Peters
 Psalms for Mixed Chorus, Op. 74 C. F. Peters
 Vier Psalmen, Op. 74   Harmonia
HAMMERSCHMIDT, ANDREAS
 Holy Is the Lord   Concordia
 How Then Shall We Find Bread? Concordia
 Now Death Is Devoured   Concordia
HANDEL, GEORGE FRIDERIC
 Acis and Galatea   Novello
 Alceste   Novello
 Autumn Day, An   Oxford
 Belshazzar   Associated
 Canticle of Praise   G. Schirmer
 Dettingen Te Deum   H. W. Gray
 Foundling Hospital Anthem   C. F. Peters
 Funeral Anthem for Queen Caroline G. Schirmer
 Israel in Egypt   G. Schirmer
 I Will Magnify You   G. Schirmer
 Joshua   Novello
 Judas Maccabaeus   G. Schirmer
 King Shall Rejoice, The   Novello
 Laudate pueri Dominum (Psalm 112) C. F. Peters
 Messiah   G. Schirmer
 O Sing unto the Lord (Psalm 96) G. Schirmer
 Samson   G. Schirmer
 Saul   H. W. Gray
 Sixth Chandos Anthem   G. Schirmer
 Solomon   Breitkopf & Härtel; H. W. Gray

Te Deum laudamus	Verlag Merseburger
Utrecht Jubilate, The	Breitkopf & Härtel
Utrecht Te Deum, The	G. Schirmer
HANSON, HOWARD	
Beat! Beat! Drums!	J. Fischer
Cherubic Hymn, The	Carl Fischer
Song of Democracy	Carl Fischer
Song of Human Rights	Carl Fischer
Songs from Drum Taps	J. Fischer
HARRIS, ROY	
Mass in C (for Male Voices and Organ)	Carl Fischer
HASSLER, HANS LEO	
Mass No. 5	Concordia
Missa Super "Dixit Maria"	Arista
HAYDN, JOSEPH	
Creation, The	G. Schirmer
Der Strum (La Tempesta)	Belwin Mills
Mare Clausum	Doblinger
Mass in Time of War	G. Schirmer
Missa Brevis in F	Doblinger
Missa Sancti Nicolai	Arista
Missa Solemnis	C. F. Peters
Seasons, The	G. Schirmer
Seven Last Words of Christ, The	G. Schirmer
Sixteenth Mass	H. W. Gray
Stabat Mater	G. Schirmer
Third Mass (The Imperial or Lord Nelson)	G. Schirmer
HAYDN, MICHAEL	
Laudate populi	Breitkopf & Härtel
Timete Dominum (O Fear the Lord)	G. Schirmer
HINDEMITH, PAUL	
Apparebit repentina dies	Schott
Four Songs	Schott
Messe	Schott
114th Psalm	Novello
When Lilacs Last in the Door-Yard Bloom'd	Schott
St. Paul (oratorio)	G. Schirmer
HOLST, GUSTAV	
Coming of Christ, The	G. Schirmer
Hymn of Jesus, The	The Galaxy Music Corp.
HONEGGER, ARTHUR	
Cantate de Noël	Éditions Salabert
Danse des morts, La	Éditions Salabert
King David	E. C. Schirmer
Nicholas de Flue	E. C. Schirmer
HOVHANESS, ALAN	
Glory to God	C. F. Peters
In the Beginning Was the Word	C. F. Peters
Look toward the Sea	C. F. Peters
Make a Joyful Noise	C. F. Peters
30th Ode of Solomon	C. F. Peters
JANEQUIN, CLEMENT	
Messe La Bataille	Éditions Salabert
KODÁLY, ZOLTÁN	
Missa Brevis	Boosey & Hawkes

Psalmus Hungarieus	Universal
Te Deum	Universal
KUBIK, GAIL	
Litany and Prayer (TTBB)	Southern Music
Record of Our Time, A	MCA Music
KYR, ROBERT	
Magnificat	E. C. Schirmer
LARSEN, LIBBY	
The Settling Years	E. C. Schirmer
Three Summer Scenes	E. C. Schirmer
LASSO, ORLANDO DI	
Missa Puisque j'ay perdu	J. Fischer
LISZT, FRANZ	
Hymn to the Virgin Mary	Lawson-Gould
XIIIth Psalm, The	G. Schirmer
LOCKWOOD, NORMAND	
Ballad of the North and South, A	Associated
Carol Fantasy	Associated
Holy Birth, The	Choral Services
LOTTI, ANTONIO	
Mass VII in the Doric Mode	E. C. Schirmer
LULLY, JEAN BAPTISTE	
Te Deum	Schott
MACHAUT, GUILLAUME	
Messe Notre Dame	Éditions Salabert
MAHLER, GUSTAV	
VIII, Symphonie	Universal
Waldmärchen (Forest Legend)	Belwin Mills
MARTIRANO, SALVATORE	
O O O O That Shakespearian Rag	Schott
MATHEWS, PETER	
Missa Brevis	Southern Music Co.
MCDONALD, HARL	
Pioneers, O Pioneers	Elkan-Vogel
Songs of Conquest	Elkan-Vogel
MCKAY, GEORGE F.	
Choral Rhapsody	J. Fischer
MENDELSSOHN, FELIX	
As the Hart Pants (42nd Psalm)	G. Schirmer
Christus	G. Schirmer
Come Let Us Sing (95th Psalm)	G. Schirmer
Elijah (oratorio)	G. Schirmer
First Walpurgis Night, The, Op. 60	G. Schirmer
Hear My Prayer	Mark Foster; G. Schirmer
Hymn of Praise	G. Schirmer
Kyrie	Oxford
Magnificat	Augsburg
PSALM 115	
"Nicht unserm Namen, Herr"	Harmonia
MENNIN, PETER	
Christmas Story, The	Carl Fischer
Cycle, The (Symphony No. 4)	Carl Fischer
MENOTTI, GIAN CARLO	
Death of the Bishop of Brindisi, The	G. Schirmer

MILHAUD, DARIUS
  Cantate pour louer le Seigneur — Universal
  Cantique du Rhône — Elkan-Vogel
  Château du Feu, Le — Associated
  Miracles of Faith — G. Schirmer
  Naissance de Vénus — Heugel
  Pan et Syrinx — Éditions Salabert
  Three Psalms of David — Associated
MOLLICONE, HENRY
  A Christmas Celebration — E. C. Schirmer
MONTEVERDI, CLAUDIO
  Laetatus sum — Mark Foster
  Lagrime d'Amante al Sepolcro dill'Amata — Lawson-Gould
  Magnificat Primo — Lawson-Gould
MOZART, WOLFGANG A.
  Davidde penitente (K. 459) — Broude Bros.
  Glory, Praise and Power — H. W. Gray
  Grand Mass in C Minor — G. Schirmer
  Litania in E Flat (K. 243) — Edwin F. Kalmus
  Mass in C (K. 317. "Coronation") — Breitkopf & Härtel; G. Schirmer
  Misericordias offertorium de tempore — G. Schirmer
  Missa Brevis in C (K. 220) — Associated
  Missa Brevis in D (K. 194) — Edw. B. Marks
  Missa Brevis in F Major (K. 192) — G. Schirmer
  Regina coeli — Lawson-Gould; E. C. Schirmer
  Requiem Mass — H. W. Gray; C. F. Peters; G. Schirmer
  Vesperae Solennes de Dominica (K. 321) — E. C. Schirmer
ORFF, CARL
  Carmina Burana — Schott
  Catulli Carmina — Schott
  Trionfo di Afrodite — Schott
PACHELBEL, JOHANN
  Deus in adjutorium — Edw. B. Marks
  Herr ist König, Der — Concordia
  Jauchzet dem Herrn (Shout Forth to the Lord) — Concordia
  Magnificat in C — Summy-Birchard
PALESTRINA, GIOVANNI
  Assumpta est Maria — Breitkopf & Härtel
  Leichte Chore — Breitkopf & Härtel
  Missa Aeterna Christi Munera — Arista
  Missa Brevis — Breitkopf & Härtel; G. Schirmer
  Missa Iste Confessor — Breitkopf & Härtel; Edw. B. Marks
  Missa Papae Marcelli — J. Fischer; G. Schirmer
  Missa Tu es Petrus — Breitkopf & Härtel
  Pater Noster — Breitkopf & Härtel
  Stabat Mater — Belwin Mills; G. Schirmer
PENDERECKI, KRZYSZTOF
  Canticum Canticorum Salomonis (Song of Songs) — Schott
  Kosmogonia — Schott

Passion According to St. Luke	Belwin Mills
Utrenja	
Entombment of Christ, The	Schott
Resurrection of Christ, The	
PERGOLESI, GIOVANNI	
Magnificat, The	Walton Music
PERSICHETII, VINCENT	
Celebrations	Elkan-Vogel
Mass	Elkan-Vogel
Stabat Mater	Elkan-Vogel
PIERNÉ, GABRIEL	
Children at Bethlehem, The	G. Schirmer
PINKHAM, DANIEL	
Ascension Cantata	E. C. Schirmer
Canticle of Praise	E. C. Schirmer
Christmas Cantata	E. C. Schirmer
Daniel in the Lions' Den	E. C. Schirmer
Easter Cantata	C. F. Peters
Emily Dickinson Mosaic, An (SSAA)	C. F. Peters
Fanfares	E. C. Schirmer
Four Elegies	E. C. Schirmer
Jonah	E. C. Schirmer
Jubilate Deo	E. C. Schirmer
Mass of the Word of God	E. C. Schirmer
Requiem	C. F. Peters
Saint Mark Passion	C. F. Peters
Wedding Cantata	C. F. Peters
POULENC, FRANCIS	
Gloria	Éditions Salabert
Messe en sol majeur	Éditions Salabert
Stabat Mater	Éditions Salabert
PRAETORIUS, MICHAEL	
Canticum trium puerorum	Sam Fox
PROKOFIEFF, SERGE	
Alexander Nevsky	Leeds Music
PUCCINI, GIACOMO	
Gloria (from Messa di Gloria)	Lawson-Gould
Messa di Gloria	Belwin Mills
PURCELL, HENRY	
Te Deum laudamus and Jubilate Deo	G. Schirmer
RACHMANINOFF, SERGEI	
The Bells, Op. 35	Kalmus; Boosey & Hawkes (rental)
The Liturgy of St. John Chrysostom	Galaxy Music Corp.
Springtide	G. Schirmer
RAMIREZ, ARIEL	
Misa Criolla	G. Schirmer
Navidad Nuestra (The Nativity)	G. Schirmer
REIZENSTEIN, FRANZ	
Voices of Night	H. W. Gray
RESPIGHI, OTTORINO	
Laud to the Nativity	Franco Colombo
RIMSKY-KORSAKOV, NIKOLAI	
Polonaise with Chorus	Boosey & Hawkes

RINCK, JOHANN CHRISTIAN HEINRICH
  Todten-feyer — Harmonia (Foreign Music Distributors)

ROGERS, BERNARD
  Letter from Pete, A — Southern Music
  Prophet Isaiah, The — Southern Music

ROREM, NED
  From an Unknown Past — Southern Music
  Two Psalms and a Proverb — E. C. Schirmer

ROSSINI, GIOACCHINO
  Messa di Gloria — G. Schirmer
  Stabat Mater — Edition Kunzelmann

ROZSA, MIKLOS
  To Everything There Is a Season — Broude Bros.; Breitkopf & Härtel

SAINT-SAËNS, CAMILLE
  Christmas Oratorio — G. Schirmer

SCARLATTI, ALESSANDRO
  Salve Regina — Walton
  Te Deum laudamus — Presser

SCHOENBERG, ARNOLD
  De profundis (Psalm 130) — MCA Music
  Gurre-Lieder — Universal
  Kol Nidre — Boelke-Bomart
  Ode to Napoleon (for speaker and string orchestra) — G. Schirmer
  Peace on Earth — Schott
  Survivor of Warsaw, A — Boelke-Bomart

SCHUBERT, FRANZ
  Gesang der Geister über den Wassern (for male voices) — Carl Fischer
  Mass in A-flat — Breitkopf & Härtel; Novello
  Mass in F — G. Schirmer
  Mass in G — H. W. Gray; G. Schirmer
  Mass No. 3 in B-flat — Arista
  Miriam's Song of Triumph — G. Schirmer
  Rosamunde — G. Schirmer

SCHUMAN, WILLIAM HOWARD
  Free Song, A — G. Schirmer
  This Is Our Time — Boosey & Hawkes

SCHÜTZ, HEINRICH
  Annunciation According to St. Luke, The — J. Fischer; G. Schirmer
  Christmas Story, The — G. Schirmer
  Deutsches Magnificat — Bärenreiter-Ausgabe
  84th Psalm — G. Schirmer
  German Requiem, A — G. Schirmer
  Magnificat — Breitkopf & Härtel
  Mein Sohn, warum hast du uns das getan? — Oxford
  Nativity — Bärenreiter
  Passion According to St. John, The — Oxford
  St. Luke Passion, The — Oxford
  St. Matthew Passion, The — Augsburg; Breitkopf & Härtel; Oxford
  Seven Last Words, The — Oxford; G. Schirmer; E. C. Schirmer
  Symphonia Sacra No. 4 — Oxford

SENFL, LUDWIG
  Ave Maria, gratia plena   Associated
  Ich stund an einem Morgen   Lawson-Gould
SHOSTAKOVICHH, DIMITRI
  Song of the Forests (cantata)   Leeds
SOWERBY, LEO
  Ark of the Covenant, The   H. W. Gray
  Canticle of the Sun, The   H. W. Gray
  Christ Reborn   H. W. Gray
  Forsaken of Man   H. W. Gray
  Great Is the Lord   H. W. Gray
  Throne of God, The   H. W. Gray
SPOHR, LOUIS
  Mass, Op. 54   Arista
STAINER, JOHN
  Crucifixion, The   G. Schirmer
  Daughter of Jairus, The (cantala)   G. Schirmer
STEVENS, HALSEY
  Magnificat   Mark Foster
STRAVINSKY, IGOR
  Cantata   Boosey & Hawkes
  Canticum Sacrum   Boosey & Hawkes
  Flood, The   Boosey & Hawkes
  Mass   Boosey & Hawkes
  Noces, Les   Boosey & Hawkes
  Oedipus Rex   Boosey & Hawkes
  Perséphone (ballet with chorus)   Boosey & Hawkes
  Symphony of Psalms   Boosey & Hawkes
  Threni   Boosey & Hawkes
SURINACH, CARLOS
  Cantata of St. John   Associated
SWEELINCK, JAN PIETERSZOON
  Psalm 150   E. C. Schirmer
TALLIS, THOMAS
  Lamentations (Parts I and II)   Oxford
TELEMANN, GEORG PHILIPP
  Jesu, Joyous Treasure   Augsburg
THOMPSON, RANDALL
  Americana   E. C. Schirmer
  Concord Cantala, A   E. C. Schirmer
  Feast of Praise, A   E. C. Schirmer
  Mass of the Holy Spirit   E. C. Schirmer
  Nativity According to St. Luke   E. C. Schirmer
  Ode to the Virginian Voyage   E. C. Schirmer
  Passion According to St. Luke   E. C. Schirmer
  Peaceable Kingdom, The   E. C. Schirmer
  Place of the Best, The   E. C. Schirmer
  Psalm of Thanksgiving, A   E. C. Schirmer
  Requiem   E. C. Schirmer
  Testament of Freedom   E. C. Schirmer
THOMSON, VIRGIL
  Mass (unison)   G. Schirmer
  Missa pro defunctis   H. W. Gray
TULL; FISCHER
  Missa Brevis   Southern Music Co.

VAUGHAN WILLIAMS, RALPH
  Dona nobis pacem — Oxford
  Epithalamion — Oxford
  Fantasia on Christmas Carols — Galaxy
  First Nowell, The — Oxford
  Five Mystical Songs — Galaxy Music Corp.
  Five Tudor Portaits — Oxford
  Four Songs of the Four Seasons — Oxford
  Hodie — Oxford
  Mass in G Minor — G. Schirmer
  Pilgrim's Journey — Oxford
  Sancta civitas — Oxford; G. Schirmer
  Sea Symphony, A — Galaxy; Oxford; Stainer & Bell
  Serenade in Music — Oxford
  Song of Thanksgiving, A — Oxford
  Thanksgiving for Victory — Oxford
  This Day — Oxford
  Toward the Unknown Region — Galaxy
  Vision of Aeroplanes, A (Motet) — Oxford

VERDI, GIUSEPPE
  Four Sacred Pieces — Franco Colombo
  Requiem — G. Schirmer
  Te Deum — C. F. Peters

VICTORIA, TOMÁS LUIS DE
  O magnum mysterium — Associated; J. Fischer & Bros.
  Missa "O Quam Gloriosum" — Arista

VIERNE, LOUIS
  Solemn Mass — Mark Foster

VIVALDI, ANTONIO
  Chamber Mass — Lawson-Gould
  Gloria — Ricordi

WALTON, WILIAM
  Belshazzar's Feast — Oxford
  Coronation Te Deum — Oxford
  Gloria — Oxford
  In Honor of the City of London — Oxford

WEBER, CARL MARIA VON
  Mass No. 1 in G — Lawson-Gould

WEBERN, ANTON
  Das Augenlicht, Op. 26 — Universal
  Kantate, Op. 29 — Universal

APPENDIX D

Music Publishers and Distributors

As in any business, publishers may change addresses or make new arrangements for the sales and distribution of their music. Generally, music dealers are aware of these changes; however, choral directors desiring up-to-date information may request a copy of the latest *Music Publishers Sales Agency List,* available from the Music Publishers' Association of the United States, 205 East 42nd Street, New York, NY, 10017.

Aberdeen Music, Inc. (order from Plymouth Music Co.)
Addington Press (order from Hinshaw Music, Inc.)
Agape (order from Hope Publishing Co.)
Alexandria House, 468 McNally Dr., Nashville, TN 37211.
Alfred Publishing Co., P.O. Box 10003, 16380 Roscoe Blvd., Van Nuys, CA 91410-0003.
Altam Music Corporation, 9301 Wilshire Blvd., Beverly Hills, CA 90210.
Antara Music Group, 468 McNally Dr., Nashville, TN 37211.
Art Masters Studios, Inc., 2710 Nicollet Ave., Minneapolis, MN 55408-1630.
Associated Music Publishers, Inc., 24 E. 22nd St., New York, NY 10010 (order from Hal Leonard Corp.)
Augsburg Fortress Publishing House, 426 S. Fifth St., Box 1209, Minneapolis, MN 55440.
Bärenreiter Music Publishers (order from Foreign Music Distributors)
Beckenhorst Press, P.O. Box 14273, Columbus, OH 43214.
Belmont Music Publishers, P.O. Box 231, Pacific Palisades, CA 90272.
Irving Berlin Music Corp., 29 West 46th Street, New York, NY 10019
Big 3 Music Corp. (order from CPP/Belwin Music)
Birch Tree Group, Ltd., 180 Alexander St., Princeton, NJ 08540
Fred Bock Music Company, P.O. Box 570567, Tarzana, CA 91357
Boelke-Bomart, Inc., and Mobart Music Publications (order from Jerona Music Corp.)
Boosey & Hawkes, Inc., 24 East 21st Street, New York, NY 10010-7200
The Boston Music Company, 172 Tremont St., Boston, MA 02111
Bote & Bock Musikverlag (order from Hal Leonard Publishing Corp.)
Bourne Company, 5 West 37th St., New York, NY 10018
Breitkopf & Härtel (order from Hal Leonard Publishing Corp.)
Broadman Press, 127 Ninth Ave. N., Nashville, TN 37234
Broude Brothers, Ltd., 141 White Oaks Rd., Williamstown, MA 01267
Cambiata Press, P.O. Box 1151, Conway, AR 72032
Carus-Verlag, Stuttgart (order from Mark Foster Music Co.)

Chantry Music Press, 32 N. Center St., Springfield, OH 45502
Chappell Music Co. (order from Hal Leonard Publishing Corp.)
Charter Publications (order from J. W. Pepper & Son, Inc.)
Cherry Lane Music Co., Inc., 10 Midland Ave., Port Chester, NY (order from Alfred Publishing Co.)
John Church Company (order from Theodore Presser Co.)
Franco Columbo Publications (order from CPP/Belwin Music)
Concordia Publishing House, 3558 S. Jefferson Ave., St. Louis, MO 63118
Consolidated Music Publishers, Inc., (order from Music Sales Corp.)
Coronet Press (order from Theodore Presser Co.)
CPP/Belwin Music, 15800 N.W. 48th Ave., P.O. Box 4340, Miami, FL 33014-9969
Creative World Music Publications (order from Warner Brothers Publications, Inc.)
Curtis Music Press (order from Neil A. Kjos Music Co.)
J. Curwen & Sons (order from Hal Leonard Publishing Corp.)
Dartmouth Collegium Musicum (order from Shawnee Press, Inc.)
Roger Dean Publishing Company (order from The Lorenz Corporation)
Oliver Ditson (order from Theodore Presser Co.)
Editio Musica, Budapest, Hungary (order from Boosey & Hawkes, Inc.)
Edition Musicus, P.O. Box 1341, Stamford, CT 06904
Editions Salabert (order from Hal Leonard Publishing Corp.)
Edizione Suvini Zerboni, Milan, Italy (order from Boosey & Hawkes, Inc.)
Elkan-Vogel, Inc. (order from Theodore Presser Co.)
European American Music Distributors Corp., 2480 Industrial Rd., Paoli, PA 19301
The Evangel Press (order from Art Masters Studios, Inc.)
Carl Fischer, Inc., 62 Cooper Sq., New York, NY 10003
J. Fischer & Bros. (order from CPP/Belwin Music)
H. T. Fitzsimons Co., P.O. Box 570567, Tarzana, CA 91357 (order from Antara Music Group)
Harold Flammer, Inc. (order from Shawnee Press, Inc.)
Foreign Music Distributors, 13 Elkay Drive, Chester, NY 10918
Mark Foster Music Company, Box 4012, Champaign, IL 61820
Sam Fox Music Sales Corp. (order from Plymouth Music Co., Inc.)
Frank Music Corp. (order from Hal Leonard Publishing Corp.)
Galaxy Music Corporation (order from E. C. Schirmer Music Co.)
Galleon Music, Inc. (order from Altram Music Corp.)
Galleria Press (order from Plymouth Music Co.)
Genesis III Music Corp. (order from Plymouth Music Company, Inc.)
Gentry Publications, P.O. Box 570567, Tarzana, CA 91357 (order from Antara Music Group)
G.I.A. Publications, 7404 S. Mason Ave., Chicago, IL 60638
Glory-Sound (order from Shawnee Press, Inc.)
H. W. Gray Company, Inc. (order from CPP/Belwin Music)
Greystone Press (order from Plymouth Music Co.)
Hansen House, 1804 West Avenue, Miami Beach, FL 33139
Harmonia (order from Foreign Music Distributors)
T. B. Harms Co. (order from Warner Brothers Publications)
The Frederick Harris Music Co., Ltd., 340 Nagel Drive, Buffalo, NY 14225-4731
Heritage Music Press (order from The Lorenz Corporation)
Heugel and Cie (order from Theodore Presser Co.)
Hinrichsen Edition (order from C. F. Peters Corp.)
Hinshaw Music, Inc., P.O. Box 470, Chapel Hill, NC 27514-0470
The Raymond A. Hoffman Co. (order from Antara Music Group)
Charles W. Homeyer & Co. (order from Carl Fischer, Inc.)
Hope Publishing Co., 380 S. Main Place, Carol Stream, IL 60188
Ione Press (order from E. C. Schirmer Music Co.)
Jenson Publications, Inc. 7777 W. Bluemound Rd., Milwaukee, WI 53213

Jerona Music Corp., P.O. Box 5010, Hackensack, NY 07606-4210
Joclem Music Publishing (order from Boosey & Hawkes, Inc.)
Edwin F. Kalmus & Company, Inc., P.O. Box 5011, Boca Raton, FL 33433-8011
Kenbridge Music (order from Jerona Music Corp.)
Kendor Music, Inc., P.O. Box 278, Delevan, NY 14042
E. C. Kerby, Ltd. (order from Hal Leonard Publishing Co.)
Neil A. Kjos Music Co., 4382 Jutland Dr., P.O. Box 178270, San Diego, CA 92117-0894
Laurel Press (order from The Lorenz Corp.)
Lawson-Gould Music Publishers, Inc., 250 W. 57th Street, Suite 932, New York, NY 10107
Hal Leonard Publishing Corp. 7777 W. Bluemound Rd., Milwaukee, WI 53213
The Lorenz Corporation, 501 E. Third St., Dayton, OH 45401
Malecki Music, Inc., 4500 Broadmoor, P.O. Box 150, Grand Rapids, MI 49501-0150
Manna Music, Inc., 25510 Stanford Ave, Valencia, CA 91355
Margun/Gunmar Music, Inc., 167 Dudley Rd., Newton Centre, MA 02159 (order from Jerona
   Music Corp.)
Edward B. Marks Music Company (order from Hal Leonard Publishing Co.)
MCA Music Publishing, 1755 Broadway, 8th Floor, New York, NY 10019 (order from Hal
   Leonard Publishing Co.)
McLaughlin & Reilly Company (order from Warner Brothers Publications)
Mercury Music Corp. (order from Theodore Presser Co.)
Merion Music Corp. (order from Theodore Presser Co.)
Edwin H. Morris & Co., Inc. (order from Hal Leonard Publishing Corp.)
Music Press (order from Theodore Presser Co.)
Music Sales Corp., 225 Park Avenue South, New York, NY 10003
Music 70 Publishers, 170 N.E. 33rd St., Ft. Lauderdale, FL 33334
National Music Publishers, 1326 Santa Ana, P.O. Box 8279, Anaheim, CA 92802
Novello Publications (order from Theodore Presser Co.)
Orpheus Music Co. (order from Plymouth Co., Inc.)
Oxford University Press, 200 Madison Ave., New York, NY 10016
Paterson's Publications, Ltd., London (order from Carl Fischer, Inc.)
Paull Pioneer Publications (order from Shawnee Press, Inc.)
J. W. Pepper & Son, Inc., 2480 Industrial Blvd., Paoli, PA 19301
Performers' Editions (Order from Broude Brothers, Ltd.)
C. F. Peters Corp., 373 Park Ave. South, New York, NY 10016
Plymouth Music Co., Inc., 170 NE 33rd St., P.O. Box 24330, Ft. Lauderdale, FL 33334
Theodore Presser Co., Presser Place, Bryn Mawr, PA 19010
Pro-Art Publications (order from CPP/Belwin Music)
Providence Press (order from Hope Publishing Co.)
G. Ricordi & Co. (order from Hal Leonard Publishing Corp.)
Robbins Music (order from CPP/Belwin Music)
R. D. Row Music Co. (order from Carl Fischer, Inc.)
Sacred Music Press (order from The Lorenz Corp.)
E. C. Schirmer Music Co., 138 Ipswich St., Boston, MA 02215
G. Schirmer, Inc., 225 Park Ave. South, New York, NY 10003
Arthur P. Schmidt Co. (order from Warner Brothers Publications)
Schmitt, Hall & McCreary (order from CPP/Belwin Music)
Schott & Company (order from European American Music Distributors Corp.)
The Shapiro, Bernstein Organization (order from Plymouth Music Co., Inc.)
Shawnee Press, Inc., Waring Drive, Delaware Water Gap, PA 18327-1099
John Sheppard Music Press, P.O. Box 6784, Denver, CO 80206
Somerset Press (order from Hope Publishing Co.)
Southern Music Co., 1100 Broadway, P.O. Box 329, San Antonio, TX 78292-0300
Spratt Music Publishers (order from Plymouth Music Co., Inc.)
Staff Music Publishing Co., Inc. (order from Plymouth Music Co., Inc.)
Stainer & Bell, Ltd. (order from E. C. Schirmer Music Co.)

Studio 4 (order from Alfred Publishing Co.)
Studio P/R, Inc. (order from CPP/Belwin Music)
Summa Productions (order from Art Masters Studio, Inc.)
Summy-Birchard Co. (order from Warner Brothers Publications, Inc.)
Tabernacle Publishing Co. (order from Hope Publishing Co.)
Templeton Publications (order from Shawnee Press, Inc.)
Tetra/Continuo Music Group (order from Plymouth Music Co., Inc.)
Gordon V. Thompson Music, 29 Birch Ave., Toronto, Ontario, Canada M4V IE2 (order
    from Hal Leonard Publishing Corp.)
Transcontinental Music Publications, 838 Fifth Ave., New York, NY 10021-7046
Triune Music, Inc. (order from The Lorenz Corp.)
TRO (The Richmond Organization), 11 West 19th Street, New York, NY 10011
Tuskegee Music Press (order from Neil A. Kjos Music Co.)
Twin Elm Publishing, 1626 Twenty-Seventh Avenue Court, Greeley, CO 80631.
UNC Jazz Press, College of Performing and Visual Arts, School of Music, Jazz Studies
    Division, University of Northern Colorado, Greeley, CO 80639
Universal Edition (order from European American Music Distributors Corp.)
Walton Music Corp. (order from Plymouth Music Co., Inc.)
Warner Bros. Publications, 265 Secaucus Road, Secaucus, NJ 07096-2037
Joseph Weinberger, Ltd., London (order from Boosey & Hawkes, Inc.)
Williamson Music Co., 598 Madison Ave., New York, NY 10019
Willis Music Co., 7380 Industrial Rd., Florence, KY 41042
Word Music, Inc., 5221 No. O'Conner Blvd., Suite 1000, Irving, TX 75039
World Library Publications, 3815 N. Willow Rd., P.O. Box 2701, Schiller Park, IL 60176
The Zondervan Music Group, 365 Great Circle Rd., Nashville, TN 37228

Index

The Right to Die

Recent Titles in the
CONTEMPORARY WORLD ISSUES
Series

Books in the **Contemporary World Issues** series address vital issues in today's society such as genetic engineering, pollution, and biodiversity. Written by professional writers, scholars, and nonacademic experts, these books are authoritative, clearly written, up to date, and objective. They provide a good starting point for research by high school and college students, scholars, and general readers as well as by legislators, businesspeople, activists, and others.

Each book, carefully organized and easy to use, contains an overview of the subject, a detailed chronology, biographical sketches, facts and data and/or documents and other primary source material, a forum of authoritative perspective essays, annotated lists of print and non-print resources, and an index.

Readers of books in the Contemporary World Issues series will find the information they need in order to have a better understanding of the social, political, environmental, and economic issues facing the world today.

The Right to Die

A REFERENCE HANDBOOK

Howard Ball

ABC-CLIO™

An Imprint of ABC-CLIO, LLC
Santa Barbara, California • Denver, Colorado

Library of Congress Cataloging-in-Publication Data

Names: Ball, Howard, 1937– author.
Title: The right to die : a reference handbook / Howard Ball.
Description: Santa Barbara, California : ABC-CLIO, LLC, [2017] | Series: Contemporary world issues | Includes bibliographical references.
Identifiers: LCCN 2016042041 (print) | LCCN 2016045321 (ebook) | ISBN 9781440843112 (alk. paper) | ISBN 9781440843129 (ebook)
Subjects: LCSH: Right to die—United States. | Euthanasia—United States.
Classification: LCC R726 .B255 2017 (print) | LCC R726 (ebook) | DDC 179.7—dc23
LC record available at https://lccn.loc.gov/2016042041

ISBN: 978-1-4408-4311-2
EISBN: 978-1-4408-4312-9

21 20 19 18 17   1 2 3 4 5

This book is also available as an eBook.

ABC-CLIO
An Imprint of ABC-CLIO, LLC

ABC-CLIO, LLC
130 Cremona Drive, P.O. Box 1911
Santa Barbara, California 93116–1911
www.abc-clio.com

This book is printed on acid-free paper ∞

Manufactured in the United States of America

For two persons who keep me from going off the rails:
Michael Bukanc and Jeffrey Rubman.

If we allow medicine to prolong life, should we also allow it to shorten life for the terminally ill?

Nora Zamichow and Ken Murray, 2014

It is necessary that [advocates on both sides] will need to work together and listen more closely to [each other's] concerns about end-of-life cases.

Alicia Ouellette, 2013

Whatever the limits and travails we face, we want to retain the autonomy—the freedom—to be the authors of our lives. This is the very marrow of being human.

Atul Gawande, 2014

Not one of us decided the time or manner in which we come into the world. Our life is a sacred gift from God, and only He can give it. It is therefore His right alone to take us out of the world.

Father Frank A. Pavone, 2014

The Right to Die: A Reference Handbook examines the issue as it has evolved over the past century, giving prominence to the last

50 years because of these decades' impact on how we die due to the exponential acceleration of scientific research and medical technological breakthroughs. As a result, Americans have been living much longer and, due to changes in *how* the medical community responds to accidents and illness, dying much more slowly and, frequently, in great pain. It is an examination that considers how these scientific-technological-medical advances impact the dying process.

Chapter One examines the beliefs, values, and fears of all the participants in these ongoing ethical, medical, social, legal, and political battles about *how* we live and *if* and *how* we can determine how we will die. At its core, this book is about the hardnosed battles between those who believe that a person has a constitutionally protected liberty to die with the assistance of a physician and their opponents, who maintain that a host of ethical, religious, legal, and medical principles bar such medical aid to help a terminally ill patient to die.

The first chapter examines these battles from these two ardently opposed positions, providing readers with a clear understanding of the reasons for such profound disagreements. It will also provide the reader with the historical context within which are located the roots of this contentious issue in the 21st century.

Chapter One underlines the importance of constitutional rights and liberties in the nation's history, especially the ways in which fundamental human rights have been expanded through interpretations of the idea of "liberty" found in the U.S. and state constitutions. It took judicial decisions, legislative enactments, and presidential powers to enlarge the scope of "liberty" to include blacks, women, ethnic and religious minorities, the poor, and the gay and lesbian communities. The Civil War amendments (Thirteenth, Fourteenth, and Fifteenth, added in 1865, 1866, and 1868); the Nineteenth Amendment (1919); the Civil (1964) and Voting (1965) Rights Acts; and U.S. Supreme Court decisions in the areas of women's rights, marital privacy, marriage, and free speech are but a few examples of how the Constitution has evolved over two-plus centuries to expand the meaning of individual rights and liberties.

The clashes surrounding whether there is a right to die protected by the Constitution and by laws passed by government are discussed in general terms in Chapter One. Democracy works, in great part, because of these *figurative* battles between opposing groups over how we live and die. Votes, not bullets, determine the outcome of such battles. But it is an outcome that will be challenged—again and again—by the losers. That is the core of a democracy. On any issue of public concern, groups—religious, social, economic, professional, political, and moral—are created to push for rights allegedly denied them.

As the right to die clashes illustrate, a defeat in court, or at the ballot box, does not end the fight. The victors know, too well, that the defeated opposition will rise, phoenix-like, to continue their efforts to change the public policy they believe is unconstitutional, and criminal, and immoral. Both sides in a policy dispute *generally* win some and lose some. Groups supporting the constitutional right of an autonomous person to choose to die with physician assistance have worked decades to achieve victories in five states. However, the opposing groups who believe that the right to die with a doctor's help is sacrilege, a criminal act, or a violation of medical codes of conduct, have won many more times when their efforts *defeated* right to die bills or petitions to judges.

The first chapter examines the beliefs and values of these two sets of individuals and organizations so that the specific confrontations that are discussed in Chapter Two are thoroughly understood by the reader. Chapter Two's focus is on the controversies that have taken place in America about the place of the right to die in the pantheon of citizen rights. The clashes revolve around the essential question the issue raises: is there, in the Constitution, a "liberty" enjoyed by terminally ill patients to hasten death with the assistance of their physician?

Can—should—the meaning of the Constitution's words evolve in order to address issues that were not present in 1787? Or are they to be read as the founders "originally" used them to convey ideas? Do the words of the 1787 Constitution allow Congress to pass a law that protects voting rights? Or does the 18th-century language not extend to legitimize such a bill? (The consequence: a legal judgment that the challenged bill is unconstitutional.) Can a state prohibit—in its criminal code—a doctor from aiding a terminally ill patient to hasten death? Or does "liberty" in the Constitution's due process clause permit a dying person to hasten death by receiving a prescription from a doctor for a lethal drug?

These are the general questions raised in American courts, especially the U.S. Supreme Court—regarding all important policy differences—since the beginning of the Republic. These are but a few of the difficult questions both sides argue over in the right to die battles. Chapter Two will examine specific right to die clashes that began in the 1970s and are still largely unresolved in 2016. They have taken place in state legislatures and state and federal courts, in the political arena, in the health care system, in the media, in churches and synagogues, on Twitter and Facebook, and around the dinner table.

After discussing the ebb and flow of the continuing battles over the right to die, Chapter Two will examine the problems that *still* hang over the issue and whether there are meaningful, realistic solutions to the major unresolved questions regarding the right to die.

The Right to Die is not an "advocacy" book; my task, as educator and writer, is to inform readers about the very different views Americans have expressed about "the morality, legality, and practicality of physician-assisted suicide (*Washington v. Glucksberg*, 1997) in the 21st century. My hope is that this book will inform and educate so that the right to die debates, regardless of their outcome, continue to reflect the virtues of reasonable and educated citizens in our Republic.

A number of persons have graciously assisted me in the preparation of this book. My editor at ABC-CLIO, Robin Tutt, has worked with me in the past and, once again, has enabled me to overcome obstacles that appeared during the writing of *The Right to Die*. Furthermore, Robin was extremely gentle when my "luddite" behavior kicked in as I confronted yet another digital dilemma. (Where were my grandkids when I needed them?) I also appreciate the help the librarians gave me at the Richmond Free Library in Vermont and at the Oro Valley, Arizona Library, over these past years. Also, a special thank you to my IT "maven" at the Oro Valley library, Eric Strong. He is there three times a week and I have reserved a seat next to his work station. He helps all of us with our computer problems, because, as snowbirds, we cannot draw upon the expertise of our grandkids. The two of them, Robin and Eric, have kept me sane as I wrote the book.

I must also thank all my political science students—from the University of Vermont, Dartmouth College, and the University of Szeged, Hungary—who took my class "Death and Dying." Their intense interest in the subject matter, their insightful questions, and their substantive discussions and debates about how we die never ceased to amaze—and educate—me. I must also thank the university pathologists at the Vermont and Dartmouth medical schools who provided my students with clinical information about the major causes of death in the 21st century—complete with slide shows of these "killers."

My sister, Carol Teplin, and I (along with our two other sisters, Brenda Levy and Sarah Ball), experienced the pain and sadness of watching our mother, Fay, succumb—very slowly—to dementia. During those years, and afterward, Carol and I discussed the right to die and the options available to us when we face the time—that all mortals face—when "breath becomes air" (Kalanithi 2016).

When I first began researching, teaching, and writing about physician assistance in dying, nearly two decades ago, my daughters were very insightful and shared their thoughts with me. Like my students, they had questions and observations about the subject. My oldest, Susan, continually suggested that the title for my book *must be* "My Life, My Choice." It reflected her fundamental take on the right to die. Sheryl and Melissa harped on the importance of all persons writing their medical care wishes (DNR documents, advanced directives, instructions for guardians to follow) if they survive a catastrophic injury or when confronted with a terminal illness. These wishes are guidelines for family, judges, doctors, nurses, and others to follow. Carol, my wife for more than 50 years, also expressed her views on the issue—quite clearly: *even if you can't keep going, keep going.*

All the cohorts I acknowledged above—editors, librarians, IT specialists, students, doctors, and family—are very aware of the problems, the controversies, and the finality of this issue. Given the visibility of the clash of opposing groups over physician assisted death and euthanasia, the question of reasonableness is ever-present. I take comfort in the fact that *all* my discussions about death and dying with colleagues, students, health care professionals, friends, and family were grounded in *rational engagement*; they understand the criticality of reasoned debate, especially when discussions focus on controversial subjects such as abortion, the right to die, and the right to privacy. My hope is that such conversations increase exponentially in

America, that some compromises can be discovered in these hotly contested social problems, thereby avoiding the rending of our society. Finally, any factual errors are solely my fault.

References

Gawande, Atul. 2014. *Being Mortal: Medicine and What Matters in the End.* New York: Metropolitan Books.

Kalanithi, Paul. 2016. *When Breath Becomes Air.* New York: Random House.

Ouellette, Alicia. 2014. "Context Matters: Disability, the End of Life, and Why the Conversation Is Still So Difficult." *New York Law School Review*, 58:371, 2013–2014.

Pavone, Father Frank A. 2014. "Freedom to Die?" Euthanasia. http://www.priestsforlife.org/euthanasia/index.htm

Zamichow, Nora, and Ken Murray. 2014. "The Hippocratic Oath and the Terminally Ill." *Los Angeles Times*, December 26.

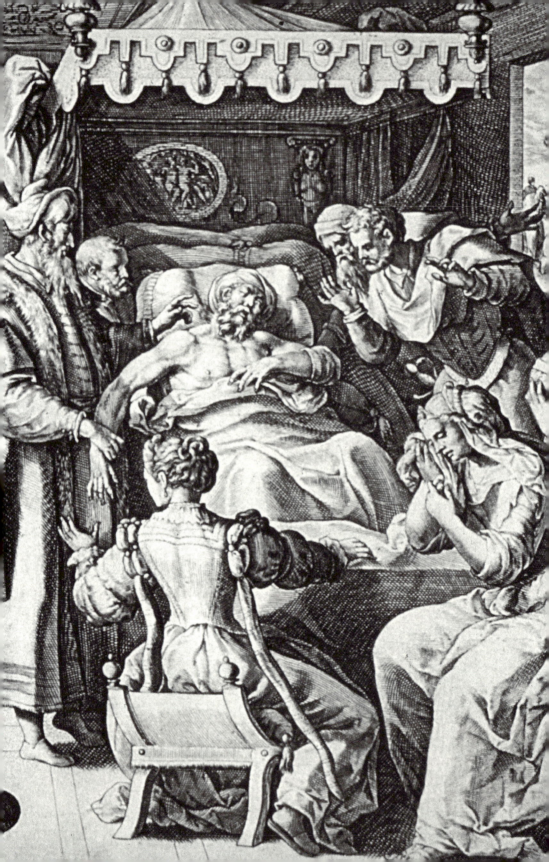

Introduction

We all die. Why has the way Americans die become so controversial in the 21st century? To answer this question, one must understand some very basic historical realities about—and major themes of—the right to die controversy. The following five topics lead unerringly to an understanding of why the right to die with the assistance of a physician has become a significant question.

1. The noteworthy changes in how we die in America over the past century.

2. The shifting doctor-patient relationship over this time.

With these two sets of topics as foundation blocks, we may

3. examine and place in context the late-19th-century-to-early-20th-century political debates and votes, articles in the press and professional journals, and public lectures about euthanasia (mercy killings, where the physician injects a lethal medication to a dying patient) and about

A 15th-16th century illustration of a man on his death bed. Through the middle of the 20th century, death generally occurred at home, with the dying person surrounded by family, clergy, and a physician. With the increase in medicalization that occurred in the 1950s, the hospital has become the primary place of death, with the dying patient surrounded by doctors, nurses, technicians, and a variety of machines and devices that artificially sustain life. (Maarten de Vos, National Library of Medicine)

the initial efforts to pass state bills legitimizing the practice of euthanizing suffering patients, leading, nearly a century later, to bills introduced in state legislatures allowing physician-assisted dying (PAD).

It is also necessary to be familiar with

4. the emergence, beginning in the mid-20th century and continuing into the 21st century, of the culture of "medicalization of death" and its dramatic impact on all discussions about dying, physician assistance in dying, the training of physicians, their relationship with patients, the health care system, and the right to die in the 21st century. This contemporary culture, some believe, has "subjected dying patients to too many treatments, denying them a peaceful death" (Lerner 2014, p. A26).

5. Finally, understanding the contours of the right to die battles requires that we know (1) the arguments put forth by advocates for PAD, (2) the various methods, other than PAD, available in the 21st century to competent, terminally ill patients who are in relentless pain and suffering but PAD is prohibited in their state (1 of 45 that bans its practice), (3) the arguments that have surfaced opposing PAD, and (4) the major groups aligned on both sides of this major societal issue.

The controversy surrounding the question of whether a dying person has a right to choose to die and who can provide assistance to the patient is one that has grown dramatically in the 21st century.

Changes in How We Die

In 1900, the 10 major causes of Americans dying were largely infectious diseases such as pneumonia, bronchitis, and, the number one killer, tuberculosis. (While cancer and stroke appeared near the bottom of the list, tuberculosis accounted for triple the number of deaths than cancer.)

After the onset of these illnesses, death came quickly because of the inability of the medical profession to treat and save people who succumbed to these illnesses. In the absence of antibiotics to treat the illness and morphine to relieve the pain, the malady rapidly became terminal—generally a matter of weeks to months between the onset of the illness and death. A doctor could do very little for the patient except prescribe bed rest, fresh air, sunshine, and nutrition! Consequently, Americans did not live very long; the average life expectancy in 1900 was 47 years.

In 1900, the overwhelming majority of people died in their homes, surrounded by friends, family, and clergy. The grieving process following death was one that reflected the family's and the community's social and religious norms. The health of persons in industrial societies slowly improved with the invention of vaccines, antibiotics, diagnostic equipment; the elimination of horrendous working conditions that adversely affected the health of the vast majority of laborers, especially women and children; better nourishment; improved sanitation; and, in the second half of the 19th century through the first third of the 20th century, improvement in the safety of industrial workers on the job, as well as the increased use of morphine and other analgesics that enabled doctors to dramatically lessen a patient's pain and suffering after an accident. In addition, the development of state-funded public health service agencies focusing on prevention of disease and the promotion of good community health practices greatly enhanced the lives of persons.

As a consequence, in the 21st century, Americans are living longer—the average life expectancy in 2015 is nearly 80 years—and how we are dying has changed significantly. Longevity enables protracted illnesses to emerge in the population, and they have become the major killers. In 2015, 7 out of 10 lived long enough to die from chronic conditions like heart disease, stroke, emphysema, dementia, diabetes, cancer, and kidney failure (Butler 2015).

A century earlier, most of us did not live long enough to contract chronic illnesses such as cancer or heart disease.

A look at the 21st century's top 10 causes of death according to the Centers for Disease Control and Prevention (CDC 2015) presents a very different portrait of the major causes of death: heart disease is the number one cause of death (30%), followed, in order, by cancer (23%), stroke (7%), and chronic lower respiratory disease (5%). Pneumonia and influenza combined account for less than 3 percent of annual deaths, and tuberculosis is not on the list at all! One looks in vain, however, for the third of the top causes of death; the CDC does not list it because it is caused by doctors. "Few things are deadlier than doctors' screw-ups. . . . Medical error kills between 210,000 and 440,000 Americans each year. Only heart disease and cancer have a higher body count" (Lieber, 2016).

In the 21st century, for the majority of the dying, the end is slow in coming, and in many instances, escorted by relentless pain and varieties of suffering. Death in the 21st century generally takes place in the modern hospital, not the home. These changes in how we die signal a fundamental change in the role and function of the physician in the dying process and how the relationship between doctor and patient has evolved.

The Changing Doctor-Patient Relationship

In 1900, the doctor's function in caring for patients was minimal: comforting the patient while participating in a ritual death watch along with the dying patient's family, friends, and clergy in the home, not in a hospital. There was little a doctor could do to halt a patient's march to death; moreover, many doctors did not have the use of drugs—morphine and other anesthetics—to manage the pain and suffering of the disabled and dying. Diagnostic instruments and devices to artificially prolong a life were nonexistent in 1900; there were very few medical laboratories that could assist the doctor by providing a scientific diagnosis to better care for a sick patient.

However, over the past century, there have been dramatic changes in the doctor-patient relationship. This has come about because of the cojoining of the changing reality of when and how we die with dramatic, exciting scientific, diagnostic, and technological breakthroughs in how we treat the major 21st-century maladies and how managing death has clearly become the province of the medical professionals, not the priest, imam, or rabbi—and, in many instances, not even the dying patient and family members.

The setting for these major transformations is no longer the private home of the patient. There has been a dramatic—indeed, profound—transformation in how and where people die and how dying rituals have changed that reflect these changes. During this time, the hospital has evolved from a kind of poorhouse where impoverished persons came to die, prayed over by clergy, to a modern institution where medical researchers deconstruct the etiology of disease using space-age technological and diagnostic equipment, where medical professionals bring their sick and dying patients to be treated and released in much improved health, and where death generally occurs.

Most deaths occurred in the home at the beginning of the 20th century. By 1950, nearly half of all deaths took place in hospitals and nursing homes; in the 1990s, over 80 percent of patients (mostly elderly) died in a hospital's intensive care ward. In 2015, nearly all deaths occur in a hospital, nursing home, or hospice, not at home. In America, this is an especially impactful change. Americans in the 21st century have "lost loss. Death as a community event, and mourning as a communal practice, has been steadily killed off" (Schillace 2016).

The First Efforts to Pass Euthanasia Bills in America

In 1997, Chief Justice William Rehnquist, writing for a unanimous Supreme Court in *Washington v. Glucksberg*, concluded that euthanasia, also tagged as physician-assisted death, was alien to the "history, legal traditions, and practices" of the United States. However, the justices and *all* 17 amicus curiae groups filing briefs opposing a terminal patient's right to die with medical assistance ignored the nation's historical reality.

For nearly 150 years there have been political, legal, and social acts and the creation of pressure groups in America's history that championed changes in the way we think about death and dying. As early as 1870, in Alabama, Samuel Williams began his decades-long journey to convince educators, doctors, and legislators that euthanasia, "mercy killing" or "merciful death," be permitted "in all cases of hopeless and painful illness [to bring about] a quick and painless death" (Emanuel 1997).

Williams's views emerged in response to two events that dramatically impacted society: the invention and growing use of morphine and other analgesics to relieve pain in gravely injured and terminally ill patients, and the brutal reality of the industrial revolution. The new drugs relieved pain, wrote Williams, and could also "painlessly induce death."

The mechanization of manufacturing, the expansion of coal mining and iron and steel mills, and the increased use of railroads to transport these goods—as well as the inordinate number of hours men, women, and children worked weekly in the factories, in the mines, and on the trains—led to terrible accidents that maimed, burned, and left many who did not die in unbelievable agony. In the decades after the discovery of morphine, it was used largely to alleviate the injured person's overwhelming pain.

Williams's proposal was a call for euthanasia, where the physician deliberately injects morphine in sufficient quantity to relieve the pain but also end the life of the gravely injured and suffering or terminally ill patient. It was neither a new nor a novel strategy for ending the tormented, painful life of a severely injured patient. The ancient Greeks and Romans accepted the merits of euthanasia, abortions, and suicide.

The Hippocratic Oath, taken by doctors, instructed them to *do no harm* when treating patients. However, few ancient Greek and Roman physicians followed this behavioral rule. "Throughout classical antiquity, there was widespread support for voluntary death as opposed to prolonged agony, and physicians complied by often giving their patients the poison they requested" (Dowbiggin 2003). (Interestingly, among the newspapers that condemned the 1906 euthanasia bills, *The Philadelphia Inquirer* editorialized that Williams "spoke like a Greek and not a human being.")

The euthanasia debates initiated by Williams in 1870 and continuing during the two decades prior to World War I, however, were fundamentally different from those surrounding the right to die and PAD today (Appel 2004). Unlike today's battles between the "sanctity of life" groups and the "personal autonomy" and "individual liberty" organizations, the earlier debates, legislative acts, news reports, editorials, and articles in medical journals focused on the question of whether euthanasia was an idea that would benefit the "collective welfare" of society in the industrial era.

"Humanity should not suffer," editorialized *The Washington Post*; use morphine to humanely end a tortured existence for the many severely injured and crippled patients across the nation. The early euthanasia clashes were fought only over whether or not the practice would benefit society. At the turn of the 20th century, the dominant attitude toward relations between individuals and the state was axiomatic: "One's life is not one's own. One's life belongs to society" (Appel 2004). Consequently, the "right to die" was never mentioned in these early discussions of euthanasia.

Euthanasia struck a chord with Americans across the nation. They knew of the ghastly aftermath of the accidents brought on in this new age of "gilded wealth." Over the next three decades (1870–1900) Williams's ideas were reprinted in popular magazines and books, discussed in the pages of prominent literary and political journals, and debated at the meetings of American medical societies and nonmedical professional associations (Emanuel 1997). Euthanasia, advanced as a remedy by Williams and others in the late 19th century to deal with painful consequences of industrialism, was a natural outcome of the immense popularity of eugenics in America.

The eugenics ("good birth" or "wellborn") movement was a radical late-19th-to-early-20th-century social movement that applied Charles Darwin's theories of natural selection to account for the evolution—and improvement—of human societies. Darwin found in his examinations of plants and animals how evolution occurred—through natural selection. In 1883, Darwin's half-cousin Francis Galton transplanted the theory of natural selection into a "science of eugenics," which would eventually eradicate the lower class, that is, all those impure residents—*untermenschen*—living in society.

This class—"imbeciles," feeble minded, criminals, and other unfit persons—was a plague on society. They had to be removed through the activation of eugenics policies and laws by the states which would improve the human species through selective breeding. In America, eugenics became the zeitgeist of the Progressive era. Leading figures in politics (Theodore Roosevelt), commerce (Alexander Graham Bell, John D. Rockefeller), and law (Oliver Wendell Holmes) were ardent supporters of this method of improving society. The science of eugenics became a popular major in colleges, universities, and law schools. It was supported by naturalists and the ministry. And, quite quickly, laws were passed that would, according to Galton, lead to the emergence of a virile, moral, and a dominant society. Thirty-two states passed such laws in the 20th century; between 60,000 and 70,000 men and women were sterilized, including, in the 21st century, hundreds of female prisoners in California.

The primary method chosen by the states was forced sterilization of these social undesirables. Sterilization became an integral part of the legal machinery; criminals convicted of a third offence were, at a prosecutor's discretion, sterilized. Slow-witted, retarded persons, residents of insane asylums, and prostitutes were prime candidates for sterilization. In 1927, the U.S. Supreme Court, in an 8-1 decision written by Justice Oliver Wendell Holmes (*Buck v. Bell*), concluded that a Virginia sterilization bill was constitutional because "three generations of imbeciles is enough." (The case has never been overturned. It was cited as precedent by the defense at the 1946 Nuremberg War Crimes Tribunal and more recently in a 2001 case.) Eugenics legislation would quickly, in the words of one of its early enthusiasts, "dry up the springs that feed the torrent of defective and degenerate protoplasm" (Cohen 2016).

Euthanasia was linked to the eugenics movement during the first decade of the 20th century, when, in 1906, radical euthanasia bills were introduced in two Midwestern states. For the first time in American history, bills were introduced in Iowa and Ohio—with accompanying intense debates in, and beyond, the legislative bodies—to legalize euthanasia so that doctors could "painlessly induce death" without fear of subsequent criminal indictment by the state. The "beneficiaries" covered by legalizing euthanasia included grievously injured workers as well as "those suffering hopelessly from paralysis, cancer, and imbecility" (Appel 2004).

In Ohio, the bill was labeled "an Act Concerning the Administration of Drugs, etc. to Mortally Injured and Diseased Persons" (Ohio H.B. 145, 1906). It provided that

> any person of lawful age and of sound mind, who is fatally injured or is so ill of disease that recovery is impossible, or who is suffering great physical pain or torture, may be treated by a physician, not a relative or interested in his or her estate, and in the presence of three witnesses he may ask the patient if he or she cared to be put to death according to law. Should the patient's answer be in the affirmative then three reputable physicians are to be called in, and if they concur—that is, if they decide there is no chance for a recovery—then an anesthetic is administered until death ensues.

In Iowa, the euthanasia proposal was called "A Bill for an Act Requiring Physicians to Take Human Life" (Iowa House File No. 367, March 1906). It was a much more radical proposal than the Ohio bill. "It shall be the duty of such physician" if the diagnosis was that it was impossible "to avert the patient's death" and "that extreme physical pain must characterize the remainder of said patient's natural life," then the "duty" of the physician was to "administer an anesthetic until death shall have ensued."

Reflecting, in part, the strength of the emergent and growing-in-popularity eugenics movement, the euthanasia bill "allowed parents to ask physicians to end the lives of their offspring in order to prevent 'the rearing of children who are hideously deformed or hopelessly idiotic,' and permitted guardians of sick and mentally 'unsound' individuals to request euthanasia on their behalf."

The initial euthanasia advocates joined humane euthanizing of terribly injured workers and incurably ill patients with involuntary euthanizing of the physically disabled, the mentally handicapped, "lunatics and idiots," and other state dependents. As one of the sponsors of the Iowa bill said during the debates: "Many of the hideously deformed were better off out of this world than in it. If at birth they could have been legally removed, they would have been better off" (Appel 2004, 629).

The most radical feature of the Iowa bill was the imposition of an affirmative duty on physicians. If asked by a patient, and the diagnosis was death, a physician *had the duty* to euthanize the person. The bill enumerated the penalty imposed on doctors and coroners for rebuffing such aid: if the doctor fails or refuses to perform euthanasia, and is convicted, he "shall be adjudged guilty of a misdemeanor and imprisoned in the county jail not less than six months or more than one year, and fined not less than $200 dollars or more than $1000 dollars" ("Physicians May Take Human Life" 1906).

Unlike the sponsors of the Ohio bill, who were nonmedical social advocates for the humane final treatment of people suffering from a terminal illness or were in great agony, the three Iowa cosponsors "were among the most prominent physicians in the region" (Appel 2004). They were rebels for a cause—the eugenics/euthanasia movement—that went counter to the position of their own professional organization, the American Medical Association (AMA)!

The proposals were fervently debated. There was, in 1906 and remains so over a century later, cacophonous shouting between the opposing sides. Some supporters of the 1906 euthanasia bills wanted a more draconian law, one that allowed ending the lives of the "hopelessly insane in padded cells." Other supporters argued for a narrower bill that would allow euthanasia only when the patient consented to the action. Opponents were similarly unable to agree on a focused argument for rejecting the bill. There were concerns that passage would adversely impact—ethically and legally—the medical profession; that physicians, because of the shortcomings of medical diagnosis, could never be certain that an ill person was terminal; that there might be opportunities for doctors to abuse the use of euthanasia; or that "a cunning murderer" would take sinister advantage of a euthanasia bill to evade homicide statutes. Unlike the contemporary right to die battles, the early-20th-century controversy "featured practical men and women negotiating desirable social policy. 'God's will' and 'individual rights' did little to shape the terms of the debate during this period" (Appel 2004).

A most revealing argument against the bill was that, if it became law, one of the legislators said, "the world would lose the 'exhibitions of heroism' and the 'inspiration that a society gains' from watching the dying man bravely endure his deathbed." Missing from the opposition to euthanasia bills in 1906 were the representatives from religious organizations, especially the Roman Catholic Church. These groups play a major role in their contemporary battles against personal autonomy, the right to die, and physician-assisted death.

Although there were angry words and equally heated retorts in the legislative chambers, both proposals failed to garner support for their passage. However, the debates and discussions about eugenics and euthanasia—its rightness and who would be euthanized—continued. For decades, there were essays about the issue in a variety of medical, nursing, political, and philosophical journals and magazines. The issue was viewed by editors and publishers as above-the-fold-page-one newsworthy in newspapers, both national (*The New York Times, New York Herald, Washington Post, Boston Herald, Philadelphia Inquirer, San Francisco Chronicle, Chicago Tribune*, among others) and in state and local media. The early-20th-century euthanasia bills and the ensuing debates continued a national discussion about death and dying that began in the 1870s, one that still remains an animated part of the public's social agenda in the 21st century—although with very different foundation values in play.

The organization representing the medical profession was one of the initial opponents of euthanasia. In 1885, reacting to the continuing glut of articles and debates about euthanasia, and fearful of the adverse impact of this idea on the practice and the ethics of the medical profession, the AMA forcefully opposed the notion. Since then, the AMA has not changed its position opposing legalizing euthanasia and its modern incarnation: physician-assisted death. It is curious that one of the first organizations to endorse legalizing euthanasia was a medical group, the American Association of Progressive Medicine. In 1917, by a vote of 87–24, the association, rebuffing the AMA, approved the legalization of euthanasia.

Although the focus of the debates has shifted because of tectonic changes in how we live and die, and on the primacy of the community over the individual, the right to die continues to be read and discussed and voted on and litigated over for almost 150 years. Justices and judges, from the county courts to the U.S. Supreme Court, "should no longer . . . ignore or dismiss the heritage of 1906" (Appel 2004, 634). Euthanasia, physician assistance in dying, and public policy battles over the right to die have been a substantial—and controversial—part of America's social, religious, political, and medical histories for a century and a half.

By the 20th century, punishing a person for attempting suicide was no longer prohibited in any state. By the century's end, euthanasia was prohibited in every state. However, passively assisting a person to end his life is another story, one that continues to agitate people and groups across the nation in the 21st century. As early as 1828, the first state law prohibiting assisting suicide was passed in New York State. By 1865, that state's criminal code was expanded to provide punishment for a person "aiding a suicide, furnishing another person with any deadly weapon or poisonous drug, knowing that such person intends to use such weapon or drug in taking his own life" (Appel 2004). Other state legislators mimicked New York's prohibition against abetting a suicide.

By the sixth decade of the 20th century, a physician assisting a terminally ill patient to die was committing a criminal offense in every state. At this time, there was seen and heard a chorus of demands and actions, across the nation, from discriminated and marginalized groups living in America, including the disabled, blacks, Hispanics, women, gays and lesbians, criminal defendants, Native Americans, and anti–Vietnam War protesters. Their complaints had been simmering, without redress, for more than 100 years. They crested and boiled over beginning in the 1960s. These angry citizens demanded the return of basic, inalienable rights guaranteed by the U.S. Constitution but denied to them: liberty, due process, justice, and freedom from discrimination—fundamental rights presumably guaranteed to all persons in America in the Fourteenth Amendment.

Their pleas and their protests, over time, were heard by influential political decision makers, and changes were made in the laws and customs that had been responsible for the discrimination and inequality that existed. These watershed actions were taken in court opinions (*Brown v. Board of Education*, 1954), in congressional legislation (1964 Civil Rights Act; 1965 Voting Rights Act), and in executive actions (broadening of the Department of Justice to deal with discrimination, issuance of executive orders integrating the military services).

In this era, in the beginning called by many the "Age of Camelot"—John F. Kennedy's presidency (1961–1963)—the emerging primacy of constitutional rights and liberties gave sustenance to the earliest advocates of physician assistance in dying groups. The mantra of these years was clear: individual rights and liberties is the bedrock of a viable democracy. The other critical societal change that led to the emergence of the right to die groups was the changing, and quite controversial, dynamics of the relationship between doctors and patients: the medicalization of death paradigm.

The Medicalization of Death

These changes in the manner of how and where people die are linked segments in a new, quite controversial health paradigm that explains how society manages death in the 21st century and accounts for a number of major questions about the doctor-patient relationship: the medicalization of death.

Medicalization of death reflects the change from dying as a private, communal event managed by the patient, family, and clergy in the home to, now, a dying event primarily involving the aggressive actions of doctors and other medical personnel in hospitals utilizing the latest medical technologies to forestall death because they can do so and, to date, for some doctors, without too much concern for the patients they are treating.

When these new technologies—the innovative emergency treatment tactics used on patients who suffered an acute injury, or inventions such as dialysis machines, respirators, and feeding tubes—and new drugs were introduced around the middle of the 20th century, the responses were elated. Lives were saved by transplanting hearts and kidneys; by CPR and other tactics employed by emergency department responders; and by new discoveries that eradicated polio and managed heart failure, some cancers (childhood leukemia), diabetes, and other once-deadly illnesses.

There was an infectious excitement in the medical community, one that dramatically changed the physician's perceptions of death and dying. The medicalization of death standard ushered in the profound belief that the physician could cure the patient and put off death for an indeterminate length of time. And the physician-as-healer became the super person who could save the world—one patient at a time.

These events, however, illuminated an emergent problem: In the 1960s, the education of the new doctors did not include any courses—medical, along with social psychology and palliative care coursework—on how to help a dying patient cope with death. Medical students lacked any mentoring or on-the-job experience with how to counsel patients about end-of-life choices. "Dying was hardly mentioned in med school or training programs, except as a failure of treatment. It was rarely spoken of to families, let alone patients, who were never to be denied hope for a recovery, no matter how dire the prognosis" (Angell 2012). Young physicians were expected to do all they could to save a life. A patient who died after aggressive medical work was seen as a medical failure.

There were, however, some physicians who abhorred such behavior. For these, generally senior, physicians, many involved in the medical futility movement (Heft et al. 2000), the medicalization of death standard dehumanized patients: "[they] had become things that needed to be treated" (Lerner 2014). One doctor, mirroring the final scene in the powerful movie *Wit*, "covered [his] newly dead patient—who had been hospitalized for months and was in constant agony—to stop his colleagues from trying to revive her" (Lerner 2014).

These physicians were not the only people upset with the new medical standard. Families of dying patients were bewildered and then angry with the behavior of their doctors in this new medical era. Chris Bohjalian is a novelist who has written nearly one dozen best-selling novels in the past two decades. Recently, in one of his final weekly columns, "Idyll Banter," in Vermont's largest daily newspaper, he spoke about his father's last days in an assisted living facility, fighting "that good fight against aging and death." For his father, the new devices and surgical and pharmaceutical inventions employed in the management of death confounded and angered him. "Technology prolongs our lives," wrote Bohjalian (2015), "but it now moves so quickly and changes so fast that my father . . . felt humiliated and [captured] by [medicine's] new 'gadgets.'"

Theresa Brown, an experienced clinical oncology and hospice nurse, provides a frank clinical definition of Bohjalian's father's frustration: "Pursuing the most aggressive treatment is far and away the [medical] norm. . . . The reigning presumption in our health care system is that treatment, no matter how hopeless or torturous, must be pursued, and that life, no matter how compromised, must be preserved" (T. Brown 2015).

There is also a second terrible result of physicians applying every new technological change onto seriously ill patients: most of the time they do not make the person treated live longer or feel better! Dr. Gawande wrote in his diary, after a futile eight-hour surgery on a dying cancer patient, that although the operation was a "technical success," it did not help the man at all. "The chances that he would return to anything like the life he had even a few weeks earlier were zero. But admitting this and helping him cope with it seemed beyond us. We offered no acknowledgement or comfort or guidance. We just had another treatment he could undergo. Maybe something very good would result" (Gawande 2014).

Sadly, death has become a technical event—a *medical experience*—one that sees the aggressive implementation by physicians of new techniques that prolong a dying patient's life. And for too many patients and their family caregivers and legal surrogates, this generally fruitless prolongation of life by the medical doctors is not what they wanted.

The medicalization of death phenomenon is premised on the principle of doctors applying aggressive healing protocols to patients who are close to death, even though these new cutting-edge procedures used to prolong life also impair life afterward—if the patient survives the procedure. Too many times, especially with cancer patients, the aftermath of the life-saving surgery or radiation or chemotherapy (usually all three strategies are employed) leaves a patient in far greater pain than experienced before the operation.

The 2015 findings of a major research center reviewing the impact of using chemotherapy to help end-stage cancer patients underscore medical reality in this new age. The Center for Research on End-of-Life Care at the Weill Cornell Medical College in New York "found no evidence that chemo improved [terminally ill] patients' quality of life. . . . Of those receiving chemotherapy, 56% were reported to have lower quality of life in their last week, compared with 31% of those who did not have chemotherapy. [A director of the research center said,] 'The real kicker is it's the people who are performing well, who are thinking they're going to benefit, that didn't'" (Szabo 2015). Indeed, for the healthiest of the dying cancer patients, the quality of life "actually got worse after chemo" (Belluck 2015).

This medicalization of death paradigm has been the preeminent standard of health care since the middle of the last century. However, it has come under increasing attack and has been condemned by many physicians who offer another view of how sick and dying patients should be cared for. They believe that when healing a patient is no longer possible, "when death is imminent and patients find their suffering unbearable, then the physician's role should shift from healing to relieving suffering in accord with the patient's wishes" (Angell 2012).

This respectful alternative concept of a patient-centered care system rather than a system grounded in the physician's medicalizing care has been accompanied by two major events in how a society should care for its sick and dying: the emergence of the hospice and palliative care movements and the advent of state court decisions addressing the futility of the applicability of medicalization of death innovations in every treatment of a dying patient.

The first significant occurrence was the re-introduction in our time of the ideas of "hospice" and "palliative care." During "medieval times [11th century], [hospice] referred to a place of shelter and rest for weary or ill travelers on a long journey" (History of Hospice Care 2016). It entered the medical comfort care lexicon due to the singular efforts of a British medical doctor, Dame Cicely Saunders, who began her work with terminally ill patients in 1948. From the very beginning of her medical practice, she focused on what was, for her, the essence of hospice in the 20th century: a team-oriented approach (including physicians, nurses, and specialists providing emotional, psychological, and spiritual support tailored to the patient's needs) to "compassionately caring, not curing," terminally ill patients in the patient's home, or in free-standing hospice wings in hospitals, and in other long-term care facilities (History of Hospice Care 2016).

Dr. Saunders eventually created a model of the hospice system of specialized care for dying patients. She was able, by 1967, to establish the first modern hospice—St. Christopher's Hospice—in London. She introduced the hospice care concept in America when she visited Yale University's School of Nursing in 1963. Her talks led to the launching of the hospice movement in America. By 1974, Professor Florence Wald, Dean of the Yale School of Nursing, and Dr. Saunders' colleague, founded the first American hospice, Connecticut Hospice in Branford, Connecticut.

By the first decade of the 21st century, over 40 percent of deaths occurred in hospice and palliative care centers (Ball 2012). Hospice was supported by palliative care physicians working in palliative care centers treating seriously ill patients in great pain but not yet dying. (When a patient in palliative care is diagnosed as terminally ill, then that person can be admitted to hospice.) Hospice, palliative care, and PAD all share the belief that seriously ill and dying patients must be compassionately cared for and treated as sentient, unique, and autonomous human beings; their questions and fears must not be ignored by their doctors.

The second event that had a major impact on the right to die issue took place in the New Jersey state Supreme Court

where, for the first time since 1906, a case gave "explicit attention to whether and how to bring about an earlier death in
permanently unconscious patients or in patients who were suffering unbearably at the end of life" (Angell 2012). The case, *In
Re Quinlan* (1976), was a landmark judicial decision allowing
guardians of an unconscious patient in a permanent vegetative state (PVS) to have all life-sustaining procedures removed
in order to hasten death; it became the opening round of the
four decades-long-and-still-counting PAD movement's effort
to establish the right to die as a fundamental liberty owned by
all persons living in America.

The public was made vividly aware of the issue after *Quinlan*, when new cases raising that issue were litigated in state
courts across America. Beginning in that decade, the media
latched onto these cases and American listeners, readers, and
viewers were bombarded with heartbreaking human interest
stories about the tragedies that befell families when a daughter,
a wife, or a husband suffered a devastating injury that left the
individual unconscious, with medical devices artificially providing the person with oxygen, nutrition, and hydration.

Since then, the media has not stopped covering these right
to die clashes. Given the breadth, the speed with which the
stories are covered, written, and published, and the number
of reporters covering the news since the 1970s, a considerable
number of these stories regularly flood the eyes and ears of the
people in the nation and beyond. It was the post-1906 press
coverage of the euthanasia bills, but with one thousand times
more coverage by the press, on radio and television, in news
weeklies and journals, on Facebook, Twitter, and Instagram,
and in books, and has continued since then.

The Basic Arguments Supporting and Opposing PAD

Physician aid in dying has become an intensely felt issue, from
the *Quinlan* case to the present time, forcing Americans to pick
a side in the clash. One either uncompromisingly supports

PAD or ferociously opposes all efforts to legalize PAD. There is no middle ground; there is, to date, no possibility of developing a compromise. This issue has been, since the 1970s, a take-no-prisoners battle between true believers. It joined abortion, stem cell, and other controversial issues associated with privacy, autonomy, sanctity of life, and "do no harm."

The Arguments of Supporters of PAD

The essence of the advocate's attachment to PAD is the deeply held view that a terminally ill, competent person has the unconditional right to choose when, how, and where to die. It is my life; it is, therefore, my choice how I end it! The American Psychological Association's mission statement reflects this view: "No person should have to endure terminal suffering that is unremitting, unbearable, or prolonged. . . . When the circumstances are not remediable, the dying person should be able to ask for and receive help in [PAD]" (Working Group Report, 2000).

A small number of PAD advocates, early on, included voluntary euthanasia in their drafts of PAD bills. Most right to die believers, however, support passive physician assistance in dying that is the basis of PAD legislation (and court orders) in six states: the physician provides the terminally ill patient with a prescription for the lethal drug which the patient self-administers (or not). If that path is not taken, the person dies of the underlying disease.

There are a number of reasons that amplify a dying person's right to choose death:

1. **Respect for autonomy**: The choice of PAD is a personal one, and the autonomous individual who is dying has the liberty to make such a choice. Competent, terminally ill people have an inalienable right—constitutional or common law—to choose the time, place, and manner of death.

2. **Justice**: Justice requires that we treat like cases alike. The Fourteenth Amendment's equal protection clause, which

says that state actions that "deny any person within its jurisdiction of the equal protection of the laws" are unconstitutional, has been employed by PAD advocates in legal battles. Their argument: terminally ill competent patients who have no life-sustaining artificial medical devices they can have withdrawn in order to die are denied "equal protection" unless the state allows them to choose PAD. Withdrawing or withholding artificial means that sustains the life of a dying patient is the same as a terminally ill patient not on such a life-maintaining device requesting physician-aid-in-dying. Distinguishing these situations is a violation of the equal protection clause.

3. *Compassion*: A dying patient's suffering is more than physical pain; there are also mental, emotional, social, and psychological infirmities, such as the loss of independence, the loss of sense of self-hood, and an intolerable quality of life, all incapacities that devastate the dignity of some dying patients. PAD is a compassionate response to unremitting pain and suffering of a terminally ill patient.

4. *The individual's liberty to die outweighs a state interest in preserving life*: When a competent, terminally ill patient's pain and suffering is intolerable, using PAD trumps the state's interest in preserving that patient's life. The state's commitment to preserving the life of a dying resident is secondary to that person's liberty to use PAD. Such a state police power unconstitutionally deprives a person of the right to PAD.

5. *PAD—Patient choice, not coercion*: Every PAD bill that has become law provides the terminally ill patient with a critically important option after the person receives a prescription and fills it: she does not have to take the lethal pill! The Oregon PAD law has been in effect since late 1997. Statistics through 2014 show that doctors in Oregon have written 1,173 prescriptions. However, choices were made by every one of the terminal patients—to take the lethal

medication or not to take it and let nature take its course. Of the 1,173 persons, 752 chose to use the medication to end their lives; but 421 terminally ill patients chose not to hasten their death.

In the states that allow PAD, with the Oregon law serving as a template, the law underscores the basic principle of self-autonomy: all competent patients who meet the requirements can legally obtain lethal medication; it provides a great deal of comfort for a patient to know that if the pain and suffering is unbearable, he can choose to use the medication. As Governor Jerry Brown said to the California Assembly members explaining his decision to sign California's PAD law: "I do not know what I would do if I were dying in prolonged and excruciating pain. I am certain, however, that it would be a comfort to be able to consider the options afforded by this bill. And I wouldn't deny that right to others" (E. Brown, 2015).

6. ***Countering the opposition's slippery slope argument***: The supporters of PAD have confronted this argument from the very beginning of their efforts to legitimize PAD through legislation or court interpretations of the language found in state laws or the U.S. Constitution. They maintain that the PAD model, which has been the archetype in the five states allowing it through the political process—the Oregon Death with Dignity Act—has a set of stringent protections built into the act that prevent intentional or unintentional acts of euthanasia. They point to the statistics compiled annually by the PAD states' health departments illustrating the fact that the constraints are working and that there is no evidence of the existence of the slippery slope. In Montana, the state Supreme Court interpret the Montana Constitution to immunize doctors from criminal indictment if they assisted a patient to hasten death. The state legislature, however, has not moved to pass a right to die law.

7. ***Other benefits of PAD***: The legalization of PAD would encourage open discussion and may promote better

end-of-life care as patient and MD could more directly talk about concerns and options available to the patient. Also, public awareness of PAD can lead to more people writing "advanced directives" describing the medical treatment they want—and do not want—in the event they are incapacitated and no longer able to provide "informed consent" to their physician and their loved ones.

The Major Groups Supporting PAD

The primary advocates of PAD are doctors who believe that the fundamental ethical norm of the profession—the "first, do no harm" mantra in the Hippocratic Oath (created in the fifth century BCE.)—is not violated when they assist a terminally ill patient to die. Indeed, they maintain the doctor does harm when she does nothing to help, thereby allowing the dying patient to live with agonizing pain and suffering. If the patient's malady is beyond curing, the doctor must then care for that person. And if the patient asks for physician assistance to die the doctor's duty is to act to alleviate further pain and suffering.

While the major group representing physicians, the AMA, continues to reject PAD, it does not speak for a majority of doctors. Only a bit more than 30 percent of practitioners are members of the AMA (Angell 2012), and some of them disagree with the organization's position on PAD. There are two PAD physician types: the zealots and the conventional physicians.

Doctors as "Indiscriminate Zealots"

There are PAD doctors who are called indiscriminate zealots. Some act spontaneously to alleviate the pain and suffering of a patient; others support PAD but see it as a means to achieving their ultimate goal: legitimizing euthanasia. Examples of these PAD physicians follow.

In 1988, *The Journal of the American Medical Association* (*JAMA*) published a short essay "It's Over Debbie," written by an anonymous doctor on duty at a large, private hospital (Anonymous, 1988). While on call in the middle of the night, the gynecology intern was awakened by a nurse's call. He was asked to see a young female patient in the gynecological-oncology unit. She was not the doctor's patient, and the ward she was in was not his "usual duty station."

The doctor responded and noted that the 20-year-old patient, whose name was Debbie, was dying of ovarian cancer. "She was sitting in bed suffering . . . the room seemed filled with the patient's desperate effort to survive. . . . It was a gallows scene, a cruel mockery of her youth and unfulfilled potential. Her only words to me were, 'Let's get this over with.'" After "retreating with [his] thoughts" to the nurse's station, he asked the nurse "to draw 20 mg of morphine sulfate into a syringe. Enough, I thought, to do the job." He joined Debbie and an older woman and told them he was "going to give Debbie something that would let her rest and to say good-bye."

He injected the morphine intravenously, and he and the visitor waited and watched for the inevitable result: Debbie's breathing soon ceased. The visitor, holding Debbie's hand until she died, "stood erect and seemed relieved. It's over, Debbie." The short two-page essay appeared in *The JAMA* in 1988 and sparked a national firestorm of outrage from medical and nursing associations, religious groups, spokespersons for the disabled, and many of the general public.

For some time the "Debbie" essay, which had instantly been reprinted in many media outlets, was talked about in editorials, in letters to the editor, in talk shows, and by persons gathered around the water fountain. The local prosecutor spent many months, ultimately unsuccessful, trying to uncover the name of the anonymous intern who killed Debbie so that criminal charges could be filed by the state. It became the signal event in the opening up of an issue that had never been discussed publicly until this period of American history: PAD.

The Michigan pathologist who characterized these medical zealots was Dr. Jack Kevorkian (called "Dr. Death" in the media although he labeled himself a "death consultant"). He was an uncompromising believer in the morality of active voluntary euthanasia by doctors. In 1990, he began assisting people to die. He invented a traveling death-inducing machine and installed it in his vintage VW van. Kevorkian purchased newspaper ads in Michigan papers and solicited persons who were in pain and who wished to die with his assistance (Kevorkian 1991).

For nearly a decade, he traveled in his VW, assisting more than 130 people to enter his van and, after hooking themselves up to his machine, to die—a majority of them not terminally ill. His continuing actions and state criminal court trials received national and international attention; since his first appearance as Dr. Death in 1990, Kevorkian remains an icon for some in the right to die clashes—although he died in 2011. Books, movies, television documentaries, news reports, and segments on shows such as *60 Minutes* provided the public with new and, for many, disturbing information about his belief in active voluntary euthanasia and how he was putting his values to work. He was, in 1999, after acquittals or mistrials in earlier trials, convicted of 2nd degree murder and sentenced to 10 to 25 years in prison.

Other intensely committed PAD/euthanasia advocates who founded organizations to publicize their beliefs were Derek Humphry, who created the Hemlock Society, and, in New Zealand, Dr. Philip Nitschke, the founder of the international Final Exit Network. Nitschke's group's "guiding principles and mission" holds that mentally competent adults who are *not* terminally ill, who suffer "intractable physical pain, or [suffer] from a constellation of chronic, progressive physical disabilities, have a basic human right to choose to end their lives when they judge the quality of life to be unacceptable" (Mission 2016). It is the only organization functioning in America that provides help to non-terminally-ill patients.

The Conventional Physician/Supporter of PAD

The second type of physician believes in PAD but, unlike Kevorkian, is a respected member of the profession because of the compassionate care and counseling practiced by him in interactions with patients. This type is exemplified by the behavior of Dr. Timothy Quill. He differs from Kevorkian and other "enthusiasts" in three ways: he cares for his patients, many he has known for years; he does not advertise in newspapers or television for dying patients; and, because he believes that physicians should always engage in "comfort care," Quill presents PAD as one option among others for physicians to discuss with their dying patients.

Quill became familiar to the public in 1991 after an essay he wrote about one of his patients came to the attention of the medical community, the district attorney's office, and the public. It appeared in *The New England Journal of Medicine* and it too, like the Kevorkian stories in the press at the same time, angered and informed the public about how we die when it became public. His account, "Diane" (Quill 1991), described why he gave a prescription of lethal drugs to a leukemia patient.

Diane was Dr. Quill's patient. He had been her doctor for nearly a decade when acute myelomonocytic leukemia was discovered in Diane by the doctors. After Quill provided her with a bleak assessment of the outcome of a series of painful, dangerous, and debilitating proposed treatments for her cancer (25% chance of survival after the series of two treatments and a bone marrow transplantation ended), she told Quill that she would rather die at home—at a time of her choosing—by self-medicating a lethal dose of a drug. She believed it was better than dying alone, in a hospital room, hooked up to medical devices that were not making her pain and suffering better.

After many tear-producing conversations with Diane about her choices, Quill gave her a prescription for a lethal dose of barbiturates. To avoid possible criminal action against him for assisting her to die, Quill prescribed the medicine for Diane to use for sleeping and cautioned her to avoid taking too many pills lest she unintentionally commit suicide.

She picked up the medication and, at a time of her choosing because of the unremitting pain, took the pills and died alone in her own bed. (To avoid her family from possible charges of assisting a suicide, Diane chose to die alone. Before she took the lethal dose, however, she spent many hours with friends and family sharing memories of their lives together.)

The ensuing uproar over these doctor-patient conversations and Diane's final act triggered (unsuccessfully) efforts to take away Quill's license to practice in New York State as well as the possibility of Quill facing a criminal indictment. It also made the public, once again, acutely aware of the consequence of chronic illness's impact on the dying process and on the new type of doctor-patient relationship.

Professional Medical Groups Supportive of PAD

There have been a number of health care groups that have supported a dying patient's right to die. In taking this position in the controversy, the members are at odds with the major professional medical organization, the AMA. They believe that the compassionate care and counseling exhibited by Dr. Quill is the hallmark of how doctors must act in physician assistance to their dying patient. These groups include the American Medical Students Association (30,000 members), the American Medical Women's Association (4,000 members), the American Association of Hospice and Palliative Medicine (5,000 members), the American Pharmacists Association (62,000 members), the American College of Legal Medicine (1,000 members), and a number of state chapters of the AMA, for example, the California Medical Association (40,000 members) and the American Public Health Association (50,000 members).

Nonmedical Groups Supporting PAD

A wide variety of nonmedical groups supporting physician-assisted-dying legislation can be identified by simply viewing the amicus curiae petitions supporting PAD filed in litigation in state and federal courts. For example, in the critically important Ninth Circuit U.S. Court of Appeals decision, *Compassion in Dying v. State of Washington* (1996), there were AIDS support groups, gay and lesbian groups, women's groups, senior citizens groups, legal groups, humanistic and religious groups, euthanasia organizations, as well as labor unions and groups that acted to defend the rights of all persons found in the Bill of Rights.

These support organizations included the Americans for Death with Dignity; Euthanasia Research and Guidance Organization; the ACLU of Washington; Seattle Chapter; Japanese American Citizens League; Northwest Women's Law Center; Lambda Legal Defense and Education Fund (a gay rights support group); AIDS Action Council; Northwest AIDS Foundation; Seattle AIDS Support Group; Grey Panthers Project Fund; Older Women's League; Seattle Chapter of National Organization for Women; The American Humanist Association; Temple De Hirsch Sinai; Unitarian Universalist Association; National Lawyers Guild; and Local 6, Service Employees International Union.

The Two Major PAD Pressure Groups

For the past three decades, two major national organizations (joined by affiliated state chapters) have been involved in all the right to die battles, in state legislatures and in state and federal courts: Compassion and Choices and Death with Dignity National Center.

Compassion and Choices

Compassion and Choices is one of the earliest groups advocating euthanasia for terminally ill patients. Initially, the group, founded in 1980 by Derek Humphry, was called the Hemlock Society. Its mission was to provide information about how to die to terminally ill patients and others and supporting legislation that would legitimize physician-assisted dying. Hemlock Society members supported the initial—unsuccessful—efforts in California, Washington, Michigan, and Maine to pass right to die bills in the early 1990s. Humphry's intense fervor about the essentiality of voluntary euthanasia, however, led to his hasty removal (by the leaders of the PAD movement) from any public forum whose subject was a proposed right to die bill.

(Supporting the idea of a physician administering a lethal dose of medicine to a dying patient who asked for that action was, and remains, a kiss of death for any proposed legislation to legitimatize the right to die.)

At the time of its first name change in 2002 (to End of Life Choices), the organization had nearly 90 chapters across America with close to 50,000 members. In 2003, it merged with the Compassion in Dying Federation to become the national Compassion and Choices organization. Its motto is its mission: "Expanding Choices and Improving Care at the End of Life." Mirroring the primary functions of the Hemlock Society, the merged advocacy organization—working with state chapters—participates in preparing legal briefs for PAD plaintiffs in state and federal courts. It is also a major advocacy group working with PAD groups in dozens of states in the continuous effort to pass right to die bills.

It also provides end-of-life help to terminally ill patients and their families through conversations with them and with clergy, with palliative care professionals, and through providing books and articles that enable the patient to continue to explore the options available at this critical stage of life. Trained *client support volunteers* provide counsel and information to the patients and their family: advanced directives, living will, and Do Not Resuscitate documents; help with admission to a hospice; linking the patient with illness-specific support groups; providing information to the patient and family members on the legal options available to assist in dying; and other services.

Since the merger, Compassion and Choices' main office is in Denver, Colorado. It has a smaller number of staff in other states, including California, Colorado, the District of Columbia, Washington State, Oregon, Connecticut, Massachusetts, Montana, New Mexico, New York, and Vermont.

Death with Dignity National Center

The Death with Dignity National Center, initially partnered with the Oregon Death with Dignity Legal Defense and Education

Center in 1997, began life in Oregon in 1993 as Oregon Right to Die, a political action committee. Its mission was, and remains in 2016, "to promote Death and Dignity laws based on our model legislation, the Oregon Death with Dignity Act, both to provide an option for dying individuals and to stimulate nationwide improvements in end-of-life care."

Its members actually drafted and then led the fight to pass the nation's first PAD bill, the 1994 Oregon Death with Dignity Law (which was a ballot initiative, not a bill passed by the legislature).

The mission statement also underscores the symbiotic relationship between PAD organizations and the important and growing hospice and palliative care movements in America. (A major group, the National Hospice and Palliative Care Organization, passed a resolution in 2005 opposing all efforts to legitimize physician-assisted dying.) Generally, terminally ill patients who have legally received PAD were in palliative care centers in hospital and then in hospice care in a hospital or at home once they were diagnosed as terminal.

In 2004, the Oregon Death with Dignity and the Oregon Death with Dignity Legal Defense and Educational Council merged to become the nonprofit Death with Dignity National Center (DDNC) and the Oregon Death with Dignity Political Action Fund. In the first decade of the 21st century, the DDNC began working with DDNC groups in Maine (2000), Hawaii (2002), Vermont (2001–2013), California (2002–2015), Washington State (2006–2008), Massachusetts (2012), and other states to plan strategy for passing PAD legislation in these states. These organizations, along with Compassion and Choices, are the primary national groups leading the battles—state by state—for PAD legislation.

The Alternatives Available to Terminally Ill Patients if PAD Is Not Legal

Before—and after—the advent of the right to die in six states, there were a number of alternative actions, taken by doctors, nurses, and other medical professionals, that addressed the needs of terminally ill patients. None of these paths to compassionate care of dying patients excluded the use of PAD where it was legally available. Some of them were also supported by groups that were absolutely opposed to PAD. The Catholic Church's acceptance of the double effect alternative, and the distinctions it draws between ordinary means to extend a life (which must be used) and extraordinary means to save the dying patient (which must not be employed), is one example.

Withholding/withdrawing life-sustaining remedies and refusing life support treatments: This alternative, useful only when a patient either is on a device or could be placed on a device that would extend life (but not the pain and suffering), became another possibility only after new innovative techniques (CPR) and devices (ventilators, defibrillators, dialysis machines) became available in the 20th century. Patients on dialysis, for example, at some point in their cycle of life-saving care on the machine, can request withdrawal of the treatment. Death occurs within a week because of that choice. A competent patient can also refuse to begin dialysis.

Courts, both state and federal, accept the right of a competent patient to withdraw, withhold, or refuse to use such devices even though death would follow. Religious institutions and other anti-PAD groups accepted the validity of such a choice, because the disease is the direct cause of death, not the physician.

Double effect: This is an alternative that has been used by physicians and nurses for centuries. It was written about by Catholic theologian Thomas Aquinas in the 13th century. He wrote, in *Summa Theologica*, that "nothing hinders one act from having two effects, one of which is intended, while the other is beside the intention." Essentially, it is the use of medications in a sufficient quantity to relieve the pain and suffering of a patient whose death is imminent. The large amount of medication will relieve the pain but might indirectly lead to the death of the terminally ill patient. The double effect protocol directly treats the patient's pain and suffering, while at the same time it indirectly causes the patient to die from the cancer, or from AIDS, and so on.

A wink and a nod: A secular corollary to the double effect convention is the *wink and a nod* practice. In *Vacco v. Quill*, one of the two major 1997 U.S. Supreme Court decisions addressing PAD, Associate Justice Ruth Bader Ginsberg spoke of this alternative to PAD. "Sometimes," she wrote, "a covert dialogue takes place between doctor and patient that result[s] in an unspoken agreement. . . . A doctor will tell a nurse, 'start the morphine and go ahead and be generous, *if you know what I mean*" (Schwartz 2005). This practice, very familiar to the medical community, consists of "veiled conversations between medical professionals and overwhelmed families. Doctors and nurses want to help but also want to avoid prosecution, so they speak carefully, parsing their words" (Dembosky 2015).

Palliative sedation: This option is used by physicians to "relieve the burden of otherwise intolerable suffering for terminally ill patients pain by sedating [the patient] and to do so in such a manner so as to preserve the moral sensibilities of the patient" (Cherny 2016). It is generally initiated by the patient because of intense pain and discomfort. Palliative sedation is employed to induce a state of decreased awareness or absent awareness (unconsciousness). It leads to patient unconsciousness for a short time (until pain is lessened). Indirectly, it may lead to death. There is also the controversial variant, terminal sedation.

Terminal sedation: It is used in cases involving dying patients "where normal medical treatments cannot relieve severe symptoms such as pain and agitation, and no option is left but to take away the perception of these symptoms." Death of the terminally ill patient is the purpose of this protocol. This extreme alternative to PAD has been "the subject of fierce ethical debates." The central claim of the critics is that it is a "slow euthanasia [requested by the patient]; it is not a good palliative intervention" (van Delden 2007).

Palliative care and hospice care: These have been, since the opening of the first hospice in America in 1974, team-oriented ways of providing compassionate, comfort care for severely ill or terminally ill patients. One difference between them is that hospice care is available—either inpatient (hospital) or home care (the venue of more than 80% of patients)—only after a team of physicians has estimated that the patient has six months or less left to live, and the doctor and patient have "decided to move from active curative treatment to a regimen more focused on quality of life" (Stages of Hospice Care 2016). Palliative care, now a medical sub-specialty taught in many medical schools, is not triggered by an estimate of a patient's time of death. It is available to all patients who are in pain, and while care is the primary goal, curative medical treatments can continue if the patient wishes. A seriously ill patient in a palliative care hospital wing *must* leave that wing when there is a terminal diagnosis. The now-terminal patient can be admitted into a hospice program and, if a resident in one of the five PAD states, can ask for PAD while in hospice.

Becoming a "Death Tourist"

Although Switzerland has had an "assisted suicide" law (for altruistic reasons) since 1937, other countries that allow PAD and euthanasia passed their laws in recent decades. The "death tourist" method of dying has been allowed in Europe. (Belgium [2002], Luxembourg [2009], and the Netherlands [2002] permit PAD and voluntary euthanasia.) In North America, Canada (2015) and five states in the United States allow PAD, while Columbia in South America authorized PAD in 1997; in 2015, euthanasia was made part of Columbia's law. When a society legalizes PAD or euthanasia, dying people who live in states or countries where PAD is illegal can travel to that location, meet residency requirements and medical requirements, and then receive PAD.

The Arguments in Opposition to PAD

Countering the supporters of PAD are individuals and organizations who base their condemnation of PAD and euthanasia on medical, ethical, and religious values. The medical community's *oath of medical ethics* calls on physicians to preserve life and to do no harm. PAD is fundamentally incompatible with the physician's role as healer. The major religious denominations renounce PAD because of rock-solid belief in the central maxim of all religion: Life is a gift of God. It must not be prematurely and criminally shortened by PAD; that's the Creator's decision. Following are the basic beliefs and values of those who believe that PAD is unconstitutional and/or criminal, immoral, or an unethical medical practice.

Religious belief in the sanctity of life: Organized religion disdains PAD and euthanasia; they are sins against the sanctity of life, against God. Pope Francis, the leader of the world's Roman Catholics, denounced the right to die movement, saying it is "a false sense of compassion to consider euthanasia as an act of dignity when in fact it's a sin against God and creation" (Pope Says 2014). The most powerful arguments against PAD and euthanasia "come from the religious beliefs that life is sacred and that humans are the stewards and not the absolute masters of life," noted a Catholic physician/nun working in Canada (Kenny 2015).

Medical arguments against PAD: There are a number of reasons why the medical establishment opposes physician-assisted death and euthanasia. First, there is the problem all humans face: fallibilism—the reality of physician misdiagnosis of the patient's medical problem, an erroneous prognosis, or an incorrect treatment. The lack of information about new curative approaches/treatments to help the patient is also a possibility; it can lead to dire consequences if the patient is told that the malady is terminal and incurable. We are all fallible, even doctors; PAD ignores this basic human condition.

There are also ethical reasons that lead physicians to oppose PAD. The right to die is fundamentally at odds with the ethical norm that pervades the medical community: the doctor's role is curative; he is a healer. And one piece of the Hippocratic Oath is an essential barrier to a physician's assisting a patient to die:

"I will neither give a deadly drug to anybody if asked for it, nor will I make a suggestion to this effect."

The AMA's modern version of the Hippocratic Oath, the Code of Medical Ethics, published in 1994, absolutely prohibits PAD and euthanasia. Opinion E-2.21 states that "allowing physicians to participate in assisted suicide would cause more harm than good. Physician assisted suicide is fundamentally incompatible with the physician's role as healer, would be difficult or impossible to control, and would pose serious societal risks."

Distinguishing Passive "Letting Die" from Active "Killing"

Critics of PAD distinguish between passive and active actions or inactions of a physician working with a terminally ill patient. They maintain that there is a major difference between justifiable "letting die" (e.g., at the behest of the dying patient, withholding/withdrawing life-sustaining treatment or stopping dialysis treatment) and non-justifiable active "killing" of the patient by PAD or euthanasia. The physician who assists a terminal patient to die is killing that patient and should be subjected to criminal prosecution and loss of license to practice medicine.

Potential for abuse: There is a fear held by opponents of PAD that a seriously ill patient who is in one of society's vulnerable groups (disabled, poor, women, the aged, and minorities), and without the ability to pay for health care, may be pushed into PAD. More generally, *regardless of socio-economic status*, given the "secular, death-denying, death-defying culture," legalizing PAD will "cause pressure on [*all*] terminal patients who fear their illness is burdensome—physically, emotionally, or financially—to their families and caregivers" (Lagay 2001).

Personal integrity: There are, accompanying the historical ethical traditions associated with oaths and codes, concerns about the professional integrity of the medical community if physicians participate in assisting patients to die. The AMA and the American Geriatrics Society, for example, oppose linking medicine with PAD and euthanasia because the linkage would harm both the integrity of the profession and the public's image of the profession.

The slippery slope: This is a major concern—and deep fear—of all the individuals and groups that oppose PAD. Beyond the medical, ethical, and religious arguments, there is the belief that there are no procedural protections preventing the society from moving—inexorably—from PAD to voluntary euthanasia and then to involuntary euthanasia carried out by agents of the government. The slide-to-eugenics argument is a strategic part of the anti-PAD strategy presented by the opposition. They point to the Nazi regime's actions euthanizing all those the state thought *unfit to live* as the final end for a society that adopts a policy that, in the beginning, allows PAD.

Religious Groups Opposed to PAD

The Pew Research Center annually presents its findings about the beliefs and values of the mainstream religions functioning in America (Pew Research Center 2014). With but two exceptions, all the religious organizations participating in the survey reject PAD and euthanasia. "God is the sole giver of life and only God is the taker of life," summarizes their opposition. These religious bodies also believe that it's morally acceptable for a dying patient not to take extraordinary measures to preserve life. Allowing a terminal patient to die from natural causes is not euthanasia or PAD. Allowing is vastly different from actively speeding up death.

The following religions, featured in annual Pew Research surveys, agree on these two general principles: Assemblies of God, Buddhism, Catholicism, Evangelical Lutheran Church America, Episcopal Church, Hinduism, Islam, Judaism, Mormonism, National Baptist Convention, Presbyterian Church U.S.A., Seventh-day Adventist Church, Southern Baptist Convention, and the United Methodist Church.

However, the most active of all these religious institutions in the battles to defeat legislative efforts to pass PAD as well as present legal briefs that argue against the constitutionality of PAD when the issue is litigated is the Roman Catholic Church. Leaders, including the pope, condemn PAD. Their messages are transmitted to the faithful through state Catholic organizations, the national Catholic Church, and the Vatican. They use the Church's professional organizers, media experts, and millions of dollars of church funds to defeat every effort made by PAD advocates to advance their cause.

As noted earlier, the *sanctity of life* principle is the central motivating norm, whether the Church is battling abortion, the death penalty, suicide, euthanasia, or PAD. "Life should not be prematurely shortened because it is a gift of God. We don't have the authority to take into our hands when life will end. That's the Creator's decision" (Pew Research Center 2013). Death "is not an unmitigated evil, nor is it the enemy. Rather it is but a stage in the pilgrimage of life." Suicide, PAD, and euthanasia are all violations of "God's Dominion. [They] are the ultimate act of defiance—the assertion of self over divine sovereignty" (Paris and Moreland 1998).

Medical Groups Opposed to PAD

The AMA was founded in 1847 and, although membership has declined in the past decade since its high in 2002 (278,000), there is an upward swing of new membership (2011–2015). In 2016, the AMA still remains the largest association of doctors in the nation (about 226,000 members).

The AMA's Code of Medical Ethics, written in 1847, stands as the organization's moral foundation regarding medical ethics and standards for a physician's ethical behavior. The prime duty of care for the doctor (which persists until the death of a patient) is to provide the patient with "specialty consultation, hospice care, pastoral support, family counseling, and other modalities. Patients near the end of life must continue to receive emotional support, comfort care, adequate pain control, respect . . . and good communication" (AMA Code of Medical Ethics, Opinion E 2.21).

As the world's largest medical professional association, the AMA's policies and budgets have supported its motto: "Helping Doctors Helping Patients." Its professional lobbyists spend many millions of dollars annually to work in the halls of Congress, in the halls of all state legislative chambers, and in state and federal courtrooms to advance the interests of medical students, physicians, and their patients.

Their activities are in controversial policy areas relating to the medical profession. The AMA was an aggressive opponent of Medicare until its emergence in the mid-1960s as a national policy. It has championed Medicare and Medicaid since then. It also supported President Barack Obama's (2009–2017) extremely controversial Patient Protection and Affordable Care Act (Obamacare). A portion of its political activities and expenditures is used annually to pay for the organization's clashes with PAD movements across the nation.

The American Nurses Association (ANA) is the major organization representing registered nurses in America, through its 54 local and state member associations. In 2015, the ANA represented nearly 175,000 members. Like the AMA, the ANA has a Code of Ethics for Nurses with Interpretive Statements (Code) (2001), and it prohibits PAD and euthanasia. Its revised Position Statement on Euthanasia, Assisted Suicide, and Aid in Dying, dated April 24, 2013, states that the organization "prohibits nurses' participation in assisted suicide and euthanasia because these acts are in direct violation of the Code, the ethical traditions and goals of the profession, and its covenant with society."

> Nurses have an obligation to provide humane, comprehensive, and compassionate care that respects the rights of patients but upholds the standards of the profession in the presence of chronic, debilitating illness and at end-of-life. . . . Nurses may not act with the sole intent of ending a patient's life even though such action may be motivated by compassion, respect for autonomy

and quality of life considerations. (American Nurses Association, 2015)

For the ANA, palliative care and hospice are the avenues that should be suggested by nurses when a patient initiates a conversation about end-of-life choices. Palliative care and hospice "provide individualized, comprehensive, holistic care to meet patient and family needs predicated on goals of care from the time of diagnosis, through death." The Code states that such care "affirms life and neither hastens nor postpones death." The primary responsibility of the nurse, when a terminal patient requests aid in dying, is to "create environments where patients feel comfortable to express thoughts, feelings, conflict, and despair. . . . It is crucial to listen to and acknowledge the patient's expressions of suffering, hopelessness, and sadness" (ANA Code, 2013).

Subsequently, the nurses, along with the patient, the patient's family, palliative care doctors, can develop a plan of care "initiated to address the patient's physical and emotional needs" (ANA Code, 2013). One study found that, on the basis of inputs from nurses who work with terminally ill patients, these caregivers "used similar, established palliative care strategies to lessen suffering in this ethically troubling situation. . . . [The study concluded that] nurses' support of patient autonomy did not necessarily mean they were supportive of euthanasia" (Lachman 2010).

Vulnerable Groups' Opposition to PAD

Another cohort of groups and individuals opposed to the legalization of PAD are generally incorporated under the phrase *vulnerable*. These include the poor, the frail, the ill, the elderly, the disabled, black Americans, and other racial and ethnic minorities living in America. They "worry that if PAD becomes widely available they will be viewed as 'throwaway people.' They fear coercion, stigmatization, and discrimination, understandingly believing that the societal indifference prevalent throughout their lives will also infect their end-of-life care" (King 2012).

Study after study about the attitudes of these politically powerless groups concludes that a major concern all these groups
share is that their "rights are not valued in society; they fear
they will not have access to life-prolonging treatment or palliative care that for them represents death with dignity" (King
2012). Members of these groups have been treated with disre-
spect, with disdain, with derision, and as inferior members of
the society all their lives.

In 1989, illustrating this reality, the U.S. Civil Rights Commission published a 153-page report entitled "Medical Discrimination against Children with Disabilities." The report, in
part, described an experiment conducted from 1977 to 1982
in the Children's Hospital, Oklahoma:

> Doctors there developed a "quality of life" formula for
> babies with spina bifida ["split spine," the most common
> permanently disabling birth defect in the United States],
> taking into account the socioeconomic status of the baby's
> family to determine what to advise families about a simple
> but life-and-death procedure. Better-off families were
> provided a realistic and optimistic picture of their child's
> potential. Poor families were provided a pessimistic picture.
> All the families who were given an optimistic picture asked
> for medical care for their children. Conversely, four out of
> five poor families agreed not to treat their children, and
> twenty four babies died. (Coleman n.d.)

The report concluded that the doctors' "projection of a negative quality of life . . . based on the difficulties society will
cause, rather than tackling the difficulties themselves, is unacceptable" (Coleman n.d.).

For advocates for vulnerable populations, this behavior,
unfortunately, is the norm when medical professionals "counsel" the patients and their families. Nonverbal discomfort and
implicit biases are regrettably present in these physician consultations with a vulnerable patient—whether the person is

ill, dying, or just fine at that moment—but who are on the "wrong side" of the lines of race, ethnicity, and class. For most of America's history they have been powerless.

Blacks, especially, must view "the legalization of PAD with suspicion. Rather than see it as an opportunity to exercise their autonomy at the end of life, African Americans . . . sense that this is another way through which less valued African American lives can be eliminated" (King and Wolf 1998).

Their history—from slavery, to Jim Crow, to lynching, to discrimination, to substandard public health care, and to public health agencies using them as guinea pigs for questionable medical trials—certainly does not give a great many blacks confidence that PAD will give them a death with dignity.

The Tuskegee, Alabama, syphilis "research" project, which lasted 40 years, is an arch example of blacks being unknowing medical specimens. In 1932, the U.S. Public Health Service, working with the Tuskegee Institute, in Alabama, began what turned out to be a *40-year study* of 600 black men, 400 with syphilis, and 200 men who did not have the disease. It was called the "Tuskegee Study of Untreated Syphilis in the Negro Male" and was an effort to examine syphilis's pathogenesis in an effort to develop a treatment program. The men did not give their consent to the research; they were told that they were being treated for "bad blood." They did not receive proper treatment (penicillin) but received free medical exams, free meals, and burial insurance (Jones 1993). These cruel experiences felt by blacks "have fostered distrust of physicians and the health care system." These "racial disparities in health care persist, and they exist in the broader context of historical and contemporary social and economic inequalities in American life" (King 2012).

All black community members have to do is look at the sad state of health care for them and other minorities in America in the second decade of the 21st century. Sadly, there is still—because of both attitude and practice—a social and medical devaluation of the lives of vulnerable cohorts. In 1998, *The*

JAMA published the results of a study, involving over 13,000 cancer patients. "People of color" were treated as second-class citizens: they were "significantly less likely to receive pain medication than whites, even aspirin" (Coleman n.d.).

In 1997, the American Bar Association's Commission on the Legal Problems of the Elderly introduced a resolution to the organization's members, which was passed, that addressed this issue. The American Bar Association wanted to "ensure that information and reporting systems are established to achieve close monitoring of the impact of physician-assisted death, especially with respect to vulnerable populations who may be particularly at risk if PAD is authorized" (Francis 1998).

Another organization representing the elderly population is the American Geriatrics Society (AGS). The AGS is a national organization of geriatrics health care professionals, research scientists, and others dedicated to "improving the health, independence and quality of life of all older people" (American Geriatrics Society n.d.). A general concern of the elderly addresses the impact of the primacy of personal autonomy in the decision to use PAD.

At the heart of this group's trepidation about PAD lies the following question: does it take into account the vulnerabilities of the elderly? These, at a minimum, must include physical disability; reduced independence; the loss of loved ones (including pets); economic insecurity (having to choose between medicine or food); moving into new, smaller, quarters; and leaving the comfort of an old neighborhood and friends. These factors, separate or combined, all account for the onset of chronic depression. And depression is the major cause of elderly suicide (Francis 1998). Decriminalizing PAD and euthanasia is a frightening development for elderly advocates who are struggling with the general problem of suicide.

In late 2002, the AGS issued a position paper on PAD and voluntary active euthanasia. It set out the position of the AGS with regard to the question: "should euthanasia or physician-assisted suicide be legal?" The answer was a resounding *no*.

Introducing these options creates unmanageable problems for the elderly (American Geriatrics Society 2007).

For the AGS, the traditional, essential goal of the physician "has been to comfort and to cure [the patient]. To change the physician's role to one in which comfort includes the intentional termination of life is to alter this alliance and could undermine the trust between physician and patient" (American Geriatrics Society 2007). The existence of PAD "encourages the elderly to accept death prematurely rather than burden society and family."

The AGS strongly believes that the elderly would overwhelmingly want to receive quality palliative care so that they would be comfortable—"which might require sedation"—and "potentially could find meaning in the last phase of life. . . . Most would choose to live if they had full confidence that the care system would serve them well" (American Geriatrics Society 2007). Because of the sorry history of society's treatment of them, the elderly population, with few exceptions, lacks the certainty that they will be treated equitably.

Not Dead Yet: The Disabled Community's Vocal Advocate

"Disabled persons have been historically victimized by stereotypical attitudes about their abilities and worth, coupled with a paternalism that has undercut their right to self-determination" (Bickenbach 1998). Retired Judge Ted Knuck, the father of a 40-year-old developmentally disabled woman, put it tersely: "Those of us who are not disabled tend to impose our way of thinking on people who are disabled" (Machelor 2015).

The most visible group representing the interests of the disabled is the Not Dead Yet (NDY) organization. It is a national disability rights group, founded in early 1996, that opposes the legalization of PAD and euthanasia as deadly forms of discrimination. (Ironically, the immensely popular 1975 satiric film *Monty Python and the Holy Grail* gave the group its name. In the film, plague victims are thrown into a burial cart; however, one of the "corpses" protests that he is "not dead yet"!)

Since 1996, about one dozen other disability rights groups have joined NDY in the battles against PAD and euthanasia in state legislatures and in state and federal courts. Some of them are the Disability Rights Center, Justice for All, the Autistic Self-Advocacy Group, the National Council on Disability, the National Spinal Cord Injury Association, the World Association of Persons with Disabilities, Second Thoughts, and the United Spinal Association.

For NDY, PAD's claim that it is a compassionate way to exit life is categorically false. "This is not compassion, it's contempt. Legalized medical killing is really about a deadly double standard for people with severe disabilities, including both conditions that are labeled terminal and those that are not" (Coleman, 1999).

This observation underscores a cruel "catch-22" for those disabled terminally ill patients living in PAD states who want to use the process. These persons, although dying, are barred from PAD if they are unable to end their lives without assistance. And help is, by definition, voluntary euthanasia—an action prohibited by PAD strictures. There is a huge gap in the Oregon model used in the United States. Unlike Canada's 2016 assisted suicide bill, which allows doctors to assist such patients to die, in America these "paraplegic or completely paralyzed [patients] unable to control their hands, unable to self-administer the lethal cocktails that licensed physicians may not administer legally," face a despairing existence (Lief 2016).

The severely handicapped terminally ill patient is "legally prevented from pursuing a legal option [PAD] on the basis of physical disability" (Bickenbach 1998). This is discriminatory state action, arguably a violation of the Fourteenth Amendment's Equal Protection Clause. But this is only the very tip of the iceberg of inequitable health care services for this group of vulnerable persons—and others as well. NDY's actions and broadsides on their behalf expose a bitterness about "normal society"; it is based on a fundamental historical reality faced by the disabled in America: They have been marginalized, stigmatized, and discriminated against in—and outside of—the health care system throughout their lives. The disabled have "good reason to distrust the health care system in the United States and until the system is perceived as more fair and trustworthy they will continue to find inadequate the argument that procedures safeguard against abuse" (Ouellette 2014).

Many disabled patients view the contemporary doctor's office and the hospital as *dangerous* places. "Most people with a disability fear even the most routine hospitalization. We do not fear any of the commonplace indignities those without a disability worry about when hospitalized. Our fear is primal—will our lives be considered devoid of value?" (Peace 2012).

In May 2012, a disability rights organization, the National Disability Rights Network, published a searing report that detailed the two major ways "in which the U.S. health care system fails to recognize the value of life with disability" (Carlson, Smith, and Wilker 2012). There are "controversial medical innovations," devices, and protocols, used for treating illness and providing curative health services to patients, that make disabled patients either very uncomfortable or, because of the physical nature of the person's disability, unable to benefit from the use of the new, life-prolonging devices. Conversely, because of the doctor's perceived bias, there is a dismissive valuation of disabled patients; the new devices are not discussed with the patient and family, are not used, or are withdrawn from disabled children and adults.

Beyond the discriminatory employment of these innovations, the report indicated that the disabled community is "even more troubled by the day-to-day dehumanizing experience of persons with disabilities in the health care system. They experience significant health care [attitudinal] disparities and [medical equipment] barriers to care. This inequality extends to *all* vulnerable groups" (Carlson, Smith, and Wilker 2012).

Whether one is disabled, black, Hispanic, old, poor, demented, or feeble, that patient is more likely to go without needed care; such patients make more preventable emergency room visits and hospitalizations; they experience a significantly higher prevalence of secondary conditions; they get less preventive care—fewer pelvic exams, fewer pap smears, fewer prostate exams, less prenatal care; they are not as likely to be weighed when they go to the doctor; and they have poor health outcomes (see, for example, Matthew 2005).

These historical barriers to quality health care for the disabled community are the context from which emerges the vigorous rejection of PAD by all these vulnerable groups. When there is a deathly fear of any routine visit to a hospital because the person does not trust the health care personnel and the system itself, can any disabled person believe that death with dignity laws "are not targeted at them"? (Ouellette 2014).

For the protectors of the disabled, there has to be a systemic change in the health care system's weaknesses, including the explosive rise in the cost of health care. The negative perception of quality health care these vulnerable groups possess will not diminish until visible and substantive changes are made that address these problems. And this health care reality has been a major concern of NDY. What choices are left for a severely disabled person who must continually deal with the systemic problems in the health care system?

Stephen Hawkins is an internationally recognized scientific genius who is severely disabled with ALS. He revealed his desperation with the health care system when, in 2013, he spoke to a BBC reporter. Previously, he was opposed to PAD and suicide for persons confronting their medical condition. He said, in 2007, that killing oneself "would be a great mistake. However bad life may seem, there is always something you can do. While there's life, there's hope" ("Feature" 2006). In 2013 Hawking changed his mind and "offered his unqualified support to those who feel their life is no longer tolerable."

I think those who have a terminal illness and are in great pain should have the right to choose to end their lives and those that help them should be free from prosecution. We don't let animals suffer, so why humans? There must be safeguards that the person concerned genuinely wants to end their life and they are not being pressured into it or have it done without their knowledge or consent as would have been the case with me. We should not take away the freedom of the individual to choose to die. I believe one should have control of one's life, including its ending. (Boseley 2013)

Hawking and other disabled persons understand, because of their poor, personal experiences with physicians, the critical importance of proper and rigorous safeguards to protect them when they enter the public health system—and what can happen if these safeguards are not present.

Improper, discriminatory treatment of vulnerable groups lies at the core of the fears expressed by NDY advocates. However, PAD advocates are equally ardent when they assert that the PAD policy has the necessary safeguards to prevent such unasked-for final actions. There is no doubt that how physicians—and the health care system itself—treat their vulnerable patients is a key element in the generally negative perception of PAD by these individuals..

Conclusion

The foregoing examination of the organizations on both sides of the right to die issue touches only a small number of individuals and associations. There are, across the nation, in every state, many dozens of local, state, and national groups of committed persons continuously working to achieve their goals in this legal, political, ethical, religious, and medical quandary. Chapter Two examines these activities and actions that began in the 1970s and continue into the present century.

These events saw a re-awakening, aided and abetted by editors, publishers, and social media participants, of readers' interest in the issue of how we die and what options do we have about confronting death. Since 1990 there has been a major expansion of media coverage of all events that touch on a person's right to choose to die with passive assistance by a doctor. The public has been exposed to books and articles about the political, ethical, legal, and religious clashes that occurred on the floors of legislative chambers and in courtrooms; writers produced human interest stories focusing on the tragic, heart-rending stories about patients and their families facing cruel choices about living or dying. The expected consequence was sensational headlines feeding peoples' imagination and providing grist for their dinner table conversations

The creation of PAD pressure groups began in earnest in the 1980s and was fully covered in the news. Important events in the U.S. Supreme Court, in state politics, in Congress were occurring and the need for organizations to work for—and against—the passage of right to die legislation grew quickly. The absence of Advanced Directive planning in people's lives became newsworthy when, in 1990, the U.S. Congress passed the Patient Self-Determination Act.

That same year, the nation read about the politics surrounding Washington State's Initiative 119, the first ever voter referendum which, if passed, would have made physician assistance in dying a legal right that protected the participants from any criminal action in the state. (It did not pass in 1990; another version was passed by the voters in 2008.)

Needless to say, these right to die incidents, cases, and personalities were written about at length and in depth; they were discussed by doctors, nurses, ethicists, clergy, politicians, talking heads on radio and television, magazines, and the general public for many years. Hollywood has played a significant role in further exposing the general public to pervasive issues associated with death and dying. Some of the most well-known are about leukemia (*Love Story* [1970], *Dying Young* [1991]); cancer (*Brian's Song* [1971], *Wit* [2001]); disability (*Whose Life Is It Anyway* [1981]); Alzheimer's disease (*Do You Remember Love*

[1985], *Still Alice* [2014]); PAD (*Million Dollar Baby* [2004]); and Dr. Kevorkian (*You Don't Know Jack* [2010]).

These books, films, and plays are integral to the opening up of needed discussions of death, sensitizing Americans to the realities of growing old in the 21st century. We have been forced to think about, for the first time in generations, the watershed changes in how and why we are living longer but dying much more slowly, often with accompanying pain and suffering. Most important, Americans are, for the first time, thinking about how they will want to die.

For nearly a half century (1970–present), contemporary Americans have been made increasingly aware of the emotionally charged questions surrounding society's beliefs and efforts about how to cope with terminal illness. Attitudinal changes have taken place in the nation, but they are incremental and somewhat irregular. Viewing annual polls about how Americans respond to moral issues shows these changes at play in the society. The Gallup poll concluded in May 2015 that "Americans are more likely now than in the early 2000s to find a variety of behaviors morally acceptable . . . at a record-high level" (Newport 2015). The poll annually tracks the ebb and flow of Americans' attitudes on more than a dozen key moral issues, including whether doctor-assisted suicide is morally acceptable. In 2001, the response to that question was 49 percent who believed PAD was morally acceptable; by 2011, however, the response dropped to 45 percent; however, in 2015, Gallup pollsters found that 56 percent of the persons thought that physician-assisted suicide *was* morally acceptable.

How does one explain these fluctuations, especially the upsurge of support for PAD? In October 2014, there was extensive media coverage of Brittany Maynard's decision to move from California to Oregon, where PAD is legal, in order to die because of her inoperable brain cancer. In the latter part of 2014, across the globe, the story—with videos made by the young woman explaining her decision—was continuous on

Facebook, Twitter, television, radio, newspapers, magazines—all with haunting photographs of the 29-year-old recently married woman who received physician assistance to die by moving to a PAD state. In less than one year, the publicity and the public outcry over Brittany's final months of life had much to do with the passage—and signing by the governor—of California's End of Life Options Act. This substantive policy created in California, after nearly two decades of being rejected by state legislators, is the result of a "decades-long evolution in public attitudes toward how we die" (Angell 2012).

Chapter Two examines the ongoing hard-nosed battles surrounding the constitutionality of laws punishing any person assisting another to end her life. Chapter Two also addresses the problems confronting the participants in these political fights, as well as some new wrinkles about the controversy that have arisen in recent years. Finally, and the most difficult question of all, is whether there is a solution to this divisive issue.

References

American Geriatrics Society. 2002. *Position Statement: Physician-Assisted Suicide and Voluntary Active Euthanasia.* New York: American Geriatrics Society.

American Geriatrics Society. 2007. *Position Paper: Physician Assisted Suicide and Voluntary Active Euthanasia.* New York: American Geriatrics Society. November 2002, revised 2007.

American Geriatrics Society. n.d. "Who We Are." http://www.americangeriatrics.org/about_us/who_we_are/

American Nurses Association. 2015. *Code of Ethics for Nurses.* http://nursingworld.org/DocumentVault/Ethics-1/Code-of-Ethics-for-Nurses.html

American Psychological Association. 2000, May. "On Assisted Suicide and End of Life Decisions." Working Group Report. Washington, DC: American Psychological Association.

Angell, Marcia. 2012. "May Doctors Help You to Die?" *New York Review of Books*, October 11.

Anonymous. 1988. "It's Over Debbie." *JAMA*. January 8, Vol. 259, No. 2:272.

Appel, Jacob M. 2004. "A Duty to Kill? A Duty to Die? Rethinking the Euthanasia Controversy of 1906." *Bulletin of the History of Medicine*, 78:3, 610–634.

Ball, Howard. 2012. *At Liberty to Die: The Battle for Death with Dignity in America*. New York: New York University Press.

Belluck, Pam. 2015. "Benefit of End Stage Chemotherapy Is Questioned." *The New York Times*, July 23, p. A15.

Bickenbach, Jerome E. 1998. "Disability and Life-Ending Decisions." In *Physician Assisted Suicide: Expanding the Debate*, edited by Margaret P. Battin, Rosamond Rhodes, and Anita Silvers, 123–132. New York: Routledge.

Bohjalian, Chris. 2015. "A Little Too Much Like Life." *Burlington Free Press*, August 16, p. 2C.

Boseley, Sarah. 2013. "Professor Stephen Hawking Backs Right to Die for the Terminally Ill." *The Guardian*, September 17. www.guardian.org.

Brown, Edmond G., Jr. 2015. Letter to Members of the California State Assembly, October 5. https://www.gov.ca.gov/docs/ABX2_15_Signing_Message.pdf

Brown, Theresa. 2015. "Choosing How We Die." *The New York Times*, July 24.

Butler, Katy. 2015. "Aid in Dying Laws Are Just a Start." *The New York Times*, July 12, SR2.

Carlson, David, Cindy Smith, and Nachama Wilker. 2012. "Devaluing People with Disabilities: Medical Procedures That Violate Civil Rights. National Disability Rights Network." http://www.disabilityrightswa.org/devaluing-people-disabilities

Cherny, Nathan. 2016. "Palliative Sedation." UpToDate. http://www.uptodate.com/contents/palliative-sedation

Code of Ethics for Nurses With Interpretive Statements. 2013. www.nursingworld,org

Cohen, Adam. 2016. *Imbeciles: The Supreme Court, American Eugenics, and the Sterilization of Carrie Buck.* New York: Penguin Press.

Coleman, Diane. 1999. "Deadly Tactics: It's Not Compassion, It's Contempt." *Chicago Tribune*, March 17. www.chicagotribune.com

Coleman, Diane. n.d. "Assisted Suicide and Disability: Another Perspective." Disability Rights Education & Defense Fund. http://dredf.org/public-policy/assisted-suicide/assisted-suicide-and-disability/

Dembosky, April. 2015. "Doctors' Secret Language for Assisted Suicide." *The Atlantic*, May 27.

Dowbiggin, Ian. 2003. *A Merciful End: The Euthanasia Movement in Modern America.* New York: Oxford University Press.

Emanuel, Ezekiel J. 1997. "Whose Right to Die?" *The Atlantic*, March.

"Feature: There's Life, There's Hope: Stephen Hawking." 2006. *Xinhua*, June 14. http://en.people.cn/200606/14/eng20060614_273839.html

Francis, Leslie P. 1998. "Assisted Suicide: Are the Elderly a Special Case?" In *Physician Assisted Suicide: Expanding the Debate*, edited by Margaret P. Battin, Rosamond Rhodes, and Anita Silvers, 75–90. New York: Routledge.

Gawande, Atul. 2014. *Being Mortal: Medicine and What Matters in the End.* New York: Metropolitan Books.

Heft, P.R., M. Siegler, and J. Lantos. 2000. "The Rise and Fall of the Futility Movement." *New England Journal of Medicine*, 343, 293–296.

History of Hospice Care. 2016. National Hospice and Palliative Care Organization. http://www.nhpco.org/history-hospice-care

Jones, James H. 1993. *Bad Blood: The Tuskegee Syphilis Experiment.* New York: Simon and Schuster.

Kenny, Nuala. 2015. "Physician Assisted Suicide: Medicalization of Suffering and Death." *Canadian Bioethics*, February.

Kevorkian, Jack. 1991. *Prescription Medicide: The Goodness of Planned Death.* Buffalo: Prometheus Books.

King, Patricia A. 2012. "Address Inequalities before Legalizing Assisted Suicide." *The New York Times*, April 10.

King, Patricia A., and Leslie E. Wolf. 1998. "Lessons for Physician-Assisted Suicide from the African-American Experience." In *Physician Assisted Suicide: Expanding the Debate*, edited by Margaret P. Battin, Rosamond Rhodes, and Anita Silvers, 123–132. New York: Routledge.

Lachman, Vicki. 2010. "Physician Assisted Suicide: Compassionate Liberation or Murder?" *MEDSURG Nursing*, 19:2, 124, March/April.

Lagay, Faith. 2001. "Physician-Assisted Suicide: What's Legal and What's Professional?" *Virtual Mentor*, 3:1, 1.

Lerner, Barron H. 2014. "When Medicine Is Futile," *The New York Times*, September 18.

Lieber, James E. 2016. "How to Make Hospitals Less Deadly." *The Wall Street Journal*, May 18.

Lief, Donald W. 2016. "Aid in Dying." Letter to the Editor. *The New York Times*, April 30.

Machelor, Patty. 2015. "Retired Judge Warns against Forcing Integrated Work Settings on the Disabled." *Arizona Daily Star*, November 8.

Matthew, Dayna Bowen. 2005. *Just Medicine: A Cure for Racial Inequality in American Health Care.* New York: New York University Press.

Mission. 2016. Final Exit Network. http://www. finalexitnetwork.org/Mission.html

Newport, Frank. 2015. "Americans Continue to Shift Left of Key Moral Issues." Gallup, May 26. http://www.gallup.com/poll/183413/americans-continue-shift-left-key-moral-issues.aspx

Ouellette, Alicia. 2014. "Context Matters: Disability, the End of Life, and Why the Conversation Is Still So Difficult." *New York Law School Review*, 58:371, 2013–2044.

Paris, John J. and Michael P. Moreland. 1998. "A Catholic Perspective on Physician-Assisted Suicide." In *Physician Assisted Suicide: Expanding the Debate*, edited by Margaret P. Battin, Rosamond Rhodes, and Anita Silvers, 123–132. New York: Routledge.

Peace, William J. 2012. "Disability Discrimination: The Author Responds." Hastings Bioethics Forum, July 27. http://www.thehastingscenter.org/Bioethicsforum/Post.aspx?id=5935&blogid=140

Pew Research Center. 2013. Religious Groups' Views on End-of-Life Issues. http://www.pewforum.org/2013/11/21/religious-groups-views-on-end-of-life-issues/

Pew Research Center. 2014. Religious Landscape Study. http://www.pewforum.org/about-the-religious-landscape-study/

"Physicians May Take Human Life." 1906. *Des Moines Register and Leader*, March 11, p. 1.

"Pope Says Assisted Suicide Is a 'Sin Against God.'" 2014. Associated Press, November 15. www.ap.com

Quill, Timothy E. 1991. "Death and Dignity: A Case of Individualized Decision Making." *New England Journal of Medicine*, 324:10, 691–694.

Schillace, Brandy. 2016. *Death's Summer Coat: What the History of Death and Dying Teach Us about Life And Living*. New York: Pegasus Books.

Schwartz, John. 2005. "New Openness in Deciding When and How to Die." *The New York Times*, March 21.

Stages of Hospice Care. 2016. Center for Hospice Care Southeast Connecticut. https://www.hospicesect.org/hospice-and-palliative-care/stages-of-hospice-care

Szabo, Liz. 2015. "Chemo Won't Help End Stage Cancer." *USA Today*, July 24.

van Delden, Johannes J.M. 2007. "Terminal Sedation: Source of a Restless Ethical Debate." *Journal of Medical Ethics*, 33:4, 187–188.

In Loving Memory
1963 ~ 2005

Introduction

Can a competent, terminally ill, nonclinically depressed person, in pain—or not—and suffering, end life with the passive assistance of a physician? This is the central substantive issue examined in this chapter. It begins by examining the ongoing hard-nosed battles surrounding the legal efforts by physician-assisted dying (PAD) supporters—in state and federal courts—that challenged the constitutionality of state laws that criminally punish any person assisting another to end his life. There was, in 2015, a total of 45 states and the District of Columbia that considered PAD illegal: 38 have laws prohibiting PAD; 3 states (Alabama, Massachusetts, and West Virginia) and the District of Columbia prohibit PAD by common law; and 4 states (Nevada, North Carolina, Utah, and Wyoming) have no laws prohibiting PAD, may not recognize common law, and are unclear on the legality of PAD ("State-by-State

---

The Rev. Patrick Mahoney, director of the Christian Defense Coalition, holds up a picture of Terri Schiavo in front of the U.S. Supreme Court building to commemorate her death. Schiavo was a Florida resident who suffered a catastrophic medical event in 1990 that left her near brain dead, and in a permanent vegetative state. Until her death in March 2005, Terri's tragedy was a political and legal battleground for two contradictory principles: the sacredness of life and the right of her surrogate to end her life by withdrawing her feeding tube. (AP Photo/Haraz N. Ghanbari)

Guide" 2015). The chapter then investigates *political* efforts by PAD pressure groups to convince state legislators to pass legislation permitting physician aid to terminally ill patients. These two venues—the legal and the political—are the only roads available to groups who seek to change social policy in America. Beginning in the late 1980s, PAD advocates' efforts have brought every group on both sides into the right to die firestorm.

This battle has continued, unabated, since then. The latest data regarding the legislative battles in America show that a majority of states face continuing efforts by pro-PAD legislators to introduce Oregon-style death with dignity laws. In every instance, in the courts and in the legislatures, the groups opposing PAD, religious institutions—especially the Catholic Church—disabled groups, and the medical, nursing, and health care establishments, challenge the PAD supporters.

This right to die battle in the states is a national war between groups of proponents and objectors; it continues to roil the society with no sign of let-up, fatigue, or armistice. In addition to the 6 states that allow PAD as of 2017, another 25 state legislatures are continuing to debate the merits of a PAD bill, 15 of them examining the issue for the very first time during their 2015 legislative session. The expectation is that most if not all states will eventually become battlegrounds in the struggles surrounding the right to die.

The right to die conflagration joined the on-going political-religious-social fights over another very impassioned struggle: the still-continuing battle over the constitutionality of a woman's right to have an abortion. The abortion confrontation began with the Supreme Court's *Roe v. Wade* decision in 1973 and continues into the second decade of the 21st century. By a 7-2 majority, the justices concluded that a woman had a personal "liberty" interest, a right to privacy (found in the U.S. Constitution's Fourteenth Amendment's due process clause) to choose—or not—to have an abortion. Justice Harry A. Blackmun, for the majority opinion, wrote that "this right of privacy, . . . founded in the Fourteenth Amendment's concept of personal liberty and restrictions upon state action, as we feel it is, is broad enough to encompass a woman's decision whether or not to terminate her pregnancy." (In 1992, in another case involving the scope of a woman's liberty interest to have an abortion, *Planned Parenthood of Southeastern Pennsylvania v. Casey*, the judgment noted that "at the heart of liberty" is a person's right to "define one's own concept of existence . . . and of the mystery of human life." This comment was cited as a viable precedent by the PAD plaintiffs' lawyers in the watershed right to die cases before the U.S. Supreme Court in 1997: *Vacco v. Quill* and *Washington v. Glucksberg*.)

Both issues—abortion and the right to die—engage the same individuals and organizations in the battles. The moral themes—the sanctity of life versus the autonomous person's liberty to choose—are identical in these two social-religious-political clashes. The examination of these legal and political venues, where the right to die is the focus, underscores the unremitting harshness of both sides.

This chapter also investigates the continuing right to die problems that emerge from the disputes, as well as focusing on the general society's responses to the changes in how we die in this new century. Finally, the most difficult question of all is whether there are solutions to these problems or whether, like the abortion controversy, there is no resolution.

The Right to Die Battle in the Courts

The right to die controversy, like the abortion issue, began in earnest in the state and federal courts. Ultimately, the U.S. Supreme Court played a major role in addressing both issues. The right to die became a very public issue in America in the 1970s because of massive media coverage of a number of highly unusual medical cases. What was so singular about these initial cases were the patients at the center of the stories. They were not terminally ill, aging persons in great pain, suffering in a number of ways. These cases generally had once-vibrant primarily young (twenties to thirties) females at the center of the litigation. They became headline news stories because of their medical condition after they experienced a catastrophic injury. They were unconscious and incompetent, diagnosed as being in a persistent, then permanent vegetative state (PVS).

The PVS Cases: The Initial Judicial Foray into the Contemporary Right to Die Controversy

These cases involved individuals who barely survived a catastrophic medical event, but, because of a lack of oxygen to the brain for more than six to eight minutes, lost nearly all cognitive capacity, were comatose, and were diagnosed to be in a PVS. Almost every day Americans read, heard, and watched the news reports—accompanied by photographs of these poor souls—describing their plight. The despair of their families became a part of these human interest stories. Husbands, wives, parents, siblings, and family members couldn't do anything but watch, hope, and pray for some utterance or movement or tears that would indicate improvement in the health of their loved ones.

The injured were vibrant one day and, the next day, after cardio-pulmonary resuscitation (CPR) performed by EMTs rescued them from death, were left unconscious, blind, unable to communicate, and in desperate need of medical devices that artificially breathed and provided hydration and nutrition for them. A patient in a PVS, after a year with no change or, more likely, with a further deterioration of her medical condition, is diagnosed to be in a permanent vegetative state.

The doctors share this dire prognosis with the immediate family. It is grim because there is no medical treatment that will improve the patient's existence. A person in such a state simply exists; there is no quality of life. The PVS patient is in a *twilight zone*, not biologically dead yet, but without life. And, as the cases below indicate, the patients had been in a PVS for years; in one of the cases, *In Re Schiavo*, the patient remained in a PVS for 15 years (1990–2005) until the hydration and feeding tube was withdrawn from her body and she died.

If the patient prepared an advanced directive (or a do-not-resuscitate order) that laid out his or her feelings about being kept alive by artificial breathing, drinking, and eating, then action could be taken by medical professionals to honor the patient's known wishes. However, preparing such documentation was and still remains an action few people take, especially while they are young and healthy. Every case state and federal judges have had to adjudicate featured a basic set of facts: a patient in a deteriorating PVS for many years, with no written instructions, and a guardian (generally the spouse or the parents) who asks the court for permission to end the PVS patient's life.

These cases became the opening clash of opposing forces in the movement to legitimize a terminally ill patient's right to die with physician assistance. Because of them, society became acutely aware of the emotionally draining conflicts over life and death decisions, taken by doctors, parents, husbands, legislatures, and courts, in New Jersey (*Quinlan*), Virginia (*Gilmour*), Missouri (*Cruzan*), Florida (*Schiavo*), and other states regarding the care of persons in a PVS.

Three years before *Quinlan*, *Roe v. Wade* had been decided. *Roe* was a major turning point in the right to die controversy for two basic reasons: (1) The opposing forces in the abortion battles since the *Roe* decision was announced, the religious and conservative "sanctity of life" groups, pitted against those coalitions that maintain that an autonomous individual has the "liberty" to "define one's own concept of existence," are the very same organizations clashing in the right to die battles since *Quinlan*. (2) The legal and political arguments used by the adversaries in the abortion and right to die confrontations are interchangeable. A news story published in 1998 illustrates this reality quite clearly.

After standing for an hour in a local abortion protest with her Catholic parish, Nancy Supples went straight to a nursing home 1½ miles away, where a feeding tube had

just been withdrawn [from a patient in a PVS]. She found
herself leading a prayer vigil—and, through that peaceful
picket line, bringing home . . . a slice of a powerful social
movement that is starting to sweep the nation. (Goldstein
1998)

Quinlan was the first case to lay open to the public the right
to die issue in the modern era. Twenty-one-year-old Karen Ann
Quinlan, in mid-April 1975, came home from a party where
she had some drinks. She had taken prescription medicine
before the partying began. Karen collapsed, stopped breathing,
and fell into a coma. EMTs and then emergency room doctors
saved her life, but, because she had sustained two respiratory
arrests and lacked oxygen (*anoxia*) for about 15 minutes each
time, Karen suffered severe brain damage and remained comatose. She was, after one month, diagnosed to be in a PVS by
her physicians. She was kept alive by a mechanical breathing
device and a feeding tube.

After three months spent with Karen every day, coping with
the somber medical prognosis that she would never regain "any
level of cognitive function" (Clark 2006), discussing the hopelessness of Karen's existence with their parish priest (the family
was Catholic), and reviewing the Vatican's position regarding
the care of PVS patients, her parents made a decision that
opened the still-continuing right to die controversy.

They were heartbroken because of the social death of their
child; while she was physically "alive" because of the tubes,
she was no longer living. Her mother wrote that "by late
May 1975, I faced the reality that there was no medical help for
Karen" (Quinlan 2005). They, as Karen's co-guardians, signed a
statement prepared by their lawyer instructing the doctors "to
discontinue all extraordinary measures, including the use of a
respirator for our daughter Karen Quinlan" (Quinlan 2005).
The instant the document was given to the hospital administrators, the right to die issue became a part of the national,
and then, international, conversation. Hospital administrators

and the doctors, however, refused to accede to the request after being notified by the local prosecutor that homicide charges could be brought against them if the respirator was removed. The only option available to the parents was to go into state court to get an order to force the hospital to remove the device and allow Karen Ann to die.

After a lower court judge rejected the petition, the case came to the New Jersey Supreme Court in 1976. The judges took the unusual step of taking the case before the intermediate appellate court could hear and decide the issue. Oral arguments were heard in late January 1975; two months later the unanimous decision was announced.

The judges explained their unusual decision to take the case: *Quinlan* was "a matter of transcendent importance,"

> involv[ing] questions related to the definition and existence of death, the prolongation of life through artificial means developed by medical technology undreamed of in past generations of the practice of the healing arts; [and] the impact of such durationally indeterminate and artificial life prolongation on the rights of the incompetent, her family, and society in general. (*In Re Quinlan*, 355 A. 2nd 647, at 652)

The judges ordered the hospital to remove the respirator. The Court relied on the *Roe* precedent, particularly "what has been called the rights of 'personality' " for its decision. These personality rights, they concluded, "were paramount against the state's right to preserve life. [They were] broad enough to encompass a patient's decision to decline medical treatment under certain circumstances in much the same way as it is broad enough to encompass a woman's decision to terminate pregnancy."

The judges, however, emphatically stated that "the case is not to be considered euthanasia in any way; that would never be licit. [Furthermore, in cases such as *Quinlan*'s], the interruption of attempts at resuscitation, even when it causes the arrest of circulation, is no more than an indirect cause of the cessation of life." This comment mirrored the dogma of the Catholic Church in this matter. In a 1957 address to an international gathering of anesthesiologists by Pope Pius XII, he uttered words that have been a part of the right to death debates since *Quinlan*. He told the gathering that

> the doctor . . . has no separate or independent right where the patient is concerned. [He can act] only if the patient explicitly or implicitly, directly or indirectly, gives him permission. . . . Using a ventilator, however, is an *extraordinary* means of preserving life. . . . There is no [moral] *obligation* to use it or to give the doctor permission to use it. Since these forms of treatment go beyond the *ordinary means* to which one is bound, it cannot be held that there is an obligation to use them or not, consequently, that one is bound to give the doctor permission to use them. (Pope Pius XII 1957)

If the patient is incompetent, Karen's legal co-guardians, based on their understanding of her view of living, could stop the use of extraordinary means to keep her alive. The pope's address, however, indicated that nutrition and hydration tubes were "ordinary means" of caring for a severely disabled person, and that Catholics were bound to always use such conventional medical aids. To withdraw these devices was both immoral and an act of murder subject to action in criminal court.

Following the court's opinion, the doctor withdrew the breathing apparatus from Karen Ann. However, because nutrition and hydration were ordinary means of assisting a patient diagnosed with PVS, they were never withdrawn. After the respirator was disconnected, she breathed on her own; Karen lived in a nursing home for another nine years. She died of pneumonia in 1985. She never regained consciousness. An autopsy of her brain indicated that it had lost 50 percent of its size since 1975.

The *Quinlan* decision remains a milestone in the history of the right to die movement. For the first time in America, a court (unanimously) concluded that there are constitutionally protected *personality rights*; that is, the right to privacy encompassed an individual's (or guardian's) decision to decline medical treatment, even if it led to death.

However forward looking *Quinlan* was, it was law only in New Jersey. No other state is bound by it. They could modify their state laws—or not—to allow guardians to withdraw the medical devices; they were not required to do so. The initial response by other states was to do nothing. For centuries, the "sanctity of life" principle was—and still remains—a cornerstone of a state's constitutionally protected "police powers." Unless prohibited by the U.S. Constitution itself, a state can pass all laws its lawmakers thought would protect the life, liberty, and pursuit of happiness of all persons within its jurisdiction.

From 1976 on, however, because of the media coverage of these tragedies, millions of families became very familiar with the plight of the New Jersey "sleeping beauty" (Quinlan 2005) and how that story ended. When they faced a similar medical catastrophe, many requested doctors to withdraw medical devices from the body of their sleeping princesses. These demands meant that guardians of an incompetent PVS patient—a mother, father, husband, son, daughter, or granddaughter—had to petition their state court for the right to disconnect the device.

After *Quinlan*, because of the increase in the number of persons who, because of a catastrophic injury, lost oxygen for more than six to eight minutes but were kept alive in a PVS, there were many petitions to state courts to allow guardians to have artificial means of life support withdrawn. A 1988 case from Virginia reflects the right to die issue prior to the U.S. Supreme Court's entry into the issue two years later.

James Gilmore III v. Hugh Finn is an example of how a state judiciary responded to a *Quinlan*-like petition—and how quickly the case entered the political arena. (Virginia's

Republican governor, Jim Gilmore III, inserted himself in the matter in an attempt to protect the life of Hugh Finn, the incapacitated PVS patient.)

In early March 1995, 44-year-old Hugh Finn, a well-known news reporter, barely survived a car crash near his home in Louisville, Kentucky. Although EMT technicians and emergency department doctors saved his life, because his aorta ruptured and Finn was without oxygen to his brain, he was diagnosed as being in a PVS. A nutrition and hydration tube was inserted.

Because his parents and siblings lived in Virginia, in February 1996 his wife Michele Finn moved her comatose husband to a nursing home in Manassas, Virginia, to enable them to visit Hugh. After more than three years in a PVS, and after doctors once again informed Michele that there would probably be no improvement in Hugh's condition, she decided to have the physician withdraw his life-sustaining apparatus and tubes.

Hugh's parents, siblings, and family and friends initially disagreed with her decision and entered the circuit court seeking a court order blocking the removal of the tubes. Judge Frank A. Hoss heard argument in July and, on August 31, 1996, announced his ruling: the devices could be removed in 21 days. The judge concluded, on the basis of Hugh's wife's and his attorney's testimony, that "clear and convincing evidence" was provided by them that Finn "would not wish to have his life artificially prolonged." Virginia law allowed guardians of terminally ill patients or patients in a PVS to request such withdrawal if doctors, "to a reasonable degree of medical probability," believed recovery was impossible.

However, three days before the tube removal, a nurse with the Virginia Department of Medical Assistance Services visited the patient to check his condition. According to an affidavit filed with the court by Virginia Attorney General Mark Earley's office, Finn said "hi" to the nurse when she entered the room and "mumbled what appeared to be words" to her. Responding to the document on September 21, the judge postponed his order for nine days in order for the family to appeal, although he didn't believe the nurse's statement "added anything substantially new" to the case (Masters 1998a).

The family decided not to appeal the court order to the state Supreme Court. They concluded, Hugh's brother said, that "even if we kept Hugh alive, we don't think his quality of life would ever be anything to speak of" (Masters 1998b). However, Finn's sister asked Governor James Gilmore to intervene on the family's behalf to stop the withdrawal process. On October 1, the governor filed an appeal to the state Supreme Court, asking for a temporary restraining order. He said: "My job as governor and my role is to protect those people who are most frail in society and cannot necessarily protect themselves" (Masters 1998c). Gilmore told reporters that he "holds a longstanding belief that people who are in those types of frail medical conditions ought to have the best possible review of their cases by the courts. I've always felt very strongly about that" (Masters 1998c).

The next day the county judge rejected Gilmore's appeal. He concluded that state law allows the removal of hydration and nutrition tubes from a patient with a terminal illness or one in a PVS "from which, to a reasonable degree of medical probability, there can be no recovery" (Melton and Masters 1998). Two days later, the Virginia Supreme Court upheld the judge's decision. In a short, three-paragraph decision, the judges said the "withdrawal merely permits the natural process of dying" (Melton and Masters 1998). Hugh Finn died on October 9, 1998, eight days after the final court order.

This, however, was not the final act in the Finn sorrows. Less than one month later, November 5, 1998, Michele Finn filed a lawsuit asking for compensation for her court costs and punitive sanctions against the governor, the attorney general, and other state officials. Gilmore's emergency petition to the state Supreme Court, she claimed in her petition, was "ill-advised, improvident, and spurious." The governor, she claimed, was motivated by purely political reasons and did not even have "standing" to bring the emergency appeal to the court.

In late November Judge Hoss of Circuit Court of Prince William County, Virginia, ruled against Gilmore. He wrote that the governor's action "was not warranted by existing law." If Gilmore did not like the Virginia law allowing withdrawal of tubes from PVS patients, then the governor should remember a basic political fact of life: the separation of powers principle in the Constitution! Changes in laws are "made in the political arena and not in the court, certainly not in the manner that it was done in this case." Hoss awarded Finn $13,124.20 for court costs but did not award punitive damages.

This time Hoss was overturned by the state Supreme Court. They ruled—unanimously—that the governor "had a duty to intervene if he has a reasonable, good faith legal basis for suspecting that a citizen's rights may be threatened." Because they concluded that Gilmore had a legitimate reason for filing suit, he was not liable for Finn's court costs.

Coinciding with the *Finn* decision was the U.S. Supreme Court's initial entry into the right to die controversy. The case was another terrible PVS situation involving a young woman's near-fatal automobile accident in Missouri: *Cruzan v. Director, Missouri Department of Health*. In *Cruzan*, the Justices struggled—for the first time in right to die appeals—with medical, moral, and constitutional questions raised in the briefs filed in the Court.

With this decision, the Court majority moved the right to die issue further into the public arena by "enhancing" the *Quinlan* precedent in two ways: (1) the decision impacted *all* state judicial proceedings, and (2) the Court, by enabling each state to create guidelines and definitions regarding withdrawal of or preventing insertion of medical aids in PVS cases, indirectly rejected the division of medical technology into ordinary means (e.g., nutrition and hydration tubes) and extraordinary means (e.g., respirator) used to save lives.

Cruzan obliterated the distinction. After 1990, PVS guidelines were determined by an individual state; in many states, including Missouri, a competent adult, or (when a patient was incompetent) a guardian, could request that all aids to continuing life be withheld or withdrawn.

In January 1983, 27-year-old Nancy Cruzan lost control of her car and was thrown into a ditch. She suffered cardiac and respiratory arrest. When EMTs arrived, she had no vital signs but, with CPR, was resuscitated. She sustained severe, traumatic brain damage. Her brain was deprived of oxygen for over 14 minutes; she was unresponsive and in a coma. At the hospital, a gastrostomy tube was inserted to provide nutrition and hydration. She was, almost immediately, in an "unconscious state"; a CT scan of her brain when she entered the emergency department showed severe brain damage—"a nearly flat background." (A "flat" reading is a clear indication of brain death.) After a month the family and medical staff noted that Nancy's arms and legs "had started to stiffen and atrophy, drawing in slowly toward her trunk. The doctors and nurses called this stiffening 'contractures'" (Colby 2002). The medical diagnosis was very grim: no possibility of improvement. She was being kept alive by a feeding tube and round-the-clock medical care by hospital staff. Her parents, as Nancy's co-guardians, acting in their daughter's "best interest," signed a do-not-resuscitate form in the event her breathing stopped.

Inexorably, four years later, in May 1987, Mary Cruzan's parents, seeing no change in their daughter's condition, authorized the hospital to "discontinue the life support system" keeping her alive. The administrators refused to withdraw the tube because of a state law that categorically prohibited stopping the use of a feeding tube in these medical situations. Missouri legislators, in 1985, had passed a "living will" statute enabling a person to list the medical equipment that were not to be used if he or she faced a catastrophic health event and was unconscious.

The law, however, targeted a medical action that was forbidden even if the "living will" document listed it as one that was not to be used to resuscitate the person: "feeding tubes were not considered medical equipment in Missouri, and a person could not list feeding tube as a treatment to forgo in a Missouri living will" (Colby 2002). The prohibition, the Cruzan's lawyer noted later, "was the exact medical procedure our lawsuit would seek to withdraw" (Colby 2002).

They had to go into probate court to seek an order allowing doctors to discontinue use of the tube. Because Nancy was comatose and had not prepared a "living will" document, her parents had to present to the court "clear and convincing evidence" that the withdrawal reflected Nancy's wish. Friends of Nancy prepared statements attesting to her views about life and whether she would want to live in a PVS. The probate judge, balancing the right of the state to maintain life against the liberty of an "individual to refuse or direct the withdrawal of artificial death prolonging procedures," directed the hospital and the Missouri Department of Health to "cause the request . . . to be carried out" (Colby 2002).

Bypassing the lower appeals court, the hospital and Health Department lawyers asked the Missouri Supreme Court to review and overturn the judge's order. The Court accepted the petition and, in late September 1988, heard oral arguments in the case. On December 15, 1988, the opinion was announced. By a 4-3 vote, it reversed the probate judge's order, concluding that state law prohibited the co-guardians request. "In the face of this State's strongly stated policy in favor of life, we choose to err on the side of life, respecting the rights of severely incompetent persons who may wish to live despite a severely diminished quality of life" (Colby 2002).

The dissenting judges sided with the parents and the probate judge: "I am not persuaded that the State is a better decision-maker than Nancy's parents," said one. Another wrote that the probate judge's opinion "was a courageous voyage in an area not previously charted by Missouri courts" (Colby 2002).

The Cruzans, in March 1989, filed a petition for a writ of certiorari with the U.S. Supreme Court. It was granted and the Justices prepared to read the briefs and hear oral arguments during the Court's 1989 term. The Cruzans' brief asked the Justices to consider the following:

> Whether a State may, consistently with the due process clause, require clear and convincing evidence that an incompetent person would want life-supporting medical procedures withdrawn before it approves the termination of such procedures. (*Cruzan v. Director, Missouri Department of Health*)

After reading briefs, listening to oral arguments, and deliberating in chambers, the U.S. Supreme Court handed down the *Cruzan* opinion on the very last day of its 1989 term. It was, as so many Court opinions since the 1980s have been, a divided 5-4 vote to affirm the judgment of the Missouri Supreme Court. While all nine justices agreed that a competent person has a "liberty interest" under the due process clause to refuse all unwanted medical treatment—even if such a refusal led to the patient's death—they disagreed on the questions of law in the case.

The division came about because Nancy Cruzan was unconscious, was incompetent, and did not have a living will, and co-guardians acted for her. For the five-person majority, stating that a person has a liberty interest "does not end the inquiry; whether Cruzan's constitutional rights have been violated must be determined by balancing his [*sic*] liberty interests against the relevant state interests." The dissenting justices disagreed: Nancy Cruzan "has a fundamental right to be free of unwanted artificial nutrition and hydration, which right is not outweighed by any interests of the State."

Was Missouri's "clear and convincing evidence" standard a reasonable use of the state's police powers was the second issue dividing the Court. The majority said that the Missouri procedural safeguard was a "reasonably designed" one. Use of the challenged safeguard is a "permissible" exercise of the State's police powers. The dissenters had a different view of the "clear and convincing evidence" standard. It was an "improperly biased procedural obstacle which impermissibly burdens the right."

Justice Antonin Scalia's concurring opinion reflected the dramatic, complex, and frustrating questions raised in these cases—and of the Supreme Court's discomfort when answering them.

> The various opinions in this case [six] portray quite clearly the difficult, indeed agonizing questions that are presented by the constantly increasing power of science to keep the human body alive for longer than any reasonable person would want to inhabit it. . . . The answers to these heartbreaking questions are neither set forth in the Constitution nor known to the nine Justices of this Court any better than they are known to nine people picked at random from the Kansas City telephone directory.

After *Cruzan* came down on June 25, 1990, the case returned to Missouri. Cruzan's lawyer had to present "clear and convincing evidence" to the probate judge that the co-guardians' request was what Nancy Cruzan would have wanted. On November 1, 1990, her relatives, her parents, and her friends presented evidence that Nancy did not want to "live" with the aid of medical devices and tubes.

After hearing and reading these testimonies about Nancy's state of mind while competent, and reviewing the most recent medical reports that clearly showed continued "worsening" deterioration of her health, on December 13, 1990, the judge ordered the nutrition and hydration tube withdrawn from Nancy's body.

There was, he wrote, "clear and convincing evidence" presented to the court that the "intent of our ward, if mentally able, would be to terminate her nutrition and hydration" (Colby 2002). Nancy's feeding tube was removed on December 14,

1990; she died 11 days later in the hospital's hospice ward. There was no reference to the notion of restraining doctors from withdrawing ordinary means used to keep a patient in a PVS alive.

The Cruzan family tragedy, however, did not end then. The parents and their lawyer had to immediately respond to a new controversy: the actions of pro-life groups to stop the tube withdrawal. The Missouri Citizens for Life group immediately asked the governor, conservative Republican John Ashcroft, to order the state's attorney general to ask the court for a writ of prohibition. (If a court grants such an "extraordinary writ of equity," the judge's order would be rescinded and the doctors would have to reinsert the feeding tube.) The Missouri attorney general, however, did not appeal the probate judge's order. Ashcroft, who became President George W. Bush's attorney general in 2001, had an aide call the hospital administrators to request that doctors reinsert the tube. The attending doctor refused to act: "The tube's already out and there's no medical reason to put it back in." When the administrator reiterated the governor's "request," the doctor showed him the court order, said, "I have a court order," and walked away (Colby 2002). After another state-wide effort by the Citizens for Life group to stop the withdrawal failed, Nancy died. She was quietly buried. Her grave marker had three dates inscribed on it: "Born: July 20, 1957; Departed: January 11, 1983; At Peace: December 26, 1990."

Justice Sandra Day O'Connor's concurring opinion offered a suggestion regarding the benchmarks needed by judges tasked with the responsibility of making choices that could lead to withdrawal of all life support devices followed by death. It was an idea that the U.S. Supreme Court repeated in 1997, when the justices responded to arguments concerning the constitutionality of PAD. "Today," she wrote, "we decide only that one State's practice does not violate the Constitution; the more challenging task of crafting appropriate procedures for safeguarding incompetents' liberty interests is entrusted to the 'laboratory' of the States, in the first instance."

O'Connor's concurring opinion stressed the value of a federal system: every state has police powers that enable it to create a standard that reflects the cultural, moral, religious, and philosophical values of the state's residents. Each state's exploration of what principle was needed for a judge to make life or death decisions for incapacitated patients in a PVS is the essence of governance in a democracy. Elected officials work in a "laboratory" in which policies are crafted to address problems in their community.

When a law is challenged by persons who claim it is unconstitutional, the duty of the judge is to defer to the judgment of the policy makers. This lowest level of scrutiny, the "rational basis" test, is generally applied by the judges in PVS cases. The party bringing the petition to the court has the burden of proof to show that there is no governmental interest in making the policy or that there is no reasonable link between that governmental interest and the challenged law. If the burden of proof is not shown, the law stands.

However, there are exceptions that call for a higher degree of appraisal. If the litigation raises the question of whether the challenged bill or governmental action significantly abridges (1) a fundamental right protected by the Constitution or (2) involves a suspect classification, then all judges—state and federal—must employ the highest, most thorough form of analysis—strict scrutiny—to determine the law's constitutionality. To pass the strict scrutiny test, the state has the burden of showing that the law was passed to further a "compelling governmental interest" and is "narrowly tailored" to accomplish that interest.

The four *Cruzan* dissenters argued that *Cruzan* involved fundamental rights and therefore the state of Missouri had to meet the strict scrutiny standard. The five-person majority did not see a fundamental right at play in the facts; they applied the least strenuous "reasonableness" test and validated the Missouri statute. And, when the Supreme Court votes, five votes always trump four!

After *Cruzan*, states passed laws that established the necessary guidelines needed by judges adjudicating PVS cases. At least three such standards were developed by the states to be applied when a state court judge was asked to allow removal of a medical device used to artificially maintain the life of a patient in a PVS. Each state chose one of these guidelines: either (1) pursue the "clear and convincing evidence" standard; or (2) determine whether the "substituted judgement" of the guardians was acceptable; or (3) decide whether "the best interests of the PVS patient" were conclusively presented by the guardian's lawyers.

During this seminal year, 1990, a number of events happened that moved the right to die controversy to center stage in America's ongoing polarized social, religious, medical, and political wars. Efforts were made in a number of states, beginning in Washington State in 1990, to pass legislation that would permit PAD for terminally ill patients; pressure groups on both sides of the right to die controversy began to operate across the nation; stories began to appear in the media about doctors who assisted in providing terminally ill patients with the means to die. These activities continued to parade before the public, courtesy of the media. They have become a part of the national news with some degree of regularity. They still remain in the national—and international—news.

The event that captured the hearts and minds of hundreds of millions of Americans and countless millions watching and reading about it in other nations—from its beginning in 1990 to its final chapter in 2005—was a Florida case involving another patient-in-a-PVS whose guardian (her husband) requested that the medical devices keeping her alive be withdrawn: *In Re Theresa Marie (Terri) Schiavo*. As Cal Thomas said of the case: "[It] will be the beginning or the continuation on the line of death that began in the womb in 1973 with *Roe v. Wade* and will now quickly advance toward the 'retirement' villages (Thomas 2005).

This polarizing, bitter battle began on February 25, 1990, just months before Nancy Cruzan died. Terri Schiavo, a 27-year-old married woman, suffered a major cardiac arrest in her home due to a potassium imbalance. Her husband, Michael Schiavo, immediately called 911 for help. Like other PVS case histories, EMTs arrived and, using CPR, restored her heart beat. However, Terri had been without oxygen to her brain for more than 12 minutes, "nearly twice as long as is generally necessary to cause profound, irreversible brain damage" (Caplan 2006).

Terri was taken to the hospital by the EMTs and a hydration and nutrition tube was inserted; she never regained consciousness. After observing her nonresponsiveness for many months and after reviewing a host of clinical physical examination results, her doctors informed the family that she was in a PVS.

Michael, her guardian (initially with Terri's parents' assent), after eight years, petitioned the Circuit Court of Pinellas County, Florida, to authorize the removal of his wife's feeding tube. Unlike the position of the guardians in *Quinlan*, *Cruzan*, and *Finn*, Terri's parents, Robert and Mary Schindler, absolutely rejected his decision. That led to seven years of bitter enmity between the husband and the Schindler family. They "reviled" Michael (Goodnough 2005), regularly accusing him of assaulting Teresa before her collapse; they charged him with murder, calling him a "wife abuser," and accused him of refusing their requests for rehab for Terri, as well as refusing their insistent requests for their own medical doctors to examine their daughter. They never changed their minds about seeing improvements in their daughter and about their utter disdain for her husband.

Devout Catholics, they believed that their daughter's death had to come about naturally, one that occurred with God's grace. And, they maintained, Terri shared their religious beliefs and would not want the tube withdrawn. In addition, throughout the entire 15-year travail, they noted a variety of semiconscious actions by Terri, indicating that she heard, cried, saw, and attempted to speak to them and others. They continued to insist that rehabilitation specialists visit their daughter to improve her mobility.

The litigation began in Florida's courts in 1998. Before it ended seven years later (2005), the case saw dozens of decisions taken by more than 30 judges and justices sitting in the Florida county circuit court (almost 30 separate rulings by the same judge), the Florida district court of appeals (nearly one dozen rulings), the Florida Supreme Court (over one dozen orders were issued, all declined review), the U.S. District Court (MD-FL), the Eleventh U.S. Circuit Court of Appeals, and the U.S. Supreme Court (more than one dozen appeals to these federal courts, with the Supreme Court declining to review any of them).

The lower trial and appellate federal courts refused to overturn the state judge's orders. The trial judge rejected the Schindlers' argument that Terri was denied due process of law. The Eleventh Circuit appeals court upheld his decision. In the opinion, the court "admonished President Bush and Congress for acting 'in a manner demonstrably at odds with our founding fathers' blueprint for the governance of a free people.'" Three times the state circuit court judge ordered the removal of the nutrition and hydration tube; twice Florida's district court of appeals directed the hospital to reinsert the tube.

With the exception of a handful of petitions presented by Terri's husband, all the petitions to the courts were for the issuance of an order either stopping the withdrawal of the tube or, if it had been removed, requiring the reinstalling of the tube into Terri. These requests came from two groups: Terri's parents (the Schindlers) and siblings, and national conservative right to life groups, including Operation Rescue, the (Catholic) Priests for Life, and the hierarchy of the Roman Catholic Church from America and the Vatican.

Pope John Paul II, speaking in the Vatican on March 20, 2004, entered the *Schiavo* fray. He conveyed, to participants attending the International Congress on Life Sustaining Treatments and

Vegetative State: Scientific Advances and Ethical Dilemmas, his deeply held beliefs about how society must care for a patients like Terri Schiavo.

He noted, first of all, a number of documented cases of patients in a vegetative state who showed "at least partial recovery even after many years; . . . . Medical science, up until now, is still unable to predict with certainty who among patients in this condition will recover and who will not" (John Paul II 2004). The absence of medical certainty that a patient in a PVS will never recover was beside the point. Even if medical certainty was achieved, a moral person would not take the patient's life by stopping medical actions that keep the person alive. The essential principle of Catholic theology was then laid out by the pope:

> There are some who cast doubt on the persistence of the "human quality" itself [in a PVS patient, with] the adjective "vegetative" . . . applied to the sick as such, actually demeaning their value and personal dignity. . . . In opposition to such [a] trend of thought, I feel the duty to reaffirm strongly that the intrinsic value and personal dignity of every human does not change, no matter what the concrete circumstances of his or her life. A man, even if seriously ill or disabled in the exercise of his highest functions, is and always will be a man, and he will never become a "vegetable" or an "animal." (John Paul II 2004)

Pope John Paul II's address is the hallmark not only of Catholic teaching and practice; *all* individuals and groups who believe in the sanctity of life share these beliefs. The defenders of the right to life insist that, as Pope John Paul II said, "the true task of medicine is 'to cure if possible, always to care'" (John Paul II 2004). A doctor who assisted in withdrawal of a feeding tube was acting immorally and criminally. These organizations absolutely rejected the beliefs of those who maintained that withdrawal of a tube providing natural or ordinary sustenance was what the person wanted and was in the best interests of the patient.

The *Schiavo* case witnessed the reemergence, in the 1990s, of the Catholic Church's financial and strategic leadership position in the right to die battles—in courts and in state and national legislatures. The contentious case turned, in 2004, into a cacophonous political drama in Florida and Washington, D.C., legislative and executive meeting rooms. Conservative Republican Florida legislators, Florida's Republican governor Jeb Bush, conservative "sanctity of life" members of both the U.S. House of Representatives and the U.S. Senate, and the conservative Republican president of the United States George W. Bush did all they could to keep Terri Schiavo alive after the judiciary's messages were announced.

"Terri's law" bills were passed in the Florida legislature and in the U.S. Congress. They were signed by the Bush brothers: Jeb in Florida and George in the White House. On March 21, 2005, President Bush hurriedly flew into Washington, D.C., just to sign the bill. At the signing he said: "In cases like this one, where there are serious questions and substantial doubts, our society, our laws, and our courts should have a presumption in favor of life. This presumption is especially critical for those like Terri Schiavo who live at the mercy of others" (Bush 2005). On appeal to the state and federal courts, the bills were ruled unconstitutional because legislators could not constitutionally instruct a court to reinsert Terri's tube. The proposals violated the principle of separation of powers.

For many Republican conservatives in state and the national legislatures, however, the case fit perfectly into their political strategy for electoral victory. Just before the final chapter of the Schiavo tragedy in 2005, for example, the legal counsel to U.S. senator Mel Martinez (R-FL) told his boss that he authored a memorandum, sent to all Republican senators, "citing the political advantage to Republicans for intervening in the case of Terri Schiavo" (Allen 2005). It said, in part, that "this case is an important moral issue and the [party's] pro-life base will be excited that the Senate is debating this important issue" (Allen 2005).

While the 15-year Schiavo tragedy was unfolding, the U.S. Supreme Court decided to hear two cases in its 1997 term that challenged the constitutionality of state laws that prohibited "assisting in a suicide": *Washington v. Glucksberg* and *Vacco v. Quill.*

The Central Role of the U.S. Supreme Court in the Right to Die Controversy

In 1997, a watershed event took place that swiftly led to a heightening of the debates, clashes, litigation, and legislation surrounding the question of whether a terminally ill patient has a constitutional right to die with the assistance of a doctor: the U.S. Supreme Court decisions in *Washington v. Glucksberg* and *Vacco v. Quill.* They came to the Supreme Court on appeal from lower federal appellate court decisions in New York and Washington State. Their laws that made PAD a crime (49 states and the District of Columbia had similar laws at the time) were overturned in the two states by federal appeals courts (Ninth U.S. Court of Appeals in *Washington* and the Second in *Vacco*). The laws ran afoul of a terminally ill person's constitutionally protected "liberty" to seek the assistance of a doctor to die.

The liberty argument successfully employed by plaintiffs in the Ninth Circuit Court of Appeals was based on the Constitution's Fourteenth Amendment's due process clause. ("No person shall be denied life, liberty, or property without due process of law.") Both courts also heard the "equal protection arguments of the PAD attorneys in both cases and concluded that the state statutes violated that guarantee in the Fourteenth Amendment as well.

The Ninth Circuit U.S. Court of Appeals heard an appeal from the state attorneys. They appealed the 1994 decision of a U.S. District Court judge, Barbara Rothstein, who was appointed by Democratic president Jimmy Carter in 1980. She had concluded that Washington's anti-PAD statute was unconstitutional on two grounds: they violated the due process and equal protection guarantees. She found "the reasoning in *Casey* highly instructive and almost prescriptive on the issue." Both abortion and the right to die centrally touch on individual liberty; "they involve the most intimate and personal choices a person may make in a lifetime." They constitute "choice[s] central to personal dignity and autonomy" (quoting *Casey*).

Using the *Cruzan* case as precedent, the judge also ruled that the equal protection clause protection was violated by the anti-PAD criminal statute. There is no constitutional distinction between withdrawal of artificial life support which results in death (*Cruzan*) and the consequence when a terminally ill, competent patient—not on any life support mechanisms—receives physician assistance to die. The state statute, she concluded, constituted an unconstitutional "undue burden" on terminally ill patients who want to die.

The Ninth Circuit took the appeal and, following federal appellate court practice, a randomly selected three-judge panel heard the case. It voted 2-1 to overturn the district court decision. They determined that "the conclusion of the district court cannot be sustained." *Casey* was incorrectly applied; it "should not be removed from the context in which it was used [abortion]." Doing so "is to make an enormous leap . . . and to ignore the differences between the regulation of reproduction and the prevention of the promotion of killing a patient at his or her request." The district court judge's ruling was just the ranting of a judge who believed that the federal judiciary is "a floating constitutional convention." They "invent a constitutional right unknown to the past and antithetical to the defense of human life that has been a chief responsibility of our constitutional government."

The PAD lawyers took the step taken by the losing party in a three-judge panel: they asked the full Ninth Circuit to sit *en banc* to review the panel's decision. Most such appeals are denied; in *Glucksberg* the full court took the case. The majority opinion written by Judge Stephen Reinhardt, appointed by

Democratic president Jimmy Carter in 1980, overturned the panel's decision.

The majority answered the central question raised by the plaintiffs—and every group that supports PAD:

> Is there a right to die? Because we hold that there is, we must then determine whether prohibiting physicians from prescribing life-ending medication for use by terminally ill patients who wish to die violates the patients' due process right. . . . The Supreme Court has recognized that the Fourteenth Amendment affords constitutional protection to personal decisions. . . . We believe that two relatively recent decisions of the Court, *Cruzan* and *Casey*, are fully persuasive, and leave little doubt as to the final result. (*Compassion in Dying v. State of Washington* 1996)

While the state has a legitimate interest in preventing—but not punishing—suicide, that interest "is substantially diminished in the case of terminally ill, competent patients who wish to die." The state "has comparatively little weight" in blocking such an action; further, a state's "insistence on frustrating their wishes seems cruel indeed." A "liberty interest exists in the choice of how and when one dies"; the statute "violates the Due Process Clause."

Furthermore, the Ninth Circuit *en banc* majority concluded that the statute also violated the equal protection clause of the Fourteenth Amendment. "We see no ethical or constitutionally cognizable difference between a doctor's pulling the plug on a respirator and his prescribing drugs which will permit a terminally ill patient to end his own life."

After this announcement, the Washington State lawyers had one more opportunity to argue their case: appeal of the circuit court decision to the U.S. Supreme Court. They filed a timely appeal in 1996. Such appeals, when the Supreme Court receives these petitions, are not automatically heard by the justices. The Court has near-total discretion to review them and it takes a vote of four of the justices to grant a review—a grant of certiorari—to hear the case on the merits.

While the lawyers on both sides of the Washington right to die litigation were battling in the lower federal courts, a parallel case from New York State was moving through the lower federal courts. *Quill v. Vacco* began in October 1994 in the U.S. District Court, Southern District, New York. The case was put forward by the plaintiffs, doctors, and terminally ill patients who argued that the state statute criminalizing PAD was unconstitutional and was identical to the arguments of their Washington State colleagues made seven months earlier: the statute violated the Fourteenth Amendment's due process and equal protection clauses.

The U.S. District Court judge, Thomas P. Griesa, appointed to the bench in 1972 by Republican president Richard Nixon, handed down his decision on December 15, 1994, less than two months after receiving the petition. However, he reached the opposite conclusion rendered by Judge Rothstein in Washington State.

He categorically rejected the plaintiffs' claim that the due process and equal protection clauses allowed a dying patient to seek physician assistance to hasten death. The "reasoning" behind the use of *Cruzan* and *Casey* as precedent for them, he said, "is too broad." There is absolutely "no historic recognition" that PAD should be a fundamental right protected by the Constitution. It

> has never been given any kind of sanction in our legal history which would help establish it as a constitutional right. The court holds that PAD does not involve a fundamental liberty interest protected by the Due Process Clause of the Fourteenth Amendment. (*Quill v. Vacco* 1997)

Griesa set aside the plaintiffs' equal protection argument as well. There are distinctions between PAD and withdrawal of life support systems. If a state presents "reasonable and rational" arguments for an anti-PAD statute, there is no violation of the equal protection clause. He concluded: "It is hardly unreasonable or irrational for the State to recognize [the] difference. The State has obvious legitimate interests in preserving life, and in protecting vulnerable persons."

Dr. Quill and the other plaintiffs immediately appealed the decision to the Second Circuit U.S. Court of Appeals (CA2). The three-judge panel voted 3-0 to uphold only the due process segment of the Griesa decision. Judge Roger Miner, first appointed to the federal district court in 1981 and then elevated to the CA2 in 1985 (both by Republican president Ronald Reagan), wrote the opinion affirming Griesa's "due process" conclusion. PAD was not rooted in America's history and therefore was not a "fundamental liberty" protected by the due process clause.

However, the panel accepted the equal protection argument of the plaintiffs: the New York anti-PAD law did violate the equal protection clause. Miner wrote that there was no difference between "allowing nature to take its course [and] intentionally using an artificial death-producing device."

> It seems clear that New York does not treat similarly circumstanced persons alike. What interest can the state possibly have in requiring the prolongation of a life that is all but ended? What concept prompts the state to interfere with a mentally competent 'right to define one's own concept of existence, of meaning, of the universe and the meaning of life' [*Casey*] when the patient seeks to have drugs prescribed to end life during the final stages of a terminal disease? None. (*Quill v. Vacco* 1997)

There was no *en banc* review by the CA2. And so, on October 1, 1996, after the attorneys general in both states appealed their Court of Appeals losses to the U.S. Supreme Court, certiorari was granted. Both cases were consolidated and oral arguments were joined by order of the Court.

As already noted by the actions of the lower federal trial and appellate judges in these cases, there is a considerable division of views with respect to whether there is a constitutionally protected right to die. On one side are judges (most appointed by a Democratic president) who believe that PAD is a fundamental right protected by the due process and equal protection clauses of the Constitution. Standing on the other side are judges (all appointed by Republican presidents) who just as ardently argue that PAD is not a protected constitutional liberty and that a state can prohibit PAD. The justices of the U.S. Supreme Court are cut from the same cloth. Throughout the nation's history every justice appointed to the high bench by the president was thought to be "his kind" of jurist. All justices have been involved in social and political life before their appointment to the Supreme Court; they were senators, state and federal attorneys general, mayors, state and federal judges, state lawmakers, governors, and president (William Howard Taft). And all the appointees to the Court had a connection to one of the major political parties of their era. Their values and their beliefs generally reflected the values and beliefs of the sitting president.

Seven justices, in 1997, were appointed by Republican presidents Richard Nixon (William Rehnquist), Gerald Ford (John Paul Stevens), Ronald Reagan (Antonin Scalia, Sandra Day O'Connor, Anthony Kennedy), and George H.W. Bush (David Souter, Clarence Thomas). (Nearly all were conservative jurists.) Only two were appointed by Democratic president William Clinton (Ruth Bader Ginsburg, Stephen Breyer). On a number of controversial issues, including abortion, voting rights, and affirmative action, the conservative justices held a majority of the votes. (While there have been personnel changes in the Court's makeup since 1996, in the second decade of the 21st century the Court, until the death of the conservative Justice Scalia, was sharply divided between five conservative and four moderate justices.) Since Scalia's death in February 2016, the Court has functioned without a ninth justice because of the absolute refusal of the Republican majority in the Senate to hold hearings and vote to confirm or reject Democratic President Obama's nominee. The expectation is that the new president will nominate a person to replace Scalia after January 20, 2017.

All the lawyers participating in the 1997 litigation knew how the Court had acted in cases with controversial social issues at their core. The attorneys knew what arguments might work with each of the justices. This knowledge became the starting point for them when drafting their written briefs and then preparing for oral argument before the justices in 1997. Also, clearly, the lawyers for the PAD litigants knew that they faced a herculean task: arguing successfully before the Court where the majority showed no inclination to expand the meaning of the Constitution's language, especially the due process clause of the Fourteenth Amendment. One only had to look—as lawyers across the nation did—at how a majority of six justices had truncated the *Roe v. Wade* precedent in the 1980s.

Justice Harry A. Blackmun, the author of the *Roe* majority opinion, was very concerned about that precedent's future. The reason for his concern: the new personalities sitting alongside him in 1988 after certiorari was granted in *Webster v. Reproductive Health Services*. He said: "Will *Roe v Wade* go down the drain? I think there's a very distinct possibility that it will, this term. You can count the votes" ("Justice Fears for Roe Ruling" 1988). In the *Webster* case decided in 1989, the Court conservatives came one vote short of overturning *Roe*. (Justice O'Connor concurred in the Rehnquist opinion; she did not join it, thereby denying Rehnquist the necessary fifth vote to overturn *Roe*.)

The losers in both appellate courts, the petitioners, were again represented by the attorneys general of New York and Washington states. The winners, the respondents, were represented by lawyers for the physicians and their dying patients, and by the Compassion in Dying organization. The lawyers for the two sets of litigants essentially presented in their briefs the arguments made in the lower courts. For Quill's and Glucks-berg's lawyers, PAD was a fundamental right found in the due process clause of the Constitution. Denial of a person's right to PAD while allowing another terminally ill person to with-draw or withhold a device in order to die more quickly was a violation of the Constitution's equal protection clause. For the attorneys general, PAD was never considered a fundamental right, and that practice was clearly distinguishable from a dying patient ordering the withdrawal of a life-extending machine. The Fourteenth Amendment did not prohibit any state action that punished the practice of PAD.

They were not the only attorneys plotting strategic argu-ments that would be presented to the justices in written briefs. In addition, a total of 60 amicus curiae briefs were filed with the Court, of which 41 were by groups and institutions who opposed legitimation of PAD. Included in this set were briefs from Not Dead Yet, the National Hospice Association, medi-cal and nursing associations, the Catholic Church, Agudath Israel of America, and one from the U.S. Justice Department, representing the Clinton administration. On the other side, 19 groups were permitted to file briefs supporting the right to die with physician assistance. These groups included the American Civil Liberties Union (ACLU), 36 religious organizations, sur-viving family members, and the American Medical Students Association.

Oral argument is the next phase of the Supreme Court's decision-making process. Up to this point, there has been no airing of views about physician-assisted suicide among the nine justices. They have read the briefs as well as other important material their clerks provided to assist their "boss." But the readings are done in private, in chambers or at home. Until oral argument, there is no conversation between the justices. Oral argument is the first time all the justices formally talk—essentially to each other—about the case before them, voice their concerns about the issue, listen to their colleagues' argu-ments, and ask the attorneys questions.

It also provides Court watchers—reporters and the legal community beyond the building—with information about what the justices are concerned about, and how they feel about the major questions of law raised by the case. While the remarks of the justices are not final, their questions and observations provide observers with what further discussion among the brethren might focus on.

In the oral arguments, nine attorneys presented their case. Time is a precious commodity and so each side, in important cases, is given little more than one hour to present their case. In these cases, the attorneys general lawyers, the U.S. solicitor general (Walter Dellinger), and noted private attorneys representing the respondents (Kathryn L. Tucker, representing Compassion in Dying and Dr. Glucksberg, and Laurence Tribe, for Dr. Quill) participated.

There were a host of questions asked, rooted in the justices' understanding of how the Constitution must be treated, concerns about unintended consequences of their decisions, fears about the possibility of the "slippery slope," views of life and death, perceptions of what really takes place between doctor, nurse, and patient, among others.

Justice Souter, over and over again, voiced his fears—to all the attorneys facing him—about "abusing" PAD and the resulting "slippery slope" dilemma. "Will PAD," he asked, "gravitate down to those who are not terminally ill. . . . And ultimately [will it] gravitate out of PAD into euthanasia?" Can the state provide "empirical evidence" of its presence in states or nations that allowed PAD? This primal fear of PAD was echoed by other justices as well.

Chief Justice Rehnquist asked the lawyers to address the equal protection argument for PAD. Justice Scalia's most challenging questions to the respondents' lawyers (Tucker and Tribe) were premised on his view that "the dying process of all of us has begun and is underway. And it seems to me that the patient who has ten years of agony to look forward to has a more appealing case than the patient who is at the threshold of death."

Justice Ginsberg asked "General" Dellinger an interesting question: "Could you deal with the argument that's been made about winks and nods, that [PAD] is a sham because PAD goes on for anybody who is sophisticated enough to want it?" Dellinger was stumped and did not answer the question. Lawrence Tribe, however, answered Ginsberg's question: winks and nods existed, "and relate to a [reality] that we all accept—the principle of the double effect." But Tribe also said that the double effect gives "dangerous authority" to the medical profession but that PAD took the "danger" away because of the stringent protections against misuse in the Oregon PAD legislation.

For Scalia, the argument of the respondents "is a lovely philosophy. But you want us to frame a constitutional rule on the basis of that?" Justice O'Connor voiced her concern about the "increased flow of cases through the court system for Heaven knows how long" if the Court invalidated state laws prohibiting PAD. Justice Kennedy agreed with her concern when he said to one of the respondents' lawyers: "You're asking us in effect to declare unconstitutional the laws in fifty states."

The oral arguments exposed the concerns the justices had about the constitutionality of PAD. Heading into the final phase of Court activity—the actual decision-making events: discussing, voting, writing, circulating opinions, and announcing the decision—the action shifts to private discussions in conference held on about two dozen Fridays during the term of the Court. In these discussions, a standard protocol is followed: The chief speaks first, giving his take on the case and his vote. The chief is followed by each of the associate justices, from the most senior to the "freshman" justice. Once the vote is tallied, if the chief is in the majority, he has the option of writing the opinion himself or assigning one of the other justices in the majority to write the opinion. If the chief is not in the majority, the senior associate justice in the majority either writes or assigns the writing to another justice in the majority.

The U.S. Supreme Court, 9-0, overturned both Court of Appeals decisions. However, it was a byzantine set of decisions.

There were six opinions. Only four justices joined Rehnquist's opinion: Scalia, Thomas, Kennedy, and O'Connor (who was the needed fifth vote for Rehnquist's "majority opinion," but she also wrote a concurring opinion). Four other justices—Stevens, Souter, Breyer, and Ginsburg—wrote concurring opinions and probably would have voted differently—with O'Connor joining them—if the terminally ill patient-petitioners in both cases had not died.

Because they all died, the two cases were technically "facial challenges" to the anti-PAD statutes, a very difficult situation for the respondents' attorneys. In a facial challenge, the attorneys must establish that "no set of circumstances exists under which the act would be valid" (*U.S. v. Salerno*, 1987). Had they been alive when the Court heard the appeals, the cases would be heard as an "as applied challenge" to the statutes. This was an easier challenge because the attorneys had only to show that the two statutes were invalid "as applied" to the terminally ill plaintiffs.

Justice Rehnquist wrote both majority opinions. In *Glucksberg* he concluded that due process is not violated by reasonable anti-PAD statutes. He also rejected the constitutional claim of the respondents that the liberty to hasten dying with a doctor's help was a "fundamental right" found in the Constitution. In his *Vacco* opinion, based on his understanding of the equal protection clause, he maintained that that clause in the Fourteenth Amendment did not create any substantive rights. It was a general rule: equals must be treated equally; unequals must be treated unequally. Because Rehnquist rejected the respondents' claims that PAD and withdrawal of medical equipment from a patient were equal, there was no violation of the equal protection clause.

In her concurring opinion, joined in part by Ginsburg, O'Connor said that the matter might have been decided differently if the cases were "as applied" challenges to the anti-PAD statutes. In that circumstance, "there is no reason to think the democratic process will not strike the proper balance between the interests of the terminally ill, mentally competent patients who seek to end their suffering and the State's interest in protecting those who might seek to end life mistakenly or under pressure."

Justice Breyer, while concurring, said that "he did not agree with the Court's formulation of the [respondents] claimed 'liberty' interest."

> The Court describes it as a "right to commit suicide with another's assistance." [He would use] a different formulation, for which our legal tradition may provide greater support. [I] would use words roughly like "a right to die with dignity." . . . At its core would be personal control over the manner of death, professional medical assistance, and the avoidance of unnecessary and severe physical suffering—combined.

Breyer's acute observation about the politics of semantics in the right to die battles remains a major fissure point separating the pro- and anti-PAD groups. He concluded by agreeing with Justice O'Connor's observation that the Court might revisit its decisions in a future "as applied" challenge.

The senior associate justice, John Paul Stevens, also concurred but it was a harsh, critical assessment of Rehnquist's opinions.

> I write separately to make it clear that there is also room for further debate about the limits the Constitution places on the powers of the states to punish the practice [PAD]. Today, the Court decides [by applying the facial challenge standard]. . . . That holding, however, does not foreclose the possibility that some applications of the statute might well be invalid.

He also asserted that the dead patient-plaintiffs "may in fact have a liberty interest even stronger than Nancy Cruzan's because, not only were they terminally ill, they were suffering constant and severe pain. "Avoiding intolerable pain and the indignity of living one's final days incapacitated and in agony is certainly 'at the heart of the liberty to define one's own concept of existence, of meaning, of the universe, and of the mystery of human life'" (quoting from *Casey*).

Justice Souter concurred in order to voice his great fear about the possibility of the "slippery slope." "The day may come when we can say with some assurance which side is right, but for now it is the substantiality of the factual disagreement, and the alternatives for resolving it, that matter. They are, for me, dispositive of the due process claim at this time."

Rehnquist's concluding words in *Washington v. Glucksberg* directed that all decisions—whether legalizing or continuing criminalization of PAD of terminally ill patients—come about after a full airing of all positions on the controversial issue:

> Throughout the nation Americans are engaged in an earnest and profound debate about the morality, legality, and practicality of physician-assisted suicide. Our holding permits this debate to continue, as it should in a democratic society.

The two 1997 decisions of the U.S. Supreme Court ended the PAD advocates' efforts to have the U.S. Supreme Court broaden the meaning of "liberty" in the Constitution. Until there is a major shift in the makeup of the Court, or the Court grants certiorari to a number of "as applied" challenges and a majority of the Court are persuaded to invalidate anti-PAD statutes, PAD advocates must take a different approach to achieve their goal. They had to enter the de jure environment of politics, the state legislature.

Without the U.S. Supreme Court providing a national PAD principle affecting all 50 states, the consequence—at best—is an incremental patchwork of legislatively structured PAD Acts, one state at a time. As the late Speaker of the House of Representatives Tip O'Neill (D-Mass) said: "In America, all politics is local" (O'Neill and Hymel 1994).

Efforts to Pass Right to Die Legislation: 1990–2016

The essential question was very clear: does an individual's liberty to choose death with the assistance of a doctor trump a state's Tenth Amendment's "police powers" to pass "assisting suicide" laws?

These disputes have evolved—differently in each state—because of the mix of the following realities:

1. The strength of the values held by the state's voters and, more importantly, the strength of the organizations involved in these battles

2. The impact of a state's particular history on social issues

3. The state citizens' religious affiliations and the dominant religious institutions

4. The participation of key political actors in the political process that impacts the final result

5. The particular demographics—political, social, and economic—in each state

These legislative activities began in the late 1980s. The major group pushing for laws protecting PAD was the controversial Hemlock Society, founded and led by its zealous euthanasia devotee Derek Humphry. In 1991, after getting the required signatures for an initiative ballot, the group placed before the voters the Washington Initiative, Ballot 119. Reflecting Humphry's impact, the proposal contained PAD as well as voluntary euthanasia. The question on the ballot called for a yes-or-no vote by the voters. They were asked: "Shall adult patients who are in a medically terminal condition be permitted to request and receive from a physician aid-in-dying?" *Aid-in-dying* was defined in the initiative as a

medical service, provided in person by a physician that will end the life of a conscious and mentally competent patient in a dignified, painless and humane manner, when requested voluntarily by the patient through a written directive. (Tucker 2008)

In 1992, California voters were presented with the California Death with Dignity Act, Ballot Proposition 191. The Hemlock Society (now called Californians against Human Suffering) was, again, the primary organization, working with volunteers who toiled across both states to get the ballot to the voters. The California Proposition defined *aid-in-dying* very clearly, allowing euthanasia and PAD:

> [*Aid-in-dying*] means a medical procedure that will terminate the life of the qualified patient in a painless, humane, dignified manner, whether administered by the physician at the patient's choice . . . or whether the physician provides means to the patient for self-administration. (Tucker 2008)

Both proposed state PAD Acts were defeated by identical 54 to 48 percent tallies. Even though public opinion polls showed that a solid majority of the two states' populations supported the idea of terminally ill persons having the liberty to choose to die more quickly, the PAD supporters were overpowered by very organized opposition groups: the Washington and California medical associations and the Roman Catholic Church.

Clearly, the Roman Catholic Church, whose members comprise the largest religious group in America (24% of the population), has been the "primary political opponent" (Stutzman 1998) of PAD in America and across the world. It has "played a preeminent role in the evolution of end-of-life decision-making policies" (Stutzman 1998). Both financially and organizationally, it worked to defeat both ballot initiatives. In Washington State, 65 percent of the funds ($750,000) used to defeat PAD—for radio and television spots, newspaper ads, flyers, special Sunday masses—came from Catholic Church funds. In California, 80 percent of the funding ($2.1 million) came from the Church.

The basic arguments against PAD presented by the medical associations, groups representing the disabled, and the Catholic

Church were as follows: the slippery slope; a strong defense of the state's right to protect the sanctity of life of all its residents; and the fact that there were two humane alternatives to PAD that allowed dying patients to die without the assistance of a physician: palliative care and hospice.

Again and again since 1990, in every battle involving PAD—in the courts and in state legislatures—the dread of the slippery slope has been in the forefront of the largely successful efforts of PAD opponents. Organizations representing the disabled and other vulnerable persons maintain that PAD will lead to involuntary euthanasia and these defenseless, powerless people—these "others"—will be the first to be euthanized by the state. All the groups opposing PAD had to do in both states was to run fear-inducing campaigns.

A number of conclusions may be drawn from these first two PAD act defeats. First, PAD organizers, after these losses, never again linked PAD with euthanasia in their proposals. Another conclusion pointed very clearly to the fact that well-financed and well-organized professionals opposed to PAD, with sufficient funds and political "smarts," can win a clash even though state public opinion polls indicated strong support for PAD. A third conclusion is that, while these battles involved local leaders, these state groups received support, financially and organizationally, nationally. Medical, nursing, disabled persons groups, and the Catholic Church, all fighting against the PAD initiatives, received money and volunteers from other state and national organizations. The PAD groups, essentially the Hemlock Society and local volunteers, were outspent and out-organized because of the organizational, political, fund-raising, and strategic skills of their opponents. It was nearly a decade before state PAD personnel in Washington and California recovered from their defeats and renewed their efforts to pass PAD Acts.

By that time, 1999, the U.S. Supreme Court had handed down its decisions, national PAD organizations had been created, other, smaller, support groups consolidated, and the public had become more aware of the right to die issue. After 1997, only one state, Oregon, had passed a PAD initiative, the Oregon Death with Dignity Act (ODWDA). Voters supported the ODWDA twice, once in 1994 (51%–49%) and then again, after the Act was unsuccessfully challenged in state court, in 1997 when generally anti-PAD state legislators put the ODWDA before the voters as an initiative ballot (Measure 51) asking them to approve or repeal the ODWDA. Oregonians, by a huge majority, again voted to approve the Act, 60–40 percent.

The Oregon Story, 1994–2006

Hemlock Society members began their labors for a PAD Act in Oregon in 1992, a year after the defeat in California. Derek Humphry continued his zealous public advocacy of euthanasia. Just months before the November 1994 election, he publicly and repeatedly insisted that the ODWDA was only the first step and that "when people become comfortable with this form of assisted dying, we may be able to go to the second step, which is euthanasia." He was championing his version of the aid in dying proposal even though the proposed Act, as it was written and passed, was a "prescribing only" PAD proposal: in Section 3, the ODWDA specifically rejected euthanasia.

His unrepentant speech forced the two PAD groups' leaders (the Hemlock Society was joined, in 1993, with the newly organized Oregon Compassionate Choices Group) to "ask him not to attend the deliberations between campaign strategists and wary community leaders." Reluctantly, he "conceded that any level of lawful assisted suicide would be better than the *status quo*, so he agreed not to enter meetings without their permission" (Hillyard and Dombrink 2001).

Why did PAD succeed in both Oregon elections, even while being heavily outspent by the opposition (principally the Roman Catholic Church, which provided about $1 million, about 60% of the funds)? First, the supporters were dampening the fear of the slippery slope to mollify apprehensive voters.

Second, Oregon citizens have, historically, been open-minded, politically independent voters. Most importantly, however, Oregon is "the most unchurched state in the nation," wrote an Oregon journalist recently (Redden 2014). Nearly

70 percent of its residents are not affiliated with any religious institution. Many Roman Catholics, about 10 percent of the population, did not agree with the Church hierarchy (Hillyard and Dombrink 2001). And a majority of Oregon's citizens disliked religious pressure of any kind in the secular affairs of the state.

However, the anti-PAD groups were not finished. If the voters did not follow their arguments and when federal appeals court judges and the justices of the U.S. Supreme Court dismissed and denied certiorari to anti-PAD attorneys' petitions asking that a permanent injunction be issued to block enforcement of the ODWDA, they turned to the other two national political institutions, the U.S. Congress and the Executive Branch, to defeat the ODWDA.

This strategy was aggressively followed for nearly a decade, from the 1997 federal judiciary's decisions in *Lee* to 2006, when the U.S. Supreme Court concluded 6–3 in *Gonzales v. Oregon* that the U.S. attorney general's actions to prohibit physicians from implementing the ODWDA were unconstitutional.

These political efforts to destroy a right to die law were taking place at the same time when politically scandalous actions were occurring in Florida, between 1998 and 2005, regarding the issue of withdrawing life support devices from Terri Schiavo. Conservative Republicans—in the Florida legislature and in the U.S. Congress and the federal Executive Branch—joined by sanctity of life adherents, primarily the Roman Catholic Church, were battling to save Terri's life. And, in both episodes, the federal courts played a decisive role in ending them in favor of the PAD supporters.

The post-1997 anti-ODWDA strategy was essentially a twofold one: (1) an expansion-by-interpretation of the 1970 Controlled Substance Act (introduced by President Richard M. Nixon in 1970 in a national effort to deal with the emergent illicit narcotics and dangerous drug problems) through actions by the U.S. attorney general that would enable the federal Drug Enforcement Agency (DEA) to prosecute a physician who prescribed a lethal drug to a terminally ill patient because that action was not "a legitimate medical practice" and (2) passage of legislation that would expand the meaning of the Controlled Substance Act.

From 1997 to the presidential election of Republican George W. Bush in 2001, efforts were directed at convincing the DEA to block the ODWDA. Powerful, conservative Republican senators Orrin Hatch (Utah) and John Ashcroft (Missouri) and Representative Henry Hyde (Illinois) joined to pressure, successfully, the DEA administrator to interpret the CSA to prohibit enforcement of the ODWDA because PAD was not a "legitimate medical practice." In December 1997, a DEA "stop" order was issued. The U.S. attorney general, Janet Reno, appointed by Democratic president Bill Clinton, reviewed the entire matter and reversed the DEA order in June 1998.

> There is no evidence that Congress, in the CSA, intended to displace the state as the primary regulators of the medical profession, or to override a state's determination as to what constitutes "legitimate medical practice." The CSA law does not authorize the DEA to prosecute, or to revoke DEA registration of, a physician who has assisted in a suicide in compliance with the Oregon law. (Reno 1998)

Undeterred, the congressional Republicans quickly introduced (Hyde) and supported (Hatch and Ashcroft) the Lethal Drug Abuse and Prevention Act of 1998. This proposal would have Congress approve the expansion of DEA authority to prohibit implementation of the ODWDA. It was not successful in part because of the possibility of a presidential veto; more importantly, the anti-PAD organizations, especially the medical professionals, objected to providing a federal agency with power to intrude on state matters affecting physicians.

The following year, the trio proposed in both houses of Congress another piece of legislation to terminate the ODWDA: The Pain Relief Promotion Act of 1999. This bill's primary purpose was to amend the CSA to promote enhanced pain management research and to increase support for quality palliative care, "without permitting PAD and euthanasia."

Under the proposed law, physicians could use lethal, controlled substances to relieve pain, even if it resulted in death (the double effect), but they were not allowed to prescribe the same medication to a dying patient. (The Senate version added the identical proposal as an amendment to the 1998 Omnibus Spending bill.) Both the AMA and the Roman Catholic Church supported this positive-sounding expansion of the law. However, President Clinton threatened to veto the bill. The proposal was withdrawn by the Republican sponsors.

The efforts to defeat the ODWDA got underway again, immediately after Republican George W. Bush became president after the controversial 2000 presidential election. It began when the new president appointed U.S. senator John Ashcroft (R-Mo.), one of the three major conservative congressional leaders working to defeat the ODWDA since 1997, as the U.S. attorney general, succeeding Janet Reno.

In November 2001, Ashcroft issued the "Ashcroft Directive," a November 6, 2001, memorandum to the new Republican administrator of the DEA, according to which prescribing a lethal substance to a terminally ill patient was a violation of the CSA: it is not a "legitimate medical practice, regardless of whether state law authorizes or permits such conduct by practitioners or others and regardless of the condition of the person whose suicide is assisted" (66 Fed. Reg. 56608 2001).

The Catholic Church, "culture of life" individuals, and groups representing vulnerable and disabled persons applauded this executive decision. The AMA, however, was in a quandary. While the medical organization opposed the ODWDA, it was equally opposed to Ashcroft's Memo. He and the Bush administration, the organization said, were "motivated by ideology"; Ashcroft's strategy was "an unprecedented attempt by the federal government to usurp the authority of the states to regulate medical practice" (Lowenstein and Wanzer 2002).

The very next day, the Ashcroft order was challenged in a federal District Court in Oregon by state officials, a physician, and a number of dying patients. Two days later, the judge, Robert Jones, appointed by President Clinton in 2000, issued a temporary restraining order against the DEA; it became a permanent restraining order in April 2002 when Judge Jones ruled that Attorney General Ashcroft lacked authority to overturn the ODWDA: while "AG Ashcroft fired the first shot in the battle between the state of Oregon and the federal government over which government has the ultimate authority" to regulate medical practices, it was not the final salvo (*Oregon v. Ashcroft* 2002).

In late September 2002, Ashcroft appealed the ruling to the Ninth Circuit U.S. Court of Appeals. He maintained that the attorney general "has permissibly construed the CSA and its implementing regulations to prohibit the prescription of controlled substances for suicide." A physician acting in accordance with the ODWDA was not performing a "legitimate medical practice" and was thus subject to the penalties enumerated in the CSA regulations.

In March 2003, in *Ashcroft v. Oregon*, the three-judge panel ruled 2–1 that the Ashcroft Directive was "unlawful and unenforceable." Judge Richard C. Tallman (appointed by Republican president George H.W. Bush in 1990) said: "the Ashcroft directive is unlawful and unenforceable because it violates the plain language of the CSA, . . . which targets only conventional drug abuse and excludes the AG from medical policy decisions, . . . contravenes Congress' express legislative intent and oversteps the bounds of the AG's statutory authority."

The full Court of Appeals rejected the solicitor general's *en banc* appeal request. And so, on November 9, 2004, Attorney General Ashcroft filed an amicus curiae petition in the U.S. Supreme Court. He was asking the justices to overturn the lower federal court rulings and restore the Ashcroft Directive. This was one of Ashcroft's final actions as attorney general. He announced his retirement later that day.

In February 2005 the Court granted certiorari in the newly named litigation, *Gonzales v. Oregon.* (Alberto Gonzales replaced Ashcroft as attorney general.) Eight months later, oral arguments were held in open court. In January 2006, the Court issued its opinion. By a surprising 6–3 vote, Justice Kennedy's majority opinion, joined by Justices O'Connor, Stevens, Souter, Ginsburg, and Breyer, upheld the judgment of the Court of Appeals.

The question before the Court was, "Whether the AG has permissibly construed the CSA . . . to prohibit the distribution of federally controlled substances for the purpose of facilitating a person's suicide, regardless of a state law purporting to authorize such distribution." On January 17, 2006, the Court announced that the attorney general had overstepped his authority. The action taken by Ashcroft was "beyond his expertise and incongruous with the statutory purposes and design [of the CSA. When Congress passed the Act], it did not have this far-reaching intent to alter the federal-state balance." As for the question of "who decides whether a particular medical practice serves a 'legitimate medical purpose,'" the answer was brief: "not the Attorney General."

The three dissenters, recently appointed Chief Justice John Roberts, and Justices Scalia and Thomas, believed that, in cases involving administrative law, the federal courts, including the Supreme Court, must accede to administrative interpretations of the CSA. Ashcroft's interpretation of the CSA language was "clearly valid, given the substantial deference we must accord it [under prior Court precedents]" (*Auer v. Robbins* 1997).

The *Gonzales* opinion of the Court "removed an obstacle to state efforts to authorize physician-assisted suicide" (Greenhouse 2006). *The New York Times* editorialized that the six-justice majority "rejected Mr. Ashcroft's attempt to impose his religiously conservative ideology on a state whose voters had decided differently" (Greenhouse 2006). There was one final effort by a Republican senator from Kansas, Sam Brownback, to defeat ODWDA. In early 2006, after *Gonzales*, he introduced the Assisted Suicide Prevention Act of 2006. Oregon Democratic U.S. senator Ron Wyden announced that he would block the bill from advancing in the Senate. Brownback's response: pull the proposal. Later in the year, the Democrats won both houses of Congress and, for the time being, effectively ended political action to defeat death with dignity state legislation. When the Democratic presidential candidate Barack Obama won the 2008 election, it forced PAD opponents to continue the now-growing efforts by more organized pro-PAD organizations, the Death With Dignity National Center and the Compassionate Choices organizations, to pass ODWDA-model bills state by state.

The Unsuccessful State Efforts after 1997

These state actions to pass PAD initiatives began in earnest after 1997, the year Oregon voters, for the second time, supported the ODWDA. Bills and initiatives were introduced and debated in more than two dozen states between 1997 and 2008. All these efforts to pass ODWDA-model bills—through the initiative or through the legislative process—were defeated by the strong opposition to PAD, led primarily by the Catholic Church with its financial support and its politically-and-media savvy lobbyists, by the medical establishment, by groups representing the disabled, and by other vulnerable groups.

After 1997, dozens of states saw PAD supporters start the difficult process of organizing to begin the legislative struggle to legitimize PAD. Arizona, California, Connecticut, Hawaii, Maine, Michigan, Wisconsin, Vermont, Maryland, Massachusetts, Montana, New Hampshire, New Mexico, New York, Pennsylvania, and Wyoming were among a near-majority of states where the efforts led to legislation or initiatives supporting PAD. Many of these states have seen multiple efforts to pass the right to die laws fail, even though the public opinion polls were hovering between 68 and 74 percent in favor of death with dignity legislation available for dying patients.

In June 2015, the Death with Dignity National Center (DWDNC), in the face of seemingly nonrational voting behavior in nearly all the states, issued its report that focused on these defeats and on the need to continue the push for PAD. In a pep talk the organization tried to rally its supporters across the nation.

> Some consider it a failure most bills don't end up becoming law, but we view these bills as a testament to the growing support of the Death with Dignity movement. ("Right-to-Die Bill Allowing Doctor Prosecution" 2015)

After the ODWDA became law in 1997, in the four states that have since joined Oregon and passed ODWDA laws, the PAD supporters were engaged in pitched battles for at least a decade before events in their states enabled them to achieve political victory. California legislators passed a PAD law in 2015, two decades the initial PAD law was defeated. In 1991 Washington State was the site of the first defeat of a PAD initiative proposed in America; 17 years later, in 2008, voters passed another initiative that legalized PAD. Vermont does not have an initiative ballot process.

PAD advocates had to convince the state's legislators to support the right to die. In 2013, with a second sign-off by the governor ending the sunset provision, Vermont became the first state to have ODWDA-modeled PAD passed by state legislators in 2015. However, it began its uphill battles in 2003, a dozen years before.

What accounts for the victories in Washington State, Vermont, California and Colorado? (1) The appearance on the scene of key persons in each state, (2) the state's demographic and political characteristics, (3) accompanied by the much improved organizational, tactical, and strategic abilities of the state's PAD supporters, and (4) the advocates were joined in their efforts by the two much-strengthened national right to die organizations: Death with Dignity and Compassionate Choices.

Washington State's Battles to Pass a PAD Initiative, 1991–2008

In Washington State, the key actor who impacted passage of the Washington Death with Dignity Act in 2008 (Ballot Measure I-1000–2008, RCW 70.245–2009) was a much beloved former governor of the state, Booth Gardner. In January 2006, the first attempt to pass PAD legislation since 1991 was introduced in the state Senate. It died in committee. One month after the death of the proposed PAD bill, Gardner, suffering from Parkinson's disease since 1992, announced that he would head up a drive to present another PAD initiative before the state's voters. He said, in the announcement, that "when the day comes when I no longer can keep busy, and I'm a burden to my wife and kids, I want to be able to control my exit" (Ostrum 2008).

Nearly two years later, in January 2008, Gardner filed with the secretary of state the Washington Death with Dignity Initiative (Initiative 1000, or I-1000). By July 2008, the secretary of state received over 300,000 signatures, more than the 224,000 signatures necessary to get I-1000 on the November ballot.

In the preparation for the November 2008 election battle, the bill's advocates raised $1.9 million. The opposition, the Coalition against Assisted Suicide, was led by the Roman Catholic Church, and included groups such as Not Dead Yet, people of other faiths, hospice and palliative care workers, and nurses. While the state medical association was, in 2008, "passionately split" and "very much in disarray" over the issue, it ultimately joined the Coalition (Wilson 2008). However, for the very first time, the Coalition's fund raising (essentially the Roman Catholic Archdiocese of Seattle) did not match that of the I-1000 supporters: $1,900,000 versus $509,000 as of September 2008. (The supporters ultimately spent $2 million in media advertisements while the Coalition spent $1 million.)

The major argument presented by the opposition was the "slippery slope's" impact on disabled persons. The initiative, one of their pamphlets maintained, "pressures" these vulnerable, disabled people and others "without adequate insurance or financial means to think they have no choice other than assisted suicide. It provides an incentive to health plans to cut costs by encouraging assisted suicide" (Wilson 2008).

A former governor, Barbara Roberts, publicly supported I-1000, and argued that it "is *not* a Slippery Slope . . . that threatens those with disabilities of any kind" (Roberts 2008). It was a vitriolic campaign, with untruths about the initiative's impact presented by the Coalition and harsh attacks by its supporters on a "small group of out-of-state religious leaders" for trying to impose their "zealous religious beliefs on all Washingtonians, and defeat the proposed WDWDA" (Ball 2012).

On Election Day, almost 85 percent of the voters in Washington State cast their ballots. Initiative 1000 won with 58 percent of the voters (518,500) supporting it. The Coalition received 399,775 votes (42%). However, knowing that these battles never end when the ballots are counted, both sides began preparing for actions by the Coalition to overturn the result. Almost immediately, the Coalition issued a broadside: the WDWDA is "a first step toward, not only physician-assisted suicide, but ultimately euthanasia. And people shouldn't be blind to that" (Iwasaki 2008). To date, there has been no overt action to challenge the law in the courts or in the legislature.

The Vermont Effort to Pass a PAD Law, 2003–2015

In February 2014, the Gallup Poll released the result of a survey identifying the most religious and least religious states in the United States (Newport 2014). Vermont, once again, is the state with the lowest percentage of "very religious" Americans: 22 percent. Oregon is in fifth place with 31 percent; Washington is seventh place, with 32 percent "very religious" people. (Mississippi is the most religious state, with 61 percent of its residents identifying themselves as "very religious.") Vermont, like all the states, has a Christian majority (54%), with Roman Catholics the largest subset (22%). Non-Christians account for 8 percent, with Judaism the largest group (2%). The rest of the population (37%) is "unaffiliated" (atheistic, agnostic, nothing in particular, and don't know). Furthermore, on controversial social issues agitating the nation, Vermont residents hold very progressive views. Seventy percent of Vermonters believe abortion is a woman's personal right to choose; 79 percent accept homosexuality; and 76 percent accept same-sex marriage (Pew Research Center 2015). Said one observer, "basically, if you live in New England and want to join a militia, then New Hampshire is for you. But if you want to skip showering and listen to NPR, then head on up to Vermont" (Seelye 2016).

Vermont, in addition to these demographics, has been for decades a liberal Democratic Party state. Its national representatives, in 2016, are Democratic (Patrick Leahy, U.S. Senate; Peter Welsh, House) or Independent (Bernie Sanders, U.S. Senate, and, in 2016, a Democratic presidential candidate). During this same period, voters have generally elected Democratic majorities to the state legislature. Finally, given the state's historic, democratic "town meeting" setting for Vermont debates on all issues, throughout the year, there is a large contingent of politically aware Vermonters who know what to do to affect public policies in the state.

This has been the case with regard to the right to die issue. From the beginning of the effort to pass PAD legislation, the small group of experienced—and committed—local advocates organized a state-wide group, Death with Dignity Vermont in 2003 (later called Patient Choices Vermont). In their fight for PAD, they were joined by volunteers from the Vermont chapter of the Hemlock Society. Their mission statement was clear and unambiguous.

> Patient Choices Vermont is an advocacy organization that seeks to educate Vermonters about end-of-life options and to influence policy, regulations and practice that affect the terminally ill. PCV works to promote the best possible pain control, palliative and hospice care, and to enable terminally ill patients to direct their own end of life. (Patient Choice Vermont 2011)

Beginning in August 2002 there was—and still remains—a very close relationship between the DWDNC and Patient Choices Vermont. The national organization's political and legal leaders traveled regularly to Vermont to help with drafting the bills, participating in town meeting forums across the state, and meeting with stakeholders and elected officials.

Between 2003 and 2013, the DWDNC raised and donated more than $200,000 to the Vermont group for educational efforts, for constituent outreach, and for the many town forums held in that tumultuous decade. Both the national and the Vermont group developed and used electronic communications—emails, blogs, Facebook and Twitter posts—in their outreach educational efforts across the state.

Eli D. Stutsman, an Oregon lawyer who was the founder of DWDNC, was the prime author of both the Oregon and Washington State death with dignity (DWD) bills. During the first decade of the 21st century, he served as primary legal counsel for Patient Choices Vermont and helped draft the five DWD bills introduced in the Vermont legislature between 2003 and 2013.

From the very beginning Patient Choices Vermont had the support of two extremely popular former Democratic governors, Madeleine Kunin and Phil Hoff, and the support of a highly respected former lieutenant governor, Republican Barbara Snelling. Yet, with all these favorable signs and signals, it took more than a decade to achieve their objective.

The network of opposing groups included the "usual suspects": the Roman Catholic Archdiocese of Vermont; a "sanctity of life" organization, the Vermont Alliance for Ethical Healthcare, whose leader, Dr. Robert Orr, was a long-time opponent of the abortion rights movement and was, for most of the time the PAD battles were occurring, affiliated with the University of Vermont Health Care Center; the disability rights groups Not Dead Yet; and the Vermont Medical Association, whose position on PAD was obvious: Vermont must not have a law allowing physicians to hasten a terminally ill patient's death.

In a small state like Vermont (which has a little more than 630,000 people living in the state in 2016), one of the major factors in the policy-making process is personal contact between interested persons and groups and their elected representatives: speaking with legislators regularly, at the state capital, in committee hearings, at public forums, or at home; sending letters calling for support; writing letters to the editors of the local media; and appearing on local news radio and television talk shows. Both sides continually debated in town meetings, a revered New England tradition. In Vermont the key to success was staying in regular contact with their neighbors, especially those who were sitting in the House and the Senate, and convincing them that they should support—or oppose—the pending legislation.

Beginning in September 2003, a few months before the Vermont 2004 legislative session was to begin, the antagonists began a decade-long series of town meetings to openly debate the pluses and minuses of a DWD law. Through 2012, Vermonters saw legislators evade and avoid voting on the question of aid in dying. The governor, Republican Jim H. Douglas, continuously spoke against the prospect of physicians prescribing lethal drugs for a dying patient. Four PAD bills were discussed in House and Senate committees over the years but, although there was occasional support for the bills in committee, because of wary, cautious committee chairs, and the fear of losing the next election if they supported the bills, the bills were tabled, or died in committee, or one time, defeated on a full vote (January 2007).

The bill, H 044, focused on the core ideas of all proposed PAD laws: "patient choice and patient control at the end of life" (Schwartz and Estrin 2010). Two committees conducted hearings on the bill, the House Judiciary Committee and the House Human Services Committee, and both voted to support the bill. For the first time in Vermont, a vote on the merits of H 044 took place—but it was defeated 63–82.

Dr. Orr was as surprised as the supporters of H 044. He said: "This is truly amazing! . . . a resonating rejection of this unneeded and dangerous bill" (Orr 2007). Things did not begin to change until 2011, when a Democratic politician, Peter Shumlin, took office as Vermont's governor.

Although he was not a very popular leader, Shumlin was a key factor in the legislature passing the Patient Choice and Control at End of Life Act in 2013 and again in 2015, when it was strengthened. However, in Vermont, as in all the states that have passed DWD Acts, the battles continue. During the legislative debates about the future of the sunset provisions that the 2015 Act addressed, a number of House members attempted to repeal the entire 2013 Act. After a heated discussion, a vote was taken to repeal the law. It failed 60–83. The vote on not sunsetting the patient protections commenced. It passed. The message, however, was received by PAD supporters at the end of the long day: expect continuing efforts by opponents to overturn Vermont's aid in dying law.

California's Odyssey to the Passage of the End of Life Option Act, 1992–2015

In California, a major factor accounting for the passage of the End of Life Option Act in 2015 was the story of a young California wife, Brittany Maynard. Diagnosed with inoperable brain cancer, Brittany chose to self-administer lethal medication to avoid the painful death awaiting her. Oregon had a DWD law, so she and her husband moved there. As an Oregon resident, Brittany was able to apply for physician assistance in dying for terminally ill patients. Brittany met the bill's criteria and received the medicine that she took to end her life in November 2014 (Maynard 2014).

However, passage of the 2015 law, triggered by her heavily publicized death, was the pinnacle of a number of PAD actions that had begun in the state in the 1970s. These events included passage of the Natural Death Act in 1976, which protects doctors from being sued for failure to treat an incurable ill-ness at the request of a competent patient; the founding of the Hemlock Society in 1980 and the Americans against Human Suffering (which became, in 1992, Americans for Death with Dignity).

The Hemlock group joined Compassion & Choices, a new PAD organization, to draft the initial California Death with Dignity Act, which was on the ballot in 1992 (and defeated, 46%–54%). Work halted after the 1992 defeat; however, the supporters were elated when Oregon voters passed the ODWDA in 1994. In that year, one of the two national aid in dying organizations was founded, the California Death with Dignity National Center.

Oregon was, once again, the inspiration for PAD groups in California and other states. In 1997, PAD supporters won a re-election battle for the ODWDA by a 60 to 40 percent margin, and began to implement the law in late 1997. In 1999, leg-islation was introduced in the California Assembly. Although it passed the Judiciary and Appropriations committees, it was pulled from a full vote when the sponsors concluded that it would not be passed. The opposition was led by Califor-nians against Assisted Suicide, made up of Roman Catholic Church leaders, groups representing vulnerable residents, Not Dead Yet and other groups speaking for the disabled popula-tion, the California Medical Association, and other health care organizations.

In 2005, another physician aid in dying bill was introduced in the Assembly and was again approved by the Judiciary and Appropriations committees along party lines. The bill, AB 651, was scheduled for discussion and a vote in the Senate Judiciary Committee in March 2006. The committee voted 3–2 against the bill. The committee chair, Democratic senator Joe Dunn, switched sides after pressure from Coalition members who tes-tified earlier in the week.

California's religious demographics were different from Ver-mont's, Oregon's, and Washington's. Unlike California, the three other PAD states were among 2014's top ten "least religious" states (Newport 2014). In 2014, 45 percent of California's residents affiliated with a religious organization; nearly 30 percent of them were Roman Catholics, a higher percentage than the other PAD states (Pew Research Center 2015). Clearly, Democratic legislators from districts with a heavy Roman Catholic population were aware of this political reality and the possible consequence for them if they voted for a PAD bill.

The following February (2007), another bill was introduced: AB 374, the California Compassionate Choices Act. Once again, voting 7–3 on party lines, the Judiciary Committee approved the legislation. At this point, the California Catholic Conference (CCC) clergy, lay persons, and lobbyists began a barrage of letters, ads, Church "backgrounders," daily fact sheets for Roman Catholic priests, and talking points for CCC members to use in their conversations with their elected representatives. In March 2007, the Roman Catholic Blog communicated a Sunday special broadside urging Catholics "to be 'faithful citizens' and participate [by talking to their legislators] in this important issue" (RomanCatholicBlog.com 2007). The opposition effort was successful. The sponsors of the legislation saw the shift in the Assembly and again, before the vote, pulled the bill.

Undeterred, the sponsors introduced another bill the following February when the new legislative session opened. AB 2747, the California Right to Know End of Life Options Act, did not mention PAD. It was a general bill that called on physicians and other health providers to offer information to terminally ill patients regarding end-of-life options—hospice and palliative care, withholding life-sustaining apparatus, palliative sedation, and voluntarily stopping eating and drinking—available to them.

The CCC immediately began to campaign against this bill, calling AB 2747 "a stealth bill setting up a mechanism for hastened death" (California Catholic Conference 2008). However, because PAD was not included in the "options" language, the Act passed the Assembly and the Senate and, on September 3, 2008, Governor Arnold Schwarzenegger signed the bill. There was still no PAD bill that survived opposition strategy, tactics, and persuasion.

Sixteen years later, after these pitched battles between the forces arrayed on both sides of the issue led to four PAD bill defeats, and after the death of Brittany Maynard in November 2014, another bill was again debated in the legislature, SB 128, the End of Life Option Act. It was introduced in the state Senate on January 21, 2015, barely two months after Maynard's death. In March the Senate Health Committee approved the bill 6–2, with one abstention. In April the Senate Judiciary Committee propitiously voted 5–2 for the bill, and on June 2, 2015, the full Senate approved SB 128 by a vote of 23–15.

About that time, the California Medical Association (CMA) took a surprising action, the first state medical association in America to do so. It changed its decades-old organizational policy of absolute opposition to PAD. Luther F. Cobb, CMA president, said:

> Despite the remarkable medical breakthroughs we've made and the world-class hospice or palliative care we can provide, it isn't always enough. The decision to participate in the End of Life Option Act is a very personal one between a doctor and their patient. . . . We believe it is up to the individual physician and their patient to decide voluntarily whether the End of Life Option Act is something in which they want to engage. Protecting that physician-patient relationship is essential. (California Medical Association 2015)

With that action, overturning an opposition policy approved in 1987, the CMA became "officially neutral" on Senate Bill 128. It was no longer a member of the Coalition.

After Senate passage of SB 128, the Coalition, especially the CCC, feared that the bill would be passed in the wake of Maynard's death. They were keenly aware of the firestorm of affirmative media hype about PAD (including comments in a videotape made by Maynard herself, days before her death, calling on legislators to pass a California death with dignity bill). They pulled out all the stops to block the Assembly from voting favorably on the Act. Their focus, given the time press on them, was to convince Assembly legislators—especially Democratic legislators from heavily populated Roman Catholic districts sitting on the Assembly Health Committee—to vote against the Senate-passed bill.

Before the Assembly's Health Committee could vote on the Act, the bill's sponsors withdrew SB 128. Because the bill "lacked enough support to get through committees this year amid fierce religious opposition" (Nirappil 2015) their comment to the press was brief: "we have chosen not to present SB 128 today in the Assembly Health Committee" (Monning 2015). SB 128 was dead; supporters had to plot another effort to pass PAD, including an option to put the PAD bill on an initiative ballot for an up-or-down vote by California voters if the opposition continued their thus-far successful lobbying activities in the legislature.

However, California's Democratic governor Jerry Brown took an interesting step. In August, he called for an extraordinary legislative session to have the legislators deal with the state's health care funding problems, especially funding for the state's Medi-Cal program. As soon as the special session started, the SB 128 sponsors immediately changed the agenda: they reintroduced the bill in the Assembly, and it was accepted for debate and action.

There were immediate responses from opponents in the legislature. Republicans, opposed to the bill on moral grounds, were the minority in both houses of the legislature and bitterly complained about using the special session to debate SB 128. They were rebuffed by the legislature's Democratic leaders.

One Republican lawmaker, Senator Bob Huff, angrily said to the press: "Let's call this for what it really is: It's not death with dignity. This is state-assisted death, physician-assisted death and relative-assisted death" (Pedroncelli 2015).

Very quickly the full Assembly passed the bill, 42–33, on September 8, 2015. All of the Assembly's actions on the Act occurred in less than one month. The modifications Assembly legislators made to SB 128 meant that the revised bill had to return to the Senate for that body's approval of the changes. Three days later, September 11, before the opposition even got started to try to block the bill, the Senate approved the bill, 23–14.

The CCC was livid. The bill should have been presented to legislators during the regular session. Tim Rosales, the group's spokesman, said that the Act was immoral, that suicide and physician-assisted suicide were sins against God. The greatest fear of the group, however, was that the End of Life Options Act gives physicians "the power to prescribe lethal overdoses to [impoverished] patients" (Pedroncelli 2015).

SB 128 was immediately sent to liberal Democratic governor Brown for his signature. However, unlike former governors in Vermont and Washington states, and sitting Vermont governor Shumlin, who all publicly supported PAD efforts, the California governor had been noncommittal during the debates over SB 128.

Governor Brown brought to the decision table two personal issues: his health and his religious leanings. In the years immediately preceding the special session, Brown had basal cell carcinoma removed from near his right ear in 2008; in 2011 he had a cancerous growth removed from his nose. A year later he was treated for early stage prostate cancer.

In his eighth decade, the governor said, in a May 2015 speech to a business group, that it was pointless to pursue perfect solutions in an imperfect world: "It's messy, there's suffering, and in the end we all die. When you're 77, by the way, that's something that's a little more imminent" (Pedroncelli 2015).

Further playing on his thoughts about the Act, Brown, a Roman Catholic, once studied for the priesthood at the Jesuit

Seminary at Los Gatos, California. Although he left his studies, Brown remained a devout church member. In his effort to reach his judgment, the governor discussed the pending legislation with doctors, including two of his personal physicians, his bishop, Brittany Maynard (three days before she died), Brittany's family, advocates for the disabled, retired South African Archbishop Desmond Tutu (who urged the governor to sign the bill), and "former classmates and friends who take varied, contradictory and nuanced positions. In the end I was left to reflect on what I would want in the face of my own death" (Brown 2015).

Almost a year after Maynard's death, and after nearly a month of wrestling with the controversial issue, Governor Jerry Brown signed the End of Life Option Act on October 5, 2015. In his letter notifying the members of the California State Assembly of his decision, he wrote that "I do not know what I would do if I were dying in prolonged and excruciating pain. I am certain, however, that it would be a comfort to be able to consider the options afforded by this bill. And I wouldn't deny that right to others" (Brown 2015).

Immediately, the pro-life opposition—led by Not Dead Yet and the Roman Catholic Church—launched a referendum drive to overturn the as-yet-not-implemented law. (Since the act was passed in an extraordinary legislative session, it took effect in November 2016].) Their target: get 365,000 signatures, by January 3, 2016, from their supporters to get the initiative on the November 2016 ballot. On January 6, 2016, it was announced that they failed to collect enough signatures. All pro-life groups will continue to engage in political activities. In California, these groups will aggressively work in the political and in the state and federal courts to overturn the state's assisted suicide law.

In the November 2016 election, Colorado voters approved the End of Life Options Act (65%–35%), making Colorado the 6th state to allow PAD. The D.C. Commission voted 11–2 approving a Death with Dignity Law; it awaits only the Mayor's approval.

The Role of State Courts in the Right to Die Controversy

Beside the near impossibility of the presently constituted U.S. Supreme Court changing its collective mind, or other states' PAD organizations beginning decades-long struggles to get the legislature to debate, much less to pass a PAD statute, or convince state voters to pass a PAD initiative, there is only one other road PAD supporters can take to reach their goal: persuade state judges that the state Constitution is the repository of a fundamental right of a dying patient to receive assistance from a physician to hasten imminent death.

To date, only the Montana state courts, including the Montana Supreme Court, have concluded that the state Constitution does not prohibit PAD. Since all the jurists based their decisions on their reading and interpretation of only the state Constitution, there was no "federal case or controversy" involved. Therefore, the judgment of the Montana Supreme Court could not be reviewed in any federal court.

Baxter v. Montana (2009)

In October 2007, Robert Baxter, a 75-year-old Billings, Montana, retired trucker, brought a petition into the county district court in Helena. For years, Baxter suffered from lymphocytic leukemia, a terminal-but-not-"six-months-or-less" terminal cancer and, his daughter said, "yearned for death" (Johnson 2009). In his petition in his case, *Baxter v. Montana*, Baxter asked the court to prohibit Montana's homicide statutes from being used to indict, arrest, and convict physicians who acted to assist terminally ill patients to die. His complaint: criminalizing PAD violated the Montana Constitution, in particular Article II, Declaration of Rights, Sections 3 (inalienable rights), 4 (individual dignity), and 10 (right of privacy). Joining him in bringing the petition were four Montana doctors and the national PAD organization, Compassion & Choice. Montana's attorney general argued that the state's assisting suicide statutes prohibited PAD action. Both parties asked the court to issue a summary judgment.

On December 5, 2008, the judge, Dorothy McCarter, issued a summary judgment in favor of the plaintiffs. She wrote that "the right to personal autonomy included in the state constitutional right of privacy and the right to determine 'the most fundamental question of life' inherent in the state constitution's right to dignity, mandate that a competent, terminally ill patient has the right to choose to end his or her life." Physicians who assist the patient by providing a prescription are protected from criminal statutes because the dying patient "requires the assistance of [his or her] medical professional."

On December 31, 2009, the state Supreme Court affirmed the ruling 5–2, but on statutory—not constitutional—grounds. The question the court addressed was "whether the consent of the patient to the physician's aid in dying could constitute a statutory defense to a homicide charge." One exception to Montana's defense of consent argument was whether the conduct of the doctor and the dying patient was "conduct that disrupts public peace and physically endangers others." After reviewing state precedents, the judges concluded that "every step in PAD is private. [The court found no parallel between PAD] and the bar brawler, prison fighter, BB gun shooter and domestic violence aggressor [all charged with disrupting 'public peace']."

While the Montana Constitution did not protect a right to PAD, there was "nothing in [our] precedents or Montana statutes that PAD is against public policy." In reaching this conclusion, the judges drew upon Montana's 1985 Rights of the Terminally Ill Act. That law indicated "legislative respect for a patient's autonomous right to decide if and how he will receive medical treatment at the end of his life." The Act immunized doctors from criminal prosecution because the physician was acting in accordance with the dying patient's wishes. A physician who "must actively pull the plug or withhold treatment" from a terminally ill patient who wants to hasten death is not acting "against public policy." Providing a prescription to a dying patient was analogous to a physician withholding treatment from such a patient.

The Terminally Ill Act clearly prohibited mercy killing and euthanasia. The Montana judges concluded that "PAD is, by definition, neither of these. Neither is consent-based and neither involved a patient's autonomous decision to self-administer drugs that will cause his own death."

The decision did not go beyond that; there was no judicial discussion of necessary provisions and regulations for administering PAD and which state agency would be responsible for implementing these requirements. These issues form the procedural core of the Oregon, Washington, California, Vermont and Colorado PAD laws.

Montana's Supreme Court left those provisions for the legislature to create. To date, no legislative action has been taken. The Montana legislature adjourned in April 2015, without passing any PAD-related bills, including one that called for an ODWDA-type PAD bill and another bill making PAD a felony homicide. The state will not convene its next legislative session until 2017.

Until 2014, Montana was the only state that allowed PAD because of a state Supreme Court finding that the state's laws and its Constitution allowed such private *consensual* action between patient and doctor. This unique reality changed somewhat when, that year, litigation was brought into the New Mexico state courts challenging that state's prohibition of PAD.

Morris v. New Mexico (2014–2016)

In March 2012, two New Mexico oncologists, Dr. Katherine Morris and Dr. Aroop Mangalik, filed a petition in the Bernalillo County (population, 670,000) District Court in the Second Judicial District Court of New Mexico. They were joined in the lawsuit by Compassion & Choices and the ACLU of New Mexico, whose lawyers represented the doctors, and, a few months later, by a uterine cancer patient, Aja Riggs. The plaintiffs were seeking to have the New Mexico judiciary "clarify the ability of mentally competent, terminally ill patients to obtain aid in dying from their physician if they find their dying process unbearable" (McCoy 2012).

One major element of their brief is the argument that there is a substantive difference between aid in dying and suicide; the former should be available to terminally ill patients without their doctors being prosecuted for "assisting a suicide." In an amicus brief filed by the New Mexico Psychological Association in the litigation, this difference was highlighted.

[We] recognize that aid in dying and suicide are fundamentally different psychological phenomena, and that these different categories of patients must be treated differently by the law. . . . Psychologists think of suicide as their greatest challenge, and they work tirelessly to prevent their patients from committing suicide. They also recognize that [aid in dying] involves almost no substantive theoretical overlap with suicide. (ACLU New Mexico 2013)

The plaintiffs asked the court to declare that doctors who provide a prescription for lethal medication to dying patients are not subject to criminal prosecution under the existing New Mexico "assisted suicide" law. (NMSA Section 30-2-4 proscribes assisting another to "commit suicide," classifying it as a fourth-degree felony subject to an 18-month imprisonment and a $5,000 fine.)

A bench trial, before Second Judicial District Chief Judge Nan G. Nash, was scheduled on December 11 and 12, 2013. She heard testimony from patients, practitioners of PAD from Oregon, Washington State, and Vermont, and others. Briefs were filed by the plaintiffs and by Kari Brandenberg, the Bernalillo County district attorney. Judge Nash returned to her chambers to review the arguments, the challenged law, and the state constitution's precedents.

On January 13, 2014, in *Morris v. Brandenberg*, she issued a permanent injunction prohibiting the state from prosecuting physicians assisting in a dying patient's end-of-life request. PAD is not suicide; dying patients have a "fundamental" state constitutional right to obtain "aid in dying." It is a "fundamental right under the substantive due process clause of the New Mexico Constitution." The New Mexico Constitution "provides greater rights to New Mexico defendants than those rights provided in the federal constitution in many instances." Furthermore

> this court cannot envision a right more fundamental, more private or more integral to the liberty, safety and happiness of a New Mexican than the right of a competent, terminally ill patient to choose aid in dying. If decisions made in the shadow of one's imminent death regarding how they and their loved ones will face that death are not fundamental . . . then what decisions are? (*Morris v. Brandenberg* 2014)

The New Mexico Conference of Catholic Bishops bitterly disagreed with the ruling. Allen Sanchez, the executive director, pointed out the survivability of illnesses: "As long as there is a chance for human error, we can't have [PAD]. You can never reverse the decision you've made. It's the finality of it" (New Mexico Judge Rules . . . 2014).

Two months later, March 2014, Gary King, New Mexico's attorney general, appealed Nash's ruling to the state Court of Appeals. According to a spokesperson for one of the state's active right to life organizations, "King appealed the ruling at the urging of the NM Archdiocese" (WithDignity 2014). Another pro-life group, the Euthanasia Prevention Coalition, also lobbied King extensively to convince him to act. The group was "pleased" with his decision; "EPC thanks all the people who contacted Gary King, by email, phone, and through the online petition" (Schadenberg 2014).

The Court of Appeals noted jurisdiction in the case, now called *Morris v. King*, and held oral arguments on January 26, 2015. There were a number of amicus briefs filed from groups on both sides. Supporting the state's position were Not Dead Yet (joined by five other groups all representing the disabled), three New Mexico Roman Catholic Archdioceses (Las Cruces, Santa Fe, and Gallup), the Disability Rights Legal Center, the Euthanasia Prevention Coalition, and the Alliance for Defending Freedom (representing five Republican state senators, six Republican House members, and the state's Christian Medical and Dental associations).

Briefs supporting Dr. Morris came from the American Medical Women's Association, the New Mexico Public Health Association, the American Medical Student Association, Compassion & Choices, the ACLU, the New Mexico ALS (amyotrophic lateral sclerosis, commonly referred to as Lou Gehrig's disease) Association, and the New Mexico Psychological Association.

Over a year later, in August 2015, the three-judge New Mexico Court of Appeals, by a 2–1 vote, reversed Nash's decision. In three opinions, totaling nearly 150 pages, two judges, Tim Garcia and Miles Hanisee, in separate opinions, concluded that "aid in dying is not a fundamental liberty interest under the New Mexico Constitution." The dissenting judge, Linda Vanzi, agreed with Nash that there is a fundamental liberty interest in allowing terminally ill patients to receive aid in dying from their physicians.

Judge Garcia wrote the majority decision, heavily relying on *Glucksberg*. For him, that case is the only one that directly answered the question before the New Mexico courts: "whether aid in dying is a constitutional right, fundamental or otherwise."

No court, federal or state, has held that the concept of death . . . is rooted within the protections of bodily integrity under the Constitution. [*Glucksberg*] is the only precedent regarding the nearly identical constitutional question that is posed in this case. (*Morris v. King* 2015)

The concurring justice, Hanisee, based his opinion on his understanding of the state constitution. It incorporated "no right—fundamental or otherwise—to legal narcotics medically prescribed for the sole purpose of causing the immediate death of a patient." Furthermore, the legislature "is vastly better suited to consider and resolve the lawfulness of aid in dying in New Mexico than is the judiciary."

The dissenting judge, Vanzi, used a watershed—and controversial—2015 U.S. Supreme Court 5–4 opinion (*Obergefell v. Hodges*) that, by expanding the meaning of the Fourteenth Amendment's due process and equal protection clauses, discovered a fundamental right to marry for same-sex couples. Justice Anthony Kennedy—the pivotal swing vote on the Court—was the writer of the majority opinion, joined by the four moderate jurists, Justices Ginsburg, Breyer, Sotomayor, and Kagan.

Kennedy's opinion "outright reject[ed] the idea that rights must grow out of specific historical practices," wrote a Supreme Court scholar (Sullivan 2015). "Rights come not from ancient sources alone." Continuing, Kennedy wrote that rights also come from our evolving understanding of liberty. "New insights and societal understandings," he wrote, allow a judge to discover previously unnoticed and unchallenged inequalities. He concluded the opinion with the following observations.

> The fundamental liberties protected by the Fourteenth Amendment's Due Process Clause extend to certain personal choices central to individual dignity and autonomy, including intimate choices defining personal identity and beliefs. . . . [It] is a fundamental right inherent in the liberty of the person, and under the Due Process and Equal Protection Clauses of the Fourteenth Amendment couples of the same sex may not be deprived of that right and that liberty. (*Obergefell v. Hodges* 2015)

The "ruling drew strong dissents from the Court's most conservative brethren, each of whom wrote their own dissent" (Sullivan 2015). Their opinions, "ranging from resigned dismay to bitter scorn" (Liptak 2015), all argued that same-sex marriage is not "rooted in the nation's history and traditions." Chief Justice Roberts caustically wrote that "if you are among the many Americans . . . celebrat[ing] the achievement of a desired goal, celebrate [it]. But do not celebrate the Constitution. It had nothing to do with it."

Continuing, Rogers wrote that Kennedy's opinion was "an act of will, not legal judgment. The Court invalidates the marriage laws of more than half the states and orders the transformation of a social institution that has formed the basis of human society for millennia, for the Kalahari Bushmen and the Han Chinese, the Carthaginians and the Aztecs. Just who do we think we are?"

As usual, Scalia's dissent "did not shy away from histrionics" (Sullivan 2015). "Mock[ing] the soaring language of Justice Kennedy," the "o'erweening pride" in the opinion, Scalia wrote that Kennedy's "opinion is couched in a style that is as pretentious as its content egotistic." For Scalia, it was an undemocratic "judicial Putsch [which reveals] that my Ruler, and the Ruler of 320 million Americans coast-to-coast, is a majority of the nine lawyers on the Supreme Court" (*Obergefell v. Hodges* 2015).

The Constitution is an evolving document, wrote the dissenting New Mexico appeals court judge. "If rights were defined by those who exercised them in the past," wrote Vanzi, "then received practices could serve as their own continued justification and new groups could not invoke rights once denied" (*Morris v. King* 2015).

Addressing the equal protection argument, Vanzi pointed out that physicians in the state are, by statute, allowed to administer terminal sedation as well as remove life-saving devices for their patients. Her colleagues distinguished those actions from those where a doctor, providing aid in dying, violates the "assisting suicide" statute. There are no distinctions between these medical practices; if they exist in the statute, the equal protection clause is violated.

Vanzi disagreed with Hanisee's parsimonious view of the role of the judiciary in the American governmental system. The New Mexico courts—indeed, all courts—have the "obligation" to review any statute for its constitutionality when challenged by a plaintiff. To defend Hanisee's overly cautious position, she concluded, "is little more than a bald assertion that the Legislature may constitutionally criminalize conduct simply because 'twas ever this.'"

The ACLU and Compassionate Choices lawyers immediately filed an "expedited emergency petition" to the New Mexico Supreme Court. They asked the judges to issue an Extraordinary Writ of Superintending Control from the Court of Appeals, because that court's "fractured decision" calls for further review. The writ was granted, briefs filed, and oral arguments were made by the two parties on October 26, 2015. In June 2016, the New Mexico Supreme Court, in a unanimous decision, upheld the Court of Appeals decision that the "assisting a suicide" criminal law is a valid state policy, prohibiting PAD.

In the meantime, challenges to "assisting a suicide" criminal statutes have been taking place in other state courts since the 1990s, but without success. State Supreme Courts in Florida (1997), Alaska (2001), Michigan (2001), and Connecticut (2010), among others, have all upheld "assisting suicide" criminal statutes. In 2015, in New York, doctors and dying patients challenged the criminal statute that makes "assisting suicide" a felony. In October 2015, trial judge Joan Kenney on constitutional grounds, upheld the New York law. In May 2016, in *Myers v. Schneiderman*, Judge Mazzarelli, of the Appellate Division, First Department, New York Court of Appeals, rejected plaintiff Myers's petition, upholding the state's law prohibiting a physician from giving aid-in-dying.

In 2017, then, only the Montana Supreme Court has allowed PAD.

Some Unresolved Problems Linked with Aid in Dying

As already noted many times in this book, the right to die is a very controversial social policy, with the opposing forces bitterly fighting to achieve their (contradictory) goals. It is a prime example of ongoing "hard ball," "no holds barred" politics—at the local, county, state, and national levels. There has been no consensus by the warring participants on how to resolve the issue. Nor is there any likelihood of an accord emerging in the future.

One unsettling outcome of these battles—in courts, in legislatures, in the media—is an unchanging set of conflicting positions that reflect the deep commitment the two sides have to their respective beliefs and policy goals. Again and again there have been a number of near-insoluble problems and issues that have emerged over the past four decades. They involve the following:

1. *Fears*: Fear of the slippery slope, of dying in great pain and suffering, about the inadequacy of long-term health care

2. The evolving patient-doctor relationship

3. Abuses in medical treatment continue due to the continuing implicit bias held by medical professionals against certain classes of patients

4. *Semantics*: Is it physician assistance in *dying* or physician assistance in *suicide*?

5. *The Supreme Court and the Constitution*: How to make sense of the nation's fundamental law when litigating PAD?

6. *"To be Terminal, or not to be 'Terminal'"*: This predicament is probably the most distressing problem associated with PAD.

Fears

The slippery slope problem is the most feared consequence of legitimizing PAD. Even though euthanasia is prohibited in every state and every group involved in the policy battles agrees that it should be banned, opponents expect the slide to euthanasia to ensue if PAD becomes law. The opposition to

PAD, especially among the Roman Catholic Church and disability advocates, is the shared fear that some seriously ill and vulnerable patients—the poor, the disabled, minorities, and the uninsured—would want to die rather than cope with the financial burdens they and their families are facing. Oncologist Dr. Ezekiel Emmanuel fears that too many doctors "might move too readily" to bring an end to these depressed patients. "We should address what would give them purpose, not give them a handful of pills" (Haberman 2015).

Another fundamental fear-inducing dilemma is the limited number of choices dying patients living in great pain and suffering face. For those terminally ill patients coping with life without living (where surgeries, chemotherapy, and radiation keep the dying patient alive but in greater pain and immobility than before), the clashing sides offer radically different paths the suffering incurable patient can take.

The PAD opponents suggest faith in God and staying alive until God beckons is the way people should die (although the Catholic Church and other PAD opponents accept the double effect, palliative sedation, and the withdrawal of devices). PAD is a sinful, immoral practice and must be fought ceaselessly to prevent the hated "culture of death" from becoming the zeitgeist of the new century.

Joni Eareckson Tada, a quadriplegic, a disability advocate, and the founder of the Christian Institute on Disability, wrote an essay addressed to Brittany Maynard a month before Maynard died, addressing the problem that many fearful dying patients coped with fitfully. Her words summarize the religious opposition to PAD. She wrote:

If I could spend a few moments with Brittany before she swallows that prescription she has already filled, I would tell her how I have felt the love of Jesus strengthen and comfort me through my own cancer, chronic pain, and quadriplegia. I would tell her that the saddest thing of all would be for her to wake up on the other side of her tombstone only to face a grim, joyless existence not only without life, but without God." (Tada, 2014)

PAD support groups reject that road for, they believe, it is cruel and inhuman punishment to bar a competent, nondepressed, autonomous, fearful-of-the-future dying person from seeking the assistance of a physician to hasten death. For PAD advocates, a terminally ill person does not have an obligation (to the State or to God) to live.

This issue compels the society to address another emergent, much more profound long-term problem: the glaring inadequacies of long-term health care in America. Most of us will not die from one chronic, terminal illnesses but from an accumulation of assorted maladies that come with aging and which lead to an unpredictable timing of death. And confronting all but the very wealthy is the fear of running out of funds to treat these nonterminal maladies years before death.

In its amicus brief in *Vacco*, the American Geriatrics Society asked a question that goes to the heart of this common fear facing most of us as we age: what does a physician tell a patient when the patient, faced with expensive medical procedures and outrageous prescription drug bills that lead to bankruptcy and financial burdens shifted to family, asks the doctor to help him die rather than face impoverishment or institutionalization?

In the first decade and a half of the 21st century, prescription costs for new drugs have skyrocketed. A new hepatitis C drug, Sovaldi, manufactured by a large drug company, Gilead Sciences, was sold for $1,000 a pill (nearly $90,000 for a course of treatment) in 2015 (Walker 2015). The cost for existing drugs to control, for example, diabetes, high cholesterol, and cancer, has been increasing on average 10 percent a year. One existing drug, Daraprim, had a 5,000 percent price increase when the company was sold to an avaricious entrepreneur. (It went from $13.50 to $700 overnight.) (Pollack 2015)

Fear is present in all human lives. How does a fearful, terminally ill person respond to this human predicament? There are choices available, reflecting the dichotomy between the sanctity of life and the sanctity of the autonomous human being.

The Patient–Doctor Relationship

There are dynamic changes in the physician's attitude toward PAD that impact the bond between doctor and patient. Although the AMA maintains its opposition to PAD, a majority of doctors (54%) have reexamined their views and have come around to accepting PAD and issues associated with that protocol. A 2014 Medscape poll of 17,000 physicians indicated that a majority of the doctors "supported" their patient's "decision to end their life when facing an incurable and terminal disease" (31% did not support the patient's choice) (Medscape Ethics Center 2014).

There seems to be a significant attitudinal change in many American physicians regarding their behavior with their affluent, educated, generally white patients. More of them are accepting a noted doctor's view of her profession's two obligations to their patients. "One is to support the autonomy, the self-determination of their patients. And the other is to relieve suffering. If you can't extend life significantly, then you must relieve suffering" (Joyce 2012).

Doctors also know that patients, competent but seriously ill, can ask them to remove the devices that sustain life. The patients read, regularly, about once secretive physician actions—double effect, terminal sedation, the wink and nod—that are now public knowledge because of generally supportive media coverage. And interactions between patient and doctor have improved because of the increased transparency.

At the heart of this change is the primary care doctor. In the changing interaction between the two, "it is the primary care physician's obligation to lead this difficult discussion [about death]" (Belisomo 2015). Many analysts believe that "without widespread intervention of primary providers, patients will be less likely to ensure their end-of-life wishes are honored" (Belisomo 2015). This fundamental change must continue in order for patients to understand death and what they and their families can do to prepare for it.

With the 2015 changes in the Affordable Care Act, primary care physicians can now spend quality billing time with aging patients to explore health options available for them. And given these changes, there has incrementally emerged a partnership between the two: a sort of equality where conversations take place in the doctor's office; where patients are encouraged to ask end-of-life questions; where they expect to be answered truthfully; and where patient wishes are discussed and complied with by the doctor.

However, given the reality of sharp wealth differences in America, the vulnerable do not have—nor can develop—the positive, open rapport with a physician that more affluent patients have. Indeed, many poor patients do not have the financial means to go to a doctor's private office—where the bond between patient and doctor can develop over time. The emergency department is their doctor's office.

The doctor-patient relationship is nonexistent when the patient is black, or Hispanic, or poor, or old, or disabled. These groups are generally treated without any minimal due care. All physicians hold implicit biases about these others, and this "unconscious racism leads to unintentional and in some cases, even unconscious discrimination" (Matthew 2015). Physicians will truthfully claim no ill will toward racial and ethnic groups, yet, without consciously thinking about it, the doctor is likely to have made some implicit assumptions about the patient before even seeing him or her. Based on the physician's past limited experiences with these vulnerable cohorts, assumptions and stereotypes develop and form the basis of an "unconscious racism." The doctor will assume that a patient from one of these demographic groups has less education, limited means, and few opportunities to take care to eat well, to exercise regularly, and to take care of herself—all before the doctor meets the patient. Her future health and health care are quite likely to be adversely affected by these biases. The treatment choices the physician makes as a result, such as withholding complex information or deferring expensive treatments, are more likely to harm rather than improve a minority patient's health (Matthew 2015).

The 2014 Institute of Medicine report *Dying in America* provided systematic proof that health disparities are associated with the fact that minorities in this country receive unequal health care from medical providers. Hundreds of studies show that, compared to whites, minority patients are less likely to receive appropriate medical treatment for cardiovascular disease, cancer, cerebrovascular disease, renal disease, HIV/AIDS, asthma, diabetes, or pain. They are more likely to receive inferior rehab and material, pediatric and mental health services, and hospital-based medical services than their white counterparts (Institute of Medicine 2015).

This issue remains one of the major societal problems; it has a clear impact on these groups' views about physician-assisted death.

Trust and Mistrust in the Health Care System

The medicalization of death paradigm, by training physicians to focus on curing illnesses, has largely bypassed training them to specialize in geriatric medicine and palliative care. Today, a geriatrics specialty "is one of the lower paid medical specialties, in part because virtually all its patients are on Medicare, which pays doctors less than commercial insurers" (Span 2013). Medical students, whether it is the low salary or the years of intense specialty training or simply because they consider geriatrics "depressing," shy away from that specialty. Given the increasing numbers of aging, there is an annual need for 36,000 medical students training in the geriatrics specialization; in 2013, there "were fewer than 7,000 and falling" (Span 2013).

Yet, quality geriatric care makes a significant difference in the health of the aged. "Older adults whose health is monitored by a geriatrician enjoy more years of independent living, greater social and physical functioning, and lower presence of disease. In addition, these patients show increased satisfaction, spend less time in the hospital, exhibit markedly decreased rates of depression and spend less time in nursing homes" (Houle 2015).

The same problem confounds recruitment of palliative care specialists. The number of palliative care physicians falls far short of society's needs. Successfully recruiting medical students to specialize in palliative care is very difficult for the reasons geriatrics recruiters discover in their search efforts: low pay, homogeneity of the patients, depression-inducing specialty, and both specialties are time-intensive practices. A 2015 national study found that "there is only one palliative medicine physician for every 1,200 terminally ill patients" (McCoy 2015). (There is also a shortage of trained palliative care nurses, psychologists, and medical technicians.)

In the intense commitment to research and innovation to cure cancer, diabetes, heart disease, and other chronic illnesses, the new breed of physician has not been trained in carefully diagnosing illness and in dealing with death. The result of the paradigm change is good and bad. New techniques and equipment have successfully tackled many of the deadly illnesses; however, inattention to quality care for their patients has resulted in a misdiagnosis crisis, especially critical when the patient is diagnosed as terminal.

The Journal of the American Medical Association noted that the prevalence of misdiagnosis is "shocking"; there has been no improvement in missed diagnoses since the 1930s (Leonhardt 2006). How precise is a medical diagnosis of terminal illness? This is a problem repeatedly posed by PAD opponents in debates and in legislative committee meetings. They remind their audience of the times they or their friends or family were told by a doctor that they had a terminal illness—only to find out the diagnosis was incorrect. In America, they point out, doctors seriously misdiagnose serious illnesses 20 percent of the time (Leonhardt 2006). The English Royal College of Pathologists, after reviewing diagnostic data about deceased patients, concluded that more than 5 percent of terminally ill patients were misdiagnosed (Nelson 2009). Furthermore, studies show that when physicians correctly diagnosed the cancer, they regularly overestimated the survival time of terminally ill cancer patients (Glare et al. 2003).

Why, then, should a patient with an "alleged" terminal cancer take the phenobarbital? PAD supporters respond by pointing out that the physicians attending the patient must repeatedly concur on the diagnosis and the prognosis of a terminal illness. Furthermore, they point out a salient fact: the patient has two options: first, filling the prescription, and then, *actually* taking the fatal dosage.

The disagreement will not fade away. PAD opponents cite data about medical misdiagnoses, and that it has been a hidden health care crisis for decades. These statistics bolster the religious, medical, and conservative political groups' unending opposition to PAD.

PAD supporters of aid in dying know the daunting task all physicians face to improve the quality of their diagnostic analyses and the advice and counsel they proffer to their patients. However, the capable, autonomous individual is a key component in determining the success of PAD. From the data generated in Oregon since the ODWDA was implemented in 1997, patients diagnosed as terminal and who choose aid in dying are competent and generally financially comfortable (most with private health insurance); 93 percent were white; 72 percent were dying of cancer; 51 percent were men; the majority were highly educated; the median age of those who chose PAD was 73; before their terminal illness, they had an active life; they were in palliative care and then in hospice facilities; and generally they had a long-term, trusting relationship with their physician (Oregon Public Health Division 2016). The data shows a careful, qualitative diagnostic judgment reached by the consulting physicians over a period of time. Finally, whether the dying patient chooses to take the medication is up to him or her. And there has been a total absence of patients being coerced to ask for and then take the lethal dose of Seconal or phenobarbital or morphine.

Another basic problem that exists is a general mistrust of the overall national health care system by the disabled, the poor, the aged and infirm, the minorities, and other vulnerable persons living in America. They know, they feel, and they live with the unfairness brought on by the physicians' unconscious discrimination. A 2016 study validated the truth of their grim "reality." The longevity gap between the top 10 percent rich and the bottom 10 percent poor has widened sharply despite advances in medicine, technology, and education. Rich men live 14 years longer than the bottom 10 percent; rich women live 13 years longer than the poorest 10 percent (Tavernise 2016).

This lack of trust and the continuing unfairness of the health care system extends to these groups' attitude about how PAD will affect their lives if the practice becomes law. The disabled population has been discriminated against by physicians and others who treat and care for them; they believe that there is a lack of empathy and understanding and a general bias against them because of their physical limitations or ethnicity or inability to pay. For the disabled, there is another health care failure: poor hospital facilities available to them. Hospitals are very slowly addressing the physical shortcomings of the hospital environment and its inability to examine the disabled patient using medical equipment not designed for their infirmities.

Minorities have a historical mistrust of the health care system. Black, Hispanic, and Asian communities are very cognizant of the historical discriminations they and their families have experienced—used as guinea pigs for medical experiments, being cared for in separate and inferior hospitals, not treated with the latest-model equipment, nor given the most advanced new drugs, and without the benefit of cutting-edge medical information used by doctors treating them.

Given the distrust these vulnerable groups share about the health care system generally, it is no wonder that they have a deep distrust of a legalized PAD environment. Their mistrust accompanied by a dreadful fear that PAD will be used against them—against their will—underlies the intense opposition of groups such as Not Dead Yet to PAD.

Still another problem, seen by persons on both sides, is concern about doctors and nurses employing the "wink and nod" alternative to PAD. The practice, by definition, is unregulated, not transparent, and it can be—and has been—secretly used by medical professionals in response to pleas from families of the terribly suffering dying patient—and from the patients themselves. Even supporters of PAD are concerned about the wink and nod way of assisting the dying. "Making a secret process transparent makes it safer," said the president of Compassion & Choices (Editorial Board 2015). However, there is the "catch-22" quandary: making it transparent makes it a felony in 45 states!

The Semantic Problem

Is aid in dying physician-assisted *suicide* or is it physician-assisted *death*? This "value laden" semantic problem lies near the heart of the clashes between pro- and anti-PAD supporters and groups. The use of either one generally "reflect[s] the speaker or writer's political or ideological support for or objection to the practice [of physician-aid-in-dying]" (Starks et al. 2013).

For those opposed to PAD, terminally ill patients living in states where they can legally acquire a prescription for a lethal dose of medicine from their doctor, PAD is suicide, a moral sin, a violation of God's grace. Suicide is suicide, whether it is a jilted lover or an expiring cancer patient. Branding PAD as "assisted suicide" is "one of the most pervasive tactics employed by opponents" (Ryder 2015). "Suicide," as understood by health professionals, denotes "the notion of a premature death that is being hastened out of despair" (Starks et al. 2013).

David Leven is the executive director of End of Life Choices New York. In a press conference in 2015, he presented a clear example of the semantic differences between the two sides:

> The patients taking these medications are not suicidal, they don't want to die. They would prefer to keep on living but they don't have a choice, they are going to die. An analogy can be drawn to those who leapt from the World Trade Center on 9/11. [They] had a choice to make, either burn and asphyxiate to death or leap from the building. I don't think any of us would say they were committing suicide simply because they made this choice for themselves at the very end of their lives, knowing they were going to die, it only being a matter of how. That is what aid-in-dying is about, a choice people make at the very end of their lives for themselves. (Ryder 2015)

The Supreme Court and the Constitution

In every decision the U.S. Supreme Court has made since the 1970s regarding controversial social policies, there is a fundamental conflict between them over how to interpret the words in the U.S. Constitution. There is a basic reason for this judicial problem, one that determines how the Court will decide cases raising issues such as the constitutionality of aid in dying: the Constitution is "a relic . . . written . . . in vague terms that require jurists to be creative law makers" (Caplan 2016). While it was written by a group of truly brilliant men, they were writing a Constitution made to endure for centuries; and it has been open to interpretation ever since its adoption in the late 18th century.

From 1789 to the present time, the justices have had to determine what the Constitution's words mean in order to decide a case before them. Every justice " 'fall[s] back on their priors—the impulses, dispositions, attitudes, belief, and so on they bring to a case,' before they look at the facts and at the law to be applied—and then use lingo to obscure their actual grounds for deciding" (Caplan 2016).

In this judicial decision-making reality for over two centuries, two general approaches have been employed by the justices. There is, as Judge Posner writes, the "'rearview mirror syndrome,' looking backward for the answers to current issues—backward to our 18th century Constitution" (Caplan 2016). These are the originalist jurists—such as Justices Rehnquist, Scalia, Thomas, Roberts, Alito—who argue that if the phrase "assisting a terminally ill patient to die" is not in the Constitution, then a state can prohibit that activity. Recall Chief Justice Roberts's caustic comment about the majority legalizing same-sex marriage: "[The Constitution] had nothing to do with it" (*Obergefell v. Hodges* 2015).

The second general methodology used by other justices, to determine whether a practice is protected by the Constitution, is to look to present-day values and norms to answer the question. For these jurists—such as Justices William O. Douglas, William J. Brennan, Thurgood Marshall, Ginsburg, and Kagan—the document is an evolving one. The Constitution is a living basic law, growing through judicial interpretation to address societal problems never imagined by the framers.

Resolving the PAD problem in the Supreme Court, in simple political terms, is "who has five votes?" In U.S. Supreme Court decisions since 1990 (*Cruzan*), the majority of votes cast were by the "rear view mirror" jurists. As noted, so long as originalists have the votes, the problem for the PAD advocates remains. That is why changes in how aid in dying is treated now come from the election booth and from state judges, not from the U.S. Supreme Court.

The "To Be Terminal, or Not to Be 'Terminal'" Problem: An Example of the Slippery Slope?

We are all terminal, but are we "terminal"? This is a problem that will not be resolved until a state allows voluntary euthanasia (the start of the slippery slope?) or someone becomes a death tourist. It deeply troubles and frustrates all those who believe in a compassionate, humane response to the pain and suffering of patients who are dying of a terminal illness but who are not "terminal" (death within six months or less) according to the ODWDA and its progeny.

Booth Gardner, the former Washington State governor, has been afflicted with Parkinson's disease since 1992. It is a terminal illness, yet it is not "terminal." Even though he was a committed supporter of PAD and he was a key player in convincing voters to pass the WDWDA in 2009, Gardner is not able to use the protocol in the Act—assuming he wishes to—because he has not been told that he has less than six months to live: he is not "terminal."

Dr. Kevorkian was found guilty of second-degree murder in 1999 because his client, a 52-year-old man, Thomas Youk, dying of amyotrophic lateral sclerosis (Lou Gehrig's disease), was in great pain, was disabled, and wanted to hasten his death before life became even more unbearable. Kevorkian actively euthanized Youk because the patient was unable to attach and then start the death machine. Even if Youk and Kevorkian were residents of one of the six PAD states, the doctor would be charged because Youk was not "terminal." Furthermore, if Youk was diagnosed as "terminal," and a resident of Oregon, and he had the Seconal, because of his disability, Youk could not take the pills to his mouth, nor could he pick up the glass and swallow the liquid! And the physician would be committing a felony if he or she administered the medication.

For the severely disabled, there is yet another heart-rending catch-22 that advocates for the disabled have not been able to resolve. These patients, primarily young quadriplegics, are competent, are not dying, have received the finest health care since their catastrophic injury, and have not been isolated from the larger society. Some of them want to end their lives, however outstanding the medical, palliative, and rehab care has been. But they cannot—for a number of reasons. In PAD states, they would not qualify because they are not "terminal." They cannot kill themselves—even if they possessed the toxic medicine—because of their near-total immobility. And because of their legal and medical status, they have great difficulty convincing the hospital to withdraw the life-sustaining device (Ghose 2010).

The Not Dead Yet advocates and others reject the disabled patient's wish. They, in effect, offer the Hawkings remedy: "While there's life, there's hope." They argue that society is causing the patient's negative attitude because not enough resources have been expended to do a better job of caring for such a patient. A bioethicist at the University of Pennsylvania acknowledged the issue: "We don't like to see people with disabilities decide not to go on. And people will put up road blocks and try to slow that process in every way they can" (Ghose 2010).

The paralyzed patient, meanwhile, is bereft. He or she is in a twilight zone, wanting to die but unable to—even by his or her own hands. Independent living advocates for the severely disabled believe that "the underlying problem is the lack of autonomy and dignity afforded to patients with high-level disabilities. 'The reality is they shouldn't have to live that way, and we should provide the services that make people's lives bearable'" (Ghose 2010). For some non-"terminal," competent, nondepressed, severely disabled, and suffering patients whose life is unbearable who choose to end it, the problem is that they cannot!

This is no longer the case with our neighbor to the north, Canada. A major—unanimous (9–0)—Supreme Court of Canada (SCC) decision in February 2015, *Carter et al. v. Canada (Attorney General)*, answered this "terminal" problem dramatically. Kay Carter, an 89-year-old Canadian mother of seven, died at the Dignitas Clinic in Switzerland. Suffering intolerable pain because of her terminal illness—spinal stenosis—she became a death tourist because the SCC banned PAD 21 years earlier when it announced its 4–3 decision in *Rodriguez v. British Columbia* (1994).

More than a year after her death, Carter's daughter brought suit in the British Columbia (BC) courts. She was joined by BC Civil Liberties Association, a family doctor, and another dying (ALS)-but-not-"terminal" patient, Gloria Taylor. The plaintiffs won in the trial court but the BC Court of Appeal overturned the ruling. They went to the SCC, which granted them leave to appeal. Oral arguments were heard on October 14, 2014.

Less than four months later, the SCC overturned the BC appellate court and its own 1994 *Rodriguez* opinion. It found sections 241 (b) and 14 of the Criminal Code to have infringed Canadians' rights to life, liberty, and security of the person guaranteed under section 7 of the Canadian Charter of the Rights and Freedoms.

> A consenting adult's response to a grievous and irremediable medical condition [which causes] endless suffering [physical or psychological] is a matter critical to their dignity and autonomy. The law allows people in this situation to request palliative care, refuse artificial nutrition and hydration, or request the removal of life-sustaining medical equipment, but denies them the right to request a physician's assistance in dying. This interferes with their ability to make decisions concerning their bodily integrity. But leaving people to endure intolerable suffering, it impinges on their security of person. (*Carter v. Canada* 2015)

Furthermore, the decision "decriminalized both voluntary active euthanasia and physician assisted death." The SCC "accepted the claimants' definition of [PAD] as a situation where a physician provides or administers medication that intentionally brings about the patient's death, at the request of the patient." Finally, and most important for the "terminal" problem, the SCC "did not define 'grievous and irremediable,' but it is clearly not limited to terminal illness." Even a competent person with dementia, or ALS, who is grievously and intolerably suffering can request PAD or voluntary euthanasia.

The SCC opinion, however, was not immediately implemented. The Court delayed execution of the ruling for one year in order to give the Parliament an opportunity to pass PAD legislation. On April 14, 2016, the new prime minister, the ruling Liberal Party's leader, Justin Trudeau, introduced the assisted dying bill (Bill G-14), an "Act to amend the criminal code to allow medical assistance in dying for patients with a serious and incurable illness." It differed in two fundamental ways from the ODWDA model: (1) a patient does not have to be terminal to receive aid in dying and (2) voluntary euthanasia is permitted with the consent of the patient. The assisted dying bill was acted on—positively—by the end of the 2016 legislative session because the Liberal Party has a majority in both houses of Parliament.

Canada's judicial response to the issue is the exact opposite of the U.S. Supreme Court's 1997 views on PAD (and the scope of the Constitution's Fourteenth Amendment). Additionally, the response by Canada's national government is nothing like the actions of President George W. Bush, Attorney General John Ashcroft, and other conservative Republican senators and congresspersons in the first decade of the 21st century.

In a nutshell, the terminal/"terminal" existential problem (among other difficulties) is solely an American conundrum. Unlike Canada and other nations that provide assistance in dying, America continues struggling in vain with the question of whether a competent, dying patient who is not "terminal" has the right to die. An imperative question: Is the person—whether quadriplegic, suffering from Parkinson's disease or ALS, or some other chronic devastating illness—burdened with the obligation to live? A final question: Does *compassion* for these "twilight zone" patients get the better of concerns about society skidding down the slippery slope from PAD to voluntary euthanasia? Should it?

The Right to Die Dilemma: Is There a Solution?

"There is no question that [PAD] is one of the messiest areas of health ethics, policy, and practice," wrote a columnist (Friedman

2013). A number of problems surrounding the issue have been noted in this chapter. Some reflect society's inequities, but can move toward resolution if social policies—and the necessary funding—are addressed and positive changes instituted. There are, however, implacable ones; solutions are near impossible because of the black versus white dynamic at play—an unwillingness to compromise when their deeply held fundamental values are involved.

The Resolvable Problems

There is little difference between the resolvable and unresolvable problems associated with the right to die. In the former, the solutions are found in massive realignment of public and private policies regarding the issue and the larger issue of inequities in the health care system. Given the hot-blooded partisanship of elected officials and the public, this adjustment of the agenda is a herculean task. But it is not an absolutely unbending one. There are problems surrounding the medicalization of death, the doctor-patient relationship, and, generally, the grossly unjust health care situation that conceptually can be rationally examined, and change may be an outcome. The unyielding problems are another story.

Regarding the fundamental relationship between the primary care physician and the patient, Dr. Ezekiel Emanuel, a highly regarded oncologist and ethicist, offered a simple suggestion: train doctors and nurses to talk about death with the patient!

> All doctors and nurses should be trained in how to talk to patients and their families about end-of-life care. When I was starting out, I was lucky enough to be able to witness how a great oncologist communicated with patients and their families when it was clear they were going to die, but I received no formal training whatsoever. It is hard to improve care for the dying if health professionals don't know how to talk about it. (Emanuel 2013)

Another solvable problem is the lack of critical care practitioners and facilities. There is, in the second decade of the new century, a shortage of palliative care and hospice facilities and medical professionals practicing in these end-of-life centers. Emanuel, among others, noted that "over 40% of hospitals with more than 50 beds do not have palliative care services." The resolution? "Every hospital should be required to have palliative care services both in the hospital and at the homes of dying patients who are discharged" (Emanuel 2013).

Hospice statistics reflect a similar need. In 2013, nearly 60 percent of deaths occurred *without* hospice comfort care at the end. Of the 42 percent of patients who died in hospice in 2013, data shows a positive trend in hospice admissions: more dying patients entered hospice *earlier*. In 2001, 18.8 percent accessed hospice for three or more days; by 2007, the figure was 30.1 percent (Morrison 2015). More time spent in hospice by dying patients means more quality comfort care for them, making their last days easier.

Palliative care must also be introduced earlier for seriously ill patients. In one recent study of lung cancer patients, published in *The New England Journal of Medicine* in 2010, the researchers concluded that

> among patients with metastatic non–small-cell lung cancer, early palliative care led to significant improvements in both quality of life and mood. As compared with patients receiving standard care, patients receiving early palliative care had less aggressive care at the end of life but longer survival. (Temel et al. 2010)

More hospice facilities must be introduced so that every hospital has a hospice wing and the necessary medical professional teams to provide care for the dying patient in hospital or at the patient's home. Revisions in eligibility for admission into a hospice care program must include a change in the requirement that physicians certify that patients have six months or less to live. "Unless we want to insist that physicians acquire crystal balls and take up psychic prediction" (Friedman 2013), there must be a rule change where the doctor's assessment of the patient's needs for specialized care determines eligibility for entry into hospice.

These changes can go a long way toward making the end of life pain free, but to see them adopted will take significant governmental policy change—accompanied by equally substantial budgetary shifts by both the U.S. Congress and the president to finance these changes. And if these are high cost but needed changes in health care, consider the additional costs for training new palliative care doctors, new geriatrics doctors, and new nurses, medical technicians, social workers, and psychologists.

In our polarized political environment, it's not likely that, in the near term, these policy and budgetary shifts will occur. But, given the exploding number of millennials getting ready for retirement and beginning to examine the next phase of their lives, accompanied by the lack of palliative care and hospice programs with a shrinking pool of trained physicians and nurses, there will emerge new and insistent demands for change by groups representing them.

Another solvable issue—inadequate and discriminatory health care treatment for vulnerable groups—reflects a much more fundamental problem: the nation's 240-plus-year history of government and private discrimination that targeted the disabled, the elderly, the poor and lower class individuals, and ethnic and religious minorities. As a consequence of this brutal reality, these abused and discriminated groups fear the system and, as well, fear their treatment if PAD is officially permitted. The remedy, in part, is, again, a major shift in policy and budget allocations to improve the quality of health care for these "others."

But such political changes—difficult as they are—are the tip of the iceberg of discrimination. What is needed is an acknowledgment from the larger public that class, economic, racial, gender, and age discrimination in health care is a historical fact. This inequitable treatment exists in America; it must be ended by people recognizing the disparities—and the abuses—in health care because of this pervasive bias. This aspect of the problem, in sum, calls for two new behaviors by the national community: empathy and compassion.

Unless there is a change in the public's awareness of the plight of vulnerable persons in their midst, which leads to justice in action in the form of political demands for shifts in political and budgetary policy, things remain the same. Without the very real and continuing demands for policy changes through organized political activities, abuse, intolerance, and discrimination in America's health care system will not change.

The Unbending Problem

The solvable problems enumerated above are at the edge of the right to die controversy. With major changes in the American society's domestic public policies—a prodigious task that will take place only when polarizing politics are replaced with the art of political compromise—these jarring issues revolving around health care can be addressed.

However, when we turn to addressing the core problem—the "rightness" of physician assistance in dying—there is a near absolute unwillingness by people to compromise on the contradictory but very fundamental ethical, ideological, or religious beliefs. As *The Right to Die* illustrates, this collision involves absolute but divergent values. There does not seem to be a possibility of reason in action to try to accommodate these groups' differences.

Throughout history these battle lines have endured: belief in the sanctity of life versus the belief that all persons have a personal fundamental liberty to ask a physician to assist them in hastening death. There does not appear to be any common ground for the opposing sides to sit down to reason together to find a solution.

In our time, ever since the abortion case *Roe v. Wade*, unconditional views about life and death, and about the rights all persons have to determine and act on their definition of "one's own concept of existence . . . and of the mystery of human life" have been expressed (*Planned Parenthood of Southeastern Pennsylvania v. Casey*). Legislators, presidents, governors, attorneys general, judges, doctors, nurses, priests, Imans, rabbis, columnists, tweeters, advocates for the disabled, family members, terminally ill patients, and all the others, have all examined and created their own set of values about life, dying, and death.

This reality leads to perennial skirmishes—about God, about one's essence—but no clear victories. Thomas Hobbes, a 17th-century British political philosopher, wrote that life in society is "brutish and nasty." This values conflict means that both sides are continuously preparing for the next battle to overturn a PAD law or, on the other side, to fight for passage of a PAD bill in the legislature or in a court. These clashes will go round and round without any victory. Anniversaries of important events—the *Roe* decision, the passage of legislation that ends a state's assisted dying law—will be celebrated with pickets, marches, speeches, and a renewed commitment to "the right to die" or to the "sanctity of life."

References

ACLU New Mexico. 2013. "NMPA Files Amicus Brief in Morris v. New Mexico in Support of Expanded End of Life Choices." December 10. https://www.aclu.org/news/new-mexico-psychological-association-says-physician-aid-dying-no-kind-suicide

Allen, Mike. 2005. "Counsel to GOP Senator Wrote Memo on Schiavo." *The Washington Post*, April 7, p. 19.

Ball, Howard. 2012. *At Liberty to Die: The Battle for Death with Dignity in America.* New York: New York University Press.

Belisomo, Randi. 2015. "Which Doctors Should 'Own' End-of-Life Planning?" *Reuters*, February 11.

Brown, Edmond G. Jr. 2015. Letter to Members of the California State Assembly, October 5. www.brown.gov

Bush, George W. 2005. "Statement on Signing Legislation for the Relief of the Parents of Theresa Marie Schiavo." Public Papers of the Presidents of the United States: George W. Bush, 2005 Book 1. March 21, 2005. Washington, D.C.: Government Printing Office.

California Catholic Conference. 2008. *E-Newsletter*, June 27. http://www.diocese-sacramento.org/parishes/PDFs/CCC_ENewsletter.pdf

California Medical Association. 2015. "California Medical Association Removes Opposition to Physician Aid in Dying Bill." May 20. http://www.cmanet.org/news/press-detail/?article=california-medical-association-removes

Caplan, A.L. 2006. *The Case of Terri Schiavo: Ethics at the End of Life*. Amherst, NY: Prometheus Books.

Caplan, Lincoln. 2016. "Rhetoric and Law." *Harvard Magazine*, January–February.

Clark, Annette E. 2006. "The Right to Die: The Broken Road from Quinlan to Schiavo." *Loyola University Chicago Law Journal*, 37, 384.

Colby, William H. 2002. *The Long Goodbye: The Death of Nancy Cruzan*. Carlsbad, CA: Hay House.

Editorial Board. 2015. "Offering a Choice to the Terminally Ill." *New York Times*, March 14.

Emanuel, Ezekiel J. 2013. "Better, if Not Cheaper, Care." *New York Times*, January 3.

Friedman, Emily. 2013. "So Quit, Already: Futility, Faith, Family, and the Ongoing Battle over End-of-Life Care." *Hospitals & Health Networks Daily*, August 6.

Ghose, Tia. 2010. "Paralyzed Accident Victim Fights for Right to Die." *Journal Sentinel*, November 28.

Glare, Paul, Kiran Virik, Mark Jones, Malcolm Hudson, Steffen Eychmuller, John Simes, and Nicholas Christakis. 2003. "A Systematic Review of Physician's Survival Predictions in Terminally Ill Cancer Patients." *BMJ*, 327, 195.

Goldstein, Amy. 1998. "Pro-Life Activist's Take on Death: Movement Mobilizes against Issues such as Assisted Suicide." *The Washington Post*, November 10.

Goodnough, Abby. 2005. "The Schiavo Case: The Overview; Schiavo Dies, Ending Bitter Case Over Feeding Tube." *New York Times*, April 1.

Greenhouse, Linda. 2006. "Justices Reject U.S. Bid to Block Assisted Suicide." *The New York Times*, January 18, p. A1.

Haberman, Clyde. 2015. "Stigma around Physician-Assisted Dying Lingers." *New York Times*, March 22.

Hillyard, Daniel, and John Dombrink. 2001. *Dying Right: The Death with Dignity Movement*. New York: Psychology Press.

Houle, Marcy Cottrell. 2015. "An Aging Population, without the Doctors to Match." *New York Times*, September 22.

Institute of Medicine. 2015. *Dying in America: Improving Quality and Honoring Individual Preferences Near the End of Life*. Washington, D.C.: National Academy of Sciences.

Iwasaki, John. 2008. "State Second in Nation to Allow Lethal Prescriptions." *Seattle Post Intelligencer*, November 5, 1.

John Paul II. 2004. Address of John Paul II to the Participants in the International Congress "Life-Sustaining Treatments and Vegetative State: Scientific Advances and Ethical Dilemmas." *The Vatican*, http://w2.vatican.va/content/john-paul-ii/en/speeches/2004/march/documents/hf_jp-ii_spe_20040320_congress-fiamc.html

Johnson, Kirk. 2009. "Montana Court to Rule on Assisted Suicide Case." *New York Times*, September 1.

Joyce, Jaime. 2012. "The Evolving State of Physician-Assisted Suicide." *The Atlantic*, July 16.

"Justice Fears for Roe Ruling." 1988. *New York Times*, September 14.

Leonhardt, David. 2006. "Why Doctors So Often Get It Wrong." *New York Times*, February 22.

Liptak, Adam. 2015. "Supreme Court Ruling Makes Same-Sex Marriage a Right Nationwide." *New York Times*, June 26.

Lowenstein, Edward and Sidney H. Wanzer. 2002. "Sounding Board: The U.S. Attorney General's Intrusion into Medical Practice." *New England Journal of Medicine*, 346, 447.

Masters, Brooke A. 1998a. "Pt William Judge Delays Removal of Feeding Tube." *The Washington Post*, September 22.

Masters, Brooke A. 1998b. "Family Reunites to Let Hugh Finn Die." *The Washington Post*, September 29.

Masters, Brooke A. 1998c. "Judge Rejects Va. Efforts to Prevent Finn's Death." *The Washington Post*, October 1.

Matthew, Dayna Bowen. 2015. *Just Medicine: A Cure for Racial Inequality in American Health Care.* New York: New York University Press.

Maynard, Brittany. 2014. "My Decision to Die." *People*, October 27.

McCoy, Lindsey. 2015. "California Signs Death with Dignity, U.S. Behind in Palliative Care." *MedCareer News*, October 7.

McCoy, Micah. 2012. "ACLU Seeks Ruling That Physicians Can Provide Aid in Dying." American Civil Liberties Union of New Mexico, Albuquerque, NM, March 15.

Medscape Ethics Center. 2014. Ethics Report 2014, Part 1: Life, Death, and Pain. http://www.medscape.com/resource/ethics

Melton, R.H. and Brooke A. Masters. 1988. "Court Rejects Gilmore's Bid to Overturn Finn Ruling." *The Washington Post*, October 3.

Monning, Bill. 2015, July 7. "Aid-in-Dying Legislation Removed from Assembly Health Committee Calendar." http://sd17.senate.ca.gov/news/2015–07–07-aid-dying-legislation-removed-assembly-health-committee-calendar

Morrison, Ian. 2015. "Health Care Costs and Choices in the Last Years of Life." *Hospitals & Health Networks Daily*, March 3.

Nelson, Fraser. 2009. "A Welcome Rejection of Assisted Suicide." *The Spectator*, July 7.

"New Mexico Judge Rules Doctors Can Help Terminally Ill Patients Commit Suicide without Prosecution." 2014. *Associated Press*, January 14.

Newport, Frank. 2014. "Mississippi Most Religious State, Vermont Least Religious." *Gallup*, February 3.

Nirappil, Fenit. 2015. "California 'Right to Die' Bill Stalls with Catholics Opposed." *Associated Press*, July 7.

O'Neill, Tip, and Gary Hymel. 1994. *All Politics Is Local: And Other Rules of the Game*. New York: Times Books.

Oregon Public Health Division. 2016. "Oregon Death with Dignity Act: 2015 Data Summary." Oregon Health Authority. www.oregon.gov/oha

Orr, Bob. 2007, March 21. *VAEH Newsletter #44*. Vermont Alliance for Ethical Healthcare. http://www.vaeh.org/vaeh-newsletter-44/

Ostrum, Carol M. 2008. "Initiative 1000 Would Let Patients Get Help Ending Their Lives." *Seattle Times*, September 21, 1.

Patient Choice Vermont. 2011. "Death with Dignity: From Oregon to Vermont" press release, February 23. https://vtdigger.org/2011/02/23/death-with-dignity-from-oregon-to-vermon/

Pedroncelli, Rich. 2015. "After Struggling, Jerry Brown Makes Assisted Suicide Legal in California." *Los Angeles Times*, October 5.

Pew Research Center. 2015. Religious Landscape Study. http://www.pewforum.org/religious-landscape-study/

Pollack, Andrew. 2015. "Martin Shkreli's Arrest Gives Drug Makers Cover." *New York Times*, December 17.

Pope Pius XII. 1957. Address to an International Congress of Anesthesiologists, November 24.

Quinlan, Julia D. 2005. *My Joys, My Sorrows.* Cincinnati, OH: St. Anthony Messenger Press.

Redden, Jim. 2014. "Religious Yes, Churchgoers, No." *The Portland (Oregon) Tribune*, December 18.

Reno, Janet. 1998. "Statement of Attorney General Reno on Oregon's Death with Dignity Act." U.S. Department of Justice, June 5. https://www.justice.gov/archive/opa/pr/1998/June/259ag.htm.html

"Right-to-Die Bill Allowing Doctor Prosecution Fails in House." 2015. *CBS Seattle*, February 17. http://seattle.cbslocal.com/2015/02/17/right-to-die-bill-allowing-doctor-prosecution-fails-in-house/

Roberts, Barbara. 2008. "I 1000 Is Not a Slippery Slope." *Seattle Post Intelligencer*, September 15.

RomanCatholicBlog.com. 2007. "Another Effort to Legalize a New Kind of Murder: The California 'Compassionate Choices' Act." March 25. http://romancatholicblog.typepad.com/roman_catholic_blog/2007/03/california_comp.html

Ryder, Joseph. 2015. "*Dying with Dignity: A Patients Right to Die.*" Stony Brook Press, Features. May 29. http://sbpress.com/2015/05/dying-with-dignity-a-patients-right-to-die/.

Schadenberg, Alex. 2014. "New Mexico Attorney General Appeals Assisted Suicide Lower Court Decision."

Euthanasia Prevention Coalition, March 12. http://
alexschadenberg.blogspot.com/2014/03/new-mexico-
attorney-general-appeals.html

Schwartz, James, and James Estrin. 2010. "In Vermont, a Bid
to Legalize Physician-Assisted Suicide." *New York Times*,
February 11.

Seelye, Katharine W. 2016. "More Than a River Separates
Bernie Sanders's State from Primary's." *New York Times*,
February 7.

Span, Paula. 2013. "Even Fewer Geriatricians in Training."
New York Times, January 3.

Starks, Helene, Denise Dudzinski, and Nicole White. 2013.
"Physician Aid-in-Dying." Ethics in Medicine, University
of Washington School of Medicine. https://depts.
washington.edu/bioethx/topics/pad.html

Stutzman. Eli T. 1998. "Political Strategy and Legal Change."
In *Physician Assisted Suicide: Expanding the Debate*, edited
by Margaret P. Battin, Rosamond Rhodes, and Anita
Silvers, 123–132. New York: Routledge.

Sullivan, Casey C. 2015. "SCOTUS: Same-Sex Couples
Have Fundamental Right to Marriage." The FindLaw U.S.
Supreme Court News & Information Blog, June 26. http://
blogs.findlaw.com/supreme_court/2015/06/same-sex-couples-
have-fundamental-right-to-marriage-court-rules.html

Tada, Joni Eareckson. 2014. "Why Brittany Maynard's
Choice to Die Is Not Personal or Private." *Washington Post*,
October 15.

Tavernise, Sabrina. 2016. "Disparity in Life Spans of the Rich
and the Poor Is Growing." *New York Times*, February 12.

Temel, Jennifer S., et al. 2010. "Earlier Palliative Care for
Patients with Metastatic Non-Small-Cell Lung Cancer."
New England Journal of Medicine, 363, 733–742.

Thomas, Cal. 2005. "St. Theresa Sciavo." *Jewish World Review*,
April 1.

Tucker, Kathryn L. 2008. "In the Laboratory of the States: The Progress of Glucksberg's Invitation to States to Address End of Life Choices." *Michigan Law Review*, 106:8, 1593–1612.

Walker, Joseph. 2015. "Gilead's $1,000 Pill Is Hard for States to Swallow." *Wall Street Journal*, April 8.

Wilson, Adam. 2008. "What Voters Will Bring to I 1000." *Olympian*, September 21, 1.

WithDignity. 2014. "New Mexico: ADF Files Friend-of-the-Court-Brief in Morris v. King Appeal." https://withdignity. wordpress.com/tag/morris-v-king/

This chapter consists of a number of essays about the right to die written by participants in these battles in the United States and Canada. The authors are men and women with varied backgrounds: physicians, advocates for the disabled, pressure group leaders, and religious leaders. All have been involved in the political, legal, medical, and ethical discussions, most of them for decades; all make reasoned arguments defending their contrary positions on this controversial issue.

Is There a Right to Die?

Robert D. Orr

The phrase *right to die* comes up in medicine, in philosophy, in politics, and even over a cup of coffee at Dunkin Donuts. Many people who use the term assume it is a real entity and

---

Debbie Ziegler, mother of terminal brain cancer patient Brittany Maynard, receives congratulations after California passed Death with Dignity legislation in September 2015. A year earlier, since California did not have a law that allowed physicians to assist patients in hastening their death, Maynard moved to Oregon to take advantage of the state's Death with Dignity law. She died in November 2014 using medication prescribed by her physician. Maynard's story became a rallying event in the effort to get Death with Dignity legislation passed in other states. (AP Photo/Rich Pedroncelli)

further assume that everyone means the same thing when they invoke this concept. But what does it mean? Is it a valid right? Why is there controversy about it?

A good part of the controversy about this phrase is that it has at least two meanings. In contemporary usage, it was first invoked in a passive sense—a right to refuse treatment with the expectation that death would result. Recall Karen Ann Quinlan, the young woman with severe brain damage, whose parents went to court to force reluctant doctors to remove the ventilator that was sustaining her life. That passive meaning rather quickly evolved into an active meaning—a right to actually die right now, by suicide, assisted suicide, or euthanasia. This active sense is the classical meaning of this controversial "right" dating back at least to the time of Seneca, the first-century Stoic philosopher.

These two meanings are not the same; they are not even a little bit the same. To emphasize this difference, we must further recall that when Karen Quinlan's ventilator was finally removed, she did not die. She lived for another 10 years. I would posit that those who claimed her "right to die" were incorrect in looking to this ancient concept for support. What they really intended was that she had a right to be left alone, a right to not have medical treatment imposed on her against her wishes.

A thorough review of the theory of rights (a philosophical discussion that involves argumentation about whether human rights come from divinity, from natural law, from human thought, or from some other source) is beyond the scope of this essay, but let me briefly cite two influential statements. The U.S. Declaration of Independence guarantees to all citizens the inalienable right to "life, liberty and the pursuit of happiness" as "endowed by their Creator." It goes on to state that when these rights are infringed upon by government, it is proper to alter or abolish the source of infringement. The 1945 United Nations Declaration of Human Rights guarantees to all citizens of the world "the right to life, liberty and the security of person" as part of the "endowed dignity" of all persons (http://www.un.org/en/universal-declaration-human-rights/). Neither statement even hints at a right to die. And to try to reinterpret either to support a right to die would be a serious distortion of the intent of the writers.

Another way to look at this question is to focus on the issue of autonomy, a well-accepted concept in morality, political theory, developmental psychology, and bioethical thought—the capacity of a rational individual to make an informed, un-coerced decision based on his or her own values. Like the issue of a right to die, autonomy is often thought of as a monolithic concept. This too is incorrect as there is both negative auton-omy, a right to be left alone (sounds familiar?) and positive autonomy, that is, an entitlement. The bioethical principle of autonomy is about the negative variety, the almost inviolable right of a patient who has mental capacity to accept or refuse any recommended treatment, even if refusal will lead to death. This is far different from a claim of positive autonomy, a sense of entitlement to whatever treatment one chooses, or even a claim that someone else has a duty to help that individual to die because the claimant has a right to die.

As a physician and as a clinical ethics consultant, I would strongly support a patient's refusal of unwanted life-sustaining treatment, for example, the use of a ventilator or a dialysis machine or blood transfusions. I would try to understand the patient's reason for refusal; I would try to address any modifi-able reasons that led to his or her decision; I might even try to persuade the patient to reconsider. But if the patient was adequately informed and could offer a rational explanation for refusal, I would support the patient's decision, even over the objection of his or her family or health care professionals. On the other hand, if the family of a patient who had had a stroke several days ago from lack of blood supply to a por-tion of the brain that demanded hyperbaric oxygen treatment (high-pressure oxygen administered in a sealed chamber) be used to heal the dead brain tissue, I would not support this presumed entitlement since it is contrary to a clear understanding of brain pathology.

There is a huge difference between a right to refuse treatment and a demand for inappropriate treatment. There is a huge difference between a right to be left alone and a right to die. We could have a protracted discussion about a right to commit suicide. (Should individuals or society always step in to try to prevent it?) But, in my view, there is no "right" to be made dead in which another individual is thereby obligated or even allowed to assist the requestor to achieve death.

When anyone asserts a right to die, it is incumbent upon those hearing this claim to dig deeper to see if he or she is asserting a right to be left alone, free of unwanted treatment, or whether that individual really is asking to die now. If the former, we should investigate to see if the necessary parameters are present, and if they are we should then support that person's right. If the latter, we should find out the reason for the request and do our very best to modify and hopefully nullify that reason, thereby supporting the person's valid right to life, liberty, and security of person.

Robert D. Orr, MD, CM, practiced family medicine in rural Vermont for 18 years before being awarded a postdoctoral fellowship in medical ethics at the University of Chicago in 1989. Since receiving that training, he has taught and practiced clinical ethics at Loma Linda University Medical Center, California; the University of Vermont Medical Center, Vermont; the Graduate College of Union University, New York; and Trinity International University, Illinois. He has served on numerous state and national ethics committees and commissions, lectured widely, and published many articles, book chapters, and books. His most recent book is entitled Medical Ethics and the Faith Factor *(Wm. Eerdmans Pub., 2009). He and his wife are retired in Vermont.*

My Life Is Mine

Stanley Greenberg and Kay Stambler

Our thinking is guided by our knowledge and experience. Doctors are taught to heal, to look at the value of a human life, to make things right. These two, plus many other factors, place people who are disabled at a life-threatening disadvantage.

When a disabled person, child, or adult crosses our path we think about what the person cannot do. We imagine what we would want for ourselves should this disability happen to us. Usually we have no idea who the person is beyond his or her disability. This leads to making decisions for a person who is disabled without seeing who is really there and asking the person what he or she wants.

So what happens when one of us has minimal ability to take care of one's self *and* is therefore not given support to live a full and rewarding life? What is meant by dependence and guardianship? Should anyone make a decision to conclude a life because the person is not contributing in the traditional sense of the word or someone decides—many someones decide—it would be costly and useless to keep the person alive? In the United States, this has happened to people with disabilities over and over again. It happens throughout our society: in our hospitals and in our homes.

There are those who see a person and not a disability. For these people, life can be quite different. Consider the lives described here and wonder.

Barbara was disabled before she had her drowning accident. In the call from a doctor to her guardian, she was described as comatose. The doctor arranged for Barbara to be brought to the major medical center and asked the guardian to give permission for her body parts to be used to save others. Barbara's guardian said, "Get her to the major hospital." After her arrival, her guardian insisted that a neurologist be brought in, and he determined Barbara was not "brain dead." Barbara's guardian put people in her hospital room 24 hours a day. On a pad of paper that they passed to each other, they wrote who came into the room and exactly what they did. Many professionals who were treating Barbara were angry they were being watched and argued with her guardian that it was a waste of money to keep her alive. Barbara lived to go home and find her Mom, whom she adored. Her life was different, and she gave smiles and joy to all.

Michael was a very cranky man who was also disabled. When he arrived at the hospital, he was very sick. His guardian was told by the doctor that his kidneys were not working. The doctor then added, "For people like this we usually don't do dialysis." The guardian said, "Get him dialysis and then we'll talk." Michael lived another seven years. He was not less cranky, but he sure wanted to live.

Marni was born with frozen joints. Her arms and legs were put in casts to straighten them. The casts were changed every three weeks. The procedure caused her to not keep anything in her stomach for 24 hours. At three months, she went into shock, and her pediatrician sent her to the hospital saying that there was nothing he could do. Her parents had to "let nature take its course." When another pediatrician from the practice examined her, he called in a pediatric surgeon. Surgery showed her intestine was tied in a knot. With the operation she lived. Without it, she would have died.

Forty-four years later, her life was taken by cancer. Her oncology team employed every known method to postpone her death. During Marni's 44 years, her parents were her guardians. Unlike some guardians, they knew that Marni's life was hers. In the end, they supported Marni when she decided, nonverbally, to discontinue treatment, to be served by hospice and to live the remainder of her life pain free. She died surrounded by family and close friends and the singing of her rabbi.

So why is Marni's life relevant to this discussion? Simply stated, she would have been allowed to die at three months of age if the decision was in the hands of a doctor who could imagine no future for her and parents who did not know her beyond her disabilities. Instead, a pediatrician came on the scene and told her parents that she was a whole person with a disability whose life could be saved. With the operation, Marni lived a life filled with joy, sorrow, achievement, and immeasurable value.

By the way, in addition to having difficulty expressing herself, she was intellectually disabled. Her parents did whatever was necessary to keep her from being segregated and devalued and, instead, included in the middle of society. With the help of like-minded friends, progressive educators, legal intervention, and always unrelenting tenacity, she lived a normative life: folk dancing, gymnastics, summer camp, music lessons, religious school, and youth centers.

As a young adult, Marni saw her siblings leave home to be on their own, and she made it clear that she would not spend her life as a child living in the home of her family. Consequently, she was supported to be in her own home for the last 20 years of her life. She held several volunteer jobs, went to concerts and shows, listened to rock and roll radio stations and loved the music, enjoyed going to fast food restaurants and also eating lobster and shrimp. She traveled across the country for family gatherings and vacations.

At her memorial service, Marni was eulogized by her family, her longtime friends, and her rabbi. People from the day care center where she went when she was a young child came. Her fourth-grade teacher was there. Friends throughout her life came and remembered and cried. Her family received condolences from people around the country whose lives she had touched. One young man who knew her when they were 5 years old at preschool together composed a poem which concluded that his son, now 5, would know her through him. She made an indelible impression on those with whom she came into contact, and she will be missed!

Bioethicists and many physicians who seek to make judgments regarding the lives of those with disabilities question the time, energy, and resources necessary to maintain the continuing existence of people who are not productive in the traditional sense. Some postulate that if someone is "not pulling his or her weight," whose life is determined by measurement on a tally sheet and whose existence is quantified by output, that person's life should be ended sooner rather than later.

How then should a life be measured? Should it be measured by personal income, worth on a balance sheet, number of widgets produced, number of graduate degrees, or maybe something else? Perhaps another tool should be employed: perhaps the number of lives touched positively or the number of smiles counted when the person's name is mentioned. Maybe attitudes changed by the person's mere presence should be factored in. In any event, Marni, Barbara, and Michael lived when doctors advised dying. Their very existence made the world a better place, and they died with dignity. Perhaps that is enough.

For 50 years, Kay Stambler, MEd, has worked on behalf of people with intellectual disabilities as a public guardian, an advocate for educational and community services, and an evaluator of services throughout the United States and Canada. She credits her daughter with teaching her life's possibilities and the obstacles that confront people throughout their lives. These obstacles include medical directions which, if implemented, would end the lives of individuals who are intellectually disabled.

Stanley Greenberg has been blind since birth. His love of music has grown since he began studying the piano at an early age. He received a PhD in music from the Eastman School of Music, and his first career was as a phonograph record producer, arranger, and executive. In later life, he became an executive in human services, serving as a staunch advocate for people with disabilities and their quest for complete inclusion in society. He has two living children and eight grandchildren.

The Campaign to Pass the Patient Choice at End of Life Bill in Vermont

Dick and Ginny Walters

In 2013, Vermont became the first state to pass a Death with Dignity (DWD) law through the legislative process. Oregon and Washington State passed the law by referendum, but Vermont does not allow binding referendum.

By 2002, the Oregon DWD Act had been legal for five years and was working well. With the model of the Oregon Act and our long-held strong belief in freedom of choice, we believed that we could enact similar legislation in Vermont. We were both 77 years old and had no idea that it would take 11 years to pass the bill and another two years to solidify it.

We were motivated to work for a DWD law because, like many others, we had relatives who had suffered. Dick's father, after a severe stroke, begged for help. Ginny's cousin, dying of cancer, pled, "Why is it taking so long?" Among our strong supporters were a brother and sister who mourned their sibling who, in desperation, had taken his own life with a gun.

Meeting in our living room, a small group formed a 501(c)(4) corporation. Our younger daughter, an attorney, drafted a Vermont bill following the pattern of the Oregon Death with Dignity Act. Our other daughter set up our Web site.

We mention this personal family involvement because as the issue moved forward in the legislature, opponents stated that Vermont was targeted by a national organization to pass this law. Knowing that Vermonters, who see themselves as independent thinkers, would not want to be directed by outsiders, we made sure that our organization maintained and displayed its clear Vermont roots.

To find sponsors in the legislature, Dick contacted representatives and senators who were likely to be in favor of right to die legislation. Early on, 39 representatives and a number of senators agreed to cosponsor the proposed DWD bill.

We did, of course, contact national organizations to make use of their experience. Both Death with Dignity National Center and Compassion & Choices helped us with advice, telephoning, funding, and—most valuable—Oregon people who flew in to testify in legislative committee hearings. Among them were a rabbi, the head of the state hospice organization, and a researcher from Oregon Health & Science University, who worked extensively on the statistics in Oregon.

From the beginning, our board of directors included professors and medical doctors. All were committed to our mission and stuck with it; we became a warm, closely knit group. For political experience, we were fortunate to connect with a lobbying firm with which we developed a close and lasting relationship. Their steadfast dedication, invaluable expertise, and guidance in strategic planning led to our success.

Shortly after our efforts became publicly known, a Vermont doctor who was a trustee of the Tennessee-based Christian Medical and Dental Association invited the president of that organization to help form a local organization to oppose our campaign. A disability organization, Right-to-Lifers, the hierarchy of the Catholic Church, and evangelicals formed a coalition. They continued to cite so-called abuses in Oregon, but none was ever substantiated.

However, individuals with disabilities testified in our favor in the legislature because people with disabilities, like everyone else, want to control their own medical decisions when diagnosed with a terminal illness. Polls, broken down by religious belief, showed that lay Catholics favor the legislation.

Throughout Vermont the proposed legislation gained attention and supporters because of letters to the editor and media accounts. Polls showed that Vermonters favored the bill by more than 2 to 1. (Zogby poll, 2003: 72% vs. 24%; Zogby poll, 2007: 81% vs. 14%; Zogby poll, 2011: 64% vs. 26% Results are heavily dependent upon wording of a poll.)

Some legislators, because of their personal beliefs, opposed the law; others were wary because some of their colleagues had failed to be reelected after voting for the recently passed civil union law. It took time and citizen action to educate representatives about freedom of choice at the end of life.

Some of our board members spoke at Rotary Club meetings, at gatherings at the homes of supporters, and at professional meetings of health care providers. We expanded our database by setting up DWD displays and collecting signatures at town meetings, which take place throughout Vermont every March. Among our thousands of supporters were activists who contacted legislators, wrote letters to the editor, and contributed to our campaign.

Eventually, we hired a small company to activate our database by organizing telephone trees, continually updating our Web site, posting on social media, using email and snail mail, and setting up TV ads.

Although the Vermont Medical Association testified that our bill was not needed, we developed a list of 200 supporting physicians. They understood that for the terminally ill patient, just knowing that it's legal to avoid a protracted painful dying process brings peace of mind.

By 2013 we had a governor who had long been an advocate for DWD. The speaker of the House, a strong and determined leader, also was eager to see our bill passed. To achieve a majority vote in the Senate, we needed two senators who forced a compromise: a "sunset" provision was added to the bill. It would allow most of the safeguards to disappear in 2016, thereby making physician aid in dying part of standard medical practice. Our concern was that weakening the required safeguards would make the law vulnerable to repeal.

In 2015, those two senators were no longer in the legislature. The revised bill, with the sunset clause removed, was submitted, approved, and finally signed on May 20, 2015, thereby solidifying Vermont's Act 39. The governor, the House speaker, legislators, and thousands of ordinary Vermonters came together to establish the Patient Choice at End of Life Act.

Richard (Dick) Walters, 1925–2015. Dick earned his bachelor's degree at Yale. After serving in the U.S. Navy, Dick had a successful career in retail merchandising. In retirement in Vermont, his persistence, his warm personality, and his leadership were critical in achieving the passage in the legislature of Act 39, patient choice at end of life. An ardent sailor, his days on Lake Champlain gave him the perspective to strategize the route toward that goal. Diagnosed with lung cancer in 2014, Dick continued to lead the organization until his last few weeks; he was grateful to be able to direct his own end of life under the law that wouldn't have been there without him.

Virginia (Ginny) Walters, PhD, graduated from Smith College and earned her graduate degrees in physics from Western Reserve University. She has taught physics and math at Cleveland State University, community colleges, Western Reserve Academy (a prep school)—in New York and Pittsburgh as well as in Ohio. Sophisticated in computer practice, Ginny was the behind-the-scenes powerhouse of Patient Choices—a Vermont organization of which her husband, Dick, was president.

Why Disability Rights Advocates Oppose Assisted Suicide

Diane Coleman

People are often surprised to learn that all of the major national disability rights groups that have taken a position on assisted suicide oppose legalizing it (Not Dead Yet 2016). This includes organizations like the American Association of People with Disabilities, National Council on Independent Living, Autistic Self Advocacy Network, United Spinal Association, the Disability Rights Education and Defense Fund, and others.

Why do these disability rights groups oppose assisted suicide bills that are marketed under the slogans of "self-determination" and "choice," values these groups otherwise strongly support? Simply put, because the dangers of mistake, coercion, and abuse posed to old, ill, and disabled people are too great. Those of us who live with serious disabilities have good reasons to be skeptical about the mantra of choice being used to sell assisted suicide as a new treatment option in our profit-driven health care system. Anyone could ask his or her doctor for assisted suicide, but the law gives the actual authority to doctors to make the choice about who is eligible and under what circumstances.

Doctors used to exercise near-total control over the lives of people with significant disabilities, discouraging parents from raising children with disabilities at home, sentencing us to institutions, and imposing their own ideas about what medical procedures would improve our lives.

Disability groups started paying attention to the problem of doctors making life and death determinations in the 1980s in high-profile court cases involving the right to refuse treatment. One involved Elizabeth Bouvia, a 26-year-old woman with cerebral palsy who had a miscarriage and marriage breakup and wanted a hospital to make her comfortable while she starved herself to death (Johnson 1997). Other cases involved men on ventilators stuck in nursing facilities, like Larry McAfee, who wanted the right to live in their own apartments or homes, or else "pull the plug" (Longmore 1997). The doctors, courts, media, and public all viewed these severely disabled individuals as the equivalent of terminally ill. They did not get suicide prevention efforts equal to those offered to nondisabled people, nor the right to live in real homes instead of facilities, but they were granted the "right to die." These cases were a wake-up call to disability advocates.

Then the 1990s brought Dr. Jack Kevorkian, conducting assisted suicides using lethal drugs, with two thirds of his body count being people who were not terminally ill (Roscoe et al. 2000). As before, the difference between being disabled and dying was not recognized or considered relevant. As before, the difficulties disabled individuals faced in living—access to public spaces, getting a job, getting married—were not considered, or worse, were accepted as rationales for ending their lives. Put simply, assisted suicide sets up a double standard, with suicide prevention for some and suicide assistance for others, depending on one's health and functional abilities. If such distinctions were based on race or ethnicity, we'd call it bigotry.

Two decades later, some might wonder if times have changed and awareness has increased. The 18 years of reports on medically assisted suicides from the Oregon Department of Health offer a clear and deeply concerning window into motivations behind hastened deaths. The top reasons doctors give for their patients' suicides are not pain or fear of future pain but psychological issues that are all too familiar to the disability community: feelings of "being a burden on others" (40%), "loss of autonomy" (91%), or "loss of dignity" (79%) (Oregon Public Health Division 2016).

We don't know if or to what extent the assisted-suicide-prescribing doctors knew about consumer-controlled personal care services, which could address these concerns. The Oregon law doesn't require doctors to report whether such concerns were addressed or whether home care was provided to improve the patient's quality of life. But disability advocates know that being in charge of one's home care makes a critical difference.

The median duration of the relationship between the patient and the doctor who prescribed lethal drugs in Oregon was only 12 weeks, some less than 1 week (Oregon Public Health Division 2016). This is not the public image of the doctor who treated a person through a long illness and turned to assisted suicide after all else failed. Proponents acknowledge that the majority of prescribing doctors met patients who were referred by assisted suicide organizations (Golden 2016). Those physicians begin the relationship with the assumption that some conditions are worse than death.

Real disability advocacy groups also worry about the increasing prevalence of abuse of functionally impaired elders, with federal authorities estimating that 1 in 10 elders is abused, mainly by family and caregivers (Lachs and Pillemer 2015). Against this backdrop, so-called safeguards in assisted suicide bills are hollow. An heir or abusive caregiver can suggest assisted suicide to an ill person, sign as witness to the request, and pick up the drugs. No independent witness is required at the death, and in half of the Oregon cases, no such independent witness was present. So how would anyone know if the lethal dose was self-administered? If the ill person equivocated or had a change of heart, how would we ever know that the lethal drug was given with full consent (Dore 2009)? Under current reporting requirements, there's no evidence of what happened at the end. Proponents of assisted suicide claim that there's no evidence of abuse, but the lack of depth in the government reports shouldn't be taken as proof that there's nothing to see. In fact, the problem cases that have come to light through mainstream media (Disability Rights Education and Defense Fund 2015) may be the tip of the iceberg.

Disability rights advocates have become a leading voice in the public policy debate over assisted suicide. The threats to people who are recently disabled by illness or injury are especially serious. As a society, we owe it to all old, ill, and disabled people to lead the resistance against laws that sanction doctor-assisted death. State lawmakers owe it to all of us to look behind the public relations images of assisted suicide and consider the dangers to the many who are not safe from mistake, coercion, and abuse.

References

Disability Rights Education and Defense Fund. 2015. "Some Oregon and Washington State Assisted Suicide Abuses and Complications." https://dredf.org/wp-content/uploads/2015/04/Revised-OR-WA-Abuses.pdf

Dore, Margaret. 2009. "'Death with Dignity': What Do We Advise Our Clients?" May 2009 Bar Bulletin, King County Bar Association. https://www.kcba.org/newsevents/barbulletin/BView.aspx?Month=05&Year=2009&AID=article5.htm

Golden, Marilyn. 2016. "Why Assisted Suicide Must Not Be Legalized." Section C.1. Doctor Shopping: All Roads Lead

to Rome. http://dredf.org/public-policy/assisted-suicide/
why-assisted-suicide-must-not-be-legalized/#doctor-shopping

Johnson, Mary. 1997. "Right to Life, Fight to Die: The
Elizabeth Bouvia Saga." *The Ragged Edge*, January/February.
http://www.raggededgemagazine.com/archive/bouvia.htm

Lachs, Mark S. and Karl A. Pillemer. 2015. "Elder Abuse."
New England Journal of Medicine, 373, 1947–1956. DOI:
10.1056/NEJMra1404688.

Longmore, Paul. 1997. Essay. *The Ragged Edge*, January/
February. http://www.raggededgemagazine.com/archive/
p13story.htm

Not Dead Yet. 2016. "Disability Groups Opposed
to Assisted Suicide Laws." http://notdeadyet.org/
disability-groups-opposed-to-assisted-suicide-laws

Oregon Public Health Division. 2016. "Oregon Death with
Dignity Act: 2015 Data Summary." https://public.health.
oregon.gov/ProviderPartnerResources/EvaluationResearch/
DeathwithDignityAct/Documents/year18.pdf

Roscoe, Lori A., L.J. Dragovic, and Donna Cohen.
2000. "Dr. Jack Kevorkian and Cases of Euthanasia in
Oakland County, Michigan, 1990–1998." *New England
Journal of Medicine*, 343, 1735–1736. DOI: 10.1056/
NEJM200012073432315.

*Diane Coleman is the founder, president, and CEO of Not Dead
Yet, a national disability rights group organized to give voice to
disability rights opposition to legalization of assisted suicide and
euthanasia in the United States. In addition to using traditional
advocacy strategies such as public testimony, friend of the court
briefs, and community education through various media, Not
Dead Yet uses direct action tactics like rallies and protests. Diane
has a law degree, has co-taught graduate courses in medical ethics
at the University of Illinois at Chicago, and uses a motorized wheelchair as well as breathing supports.*

The Canadian Journey to Medical Assistance in Dying

Sister Nuala Patricia Kenny

On February 6, 2015, the Supreme Court of Canada (SCC) unanimously struck down the Criminal Code prohibitions against physician-assisted death (PAD) for a competent adult who clearly consents and has a grievous and irremediable medical condition (including an illness, a disease, or a disability) that causes enduring suffering that is intolerable to the individual. In this rare situation of the legalization of assisted dying through judicial decision, the Court held that the prohibition on PAD violated the right to life, liberty, and security of the person as guaranteed by the Canadian Charter of Rights and Freedoms. The decision was breathtaking in its scope; included both physician-assisted suicide and euthanasia; was not restricted to terminal illness or dying; and failed to provide a clear definition of a grievous and irremediable medical condition.

The federal government was granted a stay of the decision for 1 year, later extended to 16 months, for the complex tasks of crafting federal and provincial legislation and professional regulation. After an inexplicable four-month delay, a Federal External Panel and a Provincial-Territorial Expert Advisory Group were established to provide recommendations to governments. Provincial medical regulatory bodies began to develop guidelines and policies. On April 14, 2016, the federal government tabled Bill C-14 on medical assistance in dying (MAID) in the Canadian Parliament, and on June 17, 2016, a week after the deadline and days before Parliament adjourned for summer recess, Bill C-14 was passed. MAID came into effect in Canada without a consistent national framework of regulation and monitoring amidst a patchwork of provincial and professional regulatory guidelines.

This reflection describes some of the contentious issues addressed during the tumultuous 16 months of discussion and debate regarding the legislation and regulation. My perspective on this history is shaped by my Christian faith and my formation as a physician ethicist educated in the morality of medicine and experience in end-of-life care. It reflects my opposition to PAD and my intense personal involvement at many levels during this time to minimize the harms of this practice, especially to the vulnerable, palliative end of life care and individual practitioner and institutional conscience.

While the time between the SCC decision and access to PAD is highlighted here, the legal history of the "right to die" movement in Canada is traced to a 1993 decision of the SCC in the case of Sue Rodriguez. In a 5–4 decision, the Court recognized that the prohibition on assisted suicide infringed on Rodriguez's rights but deemed it a "justifiable infringement" in large part because of concerns regarding protection of the vulnerable. There were repeated attempts at revising federal legislation between 1992 and 2010, but all failed. MAID returned to the courts in 2012, when the British Columbia Supreme Court ruled in favor of plaintiffs Gloria Taylor and Kay Carter (both with degenerative diseases) citing violations of the Canadian Charter of Rights and Freedoms in limiting their right to MAID. British Columbia successfully appealed the ruling, and it proceeded to the highest court in Canada.

Key Contentious Issues

Four overarching themes emerged in the discussions and debates. The first related to public support of MAID as a response to suffering in conflict with deep concerns from others about the medicalization of suffering in the absence of a promised national palliative care strategy. Second was the division between those for whom the SCC criteria were clear and directive and whose priority was optimizing access and those who believed in the role of legislation in interpreting and monitoring policy. Third was the intent to normalize MAID as a practice versus the concern for robust safeguards for a uniquely serious and irrevocable decision, such as the evaluation of the request by two practitioners and a mandatory period of reflection between the request and provision of MAID and strict reporting and monitoring. Finally, and most contentious, were deep divides over any restriction of MAID to terminal illness and dying.

Specific contentious issues related to the requirement of informed and voluntary consent by a competent adult, concern for the protection of the vulnerable, and protection of conscience.

Bill C-14 confined MAID to competent adults whose deaths are "reasonably foreseen" and defined an adult as 18 years of age. The eligibility of mature minors remains a source of deep division. The social and emotional complexity of the relationship between voluntariness and vulnerability, especially for those with psychiatric disorders, the homeless, the socially disadvantaged, and the dependent elderly, is an ongoing issue for many. The acceptability of advance directives for MAID, especially in an aging society with growing populations of dependent elderly and persons with dementia, is still under debate. These contentious issues are to be the subject of independent review in the next two years.

The SCC decision and Bill C-14 state clearly that no practitioner is required to participate in MAID. However, the notion of conscience is confused and contested. Protection of conscience has been misunderstood, not as central to moral agency, but as a conflict between the physician's private beliefs and rights and the patient's right to legally sanctioned medical interventions. The bill recognizes the desirability of a consistent approach to issues related to MAID but acknowledges the province's jurisdiction over health care. The confusion over the importance of conscience and duties of conscientious objectors and jurisdictional issues and the role of professional regulatory authorities have all contributed to highly inconsistent regulations across the country and great distress to many practitioners.

This journey has brought Canada far from its founding beliefs and has revealed challenges for religion in the pluralistic, secular public space where individual rights and choice dominate. Medical morality has been replaced by principle-based bioethics. Its prioritizing of respect for autonomy has paved the way for the consumer model of the physician-patient relationship embodied in the SCC decision where the doctor is a simply a provider of information and technical expertise and where practitioners provide the technical "fix" of MAID to spiritual and emotional suffering. Canada has journeyed far but challenges for care and the education of new practitioners to any meaningful notion of professionalism are profound.

Nuala Patricia Kenny, OC, MD, FRCP (C), was a Sister of Charity of Halifax in 1962. She received her MD from Dalhousie in 1972 and fellowship in the Royal College of Physician and Surgeons of Canada in pediatrics in 1975. In 1993, she completed a fellowship in ethics at the Kennedy Institute of Ethics at Georgetown University. After a distinguished career in pediatrics, she founded the Department of Bioethics of Dalhousie University Faculty of Medicine in 1995. From 2009 through 2015 she served as Ethics and Health Policy Advisor to the Catholic Health Alliance of Canada and is presently emeritus professor, Dalhousie University, Halifax, Nova Scotia.

Physician-Assisted Death as a Legally Available Last Resort Option

Timothy E. Quill

Why might a mainstream primary care or palliative care physician who is relatively well respected in both of these fields become involved in this "edgy" domain? Even if I was personally supportive of the option of a physician-assisted death, wouldn't it be safer and better for me professionally and perhaps for the fields to keep this discussion underground? In reflecting about these questions, I came up with four potential reasons I have continued to push for PAD to become openly available as a "last resort" option (Quill et al. 1997).

1. *I have cared for a wide range of seriously ill patients who have forced me to more forthrightly address these issues throughout my practice life.* I take care of many strong-willed, very ill patients and try to help them achieve the best possible medical treatments given their medical situations, the state of medical science, and their personal views and values. For most, when they develop a serious illness, the treatment plan starts with aggressive, state-of-the-science medical treatment alongside best possible evidence-based palliative care (Morrison and Meier 2004). This has been a "both/and" proposition for me from the beginning of my career, and now a growing amount of data supports that early inclusion of palliative care improves both quality and length of life (Temel et al. 2010). When disease-directed therapy becomes less effective and more burdensome over time, this dual approach usually moves toward a more pre-dominantly palliative approach as exemplified by hospice. Although the transition to hospice often involves consid-erable psychic suffering for both patient and family (and frequently clinicians, as they must accept the inherent limits of medicine in a very personal way) (Casarett and Quill 2007), nonetheless, once the move has been made, most patients are grateful and appreciative of what hospice has to offer (Lynn 2001). I wish that was always the end of the story, but, as a hospice, palliative care, and primary care clinician, I am painfully aware that inevitably there will be a few patients whose suffering becomes unaccept-able despite excellent hospice or palliative care toward the end of life, and a few of those patients request assistance in dying (Quill 1993). Although Diane was the first patient to explicitly request and receive aid in dying in my clinical practice (Quill 1991), I had helped many previous patients who were in similar predicaments to die using indirect

methods that society finds more acceptable (e.g., stopping life supports, sedation, and voluntarily stopping eating and drinking) (Quill et al. 1997). Whether these options are significantly morally different from aid in dying is a matter of considerable dispute (Foley and Hendin 2002; Quill and Battin 2002), but for patients who are dying badly, perhaps one of them might provide a needed escape from what is experienced by the patient as unacceptable suffering.

2. *I personally would want to have the option of PAD in the future if my condition becomes unacceptable to me.* I am an adamant believer in and proponent of palliative care and hospice, but I have seen enough suffering to know the limitations of these practices to relieve all major end-of-life suffering. For all I know, I may willingly cling to life in the ICU no matter how much suffering I experience as my death approaches, but more likely than not I anticipate that I will probably accept a timely transition to hospice and hopefully die peacefully receiving standard palliative treatments when my time comes. But being fairly control oriented, as are many physicians (and others), I would find it very reassuring to know that I could potentially achieve an escape to death at a time of my own choosing should my dying become too prolonged and too filled with suffering that was unacceptable to me. I would love to have a physician with expertise in palliative care and hospice guiding and partnering with me in this process, perhaps challenging my request for an assisted death if it emerges, but ultimately listening carefully to it and responding to the best of his or her ability (Quill 1993).

3. *The likelihood of abuse with more open, predictable availability of PAD in the United States is small and could be minimized by the requirement of safeguards including second opinions by experienced palliative care providers (Quill et al. 1992).* Over 30 years ago, we had a debate in the United States about whether patients on life supports should have the ability to voluntarily discontinue them

when death is inevitable or when the suffering associated with ongoing treatment was unacceptable. The reluctance stemmed from the fact that patients on life supports are among our most expensive, and there is potential for coercion within the process of cessation. However, such abuse has not occurred. In fact, the due diligence with which life supports are stopped in the United States could be a model for PAD. At our institution, such decisions are often accompanied by second opinions from palliative care, ethics, and psychiatry (if the patient's decision-making capacity and/or the presence of confounding depression are in question.) One can look at the medical record and see exactly what happened and why. Such assessment and documentation should become a standard model for all "last resort" options, including stopping life supports, palliative sedation (potentially to unconsciousness), voluntarily stopping eating and drinking, as well as PAD (Quill et al. 1992, 1997).

4. ***The method of assistance should be adapted to the circumstances and values of the patient and family but also needs to consider the values and expertise of the assisting physicians and other clinicians.*** As a palliative care clinician with an open mind to all of these options, I frequently find myself along with our palliative care team struggling with ways to appropriately respond to severe suffering that has become unacceptable to the patient. The patient's clinical circumstances frequently define the boundaries. Patients who lack capacity cannot have PAD (where otherwise permitted), and they cannot carry out voluntary cessation of food and fluids, but they can have proportionate sedation and cessation of life-prolonging treatments (Quill et al. 2000). Terminally ill patients with decision-making capacity who cannot swallow or cannot self-administer cannot initiate PAD even if they live in environments where the practice is legally acceptable, but they can stop all life-prolonging treatments, including food and fluids, and they can have proportionate sedation. Because I practice in New

York, where PAD is illegal, I would have to consider the potential consequences (to me and/or the patient's family) of secretly providing PAD or face the legal risks of telling the truth. On the other hand, I can legally offer the possibility of stopping eating and drinking as well as the other last resort options if they fit the patient's circumstances. If a clinician cannot provide a legally available option for which the patient potentially qualifies (living in Oregon but being personally morally opposed to PAD), the clinician should let the patient and family know of this limit in a timely way but also should be clear about ways in which he or she *can* respond (perhaps with some of the other "last resort" options). Over the past several years, I have supported several patients voluntarily stopping to eat and drink on our palliative care unit who clearly would have preferred a physician-assisted death were it legal (and I would have provided it under that circumstance), but they and their families were still appreciative that mutually acceptable options for an escape could be found.

I have received a lot of attention in this domain because I openly speak and write about my advocacy for legal access to PAD as one last resort option, but this is a small but important part of a much larger movement about which I am passionate, which includes advocacy for (1) universal access to basic health care for our entire population (including more open discussion of the boundaries of what treatments might and might not be included within that universal access); (2) universal access to palliative care for all seriously ill patients as part of the standard of care (mainly provided by better trained primary care and non-palliative care specialists with palliative care specialists available to help with the most challenging cases [Quill and Abernethy 2013]); and (3) open and predictable access to a wide range of last resort options, potentially including physician-assisted death, as small but important pieces of our commitment not to abandon those who continue to suffer unacceptably despite unrestrained efforts to palliate the suffering (Quill and Cassel 1995).

References

Casarett, D.J. and T.E. Quill. 2007. " 'I'm Not Ready for Hospice': Strategies for Timely and Effective Hospice Discussions." *Annals of Internal Medicine*, 146, 443–449.

Foley, K., and H. Hendin, editors. 2002. *The Case against Assisted Suicide: For the Right to End of Life Care.* Baltimore, MD: Johns Hopkins University Press.

Lynn, J. 2001. "Perspectives on Care at the Close of Life. Serving Patients Who May Die Soon and Their Families: The Role of Hospice and Other Services." *JAMA*, 285, 925–932.

Morrison, R.S. and D.E. Meier. 2004. "Clinical Practice. Palliative Care." *New England Journal of Medicine*, 350, 2582–2590.

Quill, T.E. 1991. "Death and Dignity. A Case of Individualized Decision Making." *New England Journal of Medicine*, 324, 691–694.

Quill, T.E. 1993. "Doctor, I Want to Die. Will You Help Me?" *JAMA*, 270, 870–873.

Quill, T.E. and A.P. Abernethy. 2013. "Generalist Plus Specialist Palliative Care—Creating a More Sustainable Model." *New England Journal of Medicine*, 368, 1173–1175.

Quill, T.E. and M. Battin, editors. 2002. *Physician-Assisted Dying: The Case for Palliative Care and Patient Choice.* Baltimore, MD: Johns Hopkins University Press.

Quill, T.E and C.K. Cassel. 1995. "Nonabandonment: A Central Obligation for Physicians." *Annals of Internal Medicine*, 122, 368–374.

Quill, T.E., C.K. Cassel, and D.E. Meier. 1992. "Care of the Hopelessly Ill. Proposed Clinical Criteria for Physician-Assisted Suicide." *New England Journal of Medicine*, 327, 1380–1384.

Quill, T.E., B.C. Lee, and S. Nunn. 2000. "Palliative Treatments of Last Resort: Choosing the Least Harmful Alternative. University of Pennsylvania Center for Bioethics Assisted Suicide Consensus Panel." *Annals of Internal Medicine*, 132, 488–493.

Quill, T.E., B. Lo, and D.W. Brock. 1997. "Palliative Options of Last Resort: A Comparison of Voluntarily Stopping Eating and Drinking, Terminal Sedation, Physician-Assisted Suicide, and Voluntary Active Euthanasia." *JAMA*, 278, 2099–2104.

Temel, J.S., J.A. Greer, A. Muzikansky, et al. 2010. "Early Palliative Care for Patients with Metastatic Non-Small-Cell Lung Cancer." *New England Journal of Medicine*, 363, 733–742.

Timothy E. Quill, MD, is the Thomas and Georgia Gosnell Distinguished Professor in Palliative Care at the University of Rochester Medical Center (URMC), where he is also professor of medicine, psychiatry, medical humanities, and nursing. He was the founding director of the URMC Palliative Care Division and a past president of the American Academy of Hospice and Palliative Medicine.

Dr. Quill has published and lectured widely about various aspects of the doctor-patient relationship, with special focus on end-of-life decision making, including delivering bad news, nonabandonment, discussing palliative care earlier, and exploring last resort options. He is the author of several books on end-of-life care and over 150 articles published in major medical journals. Dr. Quill was the lead physician plaintiff in the New York State legal case challenging the law prohibiting physician-assisted death that was heard in 1997 by the U.S. Supreme Court (Quill v. Vacco).

Death with Dignity, 2016

E. James Lieberman

In Oregon, medical aid in dying has been legal since 1998, when 24 terminally ill people received prescriptions to hasten death and 16 used them. The law is known as the Death with Dignity Act (DWDA). Last year in Oregon, most people who hastened death were elderly: 78 percent over age 65, with the median age being 73. Ninety percent died at home, usually in hospice care. With age and illness come disability, pain, and limited mobility.

The main reasons for hastening death are loss of autonomy and dignity and inability to enjoy life. Religious conservatives dismiss such motives; they believe that suffering is to be endured if it cannot be ameliorated and that unearned suffering is redemptive. In a country where religious freedom is a key value, this religious minority is remarkably powerful in limiting personal choice for all. Although in principle ecclesiastical doctrine cannot be imposed on Americans, such doctrines have major influence on policy and legislation. Unlike a number of countries that have much better health statistics than the United States, we limit effective birth control in health programs as well as aid in dying, in accord with conservative religious doctrine.

The term *assisted suicide* is misleading and prejudicial. Polling shows that a larger majority of respondents favor an Oregon-type law when questions refer to physician aid in dying and patient choice rather than assisted suicide. From the psychiatric/medical standpoint, DWDA patients and the typical suicide are very different.

- The DWDA patient is terminally ill and wants to live; the suicidal patient has no terminal illness but wants to die.

- Death with dignity is chosen, peaceful, and supported by loved ones; suicide brings shock and tragedy to families and friends.

- Death with dignity is openly planned; it only changes timing to a small degree but adds significant control in a socially approved way. By contrast, suicide is secretly planned, impulsive, or violent and wastes years of potentially good life.
- Death with dignity empowers vulnerable patients and their loved ones; suicide expresses despair and futility.

Our society observes and protects separation of church and state. Citizens have freedom of choice in religious matters. Religious and political groups may practice according to their values but not impose their objections to physician aid in dying on others.

In summary, the Death with Dignity Act is consistent with

1. the right of individuals to exercise choice in a free country,

2. ethical medical practice,

3. the integrity of the doctor-patient relationship, and

4. the role of state law in regulating medical practice.

E. James Lieberman, MD, has authored articles and books on public health and mental health, including Like It Is: A Teen Sex Guide *(with Karen Lieberman Troccoli, MPH). He was influenced by the post-Freudian approach to psychotherapy developed by Otto Rank, and wrote the definitive biography,* Acts of Will, *published also in French and German.*

Medical Futility, Then and Now

Barron H. Lerner

When an article promoting the idea of medical futility appeared in the *Annals of Internal Medicine* in 1990, my father was thrilled. He believed the term was an apt description of the end-stage cases he too often saw as an infectious diseases consultant, in which he was expected to prescribe progressively more complicated antibiotic regimens to severely ill patients with no hope of recovery.

The concept of medical futility has achieved mixed success. Advocates have promoted it as a way to discourage aggressive treatment of medical conditions that are not reversible. Critics—and in some instances the courts—have seen it as an unreasonable strategy that interferes with patients' rights.

A few years ago, while writing a book on my father's and my medical careers (Lerner 2014), I had the opportunity to revisit the concept of medical futility by reading journals that my father kept during his years in practice. His stories remind us of the types of cases that have pushed physicians to try to limit the use of questionable interventions at the end of life. My dad did so as an unabashed paternalist, something that is no longer acceptable. But we should embrace new strategies that seek to achieve this goal in an era of bioethics.

Between the mid-1950s and mid-1970s, when my father first studied and practiced medicine, doctors generally decided when severely ill patients died. They quietly withheld antibiotics, respirators, and, ultimately, cardiopulmonary resuscitation. In some instances, these decisions were secretly recorded in patients' charts.

Trained as a paternalist, my father was comfortable with this approach. But times were changing. By the late 1970s, the concepts of patient autonomy and informed consent, promoted by the new discipline of bioethics, were shifting control of medical decisions to patients. When patients were dying, resuscitation became the default option unless a patient or family member had signed a do-not-resuscitate form.

Although my dad liked aspects of bioethics, he believed that—in the case of dying patients—his hands were being tied. For example, one of his demented patients had both a feeding tube and a tracheostomy, a hole in his windpipe that was connected to a ventilator. Although the patient was "never going to get better or leave a hospital-type setting," my father wrote, "his family will not accept that reality and continues to pray for a miracle, which will not be forthcoming."

In another case, an elderly man hospitalized for six months after a hip fracture had experienced countless complications, including infection after infection. "My role in all of this," my father later ruefully noted, "was to juggle his antibiotics, risk severe toxicities from the multitude of drugs employed and constantly re-adjust and re-dose according to the circumstances."

In some instances, my father not only objected to aggressive interventions but actively sought to prevent them. For example, he had treated infections for years in a woman with a bone marrow disorder that eventually became leukemia. When she dramatically deteriorated with leukemic cells throughout her body, my dad decided not to treat a pneumonia she had developed. Infection, he liked to say, was the "final straw in the deterioration of so many of the body's vital organs and functions." The patient died.

Similarly, when a young man with end-stage AIDS developed what my father suspected was lymphoma in his spleen, which was causing unbearable pain, he prescribed morphine and did not raise the possibility of treating the cancer either with the patient or with his parents.

The most jarring case was one in which my father actually physically placed his body over a recently deceased patient to prevent his colleagues from performing resuscitation. She had "agonizing" pain and been hospitalized for months and bedbound for years. Resuscitation was inappropriate, he believed, although the patient's primary physician had not obtained a do-not-resuscitate order.

In one sense, these stories raise the exact concerns raised by critics of medical futility. My dad seemed to be judging for others what was an acceptable quality of life.

But he would have argued that he was using his clinical expertise—combined with what he had learned about his patients' values and preferences by spending time with them—to make the *correct* decisions. After all, he was in the hospital seven days a week, gave his sickest patients our home phone number, and even managed their cases when we were on vacation.

Thus, after years of keeping his extremely ill AIDS patient alive, my father believed the two of them had a "tacit understanding" about when it was time to let go. After preventing the resuscitation effort, my dad wrote that he had acted "in the name of common, ordinary humanity" and based on his "30+ years as a physician responsible for caring and relieving the pain of my patients who can't be cured."

Building on the lessons of the futility movement, modern health professionals are developing more sophisticated strategies for assessing if—and how—aggressive technologies should be offered to severely ill patients. For example, a 2012 article in the *Journal of the American Medical Association* (Blinderman et al. 2012) proposed a framework in which physicians could offer CPR as a plausible option, recommend against it or not offer it at all. Palliative care specialists are not only experts in the scientific value of potential interventions but have the time—as did my father—to get to know patients and families.

These are all positive developments. I suspect my dad, who died in 2012, would also have been pleased. By the end of his career, he was becoming increasingly uncomfortable invoking the paternalistic approach that he had once so devotedly practiced. Ultimately, what mattered most was doing the right thing for dying patients, not who was in charge.

References

Blinderman, Craig D., Eric L. Krakauer, and Mildred Z. Solomon. 2012. "Time to Revise the Approach to Determining Cardiopulmonary Resuscitation Status." *JAMA*, 307, 917–918.

Lerner, Barron H. 2014. *The Good Doctor: A Father, A Son and the Evolution of Medical Ethics*. Boston: Beacon Press.

Barron H. Lerner, MD, PhD, is a professor in the Departments of Medicine and Population Health at New York University Langone Medical Center. His book The Breast Cancer Wars: Hope, Fear and the Pursuit of a Cure in Twentieth-Century America, *published by Oxford University Press, received the William H. Welch*

Medal of the American Association for the History of Medicine and was named a most notable book by the American Library Association. Dr. Lerner's fifth book, The Good Doctor: A Father, a Son and the Evolution of Medical Ethics, *was published by Beacon Press in May 2014 and came out in paperback in May 2015. In addition to his research, Dr. Lerner practices general internal medicine and teaches medical ethics and the history of medicine to both undergraduates and medical students at New York University.*

Introduction

This chapter provides information about persons and groups that have participated in the discussions, debates, and clashes surrounding the right to die controversy. The individuals on both sides of the conflict noted here are philosophers, physicians, clergy, advocates for the disabled and other vulnerable persons, professors, and politicians. The organized groups reflect the wide array of interests—political, religious, medical, elderly, disabled, nursing— engaged in support of or in opposition to legitimatizing the right to die with physician assistance in America. In this conflict-laden issue, one of a number of controversial public policy issues, there are thousands of individuals and dozens of groups participating. This chapter tries to capture the essential diversity of the people and groups engaged in the right to die battles.

Individuals Supporting Death with Dignity Laws

Marcia Angell

Marcia Angell, MD, is senior lecturer at Harvard Medical School as well as a faculty associate in the Center for

Jane Cody of Franklin County, Vermont, speaks out against a Death with Dignity bill at the statehouse in Montpelier in February 2007. Vermont opponents of a Death with Dignity law worked for over a decade to persuade legislators to defeat the bill. However, it was finally passed in 2015. (AP Photo/Alden Pellett)

Bioethics. In med school, she trained in both internal medicine and anatomic pathology, but after her academic training ended, she became an advocate for change in the relationship between patient and physician, especially when the patient confronts death. Dr. Angel is an ardent defender of the right of a terminally ill patient to receive the highest level of care from physicians and hospital professionals. Dr. Angell writes frequently in professional journals (e.g., *The New England Journal of Medicine*) and the popular media (e.g., *New York Review of Books*) on a wide range of topics, particularly medical ethics, health policy, the nature of medical evidence, the interface of medicine and the law, and care at the end of life. She lectures frequently to public and professional audiences, makes many media appearances, and consults with government agencies and congressional committees on issues such as how government should deal with pharmaceutical overcharging, medicine, and the law, and what kind of care is best for a person at the end of life. In all her writings, talks, and presentations, she defends the right of a competent, terminally ill patient residing in one of the six states that have physician-assisted dying (PAD) to hasten death in accordance with the state law.

Margaret P. Battin

Philosopher and bioethicist Peggy Battin has worked for decades to defend the right of terminally ill individuals to have greater control over the timing and manner of their deaths. As professor of philosophy and bioethics at the University of Utah, Battin tackles issues around end-of-life care, suicide, euthanasia, and religion. She has written a number of books, some with Timothy Quill, and articles, on the ethics of the right to have a physician assist a dying patient to hasten death. In 2008, her personal and professional worlds collided when her husband Brooke, an English professor at the University of Utah, broke his neck in a bicycle accident, becoming quadriplegic. When he eventually decided to die after years of struggling with his condition, Battin found herself torn when he asked her to disconnect his ventilator and other life-prolonging technologies. Her personal experience made her reexamine her beliefs around an individual's right to autonomy, as he sought to achieve the death he believed "least worst" for him. Her personal experience with grief and dying has strengthened her support for a person's right to die with the aid of a physician.

Gerald Dworkin

Dr. Gerald Dworkin is an outspoken professor of philosophy at the University of California, Davis. Dworkin's main areas of research include the nature and justification of personal autonomy, paternalism in the criminal law, and the issue of which acts may legitimately be criminalized by the state. One of Dworkin's major books is a defense of physician-assisted suicide, *Euthanasia and Physician-Assisted Suicide: For and Against*. In it, he argues against the prevailing double standard applied when treating terminally ill patients: On the one hand, doctors who approve of withdrawing patients from life support at their request, or who approve of terminal sedation, are not subject to criminal indictment. However, physicians who assist a terminally ill patient to hasten death are condemned by the medical profession, damned by the Church, and indicted and prosecuted for violation of the "assisting suicide" state criminal statute. He has been a strong advocate for legalizing euthanasia and physician-assisted suicide.

Linda Ganzini

Dr. Ganzini is a public health medical practitioner who has practiced in Oregon for decades. She has been engaged in developing regulations and guidelines for the Oregon Death with Dignity Act (ODWDA) with the Oregon Health

Administration. Dr. Ganzini's research interests are centered in the areas of geriatric mental health, end-of-life-care issues, and improving palliative care for the terminally ill. Dr. Ganzini has published extensively in peer-reviewed journals, invited articles, book chapters, editorials, and commentaries on the topics of the ODWDA, physician aid in dying, assessing mental health in the terminally ill, and medical ethics among psychiatrists and health care providers. She is active in medical, geriatric, and other medical conferences, talking about medical ethics issues involving the care of terminally ill patients, underscoring the value of palliative care as well as the value of a final option for a suffering terminally ill patient: PAD.

Booth Gardner

Booth Gardner was a very popular two-term governor of Washington whose diagnosis with Parkinson's disease after he left office helped motivate him to lead a successful voter initiative to allow physician-assisted suicide. Gardner's condition did not qualify him to use the Washington Death with Dignity Act, which the state's voters approved in 2008. The law, modeled on one passed earlier in Oregon, allows terminally ill adults to obtain a doctor's prescription for a lethal dose of medication. Gardner knew that Parkinson's was not considered terminal under the law. "I wish we could do a more liberal law, but we're going to pattern it after the Oregon law because it passed," he said during the 2008 campaign. "We're not going to go farther than that now. My goal," he said then, "is to lessen the pain of dying." The measure passed with 58 percent of the vote. Gardner died on March 16, 2013, at his home in Tacoma due to complications of Parkinson's.

Stephen Hawking

Stephen Hawking is a brilliant physicist and mathematician and author of *A Brief History of Time*, which remains an international best seller. In 1963, Hawking contracted motor neuron disease (a type of ALS) and was given two years to live, yet he went on to Cambridge and became a brilliant researcher and professorial fellow there. Hawking is now regarded as one of the most brilliant theoretical physicists since Einstein. When he was diagnosed with his ailment, Hawking became a spokesman for severely disabled persons who wished to stay alive as long as possible. He became an arch opponent of all efforts to legalize physician-assisted suicide and euthanasia. Since the middle of the first decade of the 21st century, however, he has become a prominent advocate for the legalization of physician-assisted death in England.

Derek Humphry

Derek Humphry is a British-born American journalist, author, and principal—and quite outspoken—founder in 1980 of the Hemlock Society USA, the nation's first organization promoting physician-assisted death and voluntary euthanasia. Humphry zealously argues for the right of persons to choose to die on their own terms—with the passive (PAD) or active (euthanasia) assistance of a physician. He has served as President of the World Federation of Right to Die Societies. Both the Hemlock Society and the World Federation of the Right to Die Societies aggressively support the decriminalization of voluntary euthanasia and, as the initial step toward that goal, passage of PAD laws. He is the author of a dozen books about the value of euthanasia, including *Jean's Way* (about his wife's struggle with a terminal illness) and the best seller (for many years) *Final Exit*, laying out for readers the arguments for euthanasia and the ways it can be achieved.

Jack Kevorkian

A practicing doctor (pathologist) in Michigan, in 1990 Jack Kevorkian became a worldwide notorious figure who assisted people in ending their lives. He quickly became known as "Dr. Death" and for nearly a decade he advertised in newspapers his willingness to help people end their lives. He did not determine whether the person requesting assistance was terminal, was mentally competent (or not), or was in physical or emotional pain. He merely provided a service to literal strangers who heard of him and asked him to help them end their lives. Between 1990 and 1997, he assisted more than 130 persons to end their lives. After years of conflict with the Michigan criminal justice system over the legality of his actions, Kevorkian was tried for euthanizing an ALS patient who could not operate the "death" machine Kevorkian had made and installed in his somewhat battered Volkswagen bus. (All prior deaths were instances where the person was able to start the death machine without Kevorkian's active assistance.) Convicted of second-degree murder of the ALS patient in 1999, he spent eight years in prison. Kevorkian's actions spurred national and international debate on the ethics of passive physician aid in dying, euthanasia, and hospice care. He died in Royal Oak, Michigan, on June 3, 2011.

Barbara Coombs Lee

Barbara Coombs Lee is the president of Compassion & Choices, one of the two major national organizations dedicated to expanding and protecting the rights of the terminally ill through actions in state and federal courts as well as extensive lobbying activities on behalf of state right to die groups. She practiced as a nurse and physician assistant for 25 years before beginning a career in law and health policy. Since then she has devoted her professional life to individual choice and empowerment in health care. As a private attorney, as counsel to the Oregon State Senate, as a managed-care executive, and finally as chief petitioner for the ODWDA litigation in federal courts between 1997 and 2006, she championed initiatives that enabled individuals to consider a full range of choices and be full participants in their health care decisions. Under Coombs Lee's leadership since 1996, the end-of-life choice movement has achieved many milestones. In 2008, Coombs Lee was a senior advisor for the Washington State Death with Dignity ballot initiative that voters approved by an 18-point margin, which led to Washington becoming the second state to legalize aid in dying. In 2009, the Montana Supreme Court ruled, in the landmark case brought by Compassion & Choices (*Baxter v. Montana*), that it is not against the state's public policy for a physician to provide aid in dying to a mentally competent, terminally ill adult. In 2013, her organization's decade of work with Patient Choices Vermont led to the passage of the Vermont PAD legislation. She is a tireless advocate for legislation or judicial decisions that legitimatize a terminally ill person's right to seek the assistance of a doctor to hasten death. Her work with Brittany Maynard in California in 2014 as well as her organization's support of PAD legislation in California culminated in that state becoming, in 2016, the fifth state to allow PAD.

Barron H. Lerner

Barron H. Lerner is a professor of medicine in the Divisions of General Medicine and the Medical Humanities at New York University's Langone Medical Center. He has been involved in the medical futility movement since the 1990s and has written important books (*The Breast Cancer Wars*) as well as professional journal articles discussing the importance of a physician changing from curing a dying patient to caring for the person. He views the medical profession's zealous pursuit of keeping a patient alive using the latest medical devices, drugs, and other experiments as medically futile, ethically wrong, and lacking any genuine concern for the suffering patient. In addition to his research, Dr. Lerner practices general internal medicine and teaches medical ethics and the history of medicine.

Brittany Maynard

Brittany Lauren Maynard was born on November 19, 1984, in Anaheim, California. In 2014, Maynard, when only 29 years old, was diagnosed with an inoperable brain tumor. In short order, with the help of Compassion & Choices, she became the public face for the death with dignity movement in the

United States. Because California had not yet passed a physician-assisted death bill, she and her husband moved to Oregon in order to use the ODWDA. She ended her life on November 1, 2014, at her home in Portland, Oregon. Her cause of death was recorded, in accordance with the Oregon death with dignity law, as a brain tumor.

Philip Nitschke

Philip Nitschke is, like Derek Humphry and Jack Kevorkian, an aggressive zealot for the legalization of voluntary euthanasia. He is the Founder of Exit International, a worldwide advocacy group working to decriminalize euthanasia and the use of "assisting a suicide" criminal statutes to prevent physician-assisted death from taking place. In 1996, Nitschke became the first doctor in the world to administer a legal, lethal injection (voluntary euthanasia) under the short-lived Rights of the Terminally Ill Act of 1995. Four of Nitschke's terminally ill patients used this law to have him end their suffering before the law was overturned in March 1997 by the Australian Parliament. The same year, Nitschke retired from medical practice to found the Voluntary Euthanasia Research Foundation (now called Exit International). Despite not practicing as a doctor for well over a decade, his medical registration was suspended by the Australian Medical Board in July 2014. The Northern Territory Supreme Court in July 2015 found the board's decision to be unlawful, and Dr. Nitschke's right to be registered as a medical practitioner in Australia was immediately restored. He continues to write and speak out about the importance of and the liberty of dying patients to choose euthanasia and physician-assisted death in America, New Zealand, Australia, and Europe.

Timothy E. Quill

Timothy E. Quill is a professor of medicine, psychiatry, and medical humanities at the University of Rochester School of

Medicine and Dentistry. He is also the director of the Center for Ethics, Humanities, and Palliative Care and a board-certified palliative care consultant in Rochester, New York. Quill has been at the forefront of the right to die movement in America since the late 1980s, with his seminal article about how his conversations over many years with a leukemia patient led to his providing her with a prescription for a fatal dosage of medicine. After the article appeared in *The New England Journal of Medicine*, he was indicted (but not convicted) for violating the New York State "assisting a suicide" law. Since then, Dr. Quill has published and lectured widely about various aspects of the doctor-patient relationship, with special focus on end-of-life decision making, including delivering bad news, nonabandonment, discussing palliative care earlier, and exploring last-resort options (including physician assistance in dying in those states that allow such counsel and action) with his patients. He is the author of many books on end-of-life situations and has published numerous articles in major medical journals. One of his coauthors on a few of these books is Peggy Battin, a philosophy and medical ethics professor at the University of Utah. In the mid-1990s, Dr. Quill was the lead physician plaintiff in the New York State legal case challenging the law punishing those convicted of "assisting a suicide." The U.S. Supreme Court, in 1997, heard the case (*Quill v. Vacco*) along with a case from Washington State (*Washington State v. Glucksberg*). In two 9–0 opinions, the Court, in opinions written by Chief Justice William Rehnquist, upheld the legality of "assisting a suicide" criminal laws. Dr. Quill continues to work for more extensive, nationwide palliative care and hospice systems; these substantive changes in how society cares for the elderly have come a long way since the first palliative care facility and hospice program became reality in the 1970s. Quill points out that less than half of the chronically and terminally ill patients participate in either program. Beyond that, Quill believes, is the last available option for those terminally ill patients who still are in pain and suffering: PAD.

Eli D. Stutsman

Eli Stutsman is a practicing attorney in Portland, Oregon, and secretary on the Board of Directors of the Death with Dignity National Center, a major right to die organization. Stutsman cofounded Oregon Right to Die in 1993, the political action committee that passed the ODWDA into law. He was the founding president of the Oregon Death with Dignity Legal Defense and Education Center in 1995, which later merged with the Death with Dignity National Center, as well as the Oregon Death with Dignity Political Action Fund, founded in 2001. He was the lead author of the ODWDA in 1993 and served as the lead political and legal strategist during the 1994 campaign to pass the law and again during the 1997 campaign to defeat its repeal by the state legislature. Stutsman successfully defended the death with dignity law in the first federal court challenge, *Lee v. Oregon*, spanning 1994–1997. He later prevailed against the U.S. Attorney General and the Drug Enforcement Administration in a second round of federal court litigation, *Oregon v. Ashcroft* and *Gonzales v. Oregon*, spanning 2001–2006, in which he won an injunction against the U.S. attorney general on behalf of a physician and a pharmacist, both threatened with criminal sanctions. On January 17, 2006, the U.S. Supreme Court ruled 6–3 in favor of the physician, pharmacist, and the state of Oregon.

In 2007, Stutsman authored the Washington Death with Dignity Act, passed into law by Washington voters on November 4, 2008. He was a key participant in the drafting of the Vermont PAD legislation (passed in 2013) and assisted in the decades-long effort by PAD advocates in California until a bill was passed in 2015. He continues to serve as a vital legal and political consultant in efforts by PAD supporters in other states to draft—and pass—death with dignity legislation.

Katheryn L. Tucker

Tucker is director of Legal Affairs for Compassion & Choices, the national public interest organization dedicated to improving end-of-life care and expanding and protecting the rights of the terminally ill. She served as lead counsel representing patients and physicians in two landmark 1997 U.S. Supreme Court cases (*Vacco* and *Washington*), "asserting that mentally competent terminally ill patients have a constitutional right to choose aid in dying." The cases brought much needed attention to improving care of the dying and to convince the Supreme Court to acknowledge the federal constitutional right to aggressive pain management. Between 1997 and 2006, joined by co-counsel Eli D. Stutsman, Tucker also successfully defended the ODWDA from attacks from the federal legislature and the U.S. Department of Justice, culminating in the 2006 U.S. Supreme Court decision *Oregon v. Gonzales*, in which the justices, by a vote of 6–3, concluded that the Drug Enforcement Administration unconstitutionally expanded the scope of the 1970 CSA in order to prohibit Oregon physicians from prescribing "controlled substances" to terminally ill patients. Tucker continues to address critics of the right to die in law review articles, conferences, and other outreach ways.

Dick and Ginny Walters

Inspired by passage of the ODWDA, Dick and Ginny Walters wanted the same peace of mind, choice, and control for people in their home state of Vermont. They founded the advocacy organization Patient Choices Vermont in 2002. With the help of Eli Stutsman, they translated the Oregon law into Vermont language and started calling political leaders in the legislature. After getting 30 or 35 to sign off on the idea, they began the back-breaking work of educating Vermont citizens, legislators, and others about the value of PAD. After years of diligence and persistence—and nearly a decade of legislative defeats—they succeeded in helping to pass the Patient Choice and Control at the End of Life bill in 2013. For their superlative advocacy, Compassion & Choices honored Dick and Ginny with the 2015 Hugh B. Gallagher award, which is given annually to activists who have been the most effective in communicating—especially to those of diverse age, race, religion, ethnicity, sexual orientation, or physical abilities—the importance of better health care and expanded choice at the end of life. Vermont Governor Peter Shumlin commended their tireless work to pass Vermont's aid-in-dying law in a proclamation on June 4, 2015. Dick Walters used the Vermont Patient Choice and Control at End of Life Act to die peacefully on October 16, 2015.

Samuel D. Williams

The modern debate about physician-assisted death and voluntary euthanasia can be traced to 1870, when Samuel D. Williams (a school teacher and member of a local philosophy club) argued for voluntary euthanasia in a speech at the Birmingham Speculative Club in England. He advocated the use of newly created analgesic drugs (ether, chloroform, and, especially, morphine) not only to alleviate terminal pain but to intentionally end a patient's life. His speech initiated euthanasia and assisted suicide debates when it was subsequently published in *Popular Science Monthly* in 1873. In this seminal essay, Williams was the first person in the modern era to advocate for voluntary euthanasia for workers who were grievously injured while working in dangerous professions (mining, railroads, etc.). Arguing that mercy killing and assisted suicide should be allowed for those who are "hopelessly suffering," Williams stated that

> in all cases it should be the duty of the medical attendant, whenever so desired by the patient, to administer chloroform, or any other such anesthetics as may by and by supersede chloroform, so as to destroy consciousness at once, and put the sufferer at once to a quick and painless death; precautions being adopted to prevent any possible abuse of such duty; and means being taken to establish beyond any possibility of doubt or question, that the remedy was applied at the express wish of the patient. (Williams 1873)

It was a sensational argument for euthanasia, one that became the trigger for the emergence of voluntary euthanasia defenders in nations across the globe over the next half century. Williams's euthanasia proposal quickly received serious attention in the medical journals and at scientific meetings in England, America, and Europe. Still, most physicians held to the belief that pain medication could be administered *only* to alleviate pain, not to hasten death. Shortly after his essay appeared, the American Medical Association, in its journal *JAMA*, vigorously attacked his euthanasia proposal as an attempt to turn the doctor into an executioner. This animosity between the professional medical community (doctors, nurses, hospital administrators, and others) and supporters of euthanasia and PAD has continued into the 21st century.

Individuals Opposed to Death with Dignity Laws

John Ashcroft

U.S. attorney general John Ashcroft was one of the most powerful members of President George W. Bush's cabinet. Ashcroft had served as a state attorney general, Missouri governor, and U.S. senator prior to being nominated for U.S. attorney general on December 22, 2000. Ashcroft's nomination ran into major opposition in the Senate over his extremely conservative religious and political beliefs, including his opposition to abortion and his actions from the late 1980s as governor of Missouri to prevent voters from passing a PAD law. Ashcroft was confirmed, but the 42 votes against him in the Senate was the largest number ever cast against a U.S. attorney general's confirmation.

Following the contentious confirmation, Ashcroft vowed to renew the war on drugs, reduce violence due to firearms, find a way to delegitimize the abortion business, and combat discrimination. His conservative social views made him a controversial figure in the Bush administration. Despite his long-time support for "state's rights" while a state official, he brought federal action against Oregon's law allowing assisted suicide and against California's law allowing medicinal use of marijuana.

After filing a petition in the U.S. Supreme Court, *Ashcroft v. Oregon* (2005), that defended the right of a federal administrative agency to prosecute a physician dispensing a controlled substance to a dying patient because PAD was not a legitimate medical protocol, Ashcroft resigned his position. The case was eventually decided by the Supreme Court as *Gonzales v. Oregon* (now named after Ashcroft's successor, Alberto Gonzales).

Sissela Bok

One of the best-known ethicists in the United States, Professor Sissela Bok (author of *Lying: Moral Choice in Public and Private*) has argued that the legalization of euthanasia and physician-assisted suicide entails grave risks and does not address the needs, especially palliative and comfort care, of those at the end of their lives. This tragic reality for most terminally ill persons is most pronounced in nations without universal health insurance available to all. While she believes that a competent, terminally ill patient has a right to determine his or her fate and can, therefore, order doctors to withdraw (or withhold) all medical devices that sustain life, Bok categorically rejects PAD and euthanasia. Her continuing objection to euthanasia and PAD legislation is clearly enunciated in her coauthored 1998 book *Euthanasia and Physician-Assisted Suicide (For and Against)*.

Diane Coleman

Diane Coleman is a person with neuromuscular disabilities who has used a motorized wheelchair since the age of 11. Since then, she has been an outspoken advocate for quality health care for the disabled, including writing articles and books and coauthoring petitions to state and federal courts. She has also become, alongside religious and medical professionals, a fierce opponent of physician-assisted death and voluntary euthanasia. Coleman is the president and CEO of Not Dead Yet (NDY), a national disability rights group which she founded in 1996 to give voice to disability rights opposition to legalization of assisted suicide and euthanasia. Prior to that, she served for 3 years as director of advocacy at the Center for Disability Rights in Rochester, New York, and 12 years as executive director of Progress Center for Independent Living in Forest Park, Illinois. Coleman has presented invited testimony four times before Subcommittees of the U.S. House of Representatives and Senate. She is a well-known writer and speaker on assisted suicide and euthanasia and has appeared on national television news broadcasts for CNN, ABC, CBS, MSNBC, and others, as well as National Public Radio. She continues to coauthor amicus briefs filed in the U.S. Supreme Court and various state courts on behalf of disabled persons for NDY and other national disability organizations on the topics of assisted suicide and surrogate health care decision making.

Ezekiel J. Emanuel

Dr. Ezekiel J. Emanuel is Vice Provost for Global Initiatives and chair of the Department of Medical Ethics and Health Policy at the University of Pennsylvania. From January 2009 to January 2011, he served as special advisor for health policy to the director of the White House Office of Management and Budget. From 1997 to 2011, he was chair of the Department of Bioethics at the Clinical Center of the National Institutes of Health and a breast oncologist. Dr. Emanuel received his MD from Harvard Medical School and his PhD in political philosophy from Harvard University.

Dr. Emanuel has written and edited 9 books and over 200 scientific articles. The central focus of his writing is the pressing need for health care reform, the key innovations in the Affordable Care Act (Obamacare), and how they are likely to impact the actual delivery of quality health care. Paralleling his commitment to improving the health care system by making delivery of medical services more efficient to all, he also supports the continuing expansion of quality palliative care and hospice personnel for all patients. He speaks and writes about the need to (1) revamp the medical school curriculum to provide doctors with the skills necessary to have genuine, honest one-on-one conversations with their patients and (2) strengthen palliative care as a sub-specialty that is attractive to first-year medical students. Dr. Emanuel is a vigorous opponent of all efforts to legalize physician-assisted death and euthanasia.

Atul Gawande

Dr. Gawande is an author of four best-selling books: *Complications, A Memoir of Surgery*; *Better: A Surgeon's Notes on Performance*; *The Checklist Manifesto*; and *Being Mortal: Medicine and What Matters in the End.* He is also a surgeon at Brigham and Women's Hospital in Boston, a staff writer for *The New Yorker*, and a professor at the Harvard Medical School and the Harvard School of Public Health. He is a leading figure in the ongoing effort to improve the quality of the interactions between physician and patient, especially so with regard to end-of-life conversations. In his writing and speaking about the critical importance of the doctor-elderly patient relationship in this time of modern medicine wedded to once-unimaginable technological innovations, he focuses on a difficult moral and medical issue that has become an intimate part of the right to die issue for conscientious doctors and their dying patients: "when should we try to fix and when should we not?" Like other doctors who have confronted this existential reality with their patients, Gawande believes in the enormous role that palliative care and hospice perform in enabling their patient to die without pain and in relative comfort. Unlike Dr. Quill, who supports PAD as a last option when palliative care does not ease the chronic pain and suffering, Gawande has not become a PAD advocate. However, his writing about how one should approach death is extraordinarily beautiful; any person interested in exploring the parameters of the right to die—regardless of the person's predisposition—will do well to read Gawande's ethical-medical philosophy of death and dying.

Jyl Gentzler

Jyl Gentzler is a professor of philosophy at Amherst College. Her focus in teaching and research has been to apply ancient philosophers' theories to contemporary political, medical, ethical, and philosophical thinking regarding the meaning of the good life and how we die. Her major writings grapple with the philosophical meaning of the term "dignity," as in the phrase employed by supporters of PAD legislation: "death with dignity." She argues that all such theoretical appeals to the right to die in order to validate PAD are defective. Her writings then focus on how Aristotle's understanding of "dignity," that is, how patients, their physicians, and other professionals working in palliative health care programs, working together, can help the patient to find the ingredients to achieve the best possible life. Her research and teaching is an excellent example of the association of philosophy, ethics, and compassionate health care to find dignity in living.

Herbert Hendin

Herbert Hendin, MD, is the founder and medical director of Suicide Prevention Initiatives and the American Foundation for Suicide Prevention. He is professor of psychiatry and behavioral science at the New York Medical College. His research and his practice have centered on suicide and suicide prevention. He has been the lead researcher on studies of suicide among college students, substance abusers, African Americans, and veterans (especially the relationship between veterans with PTSD and suicide) since medical school. He also spent a number of summers in Scandinavian countries studying the high levels of suicide there. On these trips, he visited the Netherlands, at the time the only nation that had passed physician-assisted-suicide laws. (In 2002, the parliament passed its present version: the "Termination of Life on Request and Assisted Suicide [Review Procedures] Act.") His research there led him to dramatically change his views about PAD. He saw—and has written about since then—how the nation's written protections for vulnerable elderly persons against abuse and coercion were easily bypassed by physicians. For Hendin, this was the real-time, not theoretical, slippery slope of physician-assisted suicide. He has called what he experienced in the Netherlands the practice of involuntary euthanasia.

Since the mid-1960s, he has written 10 books and more than 100 scholarly articles, books, and op-ed pieces critical of PAD and euthanasia. Among his published books are *Seduced by Death*, *The Dutch Experience*, *The Dutch Cure*, *PAS in Oregon*, and *The Case against Suicide*. He has testified before congressional committees in opposition to both physician-assisted suicide and euthanasia. In his 1996 congressional testimony, he raised another issue brought on by the Dutch experience with euthanasia: "pressure for improved palliative care appears to have evaporated" in the Netherlands because of assisted suicide and euthanasia (Hendin 1996). Although in his nineties, Hendin continues his opposition to PAD and his advocacy for enhanced palliative care and hospice for patients in serious, chronic pain.

Sister Nuala Kenny

Dr. Kenny was born in New York and entered the Sisters of Charity of Halifax, Canada, in 1962. She received her BA from Mount Saint Vincent University in 1967 and an MD from Dalhousie University in 1972. After an extensive career in pediatrics and medical education, Dr. Kenny founded the Department of Bioethics at Dalhousie University in 1996. She is currently a professor in the Departments of Bioethics and Pediatrics at Dalhousie. She was a founding member of the National Council for Bioethics in Human Research. She is a past president of both the Canadian Pediatric Society and the Canadian Bioethics Society. Her research interests include professional character formation, ethics in health policy and public health, pediatric ethics, and end-of-life care. Combining her faith in the Catholic Church's doctrine of the sanctity of life with her medical efforts, as physician and bioethicist, to save lives, Sister Kenny has been an active advocate, participating in conferences and writing articles in newspapers and other media outlets, against all efforts in Canada to pass legislation that allows physicians to assist in the death of their dying patients. Sister Kenny's efforts to block changes in Canada's laws regarding PAD failed when, in 2015, the Supreme Court of Canada ruled that the Canadian constitution and Charter of Rights permit PAD and voluntary euthanasia. In 2016, the Canadian parliament passed the necessary legislation to codify the decision of the Supreme Court of Canada.

Vicki D. Lachman

Vicki D. Lachman is a nursing executive with degrees in psychiatric nursing and health care organization and management. Dr. Lachman did graduate work and received a degree in bioethics—with an emphasis on ethical issues at the end of life—in 2002. Since 2008, Dr. Lachman has served on the American Nurses Association Center for Ethics and Human Rights Advisory Board. She also serves on an ethics committee and writes the quarterly Ethics, Policy and Law column in *The MedSurg Nursing Journal*. Until 2013, she was a clinical professor in graduate nursing programs teaching bioethics.

She has authored over 100 publications and a number of books in her nursing career. The majority of Dr. Lachman's research and publications deal with bioethics issues such as quality care for terminally ill patients, physician-assisted death, and euthanasia. She disdains the current defense of euthanasia and PAD using personal liberty and autonomy. It takes the "moral courage" of a medical professional to insist on the expansion of quality palliative care and hospice rather than supporting the methodology of killing oneself. There must appear such committed doctors and nurses to figure out how health care organizations can more effectively use their facilities to ensure quality care for all ill and dying patients under their care—and assisting suicide is not the appropriate way.

Joanne Lynn

Dr. Lynn is the director, Altarum Center for Elder Care and Advanced Illness, Altarum Institute. She is a geriatrician, hospice and long-term-care physician, health services researcher, quality improvement advisor, policy analyst, and policy advocate who has focused on ensuring that every American can live comfortably and meaningfully despite serious illness and disability in the last years of life, at a sustainable cost to the community.

She has been a senior researcher at RAND and a tenured professor of medicine and community health at Dartmouth Medical School and the George Washington University. Her work includes development of prognostic indices and uniform assessment tools, quality measurement, professional and public education, end-of-life care, and quality improvement in providing quality health care for elderly patients.

Dr. Lynn has published more than 250 professional articles, and her dozen books include *The Handbook for Mortals* (awarded the American Medical Writer's Association award for best medical book for the public); *The Common Sense Guide to Improving Palliative Care* (an instruction manual for clinicians and managers seeking to improve quality care for their patients); and *Sick to Death and Not Going to Take It Any More!* (an action guide for policy makers and advocates that addresses how palliative care programs can become a major research and practice field in the future—and how medical schools can improve palliative care education and training).

Robert D. Orr

Dr. Orr is co-chair of the Healthcare Ethics Council and a senior fellow with the Center for Bioethics & Human Dignity (CBHD). A growing interest and involvement in medical ethics led him to pursue a postdoctoral fellowship at the Center for Clinical Medical Ethics at the University of Chicago (1989–1990). In his role as a Christian medical bioethicist, professor of family medicine, advisor, political leader, and strategist for the CBHD in planning and implementing strategies to block passage of a Vermont death with dignity bill, Dr. Orr has long been a leading opponent of the concept of personal autonomy and physician-assisted suicide and euthanasia.

He has authored, coauthored, or edited 6 books and contributed 14 book chapters and over 150 articles related to clinical ethics and the ethics consultation process, with a major focus on his opposition to any form of PAD, including opposition to aggressive physician involvement in the killing of terminally ill patients. He has given lectures on these topics regionally, nationally, and internationally. He chaired the Council on Ethical Affairs for the California Medical Association and was vice president of the American Society for Bioethics and the Humanities. He has served on the Ethics Commission of the Christian Medical and Dental Associations and served as chairman of that commission from 1991 to 1994. For more than a decade, Dr. Orr led the PAD opposition forces in Vermont. Through his leadership, and with the help of conservative Republican governor James Douglas, the opposition succeeded in blocking or defeating PAD proposals until a new governor (who had supported PAD legislation while he was in the state Senate), Democrat Peter E. Shumlin, took office in 2010. After the bill was finally passed in 2013, Orr continues to lead in the opposition's efforts to overturn the legislation.

Frank A. Pavone

Father Frank Pavone has been active in the pro-life movement since 1976. He was ordained a priest of the Archdiocese of New York by Cardinal John O'Connor in 1988. He served for five years as a parish priest in Staten Island and taught theology at St. Joseph's Seminary and other institutions. In 1993, with the permission of Cardinal O'Connor, he became national director of Priests for Life. In this full-time position, he has traveled to all of the 50 states and to 5 continents, preaching and teaching against abortion and helping other priests to do the same. He conducts seminars on pro-life strategy and is regularly invited to speak at national and international pro-life gatherings. Father Pavone is often quoted in papers such at *The New York Times, The Washington Times,* and other national media. Under his guidance, the Priests for Life staff has grown to 45 fulltime paid employees.

Father Pavone was asked by Mother Teresa to address the clergy of India on end-of-life issues. He was also asked to speak to the pro-life caucus of the United States House of Representatives. Norma McCorvey, the "Jane Roe" of the Supreme Court's abortion decision *Roe v. Wade,* called Father Pavone "the catalyst that brought me into the Catholic Church." In 1997, he was asked by the Vatican to help coordinate pro-life activities throughout the world as an official of the Pontifical Council for the Family. In 1999, *The Daily Catholic* named Father Pavone among the Top 100 Catholics of the Century. He serves as a consultant on Dr. James Dobson's conservative organization, Focus on the Family Institute. He is the recipient, for the year 2001, of the Proudly Pro-Life Award of the National Right to Life Committee. In 2002, in recognition of his pro-life work, he was awarded an honorary doctorate from the Franciscan University of Steubenville. In 2003, Father Pavone was elected to be the president of the National Pro-Life Religious Council, a coalition of groups from many different denominations working to end abortion.

Pope Pius XII, Pope John Paul II, and Pope Francis

These three contemporary leaders of the world's Roman Catholics provide examples of the Catholic Church's hallmark belief in the sanctity of life and the immorality of abortion, the death penalty, euthanasia, and physician-assisted suicide. Pope Pius's 1957 address to anesthesiologists about the differences between ordinary and extraordinary efforts to prolong a patient's life; John Paul's 2004 address to a conference of medical professionals about how they must care for patients in a permanent vegetative state; and Francis's 2014 address to the Association of Italian Catholic Doctors about the malevolence of physician-assisted suicide after Brittany Maynard took her life clearly reflect the position of the Catholic Church about a person's right to die.

William H. Rehnquist

A conservative member of the Nixon administration, Rehnquist was appointed Associate Justice of the Supreme Court by President Richard M. Nixon in 1972; he was elevated to chief justice in 1986 by President Ronald Reagan. His 33-year tenure (1972–2005) on the court was one of the longest and most influential in the institution's history. He was a conservative dissenter on the Supreme Court from 1972 (dissenting in *Roe v. Wade*, 1973) until the early 1980s when President Reagan appointed conservatives to replace the moderate justices who left the Court. As chief justice, Rehnquist presided over a rightward move at the court as the leader of a five-justice conservative majority. Rehnquist's judicial philosophy rested on a number of principles: conflicts between the individual and the government should be resolved in favor of government; conflicts between state and federal authority should be resolved in favor of the states; and there had to be constraints on the excessive exercise of federal jurisdiction, especially the general tendency of the Warren Court majority to use their judgment to broaden the scope of the individual's right to privacy. Chief among the restraints on Court actions was the concept of "originalism," which limited the judiciary's interpretation of the Constitution to the meaning of the original 18th-century textual meaning. As chief justice in 1997, using originalism as the core concept, he wrote the majority opinions in the two major "assisting suicide" cases (*Vacco v. Quill* and *Washington v. Glucksberg*). Both opinions upheld the right of a state to punish anyone who "assisted a suicide."

The essence of his self-restraint is found in his comment written in a 1976 *University of Texas Law Review* article: "There is no conceivable way in which I can logically demonstrate to you that the judgments of my conscience are superior to the judgments of your conscience, and vice versa. Many of us necessarily feel strongly and deeply about our own moral judgments, but they remain only personal moral judgments until in some way given the sanction of law" (Rehnquist 1976).

He wrote opinions in almost every area of the law. Among his most important opinions were those that set limits on the meaning of the Constitution's due process guarantee, declining to expand the boundaries of due process in a way that would create new rights or encroach on state power. He was one of two dissenters in 1972 when the Court majority found that "liberty" in the Constitution could be broadened to include a woman's right to an abortion (*Roe v. Wade*, 1972). As chief justice he sought to narrow *Roe*'s impact and consistently rejected the notion that the right to die is guaranteed by the Fourteenth Amendment. See, for example, his majority opinions in *Cruzan* (1990), *Vacco* (1997), and *Glucksberg* (1997).

In *Glucksberg*, he reflected on his view of courts in our society: "Attitudes towards suicide have changed but our laws have consistently condemned, and continue to prohibit, assisting suicide. Despite changes in medical technology and notwithstanding the increased emphasis on the importance of end-of-life decision making, we have not retreated from this prohibition." However, given his commitment to federalism and states' rights, he concluded his 1997 opinion with this paean: "Throughout the Nation, Americans are engaged in an earnest and profound debate about the morality, legality, and practicality of physician-assisted suicide. Our holding permits this debate to continue, as it should in a democratic society." Rehnquist died in 2005.

Cicely Saunders

Dame Cicely Mary Strode Saunders was a British nurse, physician, and humanitarian. Saunders became a Red Cross war nurse in 1944 and served as a medical social worker. Her interest in palliative care and pain control developed early. From 1945, working in hospice care as a volunteer nurse, she was involved with the end-of-life quality care of patients with terminal illness. Research work in pharmacology inspired her idea to administer low, steady doses of pain relievers to terminally ill patients to keep them alert and comfortable (now called palliative sedation). She saw what was needed, particularly better pain control, and started planning a specialized hospice in the late 1950s. Having been told that she would never get such ideas accepted in medicine unless she became a doctor, Saunders qualified as a doctor at St. Thomas' Medical School in 1957. She began fundraising for a hospice in 1963 while she was working at St. Joseph's and by 1965 she had enough to start building St. Christopher's Hospice, which opened in 1967. Saunders planned that St. Christopher's would be the first research and teaching hospice linking expert pain and symptom control, compassionate care, and teaching and clinical research, pioneering the field of palliative care. She is universally recognized as the founder of the modern hospice movement and received many honors and awards for her work. In 1987, her work contributed also to the decision by The Royal College of Physicians to recognize palliative care as a new medical specialty.

Believing that her patients were entitled to a meaningful life and to death with dignity, Saunders developed a holistic approach to their care that she hoped would also meet their emotional and spiritual needs. Among the many honors Saunders received was the Conrad N. Hilton Humanitarian Prize, awarded to St. Christopher's Hospice in 2001. Saunders was made a Dame of the British Empire in 1980 and was awarded the Order of Merit by Queen Elizabeth II in 1989. Saunders died on July 14, 2005, at St. Christopher's Hospice.

Antonin Scalia

Justice Antonin Scalia has been called the most influential justice of the last quarter century. He sat on the Supreme Court for 30 years (1986–2016). He was a champion of the conservative bloc on the Court and employed a concept that has since become synonymous with Scalia—originalism. It is the theory of constitutional interpretation that seeks to apply the understanding of the words used by those who drafted and ratified the Constitution. Judges must be tethered to the original understanding of the document and cannot run at will to find new meanings to the words and phrases in the 1787 Constitution.

Scalia eschewed the view—held by a number of his colleagues—that the Constitution is an evolving document. For Scalia, the Constitution did not say anything about the right to die; it was not a fundamental right. Caustically, Scalia said in remarks in Philadelphia in 2004: "We have now determined that liberties exist under the federal Constitution—the right to abortion, the right to homosexual sodomy—which were so little rooted in the traditions of the American people that they were criminal for 200 years" (Liptak 2004).

In his concurring opinion in the 1990 *Cruzan* case, the initial venture of the Supreme Court into the right to die controversy, he expressed his originalist views, his values, and his concern about Justices "roaming at will" in the Constitution to find new rights: "The various opinions in this case [six] portray quite clearly the difficult, indeed agonizing questions that are presented by the constantly increasing power of science to keep the human body alive for longer than any reasonable person would want to inhabit it. . . . The answers to these heartbreaking questions are neither set forth in the Constitution nor known to the nine Justices of this Court any better than they are known to nine people picked at random from the Kansas City telephone directory."

"This [right to die] is lovely philosophy," Justice Scalia said in 1997 during oral arguments for *Vacco* and *Washington*. "Where is it in the Constitution?"

Scalia died in 2016.

Joni E. Tada

Joni Eareckson Tada has lived in a wheelchair as a quadriplegic for over 40 years due to a diving accident in 1967 when she was 17. Though she suffered from deep depression and lost the will to live in the aftermath of her accident, she gradually came back to a deeper relationship with God. Because of her early struggles, she has become strong in her faith and is a testimony to the world of how when we are weak, how God is strong. Following rehabilitation, when she spent long months learning how to paint with a brush between her teeth, Tada wrote of her experiences in her international best-selling biography *Joni*, and also reenacted the events in the full-length feature film with the same title.

In 1979, she established the international nonprofit organization Joni and Friends; she continues to serve as Founder and CEO. The organization offers programs to support people affected by disability around the globe through 30 years of radio outreach and a new television series; by refurbishing and delivering thousands of wheelchairs to needy families in developing countries through the Wheels for the World program; by supporting special needs families through Family Retreats; by providing a global network of disability support through Joni and Friends offices and international charter support organizations, including NGOs on every continent; and by publishing over 40 books covering topics ranging from disability outreach to the purpose for suffering.

Florence S. Wald

Florence Wald is the creator of the hospice movement in the United States. Wald envisioned the need to enhance the quality of life for the terminally ill. Following a trip to England in the late 1960s to meet with Dame Cicely Saunders (the two women became lifelong colleagues and friends) and assess the care delivered at St. Christopher's Hospice near London, Wald returned to Yale and implemented a feasibility study to determine the need for hospice in Connecticut. Since that time, her groundbreaking work with the dying through hospice care has influenced the further development of hospice—and palliative care—throughout the nation.

She received a master's degree in nursing from Yale University School of Nursing in 1941 and began her nursing career as a staff nurse with the New York Visiting Nurse Service. She joined a surgical metabolism research team as a research assistant and taught nursing at the Rutgers University School of Nursing.

By 1969, Wald was a professor and dean at Yale, and from 1970 to 1980 served as clinical associate professor. At the same time, she was a member of the board and an integral part of the planning staff of Hospice Incorporated in Branford, Connecticut, the future location of the first hospice in the United States. Recognizing that the terminally ill have unique needs, Wald developed, with continuing discussions with her British colleague Dame Cicely Saunders, a hospice model that provides holistic and humanistic care for the dying person and requires appropriate understanding of the concepts of death and dying among nurses giving care in the hospice environment. Wald's more recent work includes bringing the hospice model of compassion and dignity in death to the Connecticut Correctional Facilities. Since its implementation, hundreds of inmate volunteers have been trained to be hospice volunteers within state correctional facilities. She has published widely in medical journals and earned many distinctions, including a Founders Award from the National Hospice Association, a Distinguished Woman of Connecticut Award from the governor of Connecticut, a fellowship in the American Academy of Nursing, and three honorary doctoral degrees. Further, the Connecticut Nurses Association established the Florence S. Wald Award for Outstanding Contributions to Nursing Practice in her honor. She died in 2008.

Organizations Supporting Death with Dignity Laws

American Medical Students Association

The American Medical Student Association (AMSA), with a half-century history of medical student activism, is the oldest and largest independent association of physicians-in-training in the United States. Today, the AMSA is a student-governed, national organization committed to representing the concerns of physicians-in-training. AMSA members are medical students, premedical students, interns, residents, and practicing physicians. Founded in 1950, the AMSA continues its commitment to improving medical training and the nation's health. From the beginning of the right to die issue, the AMSA has supported the call for state legislation to allow physicians to provide passive assistance to their terminally ill patients who request such aid.

American Medical Women's Association

The American Medical Women's Association (AMWA) is the oldest multispecialty medical organization dedicated to advancing women in medicine and improving women's health. It is an organization of women physicians, medical students, and other persons dedicated to serving as the unique voice for women's health and the advancement of women in medicine. The organization was founded by Dr. Bertha Van Hoosen in 1915 in Chicago, at a time when women physicians were an under-represented minority. The AMWA has been an advocate for legitimizing the right to die with a physician's assistance.

American Pharmacists Association

The American Pharmacists Association (APhA), the oldest and largest national professional society of pharmacists in the United States, was established in 1852.

Although the APhA "discourages pharmacist participation in [state mandated] executions on the basis that such activities are fundamentally contrary to the role of pharmacists as providers of health care," it believes that pharmacists should assist in implementing PAD. The California End-of-Life Options PAD bill, signed by the governor in 2015, contains specific language that notes the symbiotic relationship between the patient, the doctors, and the pharmacists.

American Psychological Association

The APA was founded in July 1892 at Clark University by a small group of around 30 men; by 1916 there were over 300 members. During World War II, the APA merged with other psychological organizations, resulting in a new divisional structure. Nineteen divisions were approved in 1944; the divisions with the most members were the clinical and personnel (now counseling) divisions. From 1960 to 2007, the number of divisions expanded to 54. Today the APA is affiliated with 60 state, territorial, and Canadian provincial associations. It has, from the beginning of the political and medical battles over PAD, been a supporter of changing a state's criminal code to legitimize PAD by removing all "assisting suicide" statutes from the law.

American Public Health Association

The American Public Health Association (APHA) works with key decision makers to shape public policy to address today's ongoing public health concerns. The organization advocates policies that relate to the improvement of health care for all persons living in America. They have supported the need for congressional action to, for example, improve health care for the elderly and disabled and to expand quality palliative and hospice care in all medical facilities. From the 1970s to date, the APHA has supported legislation passed by state legislatures that legitimatizes physician assistance in dying for terminally ill patients who are suffering grievously from their chronic illness. In a major policy statement announced in 1981, entitled "Patient Rights to Self-Determination at End of Life," the APHA supported PAD laws that allowed terminally ill patients to seek assistance in dying from their physicians if no other options available (sedating, palliative care, hospice) will relieve their pain and suffering. As part of its support work for PAD, in 1997, the APHA filed amicus curiae briefs in *Vacco* and *Washington State* on behalf of terminally ill patients and their physicians who challenged state laws prohibiting PAD. In their briefs, the APHA lawyers argued that there are fundamental differences between "suicide" and "assisted death." PAD is one of a few options terminally ill patients select when dealing with the unremitting pain they experience. Do I die in great pain and suffering or do I die with dignity with the assistance of a physician? This is the only binary option available; the APHA policy asserts that only a patient at that crossroad can determine how he or she will die.

Compassion & Choices

Compassion & Choices is a major nonprofit organization in the United States working to improve patient rights and individual choice at the end of life, including access to medical aid in dying. Its primary function is advocating for and ensuring access to end-of-life options, including physician assistance in dying. With over 65,000 supporters and campaigns in nine states, it is the largest organization of its kind in the United States. Compassion & Choices provides end-of-life consultation for dying patients and their families at no cost. Professional consultants and trained volunteers work by phone or in person to offer assistance in completing advance directives, make referrals to local services including hospice and illness-specific support groups, advice on adequate pain and symptom management, and provide information on safe, effective, and legal methods for aid in dying. Through litigation, Compassion & Choices protects terminally ill patients' rights to receive pain and symptom management, to voluntarily stop life-sustaining treatments, to request and receive palliative sedation, and to choose aid in dying under state and federal constitutional protections. Attorneys for the organization regularly participate in litigating patient cases related to ensuring adequate end-of-life care and choice, including representing 16 terminally ill patient-plaintiffs at the U.S. Supreme Court in *Gonzales v. Oregon* and defeating the Bush administration's challenge to Oregon's Death with Dignity Act in January 2006. It has been engaged in arguing for patient rights to die on their own terms in every case brought to state and federal courts.

Compassion in Dying Federation

Formed in 1993 around the time Oregon voters were getting ready to vote on the ODWDA, the Compassion in Dying Federation began providing national leadership for client services, legal advocacy, political lobbying, and public education to improve pain and symptom management, increase patient empowerment and self-determination, and expand end-of-life choices to include aid in dying for terminally ill, mentally competent adults. They labor, in courthouses and legislative bodies, to improve care and expand options for patients facing end-of-life choices. The organization is committed to the goals of comprehensive, effective comfort care for every dying person and legal and humane aid in dying if suffering is unbearable and cannot be relieved.

Death with Dignity National Center

The Death with Dignity National Center provides advocacy experts and political strategists to assist state PAD providers with end-of-life-care policy reform that will lead to passage of Oregon-type Death with Dignity laws.

For example, in California during the many years prior to the 2015 signing of right to die legislation, DWD experts reviewed and revised every version and amendment of the bill; provided expert guidance from the experience of passing and implementing similar laws in Oregon, Washington, and Vermont; and coached sponsors and witnesses through hearings and meetings. The Death with Dignity National Center partners with local pressure groups, PAD advocates, and ad hoc citizens groups to plot out strategies and tactics to move bills through the political process.

Final Exit Network

Final Exit Network is a national nonprofit organization serving members throughout the country in all 50 states. It publicly offers education (by providing brochure, articles, and guides) and support to its members who are faced with chronic, severe pain.

Gray Panthers

Founded in 1970, the Gray Panthers is a national organization dedicated to social justice for all. However, the Gray Panthers is best known for its work on behalf of older persons. It has lobbied and litigated against age discrimination in the areas of retirement, housing, and health care. The organization has over 70,000 members in 85 chapters nationwide. Although the organization is strongest at the grassroots level, its relatively small seven-member national staff has effected significant changes in federal law. The Gray Panthers developed a broad political agenda. Among its goals were affordable housing, the creation of a national health system, nursing home reform, and consumer protection. The Gray Panthers, very early in the right to die debates and political and legal actions surrounding the issue, was a vocal supporter of the terminally ill person's right to die with a doctor's assistance. The organization participated in the very first ballot initiative vote on permitting euthanasia in Washington State in 1991. (The initiative was defeated, 54%–46%.)) However, the Gray Panthers has been one of the consistent supporters of PAD since then, including its support of the 2008 vote in Washington State (which passed this time).

Hemlock Society

The Hemlock Society USA is a national right to die organization founded in 1980 in Santa Monica by author and euthanasia activist Derek Humphry. Its primary missions include

providing information to dying persons and supporting legislation permitting physician-assisted dying. In 2003 the national
organization renamed itself to End of Life Choices, and a year
later merged with another group into a newly formed national
organization called Compassion & Choices.

Lambda Legal Defense and Educational Fund

The Lambda Legal Defense and Educational Fund (LLDEF)
was founded in 1973 as the nation's first legal organization dedicated to achieving full legal and political equality for lesbian
and gay people. When founder Bill Thom filed an application
in early 1972 to establish the LLDEF, he borrowed from the
bylaws of another newly established organization—the Puerto
Rican Legal Defense and Education Fund. Both organizations
follow in the path of the original Legal Defense and Education
Fund organization: the NAACP-LDEF.

Although the right to physician-assisted suicide is not as
immediate an issue as securing the right to affordable and
decent health care for people living with HIV, the right to
determine when meaningful life ends is a fundamental aspect
of personal autonomy and self-empowerment. On behalf of
the plaintiffs, the LLDEF's lawyers coauthored two amicus
curiae briefs, in *Vacco* and *Washington State* (1997). They have
continued to provide legal counsel in litigation brought on due
to the opposition to proposed PAD legislation. For the LLDEF,
assisting PAD groups supports the organization's fundamental belief in the historical importance of personal autonomy in
decision-making for individuals with disabilities such as AIDS.
That right, unambiguously, must apply to all significant life
decisions, including the most intimate and personal decision
of all, whether to hasten death if one's condition becomes terminal. Like so many other groups supporting PAD legislation
and the right of personal autonomy, the LLDEF rejects the use
of the term *suicide* to define physician assistance in dying. The
competent, terminally ill patient does not choose between life
and death, which are the choices a suicidal person confronts.

For the dying patient, LLDEF briefs insist, the only real choices remaining are intolerable suffering or getting physician assistance to hasten death.

Organizations Opposed to Death with Dignity Laws

American Academy of Hospice and Palliative Medicine

Since 1988, the American Academy of Hospice and Palliative Medicine (AAHPM) has dedicated itself to expanding access of patients and families to high-quality palliative care and advancing the discipline of hospice and palliative medicine through professional education and training, development of a specialist workforce, support for clinical practice standards, research, and public policy. Membership is available to physicians specializing in hospice and palliative medicine, nurses, and other health care providers, including trained volunteers, who are committed to improving the quality of life of patients and families facing serious illness. The primary function of the AAHPM is to provide assistance of all varieties for seriously ill or dying patients. It has, as a matter of policy (2007), taken a position of "studied neutrality" on the controversial issue of PAD. While the organization understands the arguments for PAD, the medical response to intolerable pain should be innovative palliative care or palliative sedation.

American Association of People with Disabilities

Since 1996, the American Association of People with Disabilities's (AAPD's) primary tasks have been to ensure that the provisions of the 1990 Americans with Disabilities Act (ADA) are implemented in a timely manner and to "unite the diverse community of people with disabilities." Paul Herne, a severely disabled student at Hofstra University in the late 1960s, was a major figure in the creation of the AAPD and was one of the key people responsible for the drafting of the ADA in the late 1980s. It was signed into law by President Bush on July 26, 1990, and provides the disabled population (more than 50 million in America) with protections against discrimination similar to the safeguards found in the 1964 Civil Rights Act. The need for access by the disabled to high-quality, comprehensive, affordable health care and the improvement of community-based supports and services for the disabled are the fundamental goals of the AAPD. The AAPD, like all other disability rights advocacy groups, opposes the legalization of assisted suicide. Although the AAPD supports the concept of patient self-determination and believes that disabled persons must be allowed to make decisions regarding all medical issues surrounding their lives, patient autonomy must not extend to the disabled person receiving physician assistance to hasten death. The AAPD's explanation for its opposition to PAD reflects the fear that all groups representing the disabled share: physician error in diagnosis, poor information provided to the disabled and their families, and coercion and abuse, preventing severely disabled persons from making reasonable and informed judgments about hastening death. To that end, the AAPD has joined with nearly one dozen other organizations representing the disabled community in filing amicus curiae briefs with the federal courts of appeals and the U.S. Supreme Court opposing all efforts to legalize PAD.

American Geriatrics Society

The American Geriatrics Society (AGS) is an organization of nearly 6,000 health professionals committed to improving the health, independence, and quality of life of all older people. The society provides leadership to health care professionals, policy makers, and the public by implementing and advocating for programs in patient care, research, professional and public education, and public policy. With regard to the care of the elderly who are gravely or terminally ill, the AGS has counseled these persons (and their families) about the many benefits of entering a quality palliative care facility. It has been a major supporter of policies that enhance and expand the availability of palliative care and hospice in America. At the same time, the

AGS has opposed—by filing amicus curiae briefs, by partici- pating in lobbying against PAD proposals introduced into the state legislature, and through publishing articles in its journal, *The Journal of the American Geriatrics Society*—PAD and eutha- nasia. The AGS's opposition to physician-assisted suicide and euthanasia rests on its concern that these processes could be abused in order to cut expensive medical costs by ending lives earlier. The AGS also fears that, because PAD is available to terminally ill patients, some caregivers would abuse them and coerce the elderly into choosing assisted suicide, particularly if the caregiver will benefit from the person's death. The organi- zation believes that changing the critically important relation- ship between doctor and patient from curing to comforting will destroy the trust necessary between them. The AGS has allied its actions with other opponents of PAD, including the American Medical Association (AMA), advocates for the dis- abled, and palliative care advocacy groups.

American Medical Association

The AMA, founded in 1847, is the largest association of physi- cians and medical students in the United States. The AMA's stated mission is to promote the art and science of medicine for the betterment of the public health, to advance the inter- ests of physicians and their patients, to promote public health, and to lobby for legislation favorable to physicians and patients as well as lobby against physician-assisted suicide. The asso- ciation publishes *The Journal of the American Medical Associa- tion*, which has the largest circulation of any weekly medical journal in the world. From the very start of the movement to allow physicians to euthanize severely injured patients, 1870, the AMA has been one of the major private groups fighting to prevent states from passing laws allowing PAD and eutha- nasia. Using its political clout, the AMA has lobbied exten- sively against such laws, in courts, in state legislatures, and in the Congress. While the AMA's leadership is always alert to any attempted legislation enabling government to intrude into the profession's domain by defining or modifying the essential norms of medical profession, it has no problem working with legislators, governors, judges, and bureaucrats to maintain the political, legal, and medical status quo.

American Nurses Association

The American Nurses Association (ANA) is the largest professional organization representing the interests of the nation's nearly three million registered nurses (RNs). Joining the AMA and other medical professional groups opposed to PAD and euthanasia, the ANA—through lobbying, joining PAD opposition briefs in courts, and publishing in *The Journal of Issues in Nursing*—has been very critical of all efforts to legalize PAD and euthanasia. As is the case with other medical professional organizations opposed to PAD, the ANA strongly supports initiatives and legislation that enhances and supports quality palliative care and hospice programs.

Autistic Self-Advocacy Network

The Autistic Self-Advocacy Network represents autistic patients. Formed in 2006, it has been an active advocate in state legislatures for additional research and support to aid their clients. Like other disabled rights organizations, the Autistic Self-Advocacy Network has joined a consortium that fights to achieve two broad goals: (1) improving the quality of care for the disabled in the grossly inequitable American health care system, and (2) defeating all attempts to legalize euthanasia and physician-assisted death. One basic strategy of the Autistic Self-Advocacy Network is to join other disability rights organizations in filing amicus curiae briefs opposing PAD. It has been lobbying the courts since its formation a decade ago. Its latest action using this tactic was a brief filed in a New York appeals court case, *Myers v. Schneiderman*, which supported the dismissal by a lower court of a lawsuit seeking to legitimize PAD through the state judiciary. The core of the legal argument reflects the greatest fear of the Autistic Self-Advocacy Network (and all other disability rights advocacy organizations): instead of improving the lives of people with disabilities and illnesses, euthanasia and physician-assisted suicide laws "solve" these problems by "advising" by ending their lives.

Disability Rights Education and Defense Fund, Inc.

The Disability Rights Education and Defense Fund (DREDF), founded in 1979, follows the organizational structure of the oldest civil rights organization in American history: the NAACP-LDF. The DREDF is a leading national civil rights law and policy center directed by individuals with disabilities and parents who have children with disabilities. Its primary mission is to advance the civil rights of people with disabilities through legal advocacy, training, education, and public policy and legislative proposals on behalf of the disabled. The primary activity of this group occurs in state and federal legislatures and in litigation that protects and improves the lives of the disabled community. A major litigation issue that consumes the DREDF lawyers are cases that address the educational dis-advantages disabled children face in trying to get a high-quality education: it has won litigation that has established the right of disabled children to be educated alongside non-disabled students in regular classes as well as legal victories that redressed unfair and abusive treatment of disabled students attending "integrated" schools.

Since the 1990s the DREDF, along with most of the other disability rights organizations, has vigorously opposed the legalization of assisted suicide and euthanasia, based on their ongoing battles with the health care system's unfairness, bias, and prejudice against the disabled. Through political participation in hearings before legislative committees discussing PAD proposals, educating the disabled about the problems they may face if PAD was law, co-filing amicus curiae briefs in state and federal courts, writing articles for and letters to powerful public policy leaders against PAD and euthanasia, the DREDF has consistently fought against PAD becoming public policy. While not disparaging the concept of personal autonomy (which is vital for the disabled person in order to continue the battle for quality health care), the organization's opposition to PAD is based on the medical community's manipulation of the idea of personal autonomy to encourage a disabled person to use PAD. The organization believes that the public policy would be cruelly implemented because of the many inequities already existing for the disabled, the poor, the elderly, and minorities in America's inequitable and discriminatory market and profit-driven health care system. For the disabled, who have already been adversely effected by health care system's slippery slope, the specter of physician-assisted suicide is readymade for sliding into coercion and then euthanasia.

National Disability Rights Network

The National Disability Rights Network (NDRN), created in 1982, is the umbrella organization for all federally mandated Protection and Advocacy Systems and Client Assistance Programs for individuals with disabilities operating in all 50 states. This network is the largest provider of legally based advocacy services to people with disabilities in the United States. The programs provide training and technical assistance, legal support, and legislative advocacy to assure that people with disabilities are afforded equality of opportunity and are able to fully participate by exercising choice and self-determination. The NDRN's primary task is advocating—in Congress, state legislatures, and state and federal courts—for equal access and accommodation for the disabled in education, in medical treatment, in health care, and in the workplace. The right to die has been an issue that concerns the leadership of the NDRN. While very sympathetic to the dilemma of the disabled person suffering painfully from a terminal illness who wishes to choose death, it fears that that person may be coerced by caretakers into using PAD or that the enormous financial expense of continuing with health care will lead that person to assisted suicide. Some state programs have addressed PAD and have taken steps to oppose PAD because of the vulnerability of many disabled people who may well be coerced into ending their lives. However, as of 2016, the national organization hasn't announced a policy on assisted suicide and euthanasia. The lack of a national policy is an acknowledgement that state protection and advocacy groups are not aligned on how to address PAD. For some, in the pantheon of issues facing disabled people, the right to die is not an issue that, at this time, should replace more fundamental challenges facing the disabled.

National Hospice and Palliative Care Organization

Formed in 1978, the primary mission of the National Hospice and Palliative Care Organization (NHPCO) is to provide quality end-of-life care to patients, families, and communities—accompanied by strong opposition to physician-assisted suicide. For many hospices, that mission extends to influencing public policy and practice. In 2005, the NHPCO formally rejected physician-assisted suicide as an option for terminally ill patients to employ in order to deal with their chronic pain and suffering.

National Spinal Cord Injury Association

Founded in 1946, the National Spinal Cord Injury Association (NSCIA) is a national medical organization that provides active-lifestyle information, peer support and advocacy, and training, information, and resources for individuals with spinal cord injuries, their family members, and professionals. The NSCIA, like most other groups representing people with disabilities, has vigorously opposed PAD and euthanasia as a remedy for terminally ill patients. Perhaps the most significant problem facing opponents of PAD is the tragic association between assisted suicide and America's profit-driven managed health care. Again and again, actuaries and accountants have replaced the physician in making health care decisions. The health maintenance organizations and managed care bureaucracies have overruled physicians' treatment decisions for their severely disabled patients, leading some to turn to PAD. (The cost of the lethal medication generally used for assisted suicide is about $35 to $50, far cheaper than the cost of treatment for most long-term medical conditions.) The incentive to save money by denying treatment already poses a significant danger. This danger would increase exponentially if physician-assisted suicide is available as an end-of-life alternative. The position of the NSCIA is unambiguous: no one should go through a catastrophic event that severely injures the spinal cord permanently paralyzing the person (the great majority of victims are young and male; motorcycle accidents account for 40% of spinal cord injuries) without support from medical, rehab, and psychological professionals and others trained to help the patient move to the next life step.

The NSCIA's goal is to provide a community of these professionals that will surround the disabled person with compassionate care and love, addressing the profound depression the patient feels by showing the patient that life with such an injury is worth living. No one should feel compelled to resort to assisted suicide as a solution. Such a solution is an indictment of the health care and social support systems in America's states and in the national health care facilities. In addition to opposing PAD in legislative committees and debating PAD supporters in public meetings, the NSCIA has been one of a number of disability rights organizations to coauthor briefs opposing PAD and file the in the U.S. Supreme Court, including participation in the two major cases the Court heard in 1997 (*Vacco* and *Washington State*).

Not Dead Yet

Not Dead Yet (NDY) is a national, grassroots disability rights group, formed in 1996, that opposes legalization of assisted suicide and euthanasia as the deadliest form of discrimination against old, ill, and disabled people. NDY helps organize and articulate opposition—in political, legal, and judicial settings—to all efforts to legalize PAD and euthanasia. In a short period of time, NDY has become the most vocal and aggressive advocate protecting the rights of all disabled people to insure that they receive the best health care possible and to block attempts by PAD to legalize the right to die across the nation.

Operation Rescue

In 1988, Operation Rescue was founded to fight against abortion rights protected by the U.S. Supreme Court since 1973 (*Roe v. Wade*). From the beginning, the group has served two purposes: demonstrating obedience to God's will and preventing abortions, PAD, and any other policy that denies the sanctity of life. From its inception, Operation Rescue has been a militant anti-choice organization functioning out of Wichita, Kansas, and, presently, California and Colorado. It is one of many religious-social action groups that engage in civil disobedience to protest abortion and, more recently, PAD and euthanasia. While it initially protested and took action to close down abortion clinics by conducting sit-ins in front of Planned Parenthood clinics, it soon turned its sights on another controversial pro-choice issue: PAD. By 1991 Operation Rescue became one of the most outspoken groups opposing abortion, PAD, and euthanasia in the United States.

Operation Rescue's activities attacking PAD began with the *Schiavo* case. The organization was active in the decade-long battle to save the life of Terri Schiavo, a young wife who suffered a catastrophic cardiac arrest and was left in a permanent vegetative state until her death in 2005. Troy Newman, the president of Operation Rescue during this time, led his group in marches, sit-ins, and prayer vigils, protesting Schiavo's treatment by her husband and state and federal judges, who declined to block her death (by the doctor withdrawing her life-sustaining hydration and nutrition tube). Additionally, Operation Rescue condemned political leaders such as Republican governor Jeb Bush, whom they felt did not do enough to keep Schiavo alive.

Priests for Life

Priests for Life, formed in 1990 in San Francisco, California, is a militant Roman Catholic pro-life organization whose members are Catholic bishops, priests, and deacons, although there is also a lay auxiliary membership. Its primary function is to show the clergy how to aggressively fight to defend the culture of life. Its activities focus on ending abortion, PAD, euthanasia, and all other public policies that enhance secular society's culture of death. It is rooted in the sacrosanct Gospel of Life doctrine of the Catholic Church, recently voiced by Pope John Paul II in his Encyclical Evangelium Vitae, March 25, 1995. Priests for Life was officially recognized as a Private Association of the Faithful on April 30, 1994, and listed in the Official Catholic Directory.

Priests for Life, led by Father Frank Pavone, has been seen as an uncompromising group within the Catholic Church. Its primary task is to assist priests across America in their efforts to end abortion and block efforts to pass PAD legislation in the states. Priests for Life provides a number of services to the clergy: (1) linking actively engaged priests in the fight across the nation; (2) publishing a Priests for Life newsletter; (3) providing priests with homilies, tapes, and other pro-life resources; and (4) helping priests speak out against abortion, contraceptive use, euthanasia, and PAD.

2016 was a watershed year for Priests for Life and other pro-life organizations due to the U.S. Supreme Court decision, on May 16, 2016, in the case of *Zubik v. Burwell*. Seven separate cases were consolidated in *Zubik*, including one in which Priests for Life was the plaintiff, *Priests for Life v. Sylvia Burwell, Secretary of Health and Human Services*. These cases challenged the Affordable Care Act's (Obamacare) exception to the contraception mandate. The law required employers (through their insurance plans) to cover contraception costs without charging their employees copays. However, there were two opt-out provisions: (1) churches and all other houses of worship were entirely exempt from offering contraception coverage if it goes against their religious beliefs, and (2) nonprofit religious organizations (the seven cases consolidated in *Zubick*), if they do not want to aid employees, must fill out a two-page form explaining why they want to opt out. If there is an opt-out, then the organization's secular insurer either works with employees directly to provide no-cost coverage or finds a secular third party to do the work. Priests for Life and the other plaintiff groups argued that the 1993 Religious Freedom Restoration Act bars government from placing a "substantial burden" on religious beliefs, and filling out the two-page form is such a substantial burden. The U.S. Courts of Appeals hearing the cases all rejected the petitioners' challenge to the contraceptive exemption procedure. The U.S. Supreme Court, in a short 8–0 unsigned order (a *per curium* opinion) vacated and remanded the cases back to the lower federal courts. Priests for Life, the Little Sisters of the Poor (a Catholic nursing home), and the other plaintiffs must now—with the HHS—return to the courts of appeal to try to work out a compromise agreement. If they cannot, the issue will be brought back to the U.S. Supreme Court in 2017.

United States Conference of Catholic Bishops

The United States Conference of Catholic Bishops (USCCB) was formed in 1966. The USCCB's task is to provide public information on the sanctity of human life and "the moral evil of intentionally killing innocent human beings," whether at the beginning of life (abortion, use of contraceptives) or at its end (death penalty, euthanasia, PAD). The USCCB strongly supports the expansion of high-quality palliative care, palliative sedation, and, when the time comes, hospice programs. The essential message conveyed by the USCCB lies at the core of Catholic doctrine: kill the pain, not the patient.

References

Hendin, Herbert. 1996. "Suicide, Assisted Suicide and Euthanasia: Lessons From the Dutch Experience," U.S. House of Representatives, Committee on the Judiciary, Oversight Hearing, April 29.

Liptak, Adam. 2004. "In Re Scalia the Outspoken v. Scalia the Reserved." *New York Times*, May 2.

Rehnquist, William. 1976. "The Notion of a Living Constitution," *University of Texas Law Review*, 29:2, 402–415.

Williams, Samuel. 1873. "Euthanasia." *Popular Science Monthly*, 3, May.

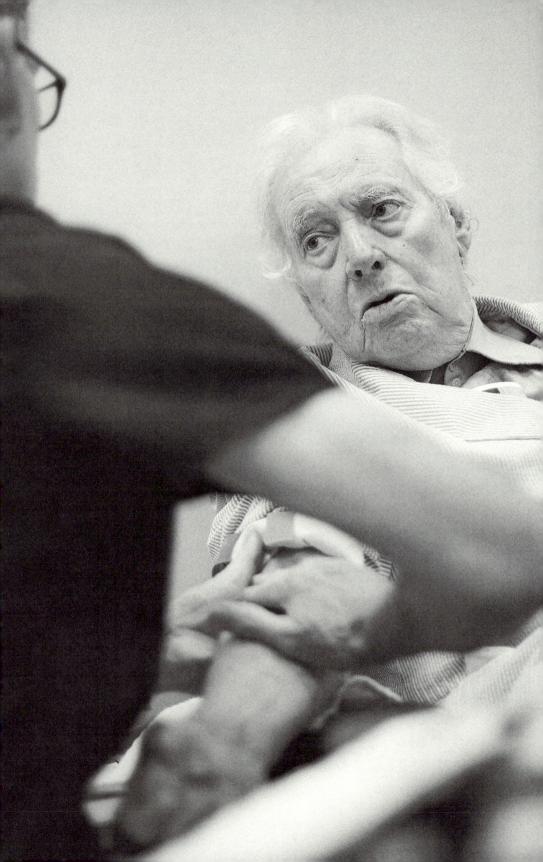

Introduction

This chapter provides data and documents about the right to die from a number of sources—political, religious, medical, and legal. The first section, Data, presents statistical and demographic information about how Americans die; how American states have dealt with assisted suicide *in their criminal codes; the framework of the Oregon Death with Dignity Act (ODWDA), which serves as the model for other states supporting PAD; and who in Oregon chooses to use the Act and what reasons they give to their family for making that choice.*

The Documents section contains letters, presidential statements, papal talks, judgments of U.S. attorney generals about the legitimacy of the ODWDA, and other documents about the right to die. The final segment of this section presents a number of judicial opinions, most from the U.S. Supreme Court, that enumerate the different views of the judiciary about the right to die.

John Jay Hooker, a veteran legislator who fought valiantly for Death with Dignity legislation in Tennessee, receives treatment for his terminal cancer during his final lobbying effort in August 2015. Hooker died shortly afterward, as did his death with dignity proposal. By 2015, after Brittany Maynard's death, more than half of the United States had proposals for Death with Dignity laws. (AP Photo/David Goldman)

Data

Top 10 Causes of Death in America (1850–2015)

The top causes of death in America have changed since the 19th century (Table 5.1). Due to dramatic changes in public health, new drugs for treating respiratory infections, and other medical innovations, people are living longer and dying from new life-style, and chronic, diseases such as cancer and heart disease. These changes in (increased) average life expectancy, accompanied by how we die, have led to the emergence of the right to die movement since the middle of the 20th century.

Legislation on Assisting Suicide (2015)

There are 40 states in which any person "assisting [a] suicide" is guilty of a criminal offence. "Assisting suicide" is a felony in most

Table 5.1   Top ten causes of death in America, 1850–2015

	1850	1900	2015
1	Tuberculosis	Pneumonia	Heart disease
2	Dysentery/diarrhea	Tuberculosis	Cancer
3	Cholera	Diarrhea	Chronic lower respiratory disease
4	Malaria	Heart disease	Unintentional injury
5	Typhoid fever	Stroke	Cerebrovascular diseases
6	Pneumonia	Liver disease	Alzheimer's disease
7	Diphtheria	Accidents	Diabetes mellitus
8	Scarlet fever	Cancer	Influenza and pneumonia
9	Meningitis	Normal aging	Nephritis
10	Whooping cough	Diphtheria	Suicide

Sources:

1850 data: Reuben H. Fleet Science Center, San Diego.
1900 data: Centers for Disease Control and Prevention. http://www.cdc.gov/nchs/data/dvs/lead1900_98.pdf.
2015 data: Centers for Disease Control and Prevention. http://www.cdc.gov/nchs/fastats/leading-causes-of-death.htm.

state criminal codes. Specifically, 40 states have laws prohibiting assisted suicide; 5 states and the District of Columbia are unclear either because the state's common law has no penalty phase or because they have no specific criminal laws regarding assisted suicide (Table 5.2).

Table 5.2   Laws on assisting a suicide: Fifty states (2015)

5 States Allow Physician-Assisted Suicide	40 States Prohibit Assisted Suicide	5 States and D.C. with No Statutory Law Nor Common Law Making Physician-Assisted Suicide Illegal
California, L	Alabama, F	Nevada
Montana, SC	Alaska, F	North Carolina
Oregon, BI	Arizona, FM	Utah
Vermont, L	Arkansas, FM	West Virginia
Washington, BI	Colorado, FM[a]	Wyoming
	Connecticut, FM	District of Columbia*
	Delaware, FM	
	Florida, F	
	Georgia, F	
	Hawaii, F	
	Idaho, F	
	Illinois, FM	
	Indiana, F	
	Iowa, F	
	Kansas, F	
	Kentucky, F	
	Louisiana, F	
	Maine, F	
	Maryland, F	
	Massachusetts, FM	
	Michigan, F	

(continued)

Table 5.2 *(continued)*

5 States Allow Physician-Assisted Suicide	40 States Prohibit Assisted Suicide	5 States and D.C. with No Statutory Law Nor Common Law Making Physician-Assisted Suicide Illegal
	Minnesota, F	
	Mississippi, F	
	Missouri, F	
	Nebraska, F	
	New Hampshire, F	
	New Jersey, F	
	New Mexico, F	
	New York, F	
	North Dakota, F	
	Ohio, M	
	Oklahoma, F	
	Pennsylvania, FM	
	Rhode Island, F	
	South Carolina, F	
	South Dakota, F	
	Tennessee, F	
	Texas, FM	
	Virginia, M	
	Wisconsin, F	

aThe Colorado "End of Life Options Act," also known as Proposition 106, is on the November 8, 2016, ballot in Colorado as an initiated state statute. A "yes" vote supports making assisted death legal among patients with a terminal illness who receive a prognosis of death within six months. A "no" vote opposes this proposal, keeping the prohibition of assisted death in Colorado. In the election, Colorado voters voted "yes" (65%–35%). It will be law in 2017.

*In November 2016, the D.C. Commissioners, 11–2, approved a Death with Dignity Bill.

BI, ballot initiative; F, felony; FM, felony/second-degree murder; L, legislature-passed bill; M, misdemeanor; SC, state Supreme Court; state with no laws addressing physician assistance and with no state common law regarding assisted suicide.

Source: Ollove, Michael. 2015. "More States Consider 'Death with Dignity' Laws." The Pew Charitable Trusts. http://www.pewtrusts.org/en/research-and-analysis/blogs/stateline/2015/3/09/more-states-consider-death-with-dignity-laws

National Public Opinion Polls on Death with Dignity (2014)

The following data summarizes public opinion regarding whether a terminally ill person should have the right to ask a physician to assist the person to die. These polls generally reflect the public's strong belief that a person should be free to make a decision of such magnitude.

Medscape Poll (December 2014)

This poll was conducted between September 18 and November 12, 2014. Medscape received many of the responses after the October 6, 2014, launch of Brittany Maynard's joint campaign with Compassion & Choices to authorize aid in dying in states nationwide.

This online survey of 17,000 U.S. doctors representing 28 medical specialties agreed by a 23 percent margin (54% vs. 31%): "I believe terminal illnesses such as metastatic cancers or degenerative neurological diseases rob a human of his/her dignity. Provided there is no shred of doubt that the disease is incurable and terminal, I would support a patient's decision to end their life, and I would also wish the same option was available in my case should the need arise." The previous Medscape survey on this issue in 2010 showed physicians supporting medical aid in dying by a 5 percent margin (46% vs. 41%).

Source: Crowley, Sean. 2014. "Post-Brittany Maynard Poll: Most U.S. Doctors Now Support Aid in Dying." Compassion & Choices. https://www.compassionandchoices.org/post-brittany-maynard-poll-most-u-s-doctors-now-support-aid-in-dying/

Harris Poll (December 2014)

This poll was conducted after the death of Brittany Maynard and found that three out of four Americans (74%) agreed that "individuals who are terminally ill, in great pain and who have no

Table 5.3   Agreement % on poll question about PAD

Demographic	Percentage
Generation	
Millennials	75
Gen X	76
Baby boomers	74
Matures	68
Education	
High school	75
Some college	74
College grad	72
Post grad	76
Political Party	
Republican	64
Democrat	78
Independent	78

chance for recovery, have the right to choose to end their own life."
Only 14 percent disagreed with this position (Table 5.3). Support
for this position cut across all generations and educational groups,
both genders, and even political affiliation.

Source: Thompson, Dennis. 2014. "Most Americans Agree
with Right-to-Die Movement." The Harris Poll. http://www.
theharrispoll.com/health-and-life/Most_Americans_Agree_
With_Right-to-Die_Movement.html

Gallup Survey (May 2014)

Seven out of 10 Americans (69%) agreed that doctors should
be allowed by law to end the life of a patient who has a disease
that cannot be cured "by some painless means if the patient
and his or her family request it." Even when Gallup asked the
same question using the language "assist the patient to commit

suicide," support dropped only 11 points, to 58 percent; the latter figure still represents a 7-point jump from this same question the previous year.

Source: McCarthy, Justin. 2014. "Seven in 10 Americans Back Euthanasia." Gallup. http://www.gallup.com/poll/171704/seven-americans-back-euthanasia.aspx

Characteristics of Those Who Used the ODWDA in 2015

This data enumerates the characteristics of all those terminally ill patients who used the lethal dose to end their lives in 2015 under the provisions of the ODWDA.

Patient Characteristics

Of the 132 Death with Dignity Act (DWDA) deaths during 2015, most patients (78.0%) were aged 65 years or older. The median age at death was 73 years. As in previous years, decedents were commonly white (93.1%) and well educated (43.1% had at least a baccalaureate degree).

While most patients had cancer, the percent of patients with cancer in 2015 was slightly lower than in previous years (72.0% and 77.9%, respectively). The percent of patients with amyotrophic lateral sclerosis was also lower (6.1% in 2015, compared to 8.3% in previous years). Heart disease increased from 2.0 percent in prior years to 6.8 percent in 2015.

Most patients (90.1%) died at home, and most (92.2%) were enrolled in hospice care. Excluding unknown cases, most (99.2%) had some form of health care insurance, although the percent of patients who had private insurance (36.7%) was lower in 2015 than in previous years (62.5% compared to 38.3%).

Similar to previous years, the three most frequently mentioned end-of-life concerns were as follows: decreasing ability to participate in activities that made life enjoyable (96.2 patients), loss of autonomy (92.4%), and loss of dignity (75.4%).

Source: Oregon Public Health Division. 2016. "Oregon Death with Dignity Act: 2015 Data Summary. http://public.health. oregon.gov/ProviderPartnerResources/EvaluationResearch/ DeathwithDignityAct/Documents/year18.pdf

Characteristics of Oregon Patients Using ODWDA: Cumulative Data (1998–2014)

Table 5.4 describes, quantitatively, the characteristics of all Oregonians who chose PAD and took the prescribed medicine to end their lives between 1998 and 2014.

Table 5.4   Characteristics and end-of-life care of 991 DWDA patients who have died from ingesting DWDA medications, by year, Oregon, 1998–2014

	2015	1998–2014	Total
Characteristics	(N = 132)	(N = 859)	(N = 991)
Sex	N (%)[1]	N (%)[1]	N (%)[1]
Male (%)	56 (42.4)	453 (52.7)	509 (51.4)
Female (%)	76 (57.6)	406 (47.3)	482 (48.6)
Age at death (years)			
18–34 (%)	1 (0.8)	7 (0.8)	8 (0.8)
35–44 (%)	5 (3.8)	18 (2.1)	23 (2.3)
45–54 (%)	2 (1.5)	61 (7.1)	63 (6.4)
55–64 (%)	21 (15.9)	184 (21.4)	205 (20.7)
65–74 (%)	41 (31.1)	247 (28.8)	288 (29.1)
75–84 (%)	30 (22.7)	229 (26.7)	259 (26.1)
85+ (%)	32 (24.2)	113 (13.2)	145 (14.6)
Median years (range)	73 (30–102)	71 (25–96)	71 (25–102)
Race			
White (%)	122 (93.1)	831 (97.1)	953 (96.6)
African American (%)	0 (0.0)	1 (0.1)	1 (0.1)
American Indian (%)	0 (0.0)	2 (0.2)	2 (0.2)
Asian (%)	4 (3.1)	9 (1.1)	13 (1.3)
Pacific Islander (%)	0 (0.0)	1 (0.1)	1 (0.1)

	2015	1998–2014	Total
Other (%)	0 (0.0)	3 (0.4)	3 (0.3)
Two or more races (%)	1 (0.8)	3 (0.4)	4 (0.4)
Hispanic (%)	4 (3.1)	6 (0.7)	10 (1.0)
Unknown	1	3	4
Marital status			
Married (including registered domestic partner) (%)	52 (39.7)	395 (46.1)	447 (45.3)
Widowed (%)	34 (26.0)	198 (23.1)	232 (23.5)
Never married (%)	9 (6.9)	69 (8.1)	78 (7.9)
Divorced (%)	36 (27.5)	194 (22.7)	230 (23.3)
Unknown	1	3	4
Education			
Less than high school (%)	7 (5.4)	51 (6.0)	58 (5.9)
High school graduate (%)	31 (23.8)	187 (21.9)	218 (22.2)
Some college (%)	36 (27.7)	224 (26.2)	260 (26.4)
Baccalaureate or higher (%)	56 (43.1)	392 (45.9)	448 (45.5)
Unknown	2	5	7
Residence			
Metro counties (Clackamas, Multnomah, Washington) (%)	64 (49.2)	361 (42.3)	425 (43.2)
Coastal counties (%)	7 (5.4)	63 (7.4)	70 (7.1)
Other western counties (%)	48 (36.9)	365 (42.7)	413 (42.0)
East of the Cascades (%)	11 (8.5)	65 (7.6)	76 (7.7)
Unknown	2	5	7
End-of-life care			
Hospice			
Enrolled (%)	118 (92.2)	747 (90.2)	865 (90.5)
Not enrolled (%)	10 (7.8)	81 (9.8)	91 (9.5)
Unknown	4	31	35
Insurance			
Private (alone or in combination) (%)	44 (36.7)	489 (60.2)	533 (57.2)

(*continued*)

Table 5.4 *(continued)*

	2015	1998–2014	Total
Medicare, Medicaid, or other governmental (%)	75 (62.5)	311 (38.3)	386 (41.4)
None (%)	1 (0.8)	12 (1.5)	13 (1.4)
Unknown	12	47	59
Underlying illness			
Malignant neoplasms (%)	95 (72.0)	667 (77.9)	762 (77.1)
Lung and bronchus (%)	23 (17.4)	154 (18.0)	177 (17.9)
Breast (%)	9 (6.8)	64 (7.5)	73 (7.4)
Colon (%)	7 (5.3)	54 (6.3)	61 (6.2)
Pancreas (%)	7 (5.3)	56 (6.5)	63 (6.4)
Prostate (%)	5 (3.8)	35 (4.1)	40 (4.0)
Ovary (%)	3 (2.3)	33 (3.9)	36 (3.6)
Other (%)	41 (31.1)	271 (31.7)	312 (31.6)
Amyotrophic lateral sclerosis (%)	8 (6.1)	71 (8.3)	79 (8.0)
Chronic lower respiratory disease (%)	6 (4.5)	38 (4.4)	44 (4.5)
Heart disease (%)	9 (6.8)	17 (2.0)	26 (2.6)
HIV/AIDS (%)	0 (0.0)	9 (1.1)	9 (0.9)
Other illnesses (%)[2]	14 (10.6)	54 (6.3)	68 (6.9)
Unknown	0	3	3
DWDA process			
Referred for psychiatric evaluation (%)	5 (3.8)	47 (5.5)	52 (5.3)
Patient informed family of decision (%)[3]	126 (95.5)	729 (93.2)	855 (93.5)
Patient died at			
Home (patient, family or friend) (%)	118 (90.1)	810 (94.6)	928 (94.0)
Long-term care, assisted living, or foster care facility (%)	9 (6.9)	37 (4.3)	46 (4.7)
Hospital (%)	0 (0.0)	1 (0.1)	1 (0.1)
Other (%)	4 (3.1)	8 (0.9)	12 (1.2)
Unknown	1	3	4

	2015	1998–2014	Total
Lethal medication			
Secobarbital (%)	114 (86.4)	466 (54.2)	580 (58.5)
Pentobarbital (%)	1 (0.8)	385 (44.8)	386 (39.0)
Phenobarbital/chloral hydrate/morphine sulfate mix (%)	16 (12.1)	0 (0.0)	16 (1.6)
Other (combination of above and/or morphine) (%)	1 (0.8)	8 (0.9)	9 (0.9)
End-of-life concerns[4]	(N = 132)	(N = 859)	(N = 991)
Less able to engage in activities making life enjoyable (%)	127 (96.2)	758 (88.7)	885 (89.7)
Losing autonomy (%)	121 (92.4)	782 (91.5)	903 (91.6)
Loss of dignity (%)[5]	98 (75.4)	579 (79.3)	677 (78.7)
Losing control of bodily functions (%)	46 (35.7)	428 (50.1)	474 (48.2)
Burden on family, friends/ caregivers (%)	63 (48.1)	342 (40.0)	405 (41.1)
Inadequate pain control or concern about it (%)	37 (28.7)	211 (24.7)	248 (25.2)
Financial implications of treatment (%)	3 (2.3)	27 (3.2)	30 (3.1)
Health care provider present (collected 2001–present)	(N = 132)	(N = 789)	(N = 921)
When medication was ingested[6]			
Prescribing physician	15	133	148
Other provider, prescribing physician not present	13	243	256
No provider	6	81	87
Unknown	98	332	430
At time of death			
Prescribing physician (%)	14 (10.8)	121 (15.7)	135 (15.0)
Other provider, prescribing physician not present (%)	13 (10.0)	268 (34.7)	281 (31.2)
No provider (%)	103 (79.2)	383 (49.6)	486 (53.9)
Unknown	2	17	19

(*continued*)

Table 5.4   (continued)

	2015	1998–2014	Total
Complications[6]	(N = 132)	(N = 859)	(N = 991)
Regurgitated	2	22	24
Other	2	1	3
None	23	506	529
Unknown	105	330	435
Other outcomes			
Regained consciousness after ingesting DWDA medications[7]	0	6	6
Timing of DWDA event			
Duration (weeks) of patient-physician relationship			
Median	9	13	12
Range	1–1004	0–1905	0–1905
Number of patients with information available	132	857	989
Number of patients with information unknown	0	2	2
Duration (days) between 1st request and death			
Median	45	47	46
Range	15–517	15–1009	15–1009
Number of patients with information available	131	859	990
Number of patients with information unknown	1	0	1
Minutes between ingestion and unconsciousness[6]			
Median	5	5	5
Range	2–15	1–38	1–38
Number of patients with information available	25	506	531
Number of patients with information unknown	107	353	460
Minutes between ingestion and death[6]			

	2015	1998–2014	Total
Median	25	25	25
Range	5 min to 34 hr	1 min to 104 hr	1 min to 104 hr
Number of patients with information available	25	511	536
Number of patients with information unknown	107	348	455
	2015	1998–2014	Total
Characteristics	(N = 132)	(N = 859)	(N = 991)
Complications[6]	(N = 132)	(N = 859)	(N = 991)
Regurgitated	2	22	24
Other	2	1	3
None	23	506	529
Unknown	105	330	435
Other outcomes			
Regained consciousness after ingesting DWDA medications[7]	0	6	6
Timing of DWDA event			
Duration (weeks) of patient-physician relationship			
Median	9	13	12
Range	1–1004	0–1905	0–1905
Number of patients with information available	132	857	989
Number of patients with information unknown	0	2	2
Duration (days) between 1st request and death			
Median	45	47	46
Range	15–517	15–1009	15–1009
Number of patients with information available	131	859	990
Number of patients with information unknown	1	0	1

(continued)

Table 5.4 (*continued*)

	2015	1998–2014	Total
Minutes between ingestion and unconsciousness[6]			
Median	5	5	5
Range	2–15	1–38	1–38
Number of patients with information available	25	506	531
Number of patients with information unknown	107	353	460
Minutes between ingestion and death[6]			
Median	25	25	25
Range	5 min to 34 hr	1 min to 104 hr	1 min to 104 hr
Number of patients with information available	25	511	536
Number of patients with information unknown	107	348	455

[1] Unknowns are excluded when calculating percentages.

[2] Includes deaths due to benign and uncertain neoplasms, other respiratory diseases, diseases of the nervous system (including multiple sclerosis, Parkinson's disease, and Huntington's disease), musculoskeletal and connective tissue diseases, cerebrovascular disease, other vascular diseases, diabetes mellitus, gastrointestinal diseases, and liver disease.

[3] First recorded beginning in 2001. Since then, 40 patients (4.4%) have chosen not to inform their families, and 19 patients (2.1%) have had no family to inform. There was one unknown case in 2002, two in 2005, one in 2009, and three in 2013.

[4] Affirmative answers only ("don't know" included in negative answers). Categories are not mutually exclusive. Data unavailable for four patients in 2001.

[5] First asked in 2003. Data available for 130 patients in 2015, 730 patients between 1998 and 2014, and 860 patients for all years.

[6] A procedure revision was made mid-year in 2010 to standardize reporting on the follow-up questionnaire. The new procedure accepts information about time of death and circumstances surrounding death only when the physician or another health care provider is present at the time of death. This resulted in a larger number of unknowns beginning in 2010.

[7] Six patients have regained consciousness after ingesting prescribed medications and are not included in the total number of DWDA deaths. These deaths occurred in 2005 (one death), 2010 (two deaths), 2011 (two deaths), and 2012 (one death). Please refer to the appropriate years' annual reports at http://www.healthoregon.org/dwd for more detail on these deaths.

Source: Oregon Public Health Division. 2016. "Oregon Death with Dignity Act: 2015 Data Summary." http://public.health. oregon.gov/ProviderPartnerResources/EvaluationResearch/ DeathwithDignityAct/Documents/year18.pdf

Family Members' Views on Why Patients Requested Physician-Assisted Death (2004–2006)

Researchers, working with data received from patients who used the ODWDA and discussed the reasons they made that choice with family members, created a list of nearly 30 responses given by dying patients explaining their reason(s) for choosing to hasten their deaths. They then asked the family to score these responses from most important to less important reasons for requesting PAD. This qualitative snapshot of the reasons (Table 5.5) why patients chose PAD substantiates the quantitative information presented above.

Table 5.5   Family members' views on why Oregon patients requested physician-assisted death (2004–2006)

Very Important (5)	(4)	(3)	(2)	Not at All Important (1)
Fear of inability to care for self in future	Fear of worsening pain in future	Lack of energy in future	Fear of loss of bowel/bladder control in future	Confusion
Fear of poor quality of life in future	Poor quality of life	Not wanting others to care for him	Inability to care for self	Depressed mood
Loss of dignity	Wanting to die at home	Perceived self as burden to others	Loss of independence at time of request	Dyspnea
Loss of independence in future	Worried about loss of sense of self	Witnessed bad deaths	Not able to pursue pleasurable activities	Fear of worsening confusion in future

(continued)

Table 5.5   (continued)

Very Important (5)	(4)	(3)	(2)	Not at All Important (1)
Wanting to control circumstances of death			Pain at time of request	Fear of worsening dyspnea in future
			Ready to die	Lack of energy
				Lack of social support
				Life tasks complete
				Loss of bowel/ bladder control
				Perceived self as financial drain

Source: Data from Ganzini, Linda, Elizabeth Goy, and Steven K. Dobscha. 2008. "Why Oregon Patients Request Assisted Death: Family Members Views." *Journal of General Internal Medicine*, 23:2, 154–157.

Documents

Summary of the 1994 Oregon Death with Dignity Act (ODWDA): Requirements

The ODWDA, initially passed in 1994 (and again in 1997), serves as a model for all other PAD advocates laboring to get their state legislature to pass a right to die bill. This summary provides the reader with all sections of the ODWDA, which has become the model used by all these groups planning for the upcoming battles in the political arena.

The DWDA allows terminally ill Oregon residents to obtain and use prescriptions from their physicians for self-administered, lethal medications. Under the Act, ending one's life in accordance with the law does not constitute suicide. The DWDA specifically prohibits euthanasia, where a physician or other person directly administers a medication to end another's life.

To request a prescription for lethal medications, the DWDA requires that a patient must be:

- An adult (18 years of age or older),
- A resident of Oregon,
- Capable (defined as able to make and communicate health care decisions), and
- Diagnosed with a terminal illness that will lead to death within six months.

Patients meeting these requirements are eligible to request a prescription for lethal medication from a licensed Oregon physician. To receive a prescription for lethal medication, the following steps must be fulfilled:

- The patient must make two oral requests to his or her physician, separated by at least 15 days.
- The patient must provide a written request to his or her physician, signed in the presence of two witnesses.
- The prescribing physician and a consulting physician must confirm the diagnosis and prognosis.
- The prescribing physician and a consulting physician must determine whether the patient is capable.
- If either physician believes the patient's judgment is impaired by a psychiatric or psychological disorder, the patient must be referred for a psychological examination.
- The prescribing physician must inform the patient of feasible alternatives to DWDA, including comfort care, hospice care, and pain control.
- The prescribing physician must request, but may not require, the patient to notify his or her next-of-kin of the prescription request.

To comply with the law, physicians must report to the Oregon Health Authority (OHA) all prescriptions for lethal medications. Reporting is not required if patients begin the request process but never receive a prescription. In 1999, the Oregon legislature added a requirement that pharmacists must be informed of the prescribed medication's intended use. Physicians and patients who adhere to the requirements of the Act are protected from criminal prosecution, and the choice of DWDA cannot affect the status of a patient's health or life insurance policies. Physicians, pharmacists, and health care systems are under no obligation to participate in the DWDA.

The Oregon Revised Statutes specify that action taken in accordance with the DWDA does not constitute suicide, mercy killing or homicide under the law.

Source: Oregon Health Department. 1997. https://public. health.oregon.gov/ProviderPartnerResources/EvaluationResearch/DeathwithDignityAct/Documents/requirements.pdf

Janet Reno's Statement about ODWDA and the CSA (1998)

Republican senators, disappointed by the 1997 Oregon referendum vote that supported the ODWDA, asked the commissioner of the Drug Enforcement Administration to interpret the 1970 Controlled Substance Act (CSA) so that physicians in Oregon could not prescribe any medications that would be used by terminally ill patients to end their lives. U.S. attorney general Janet Reno reviewed the proposed expansion of the CSA and, in the following document, overruled the planned change, noting that the CSA does not authorize the Drug Enforcement Administration to prosecute, or to revoke the Drug Enforcement Administration registration of a physician who has assisted in a suicide in compliance with Oregon law.

The Department has conducted a thorough and careful review of the issue of whether the Controlled Substances Act (CSA)

authorizes adverse action against a physician who prescribes a controlled substance to assist in a suicide in compliance with Oregon's "Death With Dignity Act." We have concluded that adverse action against a physician who has assisted in a suicide in full compliance with the Oregon Act would not be authorized by the CSA.

. . . As a matter of state law, physicians acting in accordance with the Oregon Act are immune from liability as well as any adverse disciplinary action for having rendered such assistance.

The CSA is a complex regulatory scheme that controls the authorized distribution of scheduled drugs. Physicians, for example, are authorized to prescribe and distribute scheduled drugs only pursuant to their registration with the DEA, and the unauthorized distribution of drugs is generally subject to criminal and administrative action. The relevant provisions of the CSA provide criminal penalties for physicians who dispense controlled substances beyond "the course of professional practice," and provide for revocation of the DEA drug registrations of physicians who have engaged either in such criminal conduct or in other "conduct which may threaten the public health and safety." Because these terms are not further defined by the statute, we must look to the purpose of the CSA to understand their scope.

The CSA was intended to keep legally available controlled substances within lawful channels of distribution and use. It sought to prevent both the trafficking in these substances for unauthorized purposes and drug abuse. The particular drug abuse that Congress intended to prevent was that deriving from the drug's "stimulant, depressant, or hallucinogenic effect on the central nervous system."

There is no evidence that Congress, in the CSA, intended to displace the states as the primary regulators of the medical profession, or to override a state's determination as to what constitutes legitimate medical practice in the absence of a federal law prohibiting that practice. Indeed, the CSA is essentially silent with regard to regulating the practice of medicine that involves legally available drugs except for certain specific regulations dealing with the treatment of addicts.

. . . We have concluded that the CSA does not authorize DEA to prosecute, or to revoke the DEA registration of, a physician who has assisted in a suicide in compliance with Oregon law. We emphasize that our conclusion is limited to these particular circumstances . . . . However, the federal government's pursuit of adverse actions against Oregon physicians who fully comply with that state's Death with Dignity Act would be beyond the purpose of the CSA.

Source: Reno, Janet. "Statement of Attorney General Reno on Oregon's Death with Dignity Act." June 5, 1998. https://www. justice.gov/archive/opa/pr/1998/June/259ag.htm.html

John Ashcroft's Memorandum Regarding Dispensing of Controlled Substances to Assist Suicide (2001)

The very controversial presidential election of 2000 brought into office Republican George W. Bush, a strong supporter of pro-life groups engaged in efforts to overturn Roe *and to block any state law that allowed physicians to prescribe drugs to enable a terminally ill person to hasten death. In 2001, Bush appointed former Missouri governor and U.S. senator John Ashcroft to serve as the U.S. attorney general. Ashcroft, who was governor of Missouri when* Cruzon *(1990) was heard, was a strong opponent of abortion, assisting suicide, and euthanasia. Almost immediately after his appointment, Ashcroft requested the White House Office of Legal Counsel to provide him with a legal opinion that answered a critical question: did the Oregon law's authority to allow doctors to prescribe a drug "serve a legitimate medical purpose"? If there was no legitimate purpose, then the physician could be either criminally charged or lose his or her license to practice medicine. After receiving the legal opinion, Ashcroft issued this memo, which set aside Attorney General Reno's 1998 opinion.*

Office of the Attorney General
Washington, D.C. 20530

November 6, 2001

MEMORANDUM FOR:

ASA HUTCHINSON
ADMINISTRATOR
THE DRUG ENFORCEMENT ADMINISTRATION

FROM: John Ashcroft

Attorney General
SUBJECT: *Dispensing of Controlled Substances to Assist Suicide*

Questions have been raised about the validity of an Attorney General letter dated June 5, 1998, which overruled an earlier Drug Enforcement Administration (DEA) determination that narcotics and other dangerous drugs controlled by federal law may not be dispensed consistently with the Controlled Substances Act, 21 U.S.C. §§ 801–971 (1994 & Supp. II 1996) (CSA), to assist suicide in the United States. Upon review of other relevant authorities, I have concluded that the DEA's original reading of the CSA—that controlled substances may not be dispensed to assist suicide—was correct. I therefore advise you that the original DEA determination is reinstated and should be implemented as set forth in greater detail below.

The attached Office of Legal Counsel opinion, entitled *"Whether Physician-Assisted Suicide Serves a 'Legitimate Medical Purpose' Under The Drug Enforcement Administration's Regulations Implementing the Controlled Substances Act"* (June 27, 2001) ("OLC Opinion") (attached) sets forth the legal basis for my decision.

1. *Determination on the Use of Federally Controlled Substances to Assist Suicide.* For the reasons set forth in the OLC Opinion,

I hereby determine that assisting suicide is not a "legitimate medical purpose" within the meaning of 21 C.F.R. § 1306.04 (2001), and that prescribing, dispensing, or administering federally controlled substances to assist suicide violates the CSA. Such conduct by a physician registered to dispense controlled substances may "render his registration . . . inconsistent with the public interest" and therefore subject to possible suspension or revocation under 21 U.S.C. § 824(a)(4). This conclusion applies regardless of whether state law authorizes or permits such conduct by practitioners or others and regardless of the condition of the person whose suicide is assisted.

I hereby direct the DEA, effective upon publication of this memorandum in the Federal Register, to enforce and apply this determination, notwithstanding anything to the contrary in the June 5, 1998, Attorney General's letter.

Source: Ashcroft, John. 2001. "Dispensing of Controlled Substances to Assist Suicide." *Federal Register*, November 9, 2001, 66:218, 56608. http://www.deadiversion.usdoj.gov/fed_regs/rules/2001/fr1109.htm

Pope John Paul II's Address, "Life-Sustaining Treatments and Vegetative State: Scientific Advances and Ethical Dilemmas" (2004)

The Roman Catholic Church has been in the forefront of the anti-PAD (and anti-abortion) movement ever since these issues became controversial public issues discussed in courtrooms and in legislative chambers. Leadership has come from the apex of the church: papal addresses and encyclicals addressing the sinfulness and immorality of human beings taking life away from other human beings. In this address, Pope John Paul II talks about the many ethical and religious dilemmas brought about by advances in medicine that sustain life but leave some in a very diminished state.

2. The person in a vegetative state . . . shows no evident sign of self-awareness or of awareness of the environment, and

seems unable to interact with others or to react to specific stimuli.

3. I feel the duty to reaffirm strongly that the intrinsic value and personal dignity of every human being do not change, no matter what the concrete circumstances of his or her life. *A man, even if seriously ill or disabled in the exercise of his highest functions, is and always will be a man,* and he will never become a "vegetable" or an "animal."

4. The sick person in a vegetative state, awaiting recovery or a natural end, still has the right to basic health care (nutrition, hydration, cleanliness, warmth, etc.), and to the prevention of complications related to his confinement to bed. He also has the right to appropriate rehabilitative care and to be monitored for clinical signs of eventual recovery.

I wrote in the Encyclical Evangelium Vitae, making it clear that . . . *euthanasia* . . . is always "a *serious violation of the law of God,* since it is the deliberate and morally unacceptable killing of a human person."

5. No evaluation of costs can outweigh the value of the fundamental good which we are trying to protect, that of human life. Moreover, to admit that decisions regarding man's life can be based on the external acknowledgment of its quality, is the same as . . . introducing into social relations a discriminatory and eugenic principle.

7. Distinguished Ladies and Gentlemen, in conclusion I exhort you, as men and women of science responsible for the dignity of the medical profession, to guard zealously the principle according to which the true task of medicine is "to cure if possible, always to care."

Source: Address of John Paul II to the Participants in the International Congress "Life-Sustaining Treatments and Vegetative State: Scientific Advances and Ethical Dilemmas." March 20,

2004. http://w2.vatican.va/content/john-paul-ii/en/speeches/2004/march/documents/hf_jp-ii_spe_20040320_congress-fiamc.html. © Libreria Editrice Vaticana. Used by permission.

President George W. Bush's Signing Statement on the *Terri Schiavo* Case (2005)

In the tragedy of Florida woman Terri Schiavo, who was in a permanent vegetative state since 1990 till her death in 2005, the U.S. Congress took a last-ditch gamble on a strategy they hoped would keep the comatose woman alive. They passed a bill that enabled a federal district court judge to hear and act on a petition brought by her parents who wanted to keep her alive. In the effort to stop the withdrawal of life-saving artificial means requested by Schiavo's husband, President Bush took an emergency flight from Texas to the nation's capital to sign the bill. In this signing statement, President Bush notes that his action reflects the primary value of the sanctity of life.

Statement by the President

Today, I signed into law a bill that will allow Federal courts to hear a claim by or on behalf of Terri Schiavo for violation of her rights relating to the withholding or withdrawal of food, fluids, or medical treatment necessary to sustain her life. In cases like this one, where there are serious questions and substantial doubts, our society, our laws, and our courts should have a presumption in favor of life. This presumption is especially critical for those like Terri Schiavo who live at the mercy of others. I appreciate the bipartisan action by the Members of Congress to pass this bill. I will continue to stand on the side of those defending life for all Americans, including those with disabilities.

Source: Bush, George W. 2005. *Public Papers of the Presidents of the United States: George W. Bush (2005, Book I).* March 21. Washington, D.C.: Government Printing Office, 500.

Pope Francis's Address "False Compassion" (2014)

This papal address by Pope Francis in November 2014 is one of the most recent speeches by a number of popes about an emergent very important ethical issue: how society treats—and should treat—terminally ill persons, conscious or not, in the last stage of their lives. Over the last century, many medical and technical innovations—new drugs, artificial devices that save lives, new imaging tools to diagnose patient problems, powerful electronic microscopes used in surgery—have vastly improved a physician's ability to save and extend lives. Roman Catholic doctrine has applauded these changes but has also cautioned about the ease with which society has come to accept physician-assisted suicide and euthanasia as methods of "compassionately treating" the poor, elderly, feeble, disabled, and other vulnerable persons. Given these new medical practices, it is fashionable for people to compassionately support abortion or to create new life in petri dishes. In this 2014 address to Italian Catholic physicians, Pope Francis condemns this "false compassion" and pleads with his audience to act as "good Samaritans," helping their patients to live.

There is no doubt that, in our time, due to scientific and technical advancements, the possibilities for physical healing have significantly increased; and yet, in some respects it seems that the capacity for "taking care" of the person has diminished, especially when one is sick, frail and helpless. . . . In many places, quality of life is primarily related to economic means, to "well-being," to the beauty and enjoyment of physical life, forgetting the other, more profound, interpersonal, spiritual and religious dimensions of existence. In fact, in the light of faith and right reason, human life is always sacred and always has "quality."

The predominant school of thought sometimes leads to "false compassion" which holds that it is a benefit to women to promote abortion; an act of dignity to perform euthanasia; a scientific breakthrough to "produce" a child, considered as a right rather than a gift to be welcomed; or to using human lives as laboratory animals, allegedly in order to save others. Instead, the compassion of the Gospel is what accompanies us in times of need, that compassion of the Good Samaritan, who "sees," "has compassion," draws near and provides concrete help. Your mission as doctors places you in daily contact with so many forms of suffering. I encourage you to take them on as "Good Samaritans," caring in a special way for the elderly, the infirm and the disabled. Faithfulness to the Gospel of life and respect for life as a gift from God sometimes require brave choices that go against the current, which in particular circumstances may become points of conscientious objection. . . . We are living in a time of experimentation with life. But it is harmful experimentation. Making children, rather than accepting them as a gift, as I said. Playing with life. Be careful, because this is a sin against the Creator: against God the Creator, who created things this way. Many times in my life as a priest, I have heard objections. . . . We all know that with so many elderly people in this throw-away culture, euthanasia is being performed in secret. There is also another. And this is saying to God: "No, I will end life, as I see fit". A sin against God the Creator: think hard about this.

Source: Address of His Holiness Pope Francis to Participants in the Commemorative Conference of the Italian Catholic Physicians' Association on the Occasion of Its 70th Anniversary of Foundation. November 15, 2014. https://w2.vatican.va/content/francesco/en/speeches/2014/november/documents/papa-francesco_20141115_medici-cattolici-italiani.html/ © Libreria Editrice Vaticana. Used by permission.

Excerpt from "Dear Brittany": Letter from a Terminal Brain Cancer Patient (2014)

In the fall of 2014, Brittany Maynard instantly became a world-famous name; her story and her photographs were seen in papers and magazines and on social media. She was a young terminally ill brain cancer patient who chose to hasten death with physician assistance. Philip Johnson is another young terminal brain cancer patient who disagrees with Maynard's choice. He is a Roman

Catholic Seminarian, who has continued to battle his illness. This letter shows how he is approaching his brain cancer very differently. For him, life is a gift from God; only He can take it away. Father Johnson will be ordained as a priest in January 2017.

Last week I came across the heartbreaking story of Brittany Maynard, a 29-year-old woman who was diagnosed with terminal brain cancer one year after her wedding. When doctors suggested that she might only have six months to live, she and her family moved from California to Oregon in order to obtain the prescriptions necessary for doctor-assisted euthanasia. She is devoting her last days to fundraising and lobbying for an organization dedicated to expanding the legality of assisted suicide to other States.

Brittany's story really hit home, as I was diagnosed with a very similar incurable brain cancer in 2008 at the age of twenty-four. After years of terrible headaches and misdiagnosis, my Grade III brain cancer (Anaplastic Astrocytoma) proved to be inoperable due to its location. Most studies state that the median survival time for this type of cancer is eighteen months, even with aggressive radiation and chemotherapy. I was beginning an exciting career as a naval officer with my entire life ahead of me. I had so many hopes and dreams, and in an instant they all seemed to be crushed. As Brittany said in her online video, "being told you have that kind of timeline still feels like you're going to die tomorrow."

I was diagnosed during my second Navy deployment to the Northern Arabian Gulf. . . . A few months after radiation and chemotherapy, I was discharged from the Navy and began formation for the Roman Catholic priesthood, a vocation to which I have felt called since I was nineteen years old.

I have lived through six years of constant turmoil, seizures, and headaches. I often changed hospitals and doctors every few months, seeking some morsel of hope for survival. Like Brittany, I do not want to die, nor do I want to suffer the likely outcome of this disease. I do not think anyone wants to die in this way. Brittany states relief that she does not have to die the way that it has been explained that she would—she can die "on her own terms." I have also consulted with my doctors to learn how my illness is likely to proceed. I will gradually lose control of my bodily functions at a young age, from paralysis to incontinence, and it is very likely that my mental faculties will also disappear and lead to confusion and hallucinations before my death. This terrifies me, but it does not make me any less of a person. My life means something to me, to God, and to my family and friends, and barring a miraculous recovery, it will continue to mean something long after I am paralyzed in a hospice bed. My family and friends love me for who I am, not just for the personality traits that will slowly slip away if this tumor progresses and takes my life.

There have been times over the past six years that I wanted the cancer to grow and take my life swiftly so that it would all be over. Other times, I have sought forms of escape through sin and denial just to take my mind off of the suffering and sadness, even if only for a few moments. However, deep in my heart I know that this approach is futile. My illness has become a part of me, and while it does not define me as a person, it has shaped who I am and who I will become.

Suffering is not worthless, and our lives are not our own to take. . . . There is a card on Brittany's website asking for signatures "to support her bravery in this very tough time." I agree that her time is tough, but her decision is anything but brave. I do feel for her and understand her difficult situation, but no diagnosis warrants suicide. A diagnosis of terminal cancer uproots one's whole life, and the decision to pursue physician-assisted suicide seeks to grasp at an ounce of control in the midst of turmoil. It is an understandable temptation to take this course of action, but that is all that it is—a temptation to avoid an important reality of life. By dying on one's "own terms," death seems more comfortable in our culture that is sanitized and tends to avoid any mention of the suffering and death that will eventually come to us all.

Brittany comments, "I hope to pass in peace. The reason to consider life and what's of value is to make sure you're not missing out, seize the day, what's important to you, what do you care about—what matters—pursue that, forget the rest." Sadly, Brittany will be missing out on the most intimate moments of her life—her loved ones comforting her through her suffering, her last and most personal moments with her family, and the great mystery of death—in exchange for a quicker and more "painless" option that focuses more on herself than anyone else. In our culture, which seeks to avoid pain at any cost, it is not difficult to understand why this response is so common among those who suffer.

Source: Johnson, Philip G. 2014. "Dear Brittany: Our Lives Are Worth Living, Even with Brain Cancer." The Catholic Diocese of Raleigh. October 22. http://www.dioceseofraleigh.org/content/raleigh-seminarian-terminal-brain-cancer-responds-brittany-maynard. Used by permission of the Catholic Diocese of Raleigh.

Brittany Maynard's Farewell Facebook Message (2014)

Brittany Maynard sent this Facebook message to her friends on the day she ended her life.

Goodbye to all my dear friends and family that I love. Today is the day I have chosen to pass away with dignity in the face of my terminal illness, this terrible brain cancer that has taken so much from me . . . but would have taken so much more.

The world is a beautiful place, travel has been my greatest teacher, my close friends and folks are the greatest givers. I even have a ring of support around my bed as I type. Goodbye world. Spread good energy. Pay it forward!

Source: Many news organizations reprinted Maynard's November 1, 2014, Facebook entry. See, for example, the (London) *Mirror*, http://www.mirror.co.uk/news/world-news/terminally-ill-brittany-maynard-posts-4556983. See also the *Washington Post*,

https://www.washingtonpost.com/news/morning-mix/wp/
2014/11/02/brittany-maynard-as-promised-ends-her-life-at-29/

Edmond G. Brown's Letter Supporting the End of Life Options Act (2015)

This letter was written by California governor Brown to explain to the legislators why he decided to sign the End of Life Options Act.

To the Members of the California State Assembly:

ABx2 15 is not an ordinary bill because it deals with life and death. The crux of the matter is whether the State of California should continue to make it a crime for a dying person to end his life, no matter how great his pain or suffering.

I have carefully read the thoughtful opposition materials presented by a number of doctors, religious leaders and those who champion disability rights. I have considered the theological and religious perspectives that any deliberate shortening of one's life is sinful.

I have also read the letters of those who support the bill, including heartfelt pleas from Brittany Maynard's family and Archbishop Desmond Tutu. In addition, I have discussed this matter with a Catholic Bishop, two of my own doctors and former classmates and friends who take varied, contradictory and nuanced positions.

In the end, I was left to reflect on what I would want in the face of my own death.

I do not know what I would do if I were dying in prolonged and excruciating pain. I am certain, however, that it would be a comfort to be able to consider the options afforded by this bill. And I wouldn't deny that right to others.

Sincerely,

Edmund G. Brown, Jr.

Source: Brown, Edmond G., Jr. 2015. Letter to Members of the California State Assembly, October 5. https://www.gov.ca.gov/docs/ABX2_15_Signing_Message.pdf

Excerpts from the U.S. Constitution
Tenth Amendment (1791)

The Tenth Amendment is at the core of America's system of limited and separated powers between the U.S. government and all state governments. The central government (the president, Congress, and the U.S. Supreme Court) has only those powers delegated to it in Articles 1–3 of the Constitution (and any amendments added to the constitution). All powers not delegated to the U.S. government are reserved to the states. It is the state's use of these "police powers" that triggers litigation in the federal courts. In the right to die controversies, a major question regarding the use of state powers is whether a state law that punishes any person "assisting a suicide" is a constitutional use of state power.

The powers not delegated to the United States by the Constitution, nor prohibited by it to the States, are reserved to the States respectively, or to the people.

Fourteenth Amendment (1868)

This amendment, one of three "Civil War" Amendments to the U.S. Constitution, is a major restraint on the use of state government powers. It has been the essential clause in nearly all cases involving petitions to a federal court by persons claiming that a state action has injured them and, in so doing, deprived them of life, liberty, or property without due process of law and/or denied "any person" equal protection of the laws.

Section 1

All persons born or naturalized in the United States and subject to the jurisdiction thereof, are citizens of the United States and of the State wherein they reside. No State shall make or enforce any law which shall abridge the privileges or immunities of citizens of the United States; nor shall any State deprive any person of life, liberty, or property, without due process of law; nor deny to any person within its jurisdiction the equal protection of the laws.

Source: National Archives, Charters of Freedom. http://www. archives.gov/exhibits/charters/constitution.html.

Cases Impacting the Right to Die (Excerpts)

The cases excerpts below all impact right to die litigation in state and federal courts. Some, like McCulloch, *talk about how an appellate court should interpret the Constitution when determining whether governmental powers are "constitutional." Most of these cases, however, inform the reader of how the judges and justices interpreted the Constitution in right to die petitions. A final case excerpt is a 2015 Canada Supreme Court opinion,* Carter v. Canada, *that radically changed the law regarding physician assisted death in that country.*

McCulloch v. Maryland (1819)

An important decision that strongly suggested a broad interpretation of the U.S. Constitution, with judges "deducing" the meaning of the phrase "from the nature of the objects themselves."

Opinion: Chief Justice John Marshall
A Constitution, to contain an accurate detail of all the subdivisions of which its great powers will admit, and of all the means by which they may be carried into execution, would partake of the prolixity of a legal code, and could scarcely be embraced by the human mind. It would probably never be understood by the public. Its nature, therefore, requires that only its great outlines should be marked, its important objects designated, and the minor ingredients which compose those objects be deduced from the nature of the objects themselves. . . . In considering this question, then, we must never forget that it is a Constitution we are expounding.

Source: 17 U.S. 316 (1819).

Roe v. Wade (1973)

Roe is a watershed opinion in American jurisprudence. In a 7–2 vote, the U.S. Supreme Court ruled that a woman's right to have an abortion falls in a person's "zones of personal privacy" protected by the Fourteenth Amendment. Whether this privacy right is found in the "liberty" phrase in the Fourteenth Amendment's due process clause or in the Ninth Amendment's reservation of "other rights" to the people, a state cannot prevent a woman from choosing to have an abortion.

Majority Opinion: Justice Harry A. Blackmun
The Constitution does not explicitly mention any right of privacy. In a line of decisions, however, the Court has recognized that a right of personal privacy, or a guarantee of certain areas or zones of privacy, does exist under the Constitution. In varying contexts, the Court or individual Justices have, indeed, found at least the roots of that right in the First Amendment, in the Fourth and Fifth Amendments, in the penumbras of the Bill of Rights, in the Ninth Amendment, or in the concept of liberty guaranteed by the first section of the Fourteenth Amendment. These decisions make it clear that only personal rights that can be deemed "fundamental" or "implicit in the concept of ordered liberty," are included in this guarantee of personal privacy. They also make it clear that the right has some extension to activities relating to marriage, procreation, contraception, family relationships, and childrearing and education. This right of privacy, whether it be founded in the Fourteenth Amendment's concept of personal liberty and restrictions upon state action, as we feel it is, or, as the District Court determined, in the Ninth Amendment's reservation of rights to the people, is broad enough to encompass a woman's decision whether or not to terminate her pregnancy.

Source: 410 U.S. 113 (1973).

Cruzan v. Missouri Department of Public Health (1990)

Cruzan *involves a comatose young woman in a permanent vegetative state. Her parents, after many discussions over a number of years with medical personnel and their parish priest, asked the hospital to remove all artificial means that were keeping their daughter alive. After the hospital and then Missouri courts declined their request, the parents filed a petition for certiorari with the U.S. Supreme Court. It was granted and* Cruzan *became the initial foray into the right to die controversy by the justices. The question: Does Ms. Cruzan (with surrogates acting in her best interest) have a right in the Constitution that trumps the hospital's refusal to withdraw the mechanisms from a patient?*

Opinion: Chief Justice William H. Rehnquist
We granted certiorari to consider the question whether Cruzan has a right under the United States Constitution which would require the hospital to withdraw life-sustaining treatment from her under these circumstances.

An incompetent person is not able to make an informed and voluntary choice to exercise a hypothetical right to refuse treatment or any other right. Such a "right" must be exercised for her, if at all, by some sort of surrogate. Here, Missouri has in effect recognized that under certain circumstances a surrogate may act for the patient in electing to have hydration and nutrition withdrawn in such a way as to cause death, but it has established a procedural safeguard to assure that the action of the surrogate conforms as best it may to the wishes expressed by the patient while competent. Missouri requires that evidence of the incompetent's wishes as to the withdrawal of treatment be proved by clear and convincing evidence. The question, then, is whether the United States Constitution forbids the establishment of this procedural requirement by the State. We hold that it does not.

. . . We believe Missouri may legitimately seek to safeguard the personal element of this choice through the imposition of heightened evidentiary requirements. . . . In our view, Missouri has permissibly sought to advance these interests through the adoption of a "clear and convincing" standard of proof to govern such proceedings. "The function of a standard of proof, as that concept is embodied in the Due Process Clause and in the realm of factfinding, is to 'instruct the factfinder concerning the degree of confidence our society thinks he should have in the correctness of factual conclusions for a particular type of adjudication.'"

. . . We believe that Missouri may permissibly place an increased risk of an erroneous decision on those seeking to terminate an incompetent individual's life-sustaining treatment. An erroneous decision not to terminate results in a maintenance of the status quo; the possibility of subsequent developments such as advancements in medical science, the discovery of new evidence regarding the patient's intent, changes in the law, or simply the unexpected death of the patient despite the administration of life-sustaining treatment at least create the potential that a wrong decision will eventually be corrected or its impact mitigated. An erroneous decision to withdraw life-sustaining treatment, however, is not susceptible of correction. . . . [It is] final and irrevocable.

. . . We conclude that a State may apply a clear and convincing evidence standard in proceedings where a guardian seeks to discontinue nutrition and hydration of a person diagnosed to be in a persistent vegetative state.

Source: 497 U.S. 261 (1990).

Washington v. Glucksberg (1997)

Glucksberg *and the following case (*Vacco*) were heard on the same day. Both cases centered on one of the fundamental questions raised in the right to die conflicts argued in the federal courts. The two cases began in federal district court when terminally ill patients and their doctors challenged the constitutionality of Washington and New York state laws that made a person who "assisted a suicide" guilty of a felony. The federal appellate courts heard petitions from the losing sides, and both the Second and the Ninth Courts of Appeals concluded that these two state laws violated the Fourteenth Amendment's due process and equal protection clauses. The losing parties in both cases—the state governments—immediately filed for certiorari, and the U.S. Supreme Court agreed to review (and consolidate) both cases on the same day. Chief Justice Rehnquist wrote the majority opinion in both cases (although there were a number of concurring opinions written by other justices). The* *essential question was whether either the due process clause or the equal protection clause was broad enough to protect a terminally ill person's privacy rights from a governmental law that prevents that person from receiving the assistance of a physician in order to die. Did the two state laws "offend" the Fourteenth Amendment?*

Opinion: Chief Justice William H. Rehnquist

The question presented in this case is whether Washington's prohibition against "caus[ing]" or "aid[ing]" a suicide offends the Fourteenth Amendment to the United States Constitution. We hold that it does not.

We begin, as we do in all due process cases, by examining our Nation's history, legal traditions, and practices. In almost every State—indeed, in almost every western democracy—it is a crime to assist a suicide. The States' assisted-suicide bans are not innovations. Rather, they are longstanding expressions of the States' commitment to the protection and preservation of all human life. Moreover, the majority of States in this country have laws imposing criminal penalties on one who assists another to commit suicide.

Attitudes toward suicide itself have changed since Bracton, but our laws have consistently condemned, and continue to prohibit, assisting suicide. Despite changes in medical technology and notwithstanding an increased emphasis on the importance of end-of-life decision making, we have not retreated from this prohibition. Against this backdrop of history, tradition, and practice, we now turn to respondents' constitutional claim.

The Due Process Clause guarantees more than fair process, and the "liberty" it protects includes more than the absence of physical restraint. . . . The Clause also provides heightened protection against government interference with certain fundamental rights and liberty interests.

. . . But we "ha[ve] always been reluctant to expand the concept of substantive due process because guide posts for responsible decision making in this unchartered area are scarce and open-ended."

. . . We now inquire whether this asserted right has any place in our Nation's traditions. Here we are confronted with a consistent and almost universal tradition that has long rejected the asserted right, and continues explicitly to reject it today, even for terminally ill, mentally competent adults. To hold for respondents, we would have to reverse centuries of legal doctrine and practice, and strike down the considered policy choice of almost every State.

Throughout the Nation, Americans are engaged in an earnest and profound debate about the morality, legality, and practicality of physician-assisted suicide. Our holding permits this debate to continue, as it should in a democratic society. The decision of the en banc Court of Appeals is reversed, and the case is remanded for further proceedings consistent with this opinion.

Source: 521 U.S. 702 (1997).

Vacco v. Quill (1997)

Opinion: Chief Justice William H. Rehnquist
The Court of Appeals concluded that some terminally ill people—those who are on life support systems—are treated differently than those who are not, in that the former may "hasten death" by ending treatment, but the latter may not "hasten death" through physician assisted suicide. This conclusion depends on the submission that ending or refusing lifesaving medical treatment "is nothing more nor less than assisted suicide." Unlike the Court of Appeals, we think the distinction between assisting suicide and withdrawing life sustaining treatment, a distinction widely recognized and endorsed in the medical profession and in our legal traditions, is both important and logical; it is certainly rational.

. . . Furthermore, a physician who withdraws, or honors a patient's refusal to begin, life sustaining medical treatment purposefully intends, or may so intend, only to respect his patient's wishes and "to cease doing useless and futile or degrading things to the patient when [the patient] no longer stands to benefit from them." The same is true when a doctor provides aggressive palliative care; in some cases, painkilling drugs may hasten a patient's death, but the physician's purpose and intent is, or maybe, only to ease his patient's pain. A doctor who assists a suicide, however, "must, necessarily and indubitably, intend primarily that the patient be made dead." Similarly, a patient who commits suicide with a doctor's aid necessarily has the specific intent to end his or her own life, while a patient who refuses or discontinues treatment might not.

. . . We disagree with respondents' claim that the distinction between refusing lifesaving medical treatment and assisted suicide is "arbitrary" and "irrational." Granted, in some cases, the line between the two may not be clear, but certainty is not required, even were it possible.

. . . Logic and contemporary practice support New York's judgment that the two acts are different, and New York may therefore, consistent with the Constitution, treat them differently. By permitting everyone to refuse unwanted medical treatment while prohibiting anyone from assisting a suicide, New York law follows a longstanding and rational distinction.

Source: 521 U.S. 793 (1997).

Gonzales v. Oregon (2006)

Gonzales *brought an end to many tactics, in both state legislatures and the state judiciary, as well as the Congress and the U.S. Supreme Court, to invalidate the results of a 1994 Oregon initiative that established the nation's first death with dignity law. After the voters in 1997 reaffirmed their commitment to the ODWDA, opponents sought other means to overturn the election results. One strategy, acted on by conservative Republicans in Congress, was to lobby the administrator of a federal agency, the Drug Enforcement Administration, to broaden language in a federal statute, the 1970*

Controlled Substances Act, to eviscerate the Oregon law. The Drug Enforcement Administration, after George W. Bush became president in 2001, amended the controlled substance law to bar any physician from prescribing any "regulated" drug to assist another to commit suicide. The reason: such action did not serve a "legitimate medical purpose." Oregon challenged the change in CSA regulations that would, if allowed to stand, effectively terminate the ODWDA.

Majority Opinion: Justice Anthony Kennedy

The question before us is whether the Controlled Substances Act allows the United States Attorney General to prohibit doctors from prescribing regulated drugs for use in physician-assisted suicide, notwithstanding a state law permitting the procedure.

. . . Attorney General Reno considered the matter and concluded that the DEA could not take the proposed action because the CSA did not authorize it to "displace the states as the primary regulators of the medical profession, or to override a state's determination as to what constitutes legitimate medical practice."

In 2001, John Ashcroft was appointed Attorney General. . . . He claims extraordinary authority. If the Attorney General's argument were correct, his power to deregister necessarily would include the greater power to criminalize even the actions of registered physicians, whenever they engage in conduct he deems illegitimate. This power to criminalize—unlike his power over registration, which must be exercised only after considering five express statutory factors—would be unrestrained. It would be anomalous for Congress to have so painstakingly described the Attorney General's limited authority to deregister a single physician or schedule a single drug, but to have given him, just by implication, authority to declare an entire class of activity outside "the course of professional practice," and therefore a criminal violation of the CSA.

The idea that Congress gave the Attorney General such broad and unusual authority through an implicit delegation in the CSA's registration provision is not sustainable. Congress, we have held, does not alter the fundamental details of a regulatory scheme in vague terms or ancillary provisions—it does not, one might say, hide elephants in mouseholes.

In light of the foregoing, however, the CSA does not give the Attorney General authority to issue the Interpretive Rule as a statement with the force of law. . . . To read prescriptions for assisted suicide as constituting "drug abuse" under the CSA is discordant with the phrase's consistent use throughout the statute, not to mention its ordinary meaning. . . . The text and structure of the CSA show that Congress did not have this far-reaching intent to alter the federal-state balance and the congressional role in maintaining it.

The judgment of the Court of Appeals is

Affirmed.

Source: 546 U.S. 243 (2006).

Baxter v. Montana (2009)

Baxter *is a Montana Supreme Court decision that grappled with the right to die dilemma and concluded that Montana's constitution does not prohibit a physician from providing a terminally ill patient with a prescription for a lethal drug that the patient may choose to use if the pain and suffering become unmanageable—so long as there was no coercion involved. This PAD process is a private one, between two individuals, and does not run afoul of any Montana public policy. Because the court examined the state constitution's language, there was no appeal to the U.S. Supreme Court. No "federal question" was raised in the litigation. Unlike the other four states who passed death with dignity laws that generated a specific set of guidelines for implementing the law, in Montana there are no procedures for implementing PAD. The Montana Supreme Court ruled only on the constitutionality of a private doctor-patient relationship. The legislature must establish, by law, a proper course of action to protect vulnerable patients from*

irresponsible actions by the physician or by the patient's family.
Through 2016, although there have been PAD (and anti-PAD)
bills introduced, none has made it out of committee.

LEAPHART, Judge
. . .

The bar brawler, prison fighter, BB gun-shooter, and domestic violence aggressor all committed violent acts that directly caused harm and breached the public peace. It is clear from these cases that courts deem consent ineffective when defendants directly commit blatantly aggressive, peace-breaching acts against another party.

In contrast, a physician who aids a terminally ill patient in dying is not directly involved in the final decision or the final act. He or she only provides a means by which a terminally ill patient himself can give effect to his life-ending decision, or not, as the case may be. Each stage of the physician-patient interaction is private, civil, and compassionate. The physician and terminally ill patient work together to create a means by which the patient can be in control of his own mortality. The patient's subsequent private decision whether to take the medicine does not breach public peace or endanger others.

Although the "against public policy" exception of § 45–2–211(2)(d), MCA, is not limited to violent breaches of the peace as discussed in the above cases, we see nothing in the case law facts or analysis suggesting that a patient's private interaction with his physician, and subsequent decision regarding whether to take medication provided by a physician, violate public policy. We thus turn to a review of Montana statutory law. We similarly find no indication in Montana statutes that physician aid in dying is against public policy.

The Terminally Ill Act, in short, confers on terminally ill patients a right to have their end-of-life wishes followed, even if it requires direct participation by a physician through withdrawing or withholding treatment. Section 50–9–103, MCA. Nothing in the statute indicates it is against public policy to honor those same wishes when the patient is conscious and able to vocalize and carry out the decision himself with self-administered medicine and no immediate or direct physician assistance.

In conclusion, we hold that under § 45–2–211, MCA, a terminally ill patient's consent to physician aid in dying constitutes a statutory defense to a charge of homicide against the aiding physician when no other consent exceptions apply.

Source: MT DA 09–0051, 2009 MT 449 (2009).

Morris v. New Mexico (2014)

Morris is another right to die case with a similar history (the dilemma faced by terminally ill persons living in one of 45 states that prohibits physicians from assisting such a dying person). Plaintiffs, terminally ill patients, and their doctors brought suit in a New Mexico county court, arguing that the New Mexico constitution's privacy protections allow a physician to assist a terminally ill patient to hasten death. Because "assisting suicide" is a felony in the New Mexico criminal laws, they called for the court to invalidate that section of the criminal code. The trial judge ruled in favor of the plaintiffs, and PAD was no longer considered a criminal offense. The ruling went into effect in the two counties under the court's jurisdiction. Local government officials immediately brought suit in the New Mexico Court of Appeals and, in a 2–1 vote, the appeals court overturned the trial judge's conclusions. The case excerpts that follow are the majority opinion and the dissenting opinion. The case has been appealed to the New Mexico Supreme Court; oral arguments were held in October 2015. In June 2016, the New Mexico Supreme Court, in a unanimous decision, upheld the Court of Appeals decision that the "assisting a suicide" criminal law is a valid state policy, prohibiting PAD.

Garcia, Judge. Majority opinion.
A New Mexico statute makes "assisting suicide" a fourth degree felony and defines the proscribed conduct as "deliberately

aiding another in the taking of his own life." NMSA 1978, § 30–2–4 (1963). The question presented is whether this statute may constitutionally be applied to criminalize a willing physician's act of providing a lethal dose of a prescribed medication at the request of a mentally competent, terminally ill patient who wishes a peaceful end of life (aid in dying) as an alternative to one potentially marked by suffering, pain, and/or the loss of autonomy and dignity. The district court concluded that Section 30–2–4 is invalid under two provisions of the New Mexico Constitution as applied to any physician who provides aid in dying to a patient. In reaching its conclusion, the district court determined that aid in dying is a fundamental liberty interest and that the State did not meet its burden to prove that Section 30–2–4 met a strict scrutiny standard of review.

We conclude that aid in dying is not a fundamental liberty interest under the New Mexico Constitution. Accordingly, we reverse the district court's order permanently enjoining the State from enforcing Section 30–2–4. . . . The district court concluded that Section 30–2–4 is invalid under two provisions of the New Mexico Constitution as applied to any physician who provides aid in dying to a patient. In reaching its conclusion, the district court determined that aid in dying is a fundamental liberty interest and that the State did not meet its burden to prove that Section 30–2–4 met a strict scrutiny standard of review.

We conclude that aid in dying is not a fundamental liberty interest under the New Mexico Constitution. Accordingly, we reverse the district court's order permanently enjoining the State from enforcing Section 30–2–4. In addition, we affirm the district court's determination that, for statutory construction purposes, Section 30–2–4 prohibits aid in dying.

Vanzi, Judge, dissenting.

The question presented is whether NMSA 1978, Section 30–2–4 (1963) may constitutionally be applied to criminalize a willing physician's act of providing "aid in dying" at the request of a mentally competent, terminally ill patient who wishes a peaceful end of life as an alternative to being forced to endure an unbearable dying process marked by suffering, including extreme pain and/or the loss of autonomy and dignity. I would hold that it may not and would therefore affirm the district court's order permanently enjoining the State from prosecuting under Section 30–2–4 any physician who provides aid in dying in accordance with the parties' agreed definition. I present my analysis in full, save for my recitation of the factual record and statutory interpretation, regardless of any repetition with portions of the majority opinion.

. . .

The question at the heart of this case is who has the right to decide when and how a mentally competent, terminally ill New Mexican will end her life after the options for meaningful improvement of her terminal condition have been exhausted, such that "life" means being forced to endure unbearable suffering until death arrives. I recognize that citizens may disagree about the profound implications of a terminally ill individual's decision to end her suffering by ending her life, but our judicial obligation is to give effect to the liberty interests of all New Mexicans in accordance with the guarantees of our Constitution. Other choices and decisions central to personal autonomy and dignity have long enjoyed the status of constitutionally protected liberty interests. I would hold that the New Mexico Constitution protects aid in dying as a liberty interest subject to heightened scrutiny. While it is impossible for me to conclude that governmental infringement of the right to aid in dying could be justified by any lesser interest than that required for constitutional rights previously recognized as "fundamental," the required level of scrutiny need not be determined in this case. For the State concedes that mentally competent, terminally ill citizens have a fundamental right to decide for themselves when and how to end their lives, and it provides no acceptable justification for denying them the only means available to effectuate that right in a peaceful and dignified manner—a lethal dosage of medication prescribed by a willing physician acting in accordance with the established standard of care for aid in dying. It is beyond dispute that the suffering of these citizens "is too intimate and personal for the State to insist, without more, upon its own vision [to preserve life], however dominant that vision has been in the course of our history and our culture."

Source: D-202-CV 2012–02909 (2014).

Lee Carter et al. v. Attorney General of Canada (2015)

This is a stunning decision from Canada's highest tribunal, the Supreme Court of Canada. The majority overturned an earlier decision of that court, Rodriguez v. Attorney General, British Columbia, 1993, *that rejected a petition from a patient dying of Lou Gehrig's disease. The patient argued that s241 (b) of Canada's Criminal Code which prohibits PAD was constitutionally invalid. By a 5–4 majority the Supreme Court of Canada affirmed that the challenged provision was constitutional and did not violate the Canadian Charter of Rights and Freedoms. In 1994, in* Carter et al. v. Attorney General of Canada, *the Supreme Court revisited the Rodriguez precedent and overturned it, concluding that the Canadian Charter of Rights and Freedoms does provide all persons in Canada with a right to die with the passive or active assistance of a physician. The Court suspended implementation of their order for a period of 12 months. In that period, the government introduced right to die legislation that adheres to the general conclusions of the Supreme Court of Canada.*

Majority: McLachlin C.J.
The prohibition on assisted suicide is, in general, a valid exercise of the federal criminal law power under s. 91(27) of the Constitution Act, 1867, and it does not impair the protected core of the provincial jurisdiction over health.

Insofar as they prohibit physician-assisted dying for competent adults who seek such assistance as a result of a grievous and irremediable medical condition that causes enduring and intolerable suffering, ss. 241(b) and 14 of the Criminal Code deprive these adults of their right to life, liberty and security of the person under s. 7 of the Charter. . . . Here, the prohibition deprives some individuals of life, as it has the effect of forcing some individuals to take their own lives prematurely, for fear that they would be incapable of doing so when they reached the point where suffering was intolerable. The rights to liberty and security of the person, which deal with concerns about autonomy and quality of life, are also engaged. An individual's response to a grievous and irremediable medical condition is a matter critical to their dignity and autonomy. The prohibition denies people in this situation the right to make decisions concerning their bodily integrity and medical care and thus trenches on their liberty. And by leaving them to endure intolerable suffering, it impinges on their security of the person.

The prohibition on physician-assisted dying infringes the right to life, liberty and security of the person in a manner that is not in accordance with the principles of fundamental justice. The object of the prohibition is not, broadly, to preserve life whatever the circumstances, but more specifically to protect vulnerable persons from being induced to commit suicide at a time of weakness. Since a total ban on assisted suicide clearly helps achieve this object, individuals' rights are not deprived arbitrarily. However, the prohibition catches people outside the class of protected persons. It follows that the limitation on their rights is in at least some cases not connected to the objective and that the prohibition is thus overbroad. It is unnecessary to decide whether the prohibition also violates the principle against gross disproportionality.

Having concluded that the prohibition on physician-assisted dying violates s. 7, it is unnecessary to consider whether it deprives adults who are physically disabled of their right to equal treatment under s. 15 of the Charter. . . . While the limit is prescribed by law and the law has a pressing and substantial objective, the prohibition is not proportionate to the objective. An absolute prohibition on physician-assisted dying is rationally connected to the goal of protecting the vulnerable from taking their life in times of weakness, because prohibiting an activity that poses certain risks is a rational method of curtailing the risks. However, as the trial judge found, the evidence does not support the contention that a blanket prohibition is necessary in order to substantially meet the government's objective. The trial judge made no palpable and overriding error in concluding, on the basis of evidence from scientists, medical practitioners and others who are familiar with end-of-life decision-making in Canada and abroad, that a permissive regime with properly designed and administered safeguards was capable of protecting vulnerable people from abuse and error. It was also open to her to conclude that vulnerability can be assessed on an individual basis, using the procedures that physicians apply in their assessment of informed consent and decision capacity in the context of medical decision-making more generally. The absolute prohibition is therefore not minimally impairing. Given this conclusion, it is not necessary to weigh the impacts of the law on protected rights against the beneficial effect of the law in terms of the greater public good.

The appropriate remedy is not to grant a free-standing constitutional exemption, but rather to issue a declaration of invalidity and to suspend it for 12 months. Nothing in this declaration would compel physicians to provide assistance in dying. The Charter rights of patients and physicians will need to be reconciled in any legislative and regulatory response to this judgment.

The appellants are entitled to an award of special costs on a full indemnity basis to cover the entire expense of bringing this case before the courts. A court may depart from the usual rule on costs and award special costs where two criteria are met. First, the case must involve matters of public interest that are truly exceptional. It is not enough that the issues raised have not been previously resolved or that they transcend individual interests of the successful litigant: they must also have a significant and widespread societal impact. Second, in addition to showing that they have no personal, proprietary or pecuniary interest in the litigation that would justify the proceedings on economic grounds, the plaintiffs must show that it would not have been possible to effectively pursue the litigation in question with private funding. Finally, only those costs that are shown to be reasonable and prudent will be covered by the award of special costs. Here, the trial judge did not err in awarding special costs in the truly exceptional circumstances of this case. It was also open to her to award 10 percent of the costs against the Attorney General of British Columbia in light of the full and active role it played in the proceedings. The trial judge was in the best position to determine the role taken by that Attorney General and the extent to which it shared carriage of the case.

Source: 2015 SCC 005, Date: 2015–02–06. Docket: 35591 (2015). Reproduced with the permission of the Supreme Court of Canada. 2016.

MY LIFE.

MY DECISION.

I support physician aid in dying.

Introduction

There are an untold number of resources—books, journal articles, reports, and legislative inquiries—that provide readers and researchers with every aspect of the right to die controversy. This chapter provides a very small annotated sampling of these resources—in both support of and opposition to physician assistance in dying—that have been published or are available on the Internet. The following books, articles, legislative reports, proposed physician-assisted dying (PAD) legislation (in the United States as well as in other nations), and reports published by organizations on both sides of the PAD controversy merely touch the surface of the right to die.

Books

Ralph Baergen, editor. 2000. *Ethics at the End of Life*. Belmont, CA: Wadsworth.

Right to die advocates rally in front of the New Mexico Supreme Court building in October 2015. On June 30, 2016, judges ruled that the Constitution did not allow physicians to participate in helping patients to die. To date, only one state supreme court, Montana's in 2008, has interpreted its constitution to allow doctors to help their dying patients. (AP Photo/ Russell Contreras)

This textbook of medical ethics presents all of the most common problems encountered in end-of-life medical care.

Howard Ball. 2012. *At Liberty to Die: The Battle for Death with Dignity in America*. New York: New York University Press.
A defense of a terminally ill patient's right to seek physician assistance to die and the problems the right to die movement has encountered in the legal and political processes.

Margaret Pabst Battin. 1994. *Least Worst Death: Essays in Bioethics on the End of Life*. Oxford University Press.

Margaret Pabst Battin. 1995. *Ethical Issues in Suicide*. Englewood Cliffs, N.J., Prentice-Hall.

Margaret Pabst Battin. 2005. *Ending Life: Ethics and the Way We Die*. New York: Oxford University Press.

Margaret P. Battin, Rosamond Rhodes, and Anita Silvers. 1999. *Physician-Assisted Suicide: Expanding the Debate*. New York: Routledge.
As a bioethicist, Peggy Battin writes about the right of people to end their own lives. Professor Battin's books all focus on human suffering, suicide, euthanasia, and the importance of dignified death.

Kieran Beville. 2014. *Dying to Kill: A Christian Perspective on Euthanasia and Assisted Suicide*. Cambridge, OH: Christian Publishing House.
A very sobering account of attempts to legitimate assisted suicide in our society, something which Christians must be prepared to resist. Kieran Beville discusses the issues that this raises sensitively, biblically, and uncompromisingly.

George M. Burnell. 1993. *Final Choices: To Live or to Die in an Age of Medical Technology*. New York: Insight Books.
Final Choices is an excellent presentation of the issues, options, and obstacles concerning the right and ability

of a dying person to control her future. Burnell is a psychiatrist with direct experience in grief and bereavement counseling. The book emphasizes the critical importance of the development of open communication—at the concluding stages of a patient's life—within the family and with members of the treatment staff.

Robert A. Burt. 2002. *Death Is That Man Taking Names: Intersections of American Medicine, Law, and Culture*. Berkeley: University of California Press.

Burt maintains that dying patients, their families, and their physicians are "all vulnerable to unruly psychological forces unleashed by the imminent prospect of death" and that self-determination by patients is an inadequate safeguard against the many surrounding "forces of evil." He uses legal and clinical examples of physician-assisted suicide, abortion, and capital punishment to illustrate his thesis.

A.L. Caplan, editor. 2006. *The Case of Terri Schiavo: Ethics at the End of Life*. Amherst, NY: Prometheus Press.

The ethical dilemmas that the *Schiavo* case illuminated continue to stir great controversy. This book is an in-depth examination of the dilemmas and provides information and documentation from many persons opposed to the right to die. The editors have included a foreword by Dr. Jay Wolfson, Terri Schiavo's court-appointed guardian *ad litem*, as well as Dr. Wolfson's report to Governor Jeb Bush (R-FL) on the case and Governor Bush's reply; public statements by President George Bush and Senators David Weldon, Rick Santorum, Tom DeLay, Bill Frist, and Barney Frank; statements by the pope and other representatives of the Catholic Church on this issue; plus much medical and legal background material on both precedents to the *Schiavo* case and its aftermath, including the results of the autopsy report.

William H. Colby. 2006. *Unplugged: Reclaiming Our Right to Die in America*. New York: AMACOM.

> The book addresses the fundamental questions of the right to die debate and discusses how the medical advances that brought so much hope and healing have also helped to create today's dilemma surrounding death and dignity. It illuminates the complex legal, ethical, medical, and deeply personal issues of the right to die debate and discusses the implications of current laws and proposed legislation, various medical options (including hospice), and the typical end-of-life decisions many face.

Ian Dowbiggin. 2003. *A Merciful End: The Euthanasia Movement in Modern America New York*. Oxford University Press.

Ian Dowbiggin. 2005. *A Concise History of Euthanasia: Life, Death, God, and Medicine*. Lanham, MD: Rowman & Littlefield.

> The author is an historian who has studied the euthanasia movement in history. His books examine Americans who struggled throughout the 20th century to change the nation's attitude—and its laws—regarding mercy killing. In tracing the history of the euthanasia movement, he documents its intersection with other progressive social causes: women's suffrage, birth control, abortion rights, as well as its uneasy pre–World War II alliance with eugenics. Such links brought euthanasia activists into fierce conflict with Judeo-Christian leaders who worried that "the right to die" might become a "duty to die."

Ronald Dworkin. 1993. *Life's Dominion: An Argument about Abortion, Euthanasia, and Individual Freedom*. New York: Knopf.

> The author, a highly respected lawyer and legal philosopher, argues that the key philosophical question to be resolved regarding abortion and euthanasia is how far society can go to impose a single official view upon personally held convictions of the inherent value of all life. His analysis of the right to die requires that the abstract moral

principles set out in the U.S. Constitution be interpreted to insure equal concern for the dignity of all human life.

Doris Zames Fleischer and Frieda Zanes. 2001. *The Disability Rights Movement: From Charity to Confrontation*. Philadelphia, PA: Temple University Press.

The book is a well-researched examination and analysis of the treatment of disabled persons in America for two centuries. It examines the blind, the deaf, the disabled war veterans, deinstitutionalization and independent living for disabled, push for legislation to assist the disabled community, the role of pressure groups representing the disabled, access to jobs and education for the disabled, the sorry state of the health care system, the impact of technology on the disabled, and how the disabled have impacted the culture.

Kathleen Foley and Herbert Hendin, editors. 2009. *The Case against Assisted Suicide: For the Right to End-of-Life Care*. Baltimore, MD: Johns Hopkins University Press.

The book of essays rejects arguments for patient autonomy and compassion, often used in favor of legalizing euthanasia, because they do not advance or protect the rights of terminally ill patients. The essays show the dangers that legalization of assisted suicide would pose to the most vulnerable patients. The medical profession must improve palliative care and develop and educate doctors to take a more humane response to the complex issues facing those who are terminally ill.

Atul Gawande. 2014. *Being Mortal: Medicine and What Matters in the End*. New York: Metropolitan Books.

The author, a practicing surgeon, is critical of the medical profession's aggressive commitment to curing patients rather than caring for them. He argues that quality of life is the desired goal for patients and families. He offers examples of freer, more socially fulfilling models for assisting the infirm and dependent elderly, and he explores the varieties of hospice care to demonstrate that a person's last weeks or months may be rich and dignified.

Walter Glannon. 2005. *Biomedical Ethics*. Oxford University Press.

The book is a philosophical introduction to the most important ethical positions and arguments in six areas of biomedicine: the patient-doctor relationship, medical research on humans, reproductive rights and technologies, genetics, medical decisions at the end of life, and the allocation of scarce medical resources. There is a discussion of perennial issues in medicine, such as doctors' duties to patients and recent and emerging issues in scientific innovation, including gene therapy and cloning.

Neil M. Gorsuch. 2006. *The Future of Assisted Suicide and Euthanasia*. Princeton University Press.

The book assesses the strengths and weaknesses of the arguments for assisted suicide and euthanasia. The author then builds a nuanced, novel, and powerful moral and legal argument against legalization. The argument is based on the idea that human life is intrinsically valuable and that intentional killing is always wrong.

James W. Green. 2008. *Beyond the Good Death: The Anthropology of Modern Dying*. University of Pennsylvania Press.

The book takes an anthropological approach, examining the changes in Americans' concept of death since the 1970s. The attitudes of baby boomers differ greatly from those of their parents and grandparents. The author provides an interpretation of the ways in which Americans react when death is at hand for them or for those they care about.

Herbert Hendin. 1997. *Seduced by Death: Doctors, Patients, and the Dutch Cure*. New York: Norton.

A suicide-prevention psychiatrist turns a critical eye on the Dutch experience of voluntary death with the assistance of a physician and merciful death chosen for patients no longer capable of giving consent.

Daniel Hillyard and John Dombrink. 2001. *Dying Right: The Death with Dignity Movement.* New York: Routledge.

The book provides an overview of the death with dignity movement; a history of how and why Oregon legalized physician-assisted suicide; an examination of the ethical, legal, moral, and medical complexities involved in this debate; and an analysis of the future of physician-assisted suicide. There is an excellent discussion of the question of how to balance a patient's sense about the right way to die, a physician's role as a healer, and the state's interest in preventing killing.

Derek Humphry. 1978. *Jean's Way.* Eugene, OR: Hemlock Society.

Derek Humphry. 1992. *Final Exit: The Practicalities of Self-Deliverance and Assisted Suicide for the Dying.* Eugene, OR: Hemlock Society.

Derek Humphry. 1993. *Lawful Exit: The Limits of Freedom for Help in Dying.* Junction City, OR: Norris Lane Press.

Derek Humphry. 2000. *Freedom to Die: People, Politics, and the Right-to-Die Movement.* Eugene, OR: Hemlock Society.

Derek Humphry. 2002. *Let Me Die Before I Wake, a Supplement to Final Exit.* Eugene, OR: Hemlock Society.

Derek Humphry. 2004. *The Good Euthanasia Guide: Where, What, and Who in Choices in Dying.* Eugene, OR: Hemlock Society.

Derek Humphry. 2008. *Good Life, Good Death: Memoir of an Investigative Reporter and Pro-Choice Advocate.* Eugene, OR: Hemlock Society.

The author is a major supporter of physician-assisted death and an ardent defender of euthanasia. Some of his books are guides for people who wish to hasten death; others focus on euthanasia. He has been politically active in efforts to pass right to die bills.

Stephen Jamison. 1997. *Assisted Suicide: A Decision-Making Guide for Health Professionals.* San Francisco, CA: Jossey-Bass Publishers.
    Almost all doctors and nurses who work with dying patients get asked from time to time to assist their patients to die. This book directly addresses this dilemma: what should the doctor or nurse do when asked to assist a dying patient to achieve a peaceful and painless death?

James H. Jones. 1993. *Bad Blood: The Tuskegee Syphilis Experiment,* New York: The Free Press.
    The book provides compelling answers to the questions of how and why U.S. Public Health officials systematically deceived black men in 1930s Alabama into believing they were patients in a government study of "bad blood." Tracing the evolution of medical ethics and the nature of decision making in bureaucracies, the author argues that the Tuskegee study was not, in fact, an aberration, but a logical outgrowth of race relations and medical practice in the United States. It explains the disrespect that minorities have about health care in America.

Paul Kalanithi. 2016. *When Breath Becomes Air.* New Yok: Random House.
    The author, 36 years old, on the verge of completing a decade's worth of training as a neurosurgeon, was diagnosed with stage IV lung cancer. One day he was a doctor treating the dying, and the next he was a patient struggling to live. The book traces Kalanithi's transformation from a naïve medical student "possessed by the question of what, given that all organisms die, makes a virtuous and meaningful life" into a neurosurgeon at Stanford working

in the brain, the most critical place for human identity, and finally into a patient and new father confronting his own mortality. What makes life worth living in the face of death? The book is a poignant portrayal of a human being confronting death.

David F. Kelly. 2006. *Medical Care at the End of Life: A Catholic Perspective*. Washington, D.C.: Georgetown University Press.
A medical ethicist reviews the difficult questions for end-of-life medical care from a Catholic point of view.

John Keown. 2002. *Euthanasia, Ethics, and Public Policy: An Argument against Legalisation*. Cambridge, UK: Cambridge University Press.
The author is an opponent of euthanasia. His argument against euthanasia examines both its pitfalls and answers a controversial philosophical question: are there circumstances in which withdrawal of treatment from patients should be considered euthanasia?

Jack Kevorkian. 1991. *Prescription: Medicide: The Goodness of Planned Death*. Buffalo, NY: Prometheus Books.
The world-famous "Doctor Death" tells of his lifelong efforts to permit prisoners condemned to death to donate their organs and/or give their bodies to be used in medical research and discusses his efforts to make physician-assisted voluntary death acceptable in America.

Susanne C. Knittel. 2015. *The Historical Uncanny: Disability, Ethnicity, and the Politics of Holocaust Memory*. Fordham University Press.
This book is a study of European history in the first half of the 20th century that touches eugenics, euthanasia, and the persecution of the vulnerable. It examines two discrete events that occurred during World War II: the murder of thousands of mentally ill and disabled Germans at Grafeneck and the murder of Italian Jews and partisans

in Trieste by the same German military personnel. Examined in these two histories are the relationships between disability and race, eugenics, euthanasia, ethnic persecution, and genocide.

David Kuhl. 2002. *What Dying People Want: Practical Wisdom for the End of Life*. New York: Public Affairs Press.
>   This book is based on interviews with dying people. The author addresses end-of-life realities—practical and emotional—through his own experiences as a doctor and through the words and experiences of people who knew that they were dying.

Vicki D. Lachman. 2006. *Applied Ethics in Nursing*. Springer.
>   The book is an easily understandable guide to the kind of ethical dilemmas a nurse faces in practice. Using a question-and-answer format along with numerous case studies, it offers best practices and strategies for approaching the difficult problems commonly found in clinical practice, including questions patients raise about end-of-life care and physician-assisted dying.

Edward J. Larson and Darrel W. Amundsen. 1998. *A Different Death: Euthanasia and the Christian Tradition*. Downers Grove: IVP.
>   Based on the recognition that much of the current rhetoric on physician-assisted suicide and euthanasia is lacking in appeal to historical precedent, this book reviews the history of euthanasia within Christendom.

Barbara Coombs Lee, editor. 2003. *Compassion in Dying: Stories of Dignity and Choice*. Troutdale, OR: NewSage Press.
>   The stories in the book are from individuals who sought to use the Death with Dignity Act. Most individuals have felt empowered by choice and control in how they die—whether or not they opt to use the prescribed meds to end their lives—and often experience renewed hope. The editor is the president of Compassion & Choices.

Roger S. Magnusson. 2002. *Angels of Death: Exploring the Euthanasia Underground*. New Haven, CT: Yale University Press.

> This book explores all the dynamics of helping victims of AIDS to die. The research took place in Australia and San Francisco, California. But the experiences of these doctors, nurses, social workers, and other friends can easily apply to the situations of any patients who need aid and support in the process of dying.

Lila Perl Marshall. 2007. *Cruzan v. Missouri: The Right to Die?* New York: Marshall Cavendish Benchmark.

> The book explores a controversial event, the line between the state's right to protect life versus the right of guardians of a patient in a permanent vegetative state to remove all life support. The book details, highlights, and clarifies the complex legal arguments of both sides.

Charles F. McKhann. 1999. *A Time to Die: The Place for Physician Assistance*. New Haven, CT: Yale University Press.

> A physician and professor at a medical school discusses all perspectives on physician-assisted death.

David Novak. 2007. *The Sanctity of Human Life*. Georgetown University Press.

> Novak is a Jewish theologian who digs deep into Jewish scripture and tradition to find guidance for assessing three contemporary controversies in medicine and public policy: the use of embryos to derive stem cells for research, socialized medicine, and physician-assisted suicide.

Sherwin B. Nuland. 1994. *How We Die: Reflections on Life's Final Chapter*. New York: Knopf.

> The book was a National Book Award winner; it has become the definitive text on perhaps the single most universal human concern: death. It examines the current state of health care and our relationship with life as it approaches its terminus. It also discusses how we can take control of our own final days and those of our loved ones.

Tip O'Neill and Gary Hymel. 1994. *All Politics Is Local: And Other Rules of the Game*. Holbrook, MA: Adams Media.

A small, classic book that candidly explains the nature of the political process in contemporary America.

Larry I. Palmer. 2000. *Endings and Beginnings: Law, Medicine, and Society in Assisted Life and Death*. New York: Praeger.

The book argues that legislative analysis is often more important than judicial analysis in dealing with issues that arise because of new reproductive technologies and physician-assisted suicide. A reliance on individual rights alone for answers to the complex ethical questions that result from society's faith in scientific progress and science's close alliance with medicine will be insufficient and ill advised.

Michael J. Perry. 1999. *We the People: The Fourteenth Amendment and the Supreme Court*. New York: Oxford University Press.

The book evaluates the critics' arguments that the U.S. Supreme Court, for more than eight decades, has engineered a "judicial usurpation of politics." There is an examination and analysis of a number of major Fourteenth Amendment perennial controversies—over race segregation, race-based affirmative action, sex-based discrimination, homosexuality, abortion, and physician-assisted suicide.

Tom Preston. 2007. *Patient-Directed Dying: A Call for Legalized Aid in Dying for the Terminally Ill*. New York: iUniverse Star.

The book is based on a physician's discussions with his terminally ill patients. He explains why patients—not physicians or others—should be able to make their own decisions about when and how to die. Insightful reasons about why aid in dying is not suicide when used by terminally ill patients and why physicians who help them die are not assisting suicide are presented.

Timothy E. Quill. 1993. *Death and Dignity: Making Choices and Taking Charge*. W.W. Norton.

> The last years of nine of Dr. Quill's patients are discussed. Terminal sedation was the closest Dr. Quill was willing to go toward helping patients to die. After 1997 he became an advocate for physician assistance in dying and greater use of quality palliative care.

Timothy E. Quill. 1996. *A Midwife through the Dying Process: Stories of Healing and Hard Choices at the End of Life*. Baltimore, MD: Johns Hopkins University Press.

Timothy E. Quill. 2001. *Caring for Patients at the End of Life*. Baltimore, MD: Johns Hopkins University Press.

Timothy E. Quill and Margaret P. Battin, editors. 2004. *Physician-Assisted Suicide: The Case for Palliative Care and Patient Choice*. Baltimore, MD: Johns Hopkins University Press.

> This book is a collection of articles written by various people in support of the right to die generally and more specifically in support of life-ending drugs prescribed by a physician as a means of voluntarily ending one's life under careful safeguards.

Julia D. Quinn. 2005. *My Joys, My Sorrows*. Cincinnati, OH: St. Anthony Messenger Press.

> The mother of Karen Ann Quinlan writes about the painful decision to end Karen's life by withdrawing life-saving equipment.

Betty Rollin. 1985. *Last Wish*. New York: Linden Press.

> The book is an intimate memoir of a daughter's struggle to come to terms with her terminally ill mother's decision to die. It is an examination of the ethical, spiritual, and technical aspects of assisted suicide and a compelling argument for the right of the terminally ill to a humane and dignified death.

Lois Shepherd. 2009. *If That Ever Happens to Me: Making Life and Death Decisions after Terri Schiavo*. University of North Carolina Press.

> The author opposes the right to die and looks behind labels like *starvation, care,* or *medical treatment* to consider what care and feeding really mean, when feeding tubes might be removed, and why disability groups, the faithful, and even the dying themselves often suggest end-of-life solutions that they might later regret. There is a concern about living wills and other end-of-life actions that require letter-perfect documents; they can actually weaken, rather than bolster, patient choice.

Scott Cutler Shershow. 2014. *Deconstructing Dignity: A Critique of the Right to Die Debate*. Chicago: University of Chicago Press.

> An excellent analysis of the right to die debate, from the ancient philosophers to contemporary doctors, bioethicists, and philosophers.

Wesley J. Smith. 1997. *Forced Exit: The Slippery Slope from Assisted Suicide to Legalized Murder*. New York: Random House.

> Smith is one of the strongest opponents of the right to die in the United States.

Lois Snyder and Timothy E. Quill, editors. 2001. *Physician's Guide to End-of-Life Care*. Philadelphia, PA: American College of Physicians.

> The book is a collection of articles by 27 doctors, professors, and lawyers exploring various aspects of terminal care. It was written to provide doctors who have never been trained in palliative measures and end-of-life care with important information about terminal care. It is divided into three sections containing clearly focused, practical information with illustrative cases. Topics include communications; relationship building; the goals of palliative care; evidence-based approaches to pain, depression, and delirium; intractable suffering; and legal, financial, and

quality issues. Palliative medicine should be a core clinical skill for all physicians who care for seriously ill patients.

Margaret Somerville. 2014. *Death Talk: The Cast against Euthanasia and Physician-Assisted Suicide*. Montreal, Canada: McGilll-Queen's University Press.

A professor of law examines all of the issues surrounding euthanasia and physician-assisted suicide. Legalizing the right to die would cause irreparable harm to society's value of respect for human life, which in secular societies is carried primarily by the institutions of law and medicine. Civilization should not permit the purposeful ending of human life. But all forms of making end-of-life decisions within standard medical care should be permitted.

Sigrid Sterckx, K. Raus, and F. Mortier, editors. 2013. *Continuous Sedation at the End of Life: Ethical, Clinical, and Legal Perspectives*. Cambridge, UK: Cambridge University Press.

Essays explore all dimensions of terminal sedation as a method of managing dying. Europe and North America are the most common settings, but Japan is mentioned a few times.

L.W. Sumner. 2010. *Assisted Death: A Study in Ethics and Law*. New York: Oxford University Press.

A careful philosophical exploration of end-of-life medical choices, which are intended or foreseen to shorten the process of dying: (1) "euthanasia" and "physician-assisted suicide"; (2) using pain-killers, knowing that vital functions will probably be suppressed; (3) terminal sedation—keeping the patient continuously unconscious until death; (4) terminal dehydration—giving up all food and water, supplied by any method.

Sidney Wanzer and Joseph Glenmullen. 2007. *To Die Well: Your Right to Comfort, Calm, and Choice in the Last Days of Life*. New York: Da Capo Press.

The authors provide clear legal and medical guidelines for the terminally ill and their loved ones who are facing end-of-life decisions. Drawing on case histories, they outline the rights of patients and advise them on how to appoint a health care proxy and on ways to refuse unwanted treatments. The authors also support opting for only comfort care, in which the focus is on minimizing pain and making patients comfortable. However, when someone is in uncontrollable pain with no hope of improvement, hastening death—through large doses of morphine, refusal of fluids, or inhaling helium—should be an option.

Marilyn Webb. 1999. *The Good Death: The New American Search to Reshape the End of Life.* New York: Bantam Books.

The book analyzes the consequences of lingering, debilitating diseases of old age; technology and medicine continue to dazzle, prolonging life without considering the issue of its quality. The author traveled across the country for six years, collecting stories and information that reflect every angle of the subject. She examined the range of care and values in places, ranging from tiny hospices to major metropolitan medical centers. She interviewed 300 physicians, nurses, and health care workers. She let conflicting views air: theologians versus Christian clerics; supporters of the right to die against pro-life conservatives.

Mark C. Weber. 2007. *Disability Harassment.* New York University Press.

Disability and civil rights studies lie at the core of this book written by a lawyer. The author frames his examination of disability harassment on the premise that disabled people are members of a minority group that must negotiate an artificial yet often damaging environment of physical and attitudinal barriers. The book considers courts' approaches to the problem of disability harassment, particularly the application of an analogy to race and sex harassment and the development of legal remedies and policy reforms under the Americans with Disabilities Act.

James L. Werth, Jr. 1997. *Rational Suicide? Implications for Mental Health Professionals.* Taylor & Francis.
The author argues that rational suicide is not an oxymoron; the book is an analysis of the act of suicide in history and how medical professionals, especially psychologists, have tried to work with patients to address this problem.

James L. Werth, Jr., and Dean Blevins, editors. 2009. *Decision Making Near the End of Life: Issues, Developments, and Future Directions.* New York: Routledge.
Twenty-nine authors explore various dimensions of end-of-life decision making. This book is based on extensive research and some personal experience. Doctors, nurses, professors, and some laypersons offer their perspectives.

Sue Woodman. 2000. *Last Rights: The Struggle over the Right to Die.* Da Capo Press.
The book presents the views of activists and opponents of the right to die. The author considers the complex questions that will continue to engage human beings for as long as we live and die. In the end, the book explores this question: could the right to die be humankind's ultimate civil rights struggle?

Simon Woods. 2007. *Death's Dominion: Ethics at the End of Life.* Open University Press.
Drawing on a philosophical framework, the author explores end-of-life issues in order to reflect on the nature of the good death and how this may be achieved. The book considers whether it is permissible or desirable to influence the quality of dying. Offering palliative sedation as a possible alternative to terminal sedation, the author furthers his argument to examine why some forms

of assisted dying can be shown to be compatible with the ideas of palliative care.

Kevin Yuill. 2013. *Assisted Suicide: The Liberal, Humanist Case against Legalization*. London: Palgrave Macmillan.

Yuill argues against changing the laws prohibiting assisting suicide. He presents an atheistic case against the legalization of assisted suicide. Critical of both sides in the right to die arguments, he questions the assumptions behind the discussion. Yuill shows that our attitudes toward suicide—not euthanasia—are most important to our attitudes toward assisted suicide.

Articles

Marcia Angell. 2012. "May Doctors Help You to Die?" *New York Review of Books*, October 11.

This author supports the importance of physician-assisted death.

George J. Annas. 2006. "Congress, Controlled Substances, and Physician-Assisted Suicide—Elephants in Mousehole." *The New England Journal of Medicine*, 354:10, 1079–1084.

This article is an analysis of Republican Party efforts (by Congress and the president) to use the executive branch bureaucrats and agencies to destroy the Oregon Death with Dignity Act (ODWDA).

Anonymous. 1988. "A Piece of My Mind: It's Over Debbie," *Journal of the American Medical Association*, 2, 258.

This is a watershed essay that triggered a raging debate about euthanasia. The author wrote about his euthanizing a female cancer patient in a hospital.

Jerald G. Bachman, Kirsten H. Alcser, David J. Doukas, Richard L. Lichtenstein, Amy D. Corning, and Howard Brody. 1996. "Attitudes of Michigan Physicians and the Public toward

Legalizing Physician-Assisted Suicide and Voluntary Euthanasia."
New England Journal of Medicine, 334:5, 303–309.
> This study presents an analysis of Michigan doctors' views, largely negative, of PAD.

Charles H. Baron. 2006. "Not DEA'd Yet: Gonzalez v. Oregon."
Hastings Center Report, 36:2, 8.
> This report is an analysis of the U.S. Supreme Court decision that enabled the ODWDA to remain in force.

Charles H. Baron. 2015. "Physician Aid in Dying: Wither Legalization after Brittany Maynard?" *Health Affairs*, March 12.
> This article is a discussion of the impact of Maynard's death (and the attendant publicity) on the proposed PAD bill in the California legislature.

William G. Bartholome. 1996. "Physician-Assisted Suicide, Hospice, and Rituals of Withdrawal." *Journal of Law, Medicine & Ethics*, 24:3, 233–236.
> The author argues for hospice care as the most humane way to assist a terminally ill patient.

T.L. Beauchamp. 1999. "The Medical Ethics of Physician-Assisted Suicide." *Journal of Medical Ethics*, 25:6, 437–439.
> The author supports the extension of PAD to all states. The bottom line is that PAD is the patient's choice: this decision is "compassion in its truest form."

Julie Beck. 2014. "'Going to Switzerland' as a Euphemism for Assisted Suicide." *The Atlantic*, August.
> This article is an examination of the reality of "suicide tourists" going to Switzerland to end their lives because of a fatal illness and what nations are doing to control the influx.

Philip A. Berry. 2013. "From Empathy to Assisted Dying: An Argument." *Clinical Ethics*, 8:1, 5–8.

The author argues that physicians should place patient autonomy above legal or societal objections to PAD.

Hazel Biggs. 2011. "Legitimate Compassion or Compassionate Legitimation? Reflections on the Policy for Prosecutors in Respect of Cases of Encouraging or Assisting Suicide." *Feminist Legal Studies*, 19:1, 83–91.
This article is an examination of the guidelines created by the Director of Public Prosecutions (Great Britain) that prosecutors must adhere to in cases involving PAD. It questions whether the primacy of a doctor's compassion for the patient and subsequent assistance in dying is consistent with the guidelines.

J.A. Billings and S.D. Block. 1996. "Slow Euthanasia." *Journal of Palliative Care*, www.ncbi.nih.gov
The authors examine of the use of palliative sedation to treat pain and suffering in the terminally ill patient.

Brian Bix. 2003. "Physician-Assisted Suicide and Federalism." *Notre Dame Journal of Law, Ethics and Public Policy*, 17:1, 53–70.
The author examines the ways in which the American federal system (with its separation of powers between the central and state governments and the idea that the states serve as laboratories for finding new ways to govern for the public interest) intersects with and enables states to pass—or defeat—PAD laws.

Meredith Blake. 2015. "Seeing a Proportionate Response to Personal Choice in Dying." *Health Law Central* (Canada), February.
This article is an examination of events and thoughts about the right to die that led to the Canadian Supreme Court's decision in *Carter v. Canada*.

Sandra Boodman. 2013. "Doctors Diagnostic Errors Are Often Not Mentioned but Can Take a Serious Toll." *Kaiser Health News*, May 6.

This article focuses on an issue that, in 2016, was the third leading cause of death: medical errors.

Joseph Boyle. 2004. "Medical Ethics and Double Effect: The Case of Terminal Sedation." *Theoretical Medicine and Bioethics*, 25:1, 51–60.
The author explains how the doctrine of double effect can be relied on to distinguish terminal sedation from euthanasia and PAD.

J.F. Bresnahan. 1995. "Observations on the Rejection of Physician-Assisted Suicide: A Roman Catholic Perspective." *Christian Bioethics*, 1:3, 256–284.
The author presents a critique of the efforts of pro-choice groups to pass PAD legislation from the perspective of the Roman Catholic Church.

Dan W. Brock. 1999. "A Critique of Three Objections to Physician-Assisted Suicide." *Ethics*, 109:3, 519–547
The author rebuts some major criticisms of right to die legislative proposals. He argues that patient self-determination is the fundamental ground of the right to forgo treatment in order to hasten death.

Bert Broeckaert. 2011. "Palliative Sedation, Physician-Assisted Suicide, and Euthanasia: 'Same, Same but Different'?" *American Journal of Bioethics*, 11:6, 62–64.
The author examines palliative sedation protocol, whose use in 2016 by physicians treating dying patients has exponentially increased. Are there ethical differences between palliative sedation to death and PAD and euthanasia?

JuVan D. Bruce et al. 2006. "Palliative Sedation in End of Life Care." *Journal of Hospice and Palliative Nursing*, 6, 20–27.
These authors argue that palliative care (terminal sedation) is practically and ethically more appropriate than PAD laws or euthanasia.

Robert Burt. 2003. "Why Oregon Matters: Death, Assisted Suicide and the Principle of Double Effect: The Legal Debate." *Lahey Clinic Medical Ethics Journal*, 10:2, 4–5.

>   This article is a defense of legislation that humanely addresses the final wishes of terminally ill patients.

Courtney S. Campbell. 2009. "Northwest Passages." *Philosophy in the Contemporary World*, 16:1, 66–78.

>   The article discusses the implementation of death with dignity legislation in Oregon (and its potential impact on other northwestern states Washington, Montana, and California). The author concludes that while the Oregon statute's implementation has furthered patient choice and empowered physicians, it has failed a critical test of public transparency.

Lincoln Caplan. 2016. "Rhetoric and Law" *Harvard Magazine*, January/February.

>   This article is an examination of the writings of a major American federal appeals court judge, Richard A. Posner. Posner, a highly regarded federal appellate judge and a judicial scholar, is very critical of the "originalist" judicial philosophy employed by some justices sitting on the U.S. Supreme Court.

David J. Casarett and Timothy E. Quill. 2007. "'I'm Not Ready for Hospice': Strategies for Timely and Effective Hospice Discussions." *Annals of Internal Medicine*, 146:6, 443–449.

>   The authors are supporters of palliative care and hospice for grievously suffering patients—but also believe that PAD, where legal, is a final option. The article discusses strategies doctors use to encourage dying patients to enter palliative care or hospice.

A. Chapple, S. Ziebland, A. McPherson, and A. Herxheimer. 2006. "What People Close to Death Say about Euthanasia and

Assisted Suicide: A Qualitative Study." *Journal of Medical Ethics*, 32:12, 706–710

This article is based on interviews with patients, who know they were nearing death, about PAD and euthanasia. Those who had seen others die were particularly convinced that the law should be changed to allow assisted death.

S.B. Chetwynd. 2004. "Right to Life, Right to Die and Assisted Suicide." *Journal of Applied Philosophy*, 21:2, 173–182.

The author examines, from an ethical rather than a legal point of view, how the right to life might imply a right to die, and whether this right to die can include the right of a doctor to assist the person to die.

Annette E. Clark. 2006. "The Right to Die: The Broken Road from *Quinlan* to *Schiavo*." *Loyola Law Review Chicago Law Review*, 37:383.

The author reviews the 40 years since *Quinlan* (1976), arguing that there has been a haphazard and largely ideologically driven right to die idea that ignores the reasoned arguments in the original New Jersey opinions.

Cynthia B. Cohen. 1996. "Christian Perspectives on Assisted Suicide and Euthanasia: The Anglican Tradition." *Journal of Law, Medicine & Ethics*, 24:4, 369–379.

The author reviews the basic ethical arguments against PAD and euthanasia from a Christian perspective.

A. Craig, B. Cronin, W. Eward, J. Metz, L. Murray, G. Rose, E. Suess, and M.E. Vergara. 2007. "Attitudes toward Physician-Assisted Suicide among Physicians in Vermont." *Journal of Medical Ethics*, 33:7, 400–403.

This article is an examination, based on interviews with physicians practicing in Vermont, of medical support and opposition to proposed PAD legislation in the state.

Patrick Daly. 2015. "Palliative Sedation, Foregoing Life-Sustaining Treatment, and Aid-in-Dying: What Is the Difference?" *Theoretical Medicine and Bioethics*, 36:3, 197–213.
    The author examines a number of possible choices available for terminally ill patients.

C. Delkeskamp-Hayes. 2003. "Euthanasia, Physician Assisted Suicide, and Christianity's Positive Relationship to the World." *Christian Bioethics*, 9:2–3, 163–185.
    This article is a discussion of PAD and euthanasia from a Christian perspective.

April Dembosky. 2015. "Doctors' Secret Language for Assisted Suicide." *The Atlantic*, May 27.
    The essay examines the "wink and nod" behavior of doctors and nurses in their treatment of terminally ill patients.

Charles Douglas, Ian Kerridge, and Rachel Ankeny. 2008. "Managing Intentions: The End-of-Life Administration of Analgesics and Sedatives, and the Possibility of Slow Euthanasia." *Bioethics*, 22:7, 388–396.
    The authors present a bioethical examination of the use of terminal sedation in cases where a dying patient is suffering greatly.

Gerald Dworkin. 1998. "Physician-Assisted Suicide and Public Policy." *Philosophical Studies*, 89:2–3, 133–141.
    This article by a noted philosopher supports PAD.

Gerald Dworkin, R.G. Frey, and Sissela Bok. 2000. "Euthanasia and Physician-Assisted Suicide—For and Against." *Mind*, 109:436, 893–896.
    The authors present cogent arguments for and against PAD and euthanasia.

Ezekiel J. Emanuel. 1995. "Empirical Studies on Euthanasia and Assisted Suicide." *Journal of Clinical Ethics*, 6:2, 158–160.

Ezekiel J. Emanuel. 1997. "Whose Right to Die?" *The Atlantic*, March.
This article examines the ethical questions surrounding the right to die.

G. Finlay and R. George. 2011. "Legal Physician-Assisted Suicide in Oregon and The Netherlands: Evidence Concerning the Impact on Patients in Vulnerable Groups—Another Perspective on Oregon's Data." *Journal of Medical Ethics*, 37:3, 171–174.
This essay criticizes positive interpretations by PAD supporters of post-death data about terminally ill patients.

Emily Friedman. 2013. "So Quit Already: Futility, Faith, Family and the Ongoing Battle over End of Life Care." *Hospitals and Health Networks Daily*, August 6.
This moving essay describes the problems associated with the medicalization of death, but the author is unwilling to support PAD. She fears the consequences because of the impunity inherent in legalizing assisted suicide. Physicians and, to a lesser degree, nurses have too much power; rogue members of both professions get away with murder.

Linda Ganzini, Thomasz M. Beer, Matthew Brouns, Motomi Mori, and Y.C. Hsieh. 2006. "Interest in Physician-Assisted Suicide among Oregon Cancer Patients." *Journal of Clinical Ethics*, 17:1, 27.

Linda Ganzini, D.S. Fenn, Melinda A. Lee, Ronald T. Heintz, and J.D. Bloom. 1996. "Attitudes of Oregon Psychiatrists toward Physician-Assisted Suicide." *American Journal of Psychiatry*, 153:11, 1469–1475.
The authors of the above articles examine data about the views of medical professionals regarding implementation of the ODWDA.

Linda Ganzini, Elizabeth R. Goy, Lois L. Miller, Theresa A. Harvath, Ann Jackson, and Molly A. Delorit. 2003. "Nurses'

Experiences with Hospice Patients Who Refuse Food and Fluids to Hasten Death." *New England Journal of Medicine*, 349:4, 359–365.

Linda Ganzini, Theresa A. Harvath, Ann Jackson, Elizabeth R. Goy, Lois L. Miller, and Molly A. Delorit. 2002. "Experience of Oregon Nurses and Social Workers with Hospice Patients Who Request Assistance with Suicide." *New England Journal of Medicine*, 347:8, 582–588.

Willard Gaylin, Leon R. Kass, Edmund D. Pellegrino, and Mark Siegler. 1988. "Doctors Must Not Kill." *JAMA*, 259: 2139–2140.
In this article, medical professionals critique PAD.

Jyl Gentzler. 2003. "What Is a Death with Dignity?" *Journal of Medicine and Philosophy*, 28:4, 461–487.
The author examines the different meanings of *dignity* in the phrase that describes PAD: death with dignity. However, these arguments are all defective.

Robin Gibson. 2013. "The Case for Euthanasia and Physician-Assisted Suicide." *The Australian Humanist*, 109:109, 11.
The article presents a philosophical justification of PAD and euthanasia.

Michael B. Gill. 2009. "Is the Legalization of Physician-Assisted Suicide Compatible with Good End-of-Life Care?" *Journal of Applied Philosophy*, 26:1, 27–45.
The author critiques bioethical arguments against the compatibility of palliative care and PAD.

Paul Glare et al. 2003. "A Systematic Review of Physicians' Survival Predictions in Terminally Ill Cancer Patients." *British Medical Journal*, 327:195.
This article is an examination of the data illustrating the difficulty of medical projection of a patient's death.

Fiona Godlee. 2012. "Assisted dying." *British Medical Journal*, 344, 1–9.

> The coeditor of the *BMJ* argues in favor of the passage of the right to die law in Great Britain. Doctors should be allowed to help terminally ill patients to die.

Thomas Halper. 1996. "Privacy and Autonomy: From Warren and Brandeis to Roe and Cruzan." *Journal of Medicine and Philosophy*, 21:2, 121–135.

> This interesting article examines how a person's "right to privacy" (defined by two lawyers at the turn of the 20th century) is misapplied as "personal autonomy" in right to die cases heard in contemporary Supreme Court decisions.

Theresa A. Harvath, Lois L. Miller, Elizabeth R. Goy, Ann Jackson, Molly A. Delorit, and Linda Ganzini. 2014. "Why Do Older People Oppose Physician-Assisted Dying? A Qualitative Study." *Palliative Medicine*, 28, 353–359.

> This article explores the attitudes of the elderly regarding PAD.

M.T. Harvey. 2002. "What Does a 'Right' to Physician-Assisted Suicide (PAS) Legally Entail?" *Theoretical Medicine and Bioethics*, 23:4–5, 271–286.

> The author argues that PAD legislation in America is deficient because it lacks statutory obligation that makes it legally binding on a doctor who promises to help a terminally ill patient die to carry out the promise.

P.R. Heft, M. Siegler, and J. Lantos. 2000. "The Rise and Fall of the Futility Movement." *New England Journal of Medicine*, 343, 293–296.

> The authors examine this small medical movement's rise and fall in the 1990s (objecting to the excessiveness of doctors' efforts to aggressively "cure" all their gravely ill patients by any means necessary).

Nancy S. Jecker. 2009. "Physician-Assisted Death in the Pacific Northwest." *American Journal of Bioethics*, 9:3, 1–2.
> This analysis of data generated in Oregon disproves concerns of opponents that the poor, the elderly, and the disabled would be adversely affected by PAD.

Jaime Joyce. 2012. "The Evolving State of Physician-Assisted Suicide." *The Atlantic*, July 15.
> An essay, written before Massachusetts voters narrowly defeated (51%–49%)) a proposed PAD bill, tracks the success of PAD efforts in Oregon and Washington State.

Yale Kamisar. 1995. "Against Assisted Suicide: Even a Very Limited Form." *University of Detroit Mercy Law Review*, 72, 735–69.
> A noted constitutional law scholar's important essay discusses his legal and ethical opposition to PAD.

Sister Nuala Kenny. 2015. "Physician-Assisted Suicide: Medicalization of Suffering and Death." *Impact Ethics, Canadian Bioethics*, February 13, pp. 1–5.
> A Roman Catholic Nun/MD explains why the church is opposed to PAD.

Vicki Lachman. 2010. "Physician-Assisted Suicide: Compassionate Liberation or Murder?" *Ethics, Law, and Policy, MEDSURG Nursing* (Official Journal of the Academy of Medical-Surgical Nurses), 19:2, March/April.
> The author, a nurse, expresses the belief, held by a majority in the nursing profession, that PAD is a form of killing prohibited by a state's criminal code as well as a practice that conflicts with the mission of the medical profession.

Ken Levy. 2007. "Gonzales v. Oregon and Physician-Assisted Suicide: Ethical and Policy Issues." *Tulsa Law Review*, 42, 699–729.
> This article is an analysis of the federal government's (unsuccessful) efforts to overturn the ODWDA through an expansive interpretation of the 1970 Controlled Substances Act.

Erich H. Loewy. 2004. "Euthanasia, Physician Assisted Suicide and Other Methods of Helping Along Death." *Health Care Analysis*, 12:3, 181–193.

> The author is troubled by the useless suffering (physical and emotional) of terminally ill patients yet is reluctant to argue for passage of PAD legislation because of serious—and unanswered—ethical questions about killing another person, as well as whether a physician's participation in killing a patient is ethically consistent with the oath to *do no harm.*

Edward Lowenstein and Sidney H. Wanzer. 2002. "The U.S. Attorney General's Intrusion into Medical Practice." *New England Journal of Medicine*, 346, 447.

> Another article examines Attorney General Ashcroft's efforts to use his authority to prevent doctors in Oregon from assisting terminally ill patients to hasten death.

Gunilla Lundquist, Birgit H. Rasmussen, and Bertil Axelsson. 2011. "Information of Imminent Death or Not: Does It Make a Difference?" *Journal of Clinical Oncology*, 29:29, 3927–3931.

> This article examines what occurs when doctors treating terminally ill cancer patients tell one group of patients about their imminent death but do not tell another group. Providing the information leads to improved care and an increase in the likelihood of the patient and family making decisions regarding the character, location, and quality of the final weeks of life.

Michele M. Mathes. 2004. "Assisted Suicide and Nursing Ethics." *Medicine Surgery and Nursing*, 13:4, 261–265.

> The author critiques PAD.

Brittany Maynard. 2014. "My Decision to Die." *People Magazine*, October 27.

> This essay is by a young woman dying of inoperable brain cancer who moved from California to Oregon to be able to receive physician assistance in hastening her death.

Ian Morrison. 2015. "Health Care Costs and Choices in the Last Years of Life." *Hospitals and Health Networks Daily*, March 3, pp. 5–8.

> The essay examines the impact of longevity on health care systems. There is a major focus on the need to improve the doctor-patient relationship when the patient has a terminal illness. The pain and dilemmas of dealing with mortality are examined from the perspectives of physicians, patients, and family members.

Elizabeth Morrow. 1996. "Attitudes of Women from Vulnerable Populations toward Physician-Assisted Death: A Qualitative Approach." *Journal of Clinical Ethics*, 8:3, 279–289.

> The article examines why certain women oppose PAD.

Alicia Ouellette. 2013–2014. "Context Matters: Disability, the End of Life, and Why the Conversation Is Still So Difficult." *New York Law School Law Review*, 58, 371.

> This very important essay is about the necessity of improving conversations between disabled patients and the medical professionals responsible for providing quality medical care for them.

William J. Peace. 2012. "Disability Discrimination." *Hastings Center Bioethics Forum*, July 27, pp. 1–2.

> The author, a disabled scholar, discusses the many problems the disabled confront on a daily basis within and beyond the health care system.

Carol L. Powers and Paul C. McLean. 2011. "The Community Speaks: Continuous Deep Sedation (CDS) as Caregiving versus Physician-Assisted Suicide as Killing." *American Journal of Bioethics*, 11:6, 65–66.

> This report explains why the Harvard University Community Ethics Committee concluded that CDS is an appropriate and ethical approach to care giving for terminally ill patients in great pain rather than PAD, which is criminal

and unethical. CDS is an alternative to PAD, conclude the authors, the way care giving is an alternative to killing.

Timothy E. Quill. 1991. "Death and Dignity: A Case of Individualized Decision Making." *New England Journal of Medicine*, 324:10, 691–694.

Timothy E. Quill. 2004. "Dying and Decision Making—Evolution of End-of-Life Options." *New England Journal of Medicine*, 350:20, 2029–2032.

Timothy E. Quill. 2012. "Physicians Should "Assist in Suicide" When It Is Appropriate." *Journal of Law, Medicine & Ethics*, 40:1, 57–65.

Timothy E. Quill, Bernard Lo, Dan W. Brock, and Alan Meisel. 2009. "Last-Resort Options for Palliative Sedation." *Annals of Internal Medicine*, 151:6, 421–424.
These and other articles and books by Dr. Quill and his colleagues focus on the critical role of palliative care and hospice in the care of gravely ill patients but also defend the value of PAD as a last option available—where legal—to ease the pain and suffering of dying patients.

Timothy E. Quill and Ira R. Byock. 2000. "Responding to Intractable Terminal Suffering: The Role of Terminal Sedation and Voluntary Refusal of Food and Fluids." *Annals of Internal Medicine*, 132:5, 408–414.

Terri A. Schmidt, A.D. Zechnich, Virginia P. Tilden, Melinda A. Lee, Linda K Ganzini, Heidi D. Nelson, and Susan W. Tolle. 1996. "Oregon Emergency Physicians' Experiences with, Attitudes toward, and Concerns about Physician-Assisted Suicide." *Academic Emergency Medicine*, 3:10, 938–945.
The article examines the views of emergency department doctors about PAD in Oregon, the first state to pass a PAD law.

David Shaw. 2007. "The Body as Unwarranted Life Support: A New Perspective on Euthanasia." *Journal of Medical Ethics*, 33:9, 519–521.

This interesting essay discusses differences between withdrawing (and letting die) and PAD (voluntary active euthanasia). The author presents another perspective about dying: what happens if a patient is mentally competent and wants to die but his or her body provides unwarranted life support unfairly prolonging his or her mental life?

Kenneth R. Stevens, Jr. 2006. "Emotional and Psychological Effects of Physician-Assisted Suicide and Euthanasia on Participating Physicians." *Issues in Law & Medicine*, 21, 187.

This article reviews medical and public literature regarding the reported emotional and psychological effects of participation in physician-assisted suicide and euthanasia on the physicians involved. The author concludes that the literature suggests that some doctors were adversely affected emotionally and psychologically by their experiences.

Jennifer S. Temel et al. 2010. "Earlier Palliative Care for Patients with Metastatic Small-Cell-Lung Cancer" *New England Journal of Medicine*, 363, 733.

This article emphasizes the importance of earlier palliative care so that it can have a meaningful effect on patients' quality of life and end-of-life care.

Susan W. Tolle, Virginia P. Tilden, Linda L. Drach, Erik K. Fromme, Nancy A. Perrin, and Katrina Hedberg. 2004. "Characteristics and Proportion of Dying Oregonians Who Personally Consider Physician-Assisted Suicide." *Journal of Clinical Ethics*, 15, 111–118.

All the coauthors are associated with the Oregon Department of Human Services, the state agency responsible for annual compilation and reporting of statistics about those who received a lethal prescription in accordance with the ODWDA. It is an excellent source of data.

Kathryn L. Tucker. 2008. "In the Laboratory of the States: The Progress of *Glucksberg's* Invitation to States to Address End of Life Choices." *Michigan Law Review*, 106, 1593.

> The author, one of the lawyers arguing on behalf of PAD supporters in the U.S. Supreme Court, writes about the positive impact of *Glucksberg* even though the justices rejected her arguments in support of PAD.

Johannes J.M. van Dieden. 2007. "Terminal Sedation: Source of a Restless Ethical Debate." *Journal of Medical Ethics*, 33, 187–188.

> The author asks whether terminal sedation is euthanasia or good palliative intervention. He concludes that, in most cases, they are ethically different clinical situations.

Jukka Varelius. 2012. "Ending Life, Morality, and Meaning." *Ethical Theory and Moral Practice*, 16:3, 559–574.

> The author examines how philosophical arguments about the meaning of life have figured in recent medical ethical debates on voluntary euthanasia and physician-assisted suicide. Will a terminally ill person insist on living only if there is a reason to do so?

Joseph L. Verheijde and Mohamed Y. Rady. 2011. "Justifying Physician-Assisted Death in Organ Donation." *American Journal of Bioethics*, 11:8, 52–54.

> This controversial essay examines the ethics of a new medical protocol: donation after cardiac death. Can PAD be justified when the outcome is harvesting of the decedent's organs?

James L. Werth, Jr. 1999. "When Is a Mental Health Professional Competent to Assess a Person's Decision to Hasten Death?" *Ethics and Behavior*, 9:2, 141–157.

> The author develops a set of guidelines to enable mental health professionals to determine if a professional has the training and expertise necessary to be part of a PAD medical assessment team that must determine whether or not a terminally ill patient is clinically depressed.

Susan M. Wolf. 2008. "Confronting Physician Assisted Suicide and Euthanasia: My Father's Death." *Hastings Center Report* 38:5, 23–26.

> The author, a professor of law, medicine, and public policy at the University of Minnesota, reexamines her opposition to PAD as her father lies dying.

Right to Die Legislation

Connecticut. 2014. Raised Bill No. 5326. An Act Concerning Compassionate Aid in Dying for Terminally Ill Patients.

> Bill introduced in Connecticut State Senate. Rejected.
> Find more at: www.cga.ct.gov/2014/TOB/H/2014hb-5326

Massachusetts. 2012. Massachusetts "Death with Dignity" Initiative 11–12, also known as Question 2.

> The ballot language of the measure read as follows:
> A *yes vote* would enact the proposed law allowing a physician licensed in Massachusetts to prescribe medication, at the request of a terminally ill patient meeting certain conditions, to end that person's life (48.1%).
> A *no vote* would make no change in existing laws (51.9%).
> Find at: www.ballotpedia.org/Massachusetts

Minnesota. 2015–16. SF 1880. The Minnesota Compassionate Care Act of 2015.

> PAD bill introduced in Minnesota State Senate. Failed.
> Find more at: www.revisor.mn.gov/bills/text/php?number

New York. 2015. A0 5261. Patient Self-Determination Act (Proposed).

> Following the ODWDA, the New York proposal would authorize a physician with a bona fide physician-patient relationship with a patient with a terminal illness or condition to prescribe a lethal dose of the medication to be

self-administered. The proposed statute defines *terminal illness or condition* as an illness or condition which can reasonably be expected to cause death within six months, whether or not treatment is provided. It provides legal immunity to health care providers who act in accordance with the proposed PAD law.

PADF bill introduced in New York State Assembly. No action.

Find more at: www.assembly.state.newyork.us/leg

North Carolina. 2015–2016. HB 611. Enact Death with Dignity Act. April 13, 2015.

PAD bill introduced in North Carolina House of Representatives. Failed.

Find at: www.ncleg,net/gascripts/BillLookUp/

Oklahoma. 2016. HB 2848. An Act Relating to Public Health and Safety; Creating the Oklahoma Death with Dignity Act.

Find more at: www.oklegislature.gov/BillInfo.aspx?Bill=HB%2/

United Kingdom. 2014–15. Assisted Dying Bill [HL] 2014–15. Bill 006 2014–15.

A bill to enable competent adults who are terminally ill to be provided at their request with specified assistance to end their own life and for connected purposes. The Assisted Dying Bill is a specific, focused piece of legislation that would provide safeguarded choice and control to terminally ill adults and prevent prolonged suffering among these dying adults who want to have choice over how and when they die. It will also ensure that terminally ill adults who have assistance to die do so having met clear predetermined criteria and have explored all their alternatives, rather than as at present, in secret, when checks are only made after someone dies.

Find more at: www.services.parliament.uk

Reports

American Academy of Hospice and Palliative Medicine. 2015. *Advisory Brief: Guidance on Responding to Requests for Physician-Assisted Dying.* http://aahpm.org/positions/padbrief
> This brief instructs medical providers on how to react to a request for PAD.

Center for Arizona Policy. 2014. *Physician-Assisted Suicide & Denial of Care.* http://www.azpolicypages.com/life/physician-assisted-suicide-denial-of-care/
> The report explains that proposed legislation designed to permit physician-assisted suicide has been introduced repeatedly in the Arizona legislature over the past decade. It is presented so that opposition to PAD will be better prepared to block efforts to enact any type of physician-assisted suicide measures.

Colorado Health Institute. 2016. *Aid in Dying: Colorado Confronts a Difficult Policy Question*, January. http://www.coloradohealthinstitute.org/uploads/downloads/Aid_in_Dying_report1.pdf
> This report was prepared for political actions in the Colorado state legislature, which is set to once again confront the issue in 2016 after voting down a bill in support of aid in dying during the 2015 session. The Colorado "End of Life Options Act," also known as Proposition 106, is on the November 8, 2016, ballot in Colorado as an initiated state statute. A "yes" vote supports making assisted death legal among patients with a terminal illness who receive a prognosis of death within six months. A "no" vote opposes this proposal, keeping the prohibition of assisted death in Colorado. Prepared by the Colorado Health Institute, the report offers historical context, both national and international, that is essential to understanding the debate. It highlights perspectives on both sides of the right to die.

Committee on Care at the End of Life. 1997. *Approaching Death: Improving Care at the End of Life.* Washington, D.C.: National Academy Press. http://www.nap.edu/catalog/5801/approaching-death-improving-care-at-the-end-of-life
This report argues that we can do much more to relieve suffering, respect personal dignity, and provide opportunities for people to find meaning at life's conclusion.

Director of Public Prosecutions. 2014. *Policy for Prosecutors in Respect of Cases of Encouraging or Assisting Suicide.* https://www.cps.gov.uk/publications/prosecution/assisted_suicide_policy.html
This policy presents guidance for prosecutors when a person acts to encourage or assist the suicide or attempted suicide of another person ("encouraging or assisting suicide").

F. Michael Gloth. 2003. *Physician-Assisted Suicide: The Wrong Approach to End of Life Care.* Washington, D.C.: U.S. Conference of Catholic Bishops. http://www.usccb.org/about/pro-life-activities/respect-life-program/physicianassisted-suicide-the-wrong-approach-to-end-of-life-care.cfm
This report provides information on physician-assisted suicide drawn from clinical and public policy experience. Arguments on both sides of the public debate are presented, and it is shown that as a matter of morality, medicine, and public policy, physician-assisted suicide is the wrong approach to end-of-life care. Current public policy efforts to improve the quality and availability of palliative care and hospice given to all terminally ill patients must be supported.

Hastings Center. 2016. *Bioethics Briefing Book: From Birth to Death and Bench to Clinic.* http://www.thehastingscenter.org/briefingbook/briefing-book/
This report covers issues of ethics in several fields, including abortion, end-of-life care, and PAD.

Institute of Medicine. 2015. *Dying in America: Improving Quality and Honoring Individual Preferences Near the End of Life.* Washington, D.C.: National Academies Press. http://www. nationalacademies.org/hmd/Reports/2014/Dying-In-America-Improving-Quality-and-Honoring-Individual-Preferences-Near-the-End-of-Life.aspx

> In this report, a committee of experts concludes that improving the quality and availability of medical and social services for patients and their families could not only enhance quality of life through the end of life, but may also contribute to a more sustainable care system.

Lois Snyder and Daniel P. Sulmasy. 2001. *Physician-Assisted Suicide.* Position paper of the American College of Physicians–American Society of Internal Medicine. *Annals of Internal Medicine,* 135, 209–216. https://www.acponline.org/system/files/documents/running_practice/ethics/issues/policy/pa_suicide.pdf

> In this article, The American College of Physicians–American Society of Internal Medicine states that it does not support the legalization of physician-assisted suicide. It remains thoroughly committed to improving care for patients at the end of life.

Marker, Rita L. 2013. *Euthanasia, Assisted Suicide & Health Care Decisions: Protecting Yourself & Your Family.* Steubenville, OH: Patients Rights Council. http://www.patientsrightscouncil.org/site/euthanasia-assisted-suicide-health-care-decisions-toc/

> This report discusses the reasons used by PAD activists to promote changes in the law; the contradictions that the actual proposals have with those reasons; and the slippery slope that follows when assisted suicide becomes law. The report shows the failure of so-called safeguards and outlines the impact that euthanasia and assisted suicide have on families and on a society committed to the sanctity of life.

New York State Task Force on Life and the Law. 1994. *When Death Is Sought: Assisted Suicide and Euthanasia in the Medical Context*. New York: Department of Health. https://www.health.ny.gov/regulations/task_force/reports_publications/when_death_is_sought/

In this report, one of the first published by a state, the task force unanimously recommended that New York laws prohibiting assisted suicide and euthanasia remain.

President's Commission for the Study of Ethical Problems in Medicine and Biomedical and Behavioral Research. 1981. *Defining Death: Medical, Legal and Ethical Issues in the Determination of Death*. Washington, D.C.: Government Printing Office. http://www.bioethics.gov/reports/past_commissions/defining_death.pdf

This report develops a uniform definition of *death* in the law.

Special Joint Committee on Physician-Assisted Dying. 2016. *Medical Assistance in Dying: A Patient-Centered Approach*. Parliament of Canada, 42nd Parliament, 1st Session. http://www.parl.gc.ca/HousePublications/Publication.aspx?DocId=8120006

The special committee's report calls for medical assistance in dying to be available to individuals with terminal and nonterminal grievous and irremediable medical conditions that cause enduring suffering that is intolerable to the individual in the circumstances of his condition. Further, unlike PAD guidelines in America, the Canadian report defends the views that individuals should not be excluded from eligibility for medical assistance in dying based on the fact that they have a psychiatric condition.

Task Force to Improve the Care of Terminally-Ill Oregonians. 1998, 2008. *The Oregon Death with Dignity Act: A Guidebook for Health Care Professionals*. Portland, OR: Center for Ethics in Health Care, Oregon Health & Science University.

https://www.ohsu.edu/xd/education/continuing-education/
center-for-ethics/ethics-outreach/upload/Oregon-Death-with-
Dignity-Act-Guidebook.pdf

A state agency has developed a *Guidebook for Health Care Professionals* as a collective response to its enactment. Designed to be a useful resource for health care professionals and institutions as they contemplate the Oregon Act's implications for practice, underlying the report is the assumption that regardless of the health care professionals' personal view regarding the Oregon Act, open communication, consideration of comfort needs, and respect for divergent views are necessary components of care. The report presents ethical and practical guidelines to enhance compassionate care whether or not a physician or health care system is willing to participate in providing a prescription as set forth in the Oregon Act.

United States Senate. 2005. The Consequences of Legalized Assisted Suicide. Hearing before the Subcommittee on the Constitution, Civil Rights, and Property Rights. 109th Congress, 2nd Session, May 25, 2006. Washington, D.C.: Government Printing Office. https://www.gpo.gov/fdsys/pkg/CHRG-109shrg45836/pdf/CHRG-109shrg45836.pdf

These hearings examined important issues of abortion, the death penalty, physician-assisted suicide, and euthanasia (the first two are legal in the United States, the last two considered criminal) to examine whether they promote or inhibit the culture of life.

Some Organizations Supporting Right to Die Legislation

Compassion & Choices (national)
    www.compassionandchoices.org

Compassion of Oregon (state)
    www.compassionoforegon.org

Death with Dignity National Center
   www.deathwithdignity.org

Euthanasia Research and Guidance Organization
   www.finalexit.org

Final Exit Network
   www.finalexitnetwork.org

Hawaii Death with Dignity Society
   www.hawaiidwdsociety.org

Hemlock of Illinois
   www.hemlockofillinois.org

Hemlock Society of Florida
   www.hemlockflorida.org

Hemlock Society of San Diego
   www.hemlocksocietysandiego.org

Some Organizations Opposing Right to Die Legislation

Black Americans for Life
   www.nrlc.org/outreach/bal

California: Seniors against Suicide
   www.seniorsagainstsuicide.org

Choice Is an Illusion
   www.choiceillusion.org

Disability Rights Education and Defense Fund
   www.dredf.org

Kansas against Assisted Suicide
   www.kansasagainstassistedsuicide.org

Maryland against Physician-Assisted Suicide
   www.stopassistedsuicidemd.org

Massachusetts Family Institute
www.mafamily.org

Montanans against Assisted Suicide
www.montanansagainstassistedsuicide.org

National Association of Pro Life Nurses
www.nursesforlife.org

National Right to Life
www.nationalrighttolifenews.org

Not Dead Yet
www.notdeadyet.org

Patients Rights Council
www.patientsrightscouncil.org

Second Thoughts Connecticut (disability rights)
www.second-thoughts.org

TASH (disability rights)
www.tash.org

Utah against Assisted Suicide
www.utahagainstassistedsuicide.org

Vermont Alliance for Ethical Healthcarevaeh.org
www.vaeh.org

This chapter provides the reader with an overview of major events (legislation, laws, discoveries, books, executive branch actions, appellate court decisions, organizations, etc.) in the emergence of the right to die in the past century.

1906   The first right to die/euthanasia bills are introduced in Ohio and Iowa legislatures. Both bills are rejected.

1937   The National Society for the Legalization of Euthanasia is founded; it is reorganized in 1938 as the Euthanasia Society of America

1954   The book *Morals and Medicine* (by Joseph Fletcher) is published; it forecasts the coming of right to die controversies.

1957   Pope Pius XII issues a Catholic encyclical distinguishing ordinary from extraordinary means for sustaining life.

1958   *Death of a Man* (Lael Wertenbaker) is published; it is the first book by a person who assisted her husband to die.

A drawing of Jack Kevorkian, housed at the University of Michigan's Bentley Historical Library in Ann Arbor, Michigan, in October, 2015. Between 1990 and 1998, Dr. Jack Kevorkian, a retired Michigan pathologist, assisted over 130 persons with the end of their lives. "Dr. Death," as he was referred to in the media, advocated voluntary euthanasia and solicited clients through newspaper ads in Michigan papers. Kevorkian's papers are now available to the public. (AP Photo/Carlos Osorio)

1967   A right to die bill is introduced in the Florida legislature by Dr. Walter W. Sackett. It is unsuccessful.

1969   A voluntary-euthanasia bill is introduced in the Idaho legislature. It fails.

1969   Luis Kutner develops the first living will document.

1969   *On Death and Dying* by Elisabeth Kubler-Ross is published. It has a major impact on the right to die issue.

1974   Dr. Florence Ward founds the Connecticut Hospice, in Branford, Connecticut. It is the first hospice in America.

1975   California passes the first living will law in America.

1976   A New Jersey Supreme Court decision, *In Re Quinlan*, allows parents to disconnect their daughter's respirator but not her nutrition and hydration tubes. She lives for another nine years.

1976   The California Natural Death Act is passed. This first state aid in dying law gives legal status to living wills and protects doctors from lawsuits for failing to treat incurable illnesses.

1978   The play *Whose Life Is It Anyway?*, examining a quadriplegic confronting the right to die, opens. A movie version premieres in 1981.

1980   Pope John Paul II issues the Declaration in Euthanasia encyclical opposing mercy killing but supporting palliative care and the right to refuse extraordinary means to save life.

1980   The Hemlock Society is founded by Derek Humphry in California.

1982   The U.S. Congress includes a provision to create a Medicare Hospice Benefit in the Tax Equity and Fiscal Responsibility Act of 1982. It is made permanent by Congress in 1986.

1984   Advanced Care directives are legal in 22 states and the District of Columbia.

1985   Karen Ann Quinlan dies.

1987   The California State Bar Association passes Resolution #3–4–87, becoming the first public organization to support physician-assisted dying (PAD).

1988 Americans against Human Suffering, a pro-PAD group, fails to receive sufficient signatures to place the California Humane and Dignified Death Act on the November ballot as an initiative. It is the first effort in America to have voters decide whether PAD will be legitimatized.

1988 An anonymous article, "It's Over Debbie," appears in *JAMA.*

1988 The Unitarian Universalist Association of Congregations passes a national resolution supporting PAD for terminally ill patients; it is the first national religious institution to support the right to die.

1990 This is a watershed year in the right to die controversy. Events include the following:

• *Cruzan v. Missouri Department of Health,* the initial U.S. Supreme Court opinion in the right to die controversy, is decided.

• Theresa Schiavo suffers heart stoppage and anoxia and enters into a permanent vegetative state (PVS). This is the beginning of a 15-year tragedy that ends in 2005, when she dies after life support is withdrawn.

• Washington Initiative 119, the first voter referendum on PAD and voluntary euthanasia, is filed.

• Dr. Jack Kevorkian assists in the death of his first client, Janet Atkins, who was suffering from Alzheimer's disease.

• The Hemlock Society of Oregon provides a Death with Dignity Act proposal to state legislators; the act fails to get out of committee.

• Congress passes the Patient Self-Determination Act, requiring hospitals receiving federal funds to tell patients they have a right to refuse or demand treatment.

• The American Medical Association adopts a formal position that, with informed consent, a doctor can withdraw or withhold treatment from a terminal patient and may discontinue treatment of a patient in a PVS.

1991   Dr. Timothy Quill publishes "Death and Dignity" in *The New England Journal of Medicine.*

1991   Derek Humphry's book *Final Exit* is published and appears on the *New York Times* best-seller list.

1991   Choice in Dying is formed through the merger of two PAD groups, Concern for Dying and Society for the Right to Die.

1991   Washington Ballot Initiative 119 is rejected by voters, 54 to 46 percent.

1992   Americans for Death with Dignity places the California Death with Dignity Act on the state ballot as Proposition 161. It is defeated, 54 to 46 percent (same vote percentages as in the 1991 defeat of the Washington ballot initiative).

1993   Compassion in Dying is formed in Washington State to counsel terminally ill patients and participate in lawsuits challenging assisting suicide statutes.

1993   Oregon Right to Die, a political action committee, is formed to write and work for passage of the Oregon Death with Dignity Act.

1993   Litigation challenging New York and Washington State assisted suicide statutes is brought in U.S. federal district courts.

1993   Hospice is included as a nationally guaranteed benefit in President Bill Clinton's health care reform proposal but is not passed by Congress.

1994   The Death with Dignity Education Center is formed in California to support efforts to provide compassionate care for terminally ill patients.

1994   *Compassion in Dying v. Washington* is announced by the federal district court, overturning the state assisting suicide statute. The state appeals.

1994   *Quill v. Koppell* is filed in Federal District Court (New York), challenging the state's assisting suicide statute. Quill loses and files an appeal in the federal Second Circuit Court of Appeals.

1994 Measure 16, an Oregon ballot initiative (the Oregon Death with Dignity Act), is approved by voters, 51 to 49 percent.

1995 A U.S. District Court judge rules that Oregon Measure 16, Oregon Death with Dignity Act (ODWDA), is unconstitutional.

1995 The Second Circuit Court of Appeals hears oral arguments in *Quill v. Vacco.*

1995 *Compassion v. Washington* is reheard by an 11-judge panel of the Ninth Circuit Court of Appeals.

1996 The Ninth Circuit reverses a three-judge panel decision, ruling assisting suicide statute unconstitutional. The order is stayed, pending appeal to the U.S. Supreme Court.

1996 The Second Circuit U.S. Court of Appeals reverses the district court judgment in *Quill,* ruling that the assisting suicide statute was an unconstitutional violation of the Fourteenth Amendment's equal protection clause. The order is stayed pending appeal to the U.S. Supreme Court.

1996 The U.S. Supreme Court grants certiorari in *Washington v. Glucksberg* and *Vacco v. Quill.*

1997 Oral arguments in *Glucksberg* and *Quill* are heard in the U.S. Supreme Court.

1997 The 1994 Oregon Death with Dignity Act is validated when Oregonians vote 60 to 40 percent against Measure 51, which called for the repeal of ODWDA. The law takes effect on October 27, 1997.

1997 President Bill Clinton signs the Assisted Suicide Funding Restriction Act.

1997 U.S. Supreme Court decisions are released in *Washington v. Glucksberg* and *Vacco v. Quill,* overturning the Second and Ninth U.S. Circuit Court of Appeals and upholding state "assisting suicide" criminal statutes.

1998–2005 The Schiavo tragedy unfolds in Florida, involving state and federal legislative and executive branches, including President George W. Bush.

1998   Measure B, a ballot initiative to legalize PAD, is defeated by Michigan voters, 70 to 30 percent.

1999   Dr. Jack Kevorkian is found guilty of second-degree homicide. He actively participated in the death of Thomas Youk, suffering from ALS, who could not self-administer the lethal medication.

1999   Texas passes the Futile Care Act, allowing physicians to discontinue treatment in cases where doctors believe it serves no purpose. This action is taken after consultations with patient and family indicate no opposition.

2000   A PAD ballot initiative in Maine is defeated 51 to 49 percent.

2003   U.S. Attorney General Ashcroft asks the Ninth U.S. Circuit Court of Appeals to overturn the U.S. District Court opinion that ODWDA does not run afoul of controlled substance regulations.

2004   The Hemlock Society is renamed End of Life Choices, then merges with Compassion in Dying, into Compassion & Choices.

2005   Terri Schiavo, in a permanent vegetative state since 1990, dies after removal of hydration and nutrition tubes.

2005   The U.S. Supreme Court grants certiorari in *Ashcroft v. Oregon* to decide whether the Ninth Circuit U.S. Court of Appeals decision validating the ODWDA was correct, or whether the PAD law violated the federal Controlled Substance Act.

2005   The Vermont legislature receives an initial PAD bill, House Bill 168. No action is taken.

2005   The U.S. Supreme Court hears oral arguments in *Gonzales v. Oregon* (formerly *Ashcroft v. Oregon*).

2005   California legislators receive Assembly Bill 651 (California Compassionate Choices Act). No final action is taken.

2005   The number of hospice provider institutions in America tops 4,000 for the first time.

2006   The U.S. Supreme Court votes 6–3 to uphold the ODWDA, ruling that U.S. attorney general Ashcroft overstepped his authority by interpreting the Controlled Substance Act to prevent Oregon from implementing the ODWDA.

2006   Washington Initiative 1000, the Washington Death with Dignity Act (WDWDA), is introduced (SB 684). The bill is killed in committee. Former governor Booth Gardner begins work to pass the WDWDA using the ballot initiative method.

2006   The American Board of Medical Specialties recognizes hospice and palliative care medicine as a medical specialty.

2008   Washington voters pass ballot initiative I-1000, WDWDA, on November 4 by a 58 to 42 percent margin.

2008   In *Baxter v. Montana*, the Montana Supreme Court rules that the Montana Constitution does not prohibit PAD.

2008   California passes the nation's first Terminal Patients Right to Know End of Life Options Act, which mandates that all physicians have "comprehensive information and counselling" discussions about end-of-life options available to terminally ill patients. New York becomes the second state to mandate such physician actions in consultations with their terminally ill patients.

2009   The Accreditation Council for Graduate Medical Education adds hospice and palliative medicine to its list of accredited programs.

2010   A provision in the Patient Protection and Affordable Care Act (Obamacare) requires state Medicaid programs to allow children with a life-limiting illness to receive both curative treatment and hospice care.

2010   New York, modeling legislation mirroring California's Terminal Patients Right to Know End of Life Options Act (2008), passes the Palliative Care Information Act. Hospital administrators and hospitalists must inform terminal patients about *all* options available to them at the end of life.

2010   Compassion & Choices brings a suit in the Alameda County, California, court. In *Hargett v. Vitas Hospice*, Compassion & Choices charged that hospice medical professionals working for the largest for-profit hospice corporation, Vitas Hospice, allowed a 43-year-old mother of three to die in great pain because she was not informed of the availability of palliative sedation and was not provided with adequate pain management. Compassion & Choices lawyers argued that the failure to inform the patient of all end-of-life options was "reckless and inexcusable." It deprived the woman of a "peaceful death" and was "outside the standard of care" required of all public health facilities under the 2008 California Terminal Patients Right to Know End of Life Options Act.

2013   The Vermont legislature passes the Patient Choice at End of Life Act. Governor Peter Shumlin signs the bill on May 20. The original Act 39, Patient Choices and Control at the End of Life, contained a provision sunsetting certain patient-protection safeguards on July 1, 2016. The sunset was added during the original debate in 2013 so backers could get enough votes for passage; the sunset affected a requirement for a psychiatric evaluation if there is any indication a patient requesting lethal medication has impaired judgment and a 15-day waiting period between a patient's first and second requests for the medication. Governor Shumlin signed the bill on May 20, 2015.

2014   A New Mexico trial judge rules, in *Morris v. Brandenberg*, that the New Mexico Constitution's Individual Rights section allows a competent, dying patient to seek PAD.

2014   Brittany Maynard, a terminal brain cancer patient living in California, moves residency to Oregon in order to die in accord with ODWDA. She dies in late November 2014. Media coverage of Maynard's plight is covered extensively in America and worldwide.

2015   In the Vermont legislature, SB 108, an act repealing the sunset provisions in the 2013 Patient Choices at End of

Life Act, passes both houses and is signed by Governor Shumlin on May 20.

2015   In a Special Legislative Session, California legislators pass Senate Bill 128, the California End of Life Options Act. Governor Brown signs it into law on October 5.

2015   Physician assistance in dying is law in 5 states; 45 states and the District of Columbia have laws making assisting suicide a criminal act.

2016   Colorado voters approve Colorado End of Life Options Act. Colorado is the sixth state to have a Death with Dignity Bill. The D.C. Commissioners vote 11–2 to approve a D.C. DWD bill.

Right to die debates occur in a variety of locations: political arenas, legislative chambers, courtrooms, town hall meetings, picketing on the streets, and in the press. These discussions revolve around a number of distinguishable categories that have their own lexicon: legal options for the dying, terms used in legal briefs, jurisprudential concepts, emergency medical technician language, medical illnesses, voting practices, and bioethical language. This glossary provides the reader with a brief definition of some significant terms and their connection with the right to die.

Advanced directive   An advanced directive is a legal document prepared by a person, optimally after discussions with family, clergy, and doctors, which indicates how the person wishes to be treated in the event of a medical emergency that leads to unconsciousness. It is a document that should reflect the person's health care wishes in the event a medical event leaves the patient incapable of verbally making medical decisions. It is also a document that reflects the state of a person's health at a particular point in time; as such, based on changes in a person's health, the advanced directive should reflect the person's latest instructions regarding health care.

Alzheimer's disease   Alzheimer's disease is an illness that very slowly attacks and destroys the brain's nerve cells. It leads to loss of memory, the gradual deterioration of reasoning and language skills, and stark behavioral changes. There is, at present, no cure for Alzheimer's disease. Further, because people are living longer, there will be a significant increase in the number of persons who succumb to this disease.

Amicus curiae   This Latin phrase means "friend of the court." An amicus curiae brief is prepared by lawyers for an organization interested in affecting the outcome of a substantive legal issue before a court. The argument made in an amicus brief reflects the specific view of the group and, at its best, provides the court with a helpful perspective about the issue.

Amyotrophic lateral sclerosis (Lou Gehrig's disease)   Amyotrophic lateral sclerosis, ALS, is sometimes called Lou Gehrig's disease, after baseball player Lou Gehrig, who died of it. It is generally a fatal illness, with death caused by the degeneration of the cells in the central nervous system that control voluntary muscle movement. It is a progressively debilitating disease where the patient loses all ability to move the limbs, to talk, and, in the end, to swallow. There are a few ALS patients who live beyond two to five years. Stephen Hawking, the world-famous physicist, has been living with a form of ALS for decades.

Ballot initiative   The ballot initiative is a seldom-used process that allows a group of citizens to place proposals before the general population that hadn't been addressed by state or local governments. A number of states have seen ballot initiatives to legalize physician assistance in dying placed before the voters. (The group seeking to have the initiative placed before the voters must first receive the requisite number of signatures in order to place the issue to the public.) Four ballot initiatives were employed in passing a PAD bill (Oregon, Washington State, California, and Colorado). A ballot initiative, however, differs from a referendum. A referendum is a proposal brought by the state legislature that asks the voters to approve or reject a particular existing law. For example, after the 1994 initiative for the Oregon Death with Dignity bill was passed, in 1997 the Oregon legislature introduced a referendum that, if passed, would overturn the Oregon Death with Dignity Act. It failed, 60 to 40 percent, and the Oregon bill remains state law.

Cardiac arrest   Cardiac arrest is the sudden, unexpected loss of heart function in a person. Each year, more than 420,000 emergency cardiac arrests occur in the United States. It is the major medical reason for requests for 911 assistance. First responders such as emergency medical technicians are trained in CPR and other life-saving techniques that are applied at the scene of the event and in the ambulance bringing the victim to the nearest hospital emergency department.

Cardiopulmonary resuscitation   Cardiopulmonary resuscitation (CPR) is the initial emergency treatment for cardiac arrest. CPR is continuous compressions of the chest in order to keep blood flowing through the victim's body and brain while delivering oxygen to the bloodstream. CPR is the first step in treating cardiac arrest until first responders arrive. The EMTs, once on scene, will move the patient from CPR to using a device called an electrical defibrillator to shock the heart in order to reestablish normal heart rhythms. In the past decade, technological innovations have led to the development of small, portable defibrillators; these new devices are becoming available in locations where there is heavy foot traffic so that when a person has a cardiac arrest, passersby—following instructions on the device—can rapidly assist in restoring a normal heart beat.

Case or controversy   This is a legal term found in Article III, Section 2, of the U.S. Constitution. In order for a federal court to consider whether to hear a case and reach a decision, there must be an actual dispute between the parties. If the controversy has been resolved prior to a court examination of the legal issues, it is moot and will not be heard. No federal court will provide an advisory opinion. There must be actual injury present in order for a court to note its jurisdiction to hear the case.

CAT scan   A CAT (computerized axial tomography) scan is a painless X-ray test in which a computer generates cross-section views of a segment of a patient's anatomy that seems to be the cause of the medical problem. It can identify normal and abnormal structures, and it is used to provide important information about the state of the patient's health to the physician.

Certiorari Certiorari is a written petition filed by a losing party with the U.S. Supreme Court asking the Court to review the decision of a lower federal or a state supreme court. The brief, prepared by lawyers, contains a statement of the facts of the case, the legal questions presented for review, and arguments as to why the Court should grant the writ and hear the case on the merits. Certiorari is a totally discretionary action of the Court. Most petitions (>95%) are denied. Generally, successful petitions show that a "significant federal question" is presented in the case. A "vote of four" Justices is necessary to grant certiorari.

Death tourist If a terminally ill person seeking to hasten his or her death lives in a state or country that legally prohibits physician assistance in dying, then the dying person can travel to a country or a state where medical assistance in dying is legal. Such a person is a "death tourist."

Do not resuscitate order A do not resuscitate (DNR) order is a medical order written by a doctor at the request of a patient being treated in a hospital. It instructs care givers not to do CPR or use a defibrillator if the patient's breathing stops or if the patient's heart stops beating. Any competent patient has a fundamental right to request the physician to write a DNR order.

Double effect This is a medical term that states if a doctor does something morally good (treating a terminally ill patient with a sufficient amount of a pain medication) that has a morally bad side effect (the patient dies because the drug reduced pain but caused death), the physician's action is ethical and not criminal so long as the bad side effect wasn't intentional.

EEG An electroencephalogram (EEG) is a test that detects electrical activity in the brain using small, flat metal discs (electrodes) attached to the scalp. Brain cells communicate via electrical impulses and are active all the time, even when a person is asleep. The EEG is a vital source of information for a physician treating an unconscious patient.

EMT A person trained in the use of procedures required in emergency medical care, such as cardiopulmonary resuscitation and use of an electrical defibrillator before and during transportation to a hospital. EMTs (emergency medical technicians) generally work with mobile emergency response teams, such as ambulance or fire and rescue teams. In America, a majority of EMT rescue operations are staffed by trained volunteers who reside in the town or city they serve.

En banc When all the members of a federal U.S. Court of Appeals court hear an argument, they are sitting en banc. This Latin term refers to court sessions with the entire membership of the court participating rather than the typical federal three-judge panel that initially hears petitions received by the courts. Permission to file a request for an en banc review is a discretionary power of the federal appeals courts.

Eugenics A "pseudo-science" extremely popular in America and Europe for a century (1850–1950), eugenics deals with the improvement of the hereditary qualities of new generations of citizens through tight control by the state. Central to the success of this human breeding plan is the institutionalization or forced sterilization of all "unfit" persons.

Eugenics movement This broad-based pseudo-science movement seeks to influence the emergence of a superior class of citizens by barring immigration by members of ethnic groups whom eugenicists consider biologically inferior, as well as instituting forced sterilization programs to ensure that "imbeciles" and other unfit persons cannot reproduce inferior offspring. Between 1907 and 1937, 32 American states passed statutes requiring sterilization of "unfit, inferior" persons (criminals, imbeciles, feeble minded people, prostitutes, and other defective persons). In 1927, the U.S. Supreme Court validated the practice of eugenic sterilization. In *Buck v. Bell*, a case challenging Virginia's Eugenical Sterilization Law, Carrie Buck was chosen to be sterilized because of her "feeblemindedness" and alleged sexual promiscuity. The judge ordered Carrie to be sterilized to prevent her from giving birth to more "defective" children. The U.S. Supreme Court upheld the judge's order. Justice Oliver Wendell Holmes, Jr., wrote the opinion; it reflected the eugenics philosophy: "It is better for all the world, if instead of waiting to execute degenerate offspring for crime or to let them starve for their imbecility, society can prevent those who are manifestly unfit from continuing their kind. . . . Three generations of imbeciles are enough." By the mid-1970s, nearly 70,000 persons had been sterilized by the states.

Euthanasia　Euthanasia is the practice of a physician intentionally and directly ending a patient's life in order to relieve pain and suffering, with the assent of the patient. The word *euthanasia* comes from the Greek—"eu," goodly or well, and "thanatos," death, meaning the good death.

Extraordinary means　Extraordinary means are ways of preserving human life that cannot be obtained or used without extreme difficulty in terms of pain, expense, or other burdening factors. Extraordinary means to save a life includes use of a ventilator, dialysis machine to regularly cleanse the patient's blood, chemotherapy, use of experimental drugs, and risky surgery. In addition, medical efforts to save a patient's life are considered extraordinary if, when used, they do not offer a reasonable hope of benefit to the one receiving such extraordinary treatment. For many religions (e.g., Roman Catholicism) there is no general moral obligation to use extraordinary means to keep a person alive, on the premise that God does not exact what is beyond the ordinary power of humans in general to provide.

Fallibilism　Fallibilism is a social theory that no belief (theory, view, or thesis) can ever be rationally supported or justified in a conclusive way. There always remains a possibility that the belief could be proven to be false.

Fundamental rights　Fundamental rights are a group of inalienable rights that have been recognized by various U.S.

Supreme Court majorities over the centuries and that must be afforded protection from government encroachment. These rights are specifically identified in the Constitution (especially in the Bill of Rights) or have been found in judicial interpretations of the Constitution's due process clause. Examples of fundamental rights not specifically listed in the Constitution include the right to marry and the right to privacy, which includes a right to contraception, the right to interstate travel, and a woman's right to choose to have an abortion.

Hippocratic oath   This is one of the oldest standards of professional behavior in medical history. Written in antiquity, its principles are revered by doctors to this day: treat the sick to the best of one's ability, preserve patient privacy, teach medicine to the next generation, and, its most famous axiom, "do no harm." The American Medical Association's Code of Medical Ethics proclaims that the oath "has remained in Western civilization as an expression of ideal conduct for the physician."

Hospice care   Hospice care is palliative care at the end of a terminally ill patient's life. Hospice care is a choice of a terminally ill patient when medicine cannot provide a cure for the illness; its sole purpose is to provide quality comfort care for the dying patient. The first hospice care program was introduced in Connecticut in the mid-1980s. In 2016, nearly half of all terminally ill patients are under hospice care; most of them are cared for in their homes.

Intermediate scrutiny test   Intermediate scrutiny is a test used by judges in state and federal courts in order to determine a law's constitutionality. To pass intermediate scrutiny, the challenged law must be found by the reviewing court to further an important government interest by means that are substantially related to that interest. As the name implies, intermediate scrutiny is less rigorous than the strict scrutiny test but more rigorous than the rational basis test employed by a court to determine whether the challenged statute or regulation is constitutional.

Involuntary euthanasia   This is when a physician or another medical technician takes the life of a person who is not terminally ill. It is involuntary because the person has not requested death and would not want to die.

Jim Crow laws   These laws were state and local regulations enforcing racial segregation, primarily in the American South, after the Civil War ended in 1865. They continued in force until the mid-1960s when the 1964 Civil Rights Act was passed. These de jure—state ordered—laws segregated all persons, from birth to death, on the basis of race. By the 1940s Jim Crow legislation had created two societies, black and white, separate and unequal. The U.S. Supreme Court in *Plessy v. Ferguson* (1896) had concluded that the Constitution did not forbid the establishment of "separate but equal" facilities (schools, hospitals, cemeteries, and all other social interactions) for blacks and whites. In *Brown v. Board of Education* (1954), another U.S. Supreme Court decision, the Justices unanimously overturned the *Plessy* precedent. That decision was the beginning of the end of Jim Crowism and de jure racial discrimination.

Liberty interest   Liberty interest, also referred to as fundamental rights, is a shorthand phrase encapsulating all persons' rights of individual liberty and autonomy as well as the right of privacy. In the American constitutional system, the people have

- the right to purchase and use birth control,
- the right to marry and the right to procreate,
- the right to custody of one's own children and to raise them as one sees fit,
- the right to refuse medical treatment,
- the right to freedom of speech,
- the right to travel freely among the states,

- the right the vote,
- the right to freedom of association,
- the right to freedom of religion.

These rights cannot be denied or abridged unless the government can show, in a court, that it is necessary for the government to achieve some compelling state objective. However, if the government action is challenged in the U.S. Supreme Court, the justices employ the most severe analysis—the "strict scrutiny" test—to determine whether the deprivation of a person's liberty interest serves a compelling state interest.

Medical futility movement In the 1990s, a small number of physicians, frustrated because of the profession's excessive commitment to using new innovative medical technology to save lives, using the latest powerful drugs to cure an incurable illness, or performing a lengthy surgical procedure, joined to protest these "futile" attempts to save their dying patients. They saw that many of these "cutting-edge" efforts did not extend the patient's life and left the patient in even greater pain and suffering than before the treatment. These critics are members of the medical futility movement. These physicians wrote articles in medical journals and essays in news magazines and spoke out in a variety of public gatherings about the importance of a physician going from curing a dying patient to caring for that person. Instead of trying to cure all their patients, physicians must qualitatively assess whether the patient should be subjected to yet another procedure if there is little likelihood for a meaningful existence after the procedure is concluded.

Medicalization of death In the second half of the 20th century, because of the exponential increase of new medical theories about postponing death, the invention of new mechanical devices that sustained life, and the discovery of new wonder drugs and new surgical strategies to attack cancer and other deadly diseases, medical professionals became the very center of the death experience.

The "medicalization of death" reflects the change from dying at a private, communal event managed by the patient, family, and clergy in the home to, after the 1950s, an event primarily involving the aggressive actions of doctors and other medical personnel in hospitals utilizing the latest medical technologies to forestall death because they can. The sole goal of the medicalization of death philosophy was to rid the patient of the medical problem, to cure the patient. There was not much concern for caring for the patients, nor does this practice address the consequence of doctors' aggressive attempts to cure: the poor quality of life—enhanced pain and suffering—the patient must live with after the surgery.

"Merciful death"   *Merciful death* or *good death* are two terms used to describe voluntary euthanasia. It is the action of a physician putting a terminally ill patient to death painlessly.

MRI   Magnetic resonance imaging (MRI) is one of numerous significant medical/technological innovations developed in the past few decades that physicians now rely on to significantly improve their diagnostic methods when treating their patients. The MRI is a technique that uses a magnetic field and radio waves to create detailed images of the organs and tissues within the patient's body. Use of such devices has led to longer lives for many patients. The other side of the coin is the dark side of 21st-century medical innovation: Using MRI, CAT, and other diagnostic equipment provides a doctor with information that allows a more accurate prognosis, but many patients who live longer no longer have the quality of life they experienced before the onset of the illness.

Oath of Medical Ethics   Physicians, like many other professionals, generally are members of an organization that represents them in the social and political arenas. For doctors, the oldest such association is the American Medical Association (AMA), created in the middle of the 19th century, which remains the largest medical association in the nation. It provides the medical community with a variety of benefits that improve the quality of care they provide to their patients. Through the auspices of the AMA, members share information about medical practice. Regular public meetings are held, and *The Journal of the American Medical Association*, *JAMA*, provides physicians with the latest research findings about treating illness. Equally important, the AMA, like all other professional associations, has established—with modifications made from time to time—a set of normative standards that lay out the character of doctor-patient interactions. Critically important in this litany of ethical principles is the physician's responsibility to care for the patient. The AMA's Oath of Medical Ethics is the profession's repository of standards of conduct that call for all physicians to "do no harm" to their patients.

Originalism   This theory, held by a small number of Supreme Court justices, is that the U.S. Constitution should be interpreted based on the "original intent" of its creators. U.S. Supreme Court Justice Antonin Scalia was a foremost defender of the theory. He said: "It is essential to originalism, as it is not to so-called 'evolutionary constitutional jurisprudence,' to know the original meaning of constitutional provisions." An originalist jurist will determine the constitutionality of a law based on this assessment of the original meaning.

Palliative care   Palliative care focuses on relieving a patient's pain and suffering, often triggered by a chronic illness, that adversely affects the patient's quality of life. Palliative care is a relatively new medical subspecialty; the earliest palliative care hospital wings were created in the late 1980s, to care for patients suffering grievously from illness. Palliative care is available to all patients suffering and in need of medical care that alleviates the pain. Qualitative care is the hallmark of palliative care.

Palliative medicine subspecialty   Palliative medicine is a new medical subspecialty that employs an interdisciplinary team of health care workers (physicians, nurses, medical technicians, social workers, and psychologists) practicing patient-centered care. Such care requires qualitatively addressing the patient's physical, emotional, and spiritual needs.

Palliative sedation   The primary intent of palliative sedation is to relieve a conscious patient's pain and suffering by administering a sedative such as morphine. This treatment leads to a significant reduction of pain, decreased awareness, or unconsciousness. Unlike terminal sedation, palliative sedation is not meant to take the patient's life.

Petitioner   In litigation in any state or federal court, the person presenting a petition to a court to appeal a lower court decision is called a petitioner. The opponent in such a proceeding is known as the respondent.

PVS   A person who, because of catastrophic traumatic event, is deprived of oxygen to the brain for more than six to eight minutes and remains unconscious for one month is in a persistent vegetative state. After a year in this medical condition, the patient is considered to be in a permanent vegetative state (PVS). A patient in a PVS has no awareness of the environment, nor is there any evidence of purposeful, voluntary behavioral reactions to noises, people, smells, and touch. Furthermore, when a person is in a PVS, there is no language comprehension, and the patient lacks the ability to engage in conversation. Families of patients in PVS have petitioned state courts to allow attending physicians to withdraw all artificial medical devices that keep the unconscious person alive. *Quinlan* (1976) was the first case to appear in any American court that addressed the right to die. Since then, other PVS litigation has been heard in a number of state courts. In 1990, the U.S. Supreme Court entered the discussion regarding the right to die in *Cruzan v. Director, Missouri Department of Health.*

Rational basis test for constitutionality   The "rational basis" test is used by state and federal judges to determine whether a law is constitutional. It is the lowest of three tests created and applied by a court to decide a case. (The other two levels are "strict scrutiny" and "intermediate scrutiny.") The rational basis test is employed by a court when there are no fundamental rights allegedly abridged by the law. To pass such a test, the court must conclude that the law has a "reasonable, rational relationship" to a legitimate government interest.

Sanctity of life   The principle of the "sanctity of life" is at the very heart of all groups—religious, conservative, disabled, bioethicists—opposed to physician-assisted death and euthanasia. According to this principle, human beings are the stewards of their physical bodies and souls, but God is the creator; only God can terminate the life of a human being. Humans must do all they can to preserve the sanctity of life. Abortion, physician-assisted death, and euthanasia are actions that are seen as immoral, unholy, and criminal.

Slippery slope   As employed by opponents of PAD and euthanasia, the slippery slope argument is that once such an assisted death law is passed by a legislature, there will inevitably be incremental exceptions and interpretations to the law that broaden the scope of such legislation without much reasoned debate or further political actions. Thus, opponents argue that PAD laws will be extended to cover a situation where a terminally ill quadriplegic patient, unable to self-medicate to hasten death, will be helped by a family member or a medical professional. This may be followed by extending PAD to allow patients with a terminal disease (Parkinson's, cancer, etc.) but who under the original PAD legislation are not terminal (death within six months) to receive medication they may use to take their life. Finally, there is the slide from an expanded PAD system to euthanasia. Initially, it is voluntary euthanasia, where a patient requests a physician to terminate life; then it will slide down into the monstrous practice of involuntary euthanasia, where the state orders forced euthanasia of persons determined to be unworthy of life.

State police powers   State-level police powers are granted by the Tenth Amendment to the U.S. Constitution. A state uses its police powers to pass laws to benefit, preserve, and protect the safety, health, welfare, and morals of all people within its territory. When there is a clash between a state law and federal powers, that use of state power can be challenged, often by arguing that the Fourteenth Amendment prohibits state laws that deprive people of "the equal protection of the law."

Strict scrutiny test for constitutionality   Strict scrutiny is a test used by courts to determine the constitutionality of certain laws or governmental actions. The test is employed when a petitioner claims that a law has either abridged a fundamental right (such as freedom of speech) or adversely impacted members of a suspect class (i.e., racial and ethnic) protected by the Constitution. The government's lawyers must show that the law was passed to further a "compelling governmental interest" and that it was "narrowly tailored" to "achieve that governmental interest." If the court determines that the state has not shown a compelling interest or the law was not narrowly tailored, the law is declared unconstitutional.

Sunset provision   A sunset provision in a law states that the law will no longer be valid after a specific date, unless further legislative action is taken to extend the law.

Terminal illness   A terminal illness is an irreversible illness for which there is no cure and generally leads to death within six months. All medical prognoses about how much time a patient has before death, however, are estimates and are often inaccurate.

Terminal sedation   Terminal sedation is a treatment (usually with a pain relief medication such as morphine) administered by a physician that places a terminally ill patient into a state of unconsciousness until death. In this state, the dying patient does not perceive the pain brought on by the fatal illness.

Voluntary active euthanasia   Voluntary active euthanasia occurs when a physician intentionally administers medications to hasten a patient's death at the patient's request and with full, informed consent by the terminally ill person.

Wink and nod Occasionally, doctors and nurses convey unwritten instructions and agreement about how to treat a dying patient in great pain. The "wink and nod" is a set of verbal signals between a physician and a nurse to suggest (and confirm) a medical action ("make sure you don't give the patient too much morphine") that will hasten the patient's death. Because the ensuing medical action may be considered controversial or a violation of medical ethics (as well as a violation of criminal laws), the "wink and nod" leaves no formal record that can be used to criminally charge, discharge, or decertify the medical staff involved.

Index

About the Author

Howard Ball (BA, Hunter College, CUNY, 1960; MA, PhD, Rutgers University, 1970) is a political scientist with a specialization in constitutional law, the federal judiciary, civil rights, and the international community's responses to war crimes, crimes against humanity, and genocide. Since 1965, he has taught full-time at Hofstra University, Mississippi State University, the University of Utah (Dean, SBS), and the University of Vermont (Dean, A&S). In addition, he has taught at SUNY Stony Brook, Dartmouth College, Vermont Law School, Sofia (Bulgaria) Law School (Fulbright), and Szeged University, Hungary (Fulbright). He is the author of over three dozen books (for ABC-CLIO, Oxford University Press, NYU Press, Random House, and other university presses) about American public policy, judicial biographies (Justices Hugo Black, William O. Douglas, Thurgood Marshall), the U.S. Supreme Court, and the prosecution of war crimes and genocide. He grew up in the Bronx and has lived in Vermont for the past 25 years. He has been married to Carol for 53 years, has three daughters (Sue, Sheryl, and Melissa) and three grand-kids (Lila, Nate, and Sophie), three horses, and two dogs. His next research project will examine the history, politics, and legal issues associated with the nativist movement ("America First") in America since 1789.